CW00821239

The Life and Teaching of JESUS
Explained and Applied

"This book is an excellent resource. It begins with a summary chronological presentation of the life and ministry of Christ, highlighting the various fulfillments of Old Testament prophecy. The second section covers several 'Significant Facts,' such as the identification of the various Jewish groups and institutions mentioned in the gospels, as well as Jesus' miracles and parables. The following four sections present the four gospels in canonical order dealing with each of them in this manner: distinctive features of the gospel, the Christology of the gospel, and applications of the results of that study for the use of the reader. Finally there is an outlined harmony of the gospels.

As with his *The Old Testament Explained and Applied*, Dr. Crossley has provided the reader with a substantive and reliable resource. His scholarship is impeccable and the pastoral and applicatory focus is much to be commended. I highly recommend this work."

Dr Benjamin Shaw, Professor of Old Testament, Reformation Bible College, USA

"There is nothing more important in life than to know the Lord Jesus. Even thoughtful readers of the Gospels, however, can find parts difficult to understand, or can miss important details. This book is a helpful guide for anyone who wants to deepen their knowledge of the Gospels so they can better appreciate Jesus' life and teaching. It is full of helpful insights and observations, giving the reader a fresh appreciation of the Gospels. Dr Crossley brings out the meaning of the Gospel writers, in the context of the Old and New Testaments, including useful historical details. Not only does he provide the reader with a clear explanation of the Gospels, with many helpful hints for preachers, but more importantly we find our hearts warmed as we are led to know Jesus himself more deeply."

James Poole, Executive Director, Wycliffe Bible Translators, UK

"I am delighted to commend this book to all believers and particularly those teaching others. The author loves Jesus Christ and wants everyone to know him better - and this comes across on page after page, challenging us, the readers, to also grow likewise. How often in our Christian lives and ministry do we start going astray because the main thing loses its place in our walk and service? If you read this book then you will find yourself accompanying the Saviour through the steps of his ministry, up to the cross and resurrection, gaining a sense of how it felt as each step unfolded. There is then a helpful summary of the particular, distinct contributions of each of the individual gospels to our overall understanding of his person and work, and discussion of why there are differences in their approaches and contents."

I have found the author's *The Old Testament Explained and Applied* most useful in giving pastors a 'map' for preaching Christ as the ultimate subject of the Old Testament. There are many temptations which draw pastors aside from their true work in proclaiming Christ and this book will be of great value in helping them to stand firm.

David Anderson, missionary Bible teacher West Africa.

"*The Life and Teaching of Jesus Explained and Applied,* by Gareth Crossley, is a tour de force. In it, Dr Crossley continues the task he began with *The Old Testament Explained and Applied,* that is, of showing how the whole Bible points to and find its supreme climax in the Lord Jesus Christ and his finished work of redemption.

In this he focusses on the life and ministry of the incarnate Christ as presented by the four Gospel accounts, Matthew, Mark, Luke and John. In 462 detailed, biblically well referenced and Christ-centred pages — along with maps and helpful background notes — he presents his subject in a way that is thoroughly grounded in both Testaments and in a deep grasp of biblical theology.

There is full consideration given to the author of each Gospel, and their four-fold account of the teaching and miracles of Christ and the ongoing progress of his incarnate ministry. Gareth Crossley works from two perspectives: a harmony of the Gospel accounts and the unique contribution of each Gospel. Old Testament light is brought to bear, as well as relevant, extra-biblical material concerning first century AD Israel. The author presents his subject in a way that is balanced, biblically sound and pastorally applied. Coupled with its depth of teaching, there is a simplicity of style and a clear and helpful division of subject matter that will make this work widely accessible.

Dr Crossley brings to the subject of Christ in the Gospels a long experience of pastoring and preaching to congregations, as well as mentoring preachers in the UK and other countries. This volume will edify new and mature believers alike and provide preachers with a sure foundation for expounding and applying the Gospels. I thoroughly recommend this excellent sequel to his volume on the Old Testament."

Roger Fay, previous chairman of Evangelical Press (now EP Books), former senior editor of Evangelical Times, elder of Zion Evangelical Baptist Church, Ripon, UK

The Life and
Teaching of

JESUS

Explained
and Applied

Gareth Crossley

© Gareth Crossley 2022

All rights reserved. No part of this publication may be reproduced, stored in a retrieval system, or transmitted, in any form or by any means, electronic, mechanical, photocopying, recording or otherwise, without the prior permission of the author.

First published 2022

ISBN 978-1-9998563-8-0

Unless otherwise indicated, all Scripture quotations are taken from the New King James Version. Copyright © 1994 by Thomas Nelson, Inc. All rights reserved.

email: sales@RevealingChrist.org   website: RevealingChrist.org

Dedicated to Joan Mary
for her love and service for the Lord Jesus
and her loyalty and support for her husband

Contents

Maps

Introduction

Written in plain English for pastors, Bible students and general readers this book builds on the evidence of the Gospels to create one combined account of the life and teaching of Jesus Christ.

God willing it will stimulate and encourage spiritual growth through a careful study of the Lord Jesus -

- his Life - who he was, why he came and the qualities of his unique person.
- his Teaching - understanding his sermons and miracles.
- his Explanation - how to interpret parables and to understand his life in the light of Old Testament prophecy.
- his Application - our obligations and responsibilities as followers of Jesus.

As we read of his life and teaching we gain insight into his very person. We become more conscious of his immense courage, his resilience, his humility, his compassion. In this way we get to know him, love him more and want to emulate him. We grow in grace and knowledge and glorify him in our lives.

To grow in grace and knowledge is the aim of everyone who truly believes that Jesus is the living Son of God who paid the ultimate price for sin.

Grow in the grace and knowledge
of our Lord and Saviour Jesus Christ.
To him be the glory both now and forever (2 Peter 3:18).

The aim of this book is to help the reader achieve this.

In the first two-thirds of the book the Gospel accounts are treated as one complete whole, a harmony, thus providing a chronological view of the Lord's years of public ministry and of his whereabouts when he was teaching and healing. A harmony facilitates a better understanding of how the different accounts relate to each other. The combination builds up the context of the incidents and sayings and identifies the events that occured before and afterwards which may have influenced the Lord in his words and actions: this may prove an invaluable aid to interpretation and application.

The historians Matthew, Mark, Luke and John did not attempt a biography of the Lord's life. They provide selected material, sometimes without commitment to its historical setting. Because each of the Gospel writers had a different section of society in mind, their order of events and the connection of the teachings differ; whereas in combination the four

Gospels indicate how so much of the teaching is related to the circumstances at the time.

In this book details of shared events in Matthew, Mark, Luke and John are brought together to form a complete picture with references for each Gospel included under the title of each event.

Some might challenge that if God had intended the life and teaching of the Lord Jesus to be told as one complete whole then why are there four accounts in the Bible? The answer is straightforward. The individual Gospels are essential. They are composed of eye-witness accounts. Matthew and John were personally present at many of the events they recorded. Mark is generally believed to have carefully documented the recollections of the apostle Peter. Luke makes his position very clear in his introduction; he is recording the testimony of 'eyewitnesses and ministers of the word' (Luke 1:2). Consequently the four accounts are the inspired record of eye-witnesses and as with all eye-witnesses the accounts vary; each one recalls different aspects from their perspective and memory. The non-identical descriptions validate the events and then lead the investigator to see the full picture as they are combined. This is particularly true of the four Gospels as their testimonies harmonise beautifully since they are part of the 'God-breathed' Scripture (2 Timothy 3:16) therefore trustworthy and reliable.

Faithful Bible teachers always read the relevant accounts in all the Gospels when seeking to explain the Lord's action and words in one Gospel. A harmony which highlights the significant contributions facilities study.

Following the harmony of the Life and Teaching of Jesus a chapter entitled *Significant facts* includes lists of 'Resurrection appearances', 'Parables of Jesus' etc., and explains terms often found in the four Gospels such as 'Pharisees', 'scribes' and 'Herodians'.

The concluding section is devoted to a study of the distinct contributions made by each of the authors of the four Gospels. There is therefore great value in considering the four in harmony to get the full picture and also, of equal merit, to study the four individually. In this book the aim is to do both in two separate sections.

Becoming a disciple of the Lord Jesus Christ is the beginning of the most exciting journey in life. Discovering the amazing love of God towards us in giving his only begotten Son as our Saviour is truly wonderful.

For God so loved the world that he gave his only begotten Son, that whoever believes in him should not perish but have everlasting life (John 3:16).

The eternal Son of God became Jesus of Nazareth and the only Saviour. Through him all our guilty offences before God are pardoned forever. We are welcomed into the spiritual family of God and are able to enjoy the closest possible relationship with the triune God - our heavenly Father, our Lord and Saviour, and the Holy Spirit who is the glorious and continuous Helper.

The blessings of our new relationship with God are spelt out in great detail throughout the Scriptures, so too are the obligations and responsibilities of our new status. Consequently all Christians are urged and encouraged to read, study, consider carefully, and apply the teaching of the Bible. Spiritual growth is essential. We are all to be enthusiastic and committed disciples of Jesus ever learning and applying the Word of God to our thoughts, our words and our behaviour.

May this book contribute to your growth in grace and knowledge of our Lord and Saviour Jesus Christ - to his glory!

The Four Gospels harmonised

Contents

The Peraean ministry   169

The Lord's final week in Jerusalem   213

Prophecies Jesus told to his disciples   237

The beginning

1. Prologues
Matthew 1:1; Mark 1:1; Luke 1:1-4; John 1:1-18

Though the life of Jesus began with his miraculous conception in the womb of the virgin Mary, he had existed as the Son of God long before that momentous event. In fact, as the Son of God, the second Person in the glorious Godhead, he has always existed. He is eternal, without beginning and without end, just like God the Father and the Holy Spirit. He is the Word of God, God the Son in a face-to-face relationship with God the Father (John 1:1). Miraculously the Son of God became a human being, 'the Word became flesh and lived among us' (John 1:14). Jesus is the incarnation, the human embodiment of deity, Immanuel 'God with us' (Matthew 1:23).

Not only was Jesus, in his pre-existence as the Son of God, co-equal with the Father in nature, power and glory, he was also essentially involved in the creation of all things. Nothing has come into existence without his personal involvement. He is the source and giver of all life.

In anticipation of the Son's coming into the world as one of us, God gave many prophecies about him. Spread over more than three thousand years and recorded in the Old Testament are details of the most exact and magnificent kind. The Old Testament prophets spoke from God about the Son of God who was to become Jesus the Christ.

They prophesied that he would -

- be miraculously conceived of a virgin (Isaiah 7:14; Matthew 1:21-23).
- be born in the village of Bethlehem (Micah 5:2; Matthew 2:5-6).
- descend of the tribe of Judah (Genesis 49:10; Revelation 5:5).
- be a descendant of King David (2 Samuel 7:12-14; Matthew 1:7,16).
- be preceded by a messenger (Isaiah 40:3; Malachi 3:1; Mark 1:1-3).
- be a powerful miracle worker: the blind would see, the deaf would hear, the lame would walk, and the dumb would speak (Isaiah 35:5-6; Matthew 11:4-5).
- be rejected by his own people (Isaiah 53:3; John 1:11).

- ride into Jerusalem on a donkey (Zechariah 9:9; Matthew 21:4-5).
- be betrayed by a close friend (Psalm 41:9; John 13:18; cf. 17:12).
- be betrayed for thirty pieces of silver (Matthew 27:9; Zechariah 11:12-13); which would be thrown into the temple (Zechariah 11:13; Matthew 27:3,5).
- be condemned with criminals (Isaiah 53:12; Mark 15:27-28).
- be mocked and ridiculed (Psalm 22:8; Matthew 27:39-43).
- be crucified (Psalm 22:16; Mark 15:25).
- be pierced (Zechariah 12:10; John 19:37); yet with no bones broken (Exodus 12:46; John 19:36).
- have his clothing divided, lots cast (Psalm 22:18; Matthew 27:35).
- cry out as one abandoned (Psalm 22:1; Matthew 27:46).
- suffer extreme thirst (Psalm 22:15; John 19:28).
- yield his spirit to the Father (Psalm 31:5; Luke 23:46).
- die but his body would not decompose (Psalm 16:8-11; Acts 2:25-28; 13:34-37).
- make his grave with the wicked and with the rich in his death (Isaiah 53:9; Matthew 27:38);
- rise from the dead on the third day (Hosea 6:2; 1 Corinthians 15:4).

Many more specific prophecies were given so that Israel and the world might recognise him as the promised Messiah and be certain of his true identity.

2. Introducing John the Baptist and Jesus
Luke 1:5-80

As the time drew near for God to send his Son into the world, the Holy Spirit gave further prophecies which drew together and consolidated the prophecies of the Old Testament. After 400 years of prophetic silence, there was a burst of prophecy from angels and from Elizabeth, Mary, Zacharias and Simeon culminating in the great prophet, John the Baptist. God selected Zacharias and Elizabeth to be the parents of John. John would be the herald whom the Lord promised years before through the prophet Malachi (3:1). This was the one, also promised through the prophet Isaiah, who would be the voice of one crying in the wilderness, 'Prepare the way of the Lord; make his paths straight' (Mark 1:3; Isaiah 40:3). Though the godly priest Zacharias and his godly wife Elizabeth had no children and were 'well advanced in years' (Luke 1:18) the Lord would work a miracle.

The angel Gabriel was sent to inform Zacharias the priest whilst he was engaged in his duties in the temple. It was his turn (probably once in a lifetime) to enter into the holy place and burn incense before the Lord. Here Zacharias the priest would be praying for his people Israel that the Lord would fulfil his ancient promises. This godly man could never have thought that the answer to his prayers for a Redeemer would also be the answer to the private and personal prayer of his wife and himself, a prayer prayed over many years but now no longer uttered. They would have a child, a boy, who when grown to manhood would introduce the Messiah to Israel.

The angel Gabriel prophesied that this child would be unique. He will bring joy; be great in the sight of the Lord; be filled with the Holy Spirit before his birth; will turn many to the Lord; go before the Lord and - prepare a people *for* the Lord (Luke 1:14-17). Zacharias found the announcement utterly incredible. Consequently on account of his response he was to be dumb for nine months until the child was born (Luke 1:20). He expressed unbelief with his tongue so his tongue came under discipline (Proverbs 3:11-12; Hebrews 12:6).

Six months later the angel Gabriel was sent on another prophetic mission. This time to a small town 113km (70 miles) north of Jerusalem, to Nazareth in Galilee. Here he appeared to a young woman, the chosen mother of the Son of God. Mary was 'a virgin betrothed to a man whose name was Joseph, of the house of David' (Luke 1:27). Mary demonstrated remarkable humility as she readily submitted to the Lord's will. In beautiful self-surrender she accepted the great honour from the Lord - in spite of the grief which it would also bring to her. The immediate pain which she would find hard to bear was that of having her honour and purity questioned by all who knew her, not least by her husband Joseph.

Mary was 'betrothed' (Luke 1:27; Matthew 1:18) to Joseph, that is, she was legally his wife but they had not yet established home together nor united in the marriage bond. This was the marriage practice in Israel and was evidently designed this way by God in readiness for the birth of his Son. Betrothal (legal marriage) was followed some time later with the couple establishing a home and becoming one. By this means Mary had the protection of a husband to shield her and her child from open ridicule and at the same time for her to be a true virgin until she had conceived, carried and given birth to Jesus (Matthew 1:24-25).

How long there was between the angel Gabriel's visit to Mary and Joseph being told of the expected child is not recorded. Joseph learned that his betrothed was 'with child' (Matthew 1:18). As a godly sensitive man he would no doubt be devastated, even so, he had no wish to humiliate Mary in public. The Lord graciously sent an angel to reassure Joseph that his wife had not been unfaithful. Indeed she was highly favoured by God to be the recipient of a miracle. Joseph's reaction is a fine testimony to his godliness. Reassured that this was God's work according to prophecy, Joseph did as he was directed and took Mary to his home as his wife (Mathew 1:18-22).

Having been informed that her relative Elizabeth was 'with child' Mary travelled south to the hill country of Judah and to the home of Zacharias and Elizabeth. Elizabeth welcomed her warmly. The child within 'leaped in her womb' and she 'was filled with the Holy Spirit' (Luke 1:41). Inspired she declared how much Mary had been blessed by God to be the mother of the Lord. Mary responded with her praise, 'My soul magnifies the Lord, and my spirit has rejoiced in God my Saviour…' (Luke 1:46-55) After about three months Mary returned home to Nazareth.

Elizabeth gave birth to a son. On the eighth day at his circumcision he was named 'John'. The speech of his father Zacharias returned and filled with the Holy Spirit he prophesied about his son, 'And you, child, will be called the prophet of the Highest; for you will go before the face of the Lord to prepare his ways…' (Luke 1:76-79).

John grew and became strong in spirit spending much time in the desert. In his twenties he gathered disciples around him to instruct them in the meaning of the Messianic prophecies in preparation for the coming of 'the Lamb of God who takes away the sin of the world!'

The birth and childhood of Jesus

3. The birth of Jesus (Bethlehem)
Luke 2:1-7

Six months later it so happened in the providence of Almighty God, that 'a decree went out from Caesar Augustus that all the world should be registered. This census first took place while Quirinius was governing Syria. So all went to be registered, everyone to his own city' (Luke 2:1-3). Consequently Joseph was required to leave Nazareth and journey south to Bethlehem 'because he was of the house and lineage of David' (Luke 2:4). Joseph would have known only too well that his step-Son had to be born in Bethlehem (Micah 5:2). No doubt welcoming the legitimate and publicly acknowledgeable reason to leave Nazareth, Joseph took Mary his 'betrothed' to his ancestral home in Judah. So strong was the impulse for Joseph to make a new home in Bethlehem that months later it required a message from heaven for him to leave there (Matthew 2:13).

Joseph and Mary had to travel 145km (90 miles) to the city of Joseph's ancestors: south along the flatlands of the Jordan River, then west over the hills surrounding Jerusalem, and on into Bethlehem. It was an arduous journey on foot or donkey. Taking with them also the few necessities of a Galilean household, it would take more than four days! The last 9km (6 miles) from Jerusalem to Bethlehem standing 775m (2,543ft) above sea level. involved a climb of 30m (98ft). Bethlehem ('the house of bread') is situated on the southern portion of the Judean Mountains. Herod the Great's castle, built on the highest hill south east of Bethlehem, was clearly visible for the last few miles.

Finding accommodation in a little town crowded by other visitors from the outlying district who had also come for registration, proved impossible. As a last resort, the only available shelter was a place with cattle. Hardly a conducive setting for giving birth. There is no word as to how many days they were there before Mary gave birth to 'her firstborn Son, and wrapped him in swaddling cloths, and laid him in a manger' (Luke 2:7).

The Son of God, co-Creator of all things, had become a human being. This was the most momentous event in all history. Yet there was no royal welcome, no palace or servants to attend to the mother and baby's needs. Nevertheless the Lord God provided a greeting suitable to that humble Son who was to become 'the Saviour of the world' (John 4:42). The good news was first published to nearby 'shepherds living out in the fields, keeping watch over their flock by night' (Luke 2:8). An angel, a messenger from heaven, announced to them the birth of 'a Saviour, who is Christ the Lord' (Luke 2:11). Then suddenly a huge company of heavenly beings joined the angel and said -

Glory to God in the highest, and on earth peace, goodwill toward men! (Luke 2:14)

Only once before had the hymn of the angels been heard on earth. The prophet Isaiah received a remarkable vision of the temple of God. Two angels were flying above the throne and one cried to another and said -

Holy, holy, holy is the LORD of hosts; the whole earth is full of his glory! (Isaiah 6:3)

The shepherds immediately visited the child and were so overwhelmed that they 'returned, glorifying and praising God for all the things that they had heard and seen, as it was told them' (Luke 2:20). Meanwhile 'Mary kept all these things and pondered them in her heart' (Luke 2:19).

4. Jesus taken to the temple (Jerusalem)
Luke 2:22-38

Eight days after the birth of the Lord, he was circumcised according to the instruction given to Abraham 2,000 years earlier (Genesis 17:12-13) and named 'Jesus' (Luke 2:21 meaning 'Jehovah saves'). Thirty-four days later (Leviticus 12:1-4), Joseph and Mary took the baby to the temple again. Two ceremonies were involved: the presentation of the child Jesus and the ceremonial purification of the mother Mary (Luke 2:22). The purification ceremony involved a sacrifice, 'a pair of turtle-doves or two young pigeons' (Luke 2:24; Leviticus 12:1-8). Mary and Joseph were evidently quite poor because of the offering they brought.

When the young child Jesus was taken to the temple the priests did not welcome him and give glory to God. None of the officials knew or understood the significance surrounding that little family. Yet though there was no priest to welcome the baby, there was however a godly old man to receive the child. This old man, of no official standing or prominence, received the child, praised God, blessed the parents and declared the unique glory of the Christ. Like Joseph and Mary, Zacharias and Elizabeth, Simeon was chosen for this privilege on account of his spiritual qualifications, 'For the LORD does not see as man sees; for man looks at the outward appearance, but the LORD looks at the heart' (1 Samuel 16:7).

Simeon combined the three characteristics of Old Testament spirituality: he was just, devout and waiting. He was repentant and forgiven by God. He was devoted to God by love, life and service. He had a great longing for the fulfilment of the promises of God. He was looking forward to the coming of the promised Messiah.

> Taking Jesus up in his arms he said, "Lord, now you are letting your servant depart in peace, according to your word; for my eyes have seen your salvation which you have prepared before the face of all peoples, a light to bring revelation to the Gentiles, and the glory of your people Israel." And Joseph and his mother marvelled at those things which were spoken of him (Luke 2:29-33).

Providentially another godly old saint entered the temple and met with the young family. Aged godly Anna was spiritually aware and spent most of her time in the temple serving God 'with fasting and prayers night and day'. Recognising the true identity of that six week old child, 'she gave thanks to the Lord, and spoke of him to all those who looked for redemption in Jerusalem' (Luke 2:37,38).

5. Wise men from the East
Matthew 2:1-12

Sometime after the presentation of the Saviour in the temple, wise men (magi) following a star from the east arrived in Jerusalem and made enquiry as to the whereabouts of the one born King of the Jews. When Herod the Great heard this he, and many of his subjects, were greatly troubled. He asked the chief priests and scribes where the promised King of the Jews would be born. They responded unequivocally that, according to the prophet Micah (5:2), he would be born in Bethlehem. Herod slyly found out from the wise men when the star first came to their attention. It would seem from his subsequent behaviour that the wise men first noticed the star more than a year earlier.

Leaving the palace the wise men were led by the star to the place where the family of the Lord was living. On seeing Jesus, they worshipped him and gave him gifts of gold, frankincense, and myrrh.

In Scripture gold is linked with royalty (1 Kings 10:10,21-22), for this young child is the 'King of Kings and Lord of Lords' (Revelation 19:16); frankincense is associated with the worship of God (Leviticus 2:1-2; cf. vv.15-16; Exodus 30:37), so suitable for the one who is 'Immanuel… God with us' (Matthew 1:23). Myrrh mingled with wine acted as an anaesthetic and was offered to Jesus on his way to crucifixion (Mark 15:23). It was also used with spices in preparing a body for burial (cf. John 19:39-40). It is therefore associated with pain, suffering and death, so fitting for the suffering Saviour of the world (Genesis 3:15; John 1:29; Luke 24:46; Romans 5:10).

When Herod realised that the wise men were not going to return to inform him of the child's whereabouts, he was very angry and ordered the brutal slaughter of every male child two years of age and under throughout Bethlehem and the surrounding district. Then was fulfilled what was spoken by Jeremiah the prophet, saying -

> A voice was heard in Ramah, lamentation, weeping, and great mourning, Rachel weeping for her children, refusing to be comforted, because they are no more (Matthew 2:17-18).

6. Flight to Egypt
Matthew 2:13-18

The Lord instructed Joseph, by means of an angel appearing to him in a dream, to take the young child and his mother to safety in Egypt. There they were to remain until the death of Herod the Great. Then once more under heavenly direction the family moved back to Israel. Since Herod Archelaus was reigning over Judea instead of his father Herod the Great, Joseph was afraid to go there. He was directed by heaven to return to Nazareth in Galilee. Thus a prophecy would be fulfilled, 'He shall be called a Nazarene' (Matthew 2:23). 'And the child grew and became strong in spirit, filled with wisdom; and the grace of God was upon him' (Luke 2:40).

> Education begins in the home... it is imparted by influence and example, before it comes by teaching; it is acquired by what is seen and heard, before it is laboriously learned from books; its real object becomes instinctively felt, before its goal is consciously sought.[1]

7. Jesus at twelve with the teachers in the temple
Luke 2:41-52

Nothing more is recorded of the Lord's life for a number of years until, at twelve years of age, he accompanied his mother and stepfather to the annual Feast of the Passover 'according to the custom' (Luke 2:42). The twelfth year was significant for a Jewish boy. At the end of that year a boy becomes a bar mitzvah, 'son of the commandment'. He is now treated as an adult and is committed to obedience to the commandments of God.

It would take four or five days to walk the 146km (90 miles) from Nazareth to Jerusalem. At the end of the first day of their return journey Joseph and Mary discovered the absence of the Lord Jesus and so determined to return to Jerusalem.

Was Jesus being thoughtless or inconsiderate in staying behind without consulting his parents? It is evident that Joseph and Mary had entire confidence in the behaviour of their son. For them to walk for a whole day without knowing exactly where he was and who he was with, is an indication of their trust in his maturity in looking after himself.

When Mary gave voice to their anxiety, 'Son, why have you done this to us? Look, your father and I have sought you anxiously'. Jesus was surprised, 'Why did you seek me? Did you not know that I must be about my Father's business?' (Luke 2:48,49) He was engaged with the teachers of Israel 'both listening to them and asking them questions. And all who heard him were astonished at his understanding and answers' (Luke 2:46-47).

This raises the great issue concerning the nature of Jesus. Since he is both God and Man, as God he would know all things but as a Man he had to

---

[1] Alfred Edersheim, *The Life and Times of Jesus the Messiah* (Peabody, Massachusetts: Hendrikson, 1993), p.157.

learn. 'Evidently the incarnate Christ was able somehow to bracket or limit the actual exercise of his divine powers so that he had the personality of God (basically, the motives and will of God), but the powers of knowing all and the infinite strength of God he somehow restrained.'[2]

Paul wrote to the Philippians about this glorious union of humanity and deity, a man and God in one Person: 'Christ Jesus, who, being in the form of God, did not consider it robbery [grasping] to be equal with God, but made himself of no reputation [literally, 'but himself emptied'], taking the form of a bondservant, and coming in the likeness of men' (Philippians 2:6-7). One of the things of which Christ emptied himself was omniscience (knowing everything). He said concerning the time of his return, 'Of that day and hour no one knows, not even the angels of heaven but the Father only' (Matthew 24:36).

'Then he went down with them and came to Nazareth, and was subject to them' (Luke 2:51). To Joseph and Mary, with all their weaknesses and lack of understanding, Jesus yielded continuing obedience.

For eighteen years there was silence about life in the home at Nazareth, except for the testimony that Jesus was subject to his earthly parents, his mother and step-father, and grew 'in wisdom and stature, and in favour with God and men' (Luke 2:52).

Preparation for ministry

8. John the Baptist preaching (Bethabara, Perea)[3]
Matthew 3:1-12; Mark 1:2-8; Luke 3:1-18

John the Baptist was the prophesied herald. He was to prepare the way for the Messiah, the Christ of God: 'There was a man sent from God, whose name was John' (John 1:6). He came as the forerunner of the Christ, to prepare his way before him and to introduce him to Israel and the world. He wore distinctive clothing, 'camel's hair and with a leather belt around his waist, and he ate locusts and wild honey' (Mark 1:6). The hairy mantle, 'rough garment', or coarse robe, was a mark of a prophet from Elijah onwards (2 Kings 1:8; Zechariah 13:4). The prophet's dress was a sign of his utter contempt of luxury and earthly display, and his sorrow for the nation's sins and their consequences, which it was his function to expose and confront.

---

[2] John Piper, *The Son of God at 12 years old*. Internet: *Desiring God*, 1981.
[3] See map: 'Israel in New Testament times', p.352

John came fulfilling prophecy there beyond the Jordan in Bethabara of Perea, 33km (21 miles) east of Jerusalem. He was the voice of one crying in the wilderness: 'Prepare the way of the LORD; make straight in the desert a highway for our God' (Isaiah 40:3); of whom it was foretold, 'Behold, I send my messenger, and he will prepare the way before me' (Malachi 3:1). Just as the angel of the Lord revealed to John's father Zacharias -

> ...he will turn many of the children of Israel to the Lord their God. He will also go before him in the spirit and power of Elijah, 'to turn the hearts of the fathers to the children,' and the disobedient to the wisdom of the just, to make ready a people prepared for the Lord (Luke 1:16-17; cf. Malachi 4:5-6).

Although John was commissioned to baptise with water, his foremost responsibility was that of a prophet. He was to proclaim the word of the Lord, and call the people of Israel to repentance and to prepare them for the arrival of the kingdom of heaven in the glorious form of the Messiah, the promised one. In this task John proved both faithful and fearless.

Crowds gathered to him. Many responded from Jerusalem, all Judea and the region around the Jordan where John was baptising. He showed no partiality, challenging the people, whether Pharisees or scribes, soldiers or tax collectors, king or commoners, to confess their sins. They were not to rely on their Jewish birthright but to secure a true spiritual relationship with God. Thus he urged them: 'Bear fruits worthy of repentance, and do not begin to say to yourselves, "We have Abraham as our father"' (Luke 3:8).

With a simplicity and clarity driven by a profound love for God and a deep and sincere love for the people he gave examples of the fruits of repentance: 'He who has two tunics, let him give to him who has none; and he who has food, let him do likewise.' To tax collectors he said, 'Collect no more than what is appointed for you' and to soldiers, 'Do not intimidate anyone or accuse falsely, and be content with your wages' (Luke 3:11,13,14). Crowds flocked to be baptised in the River Jordan, 'confessing their sins' (Mark 1:5). The culmination of his address was often -

> I indeed baptise you with water unto repentance, but he who is coming after me is mightier than I, whose sandals I am not worthy to carry. He will baptise you with the Holy Spirit and fire' (Matthew 3:11).

Fire illuminates and fire cleanses. The Holy Spirit does both. Of Messiah it was prophesied -

> But who can endure the day of his coming? and who can stand when he appears? For he is like a refiner's fire and like launderers'

soap. He will sit as a refiner and a purifier of silver; he will purify the sons of Levi, and purge them as gold and silver, that they may offer to the LORD an offering in righteousness (Malachi 3:2-3).

9. The baptism of Jesus (Bethabara, Peraea)
Matthew 3:13-17; Mark 1:9-11; Luke 3:21-22

To this baptism of repentance for the removal of the penalty of sin, the thirty year old Jesus came to submit (Luke 3:23). No wonder John was surprised and dumbfounded. He was aware of the incongruence when he said to the Lord, 'I need to be baptised by you, and are you coming to me?' (Matthew 3:14) John attempted to prevent the baptism of Jesus on the grounds of his own unsuitability. This was not opposition but humility and great reluctance. He already knew so much about Jesus of Nazareth.

His father would have told him of his experience in the temple years before (Luke 1:5-22). His mother would have recounted the visit of Mary and his response in her womb (Luke 1:39-45). John would probably know by heart the prophecies of Mary and of his father (Luke 1:46-55; 68-79). They were crucial to his own life and service for God. Nevertheless it was the experience at the River Jordan, when the Holy Spirit anointed Jesus at his baptism, that confirmed to him the deity and sonship of Jesus of Nazareth. Later John bore witness, saying -

> I saw the Spirit descending from heaven like a dove, and he remained upon him. I did not know him, but he who sent me to baptise with water said to me, 'Upon whom you see the Spirit descending, and remaining on him, this is he who baptises with the Holy Spirit.' And I have seen and testified that this is the Son of God (John 1:32-34).

At first glance there seems no reason in the world for the Lord Jesus Christ to be baptised. He is unique. He is without sin. He 'was in all points tempted as we are, yet without sin' (Hebrews 4:15). He 'committed no sin, nor was deceit found in his mouth' (1 Peter 2:22; cf. 1 John 3:5; Hebrews 7:26). Jesus Christ, the Only Begotten Son of God, had no sin of which to repent. Why then should the Son of God submit to water baptism, this baptism of repentance for the remission of sins?

When John humbly protested, the Saviour simply replied, 'Permit now, for thus it is fitting for us to fulfil all righteousness' (Matthew 3:15). Jesus could not say, 'I have need to be baptised by you'. For thirty years he had been holy in thought, word and deed. No word had ever come from his mouth which either dishonoured God or degraded people. His whole life was perfect in its humanness: his childhood, boyhood, youth and manhood - spotless and undefiled before God and the world.

In his submission to John's water baptism, 'a baptism of repentance for the remission of sins' (Mark 1:4), the Lord Jesus was identifying with the people he came to save. Consequently our Lord gently sets aside John's protestation with the words, 'Permit now'. These words in their plainness and dignity would be enough to terminate further resistance or questioning.

Fulfilling all righteousness

'Permit now!' The Lord's moment had come. It was fitting. There is in this baptism something outstandingly unique. 'Permit now, for thus it is fitting for us to fulfil all righteousness.' He does not mean *his* righteousness but *our* righteousness, that is, the righteousness of those he represents, those who will turn to him, believe in him and put their whole trust in him - the ones who have been his since before the foundation of the world (Ephesians 1:4).

The Holy Spirit later revealed an ideal commentary on the Lord's words, 'to fulfil all righteousness'. In the letter to the Romans, it is written -

> For the law of the Spirit of life in Christ Jesus has made me free from the law of sin and death. For what the law could not do in that it was weak through the flesh, God did by sending his own Son in the likeness of sinful flesh, on account of sin; he condemned sin in the flesh, *that the righteous requirement of the law might be fulfilled in us* who do not walk according to the flesh but according to the Spirit (Romans 8:2-4, emphasis added).

Scripture presents many meanings to Christian baptism. Baptism in water dramatically symbolises: the washing away of sins (Acts 22:16); 'the answer of a good conscience toward God' (1 Peter 3:21); burial with Christ into death 'that just as Christ was raised from the dead by the glory of the Father, even so we also should walk in newness of life' (Romans 6:3-4).

The overriding significance of baptism which embraces all the above, is the sinner's *union with Christ*. 'For as many of you as were baptised into Christ have put on Christ' (Galatians 3:26-29). Our baptism unites us with Christ: a sinner to the sinless one. His baptism unites him with us: the sinless to the sinful. He denied himself and identified wholeheartedly and completely with his sinful people.

Here at the Jordan Jesus of Nazareth was beginning his Messianic ministry. He was now initiating the process which will inevitably lead to the cross. His baptism was a major step forward on the road to Calvary. He was going to do for us what we are powerless to do for ourselves. He was going to do for us what the law of God could not accomplish. He was going to do for us what the sacrificial system and the priesthood of the Old Testament could not achieve. Jesus, and only Jesus was going to fulfil all righteousness. He is 'The LORD our Righteous-ness' (Jeremiah 23:6; cf. 1 Corinthians 1:30).

The Lord anointed by the Holy Spirit

Inseparably joined to this unique baptism was the anointing of the Saviour; his official investiture as Messiah (Christ). Here he became the Anointed (Isaiah 11:2). 'God has made this Jesus ... both Lord and Christ' (Acts 2:36). Jesus begins his ministry. Now he can say -

> The Spirit of the Lord GOD is upon me, because the LORD has anointed me to preach good tidings to the poor; he has sent me to heal the brokenhearted, to proclaim liberty to the captives, and the opening of the prison to those who are bound; to proclaim the acceptable year of the LORD (Isaiah 61:1-2; cf. Luke 4:18-21).

At one and the same time as Jesus the Son of God was baptised in the River Jordan the Holy Spirit officially anointed him as the Christ of God and the Father warmly acknowledged him, 'You are my beloved Son, in whom I am well pleased' (Mark 1:11). This was the glorious concert of the Godhead, Father, Son and Holy Spirit! Immediately Jesus was driven by the Holy Spirit into the wilderness, among wild beasts, to be tempted by Satan (Mark 1:12-13).

10. The temptations of Jesus (wilderness)
Matthew 4:1-11; Mark 1:12-13; Luke 4:1-13

Following baptism, Jesus, now filled with the Holy Spirit, was driven by the Spirit into the wilderness to be tempted by the devil (Mark 1:12; Matthew 4:1). For nearly six weeks he fasted. Then, weakened by hunger, the Lord was confronted by Satan who challenged him to prove (to himself ?) that he was the Son of God by using his new powers: (i) to feed himself by a miracle; (ii) to gain the kingdoms of the world by yielding homage to God's enemy (implied, that is, to avoid the suffering of the cross); and (iii) to test the power and willingness of God to rescue Jesus from a reckless action - throwing himself down from the highest point of the temple (Luke 4:1-13).

In each case Jesus was resolute and rebutted every one of Satan's temptations with the Word of God from the Book of Deuteronomy. Satan failed in his attempt to appeal to 'the lust of the flesh, the lust of the eyes, and the pride of life' (1 John 2:16). Many years before, Eve the first woman of creation, had yielded to a similar trio of inducements. 'So when the woman saw that the tree was good for food [the lust of the flesh], that it was pleasant to the eyes [the lust of the eyes], and a tree desirable to make one wise [the pride of life], she took of its fruit and ate' (Genesis 3:6). Jesus did not yield. All his appetites and desires were holy and directed entirely to the service of God his Father. Whether he lived or died he would depend upon God alone and readily submit to his Word and will.

11. John the Baptist's testimony about Jesus
John 1:19-34

The activity of John the Baptist was attracting vast crowds which stirred the interest of the Jewish leadership in Jerusalem. John was not part of the religious establishment, he was not involved with either the Pharisees, the Sadducees or the Herodians. He was to them an outsider. It was right that they should investigate this man with his strange attire, forceful preaching and new ritual. They therefore sent a deputation of priests and Levites to examine him.

They asked first if he was the Christ. Messiah must be of the royal line of Judah through David (Genesis 49:10; 2 Samuel 7:12-14), but John was of the priestly line, the line of Levi and Aaron. There was no way in which John could be the Christ. The question was soon resolved and John confessed, and did not deny, but confessed, 'I am not the Christ' (John 1:20).

They then asked if he was Elijah, for there was a general expectation among the Jews at that time that Elijah would once more appear on earth based on the prophecy of Malachi 4:5-6 (Matthew 16:14). Whilst there were many similarities between the Baptist and Elijah the Tishbite in their clothing and ministry, John was not actually Elijah though Jesus would later say to three of his disciples, 'If you are willing to receive it, he is Elijah who is to come' (Matthew 11;14; cf. 17:10-13). John went before Christ 'in the spirit and power of Elijah' (Luke 1:17), because he came 'to make ready a people prepared for the Lord' as Elijah had done; in other words, he was the herald calling upon people to repent and prepare for the arrival of the Christ.

The enquiry continued, 'Are you *the* Prophet?' They were referring to the prophecy given to Moses -

> The LORD your God will raise up for you a Prophet like me from your midst, from your brethren. Him you shall hear... I will... put my words in his mouth, and he shall speak to them all that I command him (Deuteronomy 18:15,18).

John was not the promised prophet for this prophecy referred to the Messiah.

Pressed to disclose himself, John said: 'I am "The voice of one crying in the wilderness: 'Make straight the way of the LORD'"', as the prophet Isaiah said' (John 1:23; Isaiah 40:3). John urged the Jews, including his examiners, to *make straight* the Lord's highway that leads into their hearts. Genuine sorrow for sin and a prayer for mercy and pardon are required.

When this prophecy of Isaiah was first given to the people of Israel they were in a wretched state and God gave a word of great comfort for he had determined to be gracious, and to give them the full blessing of his salvation. The condition for salvation was repentance. John's task was to humble the people and make them aware of their spiritual condition as wretched, condemned sinners; as the wise man years before said, 'He who covers his sins will not prosper, but whoever confesses and forsakes them will have mercy' (Proverbs 28:13).

When further challenged about his practice of baptising John immediately linked his activity with the announcement of the Coming One saying, 'I baptise with water, but there stands One among you whom you do not know. It is he who, coming after me, is preferred before me, whose sandal strap I am not worthy to loose' (John 1:26-27). Arthur Pink observes -

> No ordinary man was John the Baptist. The subject of Old Testament prophecy, the son of a priest, born as a result of the direct intervention of God's power, filled with the Holy Spirit from his mother's womb, engaged in a ministry which drew great multitudes unto him, and yet he looked up to Christ as standing on a plane infinitely higher than the one he occupied, as a Being from another world, as One before him he was not worthy to stoop down and unloose His shoes.[4]

The day following, John saw Jesus coming towards him and said, 'Behold! The Lamb of God who takes away the sin of the world!' (John 1:29) It is clear that John the Baptist had a unique understanding of Old Testament prophecy about the Messiah (Christ). Taking the words of John together with the words of four of his disciples recorded in John 1:35-51, it is evident they knew that 'the Lamb of God who takes away the sin of the world' (v.29); was also 'the Son of God' (v.34); 'the Messiah' (v.41); 'him of whom Moses in the law, and also the prophets, wrote' (v.45); and 'the King of Israel' (v.49).

From the beginning of the promises of a deliverer (Genesis 3:15) the two great themes of the Old Testament in respect to Messiah, that of his suffering and success, a cross and a crown, were difficult for Old Testament saints to harmonise. The apostle Peter noted that even the prophets who were inspired by God, found it hard to understand. He wrote -

---

[4] Arthur W. Pink, *Expositions of the Gospel of John: three volumes unabridged in one* (Grand Rapids, Michigan: Zondervan, 1970), vol. 2, pp.56-7.

Of this salvation the prophets have inquired and searched carefully, who prophesied of the grace that would come to you, searching what, or what manner of time, the Spirit of Christ who was in them was indicating when he testified beforehand the sufferings of Christ and the glories that would follow' (1 Peter 1:10-11).

The answer is now revealed. Christ will have two advents, the first for suffering the second for glory.

12. The first disciples of Jesus
John 1:35-51

Five of John the Baptist's disciples, Andrew, Simon, Philip, Nathanael and the unnamed disciple, (most likely John the brother of James - John 1:37,40), left the Baptist and became disciples of Jesus. He was the One for whom they had been waiting. The Baptist had prepared them well. He was the Bridegroom's friend and knew that once he had introduced the Bridegroom to the bride his work was joyfully completed (John 3:29). John's disciples knew the great themes of the Old Testament in relation to the promised Messiah (Christ) - King, Prophet, Son of God, and many more.

The introduction of Nathanael to Jesus is highly instructive. Philip, also studying under John the Baptist, went to Nathanael and said, 'We have found him of whom Moses in the law, and also the prophets, wrote - Jesus of Nazareth, the son of Joseph'. Nathanael responded with the question, 'Can anything good come out of Nazareth?' (John 1:45-46) This is not to be understood as racial prejudice or town rivalry as some have supposed. This was the response of a young man immersed in the study of the Old Testament prophecies who knew that the Messiah must be born in Bethlehem (Micah 5:2). In other words he questioned whether *any good purpose of God* is connected with Nazareth. Philip did not answer the question but wisely said, 'Come and see'.

As Nathanael approached Jesus, the Lord said of him, 'Behold, an Israelite indeed, in whom is no deceit!' (John 1:47) By this the Master was declaring that Nathanael was a born again, believing, penitent man. 'An Israelite indeed' indicates a man who was not only an Israelite according to the flesh but also an Israelite according to the Spirit (Romans 9:6-8; Galatians 4:28-29). The clear implication in the words of our Saviour is that Nathanael was a truly converted man! This is further confirmed by the next words spoken by Jesus, 'in whom is no deceit!' King David declared -

> Blessed is he whose transgression is forgiven, whose sin is
> covered. Blessed is the man to whom the LORD does not impute
> iniquity, and in whose spirit there is no deceit (Psalm 32:1-2).

Here is 'the Lord' Jesus crediting no deceit in the spirit of Nathanael
therefore indicating his true spiritual state. Also in the conversation with
Nathanael, Jesus identified himself with Jacob's ladder joining earth to
heaven (John 1:51; Genesis 28:12) indicating its true interpretation, as Paul
expressed it, 'For there is one God and one Mediator between God and men,
the Man Christ Jesus' (1 Timothy 2:5; cf. John 14:6).

So the first disciples of Jesus: Andrew, Simon, Philip, Nathanael and
John (?); well-taught as disciples of John the Baptist, turned to a new
Mentor, the Lord Jesus Christ. Faithful to the end, John the Baptist lived his
testimony: 'He must increase, but I must decrease' (John 3:30).

13. The first miracle: water to wine (Cana of Galilee)
John 2:1-12

Jesus and those early disciples were invited to a wedding so they travelled
north from Judah to Galilee and the city of Cana. Here Jesus was to perform
his first miracle. Whilst many miracles of Jesus were recorded by Matthew,
Mark and Luke, John records only eight. These were carefully chosen from
the hundreds of miracles that John personally witnessed during the three year
ministry of Jesus. John's purpose was specific, the eight miracles were
chosen for their spiritual significance, for each contained a profound
message -

> And truly Jesus did many other signs in the presence of his
> disciples, which are not written in this book; but these are written
> that you may believe that Jesus is the Christ, the Son of God, and
> that believing you may have life in his name (John 20:30-31).

The word translated 'sign' (John 2:11) denotes a miracle performed in the
physical realm which teaches or illustrates truth in the spiritual realm. It is a
miracle with a message. Furthermore these miracles were recorded by John
for an evangelistic purpose.

During the wedding celebrations the mother of Jesus came to him to say
that the wine had run out. She then sent servants to him with instructions to
follow everything he said. They were told to fill the six very large water jugs
with water and then draw from them and take it to the master of ceremonies
for him to taste. The water had been changed into top quality wine.

The spiritual significance of this miracle of changing water into wine is
not hard to find. There is the significance of the timing, for John noted, 'the
Passover of the Jews was at hand' (John 2:13). Later he would note the

timing of another miracle, that of the feeding of the five thousand with its multiplicity of bread, which took place near the time of the following annual Passover (John 6:4). Jesus showed the significance of bread and wine when he instituted the Lord's Supper at another Passover, his final Passover -

> Jesus took bread, blessed and broke it, and gave it to the disciples and said, 'Take, eat; this is my body'. Then he took the cup, and gave thanks, and gave it to them, saying, 'Drink from it, all of you. For this is my blood of the new covenant, which is shed for many for the remission of sins' (Matthew 26:26-28).

The timing, it is the Passover - Jesus is the Passover Lamb (1 Corinthians 5:7) who saves his people by his self-sacrifice.

Then there were the water jars: 'six waterpots of stone, according to the manner of purification of the Jews, containing twenty or thirty gallons apiece' [91-136 litres] (John 2:6). Water was needed for a number of reasons: for washing the feet of guests as they arrived (the roads were dirty and people wore sandals); for washing hands in a special ceremonial manner before eating and often between courses (Mark 7:3-4) and for washing vessels (Matthew 23:25-26). A strict Jewish home had to provide plenty of water.

Jesus gave instructions that the six jars were to be filled to the brim producing a quantity somewhere between 550-800 litres. This he turned miraculously into wine. Why did John note the number of the stone jars being six? It was because he perceived that Jesus was providing a vivid living parable.

The water symbolised all the purification ceremonies of the Old Covenant which, though they could wash feet, hands and utensils, they could do nothing for the soul. Seven is the number of completion or wholeness (Revelation 1:20; 2:1; 3:1; 4:5; cf. Isaiah 11:2). Six is the number here signifying the incomplete and ineffectiveness of the Old Covenant rituals and sacrifices to wash away sin (Hebrews 10:1-4). The only effective and everlasting means of cleansing is the blood of Jesus Christ our Saviour both for Old Testament believers as well as New Testament believers. For of the saints of the Old Covenant it is written, 'all these, having obtained a good testimony through faith, did not receive the promise, God having provided something better for us, that they should not be made perfect apart from us' (Hebrews 11:39-40).

The words of the master of ceremonies summed up the relationship of the Old and New Covenants when he said, 'You have kept the good wine until now!' (John 2:10). The imperfect is replaced by the perfect. The good wine is the best wine and denotes 'the precious blood of Christ, as of a lamb without blemish and without spot' (1 Peter 1:19). 'For indeed Christ, our Passover, was sacrificed for us' (1 Corinthians 5:7).

> To him who loved us and washed us from our sins in his own blood, and has made us kings and priests to his God and Father, to him be glory and dominion forever and ever. Amen (Revelation 1:5-6).

The early Judean ministry

14. First cleansing of the temple (Jerusalem)
John 2:13-25

After the wedding at Cana Jesus, his mother, his half-brothers (James, Joses, Jude and Simon) and his disciples spent a few days in Capernaum and then went down to Jerusalem for the Passover. On entering the temple Jesus was greatly distressed by what confronted him. The house of God was being abused. The court of the Gentiles had been turned into a cattle market and trading yard.

The temple was divided into various courts, each one inside another. The first court was for Gentile proselytes, the second was the court of the women, followed by the court of the Israelites, then the court of the priests, and finally, in the centre, the Holy of Holies where the high priest entered just once a year. The outer court, the Court of the Gentiles, was the only area where a non-Jew might enter and worship. The Jewish authorities and the Jewish traders were making this court a place of uproar, stench, argument and trade. How could a person pray in such an environment?

A visit to the temple often required the taking of a sacrifice. Many of the pilgrims would desire to thank God for his kindness and goodness. Alternatively they might need to bring a sacrifice for sin. According to the law such sacrifices had to be without blemish. Devout Jews travelling some miles would obviously prefer to obtain their animals in Jerusalem but most of the animals and birds bought outside the temple were rejected by the priests.

Everything was under the control of the high priest and his family; the priests, who inspected the offerings, and the temple authorities, who provided carefully reared animals and birds that met the requirements of the law. However the cost of the livestock and birds within the temple was exorbitant. In addition to that a significant fee had to be paid for the inspection to take place. Consequently many poor and humble folk coming to worship God and obey his commandments were being forced into buying sacrifices at grossly inflated prices. No wonder the Lord was so angry.

Every male Israelite, over the age of nineteen, was required to pay one half-shekel each year for the support of the temple services (Exodus 30:11-13). The temple tax was set at one half-shekel which was roughly equivalent to two days' wages for the average working man. This was due during the month preceding the Passover and was either sent in by those who lived at a distance or paid in person by those who attended the festival. The tax had to be paid in either Galilean shekels or shekels of the sanctuary. These were Jewish coins and could be used as a gift to the temple. Gentile money could not be used at the temple because of the graven images on it.

For all ordinary purposes throughout Israel all kinds of foreign currencies were valid. Silver coins from Rome, Greece, Egypt, Tyre and Sidon, and Israel itself, all circulated and were legal tender but they were considered polluted and unclean, unsuitable as gifts in the temple, therefore they needed to be changed.

Visitors and pilgrims arrived from all over the world; Jerusalem would be packed with Jews who had come to celebrate the Passover, perhaps numbering as many as 300,000 to 400,000. Provision for the change of currency was needed for those who came from foreign parts. So moneychangers sat in the court of the Gentiles in the temple of God. They were notorious for charging grossly inflated rates for their services (It is understood that they added 14% for every half-shekel they changed. If a pilgrim brought a two shekel coin to change they charged 14% on the whole coin). These money-changers sat at small tables, on which their coins were piled and counted.

Consumed with zeal for the honour of God's house (Psalm 69:9) Jesus made a whip of ropes and drove out traders and animals, upturning the tables and scattering the carefully piled coins. Though Jesus courageously cleared the court with a cracking swirling whip, he did not destroy any property. The sheep and oxen would be rounded up by their keepers, the scattered money would be gathered up, and the doves were still in their cages. He said to those who sold doves, 'Take these things away! Do not make my Father's house a house of merchandise!' (John 2:16) The rebuke of Jesus was addressed foremost at the priests, since the market belonged to them and the moneychangers were their agents. Malachi prophesied -

> The Lord whom you seek, will suddenly come to his temple... But who can endure the day of his coming? And who can stand when he appears? For he is like a refiner's fire and like launderers' soap... He will purify the sons of Levi, and purge them as gold and silver, that they may offer to the LORD an offering in righteousness (Malachi 3:1-3).

The Jews asked Jesus for a sign to show by what authority he behaved so outrageously. Jesus answered and said to them, 'Destroy this temple, and in three days I will raise it up' (John 2:19). Understandably they thought he was referring to the stone temple in which they stood. Even the disciples did not, at that time, grasp the meaning of the Lord's words.

Jesus was speaking of himself as a temple. Though greatly misunderstood, this was an amazing revelation linking many Old Testament prophecies (e.g. Zechariah 6:12-13[5]; Ezekiel 47:1-12; Haggai 2:7,9) and later developed by the apostles (1 Corinthians 3:16; 6:19-20; 1 Peter 2:4-5).

God had promised to fill this second temple (built at the return of the Babylonian exiles) with glory which surpassed the glory of the first temple (destroyed by King Nebuchadnezzar). He would 'shake all nations' and they would 'come to the Desire of All Nations'.

The glory of the first temple was one of unsurpassed beauty in design, presentation and furnishings. No expense had been spared in its construction. The second temple could not be compared to it for its physical proportions, design and structure. How then could its glory be greater than the former? There could only be one answer, a profoundly spiritual answer, its glory was the presence within it of the Son of God, the Saviour of the world. Jesus is the incomparable glory and also the promised, 'Desire of All Nations' (Haggai 2:6,7,9; cf. Malachi 3:1).

Jesus remained in Jerusalem throughout the Feast of the Passover. During those days, 'many believed in his name when they saw the [miraculous] signs which he did. But Jesus did not commit himself to them, because he knew all men, and had no need that anyone should testify of man, for he knew what was in man' (John 2:23-25).

The Lord has perfect knowledge of the human heart. He can recognise stony ground where there is immediate response that is only temporary, as many of these people proved to be. This is he, said Jesus later in the parable of The Sower, 'who hears the word and immediately receives it with joy; yet he has no root in himself, but endures only for a while. For when tribulation or persecution arises because of the word, immediately he stumbles' (Matthew 13:20-21).

He knows also the heart that responds well in the beginning but 'the cares of this world and the deceitfulness of riches choke the word, and he becomes unfruitful' (Matthew 13:22; cf. 7:21; John 6:66).

---

[5] Note: 'He shall build *the* temple *of* the LORD' not *a* temple *to* the Lord, for Christ will build the ultimate temple of saved humanity, Jew and Gentile (cf. 1 Corinthians 3:16; 1 Peter 2:4-5).

15. Conversation with Nicodemus
John 3:1-21

Whilst in Jerusalem, the Lord received a visitor, Nicodemus the Pharisee, a member of the Sanhedrin[6] (the ruling council of seventy, who under the oversight of Rome, exercised limited authority over the people of Israel). He had seen or heard of the miraculous signs that Jesus performed in Jerusalem and seemed convinced that no one could do the signs that he did 'unless God is with him' (John 3:2).

Jesus spoke plainly and directly to him, 'Most assuredly, I say to you, unless one is born again, he cannot see the kingdom of God' (John 3:3). The basis of all righteousness for Nicodemus and all his hope was shattered in this one terrific sentence.

The doctrines of the Pharisees[7] were built upon a false view of human nature and human righteousness. They supposed that with effort any human being could earn God's favour and be accepted into his kingdom. They relied upon a self-made holiness. Jesus put his finger on the fundamental flaw in the thinking of the Pharisees. A radical change must take place in the individual and that change must be brought about by God alone! 'Most assuredly, I say to you, unless one is born again, he cannot see the kingdom of God' (John 3:3).

Nicodemus thought only in physical terms viewing new birth as utterly impossible. Jesus challenged this professor of theology on his lack of understanding, 'Are you the teacher of Israel, and do not know these things?' (John 3:10)

As a theologian and tutor of Pharisees on the content and application of the Old Testament Scriptures he should know about spiritual rebirth. Jesus was making a reference to the Old Testament vision of the valley of dry bones when he said, 'The wind blows where it wishes, and you hear the sound of it, but cannot tell where it comes from and where it goes. So is everyone who is born of the Spirit' (John 3:8; cf. Ezekiel 37:1-10; Psalm 87:4-6).

Ezekiel 47 also teaches the new birth. In this vision the Dead Sea, where nothing could live, is fed by water flowing from the altar of the temple high up the mountain.

> This water flows toward the eastern region, goes down into the valley, and enters the [dead] sea. When it reaches the [dead] sea,

---

[6] See 'Sanhedrin' in the chapter on Significant facts, p.343

[7] See 'Pharisees' in the chapter on Significant facts, p.336

> its waters are healed. And it shall be that every living thing that
> moves, wherever the rivers go, will live (Ezekiel 47:8-9).

In this vision the new birth is connected with the death of Jesus and the
spiritual life which flows from the Saviour at Calvary for it is living water
from the altar in the temple which brings life.

Having shown the fundamental requirement of the new birth Jesus then
identified himself to Nicodemus when he said, 'No one has ascended to
heaven but he who came down from heaven, that is, the Son of Man who is
in heaven' (John 3:13). Jesus was using his favourite designation for himself
when he spoke of 'the Son of Man' (Matthew 16:13). He was also making a
clear connection to his deity for the words ascending to heaven and
descending from heaven would resonate with Nicodemus and bring to mind
the words of a proverb -

> Who has ascended into heaven, or descended? Who has gathered
> the wind in his fists? Who has bound the waters in a garment?
> Who has established all the ends of the earth? What is his name,
> *and what is his Son's name*, if you know? (Proverbs 30:4;
> emphasis added)

Jesus is the Son of Man and the Son of God. Here is revealed the divine
mystery of the two natures of Jesus - having 'the form of God' and taking
'the form of a bondservant' (Philippians 2:6,7). This is the One who has
ready access to heaven because he came from heaven.

The Lord then introduced the incident of the bronze serpent in the
wilderness which occurred nearly fifteen hundred years earlier.

After thirty years wandering in the wilderness the children of Israel were
at last heading for their new home. A further setback brought great
discouragement. There was once more a serious lack of food and water. The
people complained and spoke against God and Moses. God punished them
with an influx of fiery serpents (poisonous snakes) into their camp. Many
were bitten, many died.

Eventually the people understood the reason behind this calamity, they
repented and confessed their sin to Moses. He prayed for them and the Lord
gave the remedy for the poisonous bites. A bronze snake was to be made,
fastened to a wooden pole and erected in the camp. Anyone who was bitten
should look at that snake and they would be healed (Numbers 21:4-9).

The gospel was clearly being set forth in this Old Testament event: sin,
judgment, repentance and faith resulting in healing (salvation). Jesus linked
this incident with the significance of his own death -

> And as Moses lifted up the serpent in the wilderness, even so must
> the Son of Man be lifted up, that whoever believes in him should

not perish but have eternal life. For God so loved the world that he gave his only begotten Son, that whoever believes in him should not perish but have everlasting life. For God did not send his Son into the world to condemn the world, but that the world through him might be saved (John 3:14-17).

The linking of the Saviour with a serpent is at first sight a detestable thought for the serpent is strongly associated with Satan and all that is opposed to God (Genesis 3:14-15; Revelation 12:9,14; 20:2). Nevertheless this reveals an extraordinarily powerful message about the cross of Christ: 'For he [God the Father] made him [God's Beloved Son] who knew no sin *to be sin for us*, that we might become the righteousness of God in him' (2 Corinthians 5:21; emphasis added).

This is the very apex of the mission of Jesus the Christ. The Lord Jesus took responsibility for all the sin of all his people for 'the LORD has laid on him the iniquity of us all' (Isaiah 53:6).

Jesus concluded his conversation with Nicodemus by pointing out the root cause of unbelief. It is not a lack of evidence about the Lord nor failure to understand the message of the gospel, it is the love of darkness, the love of sin. Unbelief is a refusal to acknowledge personal guilt before God and an unwillingness to change thought and behaviour.

16. John the Baptist's final testimony
John 3:22-36

'After these things' (John 3:22) - that is, after the Passover week and the conversation with Nicodemus, Jesus went out into the country. He moved to the rural area of Judea. The disciples with him would be the first five disciples Andrew, Simon Peter, Philip, Nathanael Bartholomew and the unnamed disciple, most likely John. Jesus 'remained with them and baptised' (John 3:22), though he did not personally conduct any water baptisms (John 4:2). Meanwhile John the Baptist had moved several miles further north and was 'baptising in Aenon near Salim, because there was much water there' (John 3:23). John Calvin comments -

> From these words we may infer that John and Christ administered Baptism by total immersion, though we must not worry overmuch about the outward rite so long as it accords with the spiritual truth and the Lord's institution and rule.[8]

---

8 John Calvin, *The Gospel According to St John 1-10* (Saint Andrew Press: Edinburgh, 1959), p.78.

'John had not yet been thrown into prison' (John 3:24) indicates that the ministry of the Lord Jesus and that of John the Baptist overlapped by some months.

The disciples of John approached their mentor and complained that Jesus was engaged in baptising and the people were gathering to him rather than to John. Why were these men still disciples of John? Had not the Baptist made his position abundantly clear when he said, 'You yourselves bear me witness, that I said, "I am not the Christ", but, I have been sent before him' (John 3:28). Had he not urged their attention towards Jesus when he said -

> Behold! The Lamb of God who takes away the sin of the world! This is he of whom I said, 'After me comes a man who is preferred before me, for he was before me'. I did not know him; but that he should be revealed to Israel, therefore I came baptising with water (John 1:29-31).

These disciples of John the Baptist were clinging to John with a misplaced sense of loyalty. They were not in fact pleasing John! Far from it! Any loyalty which interferes with becoming a disciple of Jesus Christ is to be abandoned.

John explained his relationship to the Lord Jesus; he spoke of himself as the friend of the bridegroom. The friend of the bridegroom (the *shoshben*), had a unique place at a Jewish wedding. He acted as the liaison between the bride and the bridegroom and it was his duty to guard the bridal chamber and to let no false-lover in. He would only open the door when in the dark he heard the bridegroom's voice and recognised it. When he heard the bridegroom's voice he was glad and let him in, and *he went away rejoicing*, for his task was completed. When that task was done he willingly and gladly faded out of the picture.

Rather than being distressed by the increasing popularity of Jesus, John was delighted. His whole ministry was summed up when he said of the Lord, 'He must increase, but I must decrease' (John 3:30). John had achieved his goal to introduce the Messiah (Christ) to Israel and the Israelites to their Messiah (Christ).

What are some of the lessons to be learned from this outstanding man of God, John the Baptist? One lesson is to recognise and accept our God-appointed task or ministry (1 Corinthians 12:4-7,12-26). It would save us a lot of resentment and heartbreak if we realised that there are certain things which are not for us, and if we accepted with all our hearts, and did with all our might, the work that God has given us to do.

Secondly we must learn how to rejoice at other people's success (Romans 12:15). If God is pleased to give to others more ability and more favourable outcome than to us, shall we be displeased and reflect upon him as unjust, unwise, or partial? Thirdly, we must be reliable and determined to function to our utmost ability in the sphere of God's appointing.

Not long afterwards Herod Antipas arrested and imprisoned John because the Baptist had rebuked him for taking Herodias, his brother Philip's wife saying plainly, 'It is not lawful for you to have her' (Matthew 14:3,4). Herod Antipas held mixed feelings about John the Baptist. On the one hand 'although he wanted to put him to death, he feared the multitude, because they counted him as a prophet' (Matthew 14:5; Leviticus 18:16). At the same time -

> Herod feared John, knowing that he *was* a just and holy man, and he protected him. And when he heard him, he did many things, and heard him gladly (Mark 6:20).

Herod Antipas and Herodias

Herod the tetrarch [ruler of one fourth of the country] is Herod Antipas. On the death of his father, Herod the Great, he became ruler of Galilee and Peraea (the land stretching on the east from about one third of the way down the River Jordan between the Sea of Galilee and the Dead Sea to about halfway down the Dead Sea). It was Herod Antipas whom Jesus called a 'fox' (Luke 13:31-32) and it was to him that Jesus was sent by Pilate for trial (Luke 23:6-7).

> [He] had sent and laid hold of John, and bound him in prison for the sake of Herodias, his brother Philip's wife; for he had married her. For John had said to Herod, "It is not lawful for you to have your brother's wife". Therefore Herodias held it against him and wanted to kill him, but she could not; for Herod feared John, knowing that he was a just and holy man, and he protected him (Mark 6:17-20).

> Herod the tetrarch, being rebuked by him concerning Herodias, his brother Philip's wife, and for all the evils which Herod had done, also added this, above all, that he shut John up in prison (Luke 3:19-20).

Herodias was the daughter of Aristobulus, who was a son of Herod the Great by Mariamne I. Herodias had married her father's half-brother Herod Philip I, a private citizen, son of Herod the Great by Mariamne II. (Herod Philip must not be confused with his half-brother Philip the tetrarch, Herod Philip II).

> Herod Antipas on a visit to his half-brother Herod Philip, became infatuated with Herodias. The two illicit lovers left their marriage partners - Herodias left Herod Philip; Herod Antipas left his wife, the daughter of Aretas, king of the Nabatean Arabs. When John the Baptist heard about this he rebuked Herod Antipas because such a marriage between him and Herodias was incestuous (Leviticus 18:16; 20:21) and also adulterous (Romans 7:2-3).
>
> Herod's marriage to Herodias brought him nothing but trouble. He was defeated in battle by the Arabian king Aretas, father of his discarded and lawful wife and it was through the ambition of Herodias that Herod Antipas was finally deprived of his dominions and sent into exile.

17. The woman of Samaria (near Sychar)
John 4:1-42

The Lord Jesus 'left Judea and departed again to Galilee. But he needed to go through Samaria. So he came to a city of Samaria which is called Sychar' (John 4:3-5). It is interesting to note that Jews were in the practice of avoiding walking on Samaritan soil. They would extend their journey by going to the east over the River Jordan, proceeding up the east bank of the Jordan to re-cross the river higher when they could step into Galilee.

Therefore there was no literal 'need' for Jesus to go through Samaria as there was an alternative route favoured by the Jews. No doubt the simple explanation for that 'need' was in the mind and heart of the Lord Jesus. He 'needed' to go through Samaria because he planned to meet a woman from the city of Sychar, although she did not know it. The Lord has insights and abilities which were obviously greater than any other (Matthew 9:4; 12:25; Luke 5:22; 6:8; John 1:48; 2:24-25)

A contrast is presented between Nicodemus of Judea and the woman of Samaria: in race, religion, gender, social standing and morality. No doubt, in recording the two incidents, the Holy Spirit designed to show how anyone may be saved by an encounter with Jesus Christ. In his Church 'there is neither Jew nor Greek, there is neither slave nor free, there is neither male nor female; for you are all one in Christ Jesus' (Galatians 3:28; cf. Colossians 3:11).

A brief history of the Samaritans

Following the death of Solomon (931 B.C.) it was not long before the twelve tribes which composed the nation of Israel experienced civil war.

Jeroboam, one of Solomon's key leaders, a mighty man of valour and also highly industrious (1 Kings 11:28), rebelled against Solomon and fled to Egypt. When he heard of King Solomon's death and the coronation of his son Rehoboam, he returned to Israel and became a significant leader amongst the people. Jeroboam led a delegation of Israelites who visited the new king and asked for a lifting of the heavy burdens which King Solomon had imposed on the people. They assured King Rehoboam that, if he would just slacken the demands, they would willingly serve him (1 Kings 12:4).

But Solomon's son, Rehoboam, was an arrogant young man. He listened more to the young men who had grown up with him rather than to the elders who had been in close consultation with his father Solomon (1 Kings 12:6-8). The result was that Rehoboam made even heavier demands and, consequently, stirred up a rebellion among the general populace.

The kingdom of Israel split in two in 930 B.C. Rehoboam reigned as king of Judah, the small southern kingdom of the two tribes, Judah and Benjamin, whilst Jeroboam reigned as king of Israel, the northern kingdom of the remaining ten tribes.

Jeroboam was concerned to break all ties with the southern kingdom. To put an end to the religious commitment to Jerusalem, its sacrifices and its priests, he introduced a corrupted alternative place of worship and a blasphemous form of idolatry. A golden calf was erected at Bethel and at Dan, and King Jeroboam said, 'It is too much for you to go up to Jerusalem. Here are your gods, O Israel, which brought you up from the land of Egypt!' (1 Kings 12:28)

Jeroboam made shrines on the high places and appointed a priesthood from all the tribes of Israel, in violation of the law of God that priests were to come only from the tribe of Levi. He instituted sacrifices and feast days to match those that were celebrated at Jerusalem.

Two hundred years later, in 723 B.C. the Assyrians conquered the northern kingdom of Israel. The majority of the people were taken into captivity. Esarhaddon King of Assyria brought people from the five nations of Babylon, Cuthah, Ava, Hamath and

Sepharvaim (2 Kings 17:24) to inhabit the northern kingdom. They brought their own pagan religious practices with them and amalgamated them with a corrupted form of the worship of Jehovah (2 Kings 17:41).

These 'five nations each had its peculiar divinity, or, according to the ancient language of the East, its husband'.[9] This region became known as Samaria.

After the return of the Babylonian exiles into Judea, the Samaritans were described as 'the adversaries of Judah and Benjamin' (Ezra 4:1). Nehemiah recorded the separation from Israel of 'all the mixed multitude' (Nehemiah 13:3).

The building of a temple on Mount Gerizim in Samaria after the rebuilding of the Jerusalem temple illustrated the rivalry between the two peoples.

It is interesting to note the life circumstances of the woman of Samaria whom the Lord met outside the city of Sychar. Firstly there is significance in the woman's marital state. Hengstenberg notes -

> She had had five husbands; and he whom she now had was not her husband, not having deigned to connect himself with her in marriage. So with the nation. It had previously been in fivefold spiritual marriage with its idols, and this marriage had been dissolved as frivolously as it had been concluded. The people sued for marriage with Jehovah, but this was denied them, because they did not belong to Israel.'[10]

Secondly we note that she had assimilated the prevalent religious outlook in Samaria for she said, 'Sir, I perceive that you are a prophet. Our fathers worshipped on this mountain, and you Jews say that in Jerusalem is the place where one ought to worship' (John 4:19-20).

> 'The Samaritans adjusted history to suit themselves... They taught that it was on Mount Gerizim that Abraham had been willing to sacrifice Isaac; they... declared that it was on Mount Gerizim that Moses had first erected an altar and sacrificed to God when the people entered the promised land, when in fact it was on Mount Ebal that that was done (Deuteronomy 27:4). They tampered with

---

9   Charles D. Alexander, *The Gospel of John Spiritually Understood, part 5*, self-published, p.31; cf. Ernest W. Hengstenberg, *Commentary on the Gospel of St John* [1865] (Minneapolis, Minnesota: Klock and Klock, 1980), vol. 1, p.229.

10 Ernest W. Hengstenberg, *Commentary on the Gospel of St John* (Minneapolis, Minnesota: Klock and Klock, 1980), vol. 1, p.230.

the text of Scripture and with history to glorify Mount Gerizim. The woman had been brought up to regard Mount Gerizim as the most sacred spot in the world and to despise Jerusalem.'[11]

The Samaritans were taught that only the books of Moses (the first five books of the Old Testament) were the Word of God, the other books were to be rejected. How amazing, with such little information,[12] for her yet to declare, 'I know that Messiah is coming... When he comes, he will tell us all things' (John 4:25).

She was waiting for the Messiah. She knew that those things which she could not then understand and grasp would be made plain by Messiah. She believed that everything to do with her religious longing would be satisfied by Messiah when he comes. Perhaps she hoped, she expected and she desired that Messiah would come, and come soon in her lifetime. Jesus responded to her faith and her longing in a most remarkable way - with full self-disclosure: 'I who speak to you am he' (John 4:26). Messiah always reveals himself to those who long for him and seek after him (Jeremiah 29:11-14).

Jesus initiated conversation with the woman of Samaria about earthly concerns in order to lead on to the deeper pressing issues of heavenly concerns. He presented an excellent example of personal evangelism. Beginning with the earthly concern, progressing to the thirst-quenching water of spiritual life that he was able to provide, exposing the character of her past life, declaring the major changes in religious observance, describing true worship, revealing and highlighting the spiritual character of God, he concluded with his self-disclosure as the promised Messiah (John 4:10-26).

The disciples returned and were surprised that Jesus was speaking to a woman. They did not question Jesus but urged him to eat the food they had brought. He used the opportunity to turn their attention upon spiritual issues for there is a more satisfying food to share - the gospel for the salvation of sinners. They are to look for a spiritual harvest as they sow and reap for eternal life.

Meanwhile the woman testified of her encounter with Jesus. Men listened and their interest was awakened. They invited Jesus to stay in the city and talk with them further. A good spiritual harvest was gathered there at Sychar as they discovered: 'This is indeed the Christ, the Saviour of the world' (John 4:42).

---

[11] William Barclay, *The Gospel of John*, volume one (Edinburgh: Saint Andrew Press, 1955), p.150.

[12] Genesis 3:15; 12:2-3; 49:10; Deuteronomy 18:18-19

The great Galilean ministry

Galilee

In the days of Jesus Israel was divided into two - Judah in the south and Galilee in the north. Between the two was the country of Samaria. Galilee was on the west side of the Sea of Galilee[13] and was about 80km (50 miles) from north to south and 40km (25 miles) from east to west, broader to the north and narrower to the south. The Galilee region included towns such as Capernaum, Magdala, and Chorazin. The Galilee region was also home to the town Tiberias, which was built by Herod Antipas on the shoreline just over 32km (20 miles) south of Capernaum. It was named by Herod Antipas after the Roman Emperor Tiberias Caesar Augustus ruler at the time.

The people were greatly influenced by the surrounding nations. Josephus,[14] who was himself at one time governor of the area, recorded that it had 204 villages or towns, none with a population less than 15,000. It seems incredible that there could be about 3,000,000 people inhabiting Galilee. It was a land of extraordinary fertility. There was a proverb which said that, 'It is easier to raise a legion of olive trees in Galilee than to bring up one child in Judaea'. The wonderful climate and the superb water supply made it the garden of Israel. The very list of trees which grew there shows how amazingly fertile it was - vines, olives, figs, oaks, walnuts, terebinth, palms, cedars, cypress, balsam, firs, pines, sycamores, bay trees, myrtles, almonds, pomegranates and citrons.[15]

Alexander the Great conquered Israel in 332 B.C. His people, the Greeks, greatly influenced the nations which came under their control: in language, religion, morality, philosophy and government. The culture of Greece was known as 'Hellenism'.

In 63 B.C. the Romans conquered Judaea, incorporating the nation into the Roman Republic. Herod the Great (37 - 4 B.C.) was appointed governor of Galilee (47 B.C.) and ten years later he was given authority to rule as King.

---

[13] Also called Lake of Gennesaret (Luke 5:1) and Sea of Tiberias (John 21:1)

[14] Flavius Josephus a Jewish Roman historian (A.D. 37-100) was born in Jerusalem to a father of priestly descent and a mother who claimed royal ancestry. Josephus wrote *The Antiquities of the Jews* c. A.D. 93-94.

[15] William Barclay, *The Gospel of Luke* (Edinburgh: Saint Andrew Press, 1961), pp.40-41.

At the time of our Lord's ministry Galilee was ruled by Herod the Great's son Herod Antipas, the Tetrarch[16] of Galilee and Perea. Tiberias became the new capital city of the Galilee region and the place from which Herod Antipas exercised government. Religious Jews avoided Tiberias during the time of Jesus, since it was built on top of a cemetery. This made it 'unclean' under Jewish law.

Galilee was a mixed community: Jews who were religious and orthodox, together with Jews who largely accepted the Hellenised Roman culture and the Greek manner of life, and Gentiles.

Jews tried to live apart from the Gentiles whom they regarded as interlopers and corrupt. Similarly the Jews of Galilee were looked down upon by the Jews of Judaea. 'Galilee was to Judaism 'the court of the Gentiles'… The natural disposition of the people, even the soil and climate of Galilee, were not favourable to the all-engrossing passion for Rabbinic studies. In Judaea all seemed to invite to retrospection and introspection; to favour habits of solitary thought and study, till it kindled into fanaticism.'[17]

This 'Galilee of the Gentiles' (Isaiah 9:1) was in spiritual gloom and distress but it was the earthly home of 'the light of the world' (John 8:12; Matthew 4:15-16).

18. Jesus begins to preach in Galilee
Matthew 4:12,17; Mark 1:14-15; Luke 4:14-15; John 4:43-45

Having passed through Samaria Jesus arrived in Galilee, 'preaching the gospel of the kingdom of God, and saying, "The time is fulfilled, and the kingdom of God is at hand. Repent, and believe in the gospel"' (Mark 1:14-15). John the Baptist had preached 'a baptism of repentance for the remission of sins' (Luke 3:3) as a preparation for the Lord. Now that the Messiah had come the full declaration was made, 'Repent, and believe in the gospel'.

The gospel is the good news concerning 'God's Son Jesus Christ our Lord… It is the power of God to salvation for everyone who believes… For in it the righteousness of God is revealed' (Romans 1:1-4,16-17).

---

[16] A Tetrarch (in the Roman Empire) was the governor of one of four divisions of a country.

[17] Alfred Edersheim, *The Life and Times of Jesus the Messiah* (Peabody, Massachusetts: Hendrikson, 1993), p.155.

Having been anointed by the Holy Spirit at his baptism, Jesus had now 'returned in the power of the Spirit to Galilee, and news of him went out through all the surrounding region. And he taught in their synagogues, being glorified by all' (Luke 4:14-15). He was given a warm welcome for 'the Galileans received him, having seen all the things he did in Jerusalem at the feast; for they also had gone to the feast' (John 4:45).

Just how long Jesus spent travelling around and preaching in the Galilean synagogues is not recorded. During his itinerancy, however, he returned to where he had turned the water into wine at Cana just 6.5km (4 miles) from his home in Nazareth. Here he was addressed by a nobleman (an officer in the royal court, probably belonging to Herod's court) whose son was sick at Capernaum. The man pleaded with Jesus to travel to Capernaum and heal his dying son. Wonderfully Jesus healed him at a distance from where he was in Cana.

This miracle is strongly linked to the first miracle (John 2:1 with 4:46 and John 2:11 with 4:54). Bearing in mind the reason given by John for including only eight miracles of Jesus in his Gospel record (John 20:30-31) we might well form certain conclusions. The miracle of an abundance of God-given wine links with Calvary and the 'blood of the new covenant, which is shed for many for the remission of sins' (Matthew 26:28). This second miracle illustrates the need for faith in the ability of the Lord - faith alone in Christ alone for salvation without his physical presence.

Jesus knew that his greatest difficulty would be encountered at Nazareth. It was therefore wise for him to build a reputation throughout Galilee to counteract the prejudice he would face from his own townsfolk. After spending some time itinerating around the region, he then determined to visit his hometown.

19. Jesus rejected in Nazareth
Matthew 13:54-58; Mark 6:1-6; Luke 4:16-30

Nazareth stood about 19km (12 miles) southwest of the Sea of Galilee in a small hollow in the hills on the lower slopes of Galilee near the Plain of Jezreel. The land was very fertile. From the hilltop above the town an amazing panorama could be seen for miles around. The history of Israel could be traced in that landscape.

There was the Plain of Esdraelon where Deborah and Barak had fought; where Gideon had won his victories; where Saul had crashed to disaster and where Josiah had been killed in battle. There was Naboth's vineyard and the place where Jehu slaughtered Jezebel; there was Shunem where Elisha had lived; there was Carmel where Elijah had fought his epic battle with the prophets of Baal; and blue in the distance there was the Great Sea, the Mediterranean.

Jesus had left Nazareth at the age of thirty (Luke 3:23). Until then he had spent most of his life in this town where he 'increased in wisdom and stature, and in favour with God and men' (Luke 2:52). He was well known in childhood and youth as 'the carpenter's son' (Matthew 13:55). As an adult he was known as 'the carpenter, the Son of Mary' (Mark 6:3). Despite having worked no miracle there throughout those many years nor openly revealed himself as the Messiah, he will forever be known as 'Jesus of Nazareth'.

It is understood that the inhabitants of Nazareth were conservative by nature and clung to traditional Jewish values at a time when Galilee as a whole was largely influenced by Greek and Roman culture in thought and behaviour.

It would seem from Mark's account (Mark 6:1-6)[18] that Jesus and his disciples arrived at Nazareth midweek and that in the days before the Sabbath 'he laid his hands on a few sick people and healed them' (Mark 6:5). That he only healed a few was credited to the scepticism of his old townsfolk. Jesus was amazed 'because of their unbelief' (Mark 6:6). In the synagogue it will become more obvious that 'the old acquaintances of a great person are but too often his keen critics and slow to believe in his greatness'.[19]

On the Sabbath day 'as his custom was, he went into the synagogue' (Luke 4:16). He entered the place where as a child, a teenager, a man, he had often worshipped in the humble capacity of the village carpenter, sitting, not up there among the elders and the honoured, but far back. The old well-known faces were around him, the old well-remembered words and services fell on his ears. How different they had always been to him than to them with whom he had mingled in common worship! And now he was again among them, truly a stranger among his own countryfolk; this

---

[18] There seems to be no way to resolve whether Jesus was rejected once or twice by the congregation of the synagogue in Nazareth; nor, if once, whether the public rejection occurred at the time placed by Luke (4:16-30) or at the time placed by Matthew (13:54-58) and Mark (6:1-6). The Gospel writers do not always record the events in chronological order. Here it is assumed that there was one visit recorded by all three and that that visit was made immediately before Jesus moved his home base to Capernaum as positioned by Luke.

[19] Norval Geldenhuys, *Commentary on the Gospel of Luke* (London: Marshall, Morgan and Scott, 1950), p.167.

time, to be looked at, listened to, tested, tried, used or cast aside, as the case might me.[20]

Synagogues came into being during or immediately after the Babylonian captivity (605-536 B.C.).[21] It is understandable that the Jews experiencing a long exile from Jerusalem and Judah would feel the need for places for common worship on Sabbaths and feast-days. This would give rise to local assemblies.

On their return to Judah and the later dispersion of so many of the Israelites over the years, meeting houses would be essential where those who did not know the Hebrew language might hear the Scriptures read, interpreted and explained; as was undertaken by Ezra (Nehemiah 8:3,8). It would be natural for prayers and then later teaching to be added.

There was only one temple in Israel and that was in Jerusalem 135km (84 miles) from Nazareth. It was an arduous journey by foot or donkey - south along the flatlands of the Jordan River, then west over the hills surrounding Jerusalem.

The local synagogue was the real centre of religious life. Wherever a town or village had ten Jewish men a synagogue must be provided. There were no sacrifices in the synagogue; the temple was the only place for sacrifice, the synagogue was for teaching.

The service in the synagogue consisted of three parts, prayer, the reading of Scripture and teaching. The appointed lesson from the law (the first five books of the Old Testament) would be read in Hebrew. Since it was no longer widely understood, it was translated into Aramaic one verse at a time. The reading from the Prophets was translated three verses at a time and was followed by teaching. In the synagogue there was no professional ministry, but there were elders to give the address.

Before the occasion recorded by Luke the minister or attendant (Luke 4:20) would have invited Jesus to address the congregation. The people would be eager to hear him as they had heard of his reputation in Capernaum and beyond.

Jesus was handed the scroll which contained the writings of the prophet Isaiah. Whether this was providentially the appointed reading for that morning or the Scripture requested by the Lord Jesus is not recorded. Either way it was the ideal text for the carpenter to reveal his identity as the Messiah.

---

[20] Alfred Edersheim, *The Life and Times of Jesus the Messiah* (Peabody, Massachusetts: Hendrikson, 1993), p.298.

[21] There is no mention of such gatherings in the Old Testament.

So much had happened in the months since he had left his hometown not least that at his baptism and ordination God had made him 'both Lord and Christ' (Acts 2:36). That momentous event was so crucial to the people of Nazareth, Galilee, Israel and the world! He had 'returned in the power of the Spirit' (Luke 4:14) and so he read -

> 'The Spirit of the LORD is upon me, because he has anointed me to preach the gospel to the poor; he has sent me to heal the brokenhearted, to proclaim liberty to the captives and recovery of sight to the blind, to set at liberty those who are oppressed; to proclaim the acceptable year of the LORD.' Then he closed the book, and gave it back to the attendant and sat down. And the eyes of all who were in the synagogue were fixed on him. And he began to say to them, 'Today this Scripture is fulfilled in your hearing' (Luke 4:18-21).

So all bore witness to him, and marvelled at the gracious words which proceeded out of his mouth. And they said, 'Is this not Joseph's son?' (Luke 4:22) Jesus spoke with such authority and graciousness that his old townsfolk were full of admiration. But this was not to last. The Lord anticipated their reaction when once their initial enthusiasm had abated. He faced them with their own thoughts and directly confronted their inner prejudice.

Speaking of God's mercy in response to the faith of the Gentile widow at Zarephath and to the faith of the Gentile Naaman from Syria, he exposed the unbelief of the congregation there at Nazareth.

That which would have subdued any humble godly folk only served to stir up this group's anger. They rose up and drove him from the synagogue. Jesus in silence and no doubt sadness allowed himself to be pressed to the edge of the hill upon which the town stood. They would have driven him over the side to his death - but Jesus turned and facing them simply walked unhindered and unharmed through the crowd and went his way. 'He came to his own [people], and his own did not receive him' (John 1:11).

20. Jesus moves his home to Capernaum
Matthew 4:13-16; Mark 1:21-22; Luke 4:31-32

Henceforth Capernaum would be his Galilean home. Here he would preach on numerous Sabbaths in the synagogue where Jairus was one of the rulers (Mark 5:22). The synagogue was built at the expense of a Gentile Roman centurion who loved the people of Israel (Luke 7:5).

Capernaum was convenient for the Lord's purpose as it was situated on the coast of the Sea of Galilee and on the great trade route, the *via maris*, which extended from Damascus and the east to the Mediterranean coast on the west. It was easy to radiate out to all parts of Galilee from this centre. Indeed Isaiah had prophesied the mission of the Messiah to this region -

> The land of Zebulun and the land of Naphtali, by the way of the sea, beyond the Jordan, Galilee of the Gentiles: the people who sat in darkness have seen a great light, and upon those who sat in the region and shadow of death light has dawned (Matthew 4:15-16; cf. Isaiah 9:1-2).

'The light of the world' (John 8:12) had come to reside at Capernaum. The Messiah addressed them and 'they were astonished at his teaching, for he taught them as one having authority, and not as the scribes' (Mark 1:22).

21. The call of Peter, Andrew, James and John
Matthew 4:18-22; Mark 1:16-20; Luke 5:1-11

Some or all of the disciples of John the Baptist who were earlier introduced to Jesus as 'the Lamb of God who takes away the sin of the world' (John 1:29) had accompanied Jesus to the wedding in Cana of Galilee. After the wedding they would have returned home and the Lord would have continued his itinerant ministry alone. These disciples are not mentioned again until four of them met Jesus once more on the seashore at Capernaum.

The home of brothers Peter and Andrew was Bethsaida (John 1:44). Bethsaida means, 'House of fishing' and there are two places bearing that name mentioned in the New Testament. There is 'Bethsaida of Galilee' (John 12:21), a small fishing village on the western shore of the Sea of Galilee. It was a suburb of Capernaum.[22]

The other Bethsaida was 'Bethsaida Julias' on the north eastern side of the Sea of Galilee. This town was situated near where the River Jordan flowed into the Sea of Galilee. Originally a village, it had been built up into a city by Philip II (Tetrarch of Ituraea and named in honour of Julia the daughter of Emperor Augustus). It was Bethsaida of Galilee that was the home of Andrew, Peter, Philip, James and John.

As a resident of Capernaum, Jesus walked by the Lake of Gennesaret (Sea of Galilee) and people gathered round him, 'to hear the word of God' (Luke 5:1). Seeing Peter's boat by the shore, Jesus stepped in and

---

[22] Richard C.H. Lenski, *The Interpretation of St. Mark's Gospel* (Minneapolis, Minnesota: Augsburg, 1961), p.270. cf. Mark 6:45 and John 6:17,24. William Hendriksen, *A Commentary on the Gospel of John. Vols.1&2.* (London: Banner of Truth Trust, 1954), vol. 1, p.219.

asked Peter to row a short distance from land. He then sat and taught the crowd from the boat.

When he had concluded his teaching he told Peter to row further out and put down his nets. Peter informed the Lord that they had worked hard all night and had caught nothing nevertheless because he gave the instruction he would obey.

They caught so many fish in their nets that Peter and Andrew had to call James and John for assistance. Both boats became so full of fish that they were in danger of sinking. Peter reacted in humble astonishment, 'Depart from me, for I am a sinful man, O Lord!' (Luke 5:8) The Lord issued his glorious invitation and promise to all four, 'Follow me, and I will make you become fishers of men'. They immediately left their nets and followed him (Mark 1:17-18).

Later in their evangelistic work as fishers of men they would probably reflect upon that night spent in hard work with no results. Many have since toiled one night, some many nights even years, and seen little or nothing. It is the Lord who gives the increase (1 Corinthians 3:6).

One Sabbath Day there was a man in the synagogue who was demon-possessed. The evil spirit used the voice of the man to cry out at Jesus, 'Let us alone! What have we to do with you, Jesus of Nazareth. Did you come to destroy us? I know who you are - the Holy One of God!' (Luke 4:34)

It was the evil spirit who recognised the identity of Jesus. By making him known his aim would be to somehow thwart the ministry of the Lord. Jesus will not permit this, he said, 'Be quiet, and come out of him!' (Mark 1:25) This drew even more astonishment from the congregation. They were amazed at the Lord's powerful authority not only in his teaching but now also in casting out an evil spirit. His fame spread widely.

That day he privately healed Peter's mother-in-law and, as the sun began to set and the Sabbath Day came to an end, all those who had any that were sick with various diseases brought them to him; and he laid his hands on every one of them and healed them. The Scriptures were being fulfilled, 'He himself took our infirmities and bore our sicknesses' (Matthew 8:17; cf. Isaiah 53:4). Demons also came out of many, crying out, 'You are the Christ, the Son of God!' (Luke 4:41). Jesus did not allow the evil spirits to speak 'because they knew him' (Mark 1:34).

22. Jesus preaches around Galilee
Matthew 4:23; Mark 1:35-39; Luke 4:42-44

'Now in the morning, having risen a long while before daylight, [Jesus] went out and departed to a solitary place; and there he prayed; (Mark 1:35). Later the Lord resisted the crowd's insistence that he stay longer in Capernaum, saying to his disciples, 'Let us go into the next towns, that I may preach there also, because for this purpose I have come forth' (Mark 1:38).

So Jesus spent weeks preaching in the synagogues around Galilee and healing all kinds of sickness and all kinds of disease among the people.

In one city a man who was full of leprosy came to Jesus and worshipped him saying, 'Lord, if you are willing, you can make me clean' (Matthew 8:2). This remarkable plea by one so gripped by a loathsome painful disease expressed the strongest possible faith in our Lord's miraculous power and just a slight doubt about our Lord's willingness to use his power on such an outcast. He said in effect, 'If you are willing, I know you can!'

The Lord was moved with compassion. He would know that this man would cause him personal inconvenience yet he still healed him. He stretched out his hand and touched him saying, 'I am willing; be cleansed'. 'As soon as he had spoken, immediately the leprosy left him, and he was cleansed' (Mark 1:41-42).

A command would have been sufficient. That touch demonstrated the merciful heart, compassionate spirit, majestic power of the Lord. He does not contaminate himself by touching the leper, nor does he transgress the law. The healing of this man with leprosy with instruction to show himself to a priest, demonstrated the Lord's respect for the law of Moses. It also served to establish, before the priests, his authority over the natural world.

The healed man had also been strictly instructed not to tell anyone but a priest (Mark 1:43-44) so that the Jewish leaders would not be provoked. Sadly the man disobeyed the command and made the healing widely known. The circulated news quickly brought more people to the city to hear Jesus and to seek healing. The Lord moved out to a deserted place but people came from every direction and still found him.

Returning to Capernaum by boat he was able to have a few days quiet but eventually folk discovered that he was back home. Many gathered to hear him, including Pharisees and teachers of the law, from towns in Galilee, Judea and Jerusalem. The house was packed with people.

Whilst the Lord was teaching a section of the roof above was being removed. When a considerable hole had been formed, four men lowered their paralysed friend down on a stretcher right in front of the Lord. 'When Jesus saw their faith, he said to the paralytic, "Son, your sins are forgiven you"' (Mark 2:5). The scribes (teachers of the law) and Pharisees heard Jesus and said, 'Who is this who speaks blasphemies? Who can forgive sins but God alone?' (Luke 5:21)

They were absolutely right, God alone forgives sin. As God is the only one who can forgive sin, the Lord Jesus was thereby disclosing his deity! Seeing the man get up and walk out of the room the multitudes 'marvelled and glorified God, who had given such power to men' (Matthew 9:8). But they too were missing the point, for this was not just any man, this was 'Immanuel - God with us' (Matthew 1:23).

Jesus left the house where he had healed the paralysed man and later in the day he went for a walk by the Sea of Galilee. A great crowd came out to see him and he taught them there by the sea (Mark 2:13).

23. The call of Matthew Levi
Matthew 9:9-13; Mark 2:13-17: Luke 5:27-32

As Jesus returned home he passed by the tax office and saw Matthew Levi the son of Alphaeus busy at work (Mark 2:14). It would appear that the tax office was situated at the entrance to the town, possibly near the sea on the well-used trading route that came from Egypt in the west to Damascus and the east.

Tax Officers

There were three levels of tax officer:

The 'publicani' (the origin of 'publican') - wealthy men over an entire region who paid a fixed sum into the Roman state treasury.

The 'chiefs of publicans', men (like Zacchaeus) who were in charge of a segment, a tax district.

The tax collectors who dealt with the public and took the revenue.

Matthew Levi the son of Alphaeus most probably belonged to the third rank. He would collect the duty on goods that were moved into and through Capernaum. He was a customs officer, and in order to hold that position he would be well-educated and have a very good knowledge of the Greek language. But he would be despised by the Jews because he was working for the Roman government.

Taxes

There were two types of taxes:

1. The first were the stated taxes such as the poll (or head) tax, the ground tax, and income tax.

---

i. The poll (or head tax) was a yearly sum that all men from 14 to 65, and all women from 12 to 65, had to pay - just for the privilege of living.

ii. The ground tax consisted of 1/10th of all grain grown, and 1/5th of all wine and oil produced. This could be paid in kind or the value paid in cash.

iii. The third tax in this category was income tax. This was 1% of a man's income.

As these were all fixed sums or fixed percentages there was not much room for extortion through illegal inflation.

2. The second group of taxes consisted of all kinds of duties.

i. A tax was payable for using the main roads, the harbours, and the markets.

ii. A tax was payable on a cart, on each wheel of the cart, and on the animal which drew the cart.

iii. There was purchase tax on certain articles, and there were import and export duties. A tax collector could stop a man on the road, insist that he emptied all his bundles, and then charge him almost anything he wished.[23]

If the tax collector made a tax demand that a man could not pay, then the tax collector himself would usually lend him the money - at an inflated rate of interest! In Israel in New Testament times robbers, murderers and tax collectors were classed together. Tax collectors were not allowed to attend the temple or a synagogue.

This would not have been the first time Matthew had seen Jesus. He may have heard Jesus speaking more than once in the open air by the Sea of Galilee. They most likely had also talked privately for the Lord would not have issued such a highly demanding invitation without giving Matthew an understanding of just what was being expected (cf. Luke 14:25-33). When Jesus finally issued the invitation to Matthew his reaction was instant. Jesus said, 'Follow me', so he left all, rose up, and followed him (Luke 5:27-28).

The call of Matthew to give up everything and accompany Jesus in his ministry and the subsequent meal with his old colleagues and outcasts, resulted in criticism from the Pharisees. Jesus responded in gracious tones, 'I

---

[23] William Barclay, *The Gospel of Luke* (Edinburgh: St. Andrew Press, 1961), p.61.

did not come to call the righteous, but sinners, to repentance' (Matthew 9:13).

The Lord gave hope to those who were cast out from the religious community and had been given no way to return. The Lord's compassion for sinners and contempt for hypocrisy was powerfully displayed.

24. A question of fasting
Matthew 9:14-17; Mark 2:18-22; Luke 5:33-39

Criticism of the Lord's words and works came early in his ministry. It seems to have begun with the incident of the four men lowering their paralysed friend on a stretcher down in front of Jesus. The Lord healed him by saying his sins were forgiven. The scribes who were present accused Jesus of blasphemy.

The second criticism came when he ate a meal with tax collectors and sinners. The third criticism arose over the Lord's manner of life and his supposed neglect of asceticism and fasting in particular.[24]

Jesus was confronted by a group of men, some of whom were disciples of John the Baptist and others who were disciples of the Pharisees. They had been discussing the practice of fasting (for they fasted often) and in particular the fact that the disciples of Jesus were apparently not fasting (Matthew 9:14).

There was only one official religious fast day laid down under the terms of the Old Covenant and that was once a year on the Day of Atonement. On that day the Israelites were to 'afflict their souls' (Leviticus 16:29) which meant abstaining from food and from all worldly pleasures.

There were a number of other fasts recorded in Old Testament Scripture which expressed -

- deep sorrow for sin associated with repentance, tears, sackcloth and ashes (Daniel 9:3-4 and Jonah 3:5);
- deep sorrow and sadness over bereavement - as with David over Saul and Jonathan (2 Samuel 1:12; cf. 1 Samuel 31:13 and 1 Chronicles 10:12);
- deep sorrow at hearing sad news - as with Nehemiah when he heard about the terrible condition of the people and the city of Jerusalem, particularly as it was associated with God's honour and glory (Nehemiah 1:4 and context);
- deep sorrow over a plague - as with Joel (Joel 2:12-13);

---

[24] An ascetic is a person who practices great self-denial and abstains from worldly comforts and pleasures for religious reasons.

- reaction to serious threat - as with Jehoshaphat when about to be attacked by the Moabites and Ammonites when all Judah was called upon to fast (2 Chronicles 20:3);
- the reaction of the Jews following the decree issued by king Ahasuerus 'to destroy, to kill, and to annihilate all the Jews, both young and old, little children and women, in one day' (Esther 3:13; 4:3).

As time went by fasts began to be multiplied so that in the days of Jesus it was the custom, at least for the Pharisees, to fast two days each week. Jesus made reference to this in the parable of The Pharisee and the Tax Collector (Luke 18:11-12). The Pharisees were fasting as though fasting was a ritual. They did not consider fasting to be an aid to devotion or a special means of spiritual discipline.

Jesus responded to the criticism -

> Can the friends of the bridegroom fast while the bridegroom is with them? As long as they have the bridegroom with them they cannot fast. But the days will come when the bridegroom will be taken away from them, and then they will fast in those days (Mark 2:19-20).

The Lord appealed to common knowledge among the Jews. It was a question that insisted on a negative reply, 'Of course not'. The rabbis had a rule that stated, 'All in attendance on the bridegroom are relieved of all religious observances which would lessen their joy'. It is clear that the Lord assumed his disciples would fast when he was no longer on earth with them (cf. Matthew 6:16-17).

Parables played an important part in the Lord's teaching. On this occasion he brought out a lesson from the practice of not putting a new patch on an old garment nor new wine into old wineskins (Luke 5:35-38). The new order that Jesus was introducing was incompatible with Pharisaism. Indeed the whole of the Old Covenant had been superseded. As the writer to the Hebrews wrote of the work of the Lord Jesus: 'He has made the first obsolete' and 'He takes away the first that he may establish the second' (Hebrews 8:13; 10:9).

25. Healing at the pool of Bethesda (Jerusalem)
John 5:1-47

'After this there was a feast of the Jews, and Jesus went up to Jerusalem. Now there is in Jerusalem by the Sheep Gate a pool, which is called in Hebrew, Bethesda' [meaning 'House of Mercy'] (John 5:1,2).

The Sheep Gate was the first of ten gates built into the reconstructed wall of the city of Jerusalem in the days of Nehemiah (444 B.C.). The Jews who returned from exile in Babylon rebuilt the city walls in sections. Ten gates were constructed. The sections between the gates were the responsibility of different groups and individuals. The first gate was the Sheep Gate (Nehemiah 3:1) and the last section joined back to it (Nehemiah 3:32).

This is the gate through which it is thought the sacrificial lambs were brought to the nearby temple-court. The Sheep Gate therefore, immediately links with Christ and Calvary: 'the Lamb of God who takes away the sin of the world' (John 1:29).

Periodically 'an angel went down … into the pool and stirred up the water; then whoever stepped in first, after the stirring of the water, was made well of whatever disease he had' (John 5:4). Calvin comments -

> The healing of the sick was indeed God's own work. But He was accustomed to use the hand and work of angels, and so commanded an angel to perform this duty... God could have healed them all, at once and in a moment. But as His miracles have their purpose, they must also have a limit... *The troubling of the water* was a clear proof that God freely uses the elements for His own will and that He claims for Himself the result of the work.[25]

It is important to remember throughout that this miracle, along with the other seven miracles recorded by the apostle John, is a 'sign' that is, a miracle with a spiritual message (John 20:30-31). What is this miracle teaching about Jesus of Nazareth as the Christ and Son of the living God?

There is a remarkable spiritual significance in each item and every feature of this event. Five porches had been built around the pool. Five columns erected and covered by a roof to protect the sick lying around the water. These five porches may have been erected to represent the five books of the law. In the porches the people lay ill, and yet uncured. So the law could show the people their sins, but could never cleanse them (Romans 3:20); the law could uncover human weakness, but never cure it.

'Now a certain man was there who had an infirmity thirty-eight years' just like the Israelites' thirty-eight extra years of wandering in the wilderness due to disobedience and a lack of faith (Deuteronomy 2:14-15). This Bethesda incident is one where the man had evidently brought the paralysis upon himself through sin thirty-eight years before (John 5:14; Galatians

---

[25] John Calvin, *The Gospel According to St John 1-10* (Saint Andrew Press: Edinburgh, 1959), pp.118-9. cf. Psalm 104:4.

6:7-8). He was paralysed through his own guilt, paralysed under the judgment of God (Psalm 38:1-5; cf. John 9:1-3).

When Jesus saw him lying there, and knew that he had already been in that condition a long time, he gave his first challenge, 'Do you want to be made well?' (John 5:6) Then a second challenge, 'Rise, take up your bed and walk' (John. 5:8). Obeying, the man got up, picked up his bed, and walked; no doubt amazed.

However within a short while he found himself confronted by some of the Jewish leadership. Though his bed would be little more than a rolled up mat, for them carrying it constituted a breach of the Sabbath law. They interrogated him for the name of the one who had healed him and who had told him to carry his bed. The man did not know for Jesus had disappeared in the crowd. Later the Lord met the man in the temple and issued the third challenge to him, 'See, you have been made well. Sin no more, lest a worse thing come upon you' (John 5:14) - thus confirming that the man's paralysis was the result of his personal sin.

Discovering the identity of Jesus, he reported back to the Jews. Fierce hostility towards Jesus stirred within them and murder was in their hearts because of what they supposed was a violation of the Sabbath.

The hatred of the Jewish leaders for the Lord Jesus

- his breaking the Sabbath law (as they understood it);
- his claim to a special relationship with God;
- his power to work miracles they could not perform;
- his skill in discussion exposing their errors and wrong thinking;
- his teaching as he spoke with authority, with clarity and simplicity;
- his popularity as the common people heard him gladly. (Large crowds often gathered around him);
- his associations because he mixed with religious outcasts: tax collectors and sinners;
- his messianic declarations;
- his broad knowledge and use of the Scriptures;
- his challenge to the tradition of the elders;
- his public criticism of their teaching and behaviour;
- his insistence upon repentance and faith for true righteousness before God;
- his emphasis upon holiness *of heart and life.*

Confronted by the Jews Jesus justified his actions by declaring his unique relationship with God the Father: 'My Father has been working until now, and I have been working' (John 5:17). The Jews responded; rightly understanding that Jesus was revealing himself as equal with God, but wrongly concluding that he was therefore guilty of gross blasphemy and therefore worthy of death.

The Lord continued to attest his unique oneness with the Father in the works he performed: raising the dead, exercising judgment, and giving life to whomever he wills.

Then presenting proof of his unique sonship he brought evidence as though he were in a Jewish court of law (John 5:31-40). The law required two witnesses, preferably three to establish guilt of wrong doing, or right of claim (Deuteronomy 19:15; cf. John 8:14).

- The Lord's first witness: John the Baptist who testified that Jesus was the Son of God (John 1:34).
- The Lord's second witness: The works (miracles) that Jesus was doing (Isaiah 35:5-6; Acts 2:22; Hebrews 2:4) these bear witness that he is the Son of God.
- The Lord's third witness: the Heavenly Father who gives *the supreme testimony to individuals regarding the sonship of Jesus* (John 5:37-38,32; cf. 2 Corinthians 4:6).
- The Lord's fourth witness: the Old Testament Scriptures. Hundreds of Messianic prophecies were fulfilled in him, with details spread over thousands of years: his ancestry, his unique conception, his birthplace, his miracles...

The first two witnesses and the fourth are available for examination in the Scriptures. True conversion, repentance and faith are the evidence of the third witness in the heart.

26. Sabbath day controversies
Matthew 12:1-14; Mark 2:23 - 3:6; Luke 6:1-11

On the next Sabbath it happened that Jesus walked with his disciples through cornfields. His disciples were hungry so they plucked heads of corn, rubbed them in their hands, and ate the kernels (Luke 6:1). On any other day of the week their action would have raised no concern from anyone since it was permitted by the law -

> When you come into your neighbour's standing grain, you may pluck the heads with your hand, but you shall not use a sickle on your neighbour's standing grain (Deuteronomy 23:25).

On the Sabbath such action was considered by the Rabbis to be breaking the law, as the Pharisees were quick to point out to Jesus. It was not however the law of God that was being broken. The Rabbis defined 'work' under 39 headings. Four of these classifications were: reaping, winnowing, threshing and preparing a meal. To gather and rub out the ears of corn was to harvest. By reaping, winnowing, threshing and thus preparing a meal, the disciples of Jesus had broken the Sabbatic code of the Rabbis at a number of points.

With masterly skill Jesus showed the Pharisees that their understanding of the Sabbath was quite wrong. Jesus used five arguments to make his point conclusive and incontrovertible. He used the Scriptures to correct the Pharisees by their history, their temple service, their prophets and reason (Matthew 12:5-8).

- History: David did not break the law when he sought bread for his hungry men (1 Samuel 21:1-6) and obtained the showbread, which after seven days became the property of the Levites and should be eaten only by them in a holy place (Leviticus 24:9). The conduct of David rested upon a principle, that in exceptional cases, when a moral obligation clashes with a ceremonial law, the moral obligation takes priority.
- Temple service: Likewise the priests who work in the temple on the Sabbath do not break the law. Then referring to himself he said, 'But I say to you that in this place there is one greater than the temple' (Matthew 12:6).
- Prophets: The prophecy of Hosea 6:6 'For I desire mercy and not sacrifice' indicating that a moral law supersedes a ceremonial law.
- Reason: Finally Jesus revealed himself plainly, 'For the Son of Man is Lord even of the Sabbath' (Matthew 12:8). As the Sabbath gives place to the temple, so Sabbath and temple give place to the greater, the One who is Lord of the temple and Sabbath.

Probably it was on the next Sabbath when Jesus once more entered the synagogue that a man was present who had a withered hand. Scribes and Pharisees watched Jesus closely, to see 'whether he would heal him on the Sabbath, so that they might accuse him' (Mark 3:2). According to Rabbinical law all work was forbidden on the Sabbath and to heal was to work.

> Medical attention could only be given if a life was in danger... a woman in childbirth could be helped on the Sabbath. An affection of the throat might be treated... A fracture could not be attended to. Cold water might not be poured on a sprained hand or foot. A

cut finger might be bandaged with a plain bandage but not with
ointment… at the most an injury could be kept from getting worse;
it must not be made better.[26]

The scribes and Pharisees asked, 'Is it lawful to heal on the Sabbath?' - that
they might accuse him (Matthew 12:10). Jesus 'knew their thoughts' (Luke
6:8), he was well aware of the hostility in the minds and hearts of those
scribes and Pharisees so he raised a question for them, 'Is it lawful on the
Sabbath to do good or to do evil, to save life or to kill?' But they kept silent
(Mark 3:4). Any child could have answered but these men would not,
whether through shame or because they had no ready answer.

Jesus gave them a comparison. If one of their sheep had fallen into a pit
on the Sabbath, would they not take hold of it and pull it out? He then drove
home the point, 'Of how much more value then is a man than a
sheep?' (Matthew 12:12)

And when he had looked around at them with anger, being grieved
by the hardness of their hearts, he said to the man, 'Stretch out
your hand.' And he stretched it out, and his hand was restored as
whole as the other (Mark 3:5).

The Pharisees left the synagogue mad with rage and lost no time in seeking
revenge. They 'went out and immediately plotted with the Herodians[27]
against him, how they might destroy him' (Mark 3:6). Note the irony: to heal
on the Sabbath is a crime worthy of death - to plot to kill is a perfectly lawful
act!

With the murderous designs of the scribes, Pharisees and Herodians, and
knowing that the hour of his departure had not yet come, for he still had
many things to accomplish before the final conflict, Jesus withdrew from
there -

And a great multitude from Galilee followed him, and from Judea
and Jerusalem and Idumea and beyond the Jordan; and those from
Tyre and Sidon, a great multitude, when they heard how many
things he was doing, came to him. So he told his disciples that a
small boat should be kept ready for him because of the multitude,
lest they should crush him' (Mark 3:7-9).

At the same time Jesus warned them not to make him known, that it might be
fulfilled which was spoken by Isaiah the prophet, saying -

---

[26] William Barclay, *The Gospel of Mark* (Edinburgh: St. Andrew Press, 1961), p.62.
[27] See 'Herodians' in the chapter on Significant facts, p.332

Behold! my Servant whom I have chosen, my Beloved in whom my soul is well pleased! I will put my Spirit upon him, and he will declare justice to the Gentiles. He will not quarrel nor cry out, nor will anyone hear his voice in the streets. A bruised reed he will not break, and smoking flax he will not quench, till he sends forth justice to victory; and in his name Gentiles will trust (Matthew 12:18-21; cf. Isaiah 42:1-4).

This beautifully descriptive quotation was presented by Matthew to show the Lord's quiet and gentle spirit, his love for the Gentiles and his desire to avoid conflict. This contrasted sharply with his opponents' hatred and murderous intent.

Jesus continued his great Galilean ministry as he 'went about all the cities and villages, teaching in their synagogues, preaching the gospel of the kingdom, and healing every sickness and every disease among the people. But when he saw the multitudes, he was moved with compassion for them, because they were weary and scattered, like sheep having no shepherd' (Matthew 9:35-36).

This is the key to the whole ministry of Jesus, his amazing compassion, his outstanding sense of mercy. He has a keen sensitivity for the spiritual state of the people: For 'the Son of Man has come to seek and to save that which was lost' (Luke 19:10). Most if not all of these people are primarily seeking Jesus for healing for themselves, for family members or for friends.

Physical healing is at best temporary whereas spiritual healing is everlasting, eternal. They need spiritual shepherds who will care for their souls. They were 'weary and scattered, like sheep having no shepherd' because those who were their appointed shepherds were failing in their duties.

The Jewish leadership was weighing them down with 'heavy burdens hard to bear' (Matthew 23:4; cf. vv.5-36), with petty details about Sabbath observance, rituals, legalistic trivia, fasts, phylacteries and tassels. They cared more for themselves than for the people (cf. Ezekiel 34:2-5). Their concern was for externals, how they appeared to others.

They love the best places at feasts, the best seats in the synagogues, greetings in the marketplaces, and to be called by men, 'Rabbi, Rabbi' (Matthew 23:6-7).

The Lord's concern was for the heart, 'the weightier matters of the law: justice and mercy and faith' (Matthew 23:23). The people needed 'shepherds according to [God's] heart, who will feed [them] with knowledge and understanding' (Jeremiah 3:15).

He saw this multitude before him as desperately needy with no one to help. There are millions like these throughout the world, so he said to his disciples, 'The harvest truly is plentiful, but the labourers are few. Therefore pray the Lord of the harvest to send out labourers into his harvest' (Matthew 9:37-38). Instruction for future Christian shepherds (same word translated 'pastors') would come later (cf. Acts 20:28; 1 Peter 5:1-4).

27. Twelve apostles appointed
Matthew 10:1-4; Mark 3:13-19; Luke 6:12-16

During his second year of ministry Jesus appointed his apostles. Before the appointment he 'went out to the mountain to pray, and continued all night in prayer to God' (Luke 6:12). The importance that Jesus placed upon prayer is clearly evident.[28] The Lord was probably on one of the mountain ranges that stretches to the north of Capernaum. He then called the twelve to him 'that they might be with him and that he might send them out to preach, and to have power to heal sicknesses and to cast out demons' (Mark 3:14-15).

They were Simon and Andrew his brother; James the son of Zebedee, and John his brother; Philip and (Nathanael) Bartholomew; Thomas and Matthew the tax collector; James the son of Alphaeus, and Thaddaeus (also known as Judas the son of James, Luke 6:16; cf. John 14:22); Simon the Canaanite (the Zealot), and Judas Iscariot (the betrayer).

They were given 'power over unclean spirits, to cast them out, and to heal all kinds of sickness and all kinds of disease' (Matthew 10:1).

> Then his fame went throughout all Syria; and they brought to him all sick people who were afflicted with various diseases and torments, and those who were demon-possessed, epileptics, and paralytics; and he healed them. Great multitudes followed him - from Galilee, and from Decapolis, Jerusalem, Judea, and beyond the Jordan. And seeing the multitudes, he went up on a mountain, and when he was seated his disciples came to him. Then he opened his mouth and taught them ((Matthew 4:24-5:2).

28. The Sermon on the Mount
Matthew 5:3 - 7:27; cf. Luke 6:37-49

The expressions 'the kingdom of heaven' (Matthew 5:3) or 'the kingdom of God', or simply 'the kingdom' (where the context confirms that it is God's kingdom that is meant), are all interchangeable. These terms indicate God's

---

[28] For a fuller treatment see the section on 'The prayer life of Jesus' in the chapter *Understanding the Gospel of Luke: Christology No.1*, p.428

kingship, rule or sovereignty in the hearts and lives of his citizens, his people. His sovereignty brings about their complete salvation, welcomes them as born again members of his family, constitutes them as a church and ultimately settles them in the new regenerated and righteous universe.

God set his Son as King over his kingdom (Psalm 2:6-7) -

> when he raised him from the dead and seated him at his right hand in the heavenly places, far above all principality and power and might and dominion, and every name that is named, not only in this age but also in that which is to come. And he put all things under his feet, and gave him to be head over all things to the church, which is his body, the fullness of him who fills all in all' (Ephesians 1:20-23).

In the Sermon on the Mount Jesus set out 'the spiritual requirements for entrance into his kingdom, both in its spiritual and physical aspects... To enter the spiritual kingdom today and the eternal kingdom in the future, one *must not have* a Pharisaical type of righteousness; rather, one must be clothed with the imputed righteousness of God.'[29] Jesus said, 'unless your righteousness exceeds the righteousness of the scribes and Pharisees, you will by no means enter the kingdom of heaven' (Matthew 5:20).

The only righteousness acceptable to God is the perfect righteousness of Christ imputed and imparted to all who repent of sin and believe in the Lord Jesus Christ. 'For [God] made him who knew no sin to be sin for us, that we might become the righteousness of God in him' (2 Corinthians 5:21).

a. Characteristics of Christian discipleship (Matthew 5:1-16)

The opening eight sentences are called the Beatitudes, meaning 'blessings' (Matthew 5:3-12). These are the moral and spiritual qualities evident in all those who enter the kingdom of God; the virtues and graces in all Christians - all true followers and disciples of Christ. They describe citizens of God's kingdom, the distinguishing marks of the genuine Christian.

The first is the key to all that follows, 'Blessed are the poor in spirit, for theirs is the kingdom of heaven' (Matthew 5:3). They are empty, spiritually bankrupt and come to God in helplessness and desperation - 'As the deer pants for the water brooks, so pants my soul for you, O God. My soul thirsts for God, for the living God' (Psalm 42:1-2).

---

[29] Robert G. Gromacki, *New Testament Survey* (Grand Rapids, Michigan: Baker Book House, 1974), p.78.

Consequently they mourn over their sin - 'For godly sorrow produces repentance leading to salvation, not to be regretted; but the sorrow of the world produces death' (2 Corinthians 7:10);

They are meek towards others - mild, gentle and patient; they hunger and thirst for righteousness; they are merciful; pure in heart, in thought and deed; peacemakers and yet often persecuted for righteousness sake. These are the ones blessed by God.

Citizens of God's kingdom are to influence the world in which they live - as salt endeavouring to slow down moral corruption - as light to shine forth and point to the true light, to Jesus.

b. Jesus and the law of Moses (Matthew 5:17-48)

Jesus had not come to destroy the law or the prophets. In fact he accepted and promoted the Old Testament Scriptures as totally Holy Spirit inspired, without error and therefore of the highest authority. He came not to destroy, quite the opposite, he came *to fulfil* the law and the prophets.

The Pharisees emphasised outward conformity to the law of God and the laws of the Rabbis. Jesus focused his attention upon the inner being - the heart and mind. Contrasting his interpretation of the law with that of the Pharisees he said, 'You have heard that it was said to those of old... But I say to you' (Matthew 5:21-22, 27-28, 31-32, 33-34, 38-39, 43-44)

He continued each use of the phrase by dealing with the law on murder and its wider application in anger and hatred; adultery and the lustful look; divorce and remarriage; making vows; no revenge, no insisting upon one's rights; and love in the place of hatred towards enemies.

c. The godliness of Christian disciples (Matthew 6:1-18)

Jesus described the right attitude of heart and mind that pleases God. Whereas the Pharisees paraded their religion before all, disciples of Jesus are to concentrate their attention on pleasing God. Three areas were highlighted: charitable giving, prayer and fasting.

Firstly, when charitable deeds are done to impress others or gain admiration or praise, that is all that is likely to be achieved. Only charitable giving done secretly will be rewarded by the heavenly Father.

Secondly, prayer is never to be undertaken in order to impress or influence others but to be addressed to God alone. Private prayer is encouraged. Sincerity and simplicity are essential. A pattern of prayer is provided by Jesus to suggest the elements and order of our private prayers. The heart and mind must be right with God and right with others. This is a prerequisite for God to grant blessing.

Thirdly on the subject of fasting, disciples are not to behave like the Pharisees who do everything they can to draw attention to their fasting. This is hypocrisy - play acting! Fasting is to be for God's eyes only. No one should know, for when engaged in privately with a single eye to obeying and pleasing God, the Father who sees in secret will reward openly (Matthew 6:18).

d. Single-minded devotion without worry (Matthew 6:19-34)

The Pharisees believed that wealth was always a sign of God's blessing. However, health, wealth and prosperity are often not the experience of the faithful people of God -

> Others were tortured, not accepting deliverance, that they might obtain a better resurrection. Still others had trial of mockings and scourgings, yes, and of chains and imprisonment. They were stoned, they were sawn in two, were tempted, were slain with the sword. They wandered about in sheepskins and goatskins, being destitute, afflicted, tormented - of whom the world was not worthy. They wandered in deserts and mountains, in dens and caves of the earth (Hebrews 11:35-38).

These atrocities are still being perpetuated against God's faithful people in many countries of the world. There is no health, wealth and prosperity promised in the teaching of Jesus. He taught that spiritual riches are what God desires from his people.

> Do not lay up for yourselves treasures on earth, where moth and rust destroy and where thieves break in and steal; but lay up for yourselves treasures in heaven, where neither moth nor rust destroys and where thieves do not break in and steal. For where your treasure is, there your heart will be also (Matthew 6:19-21).

How then do we lay up treasures in heaven? The first step is to recognise the limitations of earthly treasures. 'Moth and rust' represent all that causes the deterioration and eventually the decomposition of earthly goods. All our earthly possessions have a restricted lifespan. Nothing in this world lasts forever.

The second step is to be fully aware of the enduring character of heavenly treasure 'what are the riches of the glory of [Christ's] inheritance in the saints' in the present and in the future (Ephesians 1:18).The apostle Peter described the treasure to come as 'an inheritance incorruptible and undefiled and that does not fade away, reserved in heaven' for all God's children (1 Peter 1:4). Anyone may gain this inheritance the moment they repent of sin and believe on the Lord Jesus Christ.

Though this inheritance is 'reserved in heaven' believers nevertheless have a sweet foretaste whilst here on earth. We enjoy forgiveness, the full pardon of our sins, a Father who loves us and hears our prayers; a Saviour who gives us peace with God and tranquility in our hearts, who even now is interceding in heaven for us: a Comforter, the Holy Spirit who indwells to inspire, lead, comfort and instruct. We are reassured that our place has been prepared for the future and when the time comes the Saviour will personally escort us 'home' (John 14:1-3).

The ultimate of all heavenly treasure is to know God - as he said to Abraham, 'I am… your exceedingly great reward' (Genesis 15:1).

Having understood the impermanence of earthly treasure and yielded our whole life to the Son of God, our third step in laying up treasure in heaven is to walk worthy of our high calling (Ephesians 4:1) by daily communion in prayer, Bible reading, meditation and study, drawing upon 'the unsearchable riches of Christ' (Ephesians 3:8).

Step four is when we commit every hour of every day to the imitation of Christ (1 Corinthians 11:1). We learn how to live for him and to him, from his example and instruction, thus we 'grow in the grace and knowledge of our Lord and Saviour Jesus Christ' (2 Peter 3:18).

In the fifth step we devote all that we have, own and are to his service and glory. If Jesus is our priceless treasure that is where our hearts will be also (Matthew 6:21).

When our minds and hearts are set upon the glory of God, the honour of our Lord Jesus Christ and the good of his people will be our priorities. Everything we have and all that we are will be devoted to him and answer to the challenge of the apostle Paul -

> If then you were raised with Christ, seek those things which are above, where Christ is, sitting at the right hand of God. Set your mind on things above, not on things on the earth (Colossians 3:1-2).

'The lamp of the body is the eye. If therefore your eye is good, your whole body will be full of light. But if your eye is bad, your whole body will be full of darkness. If therefore the light that is in you is darkness, how great is that darkness' (Matthew 6:22-23).

Jesus spoke these words in the context of two different treasures, one on earth and the other in heaven, so when he says that the eye is the lamp of the body he is referring to what attracts the attention of the eye to the treasures on earth - sumptuous food, expensive clothing, fine houses, cars, and numerous other valuables. How these things are viewed by the body will be determined by whether the eye is good or bad.

If the spiritual eye is good it will have one single focus - 'looking unto Jesus. the author and finisher of our faith' (Hebrews 12:2). The consistent effect will be that the body, guided by the mind and heart, will wholeheartedly consider Jesus (Hebrews 12:3) first and foremost.

'No one can serve two masters; for either he will hate the one and love the other, or else he will be loyal to the one and despise the other. You cannot serve God and mammon' (Matthew 6:24) for someone who is double-minded 'is unstable in all his ways' (James 1:8). Eventually there will be love for one and hatred for the other.

So Jesus urges that his followers should not worry about food and clothing but concentrate upon the major issue of life - seeking 'first the kingdom of God and his righteousness' (v.33) and trusting God for everything else. This is the true heavenly treasure.

God will take care of those who are his.

e. Judging and discrimination (Matthew 7:1-6)

When Jesus said, 'Judge not, that you be not judged' he was not contradicting John 7:24 'Do not judge according to appearance, but judge with righteous judgment'; nor 1 John 4:1 'Beloved, do not believe every spirit, but test the spirits, whether they are of God; because many false prophets have gone out into the world.' Nor is he arguing against the necessity to make judgments in church discipline (Matthew18:17-18; 1 Corinthians 5:12-13).

What he forbids is self-righteous, hypocritical judging of others. As Mounce observes -

> Human nature encourages us to pay far more attention to the shortcomings of others than to our own faults. We tend to evaluate others on the basis of a lofty standard of righteousness that somehow is not applicable to our own performance... Judging, in this context, implies a harsh and censorious spirit. If you insist on condemning others, you exclude yourself from God's forgive-ness.[30]

The Pharisees were guilty of judging others for trivial, minor issues, whilst being blind or inattentive to their own major spiritual defects. Careful righteous judgment is however necessary for Jesus said, 'Do not give what is holy to the dogs; nor cast your pearls before swine' (Matthew 7:6). Did Peter amplify this saying of Jesus when years later he wrote of those who had

---

[30] Robert H. Mounce, *New International Biblical Commentary: Matthew* (Peabody, Massachusetts: Hendrickson, 1991), p.64.

known 'the way of righteousness' and turned back as like 'a dog returns to his own vomit,' and, 'a sow, having washed, to her wallowing in the mire' (2 Peter 2:22)?

f. Persevering in prayer: ask, seek, knock (Matthew 7:7-12)

The only way decisively to leave the old corrupt way is to turn in complete sincerity to God. The Saviour graciously invites sinners to ask and they will receive, to seek and they will find, to knock and it will be opened. God will respond speedily in mercy and grace. Jesus was echoing God's earlier gracious invitation: 'You will seek me and find me, when you search for me with all your heart. I will be found by you, says the LORD' (Jeremiah 29:13-14).

> Seek the LORD while he may be found, call upon him while he is near. Let the wicked forsake his way, and the unrighteous man his thoughts; let him return to the LORD, and he will have mercy on him; and to our God, for he will abundantly pardon (Isaiah 55:6-7).

Asking, seeking and knocking are not to be confined to initial conversion or returns from backsliding, these are to be the continual endeavour of all believers.

The blessings of knowing God and being in a right relationship with God are immense. Not only is there the promise of everlasting life with the Eternal God, but life now experiencing God as Heavenly Father. God treats us as we would expect a good earthly father to treat us, only much much better! He gives 'good things to those who ask him' (Matthew 7:11). The apostle Paul summarised some of these amazingly good things experienced here and now when he wrote -

> Blessed be the God and Father of our Lord Jesus Christ, who has blessed us with every spiritual blessing... he chose us in him before the foundation of the world... having predestined us to adoption as sons by Jesus Christ to himself... he made us accepted in the Beloved. In him we have redemption through his blood, the forgiveness of sins (Ephesians 1:3-8).

The apostle Peter wrote of good things now and in eternity -

> Blessed be the God and Father of our Lord Jesus Christ, who according to his abundant mercy has begotten us again to a living hope through the resurrection of Jesus Christ from the dead, to an inheritance incorruptible and undefiled and that does not fade away, reserved in heaven for you, who are kept by the power of

God through faith for salvation ready to be revealed in the last time (1 Peter 1:3-5).

To know God as Father is to seek to emulate him as his children. 'Therefore be imitators of God as dear children. And walk in love, as Christ also has loved us and given himself for us' (Ephesians 5:1-2). So we must treat others as we would wish others to treat us.

Jesus concluded the sermon by an invitation and warnings.

g. *The narrow way and solid foundation (Matthew 7:13-27)*

Jesus has presented a standard of moral excellence in this Sermon on the Mount which is utterly unattainable by mere flesh and blood. He has piled one obligation upon another which are beyond the power of fallen human nature to fulfil.

To live as God wills takes divine help, divine power and divine assistance. It also takes commitment and utmost endeavour for the route to eternal life is through the narrow gate which leads to a difficult way (Matthew 7:14). The journey is demanding for it is no easy matter to be a follower of Jesus (cf. Matthew 16:24-26). Jeremiah made clear how important the choice was when he wrote, 'Thus says the LORD: "Behold, I set before you the way of life and the way of death"' (Jeremiah 21:8).

How vital it is to follow carefully the instructions of Jesus in all issues of life. There will be those who profess to be disciples of Jesus, even setting themselves up as genuine Christian teachers, who are 'false prophets'. Their manner of life is the test; how they behave will indicate their true heart. The discord between speech and behaviour is also an issue for everyone who professes faith in Jesus. Empty words are meaningless to the Lord and the performing of miracles unimpressive.

Living in faithful obedience is what God requires. Jesus confirmed this by describing two men who each built a house, one on sand the other on rock. He illustrated the blessing and stability of building life upon the foundation of his word, and warned of the tragedy which would ultimately result for a life built otherwise.

h. *Response to the Sermon on the Mount (Matthew 7:28-29)*

Those who listened to Jesus that day were astonished at the authority of his teaching for it was so unlike what they were used to hearing for he taught with authority.

'When he had come down from the mountain, great multitudes followed him' (Matthew 8:1). After entering Capernaum Jesus was met by a centurion who pleaded with him to heal his servant. Jesus said that he would come and heal him.

> The centurion answered and said, 'Lord, I am not worthy that you should come under my roof. But only speak a word, and my servant will be healed. For I also am a man under authority, having soldiers under me. And I say to this one, "Go", and he goes; and to another, "Come", and he comes; and to my servant, "Do this", and he does it' (Matthew 8:8-9).

Jesus noted the great faith that the centurion had in his ability and said, 'I have not found such great faith, not even in Israel!' (Matthew 8:10) Jesus then warned the Israelites that it is faith in himself not birth and ancestry that counts with God.

29. A widow's son restored to life (Nain)
Luke 7:11-17

'Now it happened, the day after, that he went into a city called Nain; and many of his disciples went with him, and a large crowd' (Luke 7:11). Another large crowd met them, a funeral procession coming out of the main gate (no one could be buried inside the city boundary). The two processions met, one a large group accompanying the Prince of Life, the other a large group escorting a victim of death. The widowed mother, according to the usual custom in that land, would be walking in front of the coffin. It was therefore quite natural for the Lord to speak to her and comfort her before touching the coffin and causing the procession to stop.

Without requiring faith from anyone the Lord Jesus commanded the young man to get up. This incident clearly revealed our Lord's tenderness of heart, and the impact which human grief has on him (cf. Psalm 146:9; James 1:27).

Whereas the power of the Lord Jesus is wonderfully displayed in raising the physically dead, his greatest work is granting spiritual, eternal life. As he would say months later to Martha on the death of her brother, 'I am the resurrection and the life. He who believes in me, though he may die, he shall live. And whoever lives and believes in me shall never die' (John 11:25-26). Those who repent of sin and believe in Jesus will enjoy the great resurrection and live forever.

30. John the Baptist sends two disciples to Jesus
Matthew 11:2-19; Luke 7:18-35

From prison John the Baptist sent two of his disciples to Jesus with the question: 'Are you the Coming One, or do we look for another?' (Matthew

11:3.) In other words, 'Are you the promised Messiah (Christ)?' These two disciples were still attached to John; they had not moved their commitment from John to Jesus as Andrew, Peter, Philip and Nathanael had done. John sent these two disciples to Jesus with the intention of passing them over to him.

It was always John's purpose to 'bridge the gap' between the Old Covenant and the New. Alexander maintains -

> Here was the secret of his office and the significance of his appearance in Israel. The old passes away in him; he must, in the name of the Old, acknowledge and recognise the Mediator of the New. Christ belonged to both Covenants that he might fulfil all things in Himself.'[31]

So John planned a strategy. He sent his two disciples to Jesus with a clear decisive question. Jesus knew instantly what John planned. He said to the two men -

> Go and tell John the things which you hear and see: The blind see and the lame walk; the lepers are cleansed and the deaf hear; the dead are raised up and the poor have the gospel preached to them (Matthew 11:4-5).

The answer is given in terms of fulfilled prophecy for Isaiah had predicted, 'Then the eyes of the blind shall be opened, and the ears of the deaf shall be unstopped. Then the lame shall leap like a deer, and the tongue of the dumb sing' (Isaiah 35:5-6).

Jesus not only referred to this fulfilled messianic prophecy, he went further by adding his greater miracles, 'lepers are cleansed and... the dead raised up'. Jesus then included reference to another messianic prophecy in his reply; Messiah will be anointed by the Holy Spirit, 'to preach good tidings to the poor' (Isaiah 61:1). This was an outstanding part of the Lord's ministry - 'the poor have the gospel preached to them'.

That *no correction was intended* for John is clear from what followed which was a remarkable tribute paid by Jesus to his imprisoned servant (Matthew 11:7-11). He asked, 'What did you go out into the wilderness to see? A reed shaken by the wind?' (v.7) 'When the wind blew fresh and fair, when the storms of Herod's rage on the other hand grew fierce and blustering, John was still the same in all weathers' (Matthew Henry). 'A prophet? Yes, I say to you, and more than a prophet' (v.9).

---

[31] Charles D. Alexander, *The Prophetism of the Gospels* (Liverpool: self-published booklet), p.15.

John acknowledged himself inferior to Christ; Christ acknowledged John as superior to all other prophets. The other prophets spoke of Christ; John pointed to him and introduced him personally. They said, 'unto us a Son is given'; he said, 'Behold, the Lamb of God!'

But Jesus went even further saying, 'among those born of women there has not risen one greater than John the Baptist; but he who is least in the kingdom of heaven is greater than he' (Matthew 11:11).

In what sense is the humblest Christian greater than John the Baptist? Because the Lord Jesus Christ has sent forth the Holy Spirit with a new and distinct commitment to New Testament believers. They do not -

> receive the spirit of bondage again to fear, but [they receive] the Spirit of adoption by whom we cry out, 'Abba, Father'. The Spirit himself bears witness with our spirit that we are children of God, and if children, then heirs of God and joint heirs with Christ, if indeed we suffer with him, that we may also be glorified together (Romans 8:15-17).

It is this 'adoption' by which we are raised to a position in this life above all Old Testament saints. It is this which makes the least in the New Covenant greater than the greatest in the Old Covenant. The Spirit declares us to be the children of God. We have immediate access to God through the Lord Jesus Christ. We need no earthly temple, earthly priesthood, ritual law or ceremony, no animal or bird sacrifices. These were but 'a shadow of things to come, but the substance is of Christ' (Colossians 2:17).

Having so graciously commended John the Baptist, Jesus drew attention to their different lifestyles, neither of which brought approval from the Jews.

Presenting the illustration of children playing their flutes or mourning in the marketplace Jesus brought home that some people are never satisfied. John was an ascetic, he came neither eating nor drinking, and they say, 'He has a demon'. Jesus was not an ascetic but quite the opposite of John, he came eating and drinking, and they say, 'Look, a glutton and a winebibber, a friend of tax collectors and sinners!' (Matthew 11:18,19)

In the end this kind of criticism achieves nothing - 'wisdom is justified by her children'. In other words, though many reject the preaching of repentance by John and the hope of salvation by Jesus, those who received their word show what it achieves in their hearts and lives when they sincerely respond. The fruit (in this case 'the children') displays the nature, quality, health and vitality of the tree.

Most of the Jews were dissatisfied whether the preaching was given by John or by Jesus. What they demanded of John they condemned in Jesus;

what they condemned in John they demanded of Jesus. There is a viciousness about the Jew's reactions to both of them.

Jesus refused to present any argument in defence but turned attention to the people of Galilee who had been so privileged by his presence and activity. For months the Saviour had engaged in itinerant evangelism around Galilee, healing and teaching in village after village and town after town, but there had been a notable lack of repentance.

Drawing a forceful comparison between Chorazin, Bethsaida and Capernaum (where he had displayed many mighty works and engaged in powerful preaching) with the towns of Tyre, Sidon and Sodom he condemned the cities of Galilee for their unbelief in the face of such a remarkable disclosure of God's grace.

31. A sinful woman from the city
Luke 7:36-50

Neither the place nor the time is indicated when the Lord Jesus accepted an invitation to a meal with Simon the Pharisee. For the meal the men reclined on couches arranged around the table with their heads close to the table, the left elbow supplying support and their legs stretched out like the beams of the radiating sun.

Whilst they were eating, a woman with a notorious reputation came in carrying 'an alabaster flask of fragrant oil'. How did she gain entry? Had she mingled with the servants, or was access free to all especially when the honoured guest was a visiting Rabbi whose words might be heard to great benefit? She had heard the Master speak before no doubt, perhaps words similar to the invitation -

> Come to me, all you who labour and are heavy laden, and I will give you rest. Take my yoke upon you and learn from me, for I am gentle and lowly in heart, and you will find rest for your souls. For my yoke is easy and my burden is light (Matthew 11:28-30).

She stood at the Lord's feet 'behind him weeping' so profusely that her tears fell upon his feet. 'She began to wash his feet with her tears, and wiped them with the hair of her head; and she kissed his feet and anointed them with the fragrant oil' (Luke 7:38). Did she see him as the promised prophet sent from God with the good news that opened the kingdom of heaven even to someone like her?

Simon the host was not impressed and said, under his breath, 'This Man, if he were a prophet, would know who and what manner of woman this is who is touching him, for she is a sinner' (Luke 7:39). Rabbis did not speak to women other than to their wives and that in private! Whatever Simon's motive in asking Jesus to dine with him, he was taken aback by the Lord's quiet acceptance of this intruder's behaviour.

Jesus graciously came to the woman's defence by telling Simon a parable concerning two debtors, one of whom owed five hundred denarii and the other fifty. 'And when they had nothing with which to repay, he freely forgave them both. Tell me, therefore, which of them will love him more?' Simon admitted the obvious, 'I suppose the one whom he forgave more' (Luke 7:42,43). The Lord was graciously indicating the motive behind the woman's behaviour.

Then the Saviour drew a further contrast between the attitude and behaviour of Simon and that of the woman. Simon had neglected the common courtesy when receiving a guest to his home: feet washing on entry, a touch of perfume on the head, and a kiss of greeting. Was Simon intentionally showing disrespect or just failing to show proper care and attention?

Jesus concluded his judgment by saying, 'Therefore I say to you, her sins, which are many, are forgiven, for she loved much. But to whom little is forgiven, the same loves little'. Then he said to her, 'Your sins are forgiven' (Luke 7:47-48). Simon was conscious of no need of forgiveness and therefore felt no love for the Saviour, and consequently received no forgiveness.

Jesus continued evangelising in Galilee as -

> he went through every city and village, preaching and bringing the glad tidings of the kingdom of God. And the twelve were with him, and certain women who had been healed of evil spirits and infirmities - Mary called Magdalene, out of whom had come seven demons, and Joanna the wife of Chuza, Herod's steward [an official responsible for the king's finances], and Susanna, and many others who provided for him from their substance' (Luke 8:1-3).

The women were as diverse as the men of the apostles. Jesus has a skill in uniting followers of very different natures, intellects, cultures, religious backgrounds and abilities and welding them into one harmonious whole. Here is the divine pattern for the local church - not perfect but 'a work in progress'!

32. Demon-possessed mute healed
Matthew 12:22-45; Mark 3:20-30; Luke 11:14-28

The Lord Jesus performed a great miracle; he healed a man who was possessed by a demon. The demon had rendered the man 'blind and mute' (Matthew 12:22). He could neither see nor speak. Jesus drove out the demon by that same authority which he had granted earlier to the apostles (Matthew 10:1). The people were clearly amazed when they saw the miracle. Many also heard of the event and were astonished. It provoked the right sort of enquiry from some who said, 'Could this be the Son of David?' (Matthew 12:23)

Scribes who came from Jerusalem to conduct an investigation into the teaching and miracles of Jesus gave a more sinister response. In the face of this great miracle came the severest criticism. Their antagonism had reached a new level. Their abuse was the worst conceivable assault upon the character of Jesus. For when the Pharisees heard it they said, 'This fellow does not cast out demons except by Beelzebub, the ruler of the demons' (Matthew 12:24). The scribes who came down from Jerusalem said, 'He has Beelzebub'. and, 'By the ruler of the demons he casts out demons' (Mark 3:22).

Beelzebub or Beelzebul means, 'Dung-god'. Of the demon world this was the worst. What could be more filthy and disgusting, more horrific and degrading than to suggest that Jesus worked by the power of the god of excrement! The scribes and Pharisees levelled two charges at the Lord: firstly he was possessed by the prince of demons, 'He has Beelzebub'; secondly his exorcisms, the driving out of demons, *was achieved by the power of the prince of demons* - 'By the ruler of the demons he cast out demons' (Mark 3:22).

'Jesus knew their thoughts' (Matthew 12:25). He called them to him and said to them in parables: 'How can Satan cast out Satan?' (Mark 3:23) By speaking in parables Jesus was able to use comparisons and analogies without going into lengthy discussion.

Jesus used a clear argument like this -

- If I really cast out demons by the power of the prince of demons, then it must mean that Satan is actually casting out Satan.
- If I cast out demons by Beelzebub, by whom do your colleagues cast them out? Are you accusing them as you accuse me?
- How can Satan cast out Satan? The accusation is nonsense.
- A kingdom or a household divided against itself cannot possibly stand. If Satan has really risen up against himself and is divided, he cannot stand. He must be finished.
- But Satan is clearly not finished. Therefore I cannot be casting out demons by the power of demons.

- On the contrary you should have realised that no one can enter a strong one's house and take his goods unless he first binds the strong one. Only when the strong one, Satan, is bound can his goods be taken. Therefore I am stronger than Satan! I am binding Satan.

Jesus concluded with a severe warning -

> Assuredly, I say to you, all sins will be forgiven the sons of men, and whatever blasphemies they may utter; but he who blasphemes against the Holy Spirit never has forgiveness, but is subject to eternal condemnation - because they said, 'He has an unclean spirit' (Mark 3:28-30).

The Lord did not say the scribes and Pharisees *had committed the unforgivable sin*. They were coming dangerously close, that is why he gave them this serious word of warning.

The Holy Spirit is called the Spirit of Truth (John 14:17; 15:26; 16:13).

- He convicts 'of sin, and of righteousness, and of judgment' (John 16:8). By him sinners are made aware of their dreadful condition and guilt before God. We are convinced of our wickedness and waywardness, our neglect to do good and failure to do right.
- He confronts us with our selfishness, self-centredness and godlessness.
- He convinces sinners of the righteousness of Jesus Christ, that all that is written about him in Scripture is trustworthy and true; that all that he said and did can be relied upon as entirely accurate: that he is holy, pure, righteous, true, just, good, gracious, merciful and forgiving - just like God his Father.
- He convinces humbled sinners that Jesus Christ is the only Saviour of sinners, the only One who can bring us to God, ransomed, healed, restored and forgiven.
- The Holy Spirit shines 'in our hearts to give the light of the knowledge of the glory of God in the face of Jesus Christ' (2 Corinthians 4:6). Through the Holy Spirit we, like Peter, are able to declare of Jesus, 'You are the Christ, the Son of the living God' (Matthew 16:16).

The reason for our Lord's severe warning was because of the grave seriousness of their words when they said, 'He has an unclean spirit' (Mark 3:30). They were calling the Holy Spirit a filthy spirit. They were coming precariously close to inverting all moral values by regarding good as evil and evil as good, as though to say, 'evil be thou my good'.

To believe that the Holy Spirit is evil is to render ourselves incapable of being convicted by him of our sinfulness and evil. We put ourselves in the position of being unforgivable. If we are never convicted then we shall never repent. If we do not repent we cannot be forgiven. The Holy Spirit cannot convict us if we regard him as evil, for evil cannot convict evil. We are shutting ourselves off from his love, mercy, truth and utter purity. We are blind to his excellent holiness. We have made ourselves unforgivable!

Jesus continued with the subject of demon possession by issuing a further warning that an evil spirit once evicted may return with evil friends to take up residence once more - 'and the last state of that man is worse than the first' (Luke 11:26). How could this be? The answer lies in the words of the evicted evil spirit when he said, 'I will return *to my house* from which I came' (Luke 11:24; emphasis added).

The man's heart is still owned by the devil. The house is swept, but it is not washed; the heart is not made holy. Sweeping takes off only the loose dirt, while the sin that besets the sinner, the beloved sin, is untouched. The house is garnished with common gifts and graces. It is not furnished with any true grace; it is all paint and varnish, not real, not lasting. It was never given up to Christ, nor dwelt in by the Spirit.

The heart, life, soul and body are to be yielded over entirely, unreservedly to Christ then the Holy Spirit will take up residence. To be indwelt by the Holy Spirit is the sure and certain way to exclude Satan from the heart (1 Corinthians 6:19; Romans 8:9; 1 Corinthians 3:16). There is a responsibility then to 'walk in the Spirit' (Galatians 5:16,25).

Some of the scribes and Pharisees responded to Jesus by challenging him to demonstrate in some conclusive way that he has God-given power and authority. They had been witness to his healings and the casting out of evil spirits but they want more. They demanded something that would be undeniably God-given. 'Such an attitude does away with faith. It originates not in a desire to know but in the decision not to believe.'[32] Years later the apostle Paul faced the same persistent problem, 'Jews request a sign' (1 Corinthians 1:22).

Jesus reacted with a severe rebuke -

> This is an evil generation. It seeks a sign, and no sign will be given to it except the sign of Jonah the prophet. For as Jonah became a sign to the Ninevites, so also the Son of Man will be to this generation (Luke 11:29-30).

---

[32] Robert H. Mounce, *New International Biblical Commentary: Matthew* (Peabody, Massachusetts: Hendrickson, 1991), p.120.

> For as Jonah was three days and three nights in the belly of the
> great fish, so will the Son of Man be three days and three nights in
> the heart of the earth (Matthew 12:40).

What happened to Jonah illustrated what the same divine love and power will do through the death and resurrection of Jesus, the Son of God. Jonah was a sign to the Ninevites because of 'the miraculous reappearance of the man thought to be dead. Had he not been cast into the sea during a raging storm, and even swallowed by a 'great fish'? Yet, here he was, alive and well.

For Christ's contemporaries the sign was going to be his glorious resurrection. This will be the greatest sign from heaven, the vindication of all that Jesus said and did, 'that promise which was made to the fathers. God has fulfilled this for us their children, in that he has raised up Jesus... And that he raised him from the dead, no more to return to corruption' (Acts 13:32,33,34).

The Queen of the South, a Gentile, travelled 1,610km (1,000 miles) to meet King Solomon and hear his wisdom. She did not hesitate at the danger, hardships, time and expense of the journey in her desire to see and hear one so renowned. Yet here was One in Galilee whose wisdom so far exceeded that of Solomon and the Jews demeaned him and dismissed the true wisdom of God proclaimed by him in the gospel of salvation which he preached. The Lord's purpose here is not to praise the Gentile but to shame the Jew!

'While he was still talking to the multitudes, behold, his mother and brothers stood outside, seeking to speak with him' (Matthew 12:46). It would have been just as easy for one of the family to go to Jesus directly, but they send a message, presumably with the intention of getting him away from the crowd in order to speak to him privately.

Jesus knew the motivation that brought his family to see him. They thought him 'out of his mind' (Mark 3:21). They had come 'to lay hold of him' and consequently take him away home, if necessary, by force. 'He came to his own, and his own did not receive him' (John 1:11). That Mary was present suggests that she was pressured into accompanying them or was taking the opportunity of seeing her Son. It is unthinkable that she would share their opinion of him.

Jesus used the circumstance to speak about his true family, his spiritual family, the family of God. He raised the question: 'Who is my mother, or my brothers?' And he looked around in a circle at those who sat about him, and said, 'Here are my mother and my brothers! For whoever does the will of God is my brother and my sister and mother' (Mark 3:33-35).

Doing the will of God means accepting Jesus of Nazareth as the Son of God and only Saviour of sinners, and yielding in devotion and service to him as the King of the Kingdom of God. To become recognised as a part of the family of God is an amazing privilege. For the Lord Jesus, Son of the living God, to call us his brothers and sisters is astounding!

33. Parables of the kingdom
Matthew 13:1-53; Mark 4:1-34; Luke 8:4-18; 13:18-21

On the same day Jesus went out of the house and sat by the sea. And great multitudes were gathered together to him, so that he got into a boat and sat; and the whole multitude stood on the shore. Then he spoke many things to them in parables (Matthew 13:1-3).

The parable was the grammatical form he often used: a simple earthly story to illustrate a spiritual heavenly truth. Yet though they were 'simple' stories they were not readily understood by all. The explanation of the general blindness to their meaning was not that it was due to any lack of intellectual ability nor failure to grasp the language, rather it was due to the providence of God. Jesus made the reason known to his disciples -

Because it has been given to you to know the mysteries of the kingdom of heaven, but to them it has not been given. For whoever has, to him more will be given, and he will have abundance; but whoever does not have, even what he has will be taken away from him. Therefore I speak to them in parables, because seeing they do not see, and hearing they do not hear, nor do they understand (Matthew 13:11-13).

The blessings and privileges of understanding the parables are not given to everyone. They are only granted to those who are followers of Jesus, to believers not to unbelievers. At this point in his ministry the Lord deliberately adopted the method of parables so that those who would not believe in him would not receive further truth about him and his kingdom.

A collection of these stories were delivered under the theme - parables of the kingdom. The kingdom is the kingdom of God or the kingdom of heaven, and it is where God's Son, King Jesus reigns supreme. What God said through his servant David, had come to pass, 'I have set my King on my holy hill of Zion' (Psalm 2:6). Jesus is King of a unique kingdom 'not of this world' (John 18:36) and entry is not by birth but by new birth for 'unless one is born again, he cannot see the kingdom of God' (John 3:3).

Through the parable of The Sower (Matthew 13:1-9,18-23) Jesus was answering the question why so few people responded positively to his ministry. Was the fault in the teacher (the sower), the teaching (the seed) or the taught (the soil)? In other words did the teacher lack the necessary skills to describe the kingdom clearly enough. If not, then was the inadequacy in the teaching; was the doctrine not good enough to make an appeal to the hearer? If that was also not the weakness, then where did it lie?

Jesus placed responsibility firmly and squarely on those who heard. He identified four conditions of the human heart in response to the good news of God's salvation -

- the hard-hearted [unresponsive] the word does not penetrate and is soon forgotten;
- the shallow-hearted [impulsive], they enthusiastically receive the word but when difficulties arise because of their connection with Jesus, they turn back;
- the half-hearted [preoccupied] also begin well but other interests, concerns or pleasures begin to take priority and draw them away;
- the wholehearted [well-prepared] who respond favourably, endure magnificently and glorify God by the quality of their lives and perseverance in his service.

In the parable of The Lamp Under a Basket (Mark 4:21-25) Jesus pointed out how the believer is to live before the world. Drawing an analogy from the positioning of a lamp he taught that disciples were not to hide themselves away but to 'shine' for the glory of God and the benefit of others. As he had taught earlier in the Sermon on the Mount, 'Let your light so shine before men, that they may see your good works and glorify your Father in heaven' (Matthew 5:16).

Followers of Jesus must be ready and willing to explain why they live as they do. Years later the apostle Peter would urge Christians: 'Always be ready to give a defence to everyone who asks you a reason for the hope that is in you, with meekness and fear' (1 Peter 3:15).

The work of God in the human heart is not always obvious in the beginning. The parable of The Seed Growing Secretly (Mark 4:26-29) showed that in some cases the initial impact of the kingdom in individuals may be almost imperceptible, but growth will come. For some disciples progress is slow.

Through the parable of The Wheat and Tares (Matthew 13:24-30,36-43) a heart-searching warning is uttered to all who profess faith in Jesus. In the early stages of growth tares are more or less indistinguishable from genuine wheat even though the tares represent the sons of the wicked one and the wheat 'the sons of the kingdom'. Jesus interpreted the parable, 'He who sows the good seed is the Son of Man' (Matthew 13:37). According to the prophecy of Daniel given to him in a vision -

> I was watching in the night visions, and behold, One like the Son of Man, coming with the clouds of heaven! He came to the Ancient of Days, and they brought him near before him. Then to him was given dominion and glory and a kingdom, that all peoples, nations, and languages should serve him. His dominion is an everlasting dominion, which shall not pass away, and his kingdom the one which shall not be destroyed (Daniel 7:13-14).

Jesus is the Son of Man, the King of an enormous kingdom. 'The field is the world, the good seeds are the sons of the kingdom, but the tares are the sons of the wicked one' (Matthew 13:38). Jesus sows the good seed of the kingdom, the message of salvation through repentance and faith. The tares are the sons of the devil. Jesus will later address the Jews who plan to have him put to death: 'You are of your father the devil, and the desires of your father you want to do. He was a murderer from the beginning' (John 8:44). These 'tares' were sown in the world 'among the wheat' at night. There was a Judas among the apostles and an Ananias and Sapphira among the early church.

Jesus challenged all who heard him to ask themselves in effect, 'Am I a son of the kingdom or a son of the wicked one? What will be my outcome at the final harvest?' (cf. Matthew 7:21-23) For those who are not sons of the kingdom but sons of wickedness there will be a dreadful end -

> The Son of Man will send out his angels, and they will gather out of his kingdom all things that offend, and those who practice lawlessness, and will cast them into the furnace of fire. There will be wailing and gnashing of teeth. Then the righteous will shine forth as the sun in the kingdom of their Father. He who has ears to hear, let him hear! (Matthew 13:41-43)

The parable of The Mustard Seed (Matthew 13:31-32) reassures the people of God that the kingdom may begin extremely small but the outcome will be enormous as is evident in the vision of the apostle John who was privileged to see at the end: 'a great multitude which no one could number, of all nations, tribes, peoples, and tongues, standing before the throne and before the Lamb, clothed with white robes, with palm branches in their hands, and crying out with a loud voice, saying, "Salvation belongs to our God who sits on the throne, and to the Lamb!"' (Revelation 7:9-10)

The parable of The Leaven (Matthew 13:33) teaches the permeating power and influence of Christian transformation. When the heart is changed by the grace of God the whole life is radically transformed: the faculties of the mind, heart and will are dramatically affected. Through the changes taking place in the individual, the home and family and then society at large are impacted. As Paul later encouraged Christians at Rome: 'I beseech you therefore, brethren, by the mercies of God, that you present your bodies a living sacrifice, holy, acceptable to God, which is your reasonable service. And do not be conformed to this world, but be transformed by the renewing of your mind, that you may prove what is that good and acceptable and perfect will of God' (Romans 12:1-2).

> All these things Jesus spoke to the multitude in parables; and without a parable he did not speak to them, that it might be fulfilled which was spoken by the prophet, saying: 'I will open my mouth in parables; I will utter things kept secret from the foundation of the world' (Matthew 13:34-35).

Jesus spoke in parables to the multitudes in fulfilment of prophecy (Psalm 78:2).

Up to this point Jesus had addressed his parables to the crowd, then he sent the multitude away and went into the house. And his disciples came to him, saying, 'Explain to us the parable of the tares of the field' (Matthew 13:36). Although understanding of the secrets of the kingdom of heaven had been given to them (Matthew 13:11-13; cf. 13:16), they still needed help to comprehend the full implications of Jesus' teaching.

The parable of The Hidden Treasure (Matthew 13:44) represents the one who 'stumbles' across the Gospel of God's grace. A number of the Lord's people were not seeking the Lord or salvation when 'by chance' (as Jesus spoke of the good Samaritan coming across the seriously injured Jew on the road down from Jerusalem to Jericho) they came into contact with both. Maybe through a friend, or receiving a tract, or a providential conversation on a train or bus. Once the heart has been gripped and the mind has become eager to know more, there is nothing that will not be given up in order to know him. As the apostle Paul testified -

> I have suffered the loss of all things, and count them as rubbish, that I may gain Christ and be found in him, not having my own righteousness, which is from the law, but that which is through faith in Christ, the righteousness which is from God by faith (Philippians 3:8-9).

That which demonstrates the other side of the salvation relationship is the parable of The Pearl of Great Price (Matthew 13:45-46). Here it is not the pearl which is likened to the Kingdom of God but the Merchant. The subject is the Merchant, the object is the costly pearl. The Saviour is the Merchant seeking his Bride, his Church, his people and to obtain her will be very costly. It will require enormous sacrifices: leaving the Father, leaving Heaven, becoming a human being forever, living life here for some years among his own creatures as one of us, suffering ill-treatment of the worst kind, and laying down his perfectly holy life for an enormous gathering of forgiven sinful, wicked, wayward, hopeless, weak and helpless individuals.

> For you know the grace of our Lord Jesus Christ, that though he was rich, yet for your sakes he became poor, that you through his poverty might become rich (2 Corinthians 8:9).

In the parable of The Dragnet (Matthew 13:47-50) Jesus re-emphasised the basis upon which the division will finally be made for those who will enjoy eternity with God and with God's people in a gloriously renewed earth. At the end of this age there will be a separation of 'the wicked from among the just' (Matthew 13:49). The just or righteous are all those who have turned to God in repentance and faith and put their lives and future in the hands of the Lord Jesus Christ who is 'the Lord our Righteousness' (Jeremiah 23:6).

34. Jesus stills the storm
Matthew 8:18,23-27; Mark 4:35-41; Luke 8:22-25

'And when Jesus saw great multitudes about him, he gave a command to depart to the other side' (Matthew 8:18), to the eastern shore of the Sea of Galilee. 'And other little boats were also with him' (Mark 4:36). He was in 'the stern' (Mark 4:38), that is, at the rear or back of the boat, in the position that was usually occupied by any distinguished person. It was common to have cushions and a carpet arranged in that section for the comfort of the traveller. Among the disciples with Jesus were Peter, Andrew, James and John who were fishermen used to sailing on that inland sea. As the boat set out and began to cross the expanse of water Jesus 'fell asleep' (Luke 8:23).

The sheltered location of 'the Sea of Galilee'[33] largely surrounded by high mountains and low elevation results in the winters being mild though subject to brief violent storms; the cool air from the uplands rushing down the gorges with great violence and tossing the waters in tempestuous waves. These storms are fairly frequent and extremely dangerous to small boats. Occasionally a tempest breaks over the sea in which a boat could hardly survive - hence the anxiety of the disciples when the storm broke out (Mark 4:35-41).

Jesus had instructed the disciples to cross over to the other side. When the boat left the shore there was no suggestion of a storm brewing 'suddenly a great tempest arose on the sea, so that the boat was covered with the

---

[33] See 'The Sea of Galilee' in the chapter on Significant facts, p.345.

waves. But he was asleep' (Matthew 8:24), 'in the stern, asleep on a pillow' (Mark 4:38). The waves beat into the boat, and 'they were filling with water, and were in jeopardy' (Luke 8:23). Yet Jesus continued to sleep whilst the tempest raged.

All through the Gospels there is testimony that Jesus always possessed a calm serenity, a tranquility of mind and heart in all circumstances, whether being threatened with his life by an angry mob, or being tossed up and down in a fierce storm.

The disciples went back to Jesus in the stern and woke him saying, 'Master, Master, do you not care that we are perishing? Lord, save us!' Jesus 'arose and rebuked the wind and the raging of the water. And they ceased, and there was a calm' (Luke 8:24; cf. Psalm 107:27-29).

He *rebuked* the wind and the waves because storms are part of the curse of God upon the earth. They are a reminder that humanity has sinned against God. It is part of the great judgment of God on account of our rebellion against him (Romans 8:19-22). He said 'to the sea, "Peace, be still!" And the wind ceased and there was a great calm' (Mark 4:39). The wise man in the Book of Proverbs asked -

> Who has gathered the wind in his fists? Who has bound the waters in a garment? Who has established all the ends of the earth? What is his name, and *what is his Son's name, if you know?* (Proverbs 30:4; emphasis added)

What were they expecting from Jesus? What did they hope he would do? They were afraid and yet also amazed at the miracle: 'Who can this be? For he commands even the winds and water, and they obey him!' (Luke 8:25)

Everything Jesus did and everything Jesus said was designed to show who he is and why he came: he is 'Immanuel', which is translated, 'God with us'; he is Jesus 'for he will save his people from their sins' (Matthew 1:23,21). Stier declares -

> The whole human life of the Son of God is in all its circumstances and details altogether symbolical, because He who is the image of the invisible God in the flesh appears... and this symbolic, typical, prophetical character meets us with special significance on some most striking occasions.[34]

---

[34] Rudolf Stier, *The Words of the Lord Jesus* (Edinburgh: T & T Clark, 1885), vol. 1. pp.349-50.

35. The Gadarene demoniacs healed
Matthew 8:28-34; Mark 5:1-20; Luke 8:26-39

In the healing miracle which follows, there is a wonderful connection with the miracle of the stilling of the storm. Meeting two men, greatly troubled and deeply distressed in body, mind and spirit, the Lord was, in effect, once more declaring: 'Peace, be still!' Once over nature; once over humanity.

It was night when Jesus and his disciples disembarked on the southeastern shore of the Sea of Galilee, in the land of the Gadarenes in Decapolis. On that section of the lake's shore there were many caves in the limestone rock. A number of those caves were being used as tombs for the dead. It would be a strange, disturbing kind of place during the day. No doubt at night it would take on a more unsettling, even frightening atmosphere. Mentally disturbed people living among those caves rendered it terrifying indeed.

Suddenly the Lord and his companions were confronted by two men. There 'met him two demon-possessed men, coming out of the tombs, exceedingly fierce, so that no one could pass that way' (Matthew 8:28). There were two men, two sufferers (Mark and Luke chose to record the striking healing and transformation of just one of them). When the Lord Jesus 'stepped out on the land, there met him a certain man from the city who had demons for a long time. And he wore no clothes' (Luke 8:27).

What is demon possession?

This is the most important, and in many respects the most perplexing of all the demoniac cures performed by the Lord Jesus and recorded in the New Testament. To identify demon-possession with other afflictions of body, mind or heart is not only to disregard the record of Holy Scripture, it also dishonours the Lord Jesus Christ. The Lord Jesus spoke of those who were demon possessed not as persons merely of a disordered mind but as subject to an alien spiritual power. Demon-possession involves the presence of two personalities - one human, the other devilish. For example, on an earlier occasion, Jesus addressed the evil spirit, as distinct from the man, when he said, 'Be quiet, and come out of him!' (Mark 1:25) Again here Jesus addresses the demon, 'Come out of the man, unclean spirit!' (Mark 5:8)

The man was 'crying out and cutting himself' - an all too familiar occurrence in our own day. Self-harm may have many causes. There are those who cut themselves to inflict great pain to distract themselves from greater emotional pain that they find intolerable. Others may cut themselves because they believe they have committed some terrible wrong and want to punish themselves. This man was being tormented by evil spirits who meant him harm. They were responsible - directly or indirectly - for his self-harm.

This man had the remarkable strength of the insane. When for his own good as well as the townsfolk's safety 'he was kept under guard, bound with chains and shackles ... he broke the bonds and was driven by the demon into the wilderness' (Luke 8:29).

He had a disorder of the mind and a disorder of the spirit. Demons were in residence who time and again exerted an evil, hurtful and vile influence and power over him.

He was a frightening and yet a pitiable man. Jesus issued a command, 'Come out of the man, unclean spirit!' (Mark 5:8) The demon reacted, 'What have I to do with you, Jesus, Son of the Most High God? I implore you by God that you do not torment me' (Mark 5:7).

How strange that on this occasion the unclean spirits did not immediately obey the Lord Jesus! There is no doubt that the Lord would be in full control and he would know exactly what he was doing. He could have ensured that his command was immediately carried out. It is evident that something further was intended by the Saviour. Lenski asserts -

> The outstanding thing is that the demons openly display their supernatural knowledge. The demoniac had never seen Jesus, yet the demons in him call Jesus by his name. The spirits always know who Jesus is and in a malicious fashion yell out their mysterious knowledge ... The demons are determined to publish the deity of Jesus as if to spite him who wanted men to arrive at this knowledge by faith in his words and his works. Jesus usually silences them at once.[35]

By their own confession these demons knew that a time was coming when light will triumph over darkness, good will conquer and dispel evil and they will be severely punished (Matthew 8:29).

Jesus asked the name of the demon who replied, 'My name is Legion; for we are many'. There followed a strange request, he begged Jesus 'earnestly that he would not send them out of the country' (Mark 5:9,10). When they then asked that they be sent into a herd of pigs the Lord gave permission. Questions immediately arise, the first is, why did the demon request to go into the pigs?

> Was it simply a yearning to destroy? Was it perhaps a sinister hope that the owners of the herd, seeing their property destroyed, would

[35] Richard C.H. Lenski, *The Interpretation of St. Mark's Gospel* (Minneapolis, Minnesota: Augsburg, 1961), p.208.

be filled with antagonism toward Jesus? The answer has not been revealed. It is, however, worthy of special attention that the demons are fully aware of the fact that without Christ's permission they will not be able to enter the pigs.[36]

Secondly, why did the Lord grant the request of Legion and his evil spirit companions? Does the Saviour perhaps want this possessed man to see a dramatic enactment of his delivery - pigs, entered by the evil spirits, in turmoil and agitation rushing headlong into the sea and perishing? As the apostle John was later to write, 'For this purpose the Son of God was manifested, that he might destroy the works of the devil' (1 John 3:8).

Another question remains: Why did the Lord Jesus permit the destruction of two thousand pigs? Since Gadara the chief town of the district was a Greek city some scholars have assumed that the owners of the pigs were Gentiles; but that would raise the moral problem of the Lord destroying the livelihood of Gentiles.

There are a number of factors which clearly indicate that the local people were not Gentiles but Jews. Firstly the name 'Lord' used by Jesus (Mark 5:19) would be readily understood by a Jew but not a Gentile. It signifies Yahweh, the Old Testament name for the covenant God. Secondly pigs were unclean animals according to the Law of Moses (Leviticus 11:7-8; Deuteronomy 14:8). It would seem therefore that God's judgment fell upon these Jews who were blatantly violating the Law of God for profit by providing forbidden meat. This loss would be a judgment against them.

The Lord had delivered Legion from possession by many evil spirits. He who was once out of his mind and could not be bound even with chains, was 'sitting and clothed and in his right mind' (Mark 5:15). The townspeople who came out to see for themselves what had happened, saw and were terrified. Of what were they so afraid; the destruction of the pigs, the reaction of the demons, or the power of this man from Galilee? They 'begged him to depart from their region' (Matthew 8:34). Instead of being drawn to Jesus they shrank from him. They were blind to his mercy, they feared only his power. This reaction was wholly abnormal and unreasonable as are all reactions of unbelief.

In appreciation the restored man wanted to accompany Jesus as he was about to sail away. His request was denied and a commission given. His assignment was to tell his friends what the Lord Jesus had done for him and the compassion shown towards him. The man took the instruction to heart.

---

[36] William Hendriksen, *The Gospel of Mark* (Edinburgh: Banner of Truth Trust, 1975), p.193.

'He departed and began to proclaim in Decapolis all that Jesus had done for him; and all marvelled' (Mark 5:20).

The region of the Decapolis (meaning 'ten cities') spread south and east from the southeast side of the Sea of Galilee. This was a region of ten Hellenistic cities loosely associated with each other, and loosely controlled by Rome. There was a large Roman military presence guarding the eastern frontier, but the cities were bastions of Greek culture (Hellenism) and places that religious Jews avoided.

Now when Jesus had crossed over again by boat to the other side they landed at Capernaum and -

> the multitude welcomed him, for they were all waiting for him. And behold, there came a man named Jairus, and he was a ruler of the synagogue. And he fell down at Jesus' feet and begged him to come to his house, for he had an only daughter about twelve years of age, and she was dying' (Luke 8:40-42).

The Jewish leadership was already hostile towards Jesus and Jairus was an elder of the synagogue. There would be considerable pressure upon Jairus not to turn to Jesus for help. Love for his dying daughter overcame any prejudice he might have felt or any fear at loosing the respect of his colleagues among the Jewish leadership. He fell at the Master's feet. Though he was a ruler in the synagogue he put aside all considerations of dignity and pleaded for his only daughter's life. 'So Jesus went with him, and a great multitude followed him and thronged him' (Mark 5:24).

36. The woman with a haemorrhage
Matthew 9:18-26; Mark 5:21-43; Luke 8:40-56

To this great crowd walking along the road to the home of Jairus, a needy woman drew near. The woman was very ill, she suffered from 'a flow of blood', the precise nature of her illness was not recorded, not even by Dr Luke the physician. Sufficient was noted to show the seriousness of her complaint. She had been suffering 'for twelve years and had suffered many things from many physicians. She had spent all that she had and was no better, but rather grew worse' (Mark 5:25-26).

Apart from the weakness and discomfort she experienced, she also suffered the stigma associated with her disease. This particular illness rendered a woman ceremonially unclean for as long as it lasted. In Leviticus 15:25-30 the law of God did not permit her participation in any religious ceremony, debarred her from entering a synagogue or the temple, and if she touched anyone they would be ceremonially unclean for the rest of that day. If, as was most likely, she shared a home with others then life would be particularly difficult as anything she touched had not to be touched by anyone else. Underlying the ceremonial law, was an important law of hygiene and the avoidance of the spread of infection.

This woman was extremely poor because she had spent everything on seeking a cure. She was excluded from the worshipping life of the community. She was a poor, ill, lonely, isolated woman and yet she loved God for Jesus called her, 'Daughter'. She 'came from behind and touched the hem of his garment. For she said to herself, "If only I may touch his garment, I shall be made well"' (Matthew 9:20-21; 14:36; Mark 6:56; Luke 6:19). It is evident that the woman had a strong faith in Jesus which he confirmed as he immediately healed her and said, 'Daughter, be of good cheer; your faith has made you well. Go in peace' (Luke 8:48).

The Lord knew she had touched his clothing. He also knew about her, who she was and that she believed and was healed. It was for her sake that the Lord said, 'Who touched me?' For her condition had rendered her an outcast in the community. If the cure had been in secret it would have been very difficult if not impossible for her to put an end to the contempt she had experienced for years. Geldenhuys concludes: 'For this reason the Saviour, who knew her in all her need and sorrows, and understood her circumstances, makes her appear before the whole multitude to testify publicly that she has been healed.'[37]

Jesus sensed the touch of this woman out of all the many people bustling about him, for he said, 'Somebody touched me, for I perceived power going out from me' (Luke 8:46; cf. 6:19). Healing power had flowed from him. Jesus made it clear that it was not the touching of his garment but his communicated power in response to her faith in him which resulted in her healing.

While he was still speaking a message came from the house of Jairus to tell him, 'Your daughter is dead. Do not trouble the Teacher' (Luke 8:49). Jesus immediately reassured Jairus not to be afraid for his daughter was going to be made well. 'When Jesus came into the ruler's house, and saw the flute players and the noisy crowd wailing, he said to them, "Make room, for the girl is not dead, but sleeping". And they ridiculed him' (Matthew 9:23-24). When the crowd was put outside, 'he permitted no one to go in except Peter, James, and John, and the father and mother of the girl' (Luke 8:51).

Jesus went to the child, took hold of her hand and said, 'Talitha, cumi,' which is translated, 'Little girl, I say to you, arise.' Immediately the girl

---

[37] Norval Geldenhuys, *Commentary on the Gospel of Luke* (London: Marshall, Morgan and Scott, 1950), p.261.

arose and walked (Mark 5:41-42). Jesus instructed the parents to tell no one what had happened, nevertheless 'the report of this went out into all the land' (Matthew 9:26).

These two miracles were recorded in an inter-connected form to show that they hold a united significance. The healing of the woman with a persistent haemorrhage and the raising of the daughter of a synagogue elder has a spiritual message. Firstly we note that both were female (Mark 5:23,25). Secondly, both had personal contact with the Lord Jesus Christ, the woman 'touched his garment' (Mark 5:27) and the Lord 'took the child by the hand' (Mark 5:41). Thirdly, the number of years in each case is no mere coincidence. The woman had been sick for twelve years (Mark 5:25; Luke 8:43). The girl was twelve years old (Mark 5:42; Luke 8:42).

Twelve indicates that both the woman and the girl represent the nation of Israel. Jacob, the son of Isaac, the grandson of Abraham, had his name changed by God from Jacob to Israel and he had twelve sons who became the heads of the twelve tribes of the nation Israel. On Mount Carmel 'Elijah took twelve stones, according to the number of the tribes of the sons of Jacob, to whom the word of the LORD had come, saying, "Israel shall be your name"'(1 Kings 18:31). The Lord Jesus appointed twelve apostles 'and gave them power and authority over all demons, and to cure diseases. He sent them to preach the kingdom of God and to heal the sick' (Luke 9:1-2). The number twelve symbolises Israel.

The twelve year old girl who is the daughter of an elder in the synagogue represents the spiritually dead Jews who attend the synagogue to worship and pray. Only the touch of Jesus through his glorious Gospel can bring such people to spiritual life and true faith. Here is a promise that the Gospel of Jesus Christ will raise up many from Judaism.

The Israelite woman who had been ill for twelve years represents the believing Jews - for she is called 'daughter' by the Lord Jesus Christ (Mark 5:34). These believing Jews have suffered much under their physicians (teachers: Rabbis, scribes and Pharisees) who had been unable to affect a cure. In fact their condition 'was no better, but rather grew worse' (Mark 5:26).

Jeremiah the prophet cried out -

> For the hurt of the daughter of my people I am hurt. I am mourning; astonishment has taken hold of me. Is there no balm in Gilead, is there no physician there? Why then is there no recovery for the health of the daughter of my people? (Jeremiah 8:21-22)

Thank God there is a Physician, there is healing! Jesus, the Son of God and the Christ of God, he is the Great Physician!

When Jesus went from there two blind men followed him, crying out and saying, 'Son of David, have mercy on us!' They followed Jesus into the house and he challenged them, 'Do you believe that I am able to do this?' They said to him, 'Yes, Lord.' Then he touched their eyes, saying, 'According to your faith let it be to you.' And their eyes were opened (cf. Isaiah 35:5). 'And Jesus sternly warned them, saying, "See that no one knows it." But when they had departed, they spread the news about him in all that country' (Matthew 9:30-31). Again there was disobedience to the clear command of the Lord!

As they went out, behold, they brought to him a man, mute and demon-possessed' (Matthew 9:32). When Jesus cast out the evil spirit the man spoke. The crowd witnessing this wonderful miracle were astonished and declared, 'It was never seen like this in Israel!' (Matthew 9:33)

The Pharisees on the other hand, driven by blind prejudice, blurted out, 'He casts out demons by the ruler of the demons' (Matthew 9:34). Were these Pharisees not present previously when the Lord reasoned so clearly and convincingly to prove that he could not be casting out an evil spirit by the power of an evil spirit? (see Matthew 12:24) Further, are they blind to the wonderful significance of the blind being given their sight and the mute being given speech? They must have known that Isaiah's prophecy was linked to the coming of the Messiah, that 'the eyes of the blind shall be opened... and the tongue of the dumb sing' (Isaiah 35:5,6). Indisputable evidence was right before their eyes!

37. The twelve apostles sent out
Matthew 10:1,5-42; Mark 6:7-11; Luke 9:1-6

Jesus 'called the twelve to himself, and began to send them out two by two' (Mark 6:7). He 'gave them power and authority over all demons, and to cure diseases. He sent them to preach the kingdom of God and to heal the sick' (Luke 9:1-2). He told them not to go to the Gentiles or Samaritans, but to 'go rather to the lost sheep of the house of Israel... Heal the sick, cleanse the lepers, raise the dead, cast out demons' (Matthew 10:6,8). They were to take no supplies with them: no money and no change of clothing. They were to rely upon the kindness, generosity and hospitality of the people they met.

If a city or house would not receive them, they were to shake the dust from their feet as they left that place. They were warned of the dangers involved but assured of the assistance of the Holy Spirit. They were to be afraid of no one, neither human nor devil. God alone was to be feared! The message will divide families, some believing some not. The cost of discipleship was spelt out clearly. Jesus said -

> He who loves father or mother more than me is not worthy of me. And he who loves son or daughter more than me is not worthy of me. And he who does not take his cross and follow after me is not worthy of me (Matthew 10:37-38).

The question is one of priorities. Commitment to the Lord Jesus must take precedence over every other relationship. When a member of a family becomes a disciple of Christ the words of the prophet Micah come painfully true. In many godless homes there is hostility towards the follower of Christ: 'For son dishonours father, daughter rises against her mother, daughter-in-law against her mother-in-law; a man's enemies are the men of his own household' (Micah 7:6; cf. Matthew 10:35-36).

Even in a godly household, love for Jesus must always take priority - even before ourselves. Like Paul we will say, 'God forbid that I should boast except in the cross of our Lord Jesus Christ, by whom the world has been crucified to me, and I to the world' (Galatians 6:14). Stressing the importance and demands of commitment Jesus sent out his apostles whilst he himself continued to preach throughout Galilee.

The death of John the Baptist

Meanwhile King Herod Antipas the tetrarch heard of Jesus and he said, 'John the Baptist is risen from the dead, and therefore these powers are at work in him.' Others said, 'It is Elijah.' And others said, 'It is the Prophet, or like one of the prophets.' Herod Antipas said, 'This is John, whom I beheaded; he has been raised from the dead!' (Mark 6:16)

Herod was suffering with a bad conscience for his foolishness, weakness and murderous act in ordering the execution of John. Herod had arrested and imprisoned John because the Baptist had rebuked him for taking Herodias, his brother Philip's wife saying plainly, 'It is not lawful for you to have her' (Matthew 14:4).

When Herod's birthday had been celebrated, the daughter of Herodias danced before them and pleased Herod. Therefore he promised with an oath to give her whatever she might ask. No doubt heavily intoxicated with wine, he also swore to her, 'Whatever you ask me, I will give you, up to half my kingdom' (Mark 6:23). The girl went immediately to her mother Herodias who told her to ask for the head of John the Baptist.

When she told the king in front of his nobles, the high officers and the chief men of Galilee he was -

exceedingly sorry; yet, because of the oaths and because of those who sat with him, he did not want to refuse her. Immediately the king sent an executioner and commanded his head to be brought. And he went and beheaded him in prison, brought his head on a platter, and gave it to the girl; and the girl gave it to her mother (Mark 6:26-28).

The return of the apostles

The apostles returned to Jesus after fulfilling their preaching and healing commission and reported what they had done and what they had taught. He encouraged them to take a break and be refreshed. Jesus 'took them and went aside privately into a deserted place belonging to the city called Bethsaida' (Luke 9:10).

The River Jordan flowed into the Sea of Galilee at the north coast and a little further round the seashore to the east was Bethsaida Julias, so called to distinguish it from the other Bethsaida of Galilee. The distance from Capernaum to Bethsaida Julias was about 4 miles (6km) by sea. This was the Bethsaida to which Jesus was heading.

Having been impressed by the miracles which Jesus performed, and anticipating his destination by the direction of the boat, thousands decided to travel around the northwest coastland by foot. As soon as Jesus arrived with his disciples he went up a mountain to spend time alone with them (John 6:3). Near the town of Bethsaida Julias, almost on the lakeside, was a grass plain. Here the crowds gathered in their thousands. After a while Jesus came down the mountain and taught them. When he saw the great multitude he 'was moved with compassion for them, because they were like sheep not having a shepherd. So he began to teach them many things' (Mark 6:34).

They were 'like sheep having no shepherd' because those who were their appointed shepherds (pastors) were failing in their duties.

As noted before, the Jewish leadership was weighing the people down with 'heavy burdens hard to bear' (Matthew 23:4; cf. vv.5-36), with petty details about Sabbath observance, rituals, legalistic trivia, fasts, phylacteries on their foreheads and tassels on their clothing. They cared more for themselves than for the people (cf. Ezekiel 34:2-5). Their concern was for externals, how they appeared to others. 'They love the best places at feasts, the best seats in the synagogues, greetings in the marketplaces, and to be called by men, "Rabbi, Rabbi"' (Matthew 23:6-7).

The Lord's concern was the heart, 'the weightier matters of the law: justice and mercy and faith' (Matthew 23:23). The people needed 'shepherds according to [God's] heart, who will feed [them] with knowledge and under-standing' (Jeremiah 3:15).

38. Feeding five thousand (Bethsaida Julias)
Matthew 14:13-21; Mark 6:33-44; Luke 9:11-17; John 6:1-14

As evening approached Jesus raised concern about the hunger of the people. He raised the subject with Philip who told him that to feed such a crowd would take a sum something like the equivalent of six months' wages for a working man. Other apostles suggested that the people should be sent away to buy food. Jesus responded that the folk need not be sent away but that the apostles should provide the food for them. Andrew, Simon Peter's brother, said there was a boy there who had five barley loaves and two small fish, but what were they among so many? Small barley loaves were a coarse bread, the food of the very poor.

Jesus took action. He said that the people were to sit in groups of fifty. Was he going to link this miracle with a similar miracle performed by Elisha hundreds of years earlier? The bread used by the prophet Elisha was 'twenty loaves of barley bread' (2 Kings 4:42). The bread used by the Lord Jesus Christ was 'five barley loaves' (John 6:9). The five thousand (one hundred groups of fifty) miraculously fed by Jesus contrast with the one hundred miraculously fed through Elisha. One greater than Elisha was there.

The men, women and children all ate bread and fish to their satisfaction and twelve baskets of fragments were collected by the apostles.

The miracle had a marked impact on the people and they questioned whether Jesus might be the promised special prophet (John 6:14; Deuteronomy 18:18-19). Aware of this reaction among the crowd and conscious that they would try to take him by force to make him king, he immediately sent his disciples to sail round to Bethsaida of Galilee (on the outskirts of Capernaum) whilst he sent the multitude away and climbed the mountain to spend time in prayer.

Whilst Jesus is a King, indeed, the 'King of Kings and Lord of lords' (1 Timothy 6:15; Revelation 19:16), his kingship is far different from that desired by this crowd. He is not willing to submit himself to their ideas. He will be King in accordance with the will of God in manner, time and place.

The connection between this miracle, the feeding of the five thousand, and the miracle of changing water into wine (John 2:1-11) is quite striking. In the first miracle Jesus provided an abundance of wine. In this miracle Jesus provided an abundance of bread; more than enough wine; more than enough bread. Both miracles were providentially timed one year apart and thus both were just before the celebration of the Jewish Festival of Passover (John 2:13; 6:4).

Spiritually understood they point to another Passover; the Passover Jesus celebrated with his disciples shortly before his crucifixion (John 13:1). At that Passover the Old Covenant celebration was superseded by the New Covenant celebration when 'as they were eating, Jesus took bread, blessed and broke it, and gave it to the disciples and said -

> 'Take, eat; this is my body.' Then he took the cup, and gave thanks, and gave it to them, saying, 'Drink from it, all of you. For this is my blood of the new covenant, which is shed for many for the remission of sins' (Matthew 26:26-28).

Jesus drew the strongest connection between bread and his unique life and between wine and his unique death. His self-sacrifice cleanses *all* who come in repentance and faith to him.

The miracle of the feeding of the five thousand must have had a great impact on the disciples because it is the only miracle recorded in all four Gospels.

39. *Walking on the Sea of Galilee*
Matthew 14:22-33; Mark 6:45-52; John 6:15-21

The crowd had been dispersed, Jesus was at prayer, and the disciples were sailing 'toward Capernaum'[38] when a severe storm broke out. The Lord noticed his disciples struggling to row the boat to the shore. He walked down the mountainside and on to the water towards them. Seeing his form in the distance, the disciples were understandably afraid thinking they were seeing a ghost. Jesus called out to them and reassured them of his identity. Peter asked for permission to join Jesus walking on the sea. The invitation having been given Peter stepped out of the boat and began to walk towards the Lord.

In a short time Peter, becoming increasingly aware of the storm all around him, became afraid and began to sink so that he cried out, 'Lord, save me!' Jesus caught him and with a gentle rebuke helped him back into the boat. Once on board the storm ceased and they landed safely.

The account of this by the apostle John is the briefest of the three records. He restricted himself to the barest details as though he were fully aware of either Matthew's account or that of Mark. John concerned himself with the spiritual lessons of the miracle. This was one of only eight miracles recorded by him, and they were 'written that you may believe that Jesus is the Christ, the Son of God, and that believing you may have life in his name' (John 20:31).

---

[38] Jesus had instructed the disciples to sail 'to the other side, to Bethsaida' (Mark 6:45). They set sail from Bethsaida Julias to Bethsaida in Galilee which was a suburb of Capernaum, hence they were sailing 'toward Capernaum' (John 6:17).

John understood that when Jesus walked on the water he was presenting a living parable which might be interpreted to great spiritual benefit. Jesus was teaching his Church by his actions. The whole event was designed to illustrate great truths concerning the Christ, the Son of God.

Jesus, though separated by more than 5km (three miles) from his disciples, was fully aware of the situation they faced. Seeing them in distress he walked over the storm tossed sea to be with them. Job said, *God 'alone spreads out the heavens, and treads on the waves of the sea ...He does great things past finding out, yes, wonders without number. If he goes by me, I do not see him; if he moves past, I do not perceive him'* (Job 9:8,10-11; emphasis added).

These words are puzzling in their context and yet have striking connection with Jesus walking on the Sea of Galilee. Furthermore Mark wrote, 'He came to them, walking on the sea, and would have passed them by' (Mark 6:48). Was this an indication that the Lord does not intrude into the lives of his people but makes his presence felt and graciously waits to be invited in. The same point is made in Revelation 3:20 where the risen Lord says, 'Behold, I stand at the door and knock. If anyone hears my voice and opens the door, I will come in to him and dine with him, and he with me.'

It looks as though the words of Job were written in Scripture expressly for the events on the sea that night. The same seems true for another portion of Old Testament Scripture -

> Those who go down to the sea in ships, who do business on great waters, they see the works of the LORD, and his wonders in the deep. For he commands and raises the stormy wind, which lifts up the waves of the sea. They mount up to the heavens, they go down again to the depths; their soul melts because of trouble. They reel to and fro, and stagger like a drunken man, and are at their wits' end. Then they cry out to the LORD in their trouble, and he brings them out of their distresses. He calms the storm, so that its waves are still. Then they are glad because they are quiet; so he guides them to their desired haven (Psalm 107:23-30).

Where were the disciples going? They were sailing across the Sea of Galilee to their destination at Capernaum (John 6:17). Caper-Nahum, the place or village of Nahum the prophet. The name Nahum means 'comfort.' Jesus brought his disciples safely through to their destination - the place of comfort which was 'their desired haven' (Psalm 107:30).

What a beautiful symbol of spiritual reality. Jesus Christ, the eternal Son of God is 'Mighty God' (Isaiah 9:6) - who controls all things for the good of his people, his church (Ephesians 1:22) and will bring his followers safely through this life to heaven. What lessons are to be learnt from this dramatic parable! Indeed 'God is our refuge and strength, a very present help in trouble. Therefore we will not fear... though its waters roar and be troubled' (Psalm 46:1-3).

The Lord had instructed his disciples to 'get into the boat and go before him to the other side, to Bethsaida' (Mark 6:45). John records that they sailed 'toward Capernaum' (John 6:17). After the stilling of the storm they arrived at their destination (John 6:23). Jesus and his disciples disembarked at 'the land of Gennesaret' (Matthew 14:14; Mark 6:53).

Some commentators conclude that the wind prevented the boat from landing at Capernaum or at Bethsaida close by, and was forced to land further down the coast at the town of Gennesaret. There is however a stronger explanation. The name was also given to a strip of land about 5km (3 miles) long and 1.6 to 2.4km (1 to 1.5 miles) inland, stretching from just south of Capernaum around the southwest coastline of the Sea of Galilee. Consequently Matthew and Mark referring to 'the land of Gennesaret' would include the village or town of Bethsaida of Galilee.

Disembarking on the shore, the Lord was soon recognised and a great crowd quickly gathered bringing their sick for healing. This continued wherever he journeyed whether in villages, cities or the countryside (Mark 6:56).

40. The sermon on the Bread of Life (Capernaum)
John 6:22-71

Meanwhile when those who had been fed by Jesus realised that he was no longer in the vicinity, they boarded the newly arrived boats and sailed over to Capernaum in search of him. When they eventually found him they gathered in the synagogue (v.59). Linking with the recent great miracle of the feeding of the 5,000 in which so many of that vast company had participated, he began profound teaching on himself as the Bread of Life.

Jesus began by exposing their motives, 'Most assuredly, I say to you, you seek me, not because you saw the [miraculous] signs, but because you ate of the loaves and were filled' (v.26). Their attention was upon earthly, physical, temporary issues. That was why Jesus urged them not to 'labour for the food which perishes, but for the food which endures to everlasting life' (v.27). In other words, put your best energy into things that really count!

They followed Jesus because he was a *Healer* (v.2). They followed him believing him to be a *Prophet* (v.14). They followed him wanting forcibly to make him a *King* (v.15), but they were acting under serious misapprehension as to the significance of these terms in relation to Jesus the Christ.

He is a Healer but more than a healer of the body or mind, his primary concern is to heal the soul, to bring in spiritual health and spiritual vitality. The body is temporary; soon it will rest in the earth. What matters is the spiritual realm which is everlasting.

He is a Prophet, but not an ordinary prophet, he is *the Prophet* promised fifteen hundred years earlier whose words were predicted to be a matter of life and death. But the value of a prophet is not his miracle working as these people imagined. The real worth of a prophet is delivering the message which God has sent. These people wanted the Lord for his miracles but not his message. They wanted his works but not his words.

He is a King and more than a king, he is '*the King of kings*' (1 Timothy 6:15). But again their minds were set on earthly things. They wanted an earthly king. They wanted a new King David who would raise up an army, drive out the invading Romans and establish Israel as a power to be reckoned with once more. But the Lord's kingdom is not earthly, it is heavenly. It is spiritual; as Jesus was later to say to Pilate: 'My kingdom is not of this world. If my kingdom were of this world, my servants would fight, so that I should not be delivered to the Jews; but now my kingdom is not from here' (John 18:36).

The people's view of their religion, which many of them took very seriously indeed, consisted in 'working' works which (it was hoped) would be pleasing to God and merit eternal/heavenly life. Hence they asked Jesus, 'What shall we do, that we may work the works of God?' (v.28) to which Jesus replied, 'This is the work of God, that you believe in him whom he sent' (v.29). The labouring of which Jesus spoke is the expending of energy and effort in the realm of faith. Faith is not a pillow of idleness but demands a greater energy than the performance of good works.

It is indolence, laziness, lethargy, which keeps so many from believing in the Lord Jesus Christ. They will not rouse themselves from their natural state. The wisest of men cried out years ago, 'When will you rise from your sleep? A little sleep, a little slumber, a little folding of the hands to sleep' (Proverbs 6:9-10). Years later the apostle Paul cried out, 'Awake, you who sleep, arise from the dead, and Christ will give you light' (Ephesians 5:14).

The people countered the Lord's answer with a challenge. If this was the great work 'to believe in him' what sign then did he perform to authenticate his claim? They quoted the example of Moses who gave the Israelites manna from heaven. How insulting was this question when he had so recently miraculously fed over five thousand men, women and children. Even so Jesus pointed out that it was not Moses who gave them the bread from heaven. It was God who gave them that physical bread as Moses himself testified (Exodus 16:15).

It is God also who gives the 'true' bread, that is, the 'spiritual' bread.[39] 'For the bread of God is he who comes down from heaven and gives life to the world' (v.33). They immediately requested this bread and Jesus declared, 'I am the bread of life. He who comes to me shall never hunger, and he who believes in me shall never thirst' (v.35). This true bread is spiritual, saving, satisfying and sustaining!

Jesus challenged them, 'You have seen me and yet do not believe' (v.36). What Jesus is implying is that these Jews have seen more than our Lord's outward form. They have seen him in all the majesty of his life, his teaching and his works. Yet though there is such widespread unbelief the Father has nevertheless given his Son a people and Jesus promises, 'All that the Father gives me will come to me, and the one who comes to me I will by no means cast out' (John 6:37).

The question is sometimes asked, 'How can anyone know that they have been given by the Father to the Son?' No-one can look into 'the Lamb's Book of Life' (Revelation 21:27) to search for their name. For 'the secret things belong to the LORD our God, but those things which are revealed belong to us and to our children forever' (Deuteronomy 29:29). Nevertheless there is a way to know.

Sinners who turn to Jesus with heartfelt repentance and confident faith may certainly know that he will by no means cast them out and therefore *they are thereby* assured that they have been given by God to his Son for salvation. He promises, 'that under no imaginable circumstances will He ever expel anyone that has come'.[40]

Jesus developed this by saying, 'No one can come to me unless the Father who sent me draws him' (v.44). The ones *given to the Son* by the Father *are also drawn to the Son* by the Father and this is achieved through teaching. Jesus referred to the writing of the prophets when he said, 'they shall all be taught by God' (v.45; Isaiah 54:13; Jeremiah 31:31-34). 'Therefore everyone who has heard and learned from the Father comes to me' (v.45).

A beautiful and very clear illustration of this blessing is given in the case of the apostle Peter. When the apostles of Jesus were with him in the region of Caesarea Philippi, Peter responded to Jesus with a declaration of his true

---

[39] When the apostle Paul calls the bread in the wilderness 'spiritual food' (1 Cor 10:3) it was only spiritual because it served as a type or symbol of Christ.

[40] Arthur W. Pink, *Expositions of the Gospel of John: three volumes unabridged in one* (Grand Rapids, Michigan: Zondervan, 1970), vol. 2, pp.56-7.

identity, 'You are the Christ, the Son of the living God' (Matthew 16:16). The Lord replied, 'Blessed are you, Simon Bar-Jonah, for flesh and blood has not revealed this to you, *but my Father who is in heaven*' (Matthew 16:17).

Feeding upon Christ

Jesus then continued his teaching on himself as 'the living bread which came down from heaven' adding, 'if anyone eats of this bread, he will live forever; and the bread that I shall give is my flesh, which I shall give for the life of the world' (v.51). Taking this literally the people found it incredible. Jesus simply reiterated his teaching by emphasising the *necessity* of eating his flesh and drinking his blood.

He was evidently speaking metaphorically. The eating of v.51 is just like the hungering and thirsting of v.35 and the dying of v.50. Jesus is expressing spiritual reality at its most profound level. Eating the flesh of the Son of Man and drinking his blood (v.56) must surely rank as the most intense figure of speech - yet in some respects a plain expression of a great truth.

Why use such apparently unintelligible abstract ideas?

- because when spiritually understood they are extremely profound;
- because they are vivid, concise and easily remembered;
- because they bear constant reflection and meditation.

Consider the process of eating. It involves certain steps -

- we recognise the food as wholesome and nourishing;
- we take it into our mouths;
- we digest the chewed food.

In the spiritual realm there are comparable steps -

- what we read of Jesus in the Word of God must be recognised as true and reliable. We may not understand all that we read but we believe he is the Saviour;
- we must appropriate him. By this we mean we must take him as our own Saviour and trust him implicitly;
- we must commit ourselves to him. Recognising Jesus Christ for what he is and believing him to be true and reliable is not enough; there has to be personal commitment allowing him to permeate our whole being and to be nourished by him.

In many different ways we are told how we must respond to the Lord Jesus Christ. We must receive him (John 1:12), believe in his name (Acts 4:12), believe the gospel (Mark 16:16), come to him (John 6:35; Matthew 11:28), and call on his name (Acts 2:21). Here in John 6:53 there is a new instruction, to eat his flesh and drink his blood.

Adam disobeyed, ate and died. Followers of Jesus obey, eat and live, 'Christ in you, the hope of glory' (Colossians 1:27). We 'taste and see that the LORD *is* good' and know that 'blessed is the man who trusts in him' (Psalm 34:8). The testimony of every believer is -

> I have been crucified with Christ; it is no longer I who live, but Christ lives in me; and the life which I now live in the flesh I live by faith in the Son of God, who loved me and gave himself for me (Galatians 2:20).

Many would-be-disciples, hearing of the demands in following Jesus, found it hard. What Jesus taught was so far removed from what they wanted to hear and they were not willing to continue with him so that they might learn to understand. A decisive moment had come. The earlier rejections in Judah were now greatly exceeded by this great rejection in Galilee, for many turned from him.

Jesus therefore took the occasion to challenge his apostles as to their allegiance and Peter responded, 'Lord, to whom shall we go? You have the words of eternal life. Also we have come to believe *and know* that you are the Christ, the Son of the living God (John 6:67-69; emphasis added).

Peter did not say that he understood all the teaching of Jesus, nor that he always grasped the implications of the Lord's words, but he and the other disciples knew enough about Jesus to trust him implicitly. There are not a few occasions when believers are called upon to 'walk by faith, not by sight' (2 Corinthians 5:7).

41. Scribes and Pharisees rebuked (Capernaum)
Matthew 15:1-20; Mark 7:1-23; Luke 6:39-40)

Scribes and Pharisees from Jerusalem were never far away from Jesus, mingling with the crowds just waiting to hear or see something about which they could bring criticism. This time it was the issue of hand washing. They challenged Jesus, not simply with the thought that the disciples were being unwise or unhygienic, but because they were not adhering to the Jewish traditions.

The supposedly spiritual leaders of the people had issued a number of rules or laws, one of which was the detailed instruction on how hands were to be washed before taking food.

> Before every meal, and between each of the courses, the hands had
> to be washed, and they had to be washed in a certain way… First,
> the hands were held with the finger tips *pointing upwards;* the
> water was poured over them and must run at least down to the
> wrist; the minimum amount of water was one quarter of a log
> [approximately 80ml] … While the hands were still wet each hand
> had to be cleansed with the fist of the other … the fist of one hand
> was rubbed into the palm and against the surface of the other. This
> meant that at this stage the hands were wet with water; but that
> water was now itself unclean because it touched unclean hands.
> So, second, the hands had to be held with finger tips pointing
> downwards and the water had to be poured over them in such a
> way that it began at the wrist and ran off at the finger tips. After all
> that had been done the hands were ceremonially clean! …to fail to
> do this was in Jewish eyes, not to be guilty of bad manners, not to
> be dirty in the health sense, but to be unclean in the sight of God.[41]

Behind many of the laws of the Rabbis there was quite a lot of common
sense. There was an element of wisdom in so much of what was being
commanded. Why then was Jesus so offended by their concern? Why did he
take the opportunity to challenge the whole system concerning the laws or
the traditions of the elders? His criticism was based on their confusing
physical health and hygiene with *spiritual cleanliness.* Jesus said,

> There is nothing that enters a man from outside which can defile
> him; but the things which come out of him, those are the things
> that defile a man… whatever enters a man from outside cannot
> defile him, because it does not enter his heart but his stomach, and
> is eliminated, thus purifying all foods (Mark 7:15,18-19).

Spiritual impurity originates in the heart as the Lord made abundantly clear -

> What comes out of a man, that defiles a man. For from within, out
> of the heart of men, proceed evil thoughts, adulteries, fornications,
> murders, thefts, covetousness, wickedness, deceit, lewdness, an
> evil eye, blasphemy, pride, foolishness. All these evil things come
> from within and defile a man (Mark 7:20-23).

God alone is able to cleanse the heart, as Ananias confirmed when he said to
Paul, 'Arise and be baptised, and wash away your sins, calling on the name
of the Lord' (Acts 22:16). Of all Christians it can be confidently affirmed,
'such were some of you. But you were washed, but you were sanctified, but
you were justified in the name of the Lord Jesus and by the Spirit of our
God' (1 Corinthians 6:11).

---

[41] William Barclay, *The Gospel of Mark* (Edinburgh: St Andrew Press, 1961), p.167.

The Lord was not critical of procedures for cleanliness; he was concerned that these men, teachers of the people, in a position of spiritual oversight and spiritual care, should not get involved with details of hygiene but should care for the spiritual wellbeing of the people.

Human traditions are not divine commandments. Traditions are opinions, beliefs or customs handed down from one generation to another. The criticism of the Lord Jesus was most fierce against the way in which the tradition of the elders was taught and upheld. At times their laws clashed with God's law and in such cases their law was paramount, resulting in God's law being violated.

The Lord raised a pertinent example of this conflict and its resolution by the elders. It related to the Jewish practice of declaring finances as 'Corban' (Mark 7:11). The word 'Corban' is a Hebrew word found frequently in the law of Moses. It was used to describe the gifts that a worshipper devoted to God. The word came to be used among the Pharisees and scribes as a form of binding contract.

If a man committed certain funds or income to the work of God then he declared it 'Corban' which meant that under no circumstance could it be used for any other purpose! Such a commitment could be given in a rash moment or given in ideal circumstances which might then change suddenly and unexpectedly. Whatever the changes in circumstance, once the declaration 'Corban' had been given, nothing could undo the commitment of that gift as devoted to the temple.

To present a clear example Jesus spoke of a man who declared 'Corban' over that which would have been used for the support of his parents (Mark 7:11). No matter how serious became the need of the parents, the 'Corban' committed funds could not be used. Thus the word of God was violated (Mark 7:10; cf. Exodus 20:12; Deuteronomy 5:16; Exodus 21:17). Instead of correcting the man and teaching him to do his God-given duty to his parents, the Jewish leadership were actually binding him to disobedience.

Through this encounter Jesus instructs his disciples that they must resist anything which is taught contrary to the Word of God. We must oppose, refute and reject any teaching which results in the violation of the teaching of Scripture.

This encounter with the scribes and Pharisees brings to a close the almost twelve month period known as The Great Galilean Ministry (Matthew 4:12 to 15:20; Mark 1:14 to 7:23; Luke 4:14 to 9:17). It marked the conclusion of the Lord's ministry in Galilee.

The northern and Perean ministry

(This period is also known as 'the retirement ministry' because Jesus spent more time in private training his apostles).

The journey to the region of Tyre and Sidon

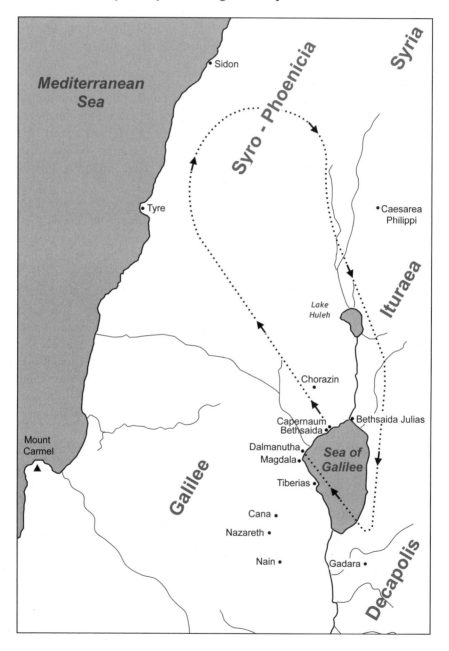

42. The Syrophoenician mother (Tyre and Sidon)
Matthew 15:21-28; Mark 7:24-30

Moving on northwest from Capernaum to the region of Tyre and Sidon, Jesus sought opportunity to be out of the public eye. He 'entered a house and wanted no one to know it' (Mark 7:24).

However, a Gentile woman, a Syro-Phoenician by birth, learned of his location and came in a state of great anxiety to Jesus. She cried out, 'Have mercy on me, O Lord, Son of David! My daughter is severely demon-possessed.' But he answered her not a word. And his disciples came and urged him, saying, 'Send her away, for she cries out after us' (Matthew 15:22-23).

The Lord did not respond to her request but said his earthly mission was to the people of Israel. His words sound harsh, 'Let the children be filled first, for it is not good to take the children's bread and throw it to the little dogs'. She took no offence however but responded with respect in a similar vein, 'Yes, Lord, yet even the little dogs under the table eat from the children's crumbs' (Mark 7:27,28). Jesus was impressed by her answer, complimented her on her 'great faith' and pronounced her daughter instantly healed.

How long Jesus stayed in the region of Tyre and Sidon is not recorded. The possibility of privacy and seclusion would be soon brought to end. News of the exorcism would probably soon become widely known and the sick, afflicted and demon-possessed brought to him.

Jesus and his disciples travelled from the coastland of Tyre and Sidon eastward out of Phoenicia and into Ituraea, the country governed by the Tetrarch Philip II. Turning south the group would pass to the east of the small Lake Huleh and then down the east coast of the Sea of Galilee eventually entering the country of Decapolis on its south-eastern shore.

Although Jesus was 'now in the territory of ancient Israel, the district and all the surroundings were essentially heathen, although in closest proximity to, and intermingled with, that which was purely Jewish.'[42] Surprisingly when the local inhabitants saw his amazing miracles, the healing of the dumb, the maimed, the blind, 'they glorified the God of Israel' (Matthew 15:31). Did any of them understand that these were the evidences of Israel's promised Messiah as Isaiah had prophesied (Isaiah 35:5-6)?

---

[42] Alfred Edersheim, *The Life and Times of Jesus the Messiah* (Peabody, Massachusetts: Hendrikson, 1993), p.504.

One sufferer was singled out for recording in the Gospels, no doubt because of the unusual procedure that the Lord employed for his healing. He was deaf and suffered a speech impediment.

> [Jesus] took him aside from the multitude, and put his fingers in his ears, and he spat and touched his tongue. Then, looking up to heaven, he sighed, and said to him, 'Ephphatha,' that is, 'Be opened.' Immediately his ears were opened, and the impediment of his tongue was loosed, and he spoke plainly (Mark 7:33-35).

Jesus was quite capable of healing even without so much as a word, but words and actions were sometimes utilised for essential teaching purposes. There were so many aids in this incident: fingers in his ears, the use of saliva, touching the tongue, looking heavenward, sighing and then the command, 'Be opened'.

Everything was Christ-centred. He was the One who was unstopping the ears, the One who enabled speech, the One connected with heaven, the One who gave the order, 'Be opened'. This was no magic; this was Messiah!

Although Jesus instructed the people not to make the miracle known they disobeyed. They were too excited at the miracle to heed the instructions given by the One who performed the miracle! Soon the news of his whereabouts became known throughout Decapolis. People from that region had flocked to hear Jesus before when he taught the Sermon on the Mount (Matthew 4:25) and no doubt many wanted to meet him once more and take neighbours and friends with them.

43. Feeding the four thousand (Decapolis)
Matthew 15:32-39; Mark 8:1-10

The land of Decapolis on the south-eastern shore of the Sea of Galilee was sparsely populated. With the arrival of Jesus a vast crowd of over four thousand men, women and children had gathered. After three days it was evident that the people were very hungry.

Jesus raised his concern with the apostles. If he dismissed them when they were so hungry many of them would not have the strength to return home, for some had travelled a considerable distance. The disciples were bewildered as to where bread to feed so many could be obtained in that wilderness region. Did any of them mention the earlier miracle of Jesus when he fed the five thousand?

When Jesus enquired about the number of loaves they had he was told seven and a few little fish. He took the bread and fish, gave thanks to God and once more multiplied the food so that the hunger of all was satisfied. There was sufficient food remaining to fill seven large baskets. Jesus dispersed the crowd and sailed across to the region of Dalmanutha on the western shore of the Sea of Galilee.

The feeding of the five thousand and the feeding of the four thousand had very marked differences: the number of participants; the size of the provision; the quantity of the leftovers; the locations; and where the people sat, in the first 'on the green grass' (Mark 6:39) and in the second (several weeks later when in the east the grass would have been scorched) 'on the ground' (Matthew 15:35).

But the most striking difference is that the one was performed before thousands of Jews, the other before thousands of Gentiles. The spiritual significance is that the Bread of Life is able to satisfy Jew and Gentile. All who come to the Saviour will be received, blessed and able to feed on the Bread of Life!

44. Pharisees and Sadducees seek a sign
Matthew 16:1-4: Mark 8:11-13

The region of Dalmanutha (also known as the region of Magdala) was on the western coast of the Sea of Galilee. On landing there Jesus was greeted by a group of hostile Pharisees and Sadducees who continued their attempts to test and trick him (Matthew 16:1; Luke 8:11). Once more they asked for a sign from heaven to confirm his credentials.

Greatly distressed by this constant request among the Jews for a sign the Lord sighed in deep sorrow of spirit. He pointed out their ability to read the signs in the sky, so that they may at times anticipate the forthcoming weather, but they could not read the signs of the times which anticipated the destruction of their temple, their city and their nation.

No sign from heaven would be given to the wayward Israelites but the sign given long before to the people of Nineveh - 'the sign of Jonah' (see 4:14). That prophet walked the length of the city for three days declaring the judgment of God upon their sin. The people repented in their thousands and the Lord had mercy (Jonah 3:1-10).

The Lord Jesus had spent *three years* preaching judgment and issuing gracious calls to repentance, but the Pharisees and Sadducees would not listen. Jesus left them at Dalmanutha and sailed north to Bethsaida Julias.

He was going to journey on to Caesarea Philippi in the northern limits of the region of Ituraea so that he might delay the final confrontation with the Jewish leadership which must begin and end in Jerusalem (John 7:1). It would start at the Feast of Tabernacles and end several months later at the Feast of the Passover with his crucifixion (John 19:14-16).

The journey to Caesarea Philippi

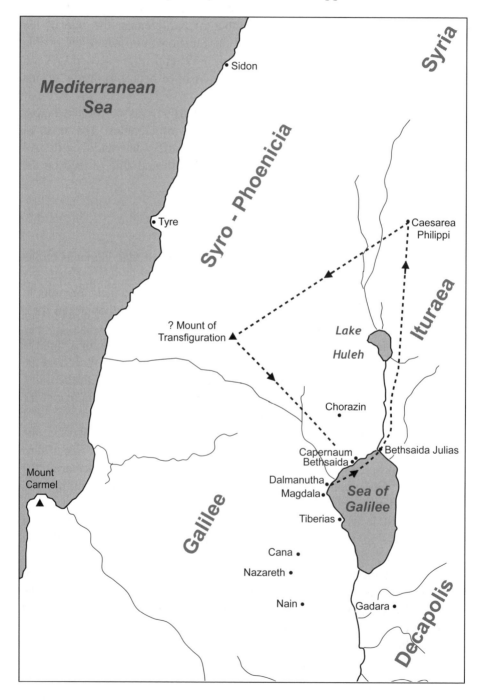

Landing at Bethsaida Julias, the disciples realised that they had forgotten to bring bread, they had only one loaf between them. Jesus took the opportunity to warn them of the 'leaven' of the Pharisees, Sadducees and Herod (Matthew 16:6; Mark 8:15). At first the disciples did not understand what Jesus meant. They could see no connection between their failure to bring bread and the subject of leaven which he raised.

Jesus challenged them for their concern about the lack of bread. He asked if they remembered the feeding of the five thousand and how many baskets of bread were left over; and the feeding of the four thousand and how many baskets of bread were gathered up afterwards. Did they now imagine that he will see them starve?

Those two miracles should have convinced the disciples that he was not concerned about any lack of bread but was drawing out an analogy through the subject of leaven. Eventually they understood that Jesus was referring to *the doctrines* of the Pharisees, Sadducees and Herod being like leaven.

Leaven is used in the Scriptures to symbolise the hidden influence that might be exerted and infiltrate, whether good or bad (Matthew 13:33; 1 Corinthians 5:6-8). The leaven of the Pharisees, the leaven of the Sadducees, and the leaven of Herod represent respectively: human religious tradition, philosophy and worldliness (Colossians 2:8-10; 1 John 2:15-16; Psalm 1:1-2).

- The leaven of the Pharisees stood for human religious tradition which appeared in many guises as legalism, ceremonialism and formalism.[43] There was an emphasis upon external order and ritual. There was an insistence upon rules and regulations. Laws of human origin as well as the law of God had to be followed with scrupulous exactness. At times the Pharisees by their traditions made people disobey the commandments of God (Matthew 15:1-9).

  To the undiscerning, Pharisees gave an appearance of piety, but to Jesus they were 'whitewashed tombs which indeed appear beautiful outwardly, but inside are full of dead men's bones and all uncleanness' (Matthew 23:27).

- The leaven of the Sadducees represented religious philosophy and materialism. Sadducees, the party to which the high priests generally belonged, denied the immortality of the soul. They rejected the truth of the resurrection (Acts 23:8). Their interest was the here and now. They came with their theories, their ideas, their doctrines, and presented them

---

[43] The use of forms of worship without regard to inner significance; the basing of ethics on the form of the moral law without regard to intention or consequences.

attractively and persuasively to the Jews. By this means they lead people away from complete confidence in the promises of God and the Word of God.

The apostle Paul called this kind of subversive system of thought and morals, of rules and regulations, 'philosophy and empty deceit'. He used expressions such as, 'the tradition of men' and 'the basic principles of the world' (Colossians 2:8) to describe this whole system of false thinking. Sadducees were worldly and thus sympathetic to Herod, his dynasty and friends.

- The leaven of Herod symbolised worldliness. Worldliness is not always evident as blatant evil and unbridled lust. It often permeates slowly and persistently into human thinking, feeling, and behaviour.

In the parable of The Sower the Lord warned of the dangers of this kind of worldliness - like a creeping paralysis of the soul. He spoke of the downfall of those who have a heart strewn with thorns; all the attractions and interests which draw away the mind and heart from God. These are many and varied: the cares of this world, the deceitfulness of riches, the pleasures of life and the desires for other things. These things may draw away those who start out as followers of the Lord Jesus.

The false teaching of these three groups: the Pharisees, Sadducees and Herodians, infiltrated and corrupted the interpretation and application of the Scriptures, the pure Word of God, and impacted heavily upon the Jewish population.

45. A blind man healed at Bethsaida Julias
Mark 8:22-26

As soon as people realised that Jesus was in town, they brought a blind man to him and begged him to heal him (Mark 8:22). This miracle was unique in three ways: it is only recorded by Mark; it is the only miracle where Jesus asked a question of the one he had healed; and it is the only miracle where the cure was achieved in two stages.

When Jesus had taken the blind man out of the town, spat on his eyes, and put his hands on him, he asked him if he saw anything. And the man looked up and said, 'I see men like trees, walking'. 'Then he put his hands on his eyes again and made him look up. And he was restored and saw everyone clearly' (Mark 8:24-25). At first the man's sight had returned only partially, 'I see men like trees, walking'. Men walking about seemed to him as trees. They were vague, indistinct. He could not differentiate them from trees except that they were moving.

It is obvious when Jesus asked the man if he saw anything, that the Lord anticipated the answer; his sight was only partially restored. There can be no explanation for the question otherwise. Jesus never asked such a question of anyone else he healed. It is evident that the Lord *intended only a partial cure* at the first touch.

After the second touch from Jesus, the man's sight 'was restored and [he] saw everyone clearly' (Mark 8:25). That his eyesight was restored indicates that he had not always been blind. He knew what men looked like. He knew what trees looked like. This was not a man 'blind from birth' (cf. John 9:1) but a man whose eyesight had been restored. Furthermore, he saw everyone clearly.

The adverb 'clearly' translates a Greek word meaning that the man had excellent far vision. He saw distant objects and people as 'clear as daylight'. The complete cure did not take long and there was no uncertainty in the end. The man's sight was totally restored.

Why then did Jesus need to touch the man's eyes twice? Neither Jesus nor Mark provide an explanation. The answer is to be found in the context, that is, the circumstances leading up to this miracle.

Jesus was on his way from Decapolis to Caesarea Philippi. In Decapolis Jesus fed over 4,000 hungry people. Just prior to that miracle he had performed another miracle, the healing of a deaf-mute. That miracle had many similarities to this healing miracle on the outskirts of Bethsaida Julias.
There a deaf-mute was brought and the people 'begged him to put his hand on him' (Mark 7:32).
Here the people 'brought a blind man to him, and begged him to touch him' (Mark 8:22).

There 'he took him aside from the multitude'.
Here he 'took the blind man by the hand and led him out of the town'.

There he 'put his fingers in his ears, and he spat and touched his tongue'.
Here he 'spat on his eyes and put his hands on him'.

There 'he commanded them that they should tell no one'.
Here he sent him away to his house, saying, 'Neither go into the town, nor tell anyone in the town'.

The first miracle was the healing of a man who was deaf.
The second miracle was the healing of a man who was blind.

Using these two miracles Jesus taught about spiritual deafness and spiritual blindness. The events surrounding these two miracles are highly significant.

After the feeding of the four thousand in Decapolis Jesus had got into a boat with his disciples to cross the Sea of Galilee. Arriving at Dalmanutha the disciples realised they had forgotten to bring bread, they only had one loaf. Jesus took the opportunity to warn them against the leaven of the Pharisees, the leaven of the Sadducees and the leaven of Herod.

The disciples thought that he was speaking about physical bread. Jesus challenged them, 'Having eyes do you not see? And having ears, do you not hear?' (Mark 8:18) Jesus then healed the blind man of Bethsaida Julias.

He performed the miracle in full consciousness of what he was doing. The Lord was teaching his disciples. He deliberately restored the man's sight in two stages to instruct the disciples about their spiritual state and condition. They were suffering from partial vision - they were spiritually shortsighted!

This would become evident again when they arrived in the region of Caesarea Philippi and Peter made his outstanding confession (considered in more detail later). He said, 'You are the Christ, the Son of the living God' (Matthew 16:16). Peter had certainly received a touch from God for Jesus declared, 'Blessed are you, Simon Bar-Jonah, for flesh and blood has not revealed this to you, but my Father who is in heaven' (Matthew 16:17).

Nevertheless in spiritual matters Peter was only partially sighted. He could not see the full picture. His understanding and perception, though real, though profound, was only partial. When the Lord then disclosed to Peter, and the others, that he was going forward to suffering and to death, Peter objected and rebuked him saying, 'Far be it from you, Lord; this shall not happen to you!' (Matthew 16:22) This brought the strongest reaction from the Lord Jesus: 'Get behind me, Satan! You are an offence to me, for you are not mindful of the things of God, but the things of men' (Matthew 16:23).

One moment Peter was giving evidence of being under the sweet impulse of God. The next moment Peter was swayed by the influence of Satan. Peter was seeing but not seeing. He understood - but only partially!

The Lord healed the blind man of Bethsaida in two stages to illustrate the spiritual state of the disciples. That is why the Lord Jesus so deliberately asked the man if he saw anything. Martyn Lloyd-Jones notes, 'He adopted this technique in the case before us, in order to enable the disciples to see themselves as they were.'[44]

---

[44] D. Martyn Lloyd-Jones, *Spiritual Depression: its causes and cure* (London: Pickering and Inglis, 1965), p.39.

46. Peter's confession of Christ (Caesarea Philippi)
Matthew 16:13-20; Mark 8:27-30; Luke 9:18-20

Leaving Bethsaida Julias Jesus and his disciples proceeded north into the district of Caesarea Philippi. Along the road Jesus raised the crucial question of his perceived identity: 'Who do men say that I am?' After giving a variety of answers: John the Baptist, Elijah, Jeremiah or one of the prophets, Jesus made the question personal, 'But who do you say that I am?' (Mark 8:29)

Peter responded wholeheartedly and with conviction, 'You are the Christ, the Son of the living God.' Jesus answered and said to him, 'Blessed are you, Simon Bar-Jonah, for flesh and blood has not revealed this to you, but my Father who is in heaven' (Matthew16:16-17).

Faith to believe the truth about Jesus Christ as to *his person* and *his mission* (the Son of the living God and the Saviour Christ) is not truly grasped from others, not even mother or father or teacher, nor is it discerned by individual endeavour. Though others may be the means of conveying the gospel to us there must be a personal revelation from the living God himself.

On another occasion Jesus thanked his Father that he had 'hidden these things from the wise and prudent and... revealed them to babes...' (Matthew 11:25-27). Though the devil has blinded the eyes of unbelievers, 'it is the God who commanded light to shine out of darkness, who has shone in our hearts to give the light of the knowledge of the glory of God in the face of Jesus Christ' (2 Corinthians 4:6; cf. John 1:12-13).

'You are Peter, and on this rock I will build my church' (Matthew 16:18), responded Jesus. A vast amount has been written about these words and a wide variety of interpretations presented.

For the Roman Catholic Church these words are the basis upon which the papacy (the office and authority of the Pope) and the church is based. There is however no evidence that Peter was ever the bishop of Rome (or even visited Rome) or that Jesus intended a succession of one man after another ruling over his church.

Was Jesus saying that Peter was the foundation of his Church? Some understand that it is the faith of Peter, his confession, which is the foundation of Christ's Church. Others have interpreted 'the rock' as the truth about the messiahship of Jesus.

In fact the church is not built upon the person of Peter or upon his confession, it is built upon the Person and Saving Work of Jesus 'the Christ, the Son of the living God' (Matthew 16:16). The Church is built and stands upon Jesus Christ alone, 'For no other foundation can anyone lay than that which is laid, which is Jesus Christ' (1 Corinthians 3:11).

In the First Letter of Peter the apostle tells all who are coming to Jesus Christ that they are coming 'as to a living stone, rejected indeed by men, but chosen by God and precious, you also, as living stones, are being built up a spiritual house, a holy priesthood, to offer up spiritual sacrifices acceptable to God through Jesus Christ' (1 Peter 2:4-5).

The apostle Peter was the first living stone to be set firm on Christ Jesus in the New Covenant Church.

The powers of Hades (hell) could not prevent the foundation being laid at Calvary and will not stop the construction of the spiritual building to completion. All sinners are under Satan's power imprisoned by the gates of hell. Jesus Christ is the only One who can release souls from the devil's clutches and set sinners free. To the Christians at Rome Paul wrote -

> God be thanked that though you were slaves of sin, yet you obeyed from the heart that form of doctrine to which you were delivered. And having been set free from sin, you became slaves of righteousness (Romans 6:17-18).

Jesus promised, 'if the Son makes you free, you shall be free indeed' (John 8:36). It is God who 'has delivered us from the power of darkness and conveyed us into the kingdom of the Son of his love, in whom we have redemption through his blood, the forgiveness of sins' (Colossians 1:13-14).

Jesus evidently raised the question of his identity to draw out the confession from Peter and then to begin to teach the apostles what the implications were for himself because he was the Messiah. It meant rejection by the chief priests and elders, suffering, death and resurrection. This first disclosure appears to have been a shock to the disciples, so much so that 'Peter took him aside and began to rebuke him' (Mark 8:32).

The Lord reacted strongly, for this was an affront to the whole plan of God to save and deliver an innumerable company of sinners that they may enjoy everlasting life with the Eternal Father, Son and Holy Spirit and all the born-again children of God.

After first revealing the demands laid upon himself, Jesus spoke of the obligations laid upon all who would follow him. Discipleship is costly: self-denial; cross-carrying; total commitment to Jesus in life or death; putting the cause of the King and his Kingdom as the number one priority; and never being ashamed of the King or embarrassed about serving in his Kingdom.

47. The transfiguration (on an unnamed mountain)
Matthew 17:1-13: Mark 9:2-13; Luke 9:28-36

Less than a week later Jesus took Peter, James, and John up a high mountain to witness an amazing event. The Holy Spirit has not recorded the name or location of the mountain. Many suggestions have been given, for example: Mount Tabor, Mount Hermon and Mount Jebel. These are all speculations and must not be allowed to divert attention from the most momentous event which took place.

The face of Jesus 'shone like the sun, and his clothes became as white as the light' (Matthew 17:2). 'His clothes became shining, exceedingly white, like snow, such as no launderer on earth can whiten them' (Mark 9:3). 'As he prayed, the appearance of his face was altered, and his robe became white and glistening' (Luke 9:29).

The root word translated 'transfigured' (Matthew 17:2; Mark 9:2) would be more accurately translated 'transformed'. Something happened to Jesus so that for a brief moment his inner form shone through his outward appearance, his deity shone in and through his humanity.

Before becoming Jesus he had always existed as true deity, 'in the form of God'. In his incarnation he took 'the form of a bondservant', a slave (Philippians 2:6,7). He who was the Son of God became also the Son of Man. The One 'being the brightness of [God's] glory and the express image of his person' identified with his human creatures completely, for 'as the children have partaken of flesh and blood, he himself likewise shared in the same' (Hebrews 1:3; 2:14).

On that mountain, in view of the three disciples, the deity of the Son of God shone throughout his whole person.

The Word that was with God, and the Word that was God had become 'flesh and dwelt among us' (John 1:1,14). There were many eyewitnesses to the incarnation but John is able to add, as only he, his brother James and Peter were able to testify, 'we beheld his glory, the glory as of the only begotten of the Father, full of grace and truth' (John 1:14).

That the apostle John was thinking about the transformation on the mountain. as he wrote the opening statements of his Gospel record, is clear from another word he used in the same sentence, the word 'dwelt'. This is an unusual word to use here, for it means 'to tabernacle' or 'to tent' or 'encamp'.

The majority of Israelites reading of 'glory' and 'tabernacle' in the same sentence would immediately think of the tabernacle in the wilderness. The purpose for that tabernacle was stated by God as a promise to Moses, 'there I will meet with you' (Exodus 25:22). When the tabernacle was completed 'the cloud covered the tabernacle of meeting, and *the glory of the LORD filled the tabernacle*' (Exodus 40:34; emphasis added).

John shares the conviction of the writer to the Hebrews that Jesus is the brightness of God's glory and the express image of God's person (Hebrews

1:3). Jesus is the very effulgence of God, the radiance, the out-shining of deity.

Peter, another eyewitness to that staggering event on the mountain, emphasised that what they saw was a reality. The three of them heard the Father honour the Son -

> For we did not follow cunningly devised fables when we made known to you the power and coming of our Lord Jesus Christ, but were eyewitnesses of his majesty. For he received from God the Father honour and glory when such a voice came to him from the Excellent Glory: 'This is my beloved Son, in whom I am well pleased.' And we heard this voice which came from heaven when we were with him on the holy mountain (2 Peter 1:16-18).

They saw Jesus speaking with Moses and Elijah about his forthcoming suffering and death which he was shortly to undergo in Jerusalem (Luke 9:30-31). Moses represented the law, Elijah represented the prophets; Jesus came to fulfil the law and the prophets (Matthew 5:17-18).

As they came down the mountain the three apostles were commanded to maintain silence about the momentous event they had witnessed until after the Lord's resurrection. This they did and when the time came they told the world that they had seen deity shine through the humanity of Jesus.

On rejoining the rest of the apostles they were faced with a problem. A desperate father had come seeking a cure for his only child who had a mute evil spirit. The boy suffered severely: being thrown to the floor, he foamed at the mouth, ground his teeth and became rigid. The disciples who had not accompanied Jesus up the mountain were approached to heal the boy but they could not. The Lord told the man that if he believed, all things were possible. He, with tears immediately responded saying, 'Lord, I believe; help my unbelief!' (Mark 9:23-24) The Lord commanded the deaf and dumb evil spirit to depart from the boy and never to return. The boy was delivered.

When the disciples were able to address Jesus privately, they asked him why they had not been able to perform the exorcism. Jesus explained that in order to cast out devils in cases so obstinate and dreadful as this, faith of the highest kind is necessary. That faith is produced and kept vigorous only by much prayer, and by such abstinence from food as trains the mind for the highest exercises of religion, and leaves it free to hold communion with God (Matthew 17:21).

For a second time Jesus predicted he was going to be killed and be raised the third day (Luke 9:22). There is a close resemblance to the first occasion following the confession of Peter in the region of Caesarea Philippi. This time however it was not so much *the necessity* but *the certainty* of his death that he stressed. Also Jesus introduced the fact that he would be betrayed but did not name the betrayer.

He had already told them that he would be 'rejected by the elders and chief priests and scribes' (Mark 8:31), by the very men who should have been foremost in welcoming him warmly with praise and thanksgiving to God. Yet in their blindness they did not recognise the promised Messiah, 'for had they known, they would not have crucified the Lord of glory' (1 Corinthians 2:8). The apostles did not understand and were afraid to ask further at this stage.

48. The coin in the fish's mouth (Capernaum)
Matthew 17:24-27

On their arrival back at Capernaum Peter was approached by an officer from the temple who asked if Jesus paid the annual temple tax. This tax had been introduced by Moses whilst the Israelites were in the wilderness (Exodus 30:12-15). There is no suggestion that the temple officials who approached Peter were hostile towards Jesus, nor that they were out to trick or trap him. It was a genuine question.

It is most likely that they knew Jesus held different opinions from the Pharisees on matters of Jewish law, such as: the observance of the Sabbath, the question of fasting, and eating with hands that had not been ceremonially washed. Peter had no hesitation in reassuring them that Jesus did pay the tax. The tax officers would not know the distinction that the Lord drew between the laws of God and the regulations the Rabbis had added to them.

Peter entered the house and was no doubt very surprised that Jesus knew about his conversation on the street with the tax collectors. There would be further evidence that the Lord was exercising his divine prerogative of knowledge when he anticipated the fish with a coin in its mouth, that the coin would be the correct amount to cover the tax for Peter and himself, and that Peter would catch that particular fish when he let down his line. Jesus was not however simply predicting events but also organising and presiding over them.

The Lord fully intended to pay the tax as he had done before, nevertheless he took the opportunity to teach a vital principle. The question he raised concerned those who were obliged to pay taxes to kings, was it sons or strangers? Peter responded saying it was strangers who were liable. Jesus thus established that sons were not under any obligation and consequently as the Son of God he was under no obligation to pay the tax which was specifically for the upkeep of his 'Father's house' (John 2:16).

Furthermore it was 'a ransom to the LORD... to make atonement for your-selves' (Exodus 30:12,15). Jesus needed no ransom for atonement, he is holy, totally without sin; *he is the ransom for atonement.* Nevertheless in order that the temple officials (and others who may hear about this matter) were not offended, the tax was paid. If Jesus and Peter (presumably the only disciple there who was over twenty years of age and liable for this tax) did not pay the tax then the people, neither knowing nor understanding the true reason, would wrongly conclude that Jesus had no respect for the temple and its worship and they would reject him and his teaching.

The Greek coin in the fish's mouth was a stater (also called a tetradrachmon) the equivalent of four drachma, exactly the sum to cover the tax for Jesus and Peter.

This is a principle continued by the apostles after the Lord's crucifixion which Paul sums up: 'Give no offence, either to the Jews or to the Greeks or to the church of God' (1 Corinthians 10:32). So that the gospel may be heard and not resisted, Paul declared -

> We give no offence in anything, that our ministry may not be blamed. But in all things we commend ourselves as ministers of God (2 Corinthians 6:3-4).

This is not a principle that overrides all other considerations. Jesus was not bound by this principle when he taught the multitude the necessity of feeding upon him as the bread of life and the doctrine of God's sovereignty in salvation. He would well know and understand the offence it caused to so many who heard him that day (John 6:57,61,65-66). The apostle Paul did not follow this principle either when he confronted the apostle Peter in the church at Antioch in Syria (Galatians 2:11-21). So the principle is, *as far as possible give no offence to anyone.*

In the home in Capernaum Jesus asked what the disciples had been discussing so passionately on the journey back down the mountain. They were evidently embarrassed, suspecting that Jesus would not approve because they had, once more, been arguing together about who would be the greatest in the kingdom of heaven.

The Lord placed a young child in the middle of the group and then taking the child in his arms said, 'Whoever receives one of these little children in my name receives me; and whoever receives me, receives not me but him who sent me' (Mark 9:37). The teaching of Jesus was once more in contrast with the prevailing attitudes and behaviour for in those days children were not held in high regard. They were often seen as no more than slaves, until twelve years of age.

Jesus taught that the way to be great among his followers is to be 'last of all and servant of all' (Mark 9:35). True greatness is also shown by simple acts of love, the giving of attention and affection, by being gentle and gracious in receiving the young (Luke 9:48) and being humble like a young child (Matthew 18:4). The Saviour was the perfect example, 'For even the Son of Man did not come to be served, but to serve, and to give his life a ransom for many' (Mark 10:45). All who love him will learn to think like him -

> Let this mind be in you which was also in Christ Jesus, who, being in the form of God, did not consider it robbery [grasping] to be equal with God, but made himself of no reputation, taking the form of a bondservant, and coming in the likeness of men. And being found in appearance as a man, he humbled himself and became obedient to the point of death, even the death of the cross (Philippians 2:5-8).

49. A stranger casting out demons
Mark 9:38-41: Luke 9:49-50

The teaching of Jesus about humility and true greatness seems to have stirred the conscience of the apostle John. Earlier the disciples had met a man who was casting out demons in the name of Jesus. Because he was not part of the recognised group of followers of Jesus, the disciples forbade him to continue. It would seem evident that the apostle John was now beginning to have second thoughts. 'Did they do right in trying to stop that man?' That is the implied question.

There are two strange things about this man and his activity. Firstly, how did one who was not a professed disciple and follower of Christ have power to cast out devils in his name? Secondly, why one who cast out devils in the name of Christ did not join himself to the apostles and follow Christ with them? For the second question there seems to be no answer but for the first there is help to be found in the Scriptures.

How did this man have such power? Evidently he performed his work by using the name of Jesus but he may not have had saving faith in him (cf. 1 Corinthians 13:2 'And though I have all faith, so that I could remove mountains, but have not love, I am nothing').

Jesus was travelling extensively. As he journeyed he preached, healed the sick, and where necessary, drove out evil spirits. This was a case in which a man evidently witnessed the work of Jesus and grasped the name of Jesus by faith and drove out evil spirits. It does not say that he performed any other kind of miracle. The effect of the teaching and the work of Jesus thus manifested itself in an unusual way. Jesus had not empowered this man as he had his disciples (Mark 3:15). In the Sermon on the Mount Jesus had issued sober warnings including these words -

> Not everyone who says to me, 'Lord, Lord,' shall enter the kingdom of heaven, but he who does the will of my Father in heaven. Many will say to me in that day, 'Lord, Lord, have we not prophesied in your name, cast out demons in your name, and done many wonders in your name?' And then I will declare to them, 'I never knew you; depart from me, you who practice lawless-ness!' (Matthew 7:21-23)

Matthew Henry asserts -

> A man might cast devils out of others, and yet have a devil, nay be a devil himself... A man may be a preacher, may have gifts for the ministry, and an external call to it, and perhaps some success in it, and yet be a wicked man; may help others to heaven, and yet come short himself.[45]

Jesus saw the good in this man's behaviour and brought out a lesson. If those who profess the name of Jesus are doing good then no-one should try to hinder them or be critical of them. Our Lord urged a generosity of spirit. His followers are to believe the best and hope the best about all who seek to promote the cause of Christ even when they do not stand where we stand in doctrine, even when they are not clear on many issues of the faith. Too often Christians react against other Christians as Barnes warns, 'They undervalue their labours, attempt to lessen the evidence of their success, and to diminish their influence'.[46]

50. Causes of offence and drastic surgery
Matthew 18:6-9; Mark 9:42-50

Jesus continued teaching on the theme of concern for others and the threat of severe punishment to anyone who causes a little one to sin. The term 'little ones' may include children, new Christian converts and the childlike believer. The punishment will be worse than the most horrid physical suffering and death. Continuing on the theme of eternal death and separation from God in a never changing condition of judgment and hell, the Lord brought out the necessity of avoiding sin.

---

[45] Matthew Henry, *The Gospel of Mark*, p.151.
[46] Albert Barnes, *Notes Explanatory and Practical on the Gospels: Matthew and Mark* (London: Routledge, 1832), p.373.

Using the analogy of the human body the importance of strict self-discipline was emphasised. The hand, the foot and the eye are extremely valuable to us. Jesus said it is far better to dispose of any one of them than to suffer eternal punishment. He was not to be understood as speaking literally about amputation and the scooping out of an eye.

As with all the writers of Scripture Jesus used ordinary rules of language and figures of speech to communicate clearly and powerfully (cf. Paul likening the Church to a human body referring to a foot, eye, ear, nose and head, 1 Corinthians 12:15-27). What then was the Lord signifying by the hand, the foot and the eye in the avoidance of sin?

The hand represents touch: unwholesome friends, associates and acquaintances real or virtual. The foot symbolises place: places of danger and evil, pursuits and interests that allure and any club or group which is likely to bring a sinful influence. The eye represents sight: salacious films, unholy television, pornography in books, magazines and on the internet. It would be far better to live without a computer than to lose our soul because of it!

> Do not love the world or the things in the world. If anyone loves the world, the love of the Father is not in him. For all that is in the world - the lust of the flesh, the lust of the eyes, and the pride of life - is not of the Father but is of the world. And the world is passing away, and the lust of it; but he who does the will of God abides forever (1 John 2:15-17).

The serious lesson is that sin must not be embraced. It must be 'put to death' (Colossians 3:5). 'For if you live according to the flesh you will die; but if by the Spirit you put to death the deeds of the body, you will live' (Romans 8:13). 'Likewise you also, reckon yourselves to be dead indeed to sin, but alive to God in Christ Jesus our Lord' (Romans 6:11).

Action must be swift and decisive. 'See how great a forest a little fire kindles!' (James 3:5). 'Each one is tempted when he is drawn away by his own desires and enticed. Then, when desire has conceived, it gives birth to sin; and sin, when it is full-grown, brings forth death' (James 1:14-15). It is worth making the most costly sacrifices rather than to lose eternal life.

Jesus repeated the warning of despising little ones and further illustrated his commitment to them, and concern in seeking for them, through the story of the shepherd seeking one lost sheep and upon finding it rejoicing greatly!

51. Forgiveness
Matthew 18:15-35

When one believer sins against another believer there is often bitter resentment, indignant complaint to other believers and avoidance of that person. Sometimes recourse is sought from the minister or another church officer but rarely it would seem is the procedure followed which the Lord presents here. The fourfold strategy of Jesus is designed to minimise hurt and division amongst believers, to limit the impact of sin, and to provide the possibility of a speedy resolution through repentance and restoration.

Step One requires the injured party to consult privately with the offender. The matter should not be raised with any other person. Gracious gentle face-to-face conversation without confrontation is to be undertaken to resolve the difficulty by receiving an apology and assuring forgiveness. The sin is then treated as over and gone, just as the Father deals with our sins (Psalm 103:12; Isaiah 43:25).

Step Two is to be taken in the event of failure in step one. The injured party now seeks one or two mature believers who will be witnesses to the discussion with the offender. Jesus based this on the law of God (Deuteronomy 19:15; John 5:31-40). These preferably should not be the elders so that no obstacle is unwittingly introduced into the reception of their teaching ministry. Great sensitivity is required of the witnesses and the injured party. Paul counselled -

> Brethren, if a man is overtaken in any trespass, you who are spiritual restore such a one in a spirit of gentleness, considering yourself lest you also be tempted (Galatians 6:1).

This means tempted to sin by a wrong attitude that is unloving, ungracious, critical, harsh, unjust or superior. The goal in dealing with sin against another is always resolution by repentance ensuring full reconciliation.

Step Three is undertaken in the event of an impasse and necessitates the problem being raised before the assembled local church. In the event that repentance is not forthcoming -

Step Four requires the offender to be no longer regarded as a believer. Nevertheless even this strong action of withdrawing fellowship from an offender is designed to bring about repentance and restoration.

Paul faced a serious situation in the church at Corinth where a believer was living with his father's wife and the church was taking no action whatsoever. When confronted by letter from the apostle Paul (1 Corinthians 5:1-11), they took the necessary action which resulted in the man being excluded from the church. This separation brought the man to his senses, he repented and was readmitted. Then the apostle counselled forgiveness and expressions of love towards the restored man (2 Corinthians 2:5-11).

The procedure sounds harsh and it is not easy to enact, but the desired outcome is the restoration of harmony. Faithful discharge of these principles is a fundamental requirement for a healthy church. Heaven is involved throughout for where even two or three are gathered together in the name of the Lord Jesus, he is present by his Spirit (Matthew 18:18-20).

Peter's question 'Lord, how often shall my brother sin against me, and I forgive him?' (Matthew 18:21) quite naturally followed on from the teaching of the Lord regarding forgiveness. Jesus had been speaking about clearing up grievances in the church and had outlined the procedure to be followed when a brother commits a sin against a brother. Peter followed this by saying, 'Lord, how often shall my brother sin against me, and I forgive him?' And as though anticipating the generosity of Jesus, he adds the speculative answer, 'Up to seven times!'

The Rabbis taught that a brother should be forgiven three times and no more. They based their teaching upon Amos 1:3; 2:1; 2:6 'For three transgressions ... and for four, I will not turn away its punishment.' Peter no doubt assumed Jesus would be more generous. But the Lord responded by saying not seven times but seventy times seven, which is tantamount to saying 'always'! He then told the parable of The Unforgiving Servant (Matthew 18:23-35) to illustrate the manner in which our forgiveness of others is to be likened to God's forgiveness of us.

It is immediately obvious that Jesus is referring to God the Father when he began 'the kingdom of heaven is like a certain king who wanted to settle accounts...' (Matthew 18:23). The first servant owed the king an astronomical amount, something like the equivalent of 13 million dollars (£10,000,000). Where did he get such an amount? Clearly he had been cheating the king, stealing from his treasury! This can be the only explanation.

A labourer in those days, if he saved all he earned without spending on food, clothing, shelter, etc., would have taken 200,000 years to repay the king. How preposterous therefore for this servant to plead, 'Master, have patience with me, and I will pay you all.' The king was moved with compassion and cancelled the whole debt (1 John 1:8-9; Colossians 2:13-14).

Jesus was demonstrating our enormous individual indebtedness to God. We have no possibility of repaying him no matter how long he might give us.

The servant goes straight from the presence of the king and finds a fellow servant who owes him a sum which might well be repaid by the equivalent of 17 weeks wages. Showing his heartless aggression, 'he laid hands on him and took him by the throat' and demanded payment. The fellow servant pleads but to no avail. He is imprisoned until he can pay. Hearing of the dealings of one who had been so graciously and generously set free of all debt, the king was angry and reversed his judgment, delivering him 'to the torturers until he should pay all that was due to him.'

The Lord drove home the vital point: 'So my heavenly Father also will do to you if each of you, from his heart, does not forgive his brother his trespasses' (Matthew 18:35). Those who have sincerely repented and are truly forgiven, forgive others who hurt them when they repent no matter how many times it may occur. Indeed, 'Blessed are the merciful, for they shall obtain mercy' (Matthew 5:7). We are also taught to pray, 'Forgive us our debts, as we forgive our debtors' (Matthew 6:12).

The later Judean ministry

52. Setting out for the Feast of Tabernacles
John 7:1-10

Up to this point the Lord Jesus had concentrated his work in Galilee. Then he had spent time journeying to the region of Tyre and Sidon, back to Decapolis and away up north to the region of Caesarea Philippi. His purpose was to avoid provoking the Jews of Judea, who were planning to kill him, by staying away from them. That was now to change. Confrontation is to be faced. As the time drew near for the Feast of Tabernacles, the Lord's step-brothers, who did not yet believe in him, tried to pressure him to attend the feast and show himself openly to his followers.

Jesus did not accept their counsel (cf. Psalm 1:1-2). He was working to a divine programme. He remained in Galilee and then after a short while he decided to travel to the feast as unobtrusively as possible. He chose the quickest way through Samaria rather than the longer but more usual way over the River Jordan and down the east bank through Perea. By this means he would avoid meeting up with the multitude of pilgrims also travelling to the capital.

Intending to pass through Samaria Jesus sent disciples ahead to find board and lodging for them (Luke 9:52-53). To find hospitality in Samaria for thirteen Jews was far from easy. There was a a state of prolonged mutual hostility between Samaritans and Jews which stretched back years as far as the rebuilding of the Jerusalem temple in the days of Nehemiah the prophet.

The Samaritan villagers refused them hospitality because they were travelling to Jerusalem for the feast.

James and John reacted very strongly and asked permission from the Lord 'to command fire to come down from heaven and consume them, just as Elijah did?' These two brothers must have been of a fiery temperament because the Lord had much earlier given them the name 'Boanerges', that is, 'Sons of Thunder' (Mark 3:17). Jesus was not impressed by their suggestion. He rebuked them and reminded them once more that his mission was to save lives not destroy them. The group moved on to another village, probably just over the border from Samaria.

As they continued their journey Jesus was approached separately by three men who spoke of their enthusiasm to join his disciples (Luke 9:57-62). The answers Jesus gave clarify even further the cost of following him. There must be: a willingness to go anywhere and accept any physical conditions (cf. Ruth's beautiful commitment to Naomi (Ruth 1:16-17); a willingness to put the service of Christ before everyone and everything else (cf. how Elisha responded to the call of God in 1 Kings 19:19-21); and no looking back with longing for the old life (cf. 'Remember Lot's wife' (Luke 17:32). There can be no place for half-hearted commitment in the Master's service.

53. The seventy sent out by the Lord
Luke 10:1-16

What a contrast, after hearing about the three would-be followers, to learn of seventy keen disciples ready to go out and serve the Lord. Seventy was a special symbolic number to the Israelites. It was the number of elders appointed to work under the direction of Moses in the wilderness (Numbers 11:16-17,24-25). It was the number of the members of the Sanhedrin (the Supreme Council of the Jews).

It was also the number of bullocks sacrificed during the Feast of Tabernacles (over the seven day period seventy bullocks were ceremonially killed (Numbers 29:12-38). Beginning on the first day with thirteen the number decreased by one each day until on the seventh day the remaining seven bullocks were sacrificed. 'It was said that the seventy bullocks were offered for the seventy nations of the earth[47] (a traditional hint of the

---

[47] Genesis 10 includes the list of the founders of 70 nations descended from Noah's three sons Shem, Ham, and Japheth. The list includes 26 descendants of Shem, 30 descendants of Ham, and 14 descendants of Japheth.

prophetical symbolism of the Feast of Tabernacles, not to be despised)'[48] This was the final harvest celebration: the Feast of First Fruits celebrated the first harvest ingathering of barley; the Feast of Weeks (Pentecost) celebrated the first harvest ingathering of wheat; and the Feast of Tabernacles (Booths) celebrated the end of all the year's harvest ingathering (Leviticus 23).

Maybe the Lord was thinking of the nations of the world when he sent out seventy disciples (v.1) for the ancient promise to Abraham and repeated to Isaac was 'in your seed all the nations of the earth shall be blessed' (Genesis 26:4). That Seed is Christ, that is, Jesus of Nazareth.

The seventy disciples were given a similar commission to that of the twelve apostles (Luke 9:1-6). The Lord begins by mentioning the harvest and wolves, the first as to its greatness, the shortage of labourers and therefore the need for urgent prayer to God; the second to the vulnerability of the disciples being as sheep among ravenous beasts. Both these concepts were included in the Lord's commission to the twelve (Matthew 9:37-38; 10:16).

Jesus gave detailed instructions for the journey. They were to travel light, no money, no travel bag (possibly for change of clothes), no sandals. They were to rely entirely and wholly upon God. Also, like Gehazi under instruction from the prophet Elisha, 'be on your way. If you meet anyone, do not greet him; and if anyone greets you, do not answer him' (2 Kings 4:29). They were not being told to be discourteous but rather to keep their calling and commission clearly in mind and not to be distracted by lesser concerns. As Paul charged his colleague Timothy -

> You... must endure hardship as a good soldier of Jesus Christ. No one engaged in warfare entangles himself with the affairs of this life, that he may please him who enlisted him as a soldier' (2 Timothy 2:3-4).

Preachers are to accept what is given to them without complaint, eat what is set before them and be satisfied with the hospitality they receive, not seeking to upgrade to more comfortable accommodation when the opportunity arises. 'The labourer is worthy of his wages' (v.7) but he does not depend upon others. It is God who will supply all their need 'according to his riches in glory by Christ Jesus' (Philippians 4:19).

They were to use their God-given power to heal the sick and proclaim that the kingdom of God had come near to them. Those who refused to receive them were to be given a dramatic demonstration of judgment, 'The very dust of your city which clings to us we wipe off against you' (v.11).

---

[48] Rudolf Stier, *The Words of the Lord Jesus* (Edinburgh: T & T Clark, 1885), vol. 5, p.278.

Jesus denounced the cities which had refused to respond appropriately to his visits and the mighty works which were performed there. Two were particularly noted for severe condemnation: Chorazin and Bethsaida. Of Bethsaida there is recorded wonderful miracles and much teaching from the Lord Jesus. Of Chorazin there is not a word of miracles or teaching, not even of one visit.

This is a clear reminder that the record of the life and teaching of the Lord Jesus is not a biography, for so much is missing. John testified that there were 'many other things that Jesus did, which if they were written one by one, I suppose that even the world itself could not contain the books that would be written' (John 21:25).

Using the example of Bethsaida and Chorazin Jesus was teaching that to hear the proclamation of the gospel and reject it is to reject Jesus the Son of God and to reject God himself.

54. Teaching at the Feast of Tabernacles
John 7:11-53

In Jerusalem opinion was divided about Jesus, whereas some said he was a good man, others said the very opposite, that he was a deceiver. Rumours circulated, misunderstandings abounded.

Towards the middle of the feast Jesus entered the temple and engaged once more in teaching. Many were impressed with his ability for they knew he had received no formal rabbinic training. He re-iterated his unique relationship with God and stressed his commission to do the Father's will.

Speaking of the Father, Jesus said, 'If anyone wills to do his will, he shall know concerning the doctrine, whether it is from God or whether I speak on my own authority' (v.17). Augustine said, 'Understanding is the reward of faith... Do not seek to understand in order to believe, but believe in order to understand.'[49]

In once more declaring his unique relationship with the Father, Jesus made reference to the murderous intentions of the Jewish leaders. He referred back to the incident at the Pool of Bethesda when he was accused of breaking the Sabbath law because he healed a paralysed man on the Sabbath. Jesus gave another justification for his action at that time by pointing out that if it was lawful for circumcision to be acceptable without violating the law of

---

[49] Augustine of Hippo, quoted in: Andreas I. Köstenberger, *Encountering John: the Gospel in Historical, Literary, and Theological Perspective* (Grand Rapids, Michigan: Baker Academic, 2002), p.112.

the Sabbath then surely healing a man on the Sabbath cannot be considered to break the Sabbath law.

He urged his listeners to judge thoughtfully and righteously and not to jump to conclusions.

There was bewilderment among the people for they had heard that the leaders intended to kill Jesus and yet here he was speaking openly. They even thought that maybe the leaders were thinking after all that he was the Christ. Jesus reiterated that he had come from God. The anger and hatred of the Pharisees remained unabated. They were determined to have him arrested, but heaven restrained them as it was not yet the right time.

The last day of the feast was a day to remember. This Feast of Tabernacles (or Booths) was the major harvest festival of the year celebrating the conclusion of the ingathering of the year's produce. There were a number of special elements which related to Israel's history: the people were instructed to live in homemade shelters in memory of the wilderness journey (Leviticus 23:42-43); to gather palm leaves and willows and to march in celebration around the great altar (Leviticus 23:40).

On the last day the ceremony was intensified as they marched seven times round the altar in memory of the sevenfold circuit around Jericho, when the walls fell down and the city was taken; also a priest would take a golden water jug to the pool of Siloam and carry water back through the Water Gate whilst the people recited Isaiah 12:3 'With joy you will draw water from the wells of salvation'.

The water was carried into the temple and poured on the altar as an offering to God. This recalled the manner in which God miraculously provided water from two rocks 38 years and about 240km (150 miles) apart (Exodus 17:6; Numbers 20:11; cf. 1 Corinthians 10:4).

On this last day of the feast, probably even at the precise moment at which the water was being poured upon the altar with shouts of praise and thanksgiving, the voice of Jesus rang out loud and clear -

> 'If anyone thirst, let him come to me and drink. He who believes in me, as the Scripture has said, out of his heart will flow rivers of living water.' But this he spoke concerning the Spirit, whom those believing in him would receive; for the Holy Spirit was not yet given, because Jesus was not yet glorified (John 7:37-39).

'Out of his heart'(literally 'out of his hollow') spiritually understood indicated an empty feeling, the longing deep within the human heart and mind, a craving for satisfaction (Psalm 42:2; 63:1; Isaiah 55:1). Jesus is the only one who can really satisfy the longing heart! Not only will the needy ones be satisfied, but they will also be vessels from which the Holy Spirit in all his graces and gifts will flow out to others, refreshing, comforting and strengthening them, even as the needy ones are refreshed by Jesus.

This blessing was dependent upon Jesus completing his unique mission and being glorified: by suffering, dying, rising, ascending and sending forth the Holy Spirit in New Covenant blessing (Acts 2:33) which would be received upon repentance (Acts 2:38).

Many, hearing him, said, 'though not with that heart-conviction which would have led to self-surrender,'[50] that he was the promised Prophet, even the Christ. Some said he could not be the Christ since he was from Galilee not Bethlehem. Jesus cried out once more repeating his personal commission from God whom he knew intimately.

Many believed in him because of the many miraculous signs he had performed, but did they possess a deep-seated, whole-hearted conviction? Theirs may have been more like the seed which fell upon stony ground rather than upon good ground.

The officers of the temple were ordered by the chief priests and Pharisees to arrest Jesus but failed to do so. They were impressed by his teaching; the Pharisees accused them of being deceived. Nicodemus, the Pharisee who came to talk with Jesus by night, urged the leaders to make a careful assessment and not judge a man before hearing and examining his actions. But they were adamant that Jesus was not a prophet, accusing Nicodemus of being a Galilean and implying therefore that he was a sympathiser. Again they brought up the objection that there is no prophecy of Messiah associated with Galilee.

55. The woman taken in adultery
John 8:1-11

The following day Jesus was once more in the temple and a woman was brought to him who had been caught in adultery. Citing Moses that adultery was a capital offence they asked Jesus for his opinion. It was a trap.

If Jesus said, 'Stone her' then he would lose forever the name he had gained for love and mercy, and never again would he be called the friend of tax collectors and sinners. Also he would immediately come into conflict with Roman law, for the Jews had no power to pass or carry out the death sentence on anyone.

If on the other hand, the Lord said, 'Do not stone her', it could be immediately pointed out that he was teaching men to break the law of Moses

---

[50] Alfred Edersheim, *The Life and Times of Jesus the Messiah* (Peabody, Massachusetts: Hendrikson, 1993), p.585.

and that he even encouraged people to commit adultery! No doubt the scribes and Pharisees who brought the woman felt confident at this point that they had Jesus trapped.

The Lord was seated (v.2) and when confronted by this woman and hearing the question raised by the scribes and Pharisees, he reacted by stooping down and writing 'on the ground with his finger, as though he did not hear' (v.6).

The Lord was confronted with sin in its worst manifestation. Not the sin of the woman but the sin in the twisted minds and hearts of the scribes and Pharisees who were so longing for his death that they were prepared to use another human being as a worthless instrument to gain their vile ends.

It may be that the leering, lustful look on the faces of the scribes and Pharisees, the bleak cruelty in their eyes, the sickening curiosity of the crowd, the shame of the woman, all combined to twist the very heart of the Lord Jesus into an agony of pity and disgust so that he hid his face, turning to the ground from this sordid event (cf. Jeremiah 17:13). He remained silent writing in the sand with his finger.

> So when they continued asking him, he raised himself up and said
> to them, 'He who is without sin among you, let him throw a stone
> at her first'. And again he stooped down and wrote on the ground
> (John 8:7-8).

Conscience-stricken the accusers all departed beginning with the oldest. Jesus then graciously dismissed the woman saying, 'Go and sin no more'.

It is always good to consider the words and actions of Jesus in the light of the Old Testament Scriptures. He came to fulfil the law and the Prophets (Matthew 5:17) and in so doing there was an underlying connection between his life and ministry and the Old Covenant Word of God.

This challenging event is a reminder of another occasion when fingers wrote words. Years before in Babylon, King Belshazzar showed his insolence towards Almighty God by using the golden and silver vessels from the temple at Jerusalem for his own use; in a feast where gods of gold, of silver, of brass, of iron, of wood and of stone, were being praised (Daniel 5:4). At that feast the fingers of a man's hand appeared which wrote on the plaster of the wall: Mene, Mene, Tekel, Upharsin. The prophet Daniel gave the interpretation of each word -

> Mene: God has numbered your kingdom, and finished it; Tekel:
> You have been weighed in the balances, and found wanting; Peres:
> your kingdom has been divided, and given to the Medes and
> Persians (Daniel 5:25-28).

Although as a reward King Belshazzar dressed Daniel with a purple robe, put a golden chain round his neck and proclaimed that he was now the third ruler in the kingdom, that very night Belshazzar, king of the Chaldeans died.

The action in stooping and writing with his finger in the sand, was therefore another of the prophetic acts of Jesus the meaning of which can only be obtained from the Old Testament Scriptures. It was a mark of that coming judgment upon the self-righteous leaders of a nation which planned and would perform the execution of the Son of God. These men would bring a wretched woman before him to trap and discredit him because their hearts were full of hatred and murder. They stood condemned and judged. They were to lose their position and their nation.

On the evening of the first day of the Feast of Tabernacles there was a ceremony called The Illumination of the Temple. It took place in the Court of the Women. The court was surrounded with deep galleries, erected to hold spectators. In the centre of the court four great candelabra, great clusters of lamp holders were prepared. During the seven days of the festival, when darkness came, the four great candelabra were lit and, it was said, that they shone such a blaze of light throughout Jerusalem that every courtyard in the city was lit up with their brilliance. This reminded the people in such a dramatic manner of the pillar of light which led the children of Israel in the wilderness (Exodus 13:21-22).

56. Jesus the light of the world
John 8:12-59

It was on the day after the Feast of Tabernacles had ended when the Lord was teaching in the temple that the woman caught in sin had been brought to him. It is therefore evident that he was standing in the Court of the Women in the very place where the oil lamps had earlier glowed so brilliantly. Against this background the wonderful force and power of the words of the Lord Jesus held a powerful significance when he declared -

> I am the light of the world. He who follows me shall not walk in darkness, but have the light of life (John 8:12).

The Jewish leaders would know only too well what the impact would be of such words from Jesus. Any Israelite well-taught in the Old Testament Scriptures could readily see the startling significance of our Lord's bold statement. He was once more linking his choice of words with revelations in the Word of God such as, 'The LORD [Yahweh/Jehovah] is my light and my salvation; whom shall I fear?' (Psalm 27:1) And again -

> Arise, shine; for your light has come! And the glory of the LORD
> is risen upon you. For behold, the darkness shall cover the earth,
> and deep darkness the people; but the LORD will arise over you,
> and his glory will be seen upon you. The Gentiles shall come to
> your light... (Isaiah 60:1-3; cf. 19-20; Micah 7:7-8).

The Jewish Rabbis accepted that one of the names of the Messiah was
'Light' therefore Jesus was clearly revealing himself to be the Messiah, God
Incarnate, 'Immanuel, God with us' (Matthew 1:23; Isaiah 7:14).

Why was there such a general lack of understanding about Jesus? Why
were the people not thoroughly convinced by the visual and audible evidence
before them? Some months earlier Jesus had explained the underlying reason
in conversation with Nicodemus the Pharisee when he said -

> This is the condemnation, that the light has come into the world,
> and men loved darkness rather than light, because their deeds were
> evil. For everyone practicing evil hates the light and does not
> come to the light, lest his deeds should be exposed (John 3:19-20).

The forefathers had followed the pillar of light. Those who had followed it
and had not rebelled against its guidance had reached Canaan. The others
had died in the desert. Likewise here the true followers of Christ not only
will not walk in the darkness of moral and spiritual ignorance, of impurity,
and of gloom, but they will reach the land of light. Yet there is more: they
will have the light! The light of the world, Jesus Christ within their hearts,
that One who is the Light of Life! (2 Corinthians 4:3-6; cf. 1 John 1:5-7).

Jesus was 'the light of the world' whilst he was here on earth, for he
said, 'As long as I am in the world, I am the light of the world' (John 9:5);
and again, 'A little while longer the light is with you. Walk while you have
the light, lest darkness overtake you; he who walks in darkness does not
know where he is going' (John 12:35).

In his physical absence the commission has been given to all his
followers: 'You are the light of the world' (Matthew 5:14-16). The apostle
Paul also urged the recognition of this responsibility. To the Ephesians he
wrote -

> For you were once darkness, but now you are light in the Lord.
> Walk as children of light (for the fruit of the Spirit is in all
> goodness, righteousness, and truth), finding out what is acceptable
> to the Lord. And have no fellowship with the unfruitful works of
> darkness, but rather expose them (Ephesians 5:8-11).

A godly life is one lived 'worthy of the Lord, fully pleasing him, being
fruitful in every good work and increasing in the knowledge of
God' (Colossians 1:10). The faithful are those who let their 'light so shine

before men, that they may see your good works and glorify your Father in heaven' (Matthew 5:16).

The Pharisees insisted that a statement such as Jesus had made about being the light of the world could not possibly be regarded as legitimate and reliable when backed by his word alone. The Jewish law, founded rightly upon the law of God, required at least two witnesses for a claim to be valid.

On an earlier occasion Jesus had presented four witnesses as proof of his sonship: the Father, John the Baptist, the miracles Jesus performed, and the Old Testament Scriptures (John 5:31-47). This time he simply indicated two witnesses, the Father and the Son, and declared that the whole root of the problem was sinfulness and wickedness in the Pharisees themselves because they did not love God in truth.

The fact that the Jews did not recognise him for who and what he is, is clear proof that they do not really know God at all. The tragedy is that the whole nation had been consistently taught what to expect in Messiah. Now he was present before them their blind unbelief was demonstrated in their rejection of him.

A love for God, knowing God in true living experience and receiving the promises of God would have meant a ready acceptance of God's Son. Instead they were blind and hostile. Furthermore, men do not want to believe in Jesus Christ because they do not want to stop sinning! (John 3:19-21)

Jesus told the Jews he was going away to somewhere where they could not go and if they do not believe in him they will die in their sins (v.21). Jesus is -

- the One sent from the Father;
- the One who is from above;
- the Son of God;
- the Son of Man;
- equal with God;
- the One who has Life in himself;
- the very essence, meaning and fulfilment of the Scriptures;
- the Bread of Life;
- the Light of the World.

If they do not believe this
it will result in their everlasting misery and death.

'When you lift up the Son of Man, then you will know that I am he, and that I do nothing of myself; but as my Father taught me, I speak these things' (v.28). Having refused to believe in him and then having crucified him they will one day realise that he was who he said he was and that all he said was indeed from God - but it will be too late.

He reiterated his special relationship with the Father, saying that he was wholly committed to saying only that which pleases God. To those who were believing in him he gave this reassurance: 'If you abide in my word, you are my disciples indeed. And you shall know the truth, and the truth shall make you free' (vv.31-32). The truth only becomes clear when tradition and preconceptions are set aside and the Lord's words are believed and acted upon. It is in abiding in his Word that the reality of faith is confirmed.

The Jews took exception to the suggestion that they were not free. They were Abraham's descendants and had never been in bondage to anyone. Had they forgotten the slavery in Egypt and the seventy years of Exile in Babylon? Jesus pointed out that they were slaves of sin from which only the Son is able make them free (v.34).

The Jews relied upon their nationality, claiming that Abraham was their father, and that God was their Father. Their behaviour indicated that their father was not God but that their father was in fact the devil (v.44). They were proving this by their murderous thoughts towards Jesus for if they were children of God they would love not hate the Son of God.

They further sought to insult Jesus by suggesting he was a Samaritan and had a demon. He responded by repeating his commitment to honour God in everything adding, 'if anyone keeps my word he shall never see death' (v.51). This claim incited the Jews and they accused Jesus of presenting himself as greater than Abraham and the prophets. He replied that he honoured God and spoke the truth. What he declared about God he knew by personal experience with God.

Furthermore he added, 'Your father Abraham rejoiced to see my day, and he saw it and was glad' (v.56). When God made the glorious promise to Abraham that in him all the families of the earth would be blessed (Genesis 12:3) Abraham knew that the Messiah of God was going to be one of his descendants and he greatly rejoiced at the greatness and glory of the promise. Then the Jews said to Jesus, 'You are not yet fifty years old, and have you seen Abraham?' (v.57)

Jesus answered with a profound and amazing self-disclosure, 'Most assuredly, I say to you, before Abraham was, I am' (v.58; cf. Exodus 3:14). They understood exactly what Jesus was saying and took up stones to throw at him, for in their view Jesus was blaspheming. No one seemed to consider that he was indeed the glorious unique Son of the living God with the utmost right to call himself the 'I am'. Knowing the truth of his divine sonship is, however, a personal revelation from God the Father (cf. Matthew 16:16-17; 2 Corinthians 4:6).

> The present interchange made one thing crystal-clear: people's opposition to the gospel is frequently not based on rational objections or intellectual argument but is at the root moral rebellion against God.[51]

Jesus withdrew from the temple. As he did so he saw a man born blind and turned the attention of his disciples to him.

57. The man born blind
John 9:1-41

Strongly connected with the Lord's declaration, 'I am the light of the world' (John 8:12) is the sixth miraculous sign recorded by the apostle John, the healing of the man born blind (v.1). Satan and sin render every human being spiritually dead and consequently spiritually blind from birth (Ephesians 2:1-2). Bringing physical light into this man's eyes powerfully illustrates the power of Jesus to bring light into the minds and hearts of those who are born spiritually blind (Isaiah 29:18; 35:5; Matthew 11:5; cf. 2 Corinthians 4:4,6).

In the midst of great criticism and much hostility and hatred from the masses and particularly from the Jewish leadership, Jesus was still able to look with graciousness and gentleness on the needy.

It must have been general knowledge for the disciples to know that this man had been blind from birth. They pose a theological question, 'Who sinned?' The thinking of the disciples was not untypical of most in their day. They probably thought that the cause of every physical affliction was sin, generally the sin of the afflicted one. But how could this be true if the man was born with a defect? In this case he could not have brought the affliction upon himself through his own misconduct. How could he sin before he was born?

The Scriptures trace sickness to four causes:

- the original sin of humanity (Romans 5:12ff.);
- the sin of parents (Exodus 20:5; 34:7). There are sins which result in the contraction of disease which may be transmitted to offspring before birth;

---

[51] Andreas I. Köstenberger, *Encountering John: the Gospel in Historical, Literary, and Theological Perspective* (Grand Rapids, Michigan: Baker Academic, 2002), pp.112,116.

- personal sin through misbehaviour (John 5:14);
- the judgment of God (Exodus 15:26; 2 Kings 5:27; 1 Corinthians 11:29-30).

Jesus responded by saying that neither the man nor his parents were the cause but rather it was so that 'the works of God should be revealed in him' (John 9:3); which was evidenced when Jesus healed him.

Whilst there are many imaginative suggestions about the medicinal value of the clay that Jesus made from saliva and dirt, it would seem there is one quite simple explanation. The man was born blind. He relied on his senses of hearing, touch and smell. The Lord's action communicated with the blind man. He heard. He felt. Jesus was doing something to him and for him, yet at the same time demanding something from him. The blind man must exercise faith and obedience. Like Naaman the Syrian he must demonstrate his faith by obeying a command (v.7; cf. 2 Kings 5:10).

The man was instructed to go and wash in the pool of Siloam. This was the pool where the golden jug from the temple had been filled only a few days earlier during the Feast of Tabernacles. At that time the people recited Isaiah 12:3 'With joy you will draw water from the wells of salvation'. Let the man consider deeply what Jesus is doing to him and for him. Upon reflection the man will have ample ground for concluding that Jesus of Nazareth is the true source of healing and salvation and that the waters of Siloam were a symbol, yet again, of the Christ of God in all his power and saving work.

The healing of the man born blind is an illustration, as John 9:5 makes clear, of what Jesus is constantly doing spiritually in his capacity as the light of the world. The man was being brought from blindness and darkness into the light of God's salvation.

The blind man went and washed and came back seeing. The people who knew him as a blind beggar were bewildered by the miracle. The man gave clear credit to 'a man called Jesus'. So they took the man who had been blind to the Pharisees and he recounted what had happened to him. Some of them responded saying Jesus could not be from God because he had performed this healing on the Sabbath Day. When pressed, the formerly blind man said he considered Jesus to be a prophet.

Unconvinced the Pharisees said they did not believe the man had been blind. His parents were called and they testified that this was their son and that he was born blind but they had no idea how he had gained sight. They were afraid of the Jewish leaders who threatened that anyone who confessed that Jesus was the Christ would be thrown out of the synagogue. This would not only debar them from worship but result in ostracism from their whole community. His parents said the Pharisees should question their son directly, he was old enough to speak for himself.

The Jews interrogated the man once more: 'Give God the glory! We know that this man is a sinner' (John 9:24). The man was extremely brave, he knew quite well what the Pharisees thought about Jesus. He knew that if he declared himself a follower of Jesus he was certain to be ex-communicated. But he made his statement, reasoned his case and took his stand -

> Since the world began it has been unheard of that anyone opened the eyes of one who was born blind. If this Man were not from God, he could do nothing (John 9:32-33).

> And they cast him out.

Years later the apostle Peter wrote -

> And who is he who will harm you if you become followers of what is good? But even if you should suffer for righteousness' sake, you are blessed. 'And do not be afraid of their threats, nor be troubled.' But sanctify the Lord God in your hearts, and always be ready to give a defence to everyone who asks you a reason for the hope that is in you, with meekness and fear; having a good conscience, that when they defame you as evildoers, those who revile your good conduct in Christ may be ashamed. For it is better, if it is the will of God, to suffer for doing good than for doing evil (1 Peter 3:13-17).

When Jesus heard that the beggar had been thrown out he searched for him and said, 'Do you believe in the Son of God?' (John 9:35) When Jesus disclosed himself, the man responded declaring his faith and worshipped him. Jesus is always true to the person who is true to him.

- Why did the Pharisees not believe in Jesus as the Son of God?

  Because they blindly and arrogantly declared: 'We know that this man is a sinner' (John 9:24);

  they judged him a Sabbath breaker (John 9:16); and

  they judged him a blasphemer (John 8:58-59)

- Why did this man, the former blind-beggar, believe in Jesus as the Son of God?

  Because he met the Lord and received his sight - 'As Jesus passed by, he saw a man' (John 9:1);

  he valued his own personal integrity (John 9:25);

  he reasoned from Scripture (John 9:30-33) - that God hears the prayers of the righteous but rejects the prayers of the wicked

(1 Samuel 8:18; Job 27:9; Psalm 18:41; Proverbs 1:28; Isaiah 59:2);

he received further revelation from Christ (John 9:35).

As Jesus said elsewhere -

> Take heed how you hear. For whoever has, to him more will be given; and whoever does not have, even what he seems to have will be taken from him (Luke 8:18).

Then Jesus said, 'For judgment I have come into this world, that those who do not see may see, and that those who see may be made blind' (John 9:39). This sounds strange, for earlier he had said that he was not sent 'into the world to condemn the world, but that the world through him might be saved' (John 3:17). The answer to this apparent dilemma is not difficult to find. 'The object of His mission was salvation; the moral effect of His life was judgment. He judged no one, and yet He judged everyone.'[52]

Some Pharisees heard Jesus speaking of blindness and asked if they too were blind. Jesus replied, 'If you were blind, you would have no sin; but now you say, "We see." Therefore your sin remains' (John 9:40-41).

When a person accepts and acknowledges blindness and need, and humbly seeks after God, then Jesus comes to dispel all darkness and bring salvation. Where a person holds on to pride and arrogance and an attitude of 'I know it all' then the light of the world will blind that one. The sinner's guilt will remain. Such people will continue under the condemnation of sin.

The former blind beggar was also spiritually blind. He received physical sight but also more importantly he received spiritual sight. He said, 'Lord, I believe!' (John 9:38) At the same time the sentence upon the Pharisees was as Isaiah predicted -

> Make the heart of this people dull, and their ears heavy, and shut their eyes; lest they see with their eyes, and hear with their ears, and understand with their heart, and return and be healed (Isaiah 6:10).

There is a very natural connection between the spiritual enlightenment of the beggar who was blind and teaching which follows, teaching about the door to the sheepfold and the good shepherd. This teaching will not only help the believing beggar to understand his experience but also help the Pharisees. Those hearing the Lord who are spiritually blind have their true spiritual

---

[52] Arthur W. Pink, *Expositions of the Gospel of John: three volumes unabridged in one* (Grand Rapids, Michigan: Zondervan, 1970), vol. 2, p.98.

condition diagnosed in order that any who will repent and believe in Jesus will be healed.

58. Jesus the door and the good Shepherd
John 10:1-21

The Pharisees were 'blind leaders of the blind' (Matthew 15:14). The leaders and pastors of Israel needed to see their true state and condition. The Lord spoke with the gracious intention of awakening some to self-knowledge and healing by illustrating their blindness with examples from shepherding.

The sheepfold (John 10:1) represents the nation of Israel. There were many sheep in the fold who were children of Israel 'according to the flesh' and only a few, as at any time in their history, who were also Israel 'according to the Spirit' (Galatians 4:29). 'For they are not all Israel who are of Israel, nor are they all children because they are the seed of Abraham' (Romans 9:6-7).

True children of Abraham are descendants who not only share his nature but also share his faith.

The sheepfold was a roofless enclosure in an open field. Usually it was situated near the village. It consisted of a wall made of rough stones and a sturdy door. A thief (one who is determined to take someone else's property) and robber (one who uses violence to take what belongs to others) would not choose to enter the sheepfold by the door. The door was locked and guarded by a doorkeeper who alone had the key. Consequently the thief and the robber must climb over the wall at another place.

By means of threats the religious leaders wanted to deprive Jesus of his disciples. They were the thieves and robbers who were out to steal the sheep of the Lord.

During the night the doorkeeper stayed with the sheep. The doorkeeper knew all the shepherds who left sheep in the fold overnight. When he heard the voice of the shepherd he opened the door. Jesus pictured himself as the true shepherd who had come to the door of the sheepfold and gained rightful entry. John the Baptist was the great doorkeeper of Israel. It was given to John to be the voice of one crying in the wilderness: 'Make straight the way of the LORD' (John 1:23) He was the one appointed to announce the arrival of the Messiah Christ (John 1:31,34).

Overnight there were quite a number of different flocks all mixed together in the one sheepfold. Separation occurred when each shepherd called his own sheep. Only his flock would follow him. It is truly an amazing picture of the way in which the Lord Jesus called out his own people to follow him. The blind beggar was one of those sheep. Jesus called him out of the sheepfold of Israel. Called out by Jesus; driven out by Pharisees. The sheep of the Lord Jesus Christ hear his voice and follow him.

The Lord warned that there would be many false christs until the true Lord returned. We have the assurance from our Lord that we shall not be deceived by any stranger (Matthew 24:23-27). We will hear and recognise the voice of the true shepherd, he will lead and his sheep will follow.

The people listening to Jesus did not understand the illustration so he presented another story to drive home his point. Still thinking of sheep and their shepherd Jesus spoke of another sheepfold.

This was not the one close to the village, with its wooden door and doorkeeper. This sheepfold was out in open country some distance from the village. In the warm season, when sheep were out on the hills, the shepherd did not lead his sheep back to the village sheepfold each night. Instead he gathered them into a hillside sheepfold. These sheepfolds in the hills were open spaces enclosed by a wall. In them there was no door, just an opening by which the sheep could enter and leave. Once the shepherd had lead his sheep into this enclosure he would lie down across the opening. None of the sheep could get out except over his body.

The shepherd was in effect 'the door'. There was no entry or exit except through him. This is what Jesus was thinking about when he said, 'I am the door'.

Jesus was a master of communication. He did not always make his words and expressions easy to understand. He made people think. He used all kinds of expressions of language: parables, metaphors, similes, analogies. Here there are metaphors. A metaphor is a figure of speech, an expression of language, in which the literal meaning is not intended. What is intended is to draw some comparison, to imply a resemblance between a word or phrase and the object or action to which it is connected. 'I am the door' is a metaphor. When Jesus uses this expression his hearers are forced to ask, 'In what sense is Jesus the door?'

Jesus is the 'door' of entry into the eternal flock of God. The evening before his death the Lord said, 'I am the way, the truth, and the life. No one comes to the Father except through me' (John 14:6). The writer to Hebrews urges his readers to take advantage of this one and only access to the living God -

> Therefore, brethren, having boldness to enter the Holiest by the blood of Jesus, by a new and living way which he consecrated for us, through the veil, that is, his flesh... let us draw near with a true heart in full assurance of faith (Hebrews 10:19-20,22).

Jesus is the only door. Anyone who enters will be saved from the penalty and power of sin and ultimately from the very presence of sin. They will also 'go in and out and find pasture' (John 10:9). To go 'in and out' is a figurative way to express perfect freedom. This is something vastly different from the experiences of even saved Israelites under the law of Moses. In Nehemiah 3 reference is made to the ten gates of the rebuilt city of Jerusalem. Only one gate, the Sheep Gate, had no locks and bars mentioned. This is a symbol of the freedom granted to all believers and correlates with the abundant life (John 10:10).

The worthless shepherds mentioned are most of the Jewish leadership who were designated thieves and robbers not caring for the sheep (cf. Zechariah 11:15-17; Ezekiel 34:1-10).

> Nothing seems so offensive to Christ as a false teacher of religion, a false prophet, or a false shepherd. Nothing ought to be so much dreaded in the Church, and if needful, be so plainly rebuked, opposed, and exposed. The strong language of our Reformers, when writing against Romish teachers, is often blamed more than it ought to be.[53]

The prophet Jeremiah faced the same problem in his day and the Lord gave a wonderful prophecy through him that God would raise up pastors (shepherds) who would genuinely care for the people and faithfully teach the Word of God (Jeremiah 23:1-6). Indeed God himself was to come and remove the worthless pastors (shepherds). He was going to come himself -

> For thus says the Lord GOD: 'Indeed I myself will search for my sheep and seek them out. As a shepherd seeks out his flock on the day he is among his scattered sheep, so will I seek out my sheep and deliver them from all the places where they were scattered on a cloudy and dark day' (Ezekiel 34:11-12).

Jesus is the Good Shepherd who owns his sheep, loves his sheep, protects his sheep, knows all his sheep and who lays down his life for them (cf. Ezekiel 34:11-16; Zechariah 13:7; 12:10; John 19:37). The Lord's sheep recognise his voice and follow him. They are called out from among the Jews and from among the Gentiles and there will be one new flock, the flock of God (John 10:16). The Father is intensely involved in the sacrificial death of his Son. He loves his Son for his extreme evidence of faithfulness, devotion and commitment. The Son will freely and willingly lay down his life for his sheep and fulfil the commission given to him (John 10:17-18).

---

[53] John Ryle in: Arthur W. Pink, *Expositions of the Gospel of John: three volumes unabridged in one* (Grand Rapids, Michigan: Zondervan, 1970), vol. 2, p.111.

A strong difference of opinion surfaced in the hearers; from those who reacted saying Jesus had a demon and was mad to others who reasoned: 'These are not the words of one who has a demon. Can a demon open the eyes of the blind?' (John 10:21)

59. The return of the seventy disciples
Luke 10:17-24

On the completion of their assignment the seventy disciples returned with great delight. They said nothing of the conversion of sinners or of the response of the people, but only of the spirits being subject to them. They had been given power to heal the sick but they evidently considered exorcism as the more wonderful experience.

Jesus said he had seen 'Satan fall like lightning from heaven' (Luke 10:18). As the prophet Isaiah declared -

How you are fallen from heaven, O Lucifer, son of the morning.
How you are cut down to the ground, you who weakened the nations (Isaiah 14:12).

Jesus regarded the success of the disciples as a sign and pledge of the complete overthrow of Satan (cf. John 12:31-32). The Lord promised more authority and power but also warned them not to be proud and excited over these things. That which should be their constant delight is to know that their names are written in God's register of the redeemed (cf. Exodus 32:32; Psalm 87:6; Hebrews 12:23; Revelation 3:5; 17:8). *Our greatest glory is not what we have done for God but what God has done for us.*

Jesus rejoiced in the Spirit and thanked the Father for choosing babes. The apostle Paul expressed the same thought when, writing to the Christians in Corinth, he declared that -

not many wise according to the flesh, not many mighty, not many noble, are called. But God has chosen the foolish things of the world to put to shame the wise, and God has chosen the weak things of the world to put to shame the things which are mighty; and the base things of the world and the things which are despised God has chosen, and the things which are not, to bring to nothing the things that are, that no flesh should glory in his presence (1 Corinthians 1:26-29).

Jesus once more delighted in the special unique relationship which exists between the Father and himself (cf. Matthew 11:25-30). Then he turned privately to his apostles and reminded them of their great privilege. They were seeing what prophets and kings longed to see, the presence and activity of the long awaited Messiah. Did Peter have these words in his mind when he wrote -

> Of this salvation the prophets have inquired and searched carefully, who prophesied of the grace that would come to you, searching what, or what manner of time, the Spirit of Christ who was in them was indicating when he testified beforehand the sufferings of Christ and the glories that would follow. To them it was revealed that, not to themselves, but to us they were ministering the things which now have been reported to you through those who have preached the gospel to you by the Holy Spirit sent from heaven - things which angels desire to look into (1 Peter 1:10-12).

As Jesus continued teaching the people, a lawyer stood up with a test question, 'Teacher, what shall I do to inherit eternal life?' (Luke 10:25) The lawyer may have been rather surprised to be directed to the Scriptures, but when challenged he came up with the appropriate answer, 'Love God and love your neighbour'. Jesus gave no new doctrine but rather confirmation, 'Do this and you will live' (Luke 10:28). The lawyer might have felt a little humiliated by this statement of the obvious so 'wanting to justify himself', and prove himself a capable legal practitioner, he asked further, 'And who is my neighbour?'

There were Jewish teachers who perverted the command of Leviticus 19:18 to mean, love your neighbour and hate your enemy. Jesus refuted this in the Sermon on the Mount (Matthew 5:43-48). Others restricted love for neighbour to mean love for neighbour Israelite. There follows one of the most well known and favourite parables. By this story the Lord showed that the question should never need to be asked. The duty of love requires neighbourliness to all.

60. The parable of The Good Samaritan
Luke 10:25-37

Jerusalem lies 754m (2,474 ft) *above* sea level. Jericho lies 258m (846 ft) *below* sea level - it is the lowest city in the world. In just under 25km (16 miles) the road drops 1,012m (3,310 ft). Consequently Jesus said, 'A certain man went down from Jerusalem to Jericho' (Luke 10:30). The road was notoriously dangerous being narrow, rocky, with many caves and hollows, and with sudden turnings which made it an ideal hunting ground for bandits. In New Testament days it was known as 'The Red Way' or 'The Bloody Way'.

Thieves attacked, beat, robbed and stripped the man, leaving him for dead. A priest came by, either on the way to the temple in Jerusalem to perform his ceremonial duties or returning. He saw the man and passed by on the other side of the road. The man looked dead. The priest knew that to touch a dead body would render him ceremonially unclean for seven days (Leviticus 21:11) so he took no risk of defilement seemingly forgetting that God had repeatedly said such things as, 'I desire mercy and not sacrifice' (Hosea 6:6; Micah 6:8).

A Levite also came by, saw the miserable condition of the seriously injured man whose life was fast ebbing away and perhaps fearing a decoy to trap him or that he might suffer a similar fate, passed by on the other side.

For the next passer-by in the story Jesus chose a despised foreigner, a descendant of the imported immigrants on the northern border of Judea. It was left to an ex-communicated Samaritan, whose very name was a byword of contempt among the Jews, and synonymous with heretic (John 8:48) to show the true nature of love. A Samaritan would know full-well that had the roles been reversed then the Jew would have left him without a second thought.

A Samaritan came by, saw the injured man and moved with compassion tended his wounds, put him on his own animal, no doubt supporting him all the way, took him to an inn and covered all his expenses. Jesus asked the lawyer, 'Which of the three was neighbour to the one who fell among the thieves?' When the lawyer answered, 'The one who showed mercy' Jesus replied, 'Go and do likewise' (Luke 10:37).

The lawyer wanted a definition. He said in effect, 'Designate my neighbour for me!' Jesus turned the question around and answered rather, 'To whom can I be a neighbour?' He taught that we must help a man even when he has brought trouble upon himself; anyone of any nation or race who is in need is our neighbour; and our help must be practical, for compassion which is real must issue in action! The challenge is clear: 'Do I behave myself as a neighbour to those who have need of my love and help?'

Beautiful as this parable is when taken in its simplest meaning, encouraging us to 'put on tender mercies' (Colossians 3:12) even though it may be painful or dangerous, there is more to learn. Trench notes -

> How much lovelier still, how much more mightily provoking to love and good work, when, with most of the [Church] Fathers, and with many of the Reformers, we trace in it a deeper meaning still,

and see the work of Christ, of the merciful Son of God Himself, portrayed to us here.[54]

Many modern-day commentators and scholars either omit reference to this interpretation or reject it in the strongest terms,[55] yet there is a compelling argument for a deeper meaning in the teaching of Jesus himself. Consider how of the forty or more recorded parables of Jesus, he interpreted only two, the parable of The Sower and the parable of The Wheat and Tares. After presenting the first of these, the disciples asked him to enable them to understand it, to which he replied, 'Do you not understand this parable? How then will you understand all the parables?' (Mark 4:13) Jesus was implying that if the method of interpretation of one parable is rightly understood, then the same approach will yield the true understanding of all parables. Jesus interpreted the two parables as allegories where most of the features in the story have a counterpart in the spiritual realm. For example, the sower is the preacher; the seed is the Word of God and the soil is the heart of the hearer.

The parable of The Sower (Matthew 13:3-9,18-23)

The sower	= The preacher
The seed	= The Word of God, the gospel
The soil	= The hearts of the hearers
The wayside	= The hard-hearted
Birds of the air	= The devil's agents - snatch away the Word
Stony ground (no roots)	= The shallow-hearted - respond quickly
Sun-scorched, withers	= Persecution comes - fall away
Among thorns, choked	= Cares of this world - choke the Word
Good ground, yields crop	= The whole-hearted - accept it, bear fruit

The same approach is used by the Lord in interpreting -

The parable of The Wheat and Tares (Matthew 13:24-30,36-43)

A man	= Son of Man
Good seed	= The sons of the kingdom
Field	= The world
Enemy	= The devil
Tares	= The sons of the wicked one

---

[54] Richard C. Trench, *Notes on The Parables of Our Lord* (London: Macmillan, 1866), pp.320-1.

[55] Frederic L. Godet, Commentary on *Luke* (Grand Rapids, Michigan: Kregel, 1981), p.309 and William Hendriksen, *The Gospel of Luke* (Edinburgh: Banner of Truth, 1978), p.594.

Servants
Harvest   = The end of the age
Reapers   = The angels
Burn   = Tares cast into the furnace of fire
Barn

Interpreting the parable of The Good Samaritan in this way does not detract from the simple meaning of the story but significantly deepens and strengthens the message and is in line with the Lord's teaching on understanding parables. Consider the following explanation of the parable of The Good Samaritan in the light of the parable of The Sower and the parable of The Wheat and Tares.

Jerusalem means, 'the place of peace' (cf. Hebrews 7:2), signifying the condition of harmony between God and humanity. Jericho symbolises the destination of the wicked. It is the profane city, a city under a curse (Joshua 6:26; 1 Kings 16:34).

The traveller has no sooner turned from the presence of God and the holy city, than he has fallen into the hands of violent thieves, that is, the devil and the fallen angels. He and his evil allies have beaten the man, stripped him of his robe of original righteousness, grievously wounded him, and left him for dead. We are all now 'dead in trespasses and sins' (Ephesians 2:1).

The priest who came by personifies the ineffective Old Covenant sacrifices (Hebrews 10:1); the Levite stands for the law which is able to diagnose the disease but cannot cure it, 'for by the law is the knowledge of sin' (Romans 3:20). 'If there had been a law given which could have offered life, truly righteousness would have been by the law' (Galatians 3:21).

Who then is represented by the Samaritan? Is it not the Lord himself? Shortly after the Feast of Tabernacles the Jews questioned Jesus, 'Do we not say rightly that you are a Samaritan?' (John 8:48) Here is the One 'despised and rejected by men' (Isaiah 53:3), who 'came to his own, and his own did not receive him'. This despised Samaritan, 'as he journeyed, came where he was'. What a glorious description of the incarnation of the Son of God.

> Inasmuch then as the children have partaken of flesh and blood, he himself likewise shared the same, that through death he might destroy him who had the power of death, that is, the devil (Hebrews 2:14; cf. Romans 8:2-4).

The Samaritan bound the wounds of the injured 'pouring on oil and wine' the beautiful symbols of the anointing of the Holy Spirit and the cleansing blood of Christ. How fitting are the words of the Lord through the prophet Ezekiel -

And when I passed by you and saw you struggling in your own blood, I said to you in your blood, 'Live!' Yes, I said to you in your blood, 'Live!' …I spread my wing over you and covered your nakedness… Then I washed you in water; yes, I thoroughly washed off your blood, and I anointed you with oil. I clothed you (Ezekiel 16:6,8,9-10).

The Samaritan then transported the wounded man to a place where he could be loved and cared for; that represents the local church where every saved sinner is to be strengthened by the preaching of the Word of God, the pastoral care of the eldership and the fellowship and support of the Lord's people. Is it not Jesus who has been so remarkably merciful and kind who comes where we are and promises to return again and to reward all those who have worked and sacrificed for his people? 'Christ was "the Samaritan," the rejected one, who was showing mercy to the spiritual and physical needs of men whereas the religious leaders were totally indifferent.'[56]

The parable of the Good Samaritan (Luke 10:30-37)

A man	=	A sinner
Jerusalem	=	Harmony between God and humanity
Jericho	=	A cursed place, the destination of the wicked
Thieves	=	The devil and fallen angels
Stripped	=	Original righteousness removed
Half dead	=	Spiritually dead in trespasses and sin
The priest	=	Representative of the sacrifices
The Levite	=	Representative of the law
A Samaritan	=	Representative of the Saviour
Oil	=	Anointing by the Holy Spirit
Wine	=	The application of the blood of Christ
Beast		
Inn	=	The Church for teaching and pastoral care
Two denarii	=	Talents and minas given to the body of Christ
'When I return'	=	The second advent of the Lord Jesus
Repayment	=	Reward to the Church for caring

61. Martha and Mary differ
Luke 10:38-42

The practical application of God's Word in the parable of The Good Samaritan is complemented by the incident which followed in the home of

---

[56] Robert G. Gromacki, *New Testament Survey* (Grand Rapids, Michigan: Baker Book House, 1974), p.123.

Mary and Martha. Here it is seen that making time for fellowship with the Saviour is more important than just serving him. The certain village referred to by Luke is Bethany, about 3km (2 miles) east of Jerusalem (John 11:18). Here Jesus visited his good friends Lazarus and his sisters Mary and Martha. It is recorded that Jesus loved these three and seems often to have stayed with them when visiting Jerusalem (John 11:5; 12:1-2; Matthew 21:17; Mark 11:11-12).

The Lord Jesus had been concerned to show the clever lawyer how to show constant neighbourliness. The emphasis was upon action. Human nature is nevertheless prone to extremes and so the Holy Spirit records a timely incident which teaches the need for balance.

Arriving at his friends' home in Bethany the Lord was greeted by Martha. Martha became involved in preparing a meal for the Lord and Mary was sitting listening to him. Martha was 'distracted with much serving' (v.40). These words suggest two important points: firstly she was 'distracted', in other words she would have liked to sit and listen to the Lord but felt the heavy responsibility to prepare food; and secondly, she was distracted 'with much serving' which suggests that she was seriously over-preparing.

She was not busy with things that were not necessary - as she understood it. Martha was not trying to make the beds, feed the hens, fix the curtains, and serve the meal. No she was concentrating upon feeding her guest. But she had committed herself to such an extent that she became flustered, frustrated and eventually annoyed at her sister.

Martha assumed that what she had chosen to do was right and therefore Mary was very much in the wrong. Martha took time from her serving to confront the Lord and Mary. 'Lord' - she began with respect but then showed discourtesy. 'Do you not care that my sister has left me to serve alone?' and then follows rudeness which will only undo all the good she intended, 'Therefore tell her to help me'.

Jesus replied, 'Martha, Martha, you are worried and troubled about many things. But one thing is needed, and Mary has chosen that good part, which will not be taken away from her' (vv.41-42). With that characteristic repeating of her name our Lord would settle her troubled mind. 'You are worried and troubled about many things.' So much of her anxiety had been brought upon herself (Proverbs 12:25; Matthew 6:21). On this occasion she was doing more than was necessary.

'Martha, Martha, you are worried' (the inward fault) and troubled (the external, restless hurrying backwards and forwards). She was in a turbulence! Martha you are losing the collectedness and calmness of thought in your misplaced zeal. You are spoiling your good work and robbing yourself of the blessing of the Lord's presence.

The placing of this incident in Holy Scripture indicates a great lesson for all. God wants action. When it comes to the great issues of life and death we are to love *'the LORD our God with all our heart, with all our soul, with all our strength, and with all our mind, and our neighbour as ourself.'* But in our great activity in serving God there is a very important place to be given regularly to spending time quietly with him - listening to him by reading his Word, thinking and praying.

62. Disciples taught to pray
Luke 11:1-13

Seeing Jesus at prayer prompted the disciples to seek his help, that he would teach them how to pray (Luke 11:1). From the request of the disciples and the gracious manner of the Lord's response we learn two helpful lessons: firstly, prayer does not come naturally or easily to most disciples of Christ; and secondly, there is the world of difference between *the desire* and *the achievement* of prayer. There was a willingness to pray in the disciples but also *a sensed inability* to pray.

The Lord provided a pattern of prayer for his disciples. It is called 'The Lord's Prayer' because he taught it but it might be more accurately called 'The Disciples' Prayer' because we are to use it as a pattern for prayer. It is sometimes called 'The Model Prayer'. The key to understanding the prayer is to see it as *a formula for composition* not *a formula for repetition*. The slavish chanting, singing or saying of this prayer will serve no purpose before God if the heart is not right with him. In The Sermon on the Mount Jesus said -

> When you pray, do not use vain repetitions as the heathen do. For they think that they will be heard for their many words. Therefore do not be like them. For your Father knows the things you have need of before you ask him (Matthew 6:7-8).

Beginning with a humble acknowledgement of the amazing privilege, the special relationship which exists with the living God, disciples of Jesus are to cry, 'Our Father' (Luke 11:2; cf. Romans 8:15; Galatians 4:6). 'Hallowed be your name' is the longing and desire that God be recognised and honoured as holy, that he be treated with the utmost reverence and respect: 'Holy, holy, holy is the Lord of hosts; the whole earth is full of his glory!' (Isaiah 6:3; cf. Revelation 4:8) Praying for his kingdom to come and his will to be done on earth is the natural outworking of love and devotion towards the Creator and Saviour who is righteous in all his ways -

Righteousness and justice are the foundation of your throne; mercy and truth go before your face. Blessed are the people who know the joyful sound! They walk, O Lord, in the light of your countenance (Psalm 89:14-15).

When God's kingdom comes and his will is done on earth, Christians will worship and praise God with great delight. For in his presence is fullness of joy and at his right hand are pleasures forevermore (Psalm 16:11). Personal needs are kept in second place to the adoration of his majesty.

The parable of The Friend at Midnight (Luke 11:5-8)

Continuing on the subject of prayer, Jesus taught a parable. A man is awakened at midnight by his friend who is travelling in the night. The man has no food to set before his guest. So he goes to another friend to ask for bread. This second friend is not pleased to be awakened at midnight, 'Do not trouble me; the door is now shut, and my children are with me in bed; I cannot rise and give to you'.

Jesus then drives home the point. 'I say to you, though he will not rise and give to him because he is his friend, *yet because of his persistence* he will rise and give him as many as he needs.' The Lord Jesus adds further comment and then concludes by declaring that the heavenly Father will 'give the Holy Spirit to those who ask him' (Luke 11:13).

This parable teaches persistence however there is a deeper meaning. There are three representative friends to be spiritually interpreted (remember the Lord's words on understanding parables).

The travelling friend had left home and was 'on his journey' or was, literally, 'out of way' (Luke 11:6; AV margin). He is 'out of way' at midnight suggesting an unbeliever who is spiritually in the dark, like Nicodemus who visited Jesus 'by night' (John 3:2). This friend arrived hungry.

The householder friend is the believer who cannot satisfy spiritual hunger from his own resources for no provision of our own will satisfy the needy sinner or the wandering saint. Nevertheless this believer knew very well where to go.

He turned to the third friend, to God who has an abundance of bread. He, the Lord, will give the Bread of Life (John 6:35) to satisfy eternally. The third friend appeared reluctant at first but was won over by persistence. Jesus was pressing home the need for determination in prayer, persistence that will not give up. Consider: Abraham praying for Sodom (Genesis 18:22-33); The Syro-Phoenician woman pleading on behalf of her sick child (Mark 7:24-30); Jacob wrestling with the Angel of the Lord (Genesis 32:28) and the parable of The Widow and the Judge (Luke 18:1-8).

How strong this friendship, how confident in their relationship is the friend who comes in the middle of the night! Jesus earned the nickname 'a friend of tax collectors and sinners' (Luke 7:34). John Wesley said, 'Pray for all your friends until they come to faith in Christ Jesus. Then find some more friends'. 'The effective, fervent prayer of a righteous man avails much' (James 5:16).

The Lord follows with teaching on ask, seek, knock! The connection with the parable is unmistakable. The word 'ask' probably alludes to the traveller's cries of distress; 'seek' links with the man's effort to find the door in the darkness; and 'knock' to his persistence in gaining the required assistance.

To ask implies humility and consciousness of need. Asking God presupposes belief in a personal God who hears and answers prayer. To seek is more than to ask, and to knock is more than to seek. In this ascending scale of earnestness there is an exhortation not merely to pray but to pray with increasing urgency - as though with all reverence to our Heavenly Father, we will not take 'No' for an answer!

What does God promise in answer to asking, seeking, and knocking? He promises the Holy Spirit to all who repent (Acts 2:38). On conversion the spirit of adoption is received so that when we cry out 'Abba, Father' the 'Spirit himself bears witness with our spirit that we are children of God' (Romans 8:15-16).

> Likewise the Spirit also helps in our weaknesses. For we do not know what we should pray for as we ought, but the Spirit himself makes intercession for us with groanings which cannot be uttered (Roman 8:26).

In many wonderful ways the Holy Spirit answers our persistent heartfelt prayers. Sometimes we see a clear and dramatic answer as when an unbelieving friend comes to faith in the Lord Jesus Christ. Sometimes the Holy Spirit teaches greater patience and greater persistence. At other times he comes simply to remind us, 'My grace is sufficient for you, for my strength is made perfect in weakness' (2 Corinthians 12:9).

63. Further criticism of scribes and Pharisees
Luke 11:37-54

As he was speaking the Lord was invited to a meal by a Pharisee. The Pharisees, for the most part, were the most bitter, stubborn, and adamant enemies of Jesus, yet he readily accepted the invitation. He took up all occasions to do good. He never shrank back from declaring the truth and making such occasions the means of spreading the gospel. There was no indication as to the reason for the invitation. At this stage in Jesus' ministry the attitude of the Pharisees in general was hostile to the point of seeking his death.

From the subsequent words of Jesus it would seem that this Pharisee wanted to argue or criticise the teaching of Jesus. The Lord's severe unrestrained rebuke of Pharisees and scribes suggests that a number were present at the meal (cf. Luke 11:53) and their manner was antagonistic. This would also help to explain why the Lord sat down to eat without first washing his hands. It seems likely that this was a deliberate act[57] to draw attention to the hypocrisy of the Pharisees and scribes.

Hand washing was something of an obsession with the Pharisees. The law of the Jewish Rabbis taught that before eating food hands should be washed in a certain way and between each course.[58] Jesus pointed out that if they were as meticulous about cleansing their hearts they would be better men! 'Now you Pharisees make the outside of the cup and dish clean, but your inward part is full of greed and wickedness' (Luke 11:39).

Whilst the Lord's words were straight to the point, his goal was the best possible one. In condemning their foolishness in emphasising external ceremonies rather than internal holiness, he was exposing their sin so that they could repent and learn true heart religion. The underlying philosophy behind all that the Saviour did and all that the Saviour taught was 'Get the inside right and the outside will take care of itself!'

> For the LORD does not see as man sees; for man looks at the outward appearance, but the LORD looks at the heart (1 Samuel 16:7).

The Pharisees (their name means 'separated') were a group that sprang up about 150 years before the birth of the Lord Jesus. They received their name because they separated themselves from all other Jews. They aimed to be more holy and more religious than others. It is very commendable to want to be more holy, but not to be more holy by comparison with others.

The apostle Peter outlines four motives for holiness of life: the grace of God, the holiness of God, the fear of God and the sacrifice of God (1 Peter 1:13-21). Unfortunately the separation of the Pharisees usually consisted in

---

[57] 'Christ deliberately neglected outward rites invented by men, in the observing of which the Jews were altogether too scrupulous' (John Calvin, *A Harmony of the Gospels Matthew, Mark and Luke* (Edinburgh: St. Andrew Press, 1972), vol. 2. p.100.

[58] See section *103. Scribes and Pharisees rebuked*, p.226.

eating different food and performing obsessive rituals. They did not lack enthusiasm but they lacked depth, faith and love.

The lawyers (scribes) also came under severe criticism for their showmanship and lack of compassion. At that point in history most scribes were also Pharisees. They were professional lawyers. Scribes knew the written law of God and the oral law of the Rabbis. Through the years, from the days of Ezra, scribes had written so many comments, enlargements and amplifications of the law of Moses that the Word of God itself was obscured. They taught the oral law and their own explanations more than they taught the pure Word of God.

Jesus criticised them in the first instance because they set standards for others to keep but not for themselves (v.46); they laid a thousand and one burdens on the people through their laws, rules and regulations. For example: A Sabbath Day's journey was set at 2,000 cubits (just over half a mile) from your home. But if a rope were tied across the end of the street, the end of the street became your home and you could walk just over half a mile from that. If, on a Friday, you put enough food for two meals at a place away from your home, that place became technically your new home and you could walk half a mile from there.

To carry a burden on the Sabbath was forbidden, but the law of the Rabbis and scribes said -

> 'he who carries anything, whether it be in his right hand, or in his left hand... or on his shoulder is guilty; but he who carries anything on the back of his hand, with his foot, or with his mouth, or with his elbow, or with his ear, or with his hair, or with his money bag turned upside down, or between his money bag and his shirt, or in the fold of his shirt or in his shoe, or in his sandal is guiltless, because he does not carry it in the usual way of carrying it out.[59]

Secondly, Jesus criticised them for a serious lack of agreement between their words and their lives. They made a great show of respect for the prophets of God; they built tombs and memorials for their dead prophets, yet on the other hand they did not follow the teaching of those prophets. What was even worse they persecuted living prophets - like the Saviour.

Thirdly, Jesus criticised them for being a hindrance to seekers: 'Woe to you lawyers! For you have taken away the key of knowledge. You did not enter in yourselves, and those who were entering in you hindered' (v.52). 'The key of knowledge', like the keys of the kingdom of heaven given to

---

[59] William Barclay, *The Gospel of Luke* (Edinburgh: St Andrew Press, 1961), p.162.

Peter after his great confession of Christ (Matthew 16:19), are the means of access to God; the Gospel and the Word of God.

> Just as today the keys of the Kingdom of Heaven are entrusted to the pastors [through their preaching] to admit the faithful to eternal life and exclude the unbelievers from any hope of it, so in former days the same responsibility was laid on the Priests and Scribes under the Law.[60]

The scribes and Pharisees reacted strongly to the Lord's criticism and their hatred grew.

A great gathering formed outside the Pharisee's house and some were injured by the crush of the crowd. Jesus turned to his disciples, warned them against hypocrisy and fear, and encouraged them to stand firm and to rely upon the Holy Spirit when confronted with animosity and hostility (Luke 12:1-12). Jesus reassured his small band of devoted followers that they had nothing to fear. The secret of life was found in fearing God - then nothing and no one need be feared!

There are two meanings in Scripture for 'the fear of the Lord'. In each case the meaning is determined by the context. There is the fear of the Lord which is found in the ungodly, a slavish fear produced by guilt from the dread of judgment or the fear of punishment. This is the fear which terrifies the heart (Deuteronomy 28:67).

There is also the fear of the Lord which is seen in the godly, a respect and reverence for God. This is the fear of which Jesus speaks here. As Solomon noted, 'In the fear of the LORD there is strong confidence, and his children will have a place of refuge' (Proverbs 14:26; cf. Psalm 112:1; 147:11). Conversion results in a dramatic change from fear which is terror and fright to fear which is reverence and respect.

> There is no fear in love; but perfect love casts out fear, because fear involves torment. But he who fears has not been made perfect in love (1 John 4:18).

64. Warning against covetousness
Luke 12:1-21

In the middle of our Lord's teaching a man interrupted with a request which indicated that his prime concerns were financial not spiritual. The burning issue on this man's mind was a felt injustice. 'Teacher, tell my brother to divide the inheritance with me' (v.13). Was his grievance legitimate? It

---

[60] John Calvin, *A Harmony of the Gospels Matthew, Mark and Luke* (Saint Andrew Press: Edinburgh, 1972), vol. 3, p.53.

would seem so, for Jesus did not deal with the subject of injustice but rather with the subject of covetousness. People can be covetous in the manner in which they keep hold of what is theirs or by reclaiming from others what is theirs by right. The man was clearly so preoccupied with his earthly inheritance that he had no ears for a sermon on heavenly inheritance.

However the man's request was not sinful. To seek out a spiritually minded man as an arbitrator in a dispute between brothers is taught by the Word of God (1 Corinthians 6:1-8). Our Lord was not saying the man's interest in matters of the world were sinful, wrong or unimportant. The wrong on this occasion was the evident priority given to this world! Hence the Lord Jesus told a parable for him.

The parable of The Rich Fool (Luke 12:16-21)

A certain rich man, said Jesus, persistently replaced his barns with bigger ones. Jesus clearly indicated that material possessions were not a sign of God's blessing. They can be a serious cause of stumbling (cf. James 5:1-3; 1 Timothy 6:9-10,17). The farmer is shown to be short-sighted. As Paul counsels, 'Set your mind on things above, not on things on the earth' (Colossians 3:2). Becoming a disciple of Jesus is an investment that brings wonderful immediate returns in this life and later in the life to come.

We are blessed 'with every spiritual blessing... in Christ' (Ephesians 1:3): loved, forgiven, adopted into the family of God and sanctified. We are indwelt by the Holy Spirit: led, comforted, encouraged and receive the wonderful fruit of 'love, joy, peace, patience, kindness, goodness, faithfulness, gentleness, self-control' (Galatians 5:22). We also have our hearts and minds guarded through Christ Jesus by the peace of God which surpasses all understanding (Philippians 4:7)

This is coupled with the glorious prospect of the heavenly 'inheritance incorruptible and undefiled and that does not fade away, reserved in heaven for [those] who are kept by the power of God through faith for salvation ready to be revealed in the last time' (1 Peter 1:4-5).

The farmer in the parable was self-absorbed. Wisdom teaches that, 'the complacency [self-satisfied feeling] of fools will destroy them' (Proverbs 1:32); and 'If riches increase, do not set your heart on them' (Psalm 62:10). The farmer showed neither gratitude to God nor concern to help others. Furthermore -

> those who desire to be rich fall into temptation and a snare, and into many foolish and harmful lusts which drown men in destruction and perdition. For the love of money is a root of all kinds of evil, for which some have strayed from the faith in their

greediness, and pierced themselves through with many sorrows (1 Timothy 6:9-10).

65. *Avoiding worry about food and clothing*
Luke 12:22-34

The parable of The Rich Fool was spoken to the crowd, but Jesus then turned his attention to the disciples. 'Therefore' connects what has just been said to what is about to be said. The disciples were poor, they had left their means of earning a living, they cannot be seeing any relevance of the rich fool in the parable and *their* condition. Jesus pointed out to them that the same driving force can exist in them as existed in the rich fool. As the rich fool was anxious to amass as much as he could, so disciples of Christ may be equally anxious about where they will see their next meal, or how they will clothe their families. Both the rich and the poor might be overwhelmed by worry.

Worry and anxiety are symptoms of a life that is not resting in God. An anxious striving after the things of this world, even necessary things, is not fitting for disciples of Jesus. We are encouraged to cast all our cares upon God. This is the right way to peace of mind and stability of heart (cf. Matthew 6:25-34). As the apostle Paul urged the Philippians -

> Be anxious for nothing, but in everything by prayer and supplication, with thanksgiving, let your requests be made known to God; and the peace of God, which surpasses all understanding, will guard your hearts and minds through Christ Jesus (Philippians 4:6-7).

'Consider the ravens' (v.24) for the Lord gives food 'to the young ravens that cry' (Psalm 147:9). As the Lord provides food *for ravens* to feed their young so the Lord provided food *by ravens* to feed the prophet Elijah (1 Kings 17:6). The one who provides the life is well able to supply the food to sustain that life. The one who provides the body is capable to deliver the clothes for that body.

Worry does no good at all, in fact it does great harm. To be gripped by anxiety instead of casting all our burdens upon the Lord demonstrates a serious lack of faith in our heavenly Father, his precious promises and his Word (v.28). It brings discredit and dishonour to our most gracious and loving Lord.

Our energy is to be directed to the primary goal of 'seeking the kingdom of God' confident that all necessary things will be provided for us: the Lord giving strength and intelligence for us to work for the essentials and where possible to be able to give to others; by giving parents to sustain the young and children to support the old; by brothers and sisters in Christ to share their resources to further the growth and development of the Church (2 Thessalonians 3:10-13; 1 Thessalonians 4:11; 1 Timothy 5`;18; Galatians 6:6).

Depending upon the Lord for provision is not a route to inactivity or laziness. It is a life of trust and confidence in God and freedom from restless, uneasy, agitated and troublesome thoughts.

66. Prepared for the Master's return
Luke 12:35-48

Jesus pictured his followers as waiting servants prepared and expecting the master's return. They are girded ready.

At night it is vitally important that the servant has a lamp to walk quickly and safely to meet the Master at the door. The lit lamp (fed by oil) signifies a vibrant spiritual life (Matthew 5:16; Philippians 2:14-16). And what does the Master do upon his return? Here is a surprise. He 'girds himself' (Luke 12:37) as they are girded and serves them with the food which they had prepared for him! This is the same Master who, in the upper room -

> rose from supper and laid aside his garments, took a towel and girded himself. After that, he poured water into a basin and began to wash the disciples' feet, and to wipe them with the towel with which he was girded (John 13:4-5).

Disciples of Jesus are to be constantly on the alert, 'looking for the blessed hope and glorious appearing of our great God and Saviour Jesus Christ' (Titus 2:13). He may return at any time!

In response to a further question from Peter, Jesus spoke of the responsibilities of Church leaders. Those found faithful and diligent in their duties will be given greater responsibilities. Selfish and self-indulgent leaders who badly treat others will be cast out completely. Others who knew the master's will and failed to do it will be punished. A less severe sentence will be past on the ones who fail but did not know the will of the master. Jesus concluded with a principle -

> Everyone to whom much is given, from him much will be required; and to whom much has been committed, of him they will ask the more (Luke 12:48).

67. Interpreting the times
Luke 12:49-59

Jesus opened his heart to his disciples, 'I came to send fire on the earth' (Luke 12:49) The mission of the Lord was to bring a new heavenly influence into the world, the Spirit of burning as John the Baptist declared, 'I indeed baptise you with water; but One mightier than I is coming... he will baptise you with the Holy Spirit and fire' (Luke 3:16). That spiritual fire descending on the Day of Pentecost was symbolised as a flame resting on every head (Acts 2:3-4).

> See how great a flame aspires,
> Kindled by a spark of grace!
> Jesu's love the nations fires,
> Sets the kingdoms on a blaze;
> Fire to bring on earth He came;
> Kindled in some hearts it is;
> O that all might catch the flame,
> All partake the glorious bliss!   Charles Wesley

The Gospel will burn through the nations 'For he is like a refiner's fire' (Malachi 3:2). The Holy Spirit will bring cleansing, for fire purifies. Disciples must take care not to put out the fire: 'Do not quench the Spirit... Test all things; hold fast what is good. Abstain from every form of evil' (1 Thessalonians 5:19,21-22). Those united to Christ display the fruit of the indwelling Holy Spirit (Galatians 5:22-25), as 'children of God without fault in the midst of a crooked and perverse generation, among whom you shine as lights in the world' (Philippians 2:15).

'I came to send fire on the earth, and how I wish it were already kindled!' Jesus longed for the dawning of the day when the Holy Spirit would come to burn through the nations of the world. But, said Jesus, he had a baptism to experience first and he was distressed until it was brought about. He spoke of the momentous events to take place leading up to and culminating at the cross of Calvary! The agonies in the Garden of Gethsemane were already present in the consciousness of the Saviour.

There is however another aspect to the arrival of the Holy Spirit and fire. Not all will receive him and be blessed. There will be those who reject the Gospel and resist the workings of the Holy Spirit. The gospel of peace will stir up antagonism, bitterness and hostility. Families will be split, divided by the faith of some and the unbelief of others. The closest of relationship will be tested and strained. Then the heavenly fire becomes a sign of 'certain fearful expectation of judgment, and fiery indignation' (Hebrews 10:27).

'For our God is a consuming fire' ... 'let us have grace, by which we may serve God acceptably with reverence and godly fear' (Hebrews 12:29,28).

Jesus addressed the multitude challenging them to recognise the signs he was fulfilling. Since they were quite capable of recognising the signs of the weather why were they not applying their minds to discerning the spiritual climate? Like Elijah's servant of old, when they saw a cloud rising from the west they knew that a shower was imminent (1 Kings 18:44).

Even in these two earthly phenomena there were spiritual signs: the dark clouds signify God's judgment and the south wind the heat of God's wrath. They could grasp and interpret the external appearances of earth and sky but their profound insincerity of heart, and wilful misunderstanding of divine things, made them incapable of seeing and discerning the signs of the time which his coming had introduced! Jesus rebuked these people because they paid far more attention to constantly changing weather conditions than to events that were announcing the most devastating and far-reaching changes for the human race!

Jesus consolidated his warnings by urging them to make every effort to settle with God before the great day of judgment (Luke 12:58). He made it distinctly personal as he addressed each one individually (In v.57 the 'you' is plural whereas in v.58 the 'you' is singular). When God passes sentence it is for eternity, with no remission, for no one is able to repay the Lord for their offences committed against him. Jesus urged all to 'be reconciled to God' (2 Corinthians 5:20).

68. Repentance is essential for all
Luke 13:1-5

There were those present who raised the subject of Pilate's sacrilege when he mingled the blood of Galileans with their sacrifices. It would appear that as some people from Galilee were offering their sacrifices in the temple they were suddenly killed upon the orders of Governor Pontius Pilate. No further information is available from any known source.

From the Lord's response it would seem that the questioners were not concerned to draw attention to Pilate's brutality but rather to present the case as evidence of God's great displeasure towards those murdered Galileans. Their reasoning went something like this: 'These Galileans killed by Pilate must have done something very wicked indeed otherwise God would not have allowed them to be killed in such a way and in such a place!' The idea that personal disaster was the direct result of personal sin was the prevalent view among the Jews.

Jesus linked this with another contemporary tragedy, that of those who were killed by a falling tower at Siloam, to urge all to repent before the judgment of God falls upon them.

In the parable of The Fruitless Fig Tree (Luke 13:6-9) the Lord pictured his own three year ministry and the following ministry of the apostles. If no fruit is then produced the nation will be judged.

Another healing on the Sabbath

The account of the Lord's activities resumed in a synagogue where he was teaching on the Sabbath. The healing of a woman who had a spirit of infirmity eighteen years, and was bent over and could in no way raise herself up demonstrated the Lord's compassion in contrast to the rigid legalism of the ruler of the synagogue. That man was indignant with Jesus because of what he considered to be the breaking of the Sabbath law. He told the crowd to come for healing on any one of six days but not on the Sabbath.

Jesus was greatly offended by the attitude of the ruler of the synagogue and called him a hypocrite for he and his colleagues would show more concern on the Sabbath for one of their animals than they would for this suffering woman. By these words his opponents were shamed and the people delighted.

69. The Feast of Dedication
John 10:22-42

About two months had passed since Jesus had left Jerusalem following the Feast of Tabernacles. He returned to the temple at the Feast of Dedication. The origin of this feast is not to be found in the Scriptures. According to Alfred Edersheim it was -

> instituted by Judas Maccabaeus in 164 B.C. when the temple, which had been desecrated by Antiochus Epiphanes, was once more purified, and re-dedicated to the Service of Jehovah.[61]

It was winter and Jesus was walking in the temple. The first court of the temple, the outer court, was the Court of the Gentiles. Along the two sides there stood rows of great pillars making a kind of walkway, portico or porch. One side was called the Royal Porch and the other Solomon's Porch. People walked along in meditation or prayer. Some would gather round a Rabbi or great teacher and listen to what he had to say.

---

[61] Alfred Edersheim, *The Life and Times of Jesus the Messiah* (Peabody, Massachusetts: Hendrikson, 1993), p.631.

Such was the situation. Jesus was in the Porch of Solomon during the eight day festival surrounded by a group of listeners. Once more the question of his identity was raised, 'How long do you keep us in doubt? If you are the Christ, tell us plainly' (John 10:24). They had been told over and over again in a variety of different ways. He had presented abundant evidence that he was the Christ the Son of the living God. Did they not know and believe the numerous Old Testament descriptions of Messiah's coming, his character and his commission that Jesus had fulfilled?

Had they known and believed the Scriptures they would have recognised him. If they loved God and enjoyed a living faith, they would have welcomed him. Jesus reminded them of his earlier teaching that his sheep hear him, recognise him and follow him. They will enjoy eternal life and no one will take them from him. Again Jesus declared his unique relationship with God: 'I and my Father are one' (John 10:30). As before (John 8:58-59), 'the Jews took up stones again to stone him'. He further challenged them and reasoned with them. They tried to seize him but he left the temple.

Jesus moved out from Jerusalem and travelled east heading for Bethabara beyond the Jordan in the land of Peraea (John 10:40). As he travelled with his disciples he went through cities and villages teaching (Luke 13:22). He stopped frequently and took opportunity to talk with those who were with him and with those who were in the area.

The Lord moved away from the controversy which surrounded him in Judah, especially in and around Jerusalem. He was seeking a quiet situation where he could further instruct his disciples and prepare them, *and himself,* for the final confrontation in Jerusalem which would result in his suffering and death.

The Peraean ministry

70. Strive to enter the narrow gate
Luke 13:22-30

Bethabara held strong associations for the Lord Jesus. Here he had been baptised by John, anointed as the Messiah by the Holy Spirit and assured of the Father's love in the hearing of others (Matthew 3:16-17). This was where his ministry as the Messiah began. He will now stay there for a while.

Hearing of his location many gathered to meet him and listen to him. As this town was also where John the Baptist conducted so much of his ministry the people naturally drew a strong connection between John and Jesus. They noted that John performed no miracles and yet everything that he said about

Jesus proved to be true, with the result that 'many believed in him there' (John 10:42).

Jesus was asked a question, 'Lord, are there few who are saved?' (Luke 13:23) Whatever could be the motive for such a question? Whatever prompted the enquiry it is clear that the Lord did not answer it but turned immediately to address the crowd and urge each one to ensure that they were saved. He issued a serious warning to everyone.

There is no automatic entry to the kingdom of God. Jews thought they were safe because of their national privilege. It was a widely held opinion, supported by the Rabbis, that all Israelites would ultimately be saved. There is a close parallel in today's institutional Christian churches where many teach universalism (the doctrine that all human beings will ultimately come to final salvation and spend an eternity with God in heaven). Unbelievers will often say, 'If there is a God of love, he will accept everyone.'

Jesus had a very different perspective. Reminding all of his early teaching about the narrow gate of entry (Matthew 7:13) which necessitates repentance and faith, he added that a time will come when many will seek entry but will be refused and it will be too late. The patriarchs will be in heaven and many others, non-Jews from all over the world will be sitting with them, but thousands of Jews will be debarred through their unbelief and sin.

'Strive to enter' - the word translated 'strive' is the word from which the English word 'agonise' is derived. The struggle to enter must be so intense that it can be described as an agony of soul and spirit. Jesus was speaking of a narrow opening which was very difficult to pass through.

In the spiritual realm he taught the pain of penitence and the struggle of conversion. Keep striving! There is no standing still for followers of Christ. The Christian way is like a climb up a mountain path. It was said of two brave climbers who died on Mount Everest, 'When last seen they were going strong for the top'. May that be our spiritual testimony.

On the very same day Pharisees came to Jesus to warn him that Herod wanted to kill him (Luke 13:31). This was King Herod Antipas, governor of Galilee and Peraea who stole Herodias, his brother Philip's wife; beheaded John the Baptist (Mark 6:16); who thought Jesus was John the Baptist risen from the dead (Matthew 14:1-2); and who will later judge Jesus at his trial (Luke 23:7-12).

When Jesus responded to the warning of the Pharisees it would seem that he detected some treachery afoot between Herod and these men. Was Herod wanting to get Jesus out of his territory? Were the Pharisees wanting to get Jesus back to Jerusalem where they or their colleagues could further intimidate, malign or trick him that they may have him condemned to death?

It is uncharacteristic of the Lord to make a comment against a civic leader. Although Herod was the puppet of Rome and not the God-appointed king over Israel it is an exception to our Lord's normal approach of avoiding political comment. Jesus called Herod 'that fox' (Luke 13:32). The fox is regarded as the craftiest animal; a most destructive animal finding pleasure in killing and destroying often without the motive of food; and when contrasted to the lion in signifying men, one is worthless or insignificant the other a strong and powerful leader.

Jesus reminded Herod and the Pharisees that he worked to a divine timetable 'today and tomorrow, and the third day I shall be perfected'. He will not be governed by the whims and wishes of Pharisees or kings. He will work until the time when he is perfected (Luke 13:32), that is, when he has reached his goal. His death will happen when the whole of his mission has been brought to a perfect and complete conclusion - in Jerusalem!

There is a beautiful but sad contrast in his lament over Jerusalem. From reference to Herod as that fox implying his craftiness, cruelty and worthlessness, the Lord spoke of himself as a hen who would readily gather her brood under her wings, signifying the loving concern and care he had for the people of Israel. He was the only One who could grant such comfort, security and eternal blessing but they were not willing. He had done his best. He had laboured hard for three years to preach the gospel and teach the truth. They will not see him again until his triumphant entry when some will say, 'Blessed is he who comes in the name of the LORD!' (Luke 13:35)

71. Dinner with a prominent Pharisee
Luke 14:1-6

It was the Sabbath Day in Bethabara and Jesus had been invited for a meal at the home of a prominent Pharisee. A number of Pharisees and lawyers were also invited. At this stage in the Lord's ministry the general reaction of the scribes and Pharisees was one of suspicion and hostility. Despite the ill-feeling of so many Pharisees Jesus still accepted the invitation to dine. He is a wonderful example of God-like love which suffers long and is kind; that does not envy; that -

> does not parade itself, is not puffed up; does not behave rudely, does not seek its own, is not provoked, thinks no evil; does not rejoice in iniquity, but rejoices in the truth; bears all things, believes all things, hopes all things, endures all things (1 Corinthians 13:4-8).

There was a man present who was afflicted with dropsy (oedema). Was he a member of the family, a friend, neighbour, or someone invited by the host just to see how Jesus would react? Dropsy (oedema) is a disease in which watery fluid collects in cavities or tissue of the body producing an over-swollen state. The man was suffering and Jesus asked the Pharisees and lawyers if it was lawful to heal on the Sabbath. They refused to answer. Jesus healed him and again drew a parallel between the way these men would treat a donkey or ox on the Sabbath. There was silence. By this action Jesus exposed the great error in their understanding of the law of God: 'Remember the Sabbath day, to keep it holy... In it you shall do no work' (Exodus 20:8,10).

Seven occasions when Jesus healed on the Sabbath -

  i.   Simon's mother-in-law in her home (Luke 4:38).
  ii. The demon-possessed man in the synagogue at
       Capernaum (Mark 1:21).
  iii. The man with the withered hand in the synagogue
       (Matthew 12:9).
  iv. The paralysed man at the pool of Bethesda (John 5:9).
  v.   The man born blind (John 9:14).
  vi. The woman in the synagogue afflicted for eighteen
       years (Luke 13:14).
  vii. The man suffering from dropsy (Luke 14:1)

At the meal the Lord changed the subject for he had noticed how the guests chose the best places as they sat down. He made direct reference to their behaviour and suggested that it was better to choose a place of less significance just in case they were asked to move because a more honoured guest arrived later. It is more honourable to be invited higher than to be asked to move lower (Proverbs 25:6-7).

Even the worldly unbeliever might well consider this wise teaching, but Luke called it 'a parable' (Luke 14:7), so it also contains a spiritual application. The dropsy (oedema) from which the man suffered is a disease affecting the physical constitution. There is a far worse spiritual disease which might well be thought of as spiritual dropsy - the over-swelling of the heart, the inflation of pride from which these Pharisees and lawyers were suffering.

Humility before God is essential: 'Blessed are the poor in spirit, for theirs is the kingdom of heaven' (Matthew 5:3). Cultivating humility involves taking great care in the regular exercise of self control and continual reflection on our lowly wretched condition before the grandeur, glory and holiness of God. 'Therefore humble yourselves under the mighty hand of God' (1 Peter 5:6).

Believers are urged to be 'kindly affectionate to one another with brotherly love, in honour giving preference to one another' (Romans 12:10). If Christians are truly humble before God and think of themselves as occupying the lowest place then there is always the possibility that God's opinion will be different. Consequently, in due time they will be exalted. 'For whoever exalts himself will be humbled, and he who humbles himself will be exalted' (Luke 14:11; cf. James 4:6).

Jesus turned to the host and made a recommendation urging him that when he next gave a feast he should invite 'the poor, the maimed, the lame, the blind' (Luke 14:13) with the reassurance that such kindness would not go unrewarded in the end.

One of the guests responded by saying, 'Blessed is he who shall eat bread in the kingdom of God!' (Luke 14:15) Jesus pursued the subject with a challenge to all to receive the invitation of God.

Through the parable of The Great Supper he illustrated how there were many who were refusing the wonderful offer God was making through him. The three rejected invitations to the supper amount to the same excuse, 'I have something more important to do'. Their place will be taken by some of the most unlikely people for -

> God has chosen the foolish things of the world to put to shame the wise, and God has chosen the weak things of the world to put to shame the things which are mighty; and the base things of the world and the things which are despised God has chosen, and the things which are not, to bring to nothing the things that are, that no flesh should glory in his presence (1 Corinthians 1:27-29).

Assessing the cost of discipleship

The Lord left the Pharisee's house and a vast company followed him. Taking the opportunity to preach he turned and declared to them the cost of discipleship. Being disciples of Jesus demands giving the Son of God prime place in the affections before all others, including self; bearing a cross; and being prepared for any sacrifice even when painful. Before taking the step of personal commitment careful thought must be given to the demands which are to be met. The gains are enormous and the cost may be high but the former greatly outweighs the latter as the apostle Paul testified -

> what things were gain to me, these I have counted loss for Christ. Yet indeed I also count all things loss for the excellence of the knowledge of Christ Jesus my Lord, for whom I have suffered the loss of all things, and count them as rubbish, that I may gain Christ

and be found in him, not having my own righteousness, which is
from the law, but that which is through faith in Christ, the
righteousness which is from God by faith (Philippians 3:7-9).

The decision to follow Jesus is to be an informed choice based on careful
consideration of the implications that result in a lifetime of wholehearted
commitment to the Master first and foremost. Jesus presents two clear and
concise illustrations of the need to carefully consider the commitment we are
making when we pledge allegiance to him.

The first is of a builder who before building a tower sits down and
calculates the cost of materials and labour. Otherwise having laid the
foundation he might find he has not sufficient funds to finish the
construction and be mocked by those who see it or hear of the folly (Luke
14:28-30). The second illustration is that of a king who intending to go to
war with another king first sits down and considers whether he has any hope
of success in taking his army against an army twice the size. If not he sends a
delegation to seek conditions for peace (Luke 14:31-32).

The point is strongly delivered: think carefully about what is involved in
becoming a disciple of Jesus. We must be ready to give up anything or
everything for him.

'Salt is good' said the Lord, using the analogy of 'salt' for the third time.
The first occasion was during the Sermon on the Mount when he said, 'You
are the salt of the earth; but if the salt loses its flavour, how shall it be
seasoned?' (Matthew 5:13). Salt counteracts corruption and has preservative
power. Those who profess allegiance to Jesus must live appropriately. Their
behaviour and speech are to exert a purifying effect on their community. In
this manner Paul exhorts believers to -

walk in wisdom toward those who are outside, redeeming the
time. Let your speech always be with grace, seasoned with salt,
that you may know how you ought to answer each one (Colossians
4:5-6).

Our Lord made a second use of the analogy when he said, 'Salt is good…
Have salt in yourselves, and have peace with one another' (Mark 9:50). In
this context the Lord warned about causing offences and maintaining a strict
self-control regarding all weaknesses towards sin. He said, have peace with
one another so that Christian harmony will impact the world. The Christian
Church is to set an example to the world of a loving, caring and amiable
community.

In this third analogy salt represents the inward power of holiness and
wholehearted commitment to the Lord Jesus. An outward profession alone
will lose its savour. Self-sacrifice, self-denial and devotion to Christ are the

hallmarks of discipleship. If the love of Jesus and the teaching of Jesus do not reach and transform the hearts of those who are called to be 'the salt of the earth' what hope is there? How shall it be seasoned? (Luke 14:34)

72. The parables of The Lost Sheep, Coin and Son
Luke 15:1-32

By his manner, attitude and teaching the Lord attracted those who had generally been rejected by the religious leaders and the Jewish community as hopeless causes; these were tax collectors and sinners. 'Tax collectors' were regarded as traitors by their own people because they gathered taxes for the occupying Romans. They had a terrible reputation. Most were crude oppressive cheats and money-grabbers. They were viewed with such hatred from the rest of the Jews that their word was never accepted as a testimony in a court of law. No gifts or donations had to be received from them; no money had to be changed by them. They were regarded as heathen, and sometimes worse than heathen, beyond all hope.

'Sinners' were those who openly flouted the law of God. They were people, whether rich or poor, who had neither the power of religion in their hearts nor the profession of it on their lips. Prostitutes came into this category (Luke 7:37-39). Seeing tax collectors and sinners gather around to hear Jesus, the Pharisees and scribes were highly critical and said, 'This man receives sinners and eats with them' (Luke 15:2).

The Lord responded by presenting three parables designed to show the love of the triune God for the lost, those who are often dismissed or forgotten -

- the Son of God who, as the Good Shepherd, seeks for his sheep;
- the Holy Spirit who is quietly and urgently seeking one who bears the image of God;
- the Father who watches and waits for the return of his child and gives a warm welcome home.

Through these parables Jesus denounced the arrogance and heartlessness of the Jewish leadership whilst extending the welcoming love and mercy of God to the lost and discounted tax collectors and sinners.

The three parables belong together, each one addresses how a sinner returns to God. The sheep had wandered away, the coin had been lost, the son had wilfully left home -

- as the Lost Sheep the sinner is portrayed as wandering away in ignorance and unable to find the way back;

- as the Lost Coin the sinner is shown as lacking spiritual-awareness and self-knowledge;
- as the Lost Son the sinner is revealed as being driven by a selfish, sinful mind and heart that resists God and runs away from him.

So in the three parables, the sinner is ignorant, foolish, blind or arrogant and opposed to God. As it is written -

> There is none righteous, no, not one; there is none who understands; there is none who seeks after God. They have all turned aside; they have together become unprofitable; there is none who does good, no, not one' (Romans 3:10-12).

Each parable contains its own emphasis, adding valuable information to complete the picture. The Lost Sheep with its persistently searching shepherd; the Lost Coin with its painstaking, resolute owner; and the Lost Son with his patiently waiting Father; each portrays different aspects of the same relationship of God and the sinner.

Taken separately each parable will lead to imbalance. The parable of The Lost Sheep and the parable of The Lost Coin represent the sinner as passive. In terms of the relationship between God and the sinner it is entirely one-sided. God is doing all the work, searching for the sheep and for the coin.

By contrast the parable of The Lost Son views God the Father as the one who is entirely passive. He waits for the sinner's return. He may long for that return and look for that return, he may run towards his son as he returns, but the onus is upon the sinner to return to God. He must come to himself, come to his senses, he must make the effort and return home, he must humble himself before the Father.

The Shepherd finds the Lost Sheep and carries it back home upon his shoulders; the Lost Son comes to himself and must make his own long and hard way back to the Father. Both perspectives though entirely different, are entirely true. Each one needs the other for a complete understanding.

The order of the parables is significant when viewed theologically. The Shepherd has first searched for and found his Lost Sheep, the Woman has first searched for and found her Lost Coin and the Son consequently comes to himself, then comes to his Father -

> Blessed be the God and Father of our Lord Jesus Christ, who has blessed us with every spiritual blessing in the heavenly places in Christ, *just as he chose us in him* before the foundation of the world (Ephesians 1:3-4).

The sovereign grace of God moves out to the sinner, the sinner becomes aware of his true spiritual predicament, and repents. Through the prophet

Isaiah the Lord said, 'I was sought by those who did not ask for me; I was found by those who did not seek me' (Isaiah 65:1). There are those however like so many of the scribes, Pharisees and Jews who resisted the overtures of God when he said -

> I have stretched out my hands all day long to a rebellious people, who walk in a way that is not good, according to their own thoughts; a people who provoke me to anger continually to my face; who sacrifice in gardens, and burn incense on altars of brick... Who say, 'Keep to yourself, do not come near me, for I am holier than you!' These are smoke in my nostrils, a fire that burns all the day (Isaiah 65: 2-3,5).

What a wonderful picture of God is presented here in these three parables. The diligent search for the lost sheep, *until he finds it*; and the woman with the lost coin who lights a lamp, sweeps the house, and searches carefully *until she finds it;* and the the father waiting, watching, running... When the shepherd finds his lost sheep 'he lays it on his shoulders, rejoicing and calls together his friends and neighbours, saying, "Rejoice with me, for I have found my sheep which was lost!" When the women finds her lost coin she calls her friends and neighbours together, saying, 'Rejoice with me, for I have found the piece which I lost!'

Look too at the welcome the lost son received when he came home. None can surely miss the delight of God over every sinners who comes in repentance and faith. There is 'joy in the presence of the angels of God over one sinner who repents'. Note these words which expressly record that *God himself rejoices* in the presence of the angels (cf. Zephaniah 3:17).

Let us consider the representations and progression in the three parables: one sheep out of a hundred is lost, one valuable coin out of ten is lost; one of two sons is lost. The numbers decrease to enhance the thought of value.

The parable of The Lost Sheep is very pertinent to the leaders of the Jews. The task of shepherding the people of God was a priority during Old Testament times (Psalm 23:1-6). Sadly the Lord had often been grieved by the failure of the appointed pastors -

> My sheep wandered through all the mountains, and on every high
> hill; yes, my flock was scattered over the whole face of the earth,
> and no one was seeking or searching for them (Ezekiel 34:6).

It is not however just scribes and Pharisees, tax collectors and sinners who are in the Lord's mind, we are all portrayed in this parable for 'all we like sheep have gone astray; we have turned, every one, to his own way' (Isaiah 53:6). The Gospel declares that the Good Shepherd loves his sheep, knows his sheep and therefore seeks for his sheep, calls his sheep, leads his sheep and will lay down his life for his sheep (John 10:1-16).

In the parable of The Lost Coin (Luke 15:8-10) it is to be noted that coins in that day bore the image of Caesar (Matthew 22:20-21). All human beings bear the image of their Maker (Genesis 1:26-27). The lost coin represents a human being who bears the image of God and is lost. The woman represents the Holy Spirit in the work of searching for a lost sinner.

This is not a picture of the Holy Spirit working alone, but rather working through the Church. This an in-house search (Luke 15:8). It is the Spirit of the living God inspiring and enabling the Church of Jesus Christ to do the searching. 'The Spirit and the bride [the Church] say, "Come!" And let him who hears say, "Come!" And let him who thirsts come. Whoever desires, let him take the water of life freely' (Revelation 22:17).

The lighting of the lamp is the clear proclamation of the Gospel: 'Your word is a lamp to my feet and a light to my path' (Psalm 119:105). The Lord Jesus is 'the true light' (John 1:9; cf. 2 Corinthians 4:5-6). So the Church is to preach nothing 'except Jesus Christ and him crucified' (1 Corinthians 2:2). The sweeping of the house suggests the removal of the confusion that is in the sinner's mind by loving confrontation and sensitive counsel, that all the hindrances might be swept away.

Seeking lost sinners requires great diligence. The church is to be engaged in this monumental and momentous endeavour. Together and individually we are to seek lost coins in the house, those mixed amongst the community of believers. God willing more lost coins will be uncovered for the Lord's treasury.

The parable of The Lost Son (Luke 15:11-32) is a word of hope for backsliders. Some of those tax collectors and sinners may once have been believers. A true faith may have burned brightly but love for God had grown cold. Whatever the reason the son in the parable was thoroughly dissatisfied with his life at home. He renounced his family. Though he wanted his father's possessions he rejected his father's love. He gained independence to be his own master. He took all that he could get and went as far away as possible from the father's influence or constraint, squandering all he had in extravagant living.

This represents not only the backslidden believer but also all who try to exclude God from their lives. A sinner away from God, lost in sin and hopelessly disillusioned with life, may readily identify with this prodigal son. Nothing had any meaning, there was no purpose to life.

> For since the creation of the world [God's] invisible attributes are
> clearly seen, being understood by the things that are made, even

his eternal power and Godhead, so that they are without excuse, because, although they knew God, they did not glorify him as God, nor were thankful, but became futile in their thoughts, and their foolish hearts were darkened (Romans 1:20-21).

With money, friends and hope gone the son eventually reached the depths of despair until an amazing change took place 'when he came to himself' (Luke 15:17). Seeing his true condition he recalled life at home and remembered the gracious character of his father. He resolved to take the long journey home, admit his stupidity and utter selfishness and hoped that his father would take him in as a hired servant.

The father waiting and watching saw his returning son in the distance and ran to meet him. Out pours the confession from the son but it was interrupted. The father called his servants and they were instructed to bring out the best robe, a ring and sandals and to prepare a grand celebration. The son who was as though dead was alive again, the son who was lost was found. Receiving 'the best robe' from the hands of the Father, a sinner reconciled to God is able to declare -

I will greatly rejoice in the LORD, my soul shall be joyful in my God; for he has clothed me with the garments of salvation, he has covered me with the robe of righteousness (Isaiah 61:10).

What rich meaning these words take when the Son of God gives himself as a sacrifice on behalf of his people in order to provide that robe (Jeremiah 23:6; 1 Corinthians 1:30; Zechariah 3:3-4). *The ring* is placed upon his finger as a mark of wealth and esteem (James 2:2); it is often used as a seal (Esther 3:10, 12; Jeremiah 22:24). How does God seal his people? The apostle Paul speaks of every Christian when he writes of the Christians at Ephesus, 'having believed, you were sealed with the Holy Spirit of promise, who is the guarantee of our inheritance' (Ephesians 1:13-14; cf. 1 Peter 1:4-5).

Sandals are the mark of a free man as distinct from a slave. Of forgiven sinners it is declared, 'God be thanked that though you were slaves of sin, yet you obeyed from the heart that form of doctrine to which you were delivered. And having been set free from sin, you became slaves of righteousness' (Romans 6:17-18). Jesus had told the Jews in Jerusalem who believed in him -

If you abide in my word, you are my disciples indeed. And you shall know the truth, and the truth shall make you free... if the Son makes you free, you shall be free indeed (John 8:31-32, 36).

'And they *began to be merry*' (Luke 15:24). Not just the loving father and the penitent son, for as the delighted shepherd 'calls together his friends and neighbours, saying to them, "Rejoice with me, for I have found my sheep which was lost" and as the thrilled woman 'calls her friends and neighbours together, saying, "Rejoice with me, for I have found the piece which I lost"', so the father calls together his household and his servants saying, 'Let us eat and be merry; for this my son was dead and is alive again; he was lost and is found.'

The delight of God and the rejoicing of his servants will never end for in God's 'presence is fullness of joy' and at his 'right hand are pleasures forevermore' (Psalm 16:11). In this parable Jesus confirmed the earlier invitation of God -

> Seek the LORD while he may be found, call upon him while he is near. Let the wicked forsake his way, and the unrighteous man his thoughts; let him return to the LORD, and he will have mercy on him; and to our God, for he will abundantly pardon (Isaiah 55:6-7).

The lost sheep, the lost coin, the lost son refer to 'the tax collectors and the sinners' who 'drew near to him to hear him' (Luke 15:1) but the context of the three parables shows that Jesus was also referring to people who wrongly thought they were righteous. They were spiritually healthy according to their own diagnosis. They were righteous in their own estimation as Jesus pointed out later in the parable of The Pharisee and the Tax Collector addressing 'some who trusted in themselves that they were righteous, and despised others' (Luke 18:9).

The older son (Luke 15:25-32) who 'was in the field (v.25), refers to the Pharisees and scribes who murmur against Jesus saying, 'This man receives sinners and eats with them' (Luke 15:2). In this second part of the third parable, the Lord makes the position of the Pharisees and scribes clear. Why did the father in the parable not send for his older son to celebrate with him? Did the father know the mind and heart of that son, that he would resent his brother's return and would spoil the celebrations?

On his return from the field the older brother heard music and dancing but he did not enter the house, rather he asked a servant the reason for the celebration. Hearing that his younger brother had returned he was angry and would not go in. However being notified of this the father went out to speak to him and pleaded with him to join the festivity.

The son reacted strongly, revealing his true heart for his brother and his father. Out poured his resentment. He had served his father, literally working like a slave, never once disobeying an instruction, yet he was never given a goat to celebrate with his friends. 'But as soon as this son of yours' (note: not 'brother of mine') comes, 'who has devoured your livelihood with harlots' (their was no mention of such behaviour) you celebrate.

The older son was a greater sinner than his younger brother. He was a hypocrite, he was a prodigal of the heart. The younger son was greedy, grasping, selfish and headstrong, but he repented. He came home, he pleaded with his father and was forgiven. He, being forgiven much, would love much, just like the woman who poured fragrant oil over the feet of the Lord Jesus (Luke 7:47-48).

The older brother had hidden a wicked, selfish heart that was now exposed. He was consumed with 'the spirit of bondage' (Romans 8:15). He had no love for the father for if he had he would have considered it a great privilege to enjoy the father's company and labour in the father's service during the long years of his brother's absence.

This was the greatest failure and sin of the Pharisees that they did not love the Lord their God with all their heart, with all their soul, with all their mind and with all their strength (Mark 12:30) for they were hypocrites. Jesus does not however leave the older brother (the Pharisees and scribes) without hope, for in the parable the father says, 'Son, you are always with me, and all that I have is yours' (Luke 15:31).

Even now the older son may enter in, for the inheritance is still there for him. It is available on the same conditions as fulfilled by his younger brother, that of repenting of his sin and his hypocrisy. He must be rid of that servile spirit thinking he can work for his inheritance and he must prove his love for God by demonstrating his love for his forgiven brother.

73. The parable of The Unjust Steward
Luke 16:1-13

This parable is firmly linked with the previous three parables: The Lost Sheep, The Lost Coin and The Lost Son for Jesus 'also said to his disciples' (Luke 16:1). His disciples would include the apostles and those tax collectors and sinners who were responding well to his teaching. The Pharisees were also listening in (Luke 16:14).

This parable is disturbing since Jesus appears to be commending a man who is blatantly dishonest and deceitful. Numerous interpretations have been suggested. In almost all other parables the individuals are either morally blameless or their immorality comes under serious criticism. Here 'an element of injustice is inseparably mixed up with the prudence which is commended in the conduct of the steward.'[62]

---

[62] William Arnot, *The Parables of our Lord* (London: Nelson, 1880), p.451.

The main point which the Lord was making was one of contrast between believers and unbelievers: the sons of this world (unbelievers) are more shrewd (having or showing sharp powers of judgment) in their generation than the sons of light (believers). He pressed home the lesson concerning the wise use of money. For his followers, faithfulness, integrity and honesty were to be paramount in their stewardship (Luke 16:10).

The steward was wasting his master's goods. He was called to give account of his stewardship and received notice that his employment would be terminated. There was no repentance, no recognition of guilt, no acknowledgment that he had abused his trust, no expression of desire to begin anew, no plea for a second chance, only a selfish anxiety for his future.

He was in a quandary, unsuited for hard work and proud. He devised a plan to gain friends who would prove useful to him later. He called in his master's debtors and tore up the old agreements and made new, considerably reduced, agreements. Though dishonest and a waster he was complimented by his master for using his intelligence and being shrewd.

Jesus recommends to all his followers: 'Make friends for yourselves by unrighteous mammon [i.e. money, wealth], that when you fail, they may receive you into an everlasting home' (Luke 16:9). The unjust steward manipulated finance to make friends for his immediate limited future in this world. Martyn Lloyd-Jones suggests -

> Now, says our Lord in effect, I am going to take that as a principle and apply it to you. If you have money, so use it while you are here in this world that, when you arrive in glory, the people who benefitted by it will be there to receive you.'[63]

The Lord's people are to use their finances in a God-honouring manner, to make friends for their eternal future in the world to come.

The shrewd Christian invests in people's lives especially their eternal future. The Lord does not look upon the size of the gift but the size of the heart giving the gift (see Mark 12:42-44). God willing there will be those converted who will go before you to heaven and welcome you to your eternal dwelling.

When Jesus said elsewhere, 'Be wise as serpents and harmless as doves' (Matthew 10:16) he was not recommending his followers to be vicious, biting, hurtful and cruel like a serpent. He was not commending the serpent's many bad characteristics but merely highlighting one that can be imitated. He was urging us to learn wisdom, not the wisdom of the world but

---

[63] D. Martyn Lloyd-Jones, *Studies in the Sermon on the Mount* (London: Inter-Varsity Fellowship, 1960), vol. 2, p.83.

that wisdom which comes 'from above [which] is first pure, then peaceable, gentle, willing to yield, full of mercy and good fruits, without partiality and without hypocrisy' (James 3:17). It is a godly wisdom in harmony with all the characteristics of righteousness.

This is the wisdom needed for rightly dispersing our finances. The wise use of our money is a mark of our faithfulness to God for 'it is required in stewards that one be found faithful' (1 Corinthians 4:2).

No one can serve God and money (Luke 16:13) for he is 'a double-minded man unstable in all his ways' (James 1:8). He oscillates, his mind fluctuates between concern for the one and concern for the other. The man who tries to love the world and love God (1 John 2:15-16) is likely to be heading for a nervous breakdown. A spiritual breakdown is inevitable.

The Pharisees had been listening in as Jesus addressed his disciples (Luke 16:14,1) and they were angered by his teaching on finance, for they were lovers of money (cf. 2 Timothy 3:2). Jesus charged them with justifying themselves before others; no doubt referring to the way they shunned tax collectors and sinners and concerned themselves with outward appearances of piety. He told them distinctly that God knew their hearts. There is a big difference between what people value and what God values.

Jesus then asserts the permanence of the law of God, illustrating it by teaching on divorce. The law on divorce was particularly pertinent for the Pharisees at that time as there was great laxity regarding commitment to marriage. The law of Moses in Deuteronomy allowed for legal divorce -

> When a man takes a wife and marries her, and it happens that she finds no favour in his eyes because he has found some uncleanness in her, and he writes her a certificate of divorce, puts it in her hand, and sends her out of his house (Deuteronomy 24:1).

The bill of divorce had to be signed by two witnesses. The problem arose however on the understanding of 'some uncleanness in her'. There were two schools of thought, that of Rabbi Shammai who held that it meant adultery and adultery alone. On the other hand the school of Hillel taught that if a wife displeased her husband by, for example, spoiling a meal, speaking disrespectfully to him, talking to another man, these were grounds for divorce.

This second view was favoured by the majority of Pharisees and people. Family life was in great danger of widespread destruction. Jesus elsewhere presented God's view on marriage when he said that divorce, even on the limited grounds of infidelity, was permitted only because of the hardness of heart. It was not part of the original design at creation (Matthew 19:8).

Jesus then tells the parable of The Rich Man and Lazarus which illustrates the rejection of those who are self righteous and the permanence of the law of God. The rejection is seen when the rich man calls out 'Father, Abraham' and receives the answer, 'they have Moses and the prophets; let them hear them'. The reply also shows the abiding nature of the law of God. The law on which the Pharisees staked their credit will nevertheless be the instrument of their eternal condemnation. This was what Jesus had said to the Jews in Jerusalem; 'Do not think that I shall accuse you to the Father; there is one who accuses you - Moses, in whom you trust' (John 5:45).

74. The parable of The Rich Man and Lazarus
Luke 16:19-31

With masterly skill the picture was presented of two men, a rich man lavishly dressed in very expensive clothing, feasting luxuriously every day, and a very poor man, a beggar 'thrown' at the rich man's gate like rotting meat, covered from head to toe in running sores and being licked by stray dogs. The beggar longed for what might fall from the rich man's table.

Both died, the beggar being carried instantly by angels to be with Abraham. The rich man, with the implied full ceremony of a funeral, arrived in the place of the ungodly dead.

Evidently the rich man knew the beggar's name and must also have known his dreadful condition. How could he not be aware of him lying at his gate. The rich man in torment saw Lazarus with Abraham afar off and cried out, 'Father Abraham, have mercy on me'. The request for relief could not be granted. No movement was possible between the two locations of Hades and Abraham's bosom.

The rich man then referred to his five brothers still alive. Was he now anxiously concerned about them? Did he want them to have the opportunity to repent before it was too late? When Abraham replied, 'They have Moses and the prophets; let them hear them' the man argued back saying it would make all the difference if a miracle of resurrection were performed.

He was claiming that the Word of God was not enough and strongly implying that *if he had experienced such a miracle himself* he would have repented and not have ended up in Hades! The essential verdict was reached in the words of Abraham, 'If they do not hear Moses and the prophets, neither will they be persuaded though one rise from the dead' (Luke 16:31). Conclusive evidence as to who Jesus was and why he came is to be found 'written in the law of Moses and the Prophets and the Psalms' (Luke 24:44; cf. vv.25-26; John 5:39-40).

Some points to note: (i) the name Lazarus is derived from the Hebrew name Eleazar meaning, 'God is my help' which suggests that Jesus was thinking of a poor believer discounted by the rich Pharisees; (ii) the Lord's good friend Lazarus died only days after this parable was spoken (John 11:14); (iii) Jesus raised that Lazarus from the dead and many Jews believed in him but the chief priests and Pharisees plotted to kill him (John 11:45-48,53).

The parable of The Rich Man and Lazarus was not intended to teach details concerning the life to come but to confront the Jewish hearers that the promises of Messiah given in the Old Testament Scriptures were now fulfilled by Jesus and they were consequently without excuse.

Nevertheless there are certainties in the story, confirmed from doctrinal instruction elsewhere in Scripture -

- the finality of death; an unalterable destiny dependent upon life here and now;
- the unspeakable happiness of believers and the dreadful misery of the ungodly;
- that the Scriptures, not miracles, are a sufficient guiding light to heaven for everyone.

75. Jesus warns of offences
Luke 17:1-4

Followers of Jesus are to be sensitive to others, not hindering a young believer or child. Jesus warned that it was impossible that no offences should arise.

Openly wicked people do not produce scandals. They are known for what they are. Scandals are caused by those who appear upright and decent citizens. A scandal is when something bad is discovered in, or arises from, someone who is thought to be good and it produces a general feeling of outrage or indignation. It may also cause another person to fall. Christians can produce scandals; in a moment of weakness or acute temptation they may fall and commit some act or speak some words which they regret for the rest of their lives.

When a church leader, loved and highly respected, falls into serious sin, it usually causes many young and vulnerable Christians to be shaken, distressed or undermined in their faith. Other scandals which may cause Christians to stumble and fall include when professing believers invite vulnerable believers to meetings where they will be exposed to false teaching, or befriend and lure them away to another church, or give CDs or DVDs with alternate teaching thus creating confusion.

Every elder must bare pastoral responsibility for his flock, 'Who is weak, and I am not weak? Who is made to stumble [scandalised], and I do not burn with indignation?' (2 Corinthians 11:29) These are the kind of problems Jesus was warning about. Scandals will certainly arise - 'but woe to him through whom they do come!'

A lot of poor, rejected, despised and outcast people were taking interest in the teaching of Jesus (Luke 15:1). But there were others listening, Pharisees and scribes who took every possible opportunity to criticise and grumble about the Lord (Luke 15:2). They were 'scandalising' the young and vulnerable. Such persons would be better drowned.

We are not permitted to turn a blind eye to scandals, offences, and death-traps. If someone is leading others astray, causing division in the Church of Christ, seeking to undermine the good order of the church or slandering a brother or sister, or you, it is your duty to face the offender personally, privately and promptly (Luke 17:3-4; cf. Matthew 18:15-17).

> And if he repents, forgive him. And if he sins against you seven times in a day, and seven times in a day returns to you, saying, 'I repent', you shall forgive him (Luke 17:4; cf. Matthew 18:21-22).

'Be kind to one another, tenderhearted, forgiving one another, even as God in Christ forgave you' (Ephesians 4:32). We are to 'resolve this, not to put a stumbling block or a cause to fall [scandal, death-trap] in our brother's way' (Romans 14:13).

This double commandment, taking care not to cause others to stumble and forgiving the penitent brother, demands real strength of character. It is no easy thing, it is not a natural trait in most people. It takes a strong faith to be alert to causing offence and to be forgiving time and time again. It takes faith in God to do what is right and not to avenge ourselves. So the apostles cried out to Jesus, 'Increase our faith'.

Jesus readily responded by saying that even a very small amount of faith is able to achieve great things. By faith Christians are able to live consistently for God. They believe in God, trust God, obey God. Faith enables Christians to face difficulties and problems in ways which honour God, encourage and edify others, and guards their own souls. Believers overcome the world outside and the world inside themselves.

> For whatever is born of God overcomes the world. And this is the victory that has overcome the world - our faith. Who is he who overcomes the world, but he who believes that Jesus is the Son of God? (1 John 5:4-5)

Faith can achieve the impossible! The sinning brother, rather than being an obstacle in the way, a cause of offence and stumbling, can be changed and transformed into a strong believer, standing firm. But faith alone is not enough. There must also be Christ-like love which God grants to his children, for 'though I have all faith, so that I could remove mountains, but have not love, I am nothing' (1 Corinthians 13:2).

Jesus issued a cautionary corrective. The removal of a scandal by the restoration of an erring brother, and the exercising of faith as Jesus instructed, might easily lead to personal pride; even to a feeling that we have earned the praise and approval of God. When the Lord is at work in us and through us there are real dangers. Paul notes the same danger, 'Brethren, if a man is overtaken in any trespass, you who are spiritual restore such a one in a spirit of gentleness, considering yourself lest you also be tempted' (Galatian 6:1). So Jesus warned his disciples with an illustration of a slave serving a meal for his master and concluded with the lesson -

> So likewise you, when you have done all those things which you are commanded, say, 'We are unprofitable servants. We have done what was our duty to do' (Luke 17:10).

Servants derive satisfaction by serving and pleasing their Master. The privilege of serving the Son of God is the highest possible reward. Thus the Lord interwove teaching about offences, sin, truth, love, faith and duty. The material of these ten verses blends perfectly.

76. The raising of Lazarus (Bethany)
John 11:1-45

Jesus was in Bethabara, Perea on the southeast coast of the River Jordan when news came to him that his good friend Lazarus was seriously ill. Jesus loved Lazarus and his two sisters Martha and Mary. He seems to have stayed often with them whenever he was in the area. The village was less than 2 miles (3km) from Jerusalem (v.18).

Combining urgency with humility these godly sisters communicated the sad and serious situation to the Lord. This was probably all that was contained in the message to Jesus. There was no familiarity, no presumption. Although Jesus had often stayed in their home and called them his friends yet it seems that they never forgot to treat him with appropriate respect. Both Mary and Martha knew that Jesus had the power to heal, in fact they were both recorded later as testifying to his ability (John 11:21,32). But they did not ask it of him, they simply brought the situation to his attention. They did not presume to suggest what the Lord might do.

'He whom you love is sick' (v.3) not 'he who loves you'. The latter would have been an appeal to merit. Rather 'he whom you love' was an appeal to grace. It was enough that Jesus should know that the one he loved was ill. Martha was confident in the authority and power of Jesus. When she saw him, after her brother's death, she boldly declared, 'Even now I know that whatever you ask of God, God will give you' (v.22).

When Jesus heard the news he said, 'This sickness is not unto death, but for the glory of God, that the Son of God may be glorified through it' (v.4). This reply, though almost as brief as the message from the sisters, had, nevertheless, sufficient within it to encourage them in their distress and anguish.

There is a surprising paradox, Jesus loved Lazarus, Mary and Martha and yet he waited two more days before doing anything. He was in Bethabara in Peraea, a distance from Bethany in Judah of 33km (20.5 miles). The Lord Jesus evidently intended that by the time he arrived at the home of Martha and Mary, Lazarus would have been dead and buried four days! Why this deliberate delay?

Because of the heat bodies were usually buried as soon as possible after death, preferably on the same day, as is seen in the case of Ananias and Sapphira (Acts 5:6,10). The Jewish Rabbis taught that the soul of a deceased person hovered around the body for three days in the hope of reunion, and that final departure came when the body had entered the state of decomposition. Scripture nowhere teaches this, in fact the very opposite is true for believers who when 'absent from the body [are] present with the Lord' (2 Corinthians 5:8). At Calvary Jesus said to the believing thief on the cross, 'Today you will be with me in paradise' (Luke 23:43).

The Lord probably had this Rabbinical superstition in mind when he delayed his journey to Bethany. He would have people know, beyond any doubt, that Lazarus was truly dead before he raised him back to life!

Lazarus was sick and would die, after four days he would be raised again from the dead. Like the blind beggar in Jerusalem whose affliction was not because of some particular sin, 'but that the works of God should be revealed in him' (John 9:3), so here it is 'for the glory of God, that the Son of God may be glorified through it' (v.4). This is the seventh of eight miracles recorded by the apostle John so that we 'may believe that Jesus is the Christ, the Son of God, and that believing [we] may have life in his name' (John 20:31). It is the crowning miracle, the greatest and most public proof of the glory of the Only Begotten Son of God; it is the climax in a history where all is miraculous: the person, the life, the teaching, the actions.

The glory of God and the faith of his people are intimately connected. The raising of Lazarus from the dead would be far more effective in strengthening the faith of the disciples than the mere restoring of one to health and strength. But more importantly still, it will consolidate for all time the words of the Lord Jesus Christ when he declared, 'I am the resurrection and the life. He who believes in me, even though he dies, he shall live. And whoever lives and believes in me shall never die' (v.25). Jesus is 'the Prince of life' (Acts 3:15). 'In him was life' (John 1:4). But what more forceful way could have been adopted to prove the power of the Lord of Glory?

Jesus decided to journey to Bethany, he told his disciples that Lazarus slept. The disciples were concerned about a return to the vicinity of Jerusalem when, on his last visit, the Jews were ready to stone the Lord. It is understandable that the disciples thought of Lazarus as just asleep (v.12-14). 'Sleep' however, is an ideal way to refer to the death of believers. When Christians die they are 'those who sleep in Jesus' (1 Thessalonians 4:14).

This is the first of three occasions when the words of the apostle Thomas were recorded. Some describe him as a pessimist, a melancholic and a doubter (v.16; John 14:5; 20:24-29). There was however no lack of love and commitment to the Lord. He did not lack courage and was ready to face death with Jesus for he said, 'Let us also go, that we may die with him'. There was no bitterness of spirit, no terror or fear, simply a quiet resignation even though he was probably loosing heart.

Loosing heart is a real danger for the people of God. The Scriptures record encouraging words to militate against a depressing outlook: in prayer (Luke 18:1-8); in evangelism and preaching (2 Corinthians 4:1-6); in Christian service (1 Corinthians 15:58); in doing good (Galatians 6:9) and when believers face trials (Ephesians 3:13). The best antidote to discouragement is to 'consider him who endured such hostility from sinners against himself, lest you become weary and discouraged in your souls' (Hebrews 12:3), consider the life and example of the Lord Jesus. Followers of Jesus are enabled to cope with enormous pressures as Paul recorded -

> We are hard-pressed on every side, yet not crushed; we are perplexed, but not in despair; persecuted, but not forsaken; struck down, but not destroyed (2 Corinthians 4:8-9).

It is relatively easy to stir up one another to doubts, fears, depression and gloom. It is altogether different when it comes to trying to 'consider one another in order to stir up love and good works' (Hebrews 10:24).

When Jesus and his disciples arrived on the outskirts of Bethany, Martha went out to meet him and express her confidence in the Lord's power: 'Lord, if you had been here, my brother would not have died. But even now I know that whatever you ask of God, God will give you' (vv.21-22). Jesus reassured her and emphasised who and what he is -

> I am the resurrection and the life. He who believes in me, though he may die, he shall live. And whoever lives and believes in me shall never die (John 11:25-26).

Martha declared her confidence in Jesus as 'the Christ, the Son of God, who is to come into the world'. She then went to tell Mary privately that the Lord had arrived and was asking to speak with her. Mary also expressed her confidence in the healing power of the Lord Jesus and was overcome with tears as were the Jews who went with her. Jesus was greatly affected by their grief. He asked for directions to the tomb of Lazarus and then wept himself.

At the tomb the Lord instructed that the stone be rolled from the entrance. Martha was concerned that there would be a strong and unpleasant smell from the decomposing body. Jesus insisted and then prayed in the hearing of the people.

It was a prayer which was so overwhelming because of its trustfulness, simplicity and sincerity. He would leave the people in no doubt as to his being the One sent from God, the true Christ. Father and Son (and no doubt the Holy Spirit too) were united to demonstrate that, 'this sickness is not unto death, but for the glory of God, that the Son of God may be glorified through it' (v.4). When Jesus is glorified the Father too is glorified (cf. Philippians 2:9-11; John 17:1).

To the disciples there had been a gradual unfolding of truth concerning the person of Jesus. His divine power and human compassion had been revealed in healings, feeding of the hungry and care for the lost. The ultimate demonstration of grace, mercy and power was when Jesus raised a man who had been dead for four days. Jesus was revealed as a far more wonderful and magnificent Messiah than ever they had been taught to expect or even imagine.

It must have been an awe-inspiring occasion, almost frightening when out from the tomb came a man who had been dead four days; a man whose body should have begun to decompose; a man who was dead and was now alive. For this man now resurrected from the tomb Jesus commanded assistance to unbind him and free him.

A number of the people were so impressed that they acknowledged Jesus to be the Messiah. Others, however, were not impressed. How could they react so badly to such a demonstration of power and mercy?

There are a number of reasons why people do not believe: there are sinners who prefer their sinful ways (John 3:18-19); sinners who prefer human popularity (John 5:44) and sinners who reject God (Psalm 14:1-3; Romans 1:18-22).

It might well be thought that a man being raised from the dead would have convinced everyone to follow the Lord Jesus but not so, the miracle had a negative impact on the authorities. The chief priests plotted to put Lazarus to death because on account of him many of the Jews went away and believed in Jesus (John 12:10-11).

The Pharisees were informed and the Sanhedrin (the Jewish Council of Seventy) was called together and presided over by Caiaphas the high priest. They were disconcerted, 'If we let him alone like this, everyone will believe in him, and the Romans will come and take away both our place and nation' (John 11:48).

Everything is not, however, always what it appears on the surface. Were the members of this ruling Jewish council truly concerned about the temple and the people or was it their own positions of power they were more concerned about? Do they fear that the people will believe in Jesus and accept him as King and Messiah and so end their rule and dominion?

Later when Jesus was brought before Pilate, Pilate was in no doubt as to the motive in the heart of the Jewish leaders: 'He knew that because of envy they had delivered him' (Matthew 27:18). They claimed an absolute authority for their human laws. They conducted themselves, not as servants but as masters, yet Jesus said, 'He who is greatest among you shall be your servant' (Matthew 23:11).

The sacrificial system was considered by them as quite sufficient for the purposes of atonement; whoever dare question their system or their authority, or the central position of their high priest, was to them an accursed heretic. Caiaphas overruled by saying -

> You know nothing at all, nor do you consider that it is expedient
> for us that one man should die for the people, and not that the
> whole nation should perish (John 11:49-50).

Disguising his true motives under a cloak of nationalism, the crafty Caiaphas was trying to remove a personal obstacle. Jesus posed a great threat to his popularity and power, so he argued that if the people followed Jesus the occupying Romans would rise up and destroy the nation, whereas if Jesus was put to death the nation would be saved. Ironically, the exact opposite was the case. When the Jews murdered Jesus they sealed their own fate and not many years later the Romans came and destroyed the city, temple and nation.

In God's amazing providence, the choice of Caiaphas' words was so directed that they were capable of expressing the essence of God's glorious plan of salvation. The Holy Spirit, without doubt, ensured that the wicked sentiments of Caiaphas were expressed in words which would testify to the saving work of the Lord Jesus Christ.

Unwittingly the high priest prophesied. He was no man of God, nor a prophet, yet he prophesied. He spoke about the profound meaning and significance of the death of Christ without realising it for one moment! As the early Christians interpreted the words of Psalm 2:1-2

> Lord, you are God, who made heaven and earth and the sea, and all that is in them, who by the mouth of your servant David have said - 'Why did the nations rage, and the people plot vain things? The kings of the earth took their stand, and the rulers were gathered together against the LORD and against his Christ.' For truly against your holy Servant Jesus, whom you anointed, both Herod and Pontius Pilate, with the Gentiles and the people of Israel, were gathered together to do whatever your hand and your purpose determined before to be done (Acts 4:24-28).

Jesus did die for a nation but not the nation of Israel that Caiaphas was claiming to be so concerned about. God's plan was for his Son to die for a nation of believers; a spiritual nation of Israelites and Gentiles from all the nations of the earth. This was God's amazing promise:

> It is too small a thing that you should be my Servant to raise up the tribes of Jacob, and to restore the preserved ones of Israel; I will also give you as a light to the Gentiles, that you should be my salvation to the ends of the earth (Isaiah 49:6; cf. 56:8; John 10:16).

The words of Caiaphas 'that one man should die for the people' spoke of Christ's death -

- its nature is *vicarious* ('for' meaning 'on behalf of');
- its power - the death of Christ does not make salvation *possible*, it makes it *certain*;
- its magnitude - Christ died for *'the people of God'* - believing Jew and believing Gentile!

So it was that 'when God displays His greatest works before the world, the world is provoked to the highest pitch of bitterness and wrath.'[64] 'From that day on, they plotted to put him to death' (John 11:53). A command was

---

[64] Anton in: Ernest W. Hengstenberg *Commentary on the Gospel of St John* (Minneapolis, Minnesota: Klock and Klock, 1980), vol. 2, pp.66-7.

issued that anyone who knew where Jesus was must report it to the authorities so that they might arrest him.

The Saviour well knew that it was appointed for him to die on the Passover Day as the Lamb that would take away the sins of the world (John 1:29). He would die neither before nor after that day. Meanwhile he will retire to Ephraim a remote country village near the wilderness. Although the location of this village is not now known it was probably not far from the city of Jerusalem. It provided further seclusion and opportunity for uninterrupted instruction of the apostles.

77. The final journey to Jerusalem
Matthew 19:1-2; Mark 10:1; Luke 17:11

After what must have been quite a brief respite, Jesus prepared for his last journey to Jerusalem. It seems strange that he should set out for Jerusalem by first going north so as to pass through Samaria (Luke 17:11), Galilee (Matthew 19:1; Luke 17:11) and 'the region of Judea by the other side of the Jordan' (Mark 10:1). It has been suggested that Jesus left Ephraim and made a brief detour north through Samaria to the southern border of Galilee perhaps to meet up with those from Galilee who were to accompany him on his final visit to Jerusalem.

At the crucifixion of the Lord there were many women who came up with him to Jerusalem (Mark 15:41). It seems highly unlikely that these 'many women' had been travelling with him since the Feast of Tabernacles in the previous autumn nor from the Feast of Dedication in the December. Now in the spring, meeting up with the women from Galilee the group would proceed southward to Jerusalem through 'the region of Judea by the other side of the Jordan' (Mark 10:1) Decapolis and Peraea. There would be nothing strange in a large company travelling to the feast in Judah. Many groups of pilgrims would be on that road.

78. The healing of ten lepers
Luke 17:12-19

As they travelled up to Jerusalem the group stopped periodically for the Lord to engage in healing (Matthew 19:2) and teaching (Mark 10:1). Matthew (8:2-4) and Mark (1:40-45) both record the healing of a leper but it is Luke alone who records the occasion when a number of lepers were healed simultaneously. When the Lord entered a village ten lepers called out loudly to him, for their condition prohibited their entering the village (Leviticus 13:45-46). They pleaded for mercy.

On a previous occasion when a leper had fallen before Jesus and pleaded, 'Lord, if you are willing, you can make me clean', the Lord responded by putting out his hand and touching him and saying, 'I am willing; be cleansed' (Luke 5:13). Yet here, without a touch or even a command of healing, Jesus simply instructed the ten men to go show themselves to the priests so that their healing might be lawfully acknowledged (Leviticus 14:1-32).

The priests must perform this function. They will announce the healing of the leper and his restoration, welcoming him back into the community. The healing by Jesus was almost casual, he avoided all ostentation, veiling his honour and this great working of his power. This was so typical of the Son of Man who is the Son of God.

One of the ten, when he saw that he was healed, returned to thank Jesus for his healing. Raising his voice he glorified God. Jesus asked him about the other nine who had not returned to give thanks. They were Jews this one was a Samaritan! The Lord made note that only a foreigner gave thanks and glorified God.

Faith in Jesus as a healer resulted in healing for ten men; faith in Jesus as the Messiah of God resulted in salvation for only one. Jesus said to him, 'Arise, go your way. Your faith has made you well' (Luke 17:19). The original word translated 'made you well' means 'to save' in the sense of 'deliver' or 'protect' and it can be used literally or figuratively. A different word is usually used for being made well after illness.

79. Predicting the Lord's return
Luke 17:20-37

Once more the Pharisees addressed the Lord with the appearance of a genuine enquiry as though truly desiring to understand and to know details of the coming of God's kingdom. Pharisees and their many followers were looking forward to the arrival of an outward, earthly, visible kingdom, one in which the Jews would occupy a very prominent place. Over against their ideas Jesus indicated that the Kingdom of God comes in two different ways: spiritually and physically.

The first is invisible, personal and internal (v.21), it is the gracious rule of God in the heart and mind of those who freely, willingly and lovingly submit to him. The second is the Lord's triumphant return in glory which will not be for some time. Jesus warned that there will be times when Christians long for his return (v.22). There will be claims that he has arrived and folk will be urged to go to him.

Jesus reassured all his followers that when he does come again it will be visible and obvious to the whole world. Before that day he must suffer many things and be rejected.

He compared the intervening period with the days of Noah when the majority took no notice of God's warning, they ate, drank, married - until the flood came and destroyed them all. Also the days of Lot when the vast majority ate, drank, bought, sold, planted, built - until the judgment of God rained fire and brimstone from heaven and destroyed them all. People will behave with the same careless attitude as they reject the warnings of God to repent and believe before it is too late.

When the final day comes there will be a separating of believer and unbeliever, those who love God and those who do not love God. Being married to a believer will not save an unbeliever, in that night there will be two in one bed: the one will be taken and the other will be left (v.34). In the same way, friendship or work association with a believer will not save an unbeliever. The all-knowing God will divide the inhabitants of the world. Judgment will fall swiftly and suddenly.

80. The parable of The Widow and the Judge
Luke 18:1-8

Perhaps in anticipating a loss of hope at the long delay of his return Jesus presented a parable with the express purpose 'that men always ought to pray and not lose heart' (v.1). The context of the parable is the return of the Lord Jesus Christ and the final establishment of the Kingdom of God on earth.

The widow represents the Church under persecution: Christians in times of acute trial and temptation longing for the return of Jesus and their relief and vindication, and the establishment of his kingdom on earth (Luke 17:22; cf. Titus 2:13). Collectively or individually members of the Church of Christ are able to identify with this widow. They are in need and in danger with no resources in themselves. They need help from elsewhere.

Who is the adversary? There is a triad of forces against the believer: the world, the flesh and the devil -

- the world attracts, threatens or persecutes (1 John 2:15-16; Luke 21:17; John 15:20);
- the old sinful nature wars against the new spiritual nature and against the Holy Spirit (Romans 7:18-19; Galatians 5:17);
- the devil is the most insidious. Behind all opposition there is this one great enemy, one great opposer of the faithful, one dreadful adversary - the devil (1 Peter 5:8-9; Job 16:10-11).

Some Christians may react that the Lord used a wicked judge to draw out lessons concerning the All-Righteous Judge, the Lord of heaven and earth. A few Christian scholars have been so anxious about this that they have tried, by elaborate means and intellectual gymnastics, to vindicate the evil and indifference of this earthly judge.

But the whole point of the parable depends upon the wickedness, self-centredness, utterly self-willed, uncaring, unfeeling, unrighteous character of this corrupt man. Had the judge been good and noble and reliably discharging his responsibilities, functioning faithfully before God and society, then the widow would have been received and her case heard and action taken with appropriate speed and efficiency.

The persistence of the widow was only evoked because of the appalling character of this man in power. Jesus presented a judge who was the opposite, in every respect and to every degree, of the heavenly Father. The righteous Judge of all the earth will always do right (Genesis 18:25; cf. 2 Timothy 4:8). The difference could not be greater. God is not *to be likened* to that wicked judge *but contrasted* with that wicked judge.

If a wicked judge vindicated an insistent widow how much more will the loving Father vindicate his persistently praying children!

The widow was being deprived of her rights. What the elect are longing for is that divine justice gives them their rights. The Church has been promised 'an inheritance incorruptible and undefiled and that does not fade away' (1 Peter 1:4). Jesus said that the meek are blessed because 'they shall inherit the earth' (Matthew 5:5). The day is to dawn when 'God will wipe every tear from their eyes; there shall be no more death, nor sorrow, nor crying; and there shall be no more pain' (Revelation 21:4). We 'look for new heavens and a new earth in which righteousness dwells' (2 Peter 3:13).

But in order that we may inherit that glorious Promised Land, the Lord Jesus must return and finally break the power of those who stand in the way of us realising our possession. He warned that it may be quite some time when he said, 'though he bears long with them' (v.7). However, what may appear to be God delaying the return of Jesus, is no delay at all, it is all according to the divine plan for 'the Lord is not slack concerning his promise as some count slackness, but is long-suffering towards us, not willing that any should perish but that all should come to repentance' (2 Peter 3:9).

Those chosen of God 'before the foundation of the world' (Ephesians 1:4) are to be brought to a saving faith in Jesus, then he will return, not a second sooner nor a second later. God will avenge his elect speedily - 'in a moment, in the twinkling of an eye, at the last trumpet' (1 Corinthians 15:52).

The question is not whether the Judge will fail in his duty but rather whether the widow will fail in hers by not being persistent in prayer!

The danger of loosing heart because the Lord has not returned is a constant danger open to believers in times of affliction (2 Corinthians 4:16), or when becoming weary in doing good (Galatians 6:9), or when engaged in evangelism (2 Corinthians 4:1) or when distressed at the sufferings of the Lord's people (Ephesians 3:13). The Lord provides the glorious antidote to sadness and despondency, as we have said before 'consider him who endured such hostility from sinners against himself, lest you become weary and discouraged in your souls' (Hebrew 12:3).

God's own chosen people correspond to the widow in the parable. The condition of the Church after the Lord's departure is like that of a widow deprived of her rights. They are like her in her suffering and in her weakness. They should be like her too in her persistent cry. God will avenge speedily. The crucial question is: 'When the Son of Man comes, will he really find faith on the earth?' (v.8) The challenge is issued and every hearer must take the words of Jesus seriously. Self-examination is essential: 'Examine yourselves as to whether you are in the faith' (2 Corinthians 13:5).

81. The parable of The Pharisee and Tax Collector
Luke 18:9-14

The Lord Jesus, continuing with the subject of prayer, related a parable for those who trust in themselves and despise others (v.9). Two men went to the temple to pray (the temple was used for teaching, offering sacrifices and for private prayers. Devout Jews observed three prayer times daily: 9am. 12 noon and 3pm. Prayer was thought to be more effective if conducted in the temple consequently quite a number of Jews visited the temple daily to pray).

The Pharisee was chosen as one of the subjects because Pharisees were normally thought of as religious and moral. The tax collector was chosen because tax collectors were thought of as religiously and morally beyond all hope. So the Lord chose two extremes and though they were quite different, there were also similarities: both were sinners and both had offended God, both prayed short prayers, both engaged in self-examination, both men stood to pray.

The one found in himself only good, the other found in himself only bad. The Pharisee either blindly failed to see his own sin or stubbornly refused to confess it. The tax collector discovered and confessed the truth regarding himself. In the end, one sinner was forgiven, and the other was not.

The Pharisee 'prayed thus with himself' (Luke 18:11). Outwardly he was addressing God but inwardly and in reality he was talking to himself about himself. Having once addressed God he never mentioned the Lord again. He was consumed with self-interest. Through his prayer the Pharisee was congratulating himself. The attitude of his mind and heart in praying was wrong. No man who is proud can truly pray to God. No man who despises other human beings can truly pray to God. Nowhere did he ask the Lord for forgiveness, mercy, or compassion.

This Pharisee who was taught the Old Testament Scripture and no doubt often referred to it in teaching others, had failed to take note of so much of its teaching, such as, 'Though the LORD is on high, yet he regards the lowly; but the proud he knows from afar' (Psalm 138:6; cf. Proverbs 29:23). His actual words were not sinful. Every child of God has reason to thank the heavenly Father that he or she is not like others. This man's sin consisted in that he gave thanks not for what he had received *from* God but for what he was and what he did *for* God.

Jesus was not implying that morality did not matter! 'Extortioners, unjust, adulterers' (v.11) are sinners. Repentance before God means turning away from sin (Isaiah 55:7; cf. Proverbs 28:13). Followers of the Lord are to 'bear fruits worthy of repentance' (Luke 3:8). Nor does the Lord wish to dismiss the virtue and value of fasting (cf. Matthew 6:16-18) or the practice of tithing (cf. Matthew 6:1-4). The Lord says, 'The one who has a haughty look and a proud heart, him I will not endure' (Psalm 101:5).

The tax collector was 'standing afar off' - at a distant. His head was bowed down. He was ashamed of his sins. He 'beat his breast' - in self-accusation and near despair. He cried, 'God be merciful to me a sinner'. He was aware of divine disapproval and longed that God's wrath and anger might be removed from him and the favour of God somehow established upon him. It was this heart-broken, self-despising prayer which resulted in his acceptance. 'A broken and a contrite heart - these, O God, you will not despise' (Psalm 51:17).

This one, and only this one of the two, 'went down to his house [having been] justified' (Luke 18:14). He left the temple with peace in his mind and tranquility in his soul (Romans 5:1-2). What blessing to know that having confessed his sins, God 'is faithful and just to forgive [his] sins and to cleanse [him] from all unrighteousness' (1 John 1:9).

82. Jesus answers about divorce
Matthew 19:3-12; Mark 10:2-12

Among the multitudes that gathered around the Lord those who sought healing were not disappointed (Matthew 19:2). The Pharisees were still however out to test Jesus with questions concerning the law of Moses. Were these the same Pharisees who were earlier rebuked on this subject by the Lord Jesus whilst he was in Perea? (Luke 16:18) Now that he had returned to Judea were they raising the issue again to continue their aim to discredit him? They turned to the interpretation of Deuteronomy 24:1-4 and asked, 'Is it lawful for a man to divorce his wife for just any reason?' (Matthew 19:3)

Moses permitted a man to divorce his wife when there was the discovery of 'some uncleanness in her'.

In Peraea Jesus had simply said, 'Whoever divorces his wife and marries another commits adultery; and whoever marries her who is divorced from her husband commits adultery' (Luke 16:18). Maybe the Pharisees were thinking further back to the Lord's earlier teaching in The Sermon on the Mount -

> It has been said, 'Whoever divorces his wife, let him give her a certificate of divorce'. But I say to you that whoever divorces his wife for any reason except sexual immorality causes her to commit adultery; and whoever marries a woman who is divorced commits adultery (Matthew 5:31-32).

The Pharisees were pressing the issue. This time Jesus answered by referring to the beginning at creation where God had made humanity male and female and declared that marriage would make them 'no longer two but one flesh'. Jesus added a solemn rider, 'Therefore what God has joined together, let not man separate' (Matthew 19:6).

The Pharisees persisted by asking why then did Moses command the giving of a certificate of divorce? Jesus pointed out that the reason for the concession was because of the hardness of the human heart. It was permitted but it was not the intention at the beginning of creation (it is thought that the certificate of divorce was introduced to protect a wife being dismissed and publicly shamed. It allowed for her remarriage without dishonour). The Lord repeated his position on divorce that it should only be on grounds of sexual immorality (Matthew 19:9).

Inside the house the disciples expressed their surprise and unease at the teaching of Jesus and concluded that it is better therefore not to marry. Jesus indicated that there are three classes of men for whom it is better to remain unmarried: those who are born without normal sexual desire, those damaged by the cruelty of others, and those who voluntarily abstain from marriage for the kingdom of heaven's sake in furthering some work for God. It has been given to them to live unmarried with celibacy and contentment, 'for this is not of nature, but of grace: it is the gift of God'.[65]

83. Jesus receives little children
Matthew 19:13-15; Mark 10:13-16; Luke 18:15-17

Parents with young children brought their offspring to him 'that he might put his hands on them and pray' (Matthew 19:13). It was a common practice to seek the blessing of a travelling Rabbi upon little ones. The Lord obviously did not regard this as superstition.

To view the action of the disciples in the best possible light it would seem they were only seeking to protect Jesus. He had recently shared with them that this was to be his last journey culminating in his death in Jerusalem. They might well have assumed that permitting young children to come to him was rather thoughtless on their part.

What followed gives a penetrating insight into the character of the Saviour. He was greatly displeased (Mark 10:14). This is the only time this strong word is used about the reaction of Jesus. When he saw the disciples rebuking those who brought little ones to him he said, 'Let the little children come to me, and do not forbid them; for of such is the kingdom of God' (Mark 10:14). He not only welcomed them but 'took them up in his arms, laid his hands on them, and blessed them' (Mark 10:16).

What a beautiful scene, the Son of the living God and Saviour of the world with gentleness and tenderness embracing little ones. Of Messiah it was prophesied, 'He will feed his flock like a shepherd; he will gather the lambs with his arm, and carry them in his bosom' (Isaiah 40:11).

God has a heart for the very young. When Jonah resisted the call of God to preach repentance to the inhabitants in the evil city of Nineveh he was made aware of the Lord's great compassion towards 'more than one hundred and twenty thousand persons who cannot discern between their right hand and their left' (Jonah 4:11).

The loving action of Jesus encourages parents everywhere to pray for their children and 'bring them up in the training and admonition of the Lord' (Ephesians 6:4), confident that even the very young may have genuine love for Jesus, 'for of such is the kingdom of heaven' (Matthew 19:14). Whatever their natural qualities they still need to come to the Saviour in repentance and faith.

---

[65] John Gill, 'Matthew 19:11' in *Exposition of the Entire Bible*, *biblehub.com*

Jesus gently reminded his disciples of his earlier teaching that in order for anyone to enter the kingdom of heaven 'turning'[66] and becoming as little children is essential (Matthew 18:3-5). Young children are dependent on others and teachable. There is a simple trustfulness and generally a readiness and willingness to obey. Followers of Jesus should 'turn' from their worldly and fleshly desires and with humility and modesty learn to be like their Master in thought, word and deed.

84. The rich young ruler
Matthew 19:16-22; Mark 10:17-22; Luke 18:18-23

'A certain ruler', this man was probably a leader in the local synagogue and evidently a principled, upright and respected young man, similar to the apostle Paul before his conversion (Philippians 3:5-6). He came running with urgency and great concern and knelt before Jesus, not in worship but in respect, with a burning question: 'Good Teacher, what good thing shall I do that I may have eternal life?' (Matthew 19:16)

Jesus responded by immediately pointing out that there is only one who is 'good' and that is God. The word 'good', a word here denoting *infinite moral perfection* should only be strictly applied to God himself. Jesus does not intend here to disclaim divinity or to say anything about his own character, but simply to correct this young man and to expose an exaggerated form of address.

The young ruler seemed aware that he lacked something with regard to eternal life. He was not confident that he was in the right relation with God and therefore feared he would not enjoy the happiness of heaven. He was hopeful that Jesus would know the answer. The Lord directed him to the Ten Commandments (Exodus 20:3-17) which he claimed to have obeyed from his youth but still was aware that something was missing. Jesus put his finger on this man's spiritual blockage - his love of money. When challenged to become a true disciple of the Lord by selling all, he turned away, 'for he had great possessions' (Mark 10:22).

The Lord was evidently intending to bring this man to an awareness of his sin. The rich young ruler had to be convinced that he had not kept the commandments. He thought he had kept them and was relying upon them for salvation so he must be brought to see that he was deceived.

---

[66] The verb translated 'convert' in Matthew 18:3 means to change or turn as from one habit of life or set of opinions to another as in Luke 22:32 and James 5:19. Conversion for salvation is 'turning' from sin to the Saviour by repentance and faith as in Acts 3:19 and 15:3.

Will anyone be saved by works of the law? That is a crucial question. Was our Lord implying such a thing? The answer is yes and no.

Yes a man or woman can be saved by keeping the law, provided they keep it entirely, completely, and perfectly for the whole of their lives! Also the law of God must be obeyed not only externally but in the heart and mind too. If the law is kept in this way without fault or failure through the whole of one's earthly existence then there would be no condemnation, no punishment from God, no need to rely on the death of the Lord Jesus Christ and no need for salvation through faith.

Nevertheless human nature being what it is, no one has ever kept the law of God in its entirety, for 'there is none righteous, no, not one' and 'by the deeds of the law no flesh will be justified in [God's] sight, for by the law is the knowledge of sin' (Romans 3:10,20). Consequently -

> what the law could not do in that it was weak through the flesh, God did by sending his own Son in the likeness of sinful flesh, on account of sin: he condemned sin in the flesh, that the righteous requirement of the law might be fulfilled in us who do not walk according to the flesh but according to the Spirit (Romans 8:3-4).

Conversation with the rich young ruler resulted in a diagnosis that his wealth was an obstacle to his spiritual life. He must be rid of that hindrance. He was given six imperatives - Go, sell all, give, come, take up the cross, follow me (Mark 10:21). Hearing this the young man 'became very sorrowful, for he was very rich' (Luke 18:23).

85. Reward for those who leave all
Matthew 19:23-30; Mark 10:23-31; Luke 18:24-30

Christian discipleship requires a particular attitude towards money and wealth. In the parable of The Sower Jesus had already warned of 'the cares of this world, the deceitfulness of riches, and the desires for other things' (Mark 4:19) which can choke spiritual desire. This was brought out dramatically in the contact with the rich young ruler. The young man lived for his possessions and was not prepared to let them all go, take up the cross of self-denial, and become a disciple of the Lord Jesus Christ.

Seeing the intense grief of the young man as he walked away, Jesus took the opportunity to expand upon the subject and said to his disciples how hard it is 'for those who have riches to enter the kingdom of God' (Mark 10:23). When the disciples heard this they were 'greatly astonished' (Matthew 19:25) for it was the popular notion among the Jews that if a man was wealthy and prosperous it was a sign of God's favour upon him.

Jesus countered this idea for he knows of the great dangers associated with riches. In the parable of The Sower he warned about the seed that fell among the thorns, interpreting this as referring to 'the ones who hear the word, and the cares of this world, the deceitfulness of riches, and the desires for other things entering in choke the word, and it becomes unfruitful' (Mark 4:18-19).

It is not being rich which is the problem but the attitude of the rich towards their riches. 'He who trusts in his riches will fall, but the righteous will flourish like foliage' (Proverbs 11:28). Abraham, Job, David and Joseph of Arimathea were rich and were faithful to God, but great possessions and wealth bring with them strange and solemn dangers, hindrances and temptations.

> Those who desire to be rich fall into temptation and a snare, and into many foolish and harmful lusts which drown men in destruction and perdition (1Timothy 6:9).

The lesson to those who are rich is not to be proud or arrogant 'nor to trust in uncertain riches but in the living God' and 'let them do good, that they be rich in good works, ready to give, willing to share' (1Timothy 6:17-18).

The disciples talked amongst themselves in bewilderment: 'Who then can be saved?' Jesus responded by pointing out a vital truth: 'The things that are impossible to men are possible to God' (Luke 18:27). This put the outcome squarely back upon the Lord God and him alone. Peter said that they have left everything to follow Jesus and added, 'Therefore what shall we have?' (Matthew 19:27) Had not the twelve done exactly what Jesus had asked the young man to do? Had they not 'left everything' and followed Jesus? The answer would therefore seem to be obvious, that the twelve would have 'treasure in heaven' (Matthew 19:21).

There are rewards for those who make sacrifices for the Lord and for the gospel. There are rewards in this life and there are rewards in the life to come. The specific reward for the apostles is given that in the regeneration, that is in the restored or renewed universe, elsewhere called 'the new heaven and earth' (Isaiah 65:17; 2 Peter 3:13; Revelation 21:1) they will rule with the Son of Man 'on twelve thrones, judging the twelve tribes of Israel' (Matthew 19:28).

The 'tribes of Israel' are not to be understood as referring to the natural or earthly tribes of Israel for that would invalidate the emphatic declaration that in Christ there is neither Jew nor Gentile (Colossians 3:11), for we are 'all one in Christ Jesus' (Galatians 3:28). It would necessitate the rebuilding of 'the middle wall of separation' which the Saviour at Calvary 'has broken down' (Ephesians 2:14-18).

Viewed then spiritually it designates the new Israel, all true believers from the beginning of creation to the end of history (Galatians 6:16; Romans 11:26). In Revelation 7 the apostle John hears the number of true believers listed as twelve tribes of Israel (v.4). He sees 'a great multitude which no one could number, of all nations, tribes, peoples, and tongues' (v.9) confirming that the term 'twelve tribes of Israel' is a spiritual symbol.

The Church of Jesus Christ is the new and true Israel, the entire people of God in their multiplicity, formed after the type of those twelve tribes.

In commitment and loyalty to Christ many believers suffer losses: houses, brothers, sisters, father, mother, wife, children or lands. Some are disowned or deserted following conversion or imprisoned through persecution. Others are servants of God who choose willingly not to have these relationships which effectively mean the loss of house, wife, children or lands in order to labour in evangelism, church planting and teaching in harsh environments. They choose celibacy 'for the kingdom of heaven's sake' (Matthew 19:12).

Being rich toward God is the best and lasting treasure (Luke 12:20-21). The persecuted Jewish Christians addressed by the writer to the Hebrews, joyfully accepted the plundering of their goods, knowing they 'have a better and an enduring possession for [themselves] in heaven' (Hebrews 10:34).

All that is relinquished for Jesus' sake and the gospel's will be repaid 'a hundredfold now in this time - houses and brothers and sisters and mothers and children and lands, with persecutions' (Mark 10:30). Here and now there are immediate real benefits.

Jesus said, 'Whoever does the will of God is my brother and my sister and mother' (Mark 3:35). The apostle Peter referred to 'Mark my son' (1 Peter 5:13). The apostle Paul regarded Timothy as his 'beloved son' (2 Timothy 1:2). To the Corinthians he wrote, 'For though you might have ten thousand instructors in Christ, yet you do not have many fathers; for in Christ Jesus I have begotten you through the gospel' (1 Corinthians 4:15). To the Romans he wrote, 'Greet Rufus, chosen in the Lord, and his mother and mine' (Romans 16:13).

To these wonderful promises that each Christian is a member of the huge worldwide family of God and will enter into the eternal kingdom, Jesus attached a warning. At the end of this present world and the establishment of the new heavens and new earth many dramatic changes are going to take place including: 'Many who are first will be last, and the last first' (Mark 10:31). One example of this will be that twelve very ordinary men, including four fishermen, a former tax collector and a former zealot (political revolutionary seeking the overthrow of the Roman government) last in the world's eyes, are going to rule with Jesus in the future.

With the promised rewards is included the greatest free gift; all followers of Jesus 'inherit eternal life' (Mathew 19:29). It is called an inheritance because it is a free gift to which the beneficiaries have contributed nothing. It is a gift that is bequeathed at death based upon legal justice and righteousness. It has been purchased on behalf of others and rightfully belongs to them. It is 'an inheritance incorruptible and undefiled and that does not fade away, reserved in heaven for you, who are kept by the power of God through faith for salvation ready to be revealed in the last time'(1 Peter 1:4-5).

All believers are 'sealed with the Holy Spirit of promise, who is the guarantee of our inheritance' until the time appointed by God (Ephesians 1:13-14). Even father Abraham looked forward to this eternal inheritance more than anything else in the world (Hebrews 11:8-10,13-16).

86. The parable of The Labourers in the Vineyard
Matthew 20:1-16

This is one of many occasions where the chapter division in the Bible should be ignored.[67] The parable will only be accurately understood when seen in its obvious connection with the preceding events: the young ruler who had 'great possessions', the teaching of Jesus concerning riches and entry into the kingdom of heaven, and the disciples concern about their reward for having given up everything.

In this parable the Lord Jesus is represented by the landowner or owner. The vineyard represents the nation of Israel in the first instance (cf. Isaiah 5:1) which the Lord had come to claim as his kingdom. The 'early morning' corresponds to the outset of the Lord's ministry and the first 'labourers' he called to be with him and work for him are the apostles. Though

---

[67] When the books of the Bible were originally written chapter divisions and verses were not included. In the fourth century a Greek manuscript, Codex Vaticanus, used paragraph divisions for convenience. In the fifth century, Jerome divided Scripture into short passages called *pericopes*. In 1227 Stephen Langton the Archbishop of Canterbury, divided the Bible into chapters in the Latin Vulgate. In 1382 the Wycliffe English Bible was the first Bible in English with this chapter format. The present verse divisions were the work of Robert Stephanus (Stephens), a French printer. He divided the Greek text into verses for his Greek New Testament published in 1551. The first entire Bible, in which these chapter and verse divisions were used, was the Stephanus' (Stephens') edition of the Latin Vulgate in 1555. The first English Bible to have both chapter and verse divisions was the Geneva Bible published in 1560.

'unprofitable servants' (Luke 17:10) they have nevertheless been promised a reward; they would inherit the eternal kingdom of heaven (Matthew 5:3,10), that kingdom of God which is 'righteousness and peace and joy in the Holy Spirit' (Romans 14:17).

The first (early) labourers agreed their reward (Matthew 20:2) but three hours later, the next group of labourers to be invited to work in the vineyard, had no such agreement. They were 'standing idle'; all activity which does not flow from a love for God and for his glory is, in God's judgment, standing idle. Those who entered the vineyard having no agreement trusted the landowner to give them 'whatever is right'. This is the humble response of the workers who are conscious that the Lord will give infinitely more than is deserved (Ephesians 3:20). On three more occasions, at three hourly intervals, the landowner went out and hired workers then, at the eleventh hour, the invitation is repeated and more were employed in the vineyard.

At the end of the day the landowner instructed his steward to pay the labourers' wages beginning with the last to be employed to the first. If the first men had been paid first they would have taken their wages and been in ignorance of the Master's gracious and generous dealings with those employed later! Each one, including those who had only worked one hour, received the same amount. The first workers complained against the landowner. They took their money and gave expression to their feelings of resentment because they expected more than the others since they had laboured longer.

Whatever stage in the ministry of Jesus, indeed whatever stage in the history of the world, all who become followers of the Lord, no matter how long they serve, will receive the same reward. In any age God is 'a rewarder of those who diligently seek him' (Hebrews 11:6). It is God himself who is the 'exceedingly great reward' (Genesis 15:1).

> The true spirit of a worker is love to the Master, and to the work for the Master's sake. The moment that a thought of merit glides into the servant's heart, it brings him down, not indeed from the number of true disciples, but from the highest to the lowest class there.[68]

What then of those who serve the longest? Do they not have a greater reward? Yes they do, for they have had the privilege and blessing of knowing and serving the Saviour for many years longer. What a favour from God to be converted in childhood or youth and look forward to a lifetime of useful service for the Master.

---

[68] William Arnot, *The Parables of our Lord* (London: Nelson, 1880), p.218.

87. The Lord's suffering: the third prediction
Matthew 20:17-19; Mark 10:32-34; Luke 18:31-34

For the third time the Saviour predicted his suffering, death and resurrection. He repeated that he would be betrayed into the hands of the chief priests and scribes and added that they would condemn him to death and deliver him to the Gentiles. They would mock, insult, scourge, spit upon and finally crucify him, so that 'all things that are written by the prophets concerning the Son of Man will be accomplished' (Luke 18:31). Though he had repeatedly warned the disciples what was ahead of him, they could not understand, indeed it was hidden from them (Luke 18:34). After three years of close and intense contact the disciples still did not grasp the great salvation plan and purpose of God. They were more concerned about their position and power in the future Kingdom.

88. James and John make a request
Matthew 20:20-28; Mark 10:35-45

James and John brought a request to Jesus that they might sit on seats of honour when the Lord's kingdom comes. Jesus asked the brothers if they were able and willing to drink the cup that he was about to drink and to be baptised with the baptism which he was to undertake. He was referring of course to the ordeal before him, that of great suffering and death. In the Garden of Gethsemane he will pray in agony of soul, 'O my Father, if it is possible, let this cup pass from me; nevertheless, not as I will, but as you will' (Matthew 26:39).

His baptism was to be an immersion of body and soul in torment as he bore the sum total of the punishment due for every sin, transgression and iniquity committed by all his people from the dawn of creation to the grand finale on the great day of the Lord.

If there is any real distinction to be drawn between the suffering described as 'drinking the cup' and that described as 'a baptism' it is in the active and passive sense of the suffering. The drinking of the cup is something in which Jesus was to be active. He will take the cup. It will not be forced to his lips. He will willingly, freely, voluntarily take the cup and drink its contents entirely. In the 'baptism' he will be passive, he will submit to what others will do to him.

Without understanding the implications the brothers both declared their willingness. Jesus told them that they would indeed drink of his cup and be baptised with his baptism. Not long afterwards James was to become the first apostle to die a martyr's death, being put to death by the sword under orders from King Herod Agrippa I (Acts 12:1-2).

John was to experience the other extreme for it would seem that he lived longest of all the apostles, labouring for the cause of Christ under the severe persecution of Rome, and in his nineties exiled to the salt mines on the Isle of Patmos. He was a worthy 'companion in the tribulation and kingdom and patience of Jesus Christ... for the word of God and for the testimony of Jesus Christ' (Revelation 1:9).

Jesus continued by saying to the brothers, 'but to sit on my right hand and on my left is not mine to give, but it is for those for whom it is prepared by my Father' (Matthew 20:23). The translation here expresses the idea that Jesus has nothing to do in bestowing rewards on his followers. This is at variance with the uniform testimony of the Scriptures (Matthew 25:31-40; John 5:22-30). A more accurate translation of the passage would be, 'To sit on my right hand and on my left is not mine to give, except to those for whom it is prepared by my Father.'

The path to glory for the Lord Jesus Christ leads through suffering and sacrifice. Likewise the path to glory for the disciples of the Lord Jesus Christ leads through suffering and sacrifice (Galatians 6:17; Philippians 3:10-11; 2 Corinthians 4:8-9).

James and John illustrate the failure of the apostles to understand the different principles and predictions being taught by Jesus. He reiterated the concept that greatness is shown by service to others, as he himself will demonstrate when he gives 'his life a ransom for many' (Mark 10:45).

89. Blind Bartimaeus (Jericho)
Matthew 20:29-34; Mark 10:46-52; Luke 18:35-43

At first glance it would appear that there is a contradiction between the record of Matthew and Luke. Matthew wrote, 'Now as they went out of Jericho...' (Matthew 20:29). Luke wrote, 'Then it happened, as he was coming near Jericho' (Luke 18:35). Christians committed to the doctrine of Scripture and convinced that it is inspired by the Holy Spirit (2 Timothy 3:16-17) and therefore trustworthy and reliable, have presented a number of plausible solutions.

The most likely seems to be that Jesus passed through Jericho and on the other side of the town he saw Zacchaeus up a tree waiting to see him. Jesus said to him, 'Zacchaeus, make haste and come down, for today I must stay at your house' (Luke 19:5). Jesus therefore then returned to Jericho with Zacchaeus. It was probably on this return that Jesus met the two blind beggars.

One of the proofs of Messiah would be his giving sight to the blind (Isaiah 35:5; Matthew 11:5; Luke 4:18-19). Blindness was widespread in

Israel and it forced many into begging for a living. There are many examples of the Lord's compassion and power in healing the blind (e.g. Matthew 9:28-29; 12:22; 15:30; 20:30-34; Mark 8:25; Luke 7:21). As the great multitude that was following Jesus drew near to Jericho they passed by the place where Bartimaeus, a blind beggar and his blind companion, were sitting begging. The Lord touched their eyes and immediately they were able to see. Bartimaeus followed Jesus, glorifying God and the crowd joined in with their praises (Luke 18:43).

90. Hospitality with Zacchaeus (Jericho)
Luke 19:1-10

Jericho was situated on the main road from Transjordan to Jerusalem. Balm, a fragrant cream or liquid used to heal or soothe the skin, produced in Jericho was widely exported consequently there were many customs officers to collect the taxes. Amongst them was Zacchaeus, who is described as 'a chief tax collector' that is, a tax inspector supervising a group of tax collectors who engage with the traders and general public.[69]

Zacchaeus had become extremely wealthy (probably by unlawful means as well as lawful). He was small of stature and despite being a wealthy leader among the tax collectors and with a total disregard to his own dignity, he ran ahead of the crowd and climbed up into a sycamore tree to be able to get a better vantage point to see the Lord. There seems no reason to assume he wanted to be seen, he was not blind, or lame, or dumb. There was no physical condition which would make him eager to meet Jesus and to experience the compassion of this Son of David.

The curiosity which he displayed would indicate some previous knowledge of the Lord's reputation as 'a friend of tax collectors and sinners' (Matthew 11:19). Maybe he knew that a fellow tax collector, Matthew, had been drawn into the close company of Jesus. However, with whatever knowledge he had, he was certainly eager to see the Lord for himself.

When Jesus came near to the tree he looked directly at Zacchaeus and calling him by name requested him to climb down because he was to welcome the Lord into his home. Jesus knew the mind and heart of this tax collector. He 'knew all men, and had no need that anyone should testify of man, for he knew what was in man' (John 2:24-25).

It would seem that others besides the scribes and Pharisees were disgusted that Jesus mixed with tax collectors (Luke 18:7). The time which

---

[69] See section 23. The call of Matthew Levi, p.60.

Jesus spent with Zacchaeus had no doubt much in common with his encounter with the woman of Samaria and the subsequent two day stay in Sychar where the people testified later, 'We ourselves have heard him and we know that this is indeed the Christ, the Saviour of the world' (John 4:42).

Jesus made the situation abundantly clear in that home in Jericho when he said -

> Today salvation has come to this house, because he also is a son of Abraham; for the Son of Man has come to seek and to save that which was lost (Luke 19:9-10; cf. John 10:27).

The close proximity of the Lord's death gives extra depth to these words to Zacchaeus. Here, only a matter of days before the crucifixion, is a beautiful example of the forgiving grace of God. The life mission of Jesus is powerfully and wonderfully illustrated.

91. The parable of The Minas
Luke 19:11-28

There are similarities, and also significant differences, between this parable and the parable of The Talents (Matthew 25:14-30) taught by Jesus a few days later. The timing of this parable is highly significant: firstly Jesus had recently brought a sinner (Zacchaeus) to salvation (Luke 19:11); secondly he was only days from his sacrificial death and thirdly because many were under the misguided view that the kingdom of God was going to appear at once, maybe even as Jesus entered Jerusalem at the end of this journey.

In the minds of the twelve apostles there was the lingering notion of Jewish supremacy in an earthly kingdom that would soon be realised. Even as late as the ascension they were asking, 'Lord, will you at this time restore the kingdom to Israel?' (Acts 1:6)

The 'certain nobleman' who was about to travel to 'a far country to receive for himself a kingdom and to return' (Luke 19:12) signifies Jesus. Through his suffering and death he will receive the Kingdom of God as prophesied a number of times in the Old Testament. Through King David God said -

> I have set my King on my holy hill of Zion. I will declare the decree: the LORD has said to me, 'You are my Son, today I have begotten you. Ask of me, and I will give you the nations for your inheritance, and the ends of the earth for your possession' (Psalm 2:7-8).

There is also the wonderful prophecy through Daniel -

I was watching in the night visions, and behold, One like the Son of Man, coming with the clouds of heaven! He came to the Ancient of Days, and they brought him near before him. Then to him was given dominion and glory and a kingdom, that all peoples, nations, and languages should serve him. His dominion is an everlasting dominion, which shall not pass away, and his kingdom the one which shall not be destroyed (Daniel 7:13-14).

Jesus receives the kingdom through his unique work on the cross of Calvary. He rules over the whole of creation for the benefit of his Church (Ephesians 1:22-23). He will return in glory from heaven.

In the parable the 'servants' (Luke 19:13) are distinguished from the 'citizens' (Luke 19:14) because they have responded to the gospel call, entered the kingdom of God, and begun service to their King. By sharp contrast the citizens said, 'We will not have this man to reign over us'.

There will be a period of waiting on the part of his servants, some time will elapse before his return. In the parable of The Ten Virgins 'the bridegroom was delayed' (Matthew 25:4). In the parable of The Talents it was 'after a long time' that 'the lord of those servants came and settled accounts with them' (Matthew 25:19). While the Master is away, his servants must work hard and be faithful until his return.

In contrast to the distribution of the unequal number of talents to three servants, 'to each according to his own ability' (Matthew 25:15), the Lord spoke here of the distribution of one mina to each of ten servants. The question is what does the Lord give to all his disciples which is identical? It is not abilities, as is clear from the parable of The Talents but grace that all receive upon conversion. 'The love of God has been poured out in our hearts by the Holy Spirit who was given to us' (Romans 5:5). It is 'our Lord Jesus Christ, through whom also we have access by faith into this grace in which we stand, and rejoice in hope of the glory of God' (Romans 5:5,1-2).

How then is the Lord's instruction to be fulfilled when he says, 'Do business till I come'? (Luke 19:13) How can the grace given to us in conversion be multiplied tenfold or even fivefold in readiness for his return?

The apostle Peter provided the answer when he wrote, 'grow in the grace and knowledge of our Lord and Saviour Jesus Christ' (2 Peter 3:18). Jesus Christ is the giver and the author of the grace and he is also the object of the knowledge. Peter shows how grace is to be multiplied 'add to your faith virtue, to virtue knowledge, to knowledge self-control, to self-control perseverance, to perseverance godliness, to godliness brotherly kindness, and to brotherly kindness love' (2 Peter 1:5-7).

Believers are able to 'grow in grace'; to develop in Christian character, to become more and more spiritually mature.

Christians are not to be content to stay as babes living on milk, 'for everyone who partakes only of milk is unskilled in the word of righteousness, for he is a babe... solid food belongs to those who are of full age, that is, those who by reason of use have their senses exercised to discern both good and evil' (Hebrews 5:13-14).

Growth in grace means not only having knowledge to discern good and evil but striving to live out the good and renounce the evil. Regular daily reading and meditation upon the Word of God is essential but equally what is learned needs to be lived out.

The goal is therefore *to learn more about Christ and to become more like Christ*, to let the word of Christ dwell in us richly in all wisdom and whatever we do 'in word or deed, to do all in the name of the Lord Jesus, giving thanks to God the Father through him' (Colossians 3:16,17).

Irrespective of our race, education, gender, intelligence or age, believers begin with the same grace from God. In the use of that grace in the growth of Christian character we all develop differently, some sadly, not at all. That is the lesson of the parable of The Minas. May 'grace and peace be multiplied to you in the knowledge of God and of Jesus our Lord' (2 Peter 1:2).

How strong and spiritually influential would each local church be if every child of God were seeking to -

> grow up in all things into him who is the head - Christ - from whom the whole body, joined and knit together by what every joint supplies, according to the effective working by which every part does its share, causes growth of the body for the edifying of itself in love (Ephesians 4:15-16).

92. Mary anoints Jesus (Bethany)
Matthew 26:6-13; Mark 14:3-9; John 12:1-11

While the Jewish pilgrims were at Jerusalem making their preparations for the Passover, Jesus visited Bethany where a supper was being given in his honour at the home of Simon the leper (Mark 14:3). It is most likely that this man had previously been healed by Jesus. Lazarus and his two sisters were present. Martha was serving the food. Lazarus talked at table with Simon and the Lord (John 12:2). Here in the town of Bethany at the tomb of Lazarus, Jesus had wept with those who weep (John 11:35). Now he rejoiced with those who rejoice (Romans 12:15).

As it was not considered proper for women to be reclining with men in public, we must assume that the guests were exclusively male. The men would be reclining on couches arranged in a U-shape around a low table.

Mary was full of thankfulness to the Lord: her brother Lazarus had been brought back from the dead; she had sat with Jesus listening to his teaching; she had turned to Jesus to unburden her heart at the anguish of her brother's death; now adoration, devotion, worship and the deepest love burst forth. In the Song of Solomon, the Shulamite said of her Beloved: 'While the king is at his table, my spikenard [that is, costly perfumed ointment] sends forth its fragrance' (Song 1:12).

She brought a flask of very expensive perfume, broke the seal and poured all the contents upon the head and feet of the Lord, wiping the surplus from his feet with her hair. The disciples, led it would seem by Judas Iscariot, regarded this as a terrible waste. Jesus supported Mary, 'Let her alone; she has kept this for the day of my burial' (John 12:7). The Lord saw this as a beautiful token of Mary's love and faith. The Bethany siblings present a picture of the future life God's people will enjoy with Jesus: like Lazarus we will sit with him; like Martha we will serve him; and like Mary we will worship him.

The whole incident displayed a most delightful expression of profound love and gratitude.

Love is not love if it cooly calculates the cost. Love gives its all. Love is also unselfconscious. Mary wiped the feet of the Lord with her hair. In Israel no respectable woman would ever appear in public with her hair unbound. On the day a girl was married her hair was bound up and never again would she be seen in public with her long tresses flowing loose. It was the sign of an immoral woman to appear in public with undone hair.

Mary clearly gave no thought to how she must appear. She was taken up in a beautiful action arising out of pure love. She was expressing her love by giving her most prized possession. Jesus was neither shocked nor embarrassed. The whole action was beautiful and moving. Only a hard-hearted, hypocritical mind like that of Judas could find fault.

The Lord's final week in Jerusalem

93. The triumphal entry (Jerusalem)
Matthew 21:1-11; Mark 11:1-11; Luke 19:29-44; John 12:12-19

The next day the Lord set out from Bethany to go the 3km (2 miles) to Jerusalem. After a short walk they drew near to the village of Bethphage on the Mount of Olives and Jesus sent two disciples to go into the village and return with a colt, the foal of a donkey. The colt was brought, the disciples threw their clothes on the animal and Jesus rode into the city. That the colt allowed Jesus to ride it was probably a miracle in itself, as it had never been ridden before.

As he travelled a great multitude cast their clothes upon the ground, cut leafy branches from the trees and spread them in his path. In sight of the city and the temple, some of the people recalled the mighty miracles he had performed, they recognised him as Messiah, and burst into loud rejoicing and praise to God (Luke 19:37-38). There is no evidence that these people were among those who, less than a week later, called for his death.

For Jesus the sight of the city brought great sadness as he recalled the resistance and unbelief of the people and their impending doom. After three years of labour and frequent visits to the city, long periods of teaching, numerous conversations, many mighty miracles, it was now too late - they had not recognised the time of their visitation (Luke 19:44; cf. 1 Peter 2:12). They did not accept and would not accept that the Messiah had come to them offering the mercy of God. It was now too late and Jesus predicted disaster for the people and the destruction of Jerusalem (Luke 19:43-44).

The following day, after spending the night back in Bethany, as Jesus was returning with his disciples to the city, he was hungry and came upon a fig-tree by the side of the road in the region of the village of Bethphage which bore nothing but leaves. There was no fruit to be found 'for it was not the season for figs' (Mark 11:13). Jesus pronounced that fruit would never grow upon it again. This seems uncharacteristic of Jesus until reflection is given to the immediately preceding events.

The day before, as he entered the city he was disheartened as he reflected upon the unbelief and rebellion of the Jews. He looked for the 'fruit' of faith in response to seeing and hearing him, the promised Messiah of God, yet what he found was hatred, hostility and rejection. The fig tree symbolised Israel - bearing no spiritual fruit.

The withering of the leafy fruitless fig tree dramatically illustrated the spiritual barrenness of Israel and her future resulting punishment by God. They were a nation which was all show and no substance. They professed to love God and to long for the promised Messiah but now that he was among them they despised and disowned him. They were 'leafy' and 'fruitless'.

The disciples witnessed the withering of the tree and were amazed.

94. Second cleansing of the temple
Matthew 21:12-13; Mark 11:15-19; Luke 19:45-48

Entering the temple Jesus once more drove out the corrupt merchants (cf. John 2:13-17). Here towards the close of his ministry he performed the same action that he performed at the beginning of his ministry, he drove out of the temple those who were selling animals and those who were changing currencies (John 2:14-16; Mark 11:15-16). Yet though there are marked similarities there are significant differences in the words of Jesus.

In both cases the Jewish authorities were trading in the court of the Gentiles thus inhibiting the non-Jewish visitors from praying in the quietness and stillness of the temple in the only area permitted to them.

In the first cleansing of the temple (John 2:13-25) the emphasis was placed upon the temple being turned into a marketplace for trade: 'Take these things away! Do not make my Father's house a house of merchandise!' (John 2:16) The word translated 'a house of merchandise' means a market, a place of buying and selling. Jesus said nothing about the corruption going on in the temple, his complaint was not that *there was dishonest buying and selling going on* but that *there was buying and selling going on at all!*

In this second cleansing of the temple Jesus said, 'It is written, "My house shall be called a house of prayer," but you have made it a "den of thieves"' (Matthew 21:13). Quoting from Isaiah 56:7 Jesus underscored God's intention that Gentiles shall have ready access to the temple in Jerusalem.

Almost a thousand years earlier King Solomon had prayed at the dedication of the first temple:

> Moreover, concerning a foreigner, who is not of your people Israel, but has come from a far country for your name's sake (for they will hear of your great name and your strong hand and your outstretched arm), when he comes and prays toward this temple, hear in heaven your dwelling place, and do according to all for which the foreigner calls to you, that all peoples of the earth may know your name and fear you, as do your people Israel, and that they may know that this temple which I have built is called by your name (1 Kings 8:41-43).

The Lord did not charge the authorities with being robbers who were *stealing* in the temple but rather being robbers *hiding* in the temple! He accused them of turning God's house into *a den of thieves* as in the days of Jeremiah when he proclaimed the Word of God and exposed their hypocrisy -

> "Behold, you trust in lying words that cannot profit. Will you steal, murder, commit adultery, swear falsely, burn incense to Baal, and walk after other gods whom you do not know, and then come and stand before me in this house which is called by my name, and say, 'We are delivered to do all these abominations'? Has this house, which is called by my name, become a den of

thieves in your eyes? Behold, I, even I, have seen it," says the
LORD (Jeremiah 7:8-11).

They are accused of having turned the temple into a 'robbers' den', meaning
a refuge for thieves – a place where sinners gather to hide from their sin.
Their problem was that they were living in all manner of sinfulness and yet
as though their presence in the temple guaranteed God's favour. Jeremiah's
message is clear - they must repent! The Lord was making the same point.

Then the blind and the lame came to Jesus in the temple and he healed
them (Matthew 21:14). The chief priests (who mostly profited from the trade
in the temple) and scribes heard his words, saw his wonderful healing
miracles and heard the children crying out in the temple, 'Hosanna to the
Son of David!' and they were very annoyed.

When they expressed their anger to Jesus he simply said, 'Have you
never read, "Out of the mouth of babes and nursing infants you have
perfected praise"' (Matthew 21:16 quoting Psalm 8:2). The Jewish leaders
had murder in their hearts but they took no action against Jesus since all the
people had a high regard for him because of his healing miracles and
teaching. Jesus and the twelve left Jerusalem to spend another night in the
village of Bethany.

The following morning they set out once more for the temple. They
passed the fruitless fig tree which was then completely dead (Mark
11:20-26). The Lord told his companions that with faith they will be able to
perform similar miracles and even greater things, and also believing prayers
will be answered (Matthew 21:21-22). 'If you have faith and do not doubt'
you will 'say to this mountain, "Be removed and be cast into the sea,' it will
be done"' (cf. 1 Corinthians 13:2).

Jesus was using a hyperbole (an exaggerated statement not meant to be
taken literally) signifying the overcoming of difficulties, even great
difficulties. There is no Biblical evidence that any apostle ever moved a
mountain literally! Jesus was reassuring them that they would perform things
much more difficult and surprising than the withering of a fig tree in their
evangelistic and missionary endeavours to promote the glory of God and the
gospel - when they have faith and do not doubt!

95. The authority of Jesus
Matthew 21:23-27; Mark 11:27-33; Luke 20:1-8

Entering the temple the Lord engaged once more in teaching the people and
preaching the gospel (Luke 20:1). The chief priests, scribes and elders
challenged him about his authority. Jesus countered their question with a
question of his own.

When he challenged them as to the origin of the baptism of John, whether it was from heaven or from men, these Jewish leaders were caught in a dilemma. The people regarded John the Baptist as a prophet of God but their leaders did not. Fearing the reaction of the people, since they held John in such high regard, the leaders answered that they did not know. Jesus therefore refused to give an answer to their question.

There were really two questions that the antagonists posed: 'To what sort of power, right, and authority, human or divine, do you lay claim?' Then secondly, 'Who has given you authority, who has commissioned and qualified you to do these things, or who authenticates you in them?'

The evidence had been before their eyes for three years. Over and over again they had been confronted with the outstanding credentials of the Lord Jesus Christ as the Son of God and the promised Messiah. But they were spiritually blind. They were not willing to accept Jesus as the Christ of God. As the Lord indicated later -

> O Jerusalem, Jerusalem, the one who kills the prophets and stones those who are sent to her! How often I wanted to gather your children together, as a hen gathers her chicks under her wings, but you were not willing! (Matthew 23:37)

That was the key to the constant questioning of those Jewish leaders. The chief priests, the scribes, and the elders 'were not willing!' And that is the key to all unbelief as Jesus makes clear: 'If anyone wills to do his [the Father's] will, he shall know concerning the doctrine, whether it is from God or whether I speak on my own authority' (John 7:17).

Jesus was not evading the question posed by the Jewish leaders. If they would but answer his question concerning John the Baptist they would know the answer to their question concerning the Lord Jesus. Whilst John the Baptist was engaged in his baptising work he had declared Jesus to be his superior (John 1:26-27), as the Son of God (John 1:34) and 'the Lamb of God who takes away the sin of the world!' (John 1:29)

To accept that John's baptism was from heaven would be to acknowledge that his testimony concerning the Lord Jesus Christ was true. The authority of Christ is from heaven.

96. The parable of The Two Sons
Matthew 21:28-32

A parable was introduced by a question from Jesus, 'But what do you think?' (Matthew 21:28) The goal of the parable was to make people think. It freed the hearers from subjective prejudices and allowed them to objectively assess the situation and their own position. The Lord sought to show them the nature of their condition with the intention that they would rectify their mistakes and turn from their sin to the Saviour.

Instead of a frontal attack making the chief priests, scribes and elders even more hostile his whole approach was gentle and disarming. His speech was 'with grace, seasoned with salt' (Colossians 4:6). He knew how he ought to answer each one.

Two sons were introduced with no indication of the elder or the younger. The first son resisted the instruction of his father to work in the vineyard with a firm, 'I will not'. This son, rebellious at heart, had not learned to disguise his disobedience under smooth and deceitful words. Nor had he learned to answer his father in respectful terms. He spoke to his father in a rude and offensive manner. 'But afterward he regretted it and went' for hard hearted as he was a great change occurred. It is clear he repented because he went into the field and began to work for his father.

Wonderful hope was being extended to all those who have openly rebelled against the Lord. Open, rebellious sinners are invited to believe in the Lord and start afresh.

> Do you not know that the unrighteous will not inherit the kingdom of God? Do not be deceived. Neither fornicators, nor idolaters, nor adulterers, nor homosexuals, nor sodomites, nor thieves, nor covetous, nor drunkards, nor revilers, nor extortioners will inherit the kingdom of God. And such were some of you… (1 Corinthians 6:9-11).

But God be thanked and praised for all these people can cease being what they are. They can turn from their ways: ' "As I live," says the Lord GOD, "I have no pleasure in the death of the wicked, but that the wicked turn from his way and live. Turn, turn from your evil ways! For why should you die?" ' (Ezekiel 33:11) 'Let the wicked forsake his way, and the unrighteous man his thoughts; let him return to the LORD, and he will have mercy on him; and to our God, for he will abundantly pardon' (Isaiah 55:7). That is the gospel in the Old Testament, the gospel which Jesus emphasised and preached. 'There is joy in the presence of the angels of God over one sinner who repents' (Luke 15:10).

The second son was so different. He responded with respect willingly saying, 'I go, sir,' but he did not go. Did he tell a blatant lie? That seems to be the weight of the parable.

All who heard the parable instantly knew the answer to the Lord's question, 'Which of the two did the will of his father?' (Matthew 21:31; cf. 7:21) They would also easily identify themselves as Jesus drove home the message: The disreputable tax collectors who collaborated with the Roman overlords and prostitutes who sold themselves for money, these responded to the preaching of John the Baptist, repented and entered the kingdom of God.

Like the first son in the parable they had wilfully refused to obey God; they lived for years in a wicked and godless manner but there came a time when they regretted their attitude towards God and their way of life. They believed the gospel, repented and obeyed. Such people were entering the kingdom of God before chief priests, scribes and elders.

97. The parable of The Wicked Tenants
Matthew 21:33-46; Mark 12:1-11; Luke 20:9-18

The Lord, in this second parable, went further in exposing the hostility and antagonism of the Jewish leaders towards him. Most likely basing his story upon Isaiah 5:1-7 he spoke of a certain landowner who built a large vineyard which required many workers. He rented out the vinery to tenants and travelled to a distant country. When harvest came he sent a servant that he might receive some of the fruit. The servant was beaten and sent away empty-handed. He sent a second servant who was stoned, wounded in the head, shamefully treated and sent away. Many servants followed at intervals, some were beaten, some were killed. He then decided to send his beloved son saying, 'They will respect my son'. But the son was killed and his inheritance stolen by the wicked vinedressers.

By this story Jesus was showing: that the Jewish authorities were hostile towards him, the Son of God, and were therefore enemies of God himself; that Jesus was quite aware of his final bloody end at the hands of the Jewish leadership; and that God was about to take away all the privileges from the Jews and give them to others.

The landowner symbolises God, for 'the vineyard of the LORD of hosts is the house of Israel, and the men of Judah are his pleasant plant. He looked for justice, but behold, oppression; for righteousness, but behold, a cry for help' (Isaiah 5:7; cf. Psalm 80:8-11). God entrusted the worship and spiritual wellbeing of the nation to a high priest with the help of priests and Levites. He favoured the nation, hedging them about; for God separated them from the world, providing for their every need, and guarding them from every oppressor. They were provided with many privileges -

> who are Israelites, to whom pertain the adoption, the glory, the covenants, the giving of the law, the service of God, and the promises; of whom are the fathers and from whom, according to the flesh, Christ came, who is over all, the eternally blessed God. Amen (Romans 9:4-5).

Yet the leaders and people were for the most part spiritually unfruitful, neither worshipping nor serving with sincerity of heart nor obedience of life. The servants of the Lord who were periodically sent to them were treated deplorably by men in office who were interested only in their own power, praise and purse without the fear of God in their hearts and minds (e.g. 1 Kings 19:10; Jeremiah 44:4; Nehemiah 9:26; Hebrews 11:32-34, 36-38).

The parable was in the nature of a warning. If the enemies of Jesus go ahead with their murderous plans there will be dreadful consequences falling upon them and their nation.

Jesus quoted the Scriptures to show that he was the stone rejected by their builders which had become the chief cornerstone (Matthew 21:42 quoting Psalm 118:22-23). In every stone building one stone was indispensable. It was the rock to ensure that the building was square and stable. Isaiah 28:16 describes this same 'precious cornerstone' as 'a sure foundation' and 'a tried stone'.

Without quoting precisely, Jesus continued by making an allusion to another Old Testament Scripture which declared that God 'will be as a sanctuary, but a stone of stumbling and a rock of offence to both the houses of Israel, as a trap and a snare to the inhabitants of Jerusalem. And many among them shall stumble; they shall fall and be broken, be snared and taken' (Isaiah 8:14-15; cf. (Luke 20:18).

The Lord Jesus was set for the division of all people - those who believe in him and enjoy his eternal salvation and those who do not believe but are disobedient and will receive eternal rejection. The apostle Peter united the Old Testament Scriptures prophesying about the cornerstone to highlight the preciousness of the Lord Jesus Christ and the futility of unbelief (1 Peter 2:6-8).

The chief priests, scribes and elders understood the point of the parable and his words of warning, yet rather than repenting and welcoming their Messiah, they became even more hostile towards Jesus.

98. The parable of The Wedding Guests
Matthew 22:2-14

'And Jesus answered' - though no question had been asked, he was responding to the situation in the temple where the officials before him were full of hostility and hatred (Matthew 21:45-46). This parable displays the generosity of God over all creation. He had graciously invited guests (the Jews) to the wedding (the enjoyment of a close and perpetual relationship) of his Son (Jesus). Most of them, particularly their leadership, were 'not willing to come' (Matthew 22:3).

When preparations for the wedding had been made and celebrations could begin, a further request was sent out to the invited guests. They treated the royal invitation with indifference: some continuing with their farm-work, others with their business, and the rest turning in violence upon the messengers and murdering them. Can anything be imagined which was more offensive than receiving such a wonderful invitation to be the wedding guest of royalty and reacting as these folk did? When the King heard he was extremely angry and sent his soldiers to destroy the murderers and their city.

With the wedding preparation all but complete, the King issued a wide invitation to all and sundry and the wedding hall was filled. When the King came in he noticed a man present who did not have the appropriate clothing for the wedding. When asked how he gained access in that condition he was speechless. The King ordered his immediate removal and punishment.

In many ways the message of this parable bears similarities with the parable of The Wicked Tenants. This time however the emphasis is placed upon the graciousness and generosity of God constantly issuing one invitation after another for sinners to be reconciled to him through sincere whole-hearted repentance and the obedience of faith (Isaiah 55:1,6-7; Psalm 32:1-6; Jeremiah 29:11-13; Ezekiel 33:11). There was also the implied invitation and welcome to tax collectors and sinners (Matthew 22:9-10).

A new note was however struck on the necessity for the appropriate wedding garment. When challenged this man was rendered speechless. He had no excuse for when a wealthy king sent out invitations to a wedding he knew that his guests would not be able to afford the appropriate clothing for such a royal occasion so he would send each guest a special free gift, a fine expensive wedding garment. This man was pouring contempt on the gift and on the giver by considering that his own clothes were sufficiently good in which to appear before the king.

The wedding garment represents the spiritual renewal which comes through salvation. By nature 'we are all like an unclean thing, and all our righteousnesses are like filthy rags' by grace we can testify -

> I will greatly rejoice in the LORD, my soul shall be joyful in my God; for he has clothed me with the garments of salvation, he has covered me with the robe of righteousness (Isaiah 64:6; 61:10; Jeremiah 23:6; Galatians 3:27; Revelation 19:6-8).

Jesus concluded the parable by saying, 'For many are called, but few are chosen' (Matthew 22:14). Many people hear the truth about Jesus. Many hear the Gospel yet do not believe and obey. Some believe and are saved, they are those chosen by God in Christ Jesus 'before the foundation of the world, that [they] should be holy and without blame before him in love' (Ephesians 1:4).

99. Paying Taxes to Caesar
Matthew 22:15-22; Mark 12:13-17; Luke 20:20-26

Pharisees collaborated once more with their old enemies the Herodians in seeking the destruction of Jesus (cf. Mark 3:6). They sent some of their disciples, most probably young Pharisees who would be unknown to Jesus and intending to pass themselves off as genuine enquirers.

The Herodians were intent on creating favourable relations with Rome so that Herod could regain rule. They preferred rule by Herod under Caesar rather than Caesar's direct rule through a procurator such as Pontius Pilate. They were in favour of paying taxes to Caesar. The Pharisees, by contrast, were constantly demanding independence from Rome and full autonomy for the Jews. They therefore objected to paying tax to Caesar.

'Pretending to be righteous' (Luke 20:20), that is, giving the appearance of being pious and upright, the conspirators sought to outwit the Lord to gain incriminating evidence which could be presented to the Sanhedrin (Jewish council) or to the Romans so that he might be put to death. Addressing the Lord with flattering remarks they sought to trap him in his words.

Raising the vexed question of Roman taxation, they thought they had him cornered for no matter what he answered he would be discredited - or so they presumed. If he supported paying taxes to Caesar he would lose favour with the people. If he was against paying taxes to Caesar he would fall foul of the Roman authorities. But Jesus perceived their wickedness, and said, 'Why do you test me, you hypocrites? Show me the tax money' (Matthew 22:18-19).

With his consummate skill he took a coin and asked whose image and inscription it bore. When they replied, 'Caesar's' Jesus resolved the quandary by saying, 'Render therefore to Caesar the things that are Caesar's, and to God the things that are God's' (Luke 20:25). The answer was amazingly simple and yet wonderfully profound. It was not a deviation or avoidance but a plain, well thought out and lucidly presented solution. It would seem that these antagonists were actually astonished and impressed by his answer.

Followers of Jesus are taught to respect and obey civil authorities (Romans 13:1-7; 1 Peter 2:13-17; Titus 3:1). It is only when there is conflict between the civil demands and God's instructions that civil disobedience is required (Acts 4:18-20). Whatever the state requires, whatever the church requires, the authority of God is supreme and never to be violated. When conflict arises we must obey God rather than men.

100. Sadducees and the Resurrection
Matthew 22:23-33; Mark 12:18-27; Luke 20:27-39

Sadducees were the next to try to humiliate Jesus. They were of the Jewish party which did not believe in the resurrection, nor did they accept the books of the Old Testament beyond the five books of Moses. They posed a question about marriage, based on Scripture, which seemed to make the notion of resurrection look utterly foolish. They quoted Moses (Deuteronomy 25:5) with the expressed intention of demonstrating that Moses had no thought of any 'resurrection'. They implied that the law concerning levirate marriage could not have been enacted if resurrection were a reality. They presented an example: seven brothers married one woman, according to the law of Moses, 'therefore, in the resurrection, whose wife of the seven will she be? For they all had her' (Matthew 22:28).

Jesus presented a clear and simple response. Firstly he said there was no relationship of marriage after the resurrection and secondly Moses himself recorded an event which proved life after death. In recording the incident of the burning bush, Moses called the Lord 'the God of Abraham, the God of Isaac, and the God of Jacob.' Jesus pointed out the significance, 'For he is not the God of the dead but of the living, for all live to him' (Luke 20:38; cf. Exodus 3:6).

Like so many the Sadducees did 'not know the Scriptures nor the power of God' (Mark 12:24). All error in doctrine (teaching) or practice (behaviour) from the days of Moses to our own day is based upon ignorance of the Scriptures or ignorance of the power of God or a combination of both. The Sadducees only accepted the first five books of the Old Testament consequently they refused the further clear and conclusive evidence for the resurrection found in the later God-given Scriptures (Job 19:25-27; Psalm 16:9-11; 17:15; Isaiah 25:8; Daniel 12:2; Hosea 13:14). That was why the Lord only quoted to them from one of the five books of Moses.

101. The first and great commandment
Matthew 22:34-40; Mark 12:28-34

One of the scribes, seemingly impressed by the Lord's answer to the Sadducees, asked Jesus which was the most important commandment of God. The Pharisees taught that Moses had listed 613 commands: 365 negative ('You shall not...') and 248 positive ('You shall...'). There was constant debate among them as to the ranking of the commandments, the most important to the least important. Jesus quoted from Deuteronomy -

> Hear, O Israel, the LORD our God, the LORD is one. And you shall love the LORD your God with all your heart, with all your soul, with all your mind, and with all your strength (Deuteronomy 6:4).

The Pharisees were very much aware of these words. In the original Hebrew, the first word of this quotation is '*Shema*' meaning, 'Hear'. The entire quotation is generally called 'the Shema'. Services in the synagogue, even in our own day, begin with the recitation of the Shema. In its longer form (Deuteronomy 6:4-9; 11:13-21) it is contained within Jewish phylacteries (small leather cases or boxes, one strapped to the forehead the other to the left arm near the heart when praying). The longer version of the Shema is also contained in the *Mezuzah,* which is a rectangular piece of inscribed parchment enclosed in a metal or wooden case and attached to the upper section of the right hand door post of a Jewish home (Deuteronomy 6:1-9).

Jesus began his answer with the fundamental requirement of God from his people. God *wills* to be loved. He is not content to be obeyed, worshipped, feared or admired, but *wills* to be loved. God is to be loved with the whole of our being, with our thoughts, words, deeds, with the emotions, with the intellect, with every disposition and attitude. The one and only God requires each person to love him wholly! God is to be loved to the full extend of our capacity. His wholehearted love must meet with the ready response of our wholehearted love. We are to reflect back his love, for 'God is love' (1 John 4:8,16).

After repeating and agreeing with the Lord's full answer, the scribe added, that this 'is more than all the whole burnt offerings and sacrifices' (Mark 12:33). By this he proved the depth of his understanding that the moral law of love to God and love to neighbour is far more important than a ceremonial law or ritual requirement.

This perception shown by the scribe brought encouragement from Jesus who said to him, 'You are not far from the kingdom of God' (Mark 12:34). It is as though the Lord said to him, 'Good, you have thought the issues through carefully and arrived at a true and right understanding. But there is still something missing. You are close to the kingdom of God but you have not yet entered in.' What was still lacking?

When, almost three years before, Jesus had begun his great Galilean ministry preaching the gospel of the kingdom of God he had said, 'The time is fulfilled, and the kingdom of God is at hand. Repent, and believe in the gospel' (Mark 1:15). The kingdom of God was at hand, was near. This scribe was near to the kingdom of God.

He had understood the necessities of a right love for God and a right love for neighbour. He saw that love was far more important than rituals or ceremonies (as in Micah 6:6-8). Were the scribe to make a real and honest attempt to love God as God required he would soon come up against a problem - his weakness and inability! His cry would often be, 'I know what is right. I know what I should do but I cannot do it (cf. Romans 7:19). I cannot love God with all my heart, with all my soul, with all my mind, and with all my strength. I cannot love my neighbour as myself. God, help me. Please forgive my failure. Please forgive my sin. Please enable me love as I ought to love.'

In other words, the man would see *the necessity for conversion on the one hand and the necessity for Christ on the other*. He must come to know and understand that he needs a Saviour.

God has demonstrated his love in creating us and loving us from the beginning. Because 'all have sinned and fall short of the glory of God' (Romans 3:23) the love of God has been further -

> manifested toward us, that God has sent his only begotten Son into the world, that we might live through him. In this is love, not that we loved God, but that he loved us and sent his Son to be the propitiation [the self-sacrifice which brings us into the full favour of God] for our sins (1 John 4:9-10).

'We love him because he first loved us' (1 John 4:19). Once saved 'the love of God' is 'poured out in our hearts by the Holy Spirit who was given to us' (Romans 5:5). We love God for who he is, what he is and what he has done, is doing and is yet to do. The Lord Jesus enables us to fulfil the greatest commandment.

102. David's Son: David's Lord
Matthew 22:41-46; Mark 12:35-37; Luke 20:40-44

Jesus took the opportunity to raise a most important subject with the Pharisees on what was to prove to be the last occasion for public discussion with them. He chose an apparent quandary in Scripture and used it as the highpoint of his self-disclosure; the humanity and deity of the promised Messiah. He began with a simple straightforward question, 'What do you think about the Christ? Whose Son is he?' (Matthew 22:42) Without hesitation they answered, 'He is the Son of David'. Jesus responded by quoting Psalm 110:1 and asking, 'If David then calls him "Lord," how is he his Son?' (Matthew 22:45) The Pharisees were silenced.

Here Jesus clearly demonstrated the divinity of the Messiah. If the Messiah (Christ) was to be only a man who would come into existence years after David's death how then could his ancestor call him Lord? The Pharisees could not answer, for no answer was to be found except to acknowledge that Messiah is the Son of God (Psalm 2:7) already existing in the days of David.

He became what he had not been when he took upon himself our human nature and as 'Immanuel - God with us' (Matthew 1:23) came and 'dwelt among us... full of grace and truth' (John 1:14). He is truly and wonderfully, the Son of God and the Son of David, Son of God, Son of Man.

No wonder 'the common people heard him gladly' (Mark 12:37) for he explained the Scriptures with such clarity and simplicity and 'no one was able to answer him a word, nor from that day on did anyone dare question him anymore' (Matthew 22:46).

103. Scribes and Pharisees rebuked
Matthew 23:1-39; Mark 12:38-40; Luke 20:45-47

Jesus continued to address the multitude and his disciples (Matthew 23:1). The Pharisees were still present, from Matthew 23:13 onwards he spoke to them directly with the eight 'woes' highlighting, with great sorrow and distress, their hypocrisy.

The scribes were also Pharisees (not all Pharisees were scribes), they were the professional students and teachers of the Old Testament and hence a distinct class. The rest of the Pharisees accepted the teaching of their scribes and made great effort to translate their teaching into instruction for the common people. In this sense they 'sit in Moses' seat' (Matthew 23:2). When the scribes and Pharisees accurately interpreted the teaching of Moses they were to be obeyed (Matthew 23:3). However, their hypocrisy hindered the work of God. The Lord made general criticism of them before declaring eight woes.

They lacked sincerity, 'for they say and do not do' (Matthew 23:3). They read the Old Testament gospel invitations without being moved with a heart response themselves. They would no doubt read passages such as -

> 'Come now, and let us reason together,' says the LORD, 'though your sins are like scarlet, they shall be as white as snow; though they are red like crimson, they shall be as wool. If you are willing and obedient, you shall eat the good of the land; but if you refuse and rebel, you shall be devoured by the sword' for the mouth of the LORD has spoken (Isaiah 1:18-20).

Or -

> Seek the LORD while he may be found, call upon him while he is near. Let the wicked forsake his way, and the unrighteous man his thoughts; let him return to the LORD, and he will have mercy on him; and to our God, for he will abundantly pardon (Isaiah 55:6-7).

These verses and many more would be read by them and taught by them but they had no personal experience of them in their heart.

They lacked sympathy, 'for they bind heavy burdens, hard to bear, and lay them on men's shoulders; but they themselves will not move them with one of their fingers' (Matthew 23:4). These 'heavy burdens' were often regarded as the Pharisaic traditions. But that cannot be so because the Pharisees themselves did try to carry those traditions. The burdens which Jesus had in mind were not lifted by the Pharisees, they did not move so much as a little finger. Their guilt is that they taught the law of Moses and their under-standing of how that law should be kept but they did not teach forgiveness and restoration. They did not point people to the way of hope, and mercy, pardon and peace with God.

> They turned everything they read from the Old Testament into law only… Blind to the gospel in the Scripture, they knew nothing but law, and this law they perverted for self-righteous purposes.[70]

They lacked humility, 'all their works they do to be seen by men' (Matthew 23:5). They drew attention to themselves: They made their phylacteries broad (their understanding of Deuteronomy 6:8) and enlarged the borders of their garments (their understanding of Deuteronomy 22:12). They made these articles very conspicuous to draw attention to their piety. They loved the best places at feasts, the best seats in the synagogues, greetings in the marketplaces, and to be called 'Rabbi, Rabbi'.

Why did Jesus issue these rebukes? There are three probable reasons: (i) because he was deeply grieved by the unbelief of so many of the scribes and Pharisees. He had given them abundant evidence in his life and teaching to prove himself beyond doubt to be the Messiah of God. Those who knew the Old Testament Scriptures as these men did ought to have recognised him easily; (ii) because he knew what influence and control these men exercised over ordinary people. It was necessary to expose these hypocrites for what they were so that the people could be warned and released from this cruel and oppressive religious rule; and (iii) because it was to be his final public address and therefore he took this last opportunity to warn the people against

---

[70] Richard C.H. Lenski, *The Interpretation of St. Matthew's Gospel* (Minneapolis, Minnesota: Augsburg, 1964), p.896.

these enemies of the truth, enemies of the gospel, and therefore enemies of God.

Hypocrites are not good people who are failing in their personal endeavours; they are not genuine people who occasionally live inconsistently in matters of life and faith; nor are they weak people who are struggling to do right. Hypocrites are deceivers, play actors, pretenders. There is an incongruence, a serious lack of agreement, between what they think and what they say or do. The people and the Lord's disciples were warned not to behave like they did. Hypocrisy is a grievous witness and turns people away from seeking God. No preacher/teacher is perfect. There are times in every leader's life when his works do not match his words, when his lip and life are in contradiction. However the criticism levelled at the scribes and Pharisees should never be applicable to a Christian leader.

The eight 'woes' are a blending of severity and compassion and form the highpoint and culmination of the Lord's appeal to the nation of Israel.

> This most eloquent, most appalling, and most terrible of all discourses ever delivered to mortals was pronounced in the temple, in the presence of multitudes. Never was there more faithful dealing, more terrible reproof, more profound knowledge of the workings of hypocrisy, or more skill in detecting the concealments of sin. This was the last of his public discourses; and it is a most impressive summary of all he ever had said, or had to say, of a wicked and hypocritical generation.[71]

The first grievous charge of hypocrisy (Matthew 23:13) levelled against scribes and Pharisees was the way in which they hindered people from entering the kingdom of heaven. They did not enter themselves and they prevented those who were taking steps to enter. They exerted a sinister influence on others. The parents of the man born blind were frightened to answer questions because the Jewish leadership 'had agreed already that if anyone confessed that he was Christ, he would be put out of the synagogue' (John 9:22; cf. 7:13; 19:38). In our own day many are hindered from believing in the Lord Jesus by those who claim to be Christians and use the media to give 'Christian' comment but whose lives and words are worldly and have nothing to commend them.

The second woe addressed blatant dishonesty. By one means or another there was corruption, they 'devour widows' houses and for a pretence make long prayers' (Matthew 23:14). Their prayers were deceitful. They were frauds, wolves in sheep's clothing. Under a cloak of piety some influenced

---

[71] Albert Barnes, *Notes, Explanatory and Practical on the Gospels: Matthew and Mark* (London: Routledge, 1832), p.282.

wealthy widows with the idea that to financially support a scribe or Pharisee was the best use of wealth. Others because of their training and skill in law might impose unjust claims against wealthy widows or encourage them to entrust their financial affairs into their hands and thus facilitate embezzlement. Others pretended that the finance received from the widows would pay for them to pray long for their benefactors. In our own day there is a plethora of TV evangelists who grow exceedingly rich on the gifts of those who seek their prayers for healing and a variety of blessings.

The third criticism (Matthew 23:15) was aimed at their missionary zeal. Jesus rebuked his opponents because they did more harm than good to those whom they won over from heathendom. At that point in time the Jews were engaged in remarkable missionary activity. In spite of the picture presented by the book of Jonah there were Israelites who were enthusiastic and dedicated in reaching out to the nations outside Judaism. Sadly they were promoting a false religion, a salvation dependent upon works of the law. The Lord's condemnation is fierce, 'you make him twice as much a son of hell as yourselves' (Matthew 23:15).

In the fourth rebuke (Matthew 23:16) Jesus showed how their logic regarding oaths was absurd. In the Sermon on the Mount the Lord made his teaching on oath taking abundantly clear - 'Let your "Yes" be "Yes," and your "No," "No." For whatever is more than these is from the evil one' (Matthew 5:33-37; cf. James 5:12).

The fifth sharp disapproval (Matthew 23:23) exposed the way in which the scribes and Pharisees paid extreme attention to less significant issues and ignored important ones. They were scrupulous when it came to matters of tithing. They went so far as to tithe their herb gardens. They were always illegitimately over-extending the law. They did the same when it came to fasting, hand-washing, Sabbath observance and a whole host of other requirements whilst being negligent in the far more serious matters of justice, mercy and faith (cf. Micah 6:8).

There is much teaching in the Old Testament Scriptures to support the Lord's sixth denunciation (Matthew 23:25) for their obsession with external appearance and failure to deal with the heart. The analogy of cleansing the outside of a cup and dish whilst their insides were 'full of extortion and self-indulgence' suggested gain by dishonest means and over-indulgence in food and drink. They appear to be good holy men yet within there was unconfessed sin. Had they not read what the Lord said to Samuel: 'For the LORD does not see as man sees; for man looks at the outward appearance, but the LORD looks at the heart' (1 Samuel 16:7).

They were without excuse for Isaiah had declared, 'we are all like an unclean thing, and all our righteousnesses are like filthy rags' (Isaiah 64:6). Through Jeremiah God had said -

> The heart is deceitful above all things, and desperately wicked; who can know it? I, the LORD, search the heart, I test the mind, even to give every man according to his ways, according to the fruit of his doings (Jeremiah 17:9-10).

The scribes and Pharisees seem totally oblivious of such teachings in the Scriptures that they read, studied and taught. Jesus told them to cleanse the inside, that is, to purity the heart, then the outward life will be transformed from within (cf. Mark 7:21-23).

The seventh sad rebuke highlighted the hidden sins within (Matthew 23:27), similar to the last but even more serious. The thought was intensified to the utmost degree. There they were accused of 'extortion and self-indulgence' due to blindness. Here they were convicted of hypocrisy of the worst order, they were 'like whitewashed tombs' full of all uncleanness, affected piety and lawlessness. Jesus was skilfully using a current event as a metaphor.

A few weeks earlier (at the beginning of March) there had been the annual repainting of family tombstones with a fresh coat of a whitewash made of lime. The purpose was not to make the tombs more attractive but to make them highly visible as a warning, for contact with a grave resulted in defilement for seven days (Numbers 19:16). Appearing righteous and godly, in an outward show of shallow piety and feigned holiness, the hearts of these scribes and Pharisees were full of hypocrisy, lawlessness and iniquity. The human heart can be a temple of the living God or a hiding place (den) for the worst kind of evil and corruption. There was no more horrible and yet more appropriate analogy to depict the huge disparity between the outside and the inside of these hypocrites.

In the eighth and last 'woe' (Matthew 23:29) Jesus charged the scribes and Pharisees with duplicity for they honour the prophets of old and criticise their persecutors yet they were perpetuating the very same evil against New Testament prophets, wisemen and scribes. The sad fact was that they were sons of those who murdered the prophets for they had inherited the same spirit, mind, attitude and behaviour; they were just like them.

At times the words of Jesus sound extremely severe, 'Serpents, brood of vipers! How can you escape the condemnation of hell?' (Matthew 23:33); yet judgment revealed beforehand is a gracious act of mercy. There is still time to repent and plead for the forgiveness of the living God.

Their sin was all the worse since they were teachers. Years later James, the half-brother of Jesus, warned men of the New Testament -

> My brethren, let not many of you become teachers, knowing that we shall receive a stricter judgment. For we all stumble in many things. If anyone does not stumble in word, he is a perfect man, able also to bridle the whole body (James 3:1-2).

God be praised there was a way to 'escape the condemnation of hell' for these men and for others even at this late point in time. The Father had sent his Son into the world, 'that whoever believes in him should not perish but have everlasting life' (John 3:16). Among the Pharisees there was a Nicodemus (John 3:1;19:39), a Joseph of Arimathea (Luke 23:50), and 'even among the rulers many believed in him, but because of the Pharisees they did not confess him, lest they should be put out of the synagogue; for they loved the praise of men more than the praise of God' (John 12:42-43).

After the sad and severe rebuking of the scribes and Pharisees (Matthew 23:1-36) the Lord's tone changed markedly with a cry of anguish and disappointment over Jerusalem -

> O Jerusalem, Jerusalem, the one who kills the prophets and stones those who are sent to her! How often I wanted to gather your children together, as a hen gathers her chicks under her wings, but you were not willing! (Matthew 23:37)

This lamentation had been heard before, a few months earlier, during his Peraean ministry (Luke 13:34). It was no doubt also on his mind during the triumphal entry when he drew near the city 'and wept over it' (Luke 19:41). This is no hard-hearted despot, he is a gracious tender-hearted Sovereign.

Compassion, infinite pity, flowed from his heart as he pronounced the rebukes and subsequent punishment of the scribes and Pharisees. This combination of overwhelming compassion and stern warning was seen in Jeremiah who was well-known as 'the weeping prophet'. God will judge all but he derives no satisfaction in punishing those who are unrepentant and unbelieving.

> "As I live," says the Lord GOD, "I have no pleasure in the death of the wicked, but that the wicked turn from his way and live. Turn, turn from your evil ways! For why should you die, O house of Israel?" (Ezekiel 33:11)

Here is a love so amazing and so divine towards an ungrateful, unbelieving and impenitent nation. With great grief in his heart Jesus warned leaders and people of the punishment they were bringing upon themselves. He might well have quoted the Book of Proverbs, 'He who sins against me wrongs his own soul; all those who hate me love death' (Proverbs 8:36). Their leadership will end; their nation will fall. Jesus will leave the world, they will not see him again until he returns and they say, 'Blessed is he who comes in the name of the LORD!' (Matthew 23:39)

104. The widow's mites
Mark 12:41-44; Luke 21:1-4

The Lord having concluded his discourse with the scribes and Pharisees did not immediately leave the temple. He sat down quietly and observed the people. It was as though he was giving yet a final opportunity for the accused leaders to speak out in their own defence or for them to turn, even now, and ask if there is any way of repentance for them. He sat opposite the treasury watching.

Jesus drew the attention of his disciples to one particular gift, two of the smallest coins in circulation being deposited in one of the thirteen boxes fixed to the pillars of the portico which surrounded the court of the women. The donor was a poor widow.

There were two words for poor in the language of the New Testament. One for those managing to make a living with difficulty and one for those who were bereft of any income or means. This widow fell into the second category. What a contrast between the selfless devotion of this widow and the corruption and greed of the scribes and Pharisees and the greed and extortion practiced in that very court by animal traders and money changers. With singleness of purpose and action she brought the two tiny symbols of her enormous devotion. Her coins would not be visible to the natural eye but Jesus knew her, he knew her circumstances, he knew her gift and he knew her heart (Hebrews 4:12-13; Psalm 139:1-3).

God does not measure the gifts and giving of his people by earthly standards. He does not measure the value in isolation but in relation to the heart and personal circumstances of the giver. The poor may consider their giving to be of little or no value, while the rich may think they have contributed greatly, though it has made little impact upon their remaining assets. This beautiful incident, so timely in the ministry of Jesus, corrected both views. A little given where only a little remains is of greater value in the sight of God than much larger sums which still leave an abundance.

Was this widow actively trusting herself and her future to God? Did many Old Testament Scriptures encourage her confidence? For example: 'The LORD... relieves the fatherless and widow' (Psalm 146:9) and David's testimony, 'I have been young, and now am old; yet I have not seen the righteous forsaken, nor his descendants begging bread' (Psalm 37:25). Was the truth of Paul's words to the Philippians sealed upon this saint's heart even before they were penned? - the assurance that her two coins were 'a sweet-smelling aroma, an acceptable sacrifice, well pleasing to God', and that God would supply all her need 'according to his riches in glory by Christ Jesus' (Philippians 4:18,19).

105. Greeks request to meet Jesus
John 12:20-50

Some Greeks who worshipped the God of the Jews, who is the true God (Acts 10:2; 13:43; 17:4), and who were attending the Feast of the Passover requested an audience with Jesus. They had an earnest and sincere desire to meet the Lord. These men from the West represented at the end of Christ's life what the wise men from the East represented at its beginning; Gentiles coming to the Messiah King. God said in prophecy to his Son -

> It is too small a thing that you should be my Servant to raise up the tribes of Jacob, and to restore the preserved ones of Israel; I will also give you as a light to the Gentiles, that you should be my salvation to the ends of the earth (Isaiah 49:6: cf. Psalm 2:8).

Old Testament prophecy was again being fulfilled with the small beginning of a mass movement from the nations of the earth coming to the Christ of God.

These Greeks in the temple were among the worshippers that the Lord was so concerned for when he drove out the traders and money-changers from the temple and stopped the carrying of goods saying, 'Is it not written, "My house shall be called a house of prayer for all nations"?' (Mark 11:17) A thousand years earlier King Solomon had prayed at the dedication of the first temple -

> Moreover, concerning a foreigner, who is not of your people Israel, but has come from a far country for your name's sake (for they will hear of your great name and your strong hand and your outstretched arm), when he comes and prays toward this temple, hear in heaven your dwelling place, and do according to all for which the foreigner calls to you, that all peoples of the earth may know your name and fear you, as do your people Israel, and that they may know that this temple which I have built is called by your name (1 Kings 8:41-43).

These Greeks had access to the temple but were restricted to the Court of the Gentiles because they had not converted to Judaism and accepted the requirements of the law of Moses. They were uncircumcised Gentiles but they were not idolatrous pagans! They had recognised the One true God, the

God of Israel. They approached Philip with the request that they might meet Jesus.

Philip went to find Andrew. He was probably hesitant to go alone directly to Jesus because he knew the Lord was committed first to 'the house of Israel' (Matthew 15:24). When Philip and Andrew informed the Lord he answered, 'The hour has come that the Son of Man should be glorified' (John 12:23; cf. 2:4; 7:30; 8:20; 12:27; 13:1; 17:1). It was the time for the Saviour to die (John 12:24). This was the purpose for which he came.

In the final public declaration of his impending death Jesus used the analogy of a grain of wheat which 'dies' to produce 'much grain'. The warmth, graciousness and earnestness of his appeal cannot go unnoticed (John 12:23-33). Less than a week remained before his execution at Calvary. He was to be the Seed (cf. Genesis 3:15) dying to give his life in order to produce much fruit. He was to die in order to bring forth a vast harvest of saved humanity (Revelation 7:9).

In the process he demonstrated outstanding self-denial and self-sacrifice. All who become his disciples must be ready and willing to follow his example and the Father will honour them.

Jesus was painfully aware of the demanding prospect before him. He was troubled in spirit but would not ask the Father to deliver him from all that was involved, for this was the ultimate reason for his coming into the world. When Jesus prayed, 'Father, glorify your name,' the Father was heard to reply, 'I have both glorified it and will glorify it again' (John 12:28).[72]

The judgment of the world had come (John 12:31). All the powers of evil were still attacking the Son of God. From his birth Satan like 'a great, fiery red dragon' had been seeking to devour him (Revelation 12:3-5). The pressure was about to intensify: Judas was to betray Jesus with a kiss; Pilate was to sentence Jesus in a phenomenal travesty of justice; the Son of God was to be unjustly scourged, and the soldiers who crucified him would mock him. The fate of the world would be sealed. In casting out the Lord Jesus, rejecting him and crucifying him, the world itself was judged and condemned. Consequently the Lord God would save people out of the world and from the world.

The tense of the verb 'will be cast out' is the same as in the following verse, 'will draw all to myself.' 'The tense of the verb here denotes that the 'casting out' of Satan would be as gradual as the 'drawing' in the next

---

[72] Three times a voice was heard from heaven during the Lord's ministry: at the beginning during his baptism; in the middle during his transfiguration and then at the end in the temple just a few days before his death (Matthew 3:17; 17:5; John 12:28).

verse.'[73] The Lord here anticipated his victory and pointed to the way in which it would be accomplished. No one would have ever dreamed of this way of fulfilling Messiah's mission. It would look as though Satan had won the victory when Jesus was put to death, yet by a momentous miracle God raised him up, 'having loosed the pains of death, because it was not possible that he should be held by it' (Acts 2:24).

The 'Seed' would die and the fruit would be immeasurable. The crucified Saviour will be the glorified Saviour. 'Having disarmed principalities and powers, he made a public spectacle of them, triumphing over them in it' (Colossians 2:15; cf. Hebrews 2: 14-15). The ruler of this world has been cast out (Revelation 12:10). One day he will be cast into 'the bottomless pit' and 'into the lake of fire and brimstone' (Revelation 20:3,10).

After the crucifixion of Jesus there was to be a great awakening, multitudes would turn away from the power of Satan and become devoted followers of Christ (e.g. Romans 6:17-18). They would hear his voice and follow him. This great Shepherd knows his sheep, loves them and lays down his life for them. He came for his sheep that were in Israel, and other sheep that are not of that fold. They must hear his voice too, and there will be one flock and one Shepherd (John 10:14-16).

The final words of Jesus in the temple were, 'While you have the light, believe in the light, that you may become sons of light' (John 12:36; cf. 3:19-21; Ephesians 5:8-10). Then he left the temple.

So much preaching and teaching had been given to the Jews by the great Teacher over his three years or so of ministry and although he had performed many miraculous signs in public view the vast majority did not believe in him; just as the prophet Isaiah predicted (John 12:37-38; Isaiah 53:1; 6:10). The second quotation John used (12:40) was taken from the vision of Isaiah in which the prophet testified -

> Woe is me, for I am undone! Because I am a man of unclean lips,
> and I dwell in the midst of a people of unclean lips; for my eyes
> have seen the King, the LORD of hosts (Isaiah 6:5).

He saw a vision of God, Yahweh of hosts. The apostle John added the staggering interpretation when he wrote: 'These things Isaiah said when he saw his glory and spoke of him' (John 12:41). The apostle John is pointing out that the prophet Isaiah actually saw a vision of the Son of God who is now Jesus the Christ (see also John 1:18). What a testimony to the deity of the Son of God!

---

[73] Alford cited by Arthur W. Pink, *Expositions of the Gospel of John: three volumes unabridged in one* (Grand Rapids, Michigan: Zondervan, 1970), vol. 2, p.273.

What the prophecy of Isaiah 6:10 had predicted that God would do, the apostle John stated that God had now done -

> He has blinded their eyes and hardened their hearts, lest they should see with their eyes, lest they should understand with their hearts and turn, so that I should heal them (John 12:40).

These form some of the most solemn words in the whole of the Scriptures! John did not include in this quotation any reference to their ears and hearing for he was showing the reason for their blindness in the face of numerous miracles performed by Jesus which proved indisputably that he was the Messiah of God (Acts 2:22; Hebrews 2:4).

The miracles that Jesus performed were many and varied. He gave sight to the blind, he gave hearing to the deaf, he healed the lame, he cured the leper, he restored withered limbs, he healed the paralysed, he drove out evil spirits, he controlled the winds, he walked on water, he turned gallons of water into best quality wine, he raised the dead: the twelve year old daughter of Jairus; the son of the widow of Nairn; and Lazarus, the brother of Mary and Martha.

Never did a man perform such miracles. Even the prophets of old, Moses, Joshua, Elijah or Elisha, never performed the number or the variety of miracles that Jesus performed.

God had now stopped the majority of the Jews from seeing the true significance behind the Messianic miracles, wonders and signs. For three years Jesus had preached the gospel and healed thousands of sick people, for 'God anointed Jesus of Nazareth with the Holy Spirit and with power, who went about doing good and healing all who were oppressed by the devil, for God was with him' (Acts 10:38).

They had hardened their hearts in the face of overwhelming evidence time and time again, now God had hardened their hearts. Just as in Egypt 1500 years earlier when Pharaoh repeatedly hardened his heart after each of the first five plagues, following the sixth plague it is recorded, 'the LORD hardened the heart of Pharaoh' (Exodus 9:12).

Jesus had preached about the love of God (e.g. John 3:16) and issued the warmest invitations: 'Come to me, all you who labour and are heavy laden, and I will give you rest' (Matthew 11:28); 'If anyone thirsts, let him come to me and drink. He who believes in me, as the Scripture has said, out of his heart will flow rivers of living water' (John 7:37-38; cf. 3:36; 6:35,47; 11:25). He often warned of the judgment of God, 'If you do not believe that I am he, you will die in your sins' (John 8:24; cf. Matthew 11:20; Mark 1:15; Luke 13:3). But the majority remained unmoved. The dreadful consequences of hardening the heart against the gracious invitations and severe warnings are clearly described by John.

There were those of the Jewish leadership who believed in Jesus (John 12:42), but through fear of being debarred from the synagogue they did not openly confess him. Joseph of Arimathea was one evidently in this position and probably also Nicodemus (John 19:38-39).

In the verses which follow (John 12:44-50) the Lord summarised his teaching ministry. This should have brought from the Jews a response of faith in him as the Son of God and Christ. Their unbelief and hardness of heart was the grounds upon which God now hardened their hearts. They had refused to believe -

- the relationship between the Father and the Son (John 12:44-45); that believing in Jesus meant believing in the Father, seeing Jesus meant seeing the Father, for the Son and the Father are one (cf. 10:38; 10:30; 14:9);
- that Jesus came as light (John 12:46); he illuminates the understanding of those who believe in him (cf. 1:4-5,9; 8:12; 9:5; 12:35-36);
- that the purpose of the first advent (coming) of Jesus was not to bring judgment but salvation (cf. John 3:17; Matthew 7:24-27);
- that rejecting Jesus and not receiving his word (John 12:48) results in judgment and disaster (cf. John 5:45-47; Matthew 7:21-27);
- that to those who believe God's promise is everlasting life (John 12:50);
- that Jesus does not speak on his own authority (John 7:16; 8:26,28).

Jesus the Son of God does not function independently but in perfect harmony of heart, mind and will with the Father. To hear Jesus, believe on him and follow him is the road to eternal life. Not to hear, not to believe and not to follow is the pathway to everlasting judgment and death.

Prophecies Jesus told to his disciples

106. Jesus reveals the future
Matthew 24:1-44; Mark 13:1-37; Luke 21:5-38

Two great issues were interwoven in this section, the destruction of Jerusalem (including the destruction of the great temple) and the final end of this age when Jesus will return in glory seen by all upon earth. Many attempts have been made to separate Matthew and its parallel passages. Divisions have been introduced to separate words referring to the destruction of Jerusalem and words referring to the last things. None of the attempts seem to work convincingly.

This raises an important question regarding the principles for the interpretation of Scripture. Three key principles are to be kept in mind. Firstly, we are to be 'rightly dividing the word of truth'. Literally according to 2 Timothy 2:15, we are 'to cut it straight' (derived from using animal skins for tents, etc., where each piece was cut to fit closely with the other pieces). One Scripture is to be interpreted so that it fits comfortably with the rest of the Scriptures. This is the comparing of Scripture with Scripture which is sometimes called *the analogy of Scripture* or *the analogy of the Faith*.

In the first place, no passage has to be interpreted in such a way as to bring tension with other passages of Scripture.

Secondly, difficult passages are to be interpreted by reference to easy and clear passages and not vice versa. Failure here has brought many divisions between equally godly, sincere believers.

Thirdly, once interpreted the explanation should be easily seen. Writing of the interpretation of parables but appropriate to all biblical interpretation, R.C. Trench said the understanding may not be easy to discover but once discovered it should be easy. In other words once explained it should appear obvious to other Christians.

Now to the Lord's prophecies: As the Lord and his disciples left the temple he told them that this magnificent temple in Jerusalem was going to be destroyed. This would have been a great shock to them. They probably continued walking in silence and bewilderment as they crossed the Kidron, and climbed the slopes of the Mount of Olives. Once seated overlooking the temple and with a panoramic view of the city, Peter, James, John and Andrew approached the Lord privately and asked when these things would take place and what would be the sign of his coming and of the end of the age.

The form of their question indicates a Jewish misconception that the fall of Jerusalem would occur *at the same time* as the end of the world. Jesus told them that considerable time would elapse between the two events but they were not unrelated.

The fall of Jerusalem which is symptomatic of the judgment of the Jewish nation as a whole is a type or example on a small scale of what will happen on a much larger scale at the end of the world. Many tests and trials will occur before the end; men will rise claiming to be the Christ, there will be wars, rumours of wars, famines, pestilences, earthquakes in various places and fearful sights.

Followers of Jesus will face great testing -

- they will be brought before religious and civil authorities, beaten in synagogues, hated and killed;
- many who profess faith will be broken by the pressure and betray one another and hate one another, even within family groups;
- false prophets will deceive many;
- 'and because lawlessness will abound, the love of many will grow cold' (Matthew 24:12; cf. 2 Timothy 3:1-5).

Despite all these disasters, catastrophes, problems and pressures, believers are urged by patience to possess their souls (Luke 21:19; cf. 2 Peter 3:10-13) that is, by their endurance, to gain their lives, because those who endure to the end will be saved, and the 'gospel of the kingdom will be preached in all the world as a witness to all the nations, then the end will come' (Matthew 24:13-14).

Jesus then turned his attention to the destruction of the city, 'when you see Jerusalem surrounded by armies, then know that its desolation is near' (Luke 21:20). The Lord indicated that the fall of Jerusalem was the fulfilment of prophecy, 'Therefore when you see the "abomination of desolation," spoken of by Daniel the prophet, standing in the holy place' (whoever reads, let him understand)... (Matthew 24:15-16). 'Let the reader understand' (Mark 13:14) refers to the prophecy of Daniel. The prophecy stated, 'forces shall be mustered by him, and they shall defile the sanctuary fortress; then they shall take away the daily sacrifices, and place there the abomination of desolation' and 'from the time that the daily sacrifice is taken away, and the abomination of desolation is set up, there shall be one thousand two hundred and ninety days' (Daniel 11:31; 12:11).

The Hebrew expression for the 'abomination of desolation' literally means 'the profanation that appals'. The Jews were of the opinion that this prophecy had been fulfilled in the intertestamental period of the Maccabeans. In 167 B.C. long before the incarnation of Jesus of Nazareth, Antiochus IV (Epiphanes), the king of Syria captured Jerusalem and desecrated the temple by offering the flesh of pigs on the great altar to Zeus and also bringing in other vile practices.

Jesus was now saying that this incident in 167 B.C. was not the fulfilment of the prophecy in Daniel. There was to be a worse desecration. This worse sacrilege took place at the siege of Jerusalem.

The siege of Jerusalem began in A.D. 66. It concluded with the destruction of the temple and city in A.D. 70. Here on the Mount of Olives Jesus gave warning that people should take immediate action as soon as the trouble began. They were to get out of the city and flee to the mountains (Mark 13:14). Jesus was particularly moved by the thought of the hardships that such a flight from the doomed city and country would bring upon pregnant and nursing women (Mark 13:17).

When Titus, who was to become Emperor of the Roman Empire, invaded Jerusalem the majority of the Jews took no notice of the words of Jesus and they crowded into the city from the countryside. Titus therefore had no alternative but to starve the people in the city into submission. The situation was complicated in that the Jews were divided against each other inside the city.

Josephus the Jewish historian and eyewitness to the siege and conquest of Jerusalem, made this record of the appalling devastation -

> Then did the famine widen its progress, and devoured the people by whole houses and families. The upper rooms were full of women and children that were dying by famine: and the lanes of the city were full of the dead bodies of the aged. The children also, and the young men wandered about the market places like shadows, all swelled with the famine, and fell down dead, wheresoever their misery seized them. As for burying them, those that were sick themselves were not able to do it; and those that were hearty and well, were deterred from doing it, by the great multitude of those dead bodies; and by the uncertainty there was how soon they should die themselves. For many died as they were burying others: and many went to their coffins before that fatal hour was come. Nor was there any lamentations made under these calamities... the famine confounded all natural passions... A deep silence also, and a kind of deadly night had seized upon the city.[74]

Josephus recorded an estimated number of Jewish deaths as 1,100,000 by slow starvation or the sword and 97,000 were taken captive.[75]

Jesus concluded his prophecy by saying, 'Jerusalem will be trampled by Gentiles until the times of the Gentiles are fulfilled' (Luke 21:24), that is, till the fulness of the Gentiles is brought in; until the Gospel is preached all over the world, and all God's elect are gathered in out of all nations.

---

[74] Flavius Josephus, *The Wars of the Jews*, Book V, Chapter 12, paragraph 3.
[75] *Ibid.,* Book VI, Chapter 9, paragraph 3.

Teaching concerning eschatology (death, judgment and the destiny of all humanity) is rooted in Old Testament prophecy that contains symbolism, allegory and metaphor and must be interpreted in that light.

> This means that an extremely literal interpretation must be avoided. Until this prophetic picture becomes history we will probably not know how much must be taken literally, how much figuratively. That at least some of it must be interpreted literally follows from 2 Peter 3:10. There will indeed be 'a new heaven and a new earth' [2 Peter 3:13; Revelation 21:1].[76]

The very least that we understand from these sober words of the Lord Jesus Christ is that his coming will be accompanied by devastating phenomena. The world as we know it is going to be brought to an end. The natural laws governing the orbit of the earth, the light of the sun and moon, and the stationing of the stars, will all be suspended. It will be horrific!

Though the experiences will be extremely difficult and demanding there is great encouragement, for Jesus foretold his glorious return, 'all the tribes of the earth will mourn, and they will see the Son of Man coming on the clouds of heaven with power and great glory' (Matthew 24:30; Revelation 1:7). When the faithful see these things begin to happen, they are to look up because their redemption draws near (Luke 21:28). 'To those who eagerly wait for him he will appear a second time, apart from sin, for salvation' (Hebrews 9:28). Jesus drew out a lesson from the fig tree; for when it puts forth leaves it is a sign of summer being near in the same way that the described events occurring in the world and church will be a sign of the impending return of the Lord. The best way to prepare for that Day is to watch and pray in readiness.

> Therefore, since all these things will be dissolved, what manner of persons ought you to be in holy conduct and godliness, looking for and hastening the coming of the day of God, because of which the heavens will be dissolved, being on fire, and the elements will melt with fervent heat? (2 Peter 3:11-12)

No one knows the day or hour of the Lord's return except the Father (Matthew 24:36). It will be a sudden shocking surprise for many, as it was in the days of Noah and the Flood. Jesus will come as a thief when least expected (Matthew 24:43; 1 Thessalonians 5:2; 2 Peter 3:10; Revelation 16:15).

---

[76] William Hendriksen, *The Gospel of Mark* (Edinburgh: Banner of Truth Trust, 1975), p.535.

107. The parable of The Faithful and Wise Servant
Matthew 24:45-51

Jesus presented four parables to clarify and enforce his warnings about the behaviour of his followers whilst he is away (the period between his ascension and second coming). He began the first by asking -

> Who then is a faithful and wise servant, whom his master made ruler over his household, to give them food in due season? Blessed is that servant whom his master, when he comes, will find so doing (Matthew 24:45-46).

Matthew highlights the responsibility of Christian teachers whilst Mark includes the words of Jesus that have a wider application to all believers: 'It is like a man going to a far country, who left his house and gave authority to his servants, and to each his work, and commanded the doorkeeper to watch' (Mark 13:34). All followers of Jesus have work committed to them (1 Corinthians 12:4-31; Ephesians 4:15-16; Romans 12:4-8).

Leaders are appointed in the church to take great care of the people of God, 'to shepherd [pastor] the church of God which he purchased with his own blood' (Acts 20:28). One of the prime duties is 'to give them food in due season', that is, they will be shepherds according to God's heart, who will feed them 'with knowledge and understanding' (Jeremiah 3:15) by the preaching of the gospel and teaching the Word of God. Through the regular preaching of the gospel they are to function as 'doorkeepers' clearly indicating who are inside the Church through sincere repentance and faith and who are still outside.

Into the hands of his followers Jesus committed the honour of his name, the care of his kingdom and the growth of his Church. They will each need wisdom, faithfulness and obedient service as the next three parables bear out.

108. The parable of The Wise and Foolish Virgins
Matthew 25:1-13

The kingdom of heaven is compared to the visible church. The virgins are those who profess faith in Christ, half are nominal Christians (that is, Christians in name only), half are true Christians and the Bridegroom is Jesus Christ. As the ten virgins were under obligation to be well prepared to meet the bridegroom so all those who profess Jesus as their Lord and Saviour should be ready to receive him when he returns 'in the glory of his Father with his angels, and then he will reward each according to his works' (Matthew 16:27).

When the Saviour returns he is coming to claim his bride, the church, the elect or chosen ones, and take her/them to be forever with him in Paradise. Foolish or wise, with or without oil, we shall all appear before 'the judgment seat of Christ. For it is written: "As I live, says the LORD, every knee shall bow to me, and every tongue shall confess to God." So then each of us shall give account of himself to God' (Romans 14:10-12). Some, like the wise virgins, will share in the wedding celebrations of the bride and groom. Others, like the foolish virgins will be excluded from all joy and celebration, cast out into outer darkness, excluded forever (cf. Matthew 7:21-23).

In order to understand the significance of this parable it is necessary to know something about marriage customs among the Jews. First comes the betrothal. This is considered more binding than an 'engagement'. Groom and bride are betrothed by their parents. The terms of the marriage are accepted in the presence of witnesses and God's blessing is pronounced upon the union. From that day groom and bride are legally husband and wife (cf. Joseph and Mary, Matthew 1:19). The apostle Paul used this type of analogy when addressing believers at Corinth when he wrote, 'I have betrothed you to one husband, that I may present you as a chaste virgin to Christ' (2 Corinthians 11:2).

After the formal betrothal there is an interval, not necessarily very long. During this interval the bridegroom pays the bride-price to the father of the bride. Sometimes the bride-price is in the form of services rendered, as in the case of Jacob working for Laban in order to receive Rachel as his wife (Genesis 29:20).

Then comes the procession at the close of the interval. The bride prepares herself and puts on a beautiful dress (Isaiah 61:10; Psalm 45:13-16). The bridegroom dresses in his best clothes and, accompanied by his friends (Matthew 9:15; John 3:29), proceeds to the home of his betrothed. As the procession is usually at night the young men carry torches as they sing through the streets. The bridegroom receives his bride and then, with the young men and young women, they walk to the bridegroom's home.

Scripture again and again compares the love-relationship between a bridegroom and his bride to that which exists between Yahweh (the LORD) and his people, or between Christ and his Church (Isaiah 54:5; Psalm 45:13-14; Ephesians 5:31-32; Revelation 19:6-9).

The spiritual interpretation is this: betrothal signifies individual conversion; the interval is the time of preparation awaiting the Lord's return (in this case the bridegroom has been delayed) (Matthew 25:5); the procession to the bride's house is the return of Jesus in glory with his angels;

and the bridegroom taking his bride to be with him forever signifies the Lord with his Church in the new heavens and new earth.

The only distinguishing feature between the virgins in the parable is that five took oil with their lamps and five did not. Lamps without oil are outward forms of Christian life without the inner spiritual substance. The Holy Spirit is often indicated by oil. Lamps without oil indicate lives with 'a form of godliness but denying its power' (2 Timothy 3:5). There is no true faith, no godliness within, they are not 'denying ungodliness and worldly lusts' and living 'soberly, righteously, and godly ... looking for the blessed hope and glorious appearing of our great God and Saviour Jesus Christ' (Titus 2:12,13).

By contrast lamps with oil symbolise lives which are indwelt by the Spirit of the living God. Anointing with oil is often used in Scripture to symbolise anointing with the Holy Spirit, for example, Samuel anointed David as king, 'and the Spirit of the LORD came upon David from that day forward' (1 Samuel 16:13; cf. 1 Corinthians 6:19; 1 John 2:20).

109. The parable of The Talents
Matthew 25:14-30

This is another parable of the kingdom of heaven. A rich man was about to leave on a long journey. He called three of his servants and divided his wealth among them according to their ability. The first received 5 talents (a very considerable sum), the second 2 talents and the third 1 talent. They were clearly intended to make good use of these assets in their master's absence. Upon his return the servants were called to render an account. Two had gained 100% profit from their prudent use of the funds entrusted to them and were praised for their faithfulness and rewarded by being given greater responsibilities. One, however, said he feared the master because he knew he would expect a good return on the one talent he had received so he buried it in the ground. He returned it to his master who called him a wicked and lazy servant. If the master was as hard as this servant claimed him to be, the very least he would have done was to put the large sum of money into the hands of someone who could have used it to advantage and produced some profit. This servant was severely punished.

Jesus was very close to the hour of his death. He was going away (to heaven) and it would be some time before he returned (at the second coming). In his absence he entrusts his servants with assets, the gifts which God graciously bestows both natural and spiritual. There is a wide variety in the gifts Christians receive, in intelligence, ability, aptitude, strength, socio-economic setting, family nurture, education, finance, experience and opportunities. Everything we have and everything we are is to be utilised for the glory and honour of God and the extension of the kingdom of Christ. Every believer also has been given spiritual gifts for the benefit and blessing of the Church and the conversion of sinners.

> There are diversities of gifts, but the same Spirit. There are differences of ministries, but the same Lord. And there are diversities of activities, but it is the same God who works all in all. But the manifestation of the Spirit is given to each one for the profit of all... one and the same Spirit works all these things, distributing to each one individually as he wills (1 Corinthians 12:4-7,11).

We have nothing that we have not first been given by God. Followers of Jesus receive disproportionate gifts and each one is judged accordingly - 'So then each of us shall give account of himself to God' (Romans 14:12). 'Having then gifts differing according to the grace that is given to us, let us use them' (Romans 12:6). 'As each one has received a gift, minister it to one another, as good stewards of the manifold grace of God' (1 Peter 4:10). 'As good stewards' reminds God's people that everything we have and everything good that we are, has been granted to us on trust to be used, not hidden away nor squandered. 'Having then gifts differing according to the grace that is given to us, let us use them... he who teaches, in teaching; he who exhorts, in exhortation; he who gives, with liberality; he who leads, with diligence; he who shows mercy, with cheerfulness' (Romans 12:6-8).

Jesus emphasises that there is work to be done during his absence. He has been delayed (Matthew 25:5) but that is no cause for inactivity and idleness in his servants. Each one had been given gifts according to ability.

The servant who hides his talent is not a true servant as he is being no use to God or to God's people. He has no love for God for he credits the Lord with being hard and by implication blames God for his indolence. The useless servant is cast into outer darkness (Matthew 25:30). He does not want a life of service for God here and he will not enjoy a life of fellowship with God hereafter. He is to be separated from God and the people of God forever!

Jesus then revealed what will happen at the close of this present world order and the beginning of the new, for - 'When the Son of Man comes in his glory, and all the holy angels with him, then he will sit on the throne of his glory' (Matthew 25:31). On the grounds of his extraordinary life, self-sacrifice, suffering and death Jesus will be highly exalted and God the Father will give 'him the name which is above every name, that at the name of Jesus every knee should bow, of those in heaven, and of those on earth, and of those under the earth, and that every tongue should confess that Jesus Christ is Lord, to the glory of God the Father (Philippians 2:9-11). The prophecy of Daniel will be fulfilled as he testified -

> I was watching in the night visions, and behold, One like the Son of Man, coming with the clouds of heaven! He came to the Ancient of Days, and they brought him near before him. Then to him was given dominion and glory and a kingdom, that all peoples, nations, and languages should serve him. His dominion is an everlasting dominion, which shall not pass away, and his kingdom the one which shall not be destroyed (Daniel 7:13-14).

110. The parable of The Sheep and Goats
Matthew 25:32-46

Sheep and goats mingle together. Israeli sheep and goats are not easy to distinguish unlike Western breeds of sheep and goats. Sheep in the parable represent those who have trusted in the Lord Jesus Christ, 'that great Shepherd of the sheep' (Hebrews 13:20); 'the good shepherd' who 'gives his life for the sheep (John 10:11); 'the Chief Shepherd' who will give 'the crown of glory that does not fade away' to all his faithful servants when he appears (1 Peter 5:4).

Jesus taught that to serve each other was to serve him and will result in a warm welcome. To the sheep he says, 'Come, you blessed of my Father, inherit the kingdom prepared for you from the foundation of the world' (Matthew 25:34). An inheritance that is 'incorruptible and undefiled and that does not fade away' (1 Peter 1:4). Followers of Jesus prove themselves genuine disciples by their love for other followers of Jesus, for, 'whoever believes that Jesus is the Christ is born of God, and everyone who loves him who begot also loves him who is begotten of him' (1 John 5:1). Indeed 'we know that we have passed from death to life, because we love the brethren. He who does not love his brother abides in death' (1 John 3:14).

Jesus identified with his needy followers when he said -

> I was hungry and you gave me food; I was thirsty and you gave me drink; I was a stranger and you took me in; I was naked and you clothed me; I was sick and you visited me; I was in prison and you came to me (Matthew 25:35-36).

Love for other believers must be intensely practical for 'whoever has this world's goods, and sees his brother in need, and shuts up his heart from him, how does the love of God abide in him?' (1 John 3:17).

> If a brother or sister is naked and destitute of daily food, and one of you says to them, 'Depart in peace, be warmed and filled;, but you do not give them the things which are needed for the body, what does it profit? (James 2;15-16).

Failure to show practical love results in exclusion, for Jesus will declare to unbelievers (symbolised by the goats), 'Assuredly, I say to you, inasmuch as you did not do it to one of the least of these, you did not do it to me'. And these will go away into everlasting punishment, but the righteous into eternal life (Matthew 25:45-46).

The Lord Jesus was particularly concerned to prepare his followers for the period between his departure and his return. The lessons from these four parables of Jesus are: *Be Wise*, have plenty of oil for your lamps, make sure you have true grace in your heart and are spiritually alive ready for the Lord's return; *Be Faithful*, use to the best advantage the talents which the Lord has given you for each one of us must give an account to God; *Be Serving*, serve your Master, the Lord Jesus Christ, in his Church and with his Church. To care for Christians is to care for Christ. The love of God is intensely practical. 'Be doers of the word, and not hearers only, deceiving yourselves' (James 1:22).

The Passover meal and betrayal

111. Judas agrees to betray Jesus
Matthew 26:1-5,14-16; Mark 14:1-2,10-11; Luke 22:1-6

Three times it is recorded that Jesus foretold his suffering and death, it was now just two days away, for he will be crucified on the day of Passover. Jesus reminded them of his predictions (Matthew 26:2).

Meanwhile the Jewish council was in discussion in the palace of the high priest as to how they might put Jesus to death secretly. Their hatred had been festering for many months (John 5:16; 7:30; 11:47; Luke 19:47). They agreed to have Jesus executed, all that remained was to decide the time and place of his arrest; they were intent on avoiding a public encounter.

The Feast of Unleavened Bread lasted for seven days. A vast multitude, possibly in excess of two million people, gathered from all parts of Judea and beyond. Many Galileans were among the crowd. The chief priests, scribes, and elders feared that if they killed Jesus during the feast week some of his many supporters and sympathisers might well create a huge public protest. There were those especially from the North who were impressed by his miracles and his answers to opponents. They might well generate serious problems for the Sanhedrin with the Roman authorities. They therefore sought how they might destroy him with subtlety and with stealth.

Judas Iscariot, one of the twelve, approached the chief priests to discover what price they would pay him to deliver Jesus to them out of public view (Matthew 26:14-15). It is staggering to think that one who had spent three years in the close company of the Son of God, seeing his many miracles of power and of compassion, hearing so much of his teaching, and seeing the abundance of grace flowing from him, was willing to sell him to death. What could possibly have been in his mind? How would he understand his proposed action? What explanation would he give to himself for such diabolical treason against the King of Kings? 'Satan entered Judas' (Luke 22:3), the die was cast.

The treachery of Judas presented the opportunity of seizing Jesus when he was well away from the people. Judas agreed to the betrayal and was paid thirty pieces of silver, no doubt totally oblivious of the words of Zechariah 11:12 and the subsequent significance of the following verse (v.13) when he returned and threw the money in the temple (Matthew 27:5-8).

The Jewish leadership was hell-bent upon killing Jesus but the timing of their dreadful deed was in higher hands. When the time came, though he was taken by lawless hands, crucified and put to death he was 'delivered by the determined purpose and foreknowledge of God' (Acts 2:23). He will die on Passover Day not before nor after, for he is 'indeed Christ, our Passover' who 'was sacrificed for us' (1 Corinthians 5:7). He is 'the Lamb of God who takes away the sin of the world' (John 1:29).

112. Preparation for the Passover
Matthew 26:17-19; Mark 14:12-16: Luke 22:7-13

In Jewish reckoning the day began and ended at sunset, which is very important in relation to the self-sacrifice of the Lord Jesus. He will eat the Passover Lamb of the Old Covenant with his disciples after sunset and become the Passover Lamb of the New Covenant the same day on the following morning. (In the beginning when God created the world he counted the days from sunset to sunset, 'the evening and the morning were the first day... the evening and the morning were the second day... the evening and the morning were the third day', and so on, Genesis 1:5,8,13).

The disciples asked Jesus where he would like to celebrate the Passover. The way in which Jesus answered this question demonstrated his desire to keep the location a secret. Presumably this was so that Judas Iscariot would not know beforehand where Jesus and his disciples would be found. The Lord would then be able to spend the time in that room without disturbance.

For the previous five or six days Jesus had been in the habit of leaving the city in the evening. This night he wanted to stay in a room in the city and celebrate privately with his apostles.

The Lord commissioned Peter and John to prepare the Passover. He sent them on a mystery tour beginning with instructions to follow the man with a jug of water. Since it was very unusual in that culture for a man to carry a jug of water the disciples would easily be able to spot him. After following him to his house Peter and John were to inform his master, 'The Teacher says, "Where is the guest room in which I may eat the Passover with my disciples?"' (Mark 14:14) The master was clearly a disciple, though unnamed in the inspired text.

What is recorded is noteworthy: he was a believer in Jesus because the simple instruction was, 'The Teacher says, "My time is at hand; I will keep the Passover at your house with my disciples"' (Matthew 26:18). The man was someone who evidently understood this language. Also he was a disciple whom Jesus knew could be trusted, willing to maintain confidentiality. Peter and John found everything just as Jesus had predicted and they went to the upper room of this man's house to prepare the Passover.

The first task before starting the preparations was to ensure that there was no leaven in the house. This involved a ceremonial search for leaven (like yeast a raising agent in bread). The master of the house would take a lit candle and search his house. This was because the first Passover in Egypt (Exodus 12:19-20) had been eaten with unleavened bread. This type of bread was used because it can be baked much more quickly than a loaf containing leaven. It is like a thin wafer biscuit which is broken rather than cut. The first Passover in Egypt was eaten in a hurry because the children of Israel were escaping captivity. Another reason for the absence of leaven was that frequently in Scripture it is used as a symbol of evil which spreads and corrupts everything with which it comes into contact (e.g. 1 Corinthians 5:6-8).

Peter and John would take a lamb along to the temple. The throat of the animal would be cut. Priests would collect the blood and pass it down a long line of priests until it reached the altar where the last priest threw the blood on the altar of sacrifice. The animal was then skinned, the entrails and the fat were extracted and the carcass handed back to the worshipper to be carried home and roasted on a spit over the fire. It has been calculated that about a quarter of a million lambs were slain annually at the Feast of the Passover.

The blood of the lamb was to remind them of the first Passover when blood on the doorposts saved them from the angel of death as it moved over Egypt. Certain other foods besides the lamb had to be specially prepared with the unleavened bread: a bowl of salt water to remind them of the tears shed in Egypt and the crossing of the Red Sea; bitter herbs - horseradish, chicory, endive - reminding them of the bitterness of slavery in Egypt; harosheth paste, a mixture of apples, dates, pomegranates and nuts into which they inserted sticks of cinnamon to remind them of the bricks made in Egypt from clay and straw; and four cups of diluted wine to be taken at different stages in the meal reminding them of the four promises of God -

> I am the LORD; I will bring you out from under the burdens of the Egyptians, I will rescue you from their bondage, and I will redeem you with an outstretched arm and with great judgments. I will take you as my people, and I will be your God (Exodus 6:6-7).

The meal followed a simple pattern: (i) The first cup of blessing: 'I will bring you out from under the burdens of the Egyptians' (Exodus 6:6); the bitter herbs to recall the bitter life in bondage; the unleavened bread, the harosheth paste and roast lamb. The head of the house dips bitter herbs in the salt water and eats, the others follow. (ii) The second cup of blessing: 'I will rescue you from their bondage' (Exodus 6:6); the head of the house washes his hands, takes two cakes of bread, breaks one and lays it on the unbroken one, breaks off a portion and eats it and all join in eating. The meal ends when the last portion of lamb has been eaten by the head of the house. (iii) The third cup of blessing: 'I will redeem you with an outstretched arm and with great judgments' (Exodus 6:6). (iv) The fourth cup of blessing: 'I will take you as my people, and I will be your God' (Exodus 6:7).

113. Sitting at table[77]
Matthew 26:20-25; Mark 14:17-21; Luke 22:14-23; John 13:1-29

The meal was prepared and the Lord sat down with his twelve disciples and told them of his strong desire to share this last Passover meal with them before he suffered (Luke 22:15).

Both the AV and the NKJV translate the opening words of John 13:2 'And supper being ended...' The word translated 'ended' is used with great latitude throughout the Greek text, consequently the ESV reads, 'During supper...' and the NIV 'The evening meal was in progress...' The meal was not ended as is clear from John 13:26, and the most natural time for the Lord to take a towel and a bowl of water to wash the disciples' feet would not be at the end of the meal but rather at its beginning.

---

[77] The order of events during the Lord's Passover meal cannot be confidently established.

The Lord Jesus, fully aware of his origin, purpose and destination (John 13:3), rose from supper, took off his outer clothing, fastened a towel round his waist, took a bowl of water and knelt before each of his disciples to wash and wipe their feet. When he came to Peter he was met by resistance. Peter thought it most inappropriate and did not want the Lord to wash his feet. The Lord used the opportunity to teach important lessons, saying, 'If I do not wash you, you have no part with me'. This of course has a wonderful spiritual significance. God alone through the sacrifice of his Beloved Son is able to wash away sin. David cried out to the Lord -

> Wash me thoroughly from my iniquity, and cleanse me from my
> sin… Wash me, and I shall be whiter than snow (Psalm 51:2,7).

As Ananias years later said to Saul of Tarsus, 'Arise and be baptised, and wash away your sins, calling on the name of the Lord' (Acts 22:16).

Peter reacted once more and this time requested the Lord to wash also his hands and his head. Jesus pointed out that once they have bathed they need only their feet to be washed and then they would be clean all over. In the Orient it was the custom to bathe before going out as guests to supper. On arrival, because of the conditions of the journey underfoot, it would only be necessary to wash the feet and the guests would then be clean all over.

There is a powerful spiritual lesson here long-established in Leviticus. In chapter 1 there is an account of the 'Atonement Offering' which is the burnt offering brought once a year under the Old Covenant institution. In Leviticus 4 there is an 'Occasional Sin Offering' which is brought at any time when an Israelite 'sins unintentionally against any of the commandments of the LORD' (Leviticus 4:2).

The Atonement offering *makes the believer right with God* by blotting out sin, transgression and iniquity at conversion, for 'if we say that we have no sin, we deceive ourselves, and the truth is not in us. If we confess our sins, he is faithful and just to forgive us our sins and to cleanse us from all unrighteousness' (1 John 1:8-9).

The Occasional Sin offering *keeps the believer right with God*, as the apostle John explains in his first letter, 'these things I write to you, so that you may not sin. And if anyone sins, we have an Advocate with the Father, Jesus Christ the righteous. And he himself is the propitiation for our sins, and not for ours only but also for the whole world' (1 John 2:1-2).

The wonderful fact is that the death of the Lord Jesus Christ is both the initial cleansing and the continual cleansing until death or glory. Indeed his death fulfils every aspect of the Old Covenant sacrificial system. As the writer to the Hebrews points out when recording how Jesus the Messiah and Son of God came into the world and said -

> Sacrifice and offering you did not desire, but a body you have
> prepared for me. In burnt offerings and sacrifices for sin you had
> no pleasure. Then I said, 'Behold, I have come - in the volume of
> the book [the Old Testament] it is written of me - to do your will,
> O God.' Previously saying, 'Sacrifice and offering, burnt
> offerings, and offerings for sin you did not desire, nor had pleasure
> in them' (which are offered according to the law), then he said,
> 'Behold, I have come to do your will, O God.' He takes away the
> first that he may establish the second. By that will we have been
> sanctified through the offering of the body of Jesus Christ once for
> all (Hebrews 10:5-10).

God, in his great mercy and love, has provided a constant means of
cleansing, healing and restoration through our Saviour Jesus Christ the Lord.

Jesus was giving a very powerful example by washing the disciples' feet.
He is the Lord of glory, their Master and Teacher, yet he willingly and freely
knelt before them and washed their feet. This is what true discipleship means
- humility to serve others. He has given an example which all his followers
are to emulate.

Having shared these thoughts with them Jesus was greatly troubled
because he must now disclose that one of them was going to betray him. He
had known from the beginning that one of them was 'a devil' (John 6:70-71).
The men were greatly distressed and began to ask, one by one, 'Lord, is it I?'
Quoting the Old Testament Scripture he spoke of one, a close friend, who ate
bread with him who has lifted up his heel against him (John 13:18; Psalm
41:9). He was letting them know about the unfaithfulness of one of them
before it happened so that when it took place they will have further
confirmation of his divine origin. The disciples were puzzled and looked at
each other wondering to whom Jesus referred.

114. The institution of the Lord's Supper
Matthew 26:26-29; Mark 14:22-25; Luke 22:17-20

As they were eating, the Lord introduced the New Covenant[78] a simple
highly significant remembrance of his death.

> He took bread, gave thanks and broke it, and gave it to them,
> saying, 'This is my body which is given for you; do this in
> remembrance of me'. Likewise he also took the cup after supper,
> saying, 'This cup is the new covenant in my blood, which is shed
> for you' (Luke 22:19-20).

---

[78] See 'Covenants' in the chapter on Significant facts, p.327.

Immediately Luke adds the words of Jesus, 'But behold, the hand of my betrayer is with me on the table. And truly the Son of Man goes as it has been determined, but woe to that man by whom he is betrayed!' (Luke 22:21-22)

Judas was present and the disciples were still perplexed and concerned to know the identity of the betrayer. Peter, sitting some distance from Jesus, motioned to John who was reclined at the Lord's side, to ask him to discover the identity of the betrayer. John leaned back close to Jesus and no doubt speaking in a whisper, made the inquiry. Jesus responded by saying that he would give a dipped piece of bread to the person responsible. As the Lord passed the bread he said directly to Judas, 'What you do, do quickly' (John 13:27). When Judas Iscariot received the morsel 'Satan entered him' (John 13:27) and he immediately left the room.

Most of those present were oblivious of the true meaning of the Lord's words to Judas. This disclosure alone ought to have pierced the conscience of Judas and brought deep repentance. The converse appears to have been the case. With a hard heart Judas went directly to meet with the Jewish leaders to inform them of the Lord's intended location so that he might betray Jesus into their hands.

Meanwhile concern about who was the guilty party, the worst, the least among them, seems to lead them to raise again the question, 'Who is the best, the greatest of them?' There is no certainty as to when this subject was brought up that night. Bearing in mind the two other recorded incidents when the disciples strongly debated who was the greatest among them (Luke 9:46-48; Mark 10:42-45), it seems likely that this issue was never far from their minds. It seems so inappropriate now when he had so recently washed their feet as an example.

In response Jesus repeated and enlarged what he had said earlier when they were near Jericho; greatness in the kingdom of God is expressed in willing and humble service to others. Jesus inverted the values of the world; in the world greatness is demonstrated by power and authority, in the giving of orders and having those orders obeyed. In the kingdom of God greatness is judged by the level of humble service.

Jesus reiterated the coming glory to himself and the Father and in anticipation of his departure he said -

> A new commandment I give to you, that you love one another; as I have loved you, that you also love one another. By this all will know that you are my disciples, if you have love for one another (John 13:34-35).

Jesus established that the hallmark of a Christian is Christ-like love and in view of his staggering love displayed at Calvary he sets an impossibly high standard, yet one to which every true Christian should aspire.

115. The last sermons of Jesus
John 14:1 - 16:33

It is a source of great amazement and wonder that the Lord Jesus Christ was so composed when his execution was so near at hand. When others would have been thrown into a state of extreme agitation and been pre-occupied with their own sufferings and anxieties, he had a mind, as ever, for his disciples. Although he was aware of all that was before him, no doubt feeling the weight of the awful load to be laid upon him, he yet concerned himself with the fears and anxieties of others. Truly 'when Jesus knew that his hour had come that he should depart from this world to the Father, having loved his own who were in the world, he loved them to the end' (John 13:1).

Going to prepare a place

The announcement that he was about to leave them and they would not be able to follow until some time later, brought considerable concern to them. Jesus reassured them by describing where he was going and why. He gave great comfort for troubled souls: 'Let not your heart be troubled; you believe in God, believe also in me' (John 14:1). He was preparing them for the coming ordeal. When the Lord was taken prisoner within a few hours and executed the following morning there would be great danger of the eleven disciples becoming thoroughly depressed and losing heart.

When trouble came, when the followers of Jesus were being persecuted, when they were abused and threatened, there was only one thing to do and that was to resolutely trust in God and trust in Christ; to be confident that God and the Saviour will keep their promises and achieve their mission. The psalmist counselled his own soul, 'Why are you cast down, O my soul? And *why* are you disquieted within me? Hope in God, for I shall yet praise him for the help of his countenance' (Psalm 42:5; cf. 27:13-14). There are times when followers of Jesus believe where they cannot prove, accept where they cannot understand, and trust where they cannot see. In issues of death and eternity in particular, 'we walk by faith, not by sight' (2 Corinthians 5:7).

Had not God spoken by the prophets about the sufferings of Christ and the glory which would follow? (1 Peter 1:11) Had he not said that Christ would be 'despised and rejected by men, a Man of sorrows and acquainted with grief... wounded for our transgressions, bruised for our iniquities'?

(Isaiah 53;3,5) Had not the Lord warned them on at least four separate occasions that he would suffer and die?

Knowing the way

Jesus was going to heaven, where there is plenty of room; he will prepare a place for them and when the time comes he will be their personal escort to take them to be with him. Jesus is the only access to God, he is the truth and the source of all truth, he is the life and the source of all life. Jesus is the only answer to the spiritual problems at the heart of everyone; alienated, cut off from God; confused, no longer able to understand God or his ways; and dead in trespasses and sins. Consequently the three basic human needs are for: *reconciliation* to deal with the alienation, *illumination* to deal with the confusion, and *regeneration* (New Birth) to deal with the spiritual death (1 John 5:20).

Our Lord had spoken very simply and plainly about the Father, his house, his many mansions, about going to prepare a place and his promise to come and receive his people to himself and share his place with them. But when Jesus said 'Where I go you know, and the way you know', Thomas could not grasp it. Jesus responded 'I am the way, the truth, and the life. No one comes to the Father except through me' (John 14:4,6). Then Philip asked that they may see the Father, and Jesus responded by declaring that the similarity is so great between the Father and the Son that to see the Son is much the same as seeing the Father (cf. John 1:18; Matthew 11:27).

Greater works

Jesus promised that those who believe in him will do the works that he did and even greater works than he did (John 14:12). What is Jesus promising?

The ability of the disciples to perform the same works is in fact the continued working of Jesus Christ (Mark 16:20). 'And whatever you ask in my name, that I will do, that the Father may be glorified in the Son. If you ask anything in my name, I will do it' (John 14:13-14), which means that their working and their greater works are still in effect his working and his greater works through them. Nevertheless the apostles did not perform greater miracles of healing; raising the dead, giving sight to the blind, walking on water... but they did perform greater miracles in another realm.

For there is something 'greater' than miracles in the physical realm and that is miracles in the spiritual realm: *conversions,* sinners being brought from spiritual death to life and from spiritual darkness to light, sinners being transformed by the power of the Lord God, sinners being born anew, brought into union with the Son of God, indwelt by the Holy Spirit of the living God.

These are the miracles that are greater than walking on water, changing water to wine, healing the sick, or even raising the dead. In contrast to hundreds of Jews coming to faith during the ministry of Jesus, there will be thousands brought to faith through the ministry of the apostles and millions upon millions through evangelists, pastors, preachers, teachers and innumerable godly witness-bearing saints down through the ages. Jesus said he would build his Church and the gates of Hades would not prevail against it (Matthew 16:18). The Lord Jesus is still building with living stones (1 Peter 2:4-5). Praise be to God.

Another Counsellor

A further blessing was promised by the Lord Jesus to those who love him and obey his commandments. He will ask the Father to grant the Holy Spirit's assistance to them; guiding them in knowing and understanding the truth, indwelling them and being constantly with them (John 14:15-31; 1 Corinthians 3:16; 6:19-20). These blessings would come once Jesus had been glorified after his crucifixion, resurrection and ascension (John 7:38-39). The Holy Spirit would also grant unusual help to the apostles in imparting further truth and assisting them in remembering the teaching of Jesus during his ministry (John 14:26; 16:12-15; 1 John 2:20).

The Saviour further promised to leave peace with them and to give his peace to them (John 14:27). This suggests that two kinds of peace are indicated, that which is *objective* and that which is *subjective*, the peace *'left'* and his peace *'given'*. Objective peace is the absence of alienation, the amazing sense of wellbeing with God; ransomed, healed, restored, forgiven. 'Therefore, having been justified by faith, we have peace with God through our Lord Jesus Christ' (Romans 5:1), and 'it pleased the Father that in him all the fullness should dwell, and by him to reconcile all things to himself, by him, whether things on earth or things in heaven, having made peace through the blood of his cross' (Colossians 1:19-20). Calvary is the place where Jesus obtained this peace for his people. He bequeathes this to all believers by the Spirit.

Subjective peace is an inner stability, a tranquility of heart and mind, 'the peace of God, which surpasses all understanding' that guards our 'hearts and minds through Christ Jesus' (Philippians 4:7; cf. Isaiah 26:3-4). It is that peace which is part of the cluster of spiritual fruit of the indwelling Holy Spirit (Galatians 5:22; cf. Romans 15:13). Jesus said, 'Not as the world gives do I give to you. Let not your heart be troubled, neither let it be afraid' (John 14:27). Let them be at peace because he is going away and will return. Let them rejoice that he is going to the Father.

Satan will be actively engaged in seeking to humiliate, tempt and destroy Jesus, nevertheless everything that that evil one attempts will be external. Jesus is holy, totally and completely without sin, he knows that Satan has nothing in him (John 14:30). Every other human being has a sinful heart which renders each one vulnerable to a satanic attack - there is an internal weakness in all - except Jesus! He reiterated his profound love for the Father and that he was about to demonstrate this by fulfilling the Father's will, suffering and dying at Calvary. This will be a testimony to the world of how much he loves the Father. At the same time Jesus will be very conscious that the Father loves him when he lays down his life (John 10:17-18).

The parable of The True Vine (John 15:1-10)

At the Lord's instigation they left the upper room (John 14:31) and he continued their final instruction. Through the parable of The True Vine he used an analogy with which the apostles would be familiar. Israel had been likened to a 'vine' on numerous occasions (Psalm 80:8-19; Isaiah 5:1-7; Jeremiah 2:21). The real value of a vine is in its fruit. It really serves no other purpose (Ezekiel 15:1-8). The vine and its branches portrays union and communion, a oneness, a common life with complete dependence of the branches upon the vine, resulting in fruit-bearing. It is in bearing much fruit that believers are able to glorify God (John 15:8).

'I am the true vine,' said Jesus (John 15:1). In using the word 'true' he is not necessarily contrasting himself with that which is 'false'. This word is often used before a metaphor. For example, Jesus is 'the true light' (John 1:9); 'the true bread from heaven' (John 6:32); 'a minister of the sanctuary and of the true tabernacle' (Hebrews 8:2). 'The true' being connected with Christ signifies that he is the perfect, essential, and enduring reality, 'the substance is of Christ' (Colossians 2:17).

This true vine 'shall grow up before [God] as a tender plant, and as a root out of dry ground. He has no form or comeliness; and when we see him, there is no beauty that we should desire him' (Isaiah 53:2). This is the vine that produces fruit which, when crushed, yields the wine 'that makes glad the heart of man' (Psalm 104:15), and 'which cheers both God and men' (Judges 9:13), the wine that symbolises supremely, the blood of Christ the Saviour (Luke 22:20).

Bearing fruit

The word which Jesus used most frequently, recorded in John 15, is the word 'abide', which appears no less than ten times in the first ten verses. 'Abiding' always has to do with bonding in fellowship; no one is capable of having fellowship with God and with his Son Jesus Christ unless he is a child of God.

This 'abiding' in Christ is linked with the words of Christ abiding in his followers (John 15:7). The word of Christ includes -

- his words given whilst on earth;
- the Scriptures of the Old Testament which are his word given before his coming from heaven;
- the Scriptures of the New Testament, beginning with *The Acts of the Apostles*, which are his word given after his return to heaven.

The whole Bible is the Son's Word (Colossians 3:16), even as it is the Father's (2 Timothy 3:16) and the Holy Spirit's (2 Peter 1:21).

Spiritual branches united to the vine have but one responsibility and that is to bear much fruit (John 15:2,4,5,8; Mark 4:20). In the days of the prophet Hosea, Israel was criticised for stripping God's vine and bringing forth 'fruit for himself' (Hosea 10:1). Those united with Christ are to bear fruit for God in order to glorify him (John 15:8). But what is the fruit which the Lord intends should be produced in such abundance? There are a number of legitimate applications of the analogy to be drawn from other Scriptures.

Fruit bearing certainly includes the responsibility to 'bear fruits worthy of repentance' (Luke 3:8). To say we repent of our sins is not enough, we must also abandon them: 'He who covers his sins will not prosper, but whoever confesses and forsakes them will have mercy' (Proverbs 28:13). 'Let the wicked forsake his way, and the unrighteous man his thoughts...' (Isaiah 55:7). Repentance includes the involvement of the will. Those who truly repent are actively engaged in forsaking sin and bearing fruit.

Fruit-bearing also includes the responsibility to live under the influence of the indwelling Holy Spirit. When he takes up residence he brings with him his own kind of fruit. As Paul declared, 'The fruit of the Spirit is love, peace, long-suffering, kindness, goodness, faithfulness, gentleness, self-control' (Galatians 5:22-23; cf. 2 Peter 1:5-9).

A further application of spiritual fruit-bearing is that for which the apostle Paul commended the Thessalonians namely, their 'work of faith, labour of love, and patience of hope in our Lord Jesus Christ in the sight of our God and Father' (1 Thessalonians 1:3). These would include feeding the hungry, giving drink to the thirsty, providing hospitality to the stranger, clothing the naked, and visiting the sick and those in prison (Matthew 25:31-40; cf. Ephesians 5:8-10). Christians are not saved *by good works* but saved *for good works*.

> For by grace you have been saved through faith, and that not of yourselves; it is the gift of God, not of works, lest anyone should boast. For we are his workmanship, created in Christ Jesus for good works, which God prepared beforehand that we should walk in them (Ephesians 2:8-10).

An essential aspect of fruit bearing is that of introducing others to the Lord Jesus Christ. In preparation for this we are to sanctify the Lord God in our hearts, and always be ready to give a clear explanation to everyone who asks a reason for the hope that is in us, with meekness and fear (1 Peter 3:15; 2:9; Matthew 5:16).

God the Father is the vine-dresser, husbandman, or cultivator, the one who alone cares for the vine and its branches. He does not delegate this task to another. In this parable the love of God for his Son and for his people are beautifully expressed. God provides protection for the weakest shoots, he waters, trains, and prunes, according to the daily needs of the plant. No branch is overlooked. None is allowed to run wild.

Branches that bear no fruit are removed whilst branches that do bear fruit are cleansed in order to produce more fruit (John 15:2). The translation 'he prunes' is misleading and hinders the flow of our Lord's reasoning. It would be better translated 'he cleanses' because the Lord uses a word from the same root in the very next verse when he says, 'You are already clean' (v.3). Translating as 'he purges' (AV) or 'he prunes' (NKJV) has led many to think of God bringing discipline upon his fruit-bearing children by affliction, chastisement and painful providence in order that they may produce more fruit. The Lord simply says that the Father 'cleanses' the fruit-bearing branch in order that it may bear more fruit. Fruit trees benefit from a 'winter wash' which removes insects, moss, and parasites which infest the trees.

The cleansing of believers which is conducted by God, is achieved through the Word of God (John 15:3). The Scriptures remove all obstructions to the flow of life and nourishment from the vine to the branches. This cleansing is not to prepare us for heaven, that has already been achieved through the blood of the Saviour. This cleansing is to fit us for better service here on earth. It is designed to make us more useful, more fruitful. Through the regular reading and study of the Scriptures, individually and collectively, we are enabled to 'grow in the grace and knowledge of our Lord and Saviour Jesus Christ' (2 Peter 3:18) as we seek to live out what we read and learn.

A distinction is to be drawn between the 'cleansing' of v.2 and the 'clean' of v.3. The first is a progressive experience, whereas the second is an accomplished fact. The first signifies sanctification and the second justification. The disciples are already spiritually clean (justified) and they are continually being spiritually cleansed (sanctified). This same distinction was made by the Lord Jesus just a little earlier when he began to wash the disciples' feet and the apostle Peter resisted. Replying to Peter's second objection Jesus said, 'He who is bathed needs only to wash his feet, but is completely clean' (John 13:10).

Abiding in Christ

What a precious state it is to abide in Christ for 'if anyone is in Christ, he is a new creation; old things have passed away; behold, all things have become new' (2 Corinthians 5:17). To abide means to remain or to continue in union. Only in this abiding are believers able to bear fruit (John 15:4). But there are many other blessings: abiding in Christ and having his words abiding in us means we abide in his love and our prayers are heard and answered (John 15:7). It also indicates that we are true disciples and are enjoying a wonderful liberty as the Lord taught earlier. He had said to believing Jews, 'If you abide in my word, you are my disciples indeed. And you shall know the truth, and the truth shall make you free' (John 8:31-32).

As we abide in him Jesus is our constant spiritual nourishment: 'He who eats my flesh and drinks my blood abides in me, and I in him' (John 6:56). By abiding in this wonderful Spiritual Vine we demonstrate our love for Jesus in our commitment and obedience to him and this is by no means a miserable servile duty - it is a delight.

As Jesus wants his disciples to share his amazing sense of peace (John 14:27), so he also wants them to experience the fulness of his joy (John 15:11). The disciples are sorrowing at the news of his departure. He has said to them, 'Let not your heart be troubled' (John 14:1) and now he wants them to have his joy, his inner delight, within their hearts. There is the joy he experienced on earth and there is the joy he anticipates in heaven. Jesus wanted his disciples to rejoice with him.

It may seem strange to learn that Jesus was joyful whilst on earth; was he not 'despised, and rejected by men, a man of sorrows and acquainted with grief'? (Isaiah 53:3) Yes, but that did not eclipse his joy. In his High Priestly prayer he said to the Father, 'But now I come to you, and these things I speak in the world, that they may have my joy fulfilled in themselves' (John 17:13). The inner life of the Lord Jesus Christ was being revealed, he was filled with joy, not miserable, never depressed. He rejoiced in his service in fulfilling the Father's will. For example, when the seventy returned after their evangelistic mission -

Jesus rejoiced in the Spirit and said, 'I thank you, Father, Lord of heaven and earth, that you have hidden these things from the wise and prudent and revealed them to babes. Even so, Father, for so it seemed good in your sight' (Luke 10:21).

There was joy in his heart even in his suffering at Calvary. His confident testimony had already been prophetically revealed -

I have set the LORD always before me; because he is at my right hand I shall not be moved. Therefore my heart is glad, and my glory rejoices; my flesh also will rest in hope. For you will not leave my soul in Sheol, nor will you allow your Holy One to see corruption. You will show me the path of life; in your presence is fullness of joy; at your right hand are pleasures forevermore (Psalm 16:8-11).

It was the anticipation of that heavenly joy that enabled the Lord Jesus to endure the cross, despising its shame (Hebrews 12:2), and all his faithful servants will one day receive a warm welcome and enter into that joy of the Lord (Matthew 25:23). Here is the experienced joy on earth and the anticipated greater joy in heaven. No matter how dark the skies and how fierce the storm the sun is always shining, just hidden from view for a while.

Calvary displayed the enormous love of Jesus for his people. Jesus revealed that he regarded them as friends when he said, 'No longer do I call you servants, for a servant does not know what his master is doing; but I have called you friends, for all things that I heard from my Father I have made known to you' (John 15:15). What an unspeakable blessing to be able to introduce him to others, 'Yes, he is altogether lovely. This is my beloved, and this is my friend' (Song of Solomon 5:16). His disciples obeyed him because they loved him. They had been chosen and appointed to go and bear fruit. The Lord Jesus will build his 'Church and the gates of Hades shall not prevail against it' (Matthew 16:18). He will continue to achieve this through the apostles for 'they went out and preached everywhere, the Lord working with them and confirming the word through the accompanying signs' (Mark 16:20).

So many Jews had heard his preaching and rejected the message and the Messenger. They had seen his unique and wonderful works which proved his origin and mission as the Messiah and yet they hated both Jesus and the Father. The hatred and persecution that Jesus faced was most likely to fall upon his disciples also for they, like him, will be hated without cause (John 15:25; Psalm 35:19; 69:4).

This hatred against Jesus was completely irrational. Who in the world had any reason to hate Jesus? What harm did he ever do to anyone? He 'went about doing good and healing all who were oppressed by the devil, for God was with him' (Acts 10:38). No one is able to provide a justification for their hatred of the Son of God. Yet he remains the most hated, despised and spurned individual who has ever lived. 'He is hated without a cause.'

There will be more warnings from Jesus of forthcoming persecutions but first he will give wonderful encouragement by speaking of the forthcoming heavenly assistance that will be given to believers.

The blessing of the Divine Helper

Interspersed throughout this last sermon that Jesus delivered to his apostles is the promise of a spiritual Helper. The Greek word translated 'Helper' is 'Paraclete' (literally meaning, 'one called alongside', John 14:16-17, 26; 15:26; and 16:7, variously translated as Comforter, Advocate, Helper, Consoler). The Lord Jesus prays that the Holy Spirit as the Divine Helper will come alongside all who love him and seek to walk in obedience to him (John 14:15,16). The Holy Spirit will be sent by Jesus from the Father (John 15:26). It is to the advantage of the apostles that Jesus goes away otherwise the Holy Spirit will not come (John 16:7).

The Holy Spirit is the Spirit of truth (John 14:17; 15:26) -

- who will indwell them;
- who will teach all things;
- who will assist their memory concerning the teaching of Jesus (John 14:26);
- who will continue to impart the teaching of Jesus to them (for the Lord still has many things to say to them but they are not able to cope with more at this time);
- who will guide them 'into all truth' including revealing things to come (John 16:13).

What a blessing the Holy Spirit will be to the Church.

The Spirit of truth will also be very active in the world, convicting the world of sin, and of righteousness, and of judgment: of sin, because they do not believe in Jesus; of righteousness, because he goes to his Father and they will see him no more; of judgment, because the ruler of this world is judged (John 16:8-11).

This unique work of conviction for sin, convincing of the righteousness of Jesus and conviction of the reality of the coming judgment of the world is beautifully illustrated in the final hours of the Lord Jesus before his death. Hanging by his side were two crucified thieves who both joined in the mockery and reviling hurled at him by those who passed by, together with the chief priests, scribes and elders who were standing there watching (Matthew 27:39-44).

After a while a change came over one of the thieves. As his colleague continued his blasphemy against Jesus he rebuked him and showed a remarkable transformation in his thinking: he readily acknowledged his wrongdoing, realised the innocence of Jesus and appealed to him saying, 'Lord, remember me when you come into your kingdom' (Luke 23:42). He was convinced that there was life after death, that Jesus had influence in the judgment that he was convinced was awaiting him. The Holy Spirit was at work in this man's life and heart. Jesus reassured him of a place in heaven, 'Today you will be with me in Paradise' (Luke 23:43).

Jesus said of the Holy Spirit, 'He will testify of me' or equally, 'He will bear witness of me' (John 15:26; cf. 1 John 5:6 'it is the Spirit who bears witness, because the Spirit is truth'. In each case the same Greek word is used and is translated either 'testify' or 'witness'). The Holy Spirit is committed to glorifying Jesus (John 16:14). With his divine help the disciples will also be witnesses for Jesus. Years later the apostle John wrote this testimony -

> That which was from the beginning, which we have heard, which we have seen with our eyes, which we have looked upon, and our hands have handled, concerning the Word of life - the life was manifested, and we have seen, and bear witness, and declare to you that eternal life which was with the Father and was manifested to us (1 John 1:1-2).

Of his Gospel record it is recorded, 'This is the disciple who testifies of these things, and wrote these things; and we know that his testimony is true' (John 21:24).

After his death and resurrection and just before his ascension Jesus told the apostles to wait a short time and they would receive power when the Holy Spirit had come upon them; and they would be his witnesses in Jerusalem, and in all Judea and Samaria, and to the end of the earth (Acts 1:8). And what fine witnesses they proved to be, indwelt, inspired, empowered and directed by the Spirit of truth, the Holy Spirit of God.

From Pentecost onward the believers were new people. They were transformed by the indwelling Holy Spirit: they were better Christians, stronger in spirit and bolder in evangelism. Believers are to God the fragrance of Christ among those who are being saved and among those who are perishing. To the one the aroma of death leading to death, and to the other the aroma of life leading to life (2 Corinthians 2:15-16).

The Holy Spirit awakened in unbelievers a consciousness of guilt which led some to true repentance (Acts 2:37-38), whilst in others the conviction led to hardening and everlasting punishment. Stephen, the first Christian martyr declared to his persecutors, 'You stiff-necked and uncircumcised in heart and ears! You always resist the Holy Spirit; as your fathers did, so do you' (Acts 7:51).

- The Holy Spirit quickens and brings us to spiritual life (John 3:6; 1:13).
- The Holy Spirit dwells within believers (1 Corinthians 6:19).
- The Holy Spirit gives believers an assurance of adoption by the Father (Romans 8:16).
- The Holy Spirit leads every believer (Romans 8:14).
- The Holy Spirit pleads for us in intercession when our words fail (Romans 8:26).
- The Holy Spirit 'seals' us 'for the day of redemption' (Ephesians 4:30).

Jesus returned to the subject of persecution, warning his disciples of the difficulties which will arise after his death so that they may be prepared and not be stumbled (John 16:1). They will be put out of the synagogues, which is tantamount to social and community ostracism. Their enemies will even be so bitter and blind as to believe that they serve God when they murder disciples of Jesus.

Again he stated clearly why he was forewarning them, it was so that when persecution comes they will remember his words and find their faith strengthened and take comfort in his spiritual presence with them (John 16:4, cf. 13:19; 14:29).

They will experience sorrow when he leaves but it will soon be turned into joy (John 16:16-22). He will be taken from them and 'delivered into the hands of sinful men, and be crucified'. They will however rejoice when on the third day he rises again (Luke 24:7; cf. v.41).

In addition the resurrection will reassure them of everything he has said and everything he has promised. They will see him again on occasions spread over a period of forty days and after his ascension into heaven they will return to Jerusalem 'with great joy' (Luke 24:52). They will go forward in the certainty of his spiritual presence always with them.

Jesus was less than twelve hours away from the most indescribable suffering, agony and death and yet he is concerned about the sorrow that his apostles will face. Not a word falls from his lips about his forthcoming personal pain. He could have quoted numerous detailed prophecies from the

Old Testament Scriptures describing his suffering but he did not. Rather he reassured his disciples of their short-lived sorrow to be followed by rejoicing with joy that no one could take away (John 16:22).

Wonderful changes were to take place after his ascension and the outpouring of the Holy Spirit. The apostles will pray to the Father in the name of Jesus and the Father will respond positively (John 16:23). Also Jesus will continue to teach them through the Holy Spirit, no longer in words which they find difficult to grasp but in plain language.

Much of what Jesus taught them was 'in figurative language', that is, in parabolic form, mysterious, enigmatic, often difficult to understand sayings (John 16:25). What Jesus taught about his suffering, death and resurrection is clear and plain to us today but to those men with all their Jewish prejudices and their great resistance to the thought of his death, they were baffling words, hard to grasp. After his resurrection they began to understand elements of his teaching (cf. John 2:20-22).

He will also teach them plainly about the Father, that is, he will reveal the will and plan of the Father for the spread of the gospel, the growth, establishment and organisation of the Church (John 16:25). Furthermore they will enjoy a deep experience of the Father's love as he watches over them, ever ready to grant their requests because they have loved Jesus and believed that he came from God (John 16:27).

They were soon to be scattered (John 16:32) and he will be left alone, but yet not alone because the Father will be with him. He had shared these things with them so that they may be at peace 'in him' even though there will be tribulation in the world. 'Be of good cheer,' he says, 'for I, I have overcome the world' (John 16:33). The savagely fierce battle was yet to begin but of the outcome there was absolutely no doubt. The Son of God, descendent of Eve, will be bruised in his heel. The arch-enemy will be bruised in his head (Genesis 3:15). The outcome of the battle is assured. Jesus the Messiah will be the Victor.

116. The prayer of the Great High Priest
John 17:1-26

It has been said that the seventeenth chapter of *The Gospel of John* is, without doubt, the most remarkable portion of the most remarkable book in the world. In it the best sermon in the world is followed by the finest prayer in the world; from preaching Jesus turned to prayer. In a sense this prayer is a pattern for all prayers. It shows that the glory of God should be the purpose, object and goal of every prayer; not the good of the one who prays, not the conversion of others, not intercession for believers in suffering, in gospel outreach nor even in spiritual crisis. Even though Jesus began by mentioning himself, his overriding concern was the glory of his Father (John 17:1-5). With less than twelve hours before crucifixion he prayed, 'Father, the hour has come. Glorify your Son, that your Son also may glorify you' (John 17:1). The glory of God is uppermost, this is the priority for all prayer as is also evidenced in 'The Lord's Prayer':

> Our Father in heaven, hallowed be your name. Your kingdom come. Your will be done on earth as it is in heaven (Matthew 6:9-10).

'Father, the hour has come' (John 17:1).

'The hour has come' the moment of crisis had arrived, the hour in which the Son of God would conclude his mission to the earth by yielding up his life on the cross. He was to be 'the Lamb of God' taking 'away the sin of the world' (John 1:29), the One to fulfil the prophecies, the types and symbols of the old order and bring in the new order. The hour of his triumph over the forces of evil and the prince of darkness was at hand.

Here are the words of the Lord Jesus facing his deepest crisis. He was about to complete his great undertaking and leave this world by means of a barbaric death on a cross. He was to be wrongly arrested, falsely accused, unlawfully judged, pitilessly mocked, crudely spat upon, viciously scourged; led away weak and bleeding, dragging a heavy wooden cross through the streets of Jerusalem to halt outside the city at the refuse tip and there be crucified as a common criminal among criminals, numbered indeed, 'with the transgressors' (Isaiah 53:12). He was to endure the physical agony of crucifixion, experience the horror of mental anguish as one 'despised and rejected by men, a man of sorrows and acquainted with grief' (Isaiah 53:3). In anticipation the Son of God described his experience prophetically in Psalm 22 -

> I am poured out like water, and all my bones are out of joint; my heart is like wax; it has melted within me. My strength is dried up like a potsherd, and my tongue clings to my jaws ... For dogs have surrounded me; the assembly of the wicked has enclosed me. They pierced my hands and my feet (Psalm 22:14-16).

This is the crisis of Christ, Son of the living God. Yet all this horror, with its bloody sweat and tears was but a fraction of his true sufferings. The excruciating agony of the cross was not the physical dimension, the pain of the body; nor the emotional, the pain of the heart; nor the mental, the agony in his mind; it was the spiritual dimension. Others have died. Others have died with terror of body and mind, but none have died like this Man *with such torment of soul*. It was the spiritual dimension in the sufferings of Jesus which mark him out as unique and mark out his sufferings as unique. Not even a soul in the everlasting torments of hell will suffer as he suffered on that cross! It is this One, facing this end, who prayed so poignantly in the upper room, 'Father, the hour has come. Glorify your Son, that your Son also may glorify you' (John 17:1).

'Glorify your Son' (John 17:1).

Jesus looked to the Father for the encouragement and support of his love, for he was to be the suffering Saviour who would be glorified in fulfilling every last detail of the Father's plan of salvation. The prayer that the Father would glorify the Son was not a selfish prayer. For the very next words demonstrate what motivated Jesus: 'That your Son also may glorify you' (John 17:1). Some days before, when Greeks wanted to see Jesus, the Lord told Philip and Andrew -

> Now my soul is troubled, and what shall I say? 'Father, save me from this hour'? But for this purpose I came to this hour. Father, glorify your name (John 12:27).

He was to be arrested, led before the high priests Annas and Caiaphas, the governor Pilate and King Herod. He was to be questioned, accused and struck, made a laughing stock before the people as he was brought out clothed in a scarlet robe with a crown of twisted thorns on his head and a reed in his right hand (Matthew 27:28-29). How could he be glorified? When the Son of God was stripped and nailed to a wooden cross, how could he then be glorified *and* glorify the Father? Through prophecy his thoughts were revealed -

> I am a worm, and no man; a reproach of men, and despised by the people. All those who see me ridicule me; they shoot out the lip, they shake the head, saying, 'He trusted in the LORD, let him rescue him; let him deliver him, since he delights in him!' (Psalm 22:6-8)

Jesus preserved his own dignity in the midst of the crude barbarism of the crucifixion. Willingly he went to death. He laid down his life that he might take it again. No one took it from him, but he laid it down of himself. He had power to lay it down, and he had power to take it again (John 10:17-18). This Son of the living God is the One 'who for the joy set before him endured the cross, despising the shame' (Hebrews 12:2).

Yes, even in this, the Son of God would be glorified -

- glorified in Gethsemane as he courageously came forward to meet the troops and officers with their swords and clubs;
- glorified in his compassion in healing the ear of Malchus;
- glorified in his humility and self-control in the Jewish Court, Pilate's Praetorium and Herod's Palace as he, the co-Creator, is ridiculed, taunted and tortured;
- glorified as he was lifted up from the earth to draw all peoples to himself;
- glorified as he successfully fulfilled the task of redemption: 'to finish the transgression, to make an end of sins, to make reconciliation for iniquity, to bring in everlasting righteousness (Daniel 9:24);
- glorified in his conduct throughout the whole of his ordeal: his composure before his inquisitors, his quiet submission to crucifixion, his concern for his mother;
- glorified in his grace, mercy and compassion: praying for forgiveness upon his executioners, welcoming the repentant thief into his kingdom and presence;
- glorified when he triumphantly cried, 'It is finished!' (John 19:30);
- glorified in his quiet confidence as he placed himself into the hands of God the Father in his final words;
- glorified in an amazing resurrection from the dead.

His is a life of obedience, love and trust, unruffled within, resolutely determined to do the will of God, the whole will of God and nothing but the will of God. The Father does glorify the Son.

'That your Son also may glorify you' (John 17:1).

He wanted, more than anything else in the world, to bring honour, praise, blessing, thanksgiving and worship to the Father in heaven. He wanted the angels to worship the Father on account of his submission and obedience. He wanted the redeemed to worship, praise and bless the Father in heaven on account of his submission and obedience.

The cross of Calvary demonstrates the perfections of the Lord God Almighty. It shows the impeccable holiness of God, the God who is light and in whom is no darkness at all (1 John 1:5), the Father of lights in whom there is no shadow due to turning (James 1:17) who cannot overlook sin. It shows the constant, inflexible righteousness of God who must punish sins, transgressions and iniquity; it shows the amazing grace of God in Christ who 'made him who knew no sin to be sin for us, that we might become the righteousness of God in him' (2 Corinthians 5:21); and it shows the magnificent love of Jesus for his Father and his people. There was no price on earth that Jesus would not pay for our salvation and the Father's glory.

The Son's eternal glory

On earth Jesus had glorified the Father by finishing the work the Father had given him to do (John 17:4). He had spoken the words of God, communicated his teaching; he had completed the mission entrusted to him, lived the life appointed for him perfectly and completed it from beginning to end. Jesus now sought to be glorified by the Father with the glory which he had with the Father before the world was created (John 17:5).

Paul in his letter to the Philippians describes the excellence of the person and work of Christ in his life here on earth which culminated in death, 'even the death of the cross'. He continues by indicating *how the Father glorified his Son* by highly exalting him and giving him -

> the name which is above every name, that at the name of Jesus every knee should bow, of those in heaven, and of those on earth, and of those under the earth, and that every tongue should confess that Jesus Christ is Lord (Philippians 2:9-11)

Everything that Jesus did and the reason for all his suffering is summed up in the words which immediately follow in Philippians 2:11 - 'to the glory of God the Father'.

The Son of God has existed eternally 'in the form of God' (Philippians 2:6), He was there in the beginning of creation with God, God with God (John 1:1-2). There was no 'Jesus' before creation, indeed he did not exist until his conception by the miraculous working of the Holy Spirit (Matthew 1:20). A humanity was prepared for the Son of God who said to his Father, 'a body you have prepared for me... Behold, I have come ... to do your will, O God' (Hebrews 10:5,7). The Son of God became flesh (John 1:14). 'Inasmuch then as the children have partaken of flesh and blood, he himself likewise shared in the same' (Hebrews 2:14).

Before his incarnation the Son of God had a wonderful glory, 'the glory as of the only begotten of the Father' (John 1:14). The apostles John, James and Peter were privileged to see that amazing phenomenon on the mount of transfiguration. Peter records that they -

> were eyewitnesses of his majesty. For he received from God the Father honour and glory when such a voice came to him from the Excellent Glory: "This is my beloved Son, in whom I am well pleased." And we heard this voice which came from heaven when we were with him on the holy mountain (2 Peter 1:17-18).

That is when John saw the intrinsic glory of Jesus the Son of God that he recorded in John 1:14.

When Jesus prayed for the same glory as he had before creation he clearly indicates his pre-existent and eternal nature 'in the bosom of the Father' (John 1:18). Here he requested the same eternal glory for himself as he now is, and forever will be, 'the God/Man'.

Knowing the only true God

The work of Jesus as the Messiah is to give eternal life to all those whom the Father gives him and this is eternal life, that they may know the only true God, and Jesus Christ whom God has sent (John 17:3; cf. 3:16). The Father of Jesus is the only true God. 'Look to me', he says, 'and be saved, all you ends of the earth! For I am God, and there is no other' (Isaiah 45:22).

> For the LORD is great and greatly to be praised; he is to be feared above all gods. For all the gods of the peoples are idols, but the LORD made the heavens. Honour and majesty are before him; strength and beauty are in his sanctuary (Psalm 96:4-6).

Jesus said, 'No one knows the Son except the Father. Nor does anyone know the Father except the Son, and the one to whom the Son wills to reveal him' (Matthew 11:27). Jesus is the only way to God and the only way to knowing God (John 14:6).

Knowing God is to know also the true Messiah, Jesus Christ. It is to know that we are loved by him, saved by him, protected by him, led by him and kept by him. It is the personal knowledge of being able to say, 'The LORD is my shepherd' and therefore, 'I shall not want' (Psalm 23:1). It is to have the highest opinion of him and with profound respect to honour, love and obey with the utmost gratitude for his grace and kindness. There is no comparison, for all other gods are dumb idols (Psalm 115:3-8). This is the God of all grace, the One who forgives all our sin, transgressions and iniquity, this is the Christ who loved us and gave himself for us (Galatians 2:20). He is everything to us. Each believer can confidently say, 'For to me, to live is Christ, and to die is gain' (Philippians 1:21).

Prayer for his disciples

Jesus had expressed his concern to glorify the Father by finishing the work entrusted to him and so gain eternal life for those whom God has given to him. He continued by praying further for those whom the Father has given to him (John 17:6-9), they have kept God's Word, which means they have received what Jesus has said as the Words of God. Years later the Christian converts in Thessalonica displayed the same reception of the Word of God and Paul prayed in gratitude -

> For this reason we also thank God without ceasing, because when you received the word of God which you heard from us, you welcomed it not as the word of men, but as it is in truth, the word of God, which also effectively works in you who believe (1 Thessalonians 2:13).

As they have kept God's Word, so Jesus prays that God will keep them, that is, guard and protect them and that they might enjoy the closest bond and union with God like Jesus enjoys (v.11; cf. 1 Peter 1:5). In praying for their protection Jesus does not ask for the disciples to be taken *out of the world* but rather to be guarded *in the world* against the evil one (John 17:15) by God sanctifying them, separating them from the weakness of the flesh, from the allurement of the world and from the influence of the devil. This sanctification, separation and distinguishing of those who belong to Jesus is to be achieved through the sanctifying power of the truth, the Word of God.

Real Christian discipleship is knowing God and knowing Jesus through a personal living relationship (John 17:3), obeying God's Word (John 17:6), belonging to God and his Son (John 17:9-10), and rejoicing with joy (John 17:13), 'joy inexpressible and full of glory' (1 Peter 1:8).

Prayer for his Church

Jesus concluded his prayer by looking beyond the small body of men gathered around him, and as in his mind's eye he looked down the years to come, he prayed for his Church (John 17:20-26). This prayer was for all those who will be saved through the preaching and teaching of the apostles. The means that is used in order to bring about faith in Jesus Christ is, as always, the Word. Jesus said it is through *their* word, not as if they had invented it, but because they heard it, accepted it and preached it. This is the message of salvation, whether spoken or written. So the Saviour prayed for everyone who will come to faith right up to his return. Through the operation of the Holy Spirit in the mind and heart of those who hear this word thousands upon thousands are to be brought to salvation in Christ.

Prayer for the unity of his Church worldwide

Jesus had prayed for the apostles to share the oneness that is between the Father and Son (John 17:11) now he asks that the oneness of *all believers* would be like that which exists eternally between the Father and the Son. Father, Son and Holy Spirit are one in essence; believers, on the other hand are one in mind, effort and purpose. God is love and when we love one another we show the very essence of God. Only those who have been born from above, and are in the Father and in the Son, are also spiritually one, and offer a united witness to the world.

> There is one body and one Spirit, just as you were called in one hope of your calling; one Lord, one faith, one baptism; in you all (Ephesians 4:4-6).

The members of the Church of Jesus Christ having a unique relationship with their Lord and with each other will be a testimony to the world. This testimony is two fold: that it is God who sent Jesus and that he loves his people as he loves his Son (John 17:23). It is staggering to learn that God loves us to this extent. What an amazing conclusion to this most wonderful prayer when Jesus says, 'that the love with which you loved me may be in them, and I in them" (v.26). What a God, what a Saviour!

117. Disciples will stumble; Peter is warned
Matthew 26:30-35; Mark 14:26-31; Luke 22:31-34; John 13:37-38

As Jesus and his disciples continued east over the Brook Kidron (in the deep ravine to the east of Jerusalem) to enter the Gethsemane grove at the foot of the Mount of Olives, Jesus told his companions that they were all going to stumble because of what was soon about to happen to him. Because of their unfaithfulness and disbelief they would be scattered! The eleven apostles would suffer a temporary set-back, a short period of backsliding. All of them would be ensnared and trapped by forthcoming events.

The Scripture to which the Lord referred is so relevant to his experience as the suffering Saviour. The fuller text in Zechariah reads -

> 'Awake, O sword, against my Shepherd, against the Man who is my Companion,' says the LORD of hosts. 'Strike the Shepherd, and the sheep will be scattered; then I will turn my hand against [rather 'upon'] the little ones' (Zechariah 13:7).

The Lord Jesus applied the latter part where it refers to the Father bringing down the sword of divine judgment upon his Beloved Son having laid 'on him the iniquity of us all', it is he who is 'pleased… to bruise him' and to 'put him to grief' (Isaiah 53:6,10), when he makes his soul an offering for sin. It is amazing, a staggering fact that God 'did not spare his own Son, but delivered him up for us all' (Romans 8:32).

The sword is the symbol of power used to uphold justice (Romans 13:3-4). Consequently this Scripture is setting forth the great doctrine that the death of Christ is an act of supreme justice in which he endured the penalty of the highest law and suffered under the wrath of Almighty God himself. The sheep deserve the death blow from the sword of justice but the shepherd interposes himself. He takes the full force of the sword and with his wounds we are healed.

A few verses earlier in Zechariah 12:10 a prophecy is recorded where God says, 'They will look on me whom they pierced', words which the apostle John sees fulfilled in the crucifixion of Christ at Calvary (John 19:37). Again it is the One who is truly God and truly Man who fulfils it. Also in Zechariah 13:1 there is another connected prophecy, 'In that day a fountain shall be opened for the house of David and for the inhabitants of Jerusalem, for sin and for uncleanness.' The two components of our salvation are assured at the cross: justification by which sinners are released from the penalty of sin (Romans 5:9) and sanctification by which sinners are cleansed from the pollution of sin (Hebrews 10:10).

When the Shepherd is struck the sheep will be scattered. The warning that Jesus gave his disciples included a great encouragement, for they would gather again. Once scattered they would be able to reflect upon this warning and the reassurance of a re-gathering. Furthermore Jesus would be raised from the dead and meet them in Galilee (Matthew 26:32).

'The scattering of the sheep' must not be limited exclusively to the dispersion of the apostles on the night the Lord was arrested. It also referred to the general dispersion that would follow the death of Messiah (see Acts 8:4; 1 Peter 1:1-2). But God would 'turn back' his hand upon [not against] the little ones (Zechariah 13:7). The Lord's promise to go before them to Galilee was the practical fulfilment of God turning back his hand by drawing them together once more.

This section of the prophecy was not exhausted in the restoration of the apostles but is also fulfilled in the gathering in of the true sheep which continued in great measure at Pentecost and has been occurring ever since (Romans 11:5). When the prophecy declared that two-thirds of the Jewish Nation will 'be cut off and die, but one-third shall be left in it' (Zechariah 13:8), the fulfilment occurred not many years after the death of Jesus when around two-thirds of the people were killed by war, pestilence, and famine.

Peter protested in the strongest terms, that even if the others fell away, he would never do so (Matthew 26:33). Jesus responded -

> Simon, Simon! Indeed, Satan has asked for you, that he may sift you as wheat. But I have prayed for you, that your faith should not fail (Luke 22:31).

In the original language the first 'you' is plural, the second 'you' does not exist and the third and fourth are in the singular. Therefore the first 'you' means that others are included in Satan's request whilst the third and fourth 'you' are addressed specifically to Peter. Furthermore the Lord used his birth name 'Simon' rather than the new name 'Peter' given to him by the Lord, no doubt to emphasise his frail humanity rather than the 'rock-like' stability of his new nature. Jesus added the most wonderful assurance for Peter: 'But I have prayed for you, that your faith should not fail; and when you have returned to me, strengthen your brethren' (Luke 22:32).

Peter insisted that he was ready to go with him to prison and to death. Jesus informed Peter that he would deny him three times before the night was out, yes, before the cock crowed. In only a few hours time Peter would be kept from utter hopelessness and dreadful despair when he recalled the words of Jesus that he had been prayed for and would be forgiven and restored.

They would all be sifted as wheat. The process of sifting separates the wheat from the chaff. Here there was an implied encouragement for them - sifted as wheat; with all their weakness and frailty they are still 'wheat', still good grain that are true disciples of Jesus.

As the group approached the Garden of Gethsemane Jesus gave them a final instruction to equip themselves with supplies. Contrasting his previous directive in sending them out to preach the kingdom of God and heal the sick when they were required not to take money, knapsack or sandals (Luke 22:35; 10:4; cf. Matthew10:9-10) he now advised them to take money, if they had it, and a knapsack too.

The comparison was raised to show the difference between the welcome they received on their first mission to that which they will receive in the future. Then they were received and given kindly hospitality, lacking nothing. The atmosphere would change when Jesus was arrested and killed as a common criminal, 'numbered with transgressors' (Luke 22:37; Isaiah 53:12). Those who were his followers would share his public disgrace (John 15:18-20). They would face hostility and rejection because of their allegiance to Christ.

The surprise here is that Jesus also included the taking of a sword, if they had one, and if they did not possess a sword then to sell some of their clothing to buy one (Luke 22:36). Bearing in mind that the Lord often used figurative, metaphorical language in his teaching such as, 'Let the dead bury their own dead' (Matthew 8:22; cf. John 2:19; 4.13-14,32; 6:51), it would seem that this was another instance of that. Jesus was therefore emphasising the hostility they would face from their own country folk. He cannot mean them to possess a physical sword since that would violate his insistence against the use of arms for the promotion of the gospel.

In the Sermon on the Mount he said, 'I tell you not to resist an evil person. But whoever slaps you on your right cheek, turn the other to him also' (Matthew 5:39). He acknowledged that he sent out gospel servants as 'lambs among wolves' (Luke 10:3). Within a few hours he would confirm his teaching when Peter, seeking to defend Jesus, took his sword and cut off the ear of Malchus, servant of the high priest (John 18:10) and Jesus then said, 'Put your sword in its place, for all who take the sword will perish by the sword' (Matthew 26:52).

When the disciples pointed out that they have two swords, Jesus said, 'It is enough' (Luke 22:38). He cannot have meant that two swords were enough to defend them against 'a great multitude with swords and clubs' (Matthew 26:47). Indeed he did not intend that physical force would be used anyway. Maybe he was not responding about the two swords but was simply indicating that the time for discussion and further teaching was at an end. 'It is enough.'

The apostle Paul certainly lived out his Christian service understanding that the cause of Christ and his Church was not to be served by violence -

> For though we walk in the flesh, we do not war according to the flesh. For the weapons of our warfare are not carnal but mighty in God for pulling down strongholds, casting down arguments and every high thing that exalts itself against the knowledge of God, bringing every thought into captivity to the obedience of Christ (2 Corinthians 10:3-5).

The Christian armoury does not include spears or clubs. The only 'weapon' permitted to us is 'the sword of the Spirit, which is the word of God' (Ephesians 6:17).

The suffering and death of the Saviour

118. Grief in the Garden of Gethsemane
Matthew 26:36-46; Mark 14:32-42: Luke 22:39-46; John 18:1

So many place names in Israel have a significance in connection to the life and ministry of the Lord: Bethlehem - 'House of Bread'; Bethesda - 'House of Mercy'; and here Gethsemane - 'The Oil-Press' which indicated the place where olives were crushed and the oil extracted. This is a fitting metaphor for the intense pressure experienced in this garden by the One soon to become the Saviour of the world.

Many of the richer citizens of Jerusalem had gardens on the slopes of the Mount of Olives probably for two reasons: there was very limited space in the city of Jerusalem and there were ceremonial prohibitions against the use of manure on the soil of the sacred city. It is probable that a rich sympathiser welcomed Jesus to use his piece of ground in the Garden of Gethsemane whenever he was in the city and wanting to be quiet and away from the noise and bustle of city life. The Lord made frequent use of this facility whenever he and his apostles visited Jerusalem. They often met there as Judas Iscariot well knew (John 18:2).

Jesus had quite a number of friends who are not mentioned in detail. There was the woman who had made Jesus a tunic that was woven without a seam. There were the women who supported him with food, clothing and shelter as he travelled from place to place preaching and healing. There was the man who loaned him a donkey to ride into Jerusalem for the triumphal entry. There was the man who loaned him the upper room for the celebration of the Passover. It is evident that there were a number of devoted followers who would willingly do whatever he requested and provide whatever he required.

By going once more to Gethsemane on the eve of Passover, Jesus was putting himself in a place where he might easily be found. The time for avoiding his enemies was past, his hour had come. He must give this opportunity to the traitor, so that there would be no doubt that Jesus laid down his life, that no one took it from him, he laid it down willingly and voluntarily (John 10:17-18). He knew that Judas would come to that place that night and so he went there deliberately to face the betrayer and his enemies openly and unashamedly. Christ our Passover (1 Corinthians 5:7) was to die on the day when the lambs for the Old Covenant sacrifice were slaughtered. This was the One of whom John the Baptist said, 'Behold! The Lamb of God who takes away the sin of the world' (John 1:29).

It was close to midnight, Jesus instructed eight of the disciples to sit just inside the garden whilst he walked a little further on to spend time in prayer. He took with him Peter, James and John. Even at this time of extreme pressure he was still concerned for others for he instructed the three colleagues to pray that they 'may not enter into temptation' (Luke 22:40). He was no doubt aware that the Sanhedrin would not be satisfied with just his arrest but would inevitably turn their venom upon his followers. Jesus had warned them earlier, 'If they persecute me they will persecute you' (John 15:20). The severe temptation in the event of such hostility would be for the disciples to disown their allegiance to him. They must pray, as he had prayed for them, to be kept by the power of God (John 17:11) that with tenacity and enduring commitment they would remain loyal.

The Lord had repeatedly told his apostles the details of his suffering and death, how he would be betrayed to the chief priests, scribes and elders, condemned to death, delivered into the hands of Gentiles, mocked, scorned, insulted, spat upon and crucified. He knew that soldiers would gamble for his clothing, offer him sour wine to drink, that one thief would be converted whilst hanging on a cross... Nothing would take him by surprise for he knew 'all things that would come upon him' (John 18:4). No wonder he began to be 'sorrowful and deeply distressed' (Matthew 26:37). Surely it was his accurate and complete knowledge of all that was before him that made his sufferings all the more intense as he thought and prayed in the garden. He shared the agony of his soul with his three closest disciples -

> My soul is exceedingly sorrowful, even to death. Stay here and watch with me (Matthew 26:38).

He was not only to face the full force of the Jewish leadership in its evil but also the cruelty and barbarity of Gentile soldiers. Even worse, beyond this horror, there was the hidden enemy behind the conflict. Satan was engaged in the final hours in his own struggle for survival. The success of Jesus, in humbly submitting to all that was before him and as 'a lamb without blemish and without spot' shedding his precious blood for the redemption of his people (1 Peter 1:19), would be the death knell for the devil (Genesis 3:15). The Son of God became a human being 'that through death he might destroy him who had the power of death, that is, the devil' (Hebrews 2:14).

As fallen creatures we all have the taste of death in our mouths from birth. This Holy Man had no such experience. Death under the judgment of God meant that he would pass through experiences which he had never known before, the worst of all being a sense of separation from his Father, a loss of the awareness of the glorious relationship with heaven. There in the garden he knew that in less than eighteen hours he would be pressed to the extreme and cry out, 'My God, my God, why have you forsaken me?' (Matthew 27:46) No wonder that when he went a little farther and fell on his face, he prayed, 'O my Father, if it is possible, let this cup pass from me; nevertheless, not as I will, but as you will' (Matthew 26:39).

When he returned to the three disciples he was disappointed to find them asleep. He acknowledged that their spirit indeed was willing but it was their flesh that was weak (Mark 14:38) and encouraged them once more to stay alert and pray. He returned to his place of private prayer and repeated his earnest plea. The Holy Spirit recorded the anguish of God's Son -

> who, in the days of his flesh, when he had offered up prayers and supplications, with vehement cries and tears to him who was able to save him from death, and was heard because of his godly fear, though he was a Son, yet he learned obedience by the things which

he suffered. And having been perfected, he became the author of eternal salvation to all who obey him (Hebrews 5:7-9).

He was about to humble himself and be 'obedient to the point of death, even the death of the cross' (Philippians 2:8) where he will bear 'our sins in his own body on the tree' and suffer 'once for sins, the just for the unjust, that he might bring us to God' (1 Peter 2:24; 3:18). 'And being in agony, he prayed more earnestly. Then his sweat became like great drops of blood falling down to the ground' (Luke 22:44).

The Lord returned once more to the three disciples and found them asleep again. Their inability to remain awake and watchful would intensify his sense of isolation. Aroused they were lost for words and so Jesus went off to spend a third period in private prayer. When he came back to find them once more 'sleeping from sorrow' he called upon them to be up and on the move because the betrayer was soon to arrive.

The true humanity of Jesus Christ, the Son of God, was nowhere more vividly displayed than during that time in the Garden of Gethsemane.

Prayer is not always answered as desired; the Lord Jesus Christ prayed earnestly (cf. James 5:16) that the cup of suffering might pass from him and yet within a few hours he went to an agonising death on the cross; King David prayed for his sick son and the child died; the apostle Paul prayed earnestly three times and his affliction was not removed. In numerous cases, today, Christians pray with fervour and with faith for the removal of some problem, stress, illness, or distress and whilst there are wonderful instances when God grants the request, yet there are not infrequent occasions when the answer is 'no' or 'not yet'. Children of God pray and plead but the Lord does not answer in the way and at the time they desire! Why? Because, although the removal of the affliction would be a blessing, the continuance of the affliction will bring greater blessing to the sufferer or to others.

The Lord Jesus poured out his heart, pleaded for delivery and concluded by repeating his life-long commitment, 'nevertheless, not as I will, but as you will' and 'your will be done' (Matthew 26:39,42). Had the Lord God granted the prayer of his agonising Son there would have been no salvation, no Church, no 'great multitude which no one could number, of all nations, tribes, peoples, and tongues, standing before the throne and before the Lamb, clothed with white robes' (Revelation 7:9). In the pain of disappointment it is wise for believers to ponder what may be the will of God in their affliction -

• the grace that will be given in the affliction may be of greater value to the individual than would be the direct answer to the prayer;

- it might not be for the good of the individual who prays that the exact thing should be granted. Afflictions and calamities may in fact keep us from more serious problems; for example, blindness is a severe affliction but the lust of the eyes may result in disaster and disgrace;

- God may have some greater purpose in mind. Bearing affliction as a good soldier of Christ gives a fine example to others and may even be the cause of another conversion to Christ;

- which of us knows what is best for ourselves? If our prayers were answered literally each time then what a burden that would place upon us. When we pray we know that a wise and loving Father knows best;

- Paul's affliction kept the apostle humble and dependent but at the same time supported by a loving glorious promise, 'My grace is sufficient for you, for my strength is made perfect in weakness' (2 Corinthians 12:9). The angels being sent to strengthen Jesus is a vivid illustration of God's support when the answer to prayer is 'No'. It is clearly evident that 'we do not have a high priest who cannot sympathise with our weaknesses, but was in all points tempted as we are, yet without sin. Let us therefore come boldly to the throne of grace, that we may obtain mercy and find grace to help in time of need' (Hebrews 4:15-16). These words have been of untold comfort to countless followers of Jesus when passing through trials and temptations.

119. Betrayal and arrest
Matthew 26:47-56; Mark 14:43-52; Luke 22:47-53; John 18:2-12

Judas knew the Lord's usual activities and where he could be found away from the crowds. The chief priests, scribes and elders were taking no chances; along with Judas and their officers they sent a detachment of troops (John 18:3). The word translated 'detachment' can have three meanings: a company of 1,000, 600 or 200 men. At the time of Passover there were always extra soldiers in Jerusalem, quartered in the Tower of Antonia which overlooked the temple. There would be hundreds of men available. So at the very least there would be 200 soldiers besides officers (a kind of temple police) all fully armed with swords and clubs and equipped with torches and lanterns, a truly formidable company.

When this 'army' arrived Jesus was not in hiding, in fact something quite astonishing took place. The Lord, 'knowing all things that would come upon him', went forward and said, "Whom are you seeking?" (John 18:4) He was not taken by surprise, nor was he cringing in some dark corner like a frightened fugitive. He stepped out before his enemies and when they replied, 'Jesus of Nazareth' he responded with a fearless declaration, 'I am' (there is no 'he' in the original. It is literally, "I, I am" which links with his earlier disclosure, 'Before Abraham was, I am' - John 8:58). Here is the matchless dignity, awesome courage, outstanding boldness of Jesus.

Suddenly at these words his would-be-captors drew back and fell to the ground. His sheer courage shocked these hardened soldiers. In the garden he pleaded with God his Father for delivery but he will not plead with soldiers, temple police or Jewish leaders. The Father had not released him from his divine commission; the Son manfully faced the humiliation and horror awaiting him at the hands of evil men.

Jesus was concerned for the safety of his disciples. He presented himself to the troops saying, 'I have told you that I am. Therefore, if you seek me, let these go their way' (John 18:8). The apostle John added, 'that the saying might be fulfilled which he spoke, "Of those whom you gave me I have lost none"' (John 18:9). This saying is not a reference to an Old Testament prophecy but to words of the Lord Jesus in his High Priestly prayer some hours earlier when he prayed, 'While I was with them in the world, I kept them in your name. Those whom you gave me I have kept; and none of them is lost' (John 17:12; cf. 6:39; 10:28).

This addition by John is noteworthy for two reasons: firstly in that it is presented in the same way as any reference to Old Testament Scripture, 'that the saying might be fulfilled...' indicating that John considered the sayings of Jesus as equally infallible to those of the prophets of old. Secondly, in the instances where Jesus spoke of guarding those given to him by the Father he was referring to the spiritual realm, guarding their souls that they may enjoy eternal life. Here John related it to keeping them safe in the physical realm. This would suggest that the present physical ordeal faced by the apostles was of such a trial and test that their faith might be destroyed. They were not ready to face this extreme ordeal so Jesus ensured their physical protection. Not one of the disciples was arrested or apprehended even when Peter injured one of their number.

Judas stepped forward and engaged in the pre-arranged signal to identify Jesus by greeting him with a kiss of friendship (Mark 14:45). This was in fact unnecessary as Jesus had already identified himself. When the Lord greeted him warmly, 'Friend, why have you come?' (Matthew 26:50) it may be that he was giving Judas a last opportunity to repent. The men laid hands upon Jesus to take him away and his disciples asked him if they were to use the two swords they had with them. Before the Lord had time to reply, Peter drew his sword and struck Malchus, a servant of the high priest, cutting off his ear. Jesus immediately ordered Peter to put his sword back into its sheath adding, 'all who take the sword will perish by the sword' (Matthew 26:52; cf. Genesis 9:6; Revelation 13:10). Jesus added that he had only to pray the Father and a host of angels would come to his assistance, but then the Scriptures and his mission would not be fulfilled. Jesus touched the injured ear and healed it (Luke 22:51).

The captain, troops and officers of the Jews arrested Jesus, bound him and led him away (John 18:12). He was not driven or dragged but led indicating his willing submission being 'led as a lamb to the slaughter' (Isaiah 53:7).

All the disciples forsook Jesus and fled (Mathew 26:56). One young man was apprehended but managed to escape by slipping out of his cloak (Mark 14:51-52).

120. Jesus taken before Annas
John 18:13-14,19-23

Why was Jesus taken first to Annas? In A.D. 6 Annas was assigned to the position of high priest by the Romans who, on their conquest of Judah, had assumed responsibility to appoint the high priest for the Jews. Annas served ten years and though officially removed from office he remained one of the nation's most influential and powerful men. Five sons, Eleazar, Jonathan, Theophilus, Matthias, and Ananus, Caiaphas his son-in-law, and a grandson followed him in the office of high priest. The Sadducean family of Annas exercised control over the religious and social life of Israel for many years. They had authority over the temple and through its trade in sacrifices and money exchange became extremely rich.

Both Annas and Caiaphas were named as high priests by Luke in the Scriptures (Luke 3:2), yet according to the law of God only one high priest was to be appointed and that for his lifetime (Exodus 40:15; Numbers 35:25); consequently pious Jews would always think of Annas as the true high priest. So although in civic affairs Caiaphas was formally recognised as high priest, in matters of religion Annas took precedence. Hence Jesus was led to Annas first. Irrespective of who happened to be holding the office of high priest at the time Annas was certainly the power behind the throne.

Annas and Caiaphas had already decided that Jesus must die long before he was arrested and brought before them. They had been on the receiving end of much clearly implied criticism from Jesus and they hated him vehemently. It had been Caiaphas who had advised the Jews that it was expedient that one man should die for the people (John 18:14; 11:50). The apostle John reminded his readers of this to make it clear that Jesus was murdered from political considerations and not issues of religion.

The Lord Jesus faced an ecclesiastical trial in three stages and a civil trial in three stages -

The ecclesiastical trial:

    i. Preliminary hearing before Annas (John 18:12-14, 19-23).

    ii. First trial before the Sanhedrin (Caiaphas, scribes and elders, Matthew 26:57).

    iii. Second trial before the Sanhedrin just after dawn (Luke 22:66).

The civil trial:

    i. Initial trial before Pilate

    ii. Trial before Herod (Luke 23:6-12)

    iii. Trial before Pilate resumed

In the preliminary hearing when Jesus stood before Annas two high priests met; a greater contrast could not have been more evident: one earthly, one heavenly; one greedy, one gracious; one filled with hate, one filled with love.

> Therefore, in all things [Jesus] had to be made like his brethren, that he might be a merciful and faithful High Priest in things pertaining to God, to make propitiation for the sins of the people. For in that he himself has suffered, being tempted, he is able to aid those who are tempted (Hebrews 2:17-18).

The greedy Annas would be very bitter against the Lord for his many verbal attacks upon the corruption and evil in the temple. There is no doubt that Annas wanted the Nazarene dead.

The dealings of Annas with Jesus were an appalling miscarriage of justice. In Jewish law no accused person could be asked a question which would incriminate himself for capital punishment. As one Jewish scholar stated, 'Our true law does not inflict the penalty of death upon a sinner by his own confession.' Annas violated the principles of Jewish justice when he questioned Jesus. This is precisely why Jesus answered him as he did. Jesus said in effect, 'Take your evidence about me in the proper and legal way. Examine your witnesses, which you have every right to do; stop examining me, which you have no right to do'.

Note how the high priest questioned Jesus firstly about his disciples then about his teaching (John 18:19). Annas was more concerned about the success of Jesus rather than the message of Jesus. Jesus said nothing about his disciples. Annas was one of those 'whitewashed tombs which indeed appear beautiful outwardly, but inside are full of dead men's bones and all uncleanness'. They, Annas and his sons and son-in-law, 'outwardly appear righteous to men, but inside [they] are full of hypocrisy and lawlessness' (Matthew 23:27-28). The words of Isaiah speak of characters like Annas and Caiaphas -

> Their works are works of iniquity, and the act of violence is in their hands. Their feet run to evil, and they make haste to shed innocent blood; their thoughts are thoughts of iniquity... and there is no justice in their ways; they have made themselves crooked paths (Isaiah 59:6-8).

Annas lived in one section of the high priest's palace and Caiaphas lived in another section, with a common courtyard. Whilst the Lord was being subjected to examination by high priest Annas, the apostle Peter was engaged in denying the Lord.

Following the arrest of Jesus and the dispersal of the apostles, Peter and an unnamed disciple plucked up courage and followed the arresting group at a distance. Within a short while they arrived at the courtyard of the high priest's palace and the unnamed disciple gained entrance because he was known to the high priest. Peter was initially denied access until the unnamed disciple spoke with the servant girl controlling the door and Peter was permitted to enter.

There would be a conflict within Peter at this time between courage and cowardice. When the servant girl doorkeeper suspected that Peter might be one of the Lord's disciples, he said, 'I am not. I do not know him'. After a short while Peter was confronted again. This time he swore with an oath that he did not know Jesus. The Lord had predicted that Peter would deny him three times. The third occasion came one hour later when the trial before the Sanhedrin was underway.

121. Trial before Caiaphas and the Jewish Council
Matthew 26:57-68; Mark 14:53-65; Luke 22:63-65; John 18:24

Meanwhile within the building Jesus was led bound from Annas to Caiaphas (John 18:24). The room where the Lord faced his second interrogation was above ground level (Mark 14:66) and visible from the courtyard (Luke 22:61). Gathered with Caiaphas were the chief priests, scribes and elders (Matthew 26:57). They were seeking grounds for putting Jesus to death and wanted false witnesses to testify against him. The law stated -

> Whoever is deserving of death shall be put to death on the testimony of two or three witnesses; he shall not be put to death on the testimony of one witness (Deuteronomy 17:6).

The problem was that they could not find two witnesses who agreed. Caiaphas the high priest stood and asked Jesus a direct question, 'Do you answer nothing? What is it these men testify against you?' (Mark 14:60) Jesus kept silent and gave no answer. There was no lawful reason why he should speak since no charge had been brought against him.

Caiaphas, presumably frustrated and annoyed, addressed the Lord Jesus directly again, 'I put you under oath by the living God: tell us if you are the Christ, the Son of God!' (Matthew 26:63) He would appear to have been using the words of Psalm 2:2,7,12 - the only place where the Christ (his Anointed) is said to be the Son of God.

It was a crafty question for although the Lord knew it was unlawful to address the accused in that way, he also knew that to remain silent to this challenge would be construed as a denial that he was the Christ. Jesus answered and confirmed his identity by saying to him, 'It is as you said. Nevertheless, I say to you, hereafter you will see the Son of Man sitting at the right hand of the Power, and coming on the clouds of heaven' (Matthew 26:64). He was using the words of the prophet Daniel which the Jews recognised as a prophecy of the coming Messiah. In full the prophecy reads -

> I was watching in the night visions, and behold, One like the Son of Man, coming with the clouds of heaven! He came to the Ancient of Days, and they brought him near before him. Then to him was given dominion and glory and a kingdom, that all peoples, nations, and languages should serve him. His dominion is an everlasting dominion, which shall not pass away, and his kingdom the one which shall not be destroyed (Daniel 7:13-14).

Caiaphas reacted by tearing his clothing (in spite of it being forbidden, Leviticus 21:10) as a faked sign of grief that God had been so dishonoured by this man who was claiming to be the Son of God. The Sanhedrin and this 'whitewashed tomb' with his outward appearance of outrage at the dishonouring of God did not stop to consider the credentials that Jesus of Nazareth had presented to the nation, numerous proofs in word and works (cf. John 5:31-40; 8:58; 10:24-30); nor did they examine his claim in the light of the abundance of Old Testament revelation. At Pentecost Peter was able to declare that this is 'Jesus of Nazareth, a Man attested by God to you by miracles, wonders, and signs' (Acts 2:22).

Caiaphas cried out,

> He has spoken blasphemy! What further need do we have of witnesses? Look, now you have heard his blasphemy! What do you think? They answered and said, 'He is deserving of death' (Matthew 26:65-66).

Members of the Jewish Council passed the sentence of death upon the Son of God in violation of the law of Moses and the principles of justice. Jesus was abused with spitting, slapping, beating, mocking and taunting; as prophesied by Isaiah, 'I gave my back to those who struck me, and my cheeks to those who plucked out the beard; I did not hide my face from shame and spitting' (Isaiah 50:6).

Meanwhile in the courtyard outside, the apostle Peter was identified by his accent as a Galilean and charged with being a follower of Jesus. In fact a relative of Malchus, whose ear Peter had severed only a few hours earlier in Gethsemane, was sure he had seen him in the garden. For the third time Peter denied all knowledge of Jesus, seeking to strengthen his objection with cursing and swearing. Even while he was protesting he heard the cockerel crow and Peter looked up. Through the window above he saw the Lord Jesus turn and look at him and Peter remembered his prediction that before the cockerel had crowed Peter would deny him three times. And Peter went out of the courtyard 'and wept bitterly' (Luke 22:62).

The whole Sanhedrin (the highest Jewish Council of seventy composed of the high priest, chief priests and elders of the people) convened at dawn. One or two hours passed to separate the two meetings; for according to Jewish practice the sentence could not be passed at the trial. The members of the council discussed how to proceed since under Roman occupation they had no power to enact the death sentence. In determining to send Jesus to the Roman governor Pilate, for him to carry out the death sentence, the charge against Jesus had to be altered. Pilate and the Romans would have no interest in Jewish religious issues of blasphemy. The charge was therefore changed to rebellion against Caesar. In the Jewish ecclesiastical court the question for Jesus was, 'Are you the Son of God?' whereas in the Roman civil court the question for Jesus was, 'Are you the King of Israel?'

Jesus was bound and led away to Pilate the Roman Governor.

122. Jesus before Pilate (the first time)
Matthew 27:2, 11-14; Mark 15:2-5; Luke 23:1-7; John 18:28-38

Roman governors of Judea normally had their residence in Caesarea with only a subordinate officer in Jerusalem supported by 4,000 to 6,000 soldiers. However at the great Jewish festivals, due to the vast influx of worshippers, the governor moved temporarily to Jerusalem with extra troops. It would have been on the authority of the governor that the detachment of troops had been despatched to accompany the officers of the temple led by Judas to arrest Jesus. It was the custom for the governor to personally preside over civic affairs whilst in the city (John 18:39). Jesus was brought to the

Praetorium (Hall of Judgment) to stand before Governor Pilate. Judging from the recorded conversation, Pilate had some prior knowledge as to the character of the Lord and the nature of his accusers (Matthew 27:18). It is possible that Nicodemus or Joseph of Arimathea had consulted with him.

The Jewish leaders sent Jesus into the Praetorium under guard but did not enter themselves. They believed that the touch of a Gentile was a defilement and that to enter a Gentile establishment would render them unable to participate in the Passover meal that day. They took great care to avoid what they considered to be moral pollution whist at the same time seeking the execution of an innocent man. They were highly religious yet spiritually blind, ceremonially punctilious yet morally bankrupt.

Consequently Pilate had to walk back and forth between the Jews and Jesus to examine him, first hearing their accusations and then going into the Praetorium to hear the answer of Jesus.

The Lord had been tried in the court of the Jews, now he was to be tried in the court of the Gentiles. Three charges were highlighted: 'perverting the nation, forbidding to pay taxes to Caesar and saying that he himself is Christ, a King' (Luke 23:2). Jesus explained to Pilate that his kingship was exercised over a spiritual realm and by implication was no threat to Caesar or any other earthly ruler.

After hearing the accusations, charges and complaints from the Jewish leaders Pilate remained totally unconvinced. He told the people, 'I find no fault in him' (John 18:38). The Jewish leadership was enraged and cried out, 'He stirs up the people, teaching throughout all Judea, beginning from Galilee to this place' (Luke 23:5). When Pilate heard the mention of Galilee he halted the proceedings. Galilee was under the jurisdiction of Herod Antipas and it so happened that he was in Jerusalem at the time, so Pilate sent the Lord Jesus to Herod (Luke 23:5-7).

Meanwhile when Judas saw that Jesus was condemned he was filled with remorse (Matthew 27:3-10). Overwhelmed with guilt for betraying an innocent man he went to the chief priests and elders in the temple to return the thirty pieces of silver. They showed no interest and dismissed him. Judas threw the money to the floor and went out and hanged himself. Probably as a consequence of the rope or branch breaking he fell headlong, burst in the middle and his internal organs gushed out (Acts 1:18).

At the same time the chief priests and elders were debating what to do with the money and since they could not put it into the treasury, because it was the price of blood (Matthew 27:6) a field was purchased to be used as a graveyard for strangers.

The potter's field (Zechariah 11:12-13) was a disused quarry close on the outskirts of the city in the Valley of Hinnom (Gehenna) on the south side of Jerusalem. The clay had been extracted for making earthenware vessels. Again the scruples of the Jewish leadership were shown to be skewed for these were the men who, in their recent dealings with the Saviour, disregarded 'the weightier matters of the law: justice and mercy and faith' (Matthew 23:23).

When Jesus and his accusers met with Herod Antipas, the king was delighted (Luke 23:8-12). He had long been interested in the Lord and hoped to see him perform a miracle. This Herod was responsible for beheading John the Baptist (Mark 6:14-29) and at one time wanted to kill Jesus (Luke 13:31). Later he was convinced that Jesus was John the Baptist risen from the dead (Matthew 14:1-2).

Herod questioned Jesus at great length but the Lord gave him no answer. He kept silent throughout the whole procedure even though the chief priests and scribes taunted him with accusations. Finally Herod and some of his soldiers treated the Lord with great contempt. Mocking him and putting a purple robe on him Herod sent him back to Pilate.

123. Jesus before Pilate (the second time)
Matthew 27:15-26; Mark 15:6-15; Luke 23:13-25; John 18:39-19:15

Pilate's attempt to pass Jesus on to Herod, that he might relinquish responsibility for making judgment, failed. The Lord was once more brought to the Praetorium to face the governor. Pilate made it quite clear to the chief priests and elders that he had examined Jesus closely in their presence and could find nothing to substantiate their accusations. Neither he nor Herod had found anything deserving of death (Luke 23:15).

Pilate's path of failure -

- he concluded that there was no charge to answer but did not acquit Jesus (Luke 23:14);
- he tried to evade passing judgment by sending Jesus to Herod Antipas (Luke 23:7);
- he appealed to the people despite saying neither Herod nor he had found fault (Luke 23:13-16);
- he appealed to the people's sympathy, 'Behold the man' (John 19:4-5);
- he appealed to the people to make a moral choice, Jesus or Barabbas (Mark 15:6);

- he ignored the warning of his wife to have nothing to do with Jesus (Matthew 27:19);
- he washed his hands insisting on the innocence of Jesus (Matthew 27:24);
- he gave in, fearing the rising tumult and to gratify the crowd (Mark 15:15).

Pilate recognised that no criminal charge had been established and sought to release Jesus. He had been told plainly the nature of the Lord's kingdom, and the purpose of the Lord's coming into the world. He had publicly confessed the Lord's innocence. Yet despite the revelation which had been given to him and being convinced himself that Jesus was without guilt, he nevertheless was ultimately responsible for him being treated in a most barbaric manner (Matthew 27:26) and with the vilest of indignities.

The Lord Jesus suffered for us, leaving us an example, that we should follow his steps -

> 'Who committed no sin, nor was guile [deceit] found in his mouth'; who, when he was reviled, did not revile in return; when he suffered, he did not threaten, but committed himself to him who judges righteously (1 Peter 2:22-23).

The crowd, spurred on by high priests Annas and Caiaphas and chief priests cried out for the release of Barabbas and the crucifixion of Jesus. Was it a coincidence that the political rebel and murderer (Luke 23:25) should be called 'Barabbas' meaning 'son of the father'? Clearly his father was the devil for 'he was a murderer from the beginning' (John 8:44). He was chosen for release. Condemned in his place was the Holy One whose Father is the All-Righteous Sovereign Lord of all creation. The predominantly Galilean pilgrims who welcomed the arrival of Jesus to Jerusalem proved no match for the citizens of Jerusalem and Judea who demanded his death. To appease the crowd Pilate yielded and granted their request. Jesus was humiliated and brutalised by soldiers then led away to be crucified. The prophecy of David was fulfilled -

> Why do the nations rage, and the people plot a vain thing? The kings of the earth set themselves, and the rulers take counsel together, against the LORD and against his Anointed [Messiah/ Christ] (Psalm 2:1-2).

Not many months later it is clear the the early Christians understood the fulfilment of that psalm when they prayed -

> You are God, who made heaven and earth and the sea, and all that is in them... For truly against your holy Servant Jesus, whom you

anointed, both Herod and Pontius Pilate, with the Gentiles and the people of Israel, were gathered together to do whatever your hand and your purpose determined before to be done (Acts 4:27-28).

There was great haste in following through the sentence of death. Jesus was taken immediately from Gabbatha to Golgotha, from judgment to execution. From Gabbatha ('the pavement') with its mockery of justice, to Golgotha ('the skull') with its stench of death and decay. It was the normal practice to give at least forty-eight hours between sentence and execution in order to give opportunity for any new witnesses or new evidence to be brought forward. In the case of the Lord this practice seems to have been intentionally overridden.

It was also the practice among the Romans to make the sentenced man walk the longest route to the place of crucifixion. An officer of the guard walked before the condemned man carrying a placard on which the man's crimes were written for all to see. There were two reasons for this procedure: firstly to act as a deterrent to any would-be criminal to demonstrate that crime does not pay; and secondly to give a final opportunity for any who could still bear witness in favour of the man, to come forward. Should new witnesses come forward then the proceedings would be immediately halted and the trial reconvened.

That the Lord Jesus was compelled to take this long journey carrying a cross added to his humiliation. He was being paraded before the eyes of sinners as a common criminal. The prophet Isaiah had well prophesied - 'he was numbered with the transgressors' (Isaiah 53:12).

Sin is so dreadful in the eyes of the All-Holy Creator God that no means can atone for it, whether a lifetime of works, obedience or sacrifice, but only the substitutionary death of his Beloved, All-Holy Eternal Son.

124. Delivered to be crucified
Matthew 27:31-34; Mark 15:20-23; Luke 23:26-33; John 19:16-17

Jesus was led out of the Palace of Pilate and out of the city of Jerusalem fulfilling yet another Old Testament type: 'The bull for the sin offering and the goat for the sin offering, whose blood was brought in to make atonement in the Holy Place, shall be carried outside the camp' (Leviticus 16:27; cf. Hebrews 13:11-13). On the way to Calvary a passer-by, Simon of Cyrene was compelled to carry the cross for Jesus for the heavy beatings had taken their toll on the Saviour -

He is despised and rejected by men, a Man of sorrows and acquainted with grief... He was oppressed and he was afflicted, yet he opened not his mouth; he was led as a lamb to the slaughter, and as a sheep before its shearers is silent, so he opened not his mouth. He was taken from prison and from judgment, and who will declare his generation? For he was cut off from the land of the living; for the transgressions of my people he was stricken (Isaiah 53:3,7-8).

Crowds followed, including sympathetic women mourners (Luke 23:27). It was a merciful Jewish practice to give those led to execution a drink of wine mingled with myrrh; a form of anaesthetic to reduce sensitivity to pain. This humanitarian act was performed by an association of devout women in Jerusalem.

Jesus refused the drink. The Lord was determined to face the cross, with all its brutality and horror, in full and complete consciousness. He will not submit himself into human hands to be drugged, but will face the whole experience in full and total awareness; for it must be seen and known that he laid down his own life freely and voluntarily, even to the very end! Jesus told the women not to mourn for him but for themselves; it will not be long before they will need comfort as tragedy falls upon them.

Jesus added, 'For if they do these things in the green wood, what will be done in the dry?' (Luke 23:31) A green tree has life, flourishes and bears fruit, just as Jesus was fruitful and useful in his preaching, teaching and healing. He was pure in nature, sinless in life and did no harm to anyone in person or property. Those who hated him and sought his death could find nothing, and prove nothing against him. It was totally unjust to cut him down and put him to death.

The metaphor highlights the innocence and righteous-ness of the Son of God. If Pilate on behalf of the Romans could unjustly sentence to death one whom he knew and declared to be totally guiltless, what will they do to a rebellious nation? A dry tree is dead wood which readily burns. The devastation brought upon a guilty people will be enormous. Jesus anticipated the siege and destruction of Jerusalem (the historian Josephus claimed that 1,100,000 people were killed during the siege, of which the majority were Jews). If the righteous suffer, how much more the wicked? Years later the apostle Peter drew a similar comparison when he wrote -

For the time has come for judgment to begin at the house of God; and if it begins with us first, what will be the end of those who do not obey the gospel of God? Now 'If the righteous one is scarcely saved, where will the ungodly and the sinner appear?' Therefore let those who suffer according to the will of God commit their souls to him in doing good, as to a faithful Creator (1 Peter 4:17-19; Proverbs 11:31).

Christ Jesus embraced the cross with its stigma and curse in wholehearted obedience to the Father and deep love for his people. He took the guilt of our sins upon himself as though it was his guilt. He made a full and eternal atonement: the condemnation has been removed, the curse has been annulled, the pollution has been purified. Christ accomplished all this upon that cross.

125. Crucifixion: six hours agony on the cross
Matthew 27:35-56; Mark 15:24-41; Luke 23:34-49; John 19:18-30

According to Roman law no Roman citizen could ever die by crucifixion. Neither was it the Jewish form of capital punishment; which was stoning not crucifixion. At the time when David prophesied, 'They pierced my hands and my feet' (Psalm 22:16) there was no nation known to practice crucifixion. It was four hundred years later that it was systematically practiced by the Persians.

The inscription on the cross

Pilate wrote an inscription to put on the cross: 'Jesus of Nazareth, the King of the Jews... and it was written in Hebrew, Greek and Latin' (John 19:19-20). There are slight differences in the wording in the four gospel accounts which are easily explained. Three languages were used to make the statement and were not intended to be translations. Hebrew was the language of religion; Greek the language of science, culture and philosophy; Latin of law. How fitting that Jesus Christ should be declared king in the three great languages of the ancient world.

He is King in the highest religious sense, King of Kings. He is King supreme over all that is beautiful of form, being and thought. He is the ultimate of all true wisdom, the glory of all right intellect. He is King as to law. In him the law of God and the Kingdom of God are perfectly displayed. He is King of the Church and King of the world (Psalm 47:2; Ephesians 1 :22-23).

The three major languages of the world declare Jesus to be King. King Jesus unites the peoples of the world. In his kingdom there are no racial distinctions and no national demarcations for we are all one in Christ Jesus our Lord (Galatians 3:28; Colossians 3:11; Revelation 5:9-10).

Why did the authorities crucify Jesus in the centre? (John 19:17-18) Was it planned by Pilate, requested by the chief priests, the final mockery of the soldiers? Whatever their reason there is certainly significance from a spiritual point of view. Jesus was not on the edge of things. He was not, as it were, touching the fringe of human existence and human suffering - he was right there in the middle - the embodiment of suffering. Prophecy was once more being fulfilled: 'He poured out his soul unto death, and he was numbered with the transgressors' (Isaiah 53:12) as the Lord predicted at the Last Supper that this prophecy would be fulfilled (Luke 22:37).

One by one prophecies were being fulfilled at the cross: David prophesied the experience of Christ -

> For dogs have surrounded me; the congregation of the wicked has enclosed me. They pierced my hands and my feet; I can count all my bones. They look and stare at me. They divide my garments among them, and for my clothing they cast lots (Psalm 22:16-18; John 19:23-24).

Five hundred years earlier Jehovah had promised, 'They will look on me whom they pierced' (Zechariah 12:10; John 19:37).

It has been said that a person who was crucified 'died a thousand deaths'. The sentenced man was stripped and laid upon a long piece of wood. His feet were positioned so that they would stand on a block of wood when the cross was lifted upright. Rope was tied around the ankles and wrists or large nails were driven through hands and feet. The rope or nails would not hold the weight so much as secure the man to the wood. The cross was lifted into the vertical position and fastened into the ground in such a manner that the criminal was not much higher than in standing. The horrors to endure were innumerable: severe inflammation, swelling of the wounds in the region of the nails, unbearable pain from torn tendons, fearful discomfort from the strained position of the body, throbbing headache and burning thirst. The crucified man had to constantly exert pressure through his legs in order to breath. Eventually, slowly and excruciatingly strength ebbs away and suffocation brings death -

> And being found in appearance as a man, he humbled himself and became obedient to death, even the death of the cross (Philippians 2:8).

The physical and mental dimension of the suffering of Jesus is not where the emphasis is found in the Scriptures of the Old and New Testament; it is the spiritual dimension that is emphasised. When God the Father 'laid on him the iniquity of us all' (Isaiah 53:6); when he 'bore our sins in his own body on the tree' (1 Peter 2:24) and 'delivers us from the wrath to come' (1 Thessalonians 1:10) the extent of his spiritual suffering is beyond our minds to comprehend.

When the soldiers shared out the clothing of the Saviour each of the four took one item. The description of the remaining article suggests a tunic like those worn by high priests. How amazing that the Lord should have this sign of his great work. He is indeed the great High Priest. He is the King/Priest forever after the order of Melchizedek who unites righteousness and peace in his glorious reign (Hebrews 7:2).

> [Jesus Christ] because he continues forever, has an unchangeable priesthood. Therefore he is also able to save to the uttermost those who come to God through him, since he always lives to make intercession for them. For such a High Priest was fitting for us, who is holy, harmless, undefiled, separate from sinners (Hebrews 7:24-26).

The Lord's words from the cross

1. 'Father, forgive them, for they do not know what they do' (Luke 23:34).

The Father honoured this prayer when the centurion and those with him came to faith at the foot of the cross (Matthew 27:54). Had not the Father said to his Son, 'Ask of me, and I will give you the nations for your inheritance, and the ends of the earth for your possession' (Psalm 2:8). Had not the Son prayed in the upper room, 'I pray for them. I do not pray for the world but for those whom you have given me, for they are yours' (John 17:9) and 'I do not pray for these alone, but also for those who will believe in me through their word' (John 17:20).

The chief priests sneered, 'He saved others; let him save himself if he is the Christ, the chosen of God'. The soldiers joined in the mocking, 'If you are the King of the Jews, save yourself' (Luke 23:35-37). Travellers on the busy road in and out of Jerusalem blasphemed, wagging their heads and saying, 'You who destroy the temple and build it in three days, save yourself! If you are the Son of God, come down from the cross' (Matthew 27:40). Even the robbers who were crucified with him reviled him (Matthew 27:44). With a collective onslaught the cry rose up, 'Save yourself! Save yourself!' The devil mustered all his forces against Jesus, tempting him to use his eternal power as the Son of God for his own ends just as Satan had done in the temptations in the wilderness. The truth is that had Jesus saved himself, he would not have saved us!

2. 'Assuredly, I say to you, today you will be with me in Paradise' (Luke 23:43).

In the midst of the reviling, mockery, sneering, derision and blasphemy the Holy Spirit was working in the heart and mind of at least one man. One of the thieves who hung crucified by the side of Jesus experienced a wonderful change of mind and heart. He came under the convicting power of the Holy

Spirit of God. Earlier in the upper room Jesus had spoken about the work of the Spirit of truth -

> When he has come, he will convict the world of sin, and of righteousness, and of judgment: of sin, because they do not believe in me; of righteousness, because I go to my Father and you see me no more; of judgment, because the ruler of this world is judged (John 16:8-11).

These three essential marks were evident in this thief. When his colleague continued in his blasphemy he said, 'Do you not even fear God [cf. Psalm 85:9], seeing you are under the same condemnation? And we indeed justly, for we receive the due reward of our deeds; but this Man has done nothing wrong' (Luke 23:40-41). He acknowledged his own sin and guilt and he recognised the righteousness of Jesus. Though the voices of the apostles were silent, God will proclaim the innocence and glory of his Son through a crucified thief.

What astonishing faith this man demonstrated in the face of the whole mocking world. In a matter of moments this man passed from spiritual death to life, from darkness to light. He was convinced that there was judgment to face after death and with surprising insight he knew that Jesus had special authority in that future court. Therefore he said to him, 'Lord, remember me when you come into your kingdom' (Luke 23:42).

In the midst of terrible spiritual darkness the light shines out brightly. 'For it is the God who commanded light to shine out of darkness, who has shone in our hearts to give the light of the knowledge of the glory of God in the face of Jesus Christ' (2 Corinthians 4:6). Jesus answered the thief, 'Assuredly, I say to you, today you will be with me in Paradise' (Luke 23:43). However bad or however good our life may be here on earth 'to depart and be with Christ... is far better' (Philippians 1:23).

3. Jesus 'said to his mother, "Woman, behold your son!" Then he said to the disciple, "Behold your mother!"'(John 19:26-27).

In English the word 'woman' sounds cold and disrespectful when addressed to one's wife or mother. In the language of the Bible the word translated 'woman' has no such connotations (cf. Matthew 15:28; 26:10; John 2:4; 4:21; 20:15). It is the general and honourable way of addressing an adult female but it lacks the familial tie of the word, 'mother'.

Many women from Galilee were present at the crucifixion of the Lord (Mark 15:40; John 19:25; Matthew 27:56). Among them Mary the mother of Jesus (not present throughout); Salome (Mary's sister, who was the wife of Zebedee and mother of James and John; this would mean that John the apostle was the cousin of Jesus); and Mary the wife of Clopas who was the mother of James the Younger and Joses. There is good non-Biblical evidence that she was Joseph's sister and therefore another aunt of Jesus; hence a very close knit family group surrounded the cross. Mary Magdalene, out of whom Jesus had cast seven demons (Mark 16:9), was also there. The apostle John is the only male disciple recorded as present at the cross.

When Jesus saw his mother he said to her, 'Woman, behold your son!' and to the disciple, 'Behold your mother!' (John 19:26,27). What amazing compassion and tenderness.

He had prayed for those who had crucified him, reassured a penitent thief of his salvation, and now he made a wonderful provision for his mother. He placed a responsibility upon the apostle John, the disciple whom he loved, for the mother whom he loved. Henceforth John was to love and care for Mary as he would his own mother.

Mary must think no longer of Jesus as her Son but of Jesus as her Saviour. She needed him to save her as much as anyone did. John fully understood the Lord's request and he took her immediately away from Calvary to his own home. She is no longer named with the women at the cross who then watched from afar.

Mary showed her true character and strength. Godly Simeon, thirty-three years earlier had prophesied her suffering, 'A sword will pierce through your own soul also' (Luke 2:35). Highly favoured she was among women (Luke 1:28), blessed indeed by the presence of God and with true godly devotion she remained faithful even with a broken heart.

4. 'My God, my God, why have you forsaken me?' (Matthew 27:46; Psalm 22:1)

For three hours the Saviour hung in agony upon the cross and it was now midday. For the next three hours there was darkness. At the heat of the day, when the sun would normally be at its hottest and brightest, darkness came upon the whole land. One of the plagues that God visited on the Egyptians was a dreadful darkness, a 'darkness which may even be felt' (Exodus 10:21). Now at Golgotha, nearly fifteen hundred years later, it is not Egypt which comes under divine judgment, it is Israel herself. Israel was committing a horrible work of darkness upon which the sun would no longer shine. This had been prophesied -

> "It shall come to pass in that day," says the Lord GOD, "that I will make the sun go down at noon, and I will darken the earth in broad daylight; I will turn your feasts into mourning, and all your songs into lamentation" (Amos 8:9-10).

Imagine the scene throughout Israel. Three hours of darkness probably a darkness like that in Egypt which could be felt. Three hours in which sinners would be inflicted with the greatest terror and fear: the disturbed meals, the confusion of the temple service, the chaos of the evening sacrifice, the interrupted lusts, the pangs of conscience. How many cries were raised to the God of heaven under that frightening experience? Yet how many soon forgot their hasty promises when the light returned?

There was an even greater darkness than that which engulfed the land, a worse darkness than in the days of Moses in Egypt. Over the soul of the Saviour was a thick darkness, even the darkness of hell! At 3.00p.m. the crucified Saviour was heard to cry, 'Eli, Eli, lama sabachthani?' that is, 'My God, my God, why have you forsaken me?'

This was not the cry of despair. It was the expression of the unfathomable depths of suffering through which the Lord passed and in which he endured faithfully and triumphantly to the end. This loud cry came at the end of the three hours of darkness. The Lord had been upon the cross six hours. The cry piercing the darkness expressed the deep anguish of his soul. He experienced a dreadful sense that he was abandoned by his Father. He felt himself rejected by God; the consciousness of divine wrath completely engulfed him yet he still cried, 'My God'. Everything had been stripped from him, Satan had done his worst, the Father had given up his Son; the sacrifice demanded of Abraham but never ratified (Genesis 22:2,12) was now enacted by God when he spared not his own Son (Romans 8:32).

He had borne the abandonment of the world, of the Jewish nation and even of his own apostles but this was the ultimate suffering, the sense that he was deserted, abandoned by God. He was tormented to the absolute limit but he still had unfaltering confidence in the Sovereign Lord and cried in humility and love, 'My God'. There never was, nor ever will be again, a death like this death.

As Jesus placed himself under the judgment of God on behalf of his sinful people, he could not be spared from experiencing God's wrath as though he were himself entirely, wholly and only guilty. This cry penetrated the wrath and ended it forever through the Saviour's perfect love and submission. Without hearing this cry from the heart and lips of the Lord we would never have known what it really cost him. Now we know. *Now we understand something of the dreadful cost. The depth of his agony defies all human comprehension.* He suffered a sense that he was forsaken, abandoned. He underwent a devastating sense of aloneness, of utter isolation, a sense of total loss. There was no word from heaven to cheer and encourage the Son of God in the hour of his greatest testing and trial, no voice from the cloud saying, 'This is my beloved Son, in whom I am well-pleased' (Matthew 3:17). No longer does he cry, 'Father', that awareness was not there. Now he has been driven to the limits of human endurance - and yet he cried in faith, 'My God!'

5. 'I thirst!' (John 19:28)

'After this, Jesus, knowing that all things were now accomplished, that the Scripture might be fulfilled, said, "I thirst!"' (John 19:28) David prophesied on behalf of the Saviour at Calvary, 'My strength is dried up like a potsherd, and my tongue clings to my jaws' (Psalm 22:15).

'After this', after prayer for his executioners, assurance to the penitent thief, provision for his mother, after the most excruciating agony, after the most appalling suffering and the dreadful sense of being abandoned, Jesus knew that all was accomplished. He had borne everything in true faithfulness; he had been tested to the very limit without wavering or sin. Everything had been combined against him. He had been hated by men, tormented and bruised by Satan (Genesis 3:15), even bruised by God his Father (Isaiah 53:10); yet there was nothing that earth, heaven, or hell could do against him to divert him from his faith and confidence in the Father. The last cry which demonstrated the depth of his agony is followed by another which showed the height of his control. Even here, at the crucial point of suffering, he was enduring the cross and he was despising the shame (Hebrews 12:2). Having endured the absolute darkness for three hours and the sense of God's wrath upon him Jesus knew that all things were accomplished. He suffered the terrible thirst which accompanies crucifixion. David again prophesied, expressing the experience of the Saviour at this moment -

Save me, O God! For the waters have come up to my neck. I sink in deep mire, where there is no standing; I have come into deep waters, where the floods overflow me. I am weary with my crying; my throat is dry; my eyes fail while I wait for my God... For my thirst they gave me vinegar to drink (Psalm 69:1-3,21).

Nothing would stop him from saying everything he wanted to say.

6. 'It is finished!' (John 19:30)

These words are a declaration of triumph, the most important triumph since the beginning of time. The confidence that was in his heart and mind he was now able to express. The moistened throat enabled him to cry out with a loud voice 'It is finished!' God was supremely honoured and Jesus was totally vindicated as the Son of God, Son of Man and the promised Messiah/Christ.

The one Greek word translated as 'It is finished' appears in a rarely used grammatical tense in the New Testament. It is the perfect tense and has no English equivalent. In Greek the perfect tense is a combination of the aorist tense and the present tense. The aorist tense denotes something which occurs at a specific moment in time whereas the present tense indicates something which occurs and continues into the future with ongoing results or implications. The Holy Spirit's guided use of the perfect tense for the verb translated 'It is finished' has wonderful implications for every Christian. Jesus is declaring that something is now completed which will remain completed. It is finished and will continue finished forever. The crucifixion of the Lord Jesus Christ has all-powerful results for time and eternity, for now and forever.

✦ 'It is finished' applies to the life of obedience of Jesus. It is completed, perfected, accomplished, brought to its appointed end, it is done and will forever remain so! When he came into the world a body was prepared for him so that as a Man he could fulfil the will of God according to the Scriptures (Hebrews 10:5-7).

From the cross Jesus was declaring that all through his life from the time of his birth, through boyhood, into manhood, as carpenter's son and carpenter, as itinerate preacher, healer, evangelist, Rabbi, teacher, Lord, miracle worker, exposer of hypocrites, encourager of the lowly poor, yes everything all through his life to the time of his death he had faithfully discharged that which the Father had given him to do. He had taken 'the form of a servant' and been 'obedient to death, even death on the cross.' He had been the Servant serving others rather than being served. He had sought out the lost. He had laid down his life for his sheep. He had given his life as a ransom for many. His personal service to Almighty God the Father had been faultless.

✦ 'It is finished' applies to the fulfilment of prophecy. Jesus did not come to destroy but rather to fulfil the law and the prophets (Matthew 5:17-18). He is the prophesied Seed of Eve (Genesis 3:15); Shiloh, Lion of the tribe of Judah (Genesis 49:9-10); the Prophet like Moses (Deuteronomy 18:18); the Son of David (2 Samuel 7:12-13); the Branch of the Lord (Isaiah 4:2); Immanuel, God with us (Isaiah 7:14); the Wonderful Counsellor, Mighty God, Everlasting Father, Prince of Peace, (Isaiah 9:6); Jehovah's Servant (Isaiah 42:1); Jehovah Tsidkenu, the LORD our Righteousness (Jeremiah 23:6); the one out of Bethlehem who would be ruler in Israel (Micah 5:2); Jehovah himself suddenly coming to his temple (Malachi 3:1).

He has finished and fulfilled his prophesied mission: as 'the Lamb of God who takes away the sin of the world' (John 1:29), Christ our Passover Lamb (1 Corinthians 5:7); through whom 'a fountain... opened... for sin and for uncleanness' (Zechariah 13:1); he is 'Messiah... cut off, but not for himself' (Daniel 9:26); the one 'to finish the transgression, to make an end of sins, to make reconciliation for iniquity, to bring in everlasting righteousness' (Daniel 9:24); the one who was 'despised and rejected by men, a Man of sorrows and acquainted with grief... smitten by God, and afflicted... wounded for our transgressions... bruised for our iniquities... the chastisement for our peace was upon him' (Isaiah 53:3-5).

He was betrayed by a close friend (Psalm 41:9), forsaken by his disciples (Psalm 31:11), falsely accused (Psalm 35:11); silent before his judges (Isaiah. 53:7); proved to be without guilt (Isaiah 53:9); numbered with transgressors (Isaiah 53:12), crucified (Psalm 22:16), mocked by spectators (Psalm 109:25); cruelly taunted (Psalm 22:7-8), soldiers gambled for his clothing (Psalm 22:18); he prayed for his enemies (Isaiah 53:12), he felt forsaken by the Father (Psalm 22:1); he thirsted (Psalm 69:21); was given vinegar to drink (Psalm 69:21); he would yield up his spirit into the hands of the Father (Psalm 31:5), his bones would not be broken (Psalm 34:20); his grave would be made with the wicked and he would be buried in a rich man's tomb (Isaiah 53:9). All these prophecies were plainly foretold centuries earlier and were fulfilled by Jesus.

✦ 'It is finished!' This is the high point of all human history. This is the moment to which all the Old Covenant principles, procedures and promises pointed and the moment from which all the New Covenant principles, procedures and promises flow forth. All history before this moment moved inescapably towards it. All history after this moment, moves irresistibly from it. The whole world is judged by its response to this momentous event. The eternal destiny of every human being is decided here at the cross. Those who disregard or reject the law of God come under the punishment of God. How much more shall those who disregard or reject the love of God on the cross, receive everlasting punishment. They are twice condemned: condemned for rejecting the law of God, condemned for rejecting the love of God. What could be more damning?

✦ 'It is finished' applies to the debt paid by the suffering servant for the eternal glorious salvation of his people. The Lamb of God, completed the once and forever offering of himself (Hebrews 10:10) 'a sacrifice to God for a sweet-smelling aroma' (Ephesians 5:2). 'Though he was a Son, yet he learned obedience by the things which he suffered. And having been perfected, he became the author of eternal salvation to all who obey him' (Hebrews 5:8-9). It was necessary that Jesus should be perfected; made entirely suitable for his great work as Saviour. He had to be righteous; by fulfilling the whole law of God. He had to be holy; by victoriously overcoming every temptation. He had to be the redeemer; by the payment of all our debts. And he had to be the mediator and reconciler; by emptying the whole cup of curse placed before him. The 'precious blood of Christ, as of a lamb without blemish and without spot' (1 Peter 1:19) is shed, for 'without the shedding of blood there is no remission' of sins (Hebrews 9:22). For 'Christ also suffered once for sins, the just for the unjust, that he might bring us to God, being put to death in the flesh' (1 Peter 3:18). He 'himself bore our sins in his own body on the tree, that we, having died to sins, might live for righteousness - by whose stripes [we] were healed' (1 Peter 2:24).

Because God laid the guilt of our sins upon the Saviour it is no longer upon us. It is as though God has cast our sins 'into the depths of the sea' (Micah 7:19). Our sins have been removed 'as far as the east is from the west' (Psalm 103:12). As God promised, 'I will be merciful to their unrighteousness, and their sins and their lawless deeds I will remember no more' (Hebrews 8:12).

The work of salvation is complete. He has done it! 'For the wages of sin is death, but the gift of God is eternal life in Christ Jesus our Lord' (Romans 6:23). Let us therefore 'draw near with a true heart in full assurance of faith, having our hearts sprinkled from an evil conscience and our bodies washed with pure water' (Hebrews 10:22).

Daniel prophesied,

> Seventy weeks are determined for your people and for your holy city, to finish the transgression, to make an end of sins, to make reconciliation for iniquity, to bring in everlasting righteousness, to seal up vision and prophecy, and to anoint the Most Holy (Daniel 9:24).

This prophecy was accomplished and achieved by the Lord Jesus Christ. The price was paid in full!

> In this the love of God was manifested toward us, that God has sent his only begotten Son into the world, that we might live through him. In this is love, not that we loved God, but that he loved us and sent his Son to be the propitiation [the full

satisfaction of the greatly offended God] for our sins (1 John 4:9-10).

✦ 'It is finished' the permanent solution to the curse on the whole of creation hinged upon the accomplishment of the Lord Jesus.

> For the earnest expectation of the creation eagerly waits for the revealing of the sons of God. For the creation was subjected to futility, not willingly, but because of him who subjected it in hope; because the creation itself also will be delivered from the bondage of corruption into the glorious liberty of the children of God. For we know that the whole creation groans and labours with birth pangs together until now (Romans 8:19-22).

The curse has gone forever (Genesis 3:17).

The piercing cry of desolation: 'My God, my God, why have you forsaken me?' (Matthew 27:46) is the opening phrase of Psalm 22. 'It is finished' are virtually the closing words of that same psalm which read, 'They will come and declare his righteousness to a people who will be born, that he has done this' (Psalm 22:31).

7. *'Father, into your hands I commit my spirit' (Luke 23:46).*

Jesus was certain of God's response and he could hand himself over in quiet confidence to his Father. During his life on earth the Father said of him, 'This is my beloved Son, in whom I am well pleased' (Matthew 3:17; 17:5). Today, upon the cross it is as though the Son delivers a glorious reply, 'You are my Father, this day I have completed your commission'.

With confidence and joy Jesus was able to entrust his body and soul to God. According to prophecy he testified -

> I have set the LORD always before me; because he is at my right hand I shall not be moved. Therefore my heart is glad, and my glory rejoices; my flesh also will rest in hope. For you will not leave my soul in Sheol, nor will you allow your Holy One to see corruption. You will show me the path of life; in your presence is fullness of joy; at your right hand are pleasures forevermore (Psalm 16:8-11).

This is the 'the joy that was set before him'; this is how he 'endured the cross, despising the shame'; this is the welcome and glory that will be his when he 'has sat down at the right hand of the throne of God' (Hebrews 12:2).

'Father' he prayed after having cried out with great anguish just minutes before, 'My God, my God, why have you forsaken me?' How wonderful to hear him calling God 'Father' once again. For some hours the joy and delight in the sense of the unique and uninterrupted eternal oneness had been taken away. The sin-bearer lost all awareness of the Father's presence. That was now over. The Son had fulfilled his God-given commission, he had now regained that glorious sense of the love of the Father. He placed himself into the Father's hands, into the protection, power and keeping of the Father; 'being put to death in the flesh but made alive by the Spirit' (1 Peter 3:18). Full propitiation, total satisfaction had been rendered. The Atonement was now completed as he placed himself into God the Father's hands. 'It is finished' announced the Lord's exit from the world. 'Father, into your hands' announced his entrance into heaven.

Upon his death the spirit of the Lord Jesus ascended to the Father, he did not descend into hell. That doctrinal error developed from a misunderstanding of 1 Peter 3:18-20 -

For Christ also suffered once for sins, the just for the unjust, that he might bring us to God, being put to death in the flesh but made alive by the Spirit, by whom also he went and preached to the spirits in prison, who formerly were disobedient, when once the Divine long-suffering waited in the days of Noah, while the ark was being prepared, in which a few, that is, eight souls, were saved through water.

The apostle Peter commenting on the letters of the apostle Paul said, 'in which are some things hard to understand, which those who are untaught and unstable twist to their own destruction, as they do also the rest of the Scriptures' (2 Peter 3:16). Peter might well have added that there were 'some things hard to understand' in his letters also.

The first step in rightly interpreting the words of 1 Peter 3:19 is to follow a golden rule of biblical interpretation; always to interpret difficult passages in the light of clear and straightforward passages, never the other way round. A clear doctrine that shines from the pages of the Scriptures is that there is no second chance for salvation *after* death. Jesus said to the Jews, 'You will die in your sins; for if you do not believe that I am he, you will die in your sins' (John 8:24). The Holy Spirit records 'it is appointed for men to die once, but after this the judgment' (Hebrews 9:27).

In the parable of The Rich Man and Lazarus Jesus taught that the permanent and eternal state of every human being is fixed at death. Jesus represented Abraham as saying to the rich man in Hades, 'between us and you there is a great gulf fixed, so that those who want to pass from here to you cannot, nor can those from there pass to us' (Luke 16:26). There is no second chance after death for anyone. Death seals the future of all humans either in heaven or in hell.

How then are the words of 1 Peter 3:19 to be explained? Peter is not declaring that Christ preached to the Antediluvians (those who lived before the Great Flood in the days of Noah) *after his death* but that he 'by the Spirit' had preached to them *years before* through the preaching of Noah. Paul writes of the Israelites in the wilderness all drinking 'the same spiritual drink. For they drank of that spiritual Rock that followed them, and that Rock was Christ' and 'nor let us tempt Christ, as some of them also tempted, and were destroyed by serpents' (1 Corinthians 10:4,9).

Christ the Son of God was, by his Spirit, present throughout the whole history of the Old Testament Scriptures. In the days of Noah Christ was preaching through Noah as surely as Christ himself would have done had he stood there visibly before them. A similar point is made after the ascension of Christ. The apostles 'went out and preached everywhere, the Lord working with them and confirming the word' (Mark 16:20).

Note the words used to describe our Lord's death - 'He breathed his last' that is, he expired, he out-spirited, out-breathed himself (Luke 23:46 and Mark 15:37). In Matthew 27:50 Jesus 'yielded up his spirit' that is he released, sent away his spirit. In John 19:30 Jesus 'gave up his spirit', he delivered up the spirit. In each case there is a sense of the active participation of the Son of God in his death.

In every other death the victim is passive; death takes hold of us. In Christ's case he must take hold of death. 'For we will surely die and become like water spilled on the ground, which cannot be gathered up again' (2 Samuel 14:14). 'No one has power over the spirit to retain the spirit, and no one has power in the day of death' (Ecclesiastes 8:8). There is however one glorious exception - Jesus Christ the Son of God. No wonder that he said of his life, 'No one takes it from me, but I lay it down of myself. I have power to lay it down, and I have power to take it again' (John 10:18).

It is not his suffering which saves but his death.

> Inasmuch then as the children have partaken of flesh and blood, he himself likewise shared in the same, that through death he might destroy him who had the power of death, that is, the devil, and release those who through fear of death were all their lifetime subject to bondage (Hebrews 2:14-15).

Praise be to the Saviour. Praise be to God.

By committing himself into the hands of God Jesus shows his people how to face death. Quoting from Psalm 31:5 he made an addition and an omission.

154

The addition is the warm, personal address to God, 'Father'; the omission are the words which follow, 'you have redeemed me, O LORD God of truth'; words that are inappropriate for him but highly appropriate for all his people as they face death.

Balaam prayed, 'Let me die the death of the righteous' (Numbers 23:10). But Balaam sinned grievously and there was a fatal flaw in his plea; he wanted to die the death of the righteous without living the life of the righteous. The fear of death and the sting of death only departs for those whose trust is in the Saviour and who walk close to God.

'For if we live, we live to the Lord; and if we die, we die to the Lord. Therefore, whether we live or die, we are the Lord's' (Romans 14:8). By the grace of God we are able to testify, 'For to me, to live is Christ, and to die is gain' (Philippians 1:21), and -

> So we are always confident, knowing that while we are at home in the body we are absent from the Lord. For we walk by faith, not by sight. We are confident, yes, well pleased rather to be absent from the body and to be present with the Lord (2 Corinthians 5:6-8).

Jesus promised his disciples, 'that where I am, there you may be also' (John 14:3). He also prayed -

> Father, I desire that they also whom you gave me may be with me where I am, that they may behold my glory which you have given me; for you loved me before the foundation of the world (John 17:24).

126. The Lord's side is pierced
John 19:31-37

The greatest demonstration of injustice had been perpetrated by fanatical Jewish leaders: high priests, chief priest, Pharisees, Sadducees and scribes, when they condemned Jesus to death. As Peter confronted the Jews on the Day of Pentecost, 'Him... you have taken by lawless hands, have crucified and put to death' (Acts 2:23). In their ignorance and arrogance they had 'crucified the Lord of glory' (1 Corinthians 2:8).

Most of those elders of the people were fanatically legalistic. They were obsessed with rules and regulations, punctilious in the extreme. They were a strange amalgam: they tried to obey the letter of the Old Testament law and developed their own rules and regulations which, with over three hundred and sixty of them, dominated their entire lives; and yet they had hatred in their hearts towards the Lord Jesus Christ. Because they did not love the Lord and believe in him as the Messiah of God it was abundantly evident that they did not really love God. They had not the faith of their godly forefathers: Abraham, Isaac, Jacob and Joseph, Moses, David, Elijah or Elisha. They were fanatical religious leaders with no real heart for God.

The Romans were accustomed to leave bodies on crosses for some time. The leaders of the Jews, with their usual attention to the details of the law, required their removal before sunset. The law stated -

> If a man has committed a sin deserving of death, and he is put to death, and you hang him on a tree, his body shall not remain overnight on the tree, but you shall surely bury him that day, so that you do not defile the land which the LORD your God is giving you as an inheritance; for he who is hanged is accursed of God (Deuteronomy 21:22-23).

Their removal was particularly important to the Jews on this particular day. The Feast of the Passover was followed by the beginning of the seven day Feast of Unleavened Bread. This year the Passover fell on the Preparation Day, the day before the weekly Sabbath. The combination of the Sabbath Day and the first day of the Feast of Unleavened Bread resulted in the day being regarded as a very special 'high day' or 'great day' (John 19:31). The Jews had good reason therefore to want the bodies removed from the crosses before sunset, which marked the beginning of the new day. They approached Pilate requesting the legs of those crucified be broken to hasten death. Pilate agreed and sent soldiers to undertake the task.

The soldiers broke the legs of one of the criminals. They then passed by Jesus, who appeared to be dead, and broke the legs of the other criminal. But one of the soldiers, presumably wanting to be sure that Jesus was dead pierced his side with his spear 'immediately blood and water came out' (John 19:34). John says that two prophecies were fulfilled: 'Not one of his bones shall be broken' (John 19:36; Exodus 12:46) and 'They shall look on him whom they pierced' (John 19:37; Zechariah 12:10).

The Old Testament prophecy reads, 'They will look on me whom they pierced' referring to God himself. Also five verses later it is written, 'In that day a fountain shall be opened for the house of David and for the inhabitants of Jerusalem, for sin [guilt] and for uncleanness [moral pollution]' (Zechariah 13:1). Washing away guilt and pollution are two blessings achieved that day at the cross and which are further expounded in the New Testament as the doctrines of justification and sanctification (Romans 3:24,28; Hebrews 10:10,14).

The apostle John made a particular point of bearing witness to what he saw: 'And he who has seen has testified, and his testimony is true; and he knows that he is telling the truth, so that you may believe' (John 19:35).

Jesus Christ the Son of the living God died on the cross. He was dead when that spear thrust released the blood and water.

There is much Old Testament teaching about blood and water in relation to our great salvation. The significance of blood may be summed up in a statement in the letter to the Hebrews, 'according to the law almost all things are purified with blood, and without shedding of blood there is no remission' (Hebrews 9:22). In other words, the guilt and penalty of sin is cancelled through the shedding of blood. All those who are saved by grace compose 'the church of God which he purchased with his own blood' (Acts 20:28) for all are redeemed 'with the precious blood of Christ, as of a lamb without blemish and without spot' (1 Peter 1:19). Water also has wonderful significance in terms of spiritual and moral cleansing -

> Then I will sprinkle clean water on you, and you shall be clean; I will cleanse you from all your filthiness and from all your idols (Ezekiel 36:25-27).

In the upper room the Lord told the disciples, 'If I do not wash you, you have no part with me' (John 13:8).

As Ananias said to Saul (Paul), 'Arise and be baptised, and wash away your sins, calling on the name of the Lord' (Acts 22:16). In the death of Jesus there is a double blessing: the blood represents the removal of guilt, pardon and acceptance; the water represents the inner cleansing, purity and holiness before God. Calvary is where the fountain was truly opened 'for sin and for uncleanness' (Zechariah 13:1).

The torn curtain in the temple

When the Saviour died the veil of the temple was torn in two from top to bottom (Mark 15:38). This main curtain in the temple was 20m (60ft) long, 10m (30ft) wide and the thickness of the palm of the hand (about 10cm (4in). It was made up of 72 squares, which were joined together like a huge patchwork quilt. A veil was part of the original design for the tabernacle in the wilderness: 'The veil shall be a divider for you between the holy place and the Most Holy' (Exodus 26:33), 'into the second part the high priest went alone once a year, not without blood, which he offered for himself and for the people's sins committed in ignorance' (Hebrews 9:7).

That a great disaster had occurred in the temple at the Lord's death is confirmed by not less than four mutually independent testimonies: the records of Tacitus, Josephus, the Talmud and the New Testament Scriptures. Alfred Edersheim, a converted Jewish scholar, examined the records and comparing them with the Scriptures then concluded -

Indeed, everything seems to indicate that, although the earthquake might furnish the physical basis, the rent of the Temple-Veil was - with reverence be it said - really made by the Hand of God.[79]

Before the evening sacrifice on that Passover Day the officiating priests would have entered the Holy Place, either to burn incense or to do other sacred duties. Suddenly the curtain tore from top to bottom. Immediately the Holy of Holies was exposed and the priests would see the Mercy Seat! The majority would have never seen it. It was only ever seen once a year by the presiding high priest but now they could all behold the Mercy Seat. What a terrifying, awe-inspiring experience. Surely those priests must have concluded that God had visited the place. Does this phenomenon account for the large number of priests who were early converted to faith in Christ? (Acts 6:7)

The writer to the Hebrews says that the temple veil symbolised the body of Jesus -

Therefore, brethren, having boldness to enter the Holiest by the blood of Jesus, by a new and living way which he consecrated for us, through the veil, that is, his flesh, and having a High Priest over the house of God, let us draw near with a true heart in full assurance of faith' (Hebrews 10:19-22).

This inner curtain of the temple separated the Holy Place from the Holy of Holies. It barred access to God. When the high priest in Israel went into the Holy of Holies, he moved the curtain aside. The writer to the Hebrews speaks of the humanity of the Lord Jesus Christ as the curtain through whom entrance to the heavenly is made. When his holy humanity was 'torn', the way was fully opened to God. Two things were made evident: Jesus Christ had now provided the actual entrance for the sinner into the presence of God, and the symbolic sacrifices were to be discontinued. The reality to whom they had pointed had come. Jesus said, 'I am the way, the truth, and the life. No one comes to the Father except through me' (John 14:6).

Other phenomena occurred besides the tearing of the veil in the temple: a number of people were raised from the dead and there was an earthquake. The centurion and the soldiers guarding the three crucified men witnessed these things and they were greatly afraid (Matthew 27:54). The centurion (leader of one hundred Roman soldiers) was responsible for everything associated with the crucifixion. Four of his men were at the foot of the cross sharing out the clothing of Jesus. There would be many more soldiers

---

[79] Alfred Edersheim, *The Life and Times of Jesus the Messiah* (Peabody, Massachusetts: Hendrikson, 1993), p.894.

surrounding the proceedings to ensure no interference or disturbance. The centurion would have witnessed the whole scene.

He heard the prayer of Jesus for himself and his men; the conversation between the Saviour and the converted criminal; the words of the Lord to his mother Mary and disciple John. He witnessed the three hours of terrifying darkness. He heard the unforgettable cries, 'My God, my God, why have you forsaken me?' 'It is finished.' 'Father, into your hands I commit my spirit'; the desperation, the glorious triumph and the calm resignation and surrender.

The centurion had not only heard the words of Jesus but witnessed also his behaviour. He had witnessed the cruelty of the Jewish leaders, noted their hostility and hatred and seen, by sharp contrast, the calm dignified, self-composed and self-controlled dying of the Lord Jesus Christ. When finally the Lord committed himself into the hands of the heavenly Father in total confidence, the centurion burst forth in confession and praise. He 'glorified God, saying, "Certainly this was a righteous man!"' (Luke 23:47) He and his men feared greatly and said, 'Truly this was the Son of God!' (Matthew 27:54)

The only reason the Lord Jesus Christ was sentenced to death by the Jews was because he had plainly acknowledged he was the Son of God. When this centurion declared Jesus to be God's Son and a righteous man he clearly understood what the Jewish leadership failed to see (it is traditionally held that he became a true follower of Jesus). Was he and the four soldiers who carried out the execution particularly in the Saviour's mind when he prayed, 'Father, forgive them, for they do not know what they are doing'? One of the many prophecies given regarding the crucifixion is found in Zechariah -

> I will pour on the house of David and on the inhabitants of Jerusalem the Spirit of grace and supplication; then they will look on me whom they pierced. Yes, they will mourn for him as one mourns for his only son, and grieve for him as one grieves for a firstborn (Zechariah 12:10).

The crowd that gathered at Calvary were also greatly affected by the phenomena that they had witnessed and they departed with heavy hearts (Luke 23:48).

127. The body of Jesus placed in Joseph's tomb
Matthew 27:57-61; Mark 15:42-47; Luke 23:50-56: John 19:38-42

As we have seen, the death of the Lord Jesus had a significant impact upon the Gentile Roman centurion and soldiers by the cross. They declared openly that he was the Son of God. Two other men, of very different race and social standing, were also greatly influenced, Joseph and Nicodemus. Both were high ranking Pharisees and members of the Sanhedrin (the seventy-strong rulers of the Jewish court). Joseph of Arimathea was a rich man, a prominent council member, a good and just man who was 'waiting for the kingdom of God' (Luke 23:51). He was 'a disciple of Jesus, but secretly, for fear of the Jews' (John 19:38).

Aware that the body of Jesus was likely to be thrown roughly into an open common grave, he realised that the time had come for him to risk his professional status and social standing and take action so that the body of Jesus would be treated with respect and dignity. On the death of Jesus, and the fast approaching sunset announcing the Sabbath, Joseph took courage and visited Pilate to obtain permission to take away the body. Pilate was surprised to hear that Jesus was already dead. He checked with the centurion who confirmed the fact.

Joseph, assisted by Nicodemus (John 3:1-21; 7:50-51; 19:39), evidently now a fellow believer in Jesus, took the body down from the cross. They carried it a short distance to a new tomb which Joseph had cut from the rock ready to receive his own body when the time came. The two disciples bound the body of Jesus in strips of linen interlaid with spices. Nothing more could be done with the body for another twenty-four hours because of the Sabbath. They then rolled a great stone over the entrance of the tomb. Mary Magdalene and Mary the mother of James and Joses observed the whole procedure.

The next day, the Sabbath Day, some of the chief priests and Pharisees, contrary to their own laws, visited the Gentile Governor Pilate again. Having discussed the prediction of Jesus, that his resurrection would follow three days after his death, they had come to make a request. They asked that a seal be fixed to the tomb and a guard placed at the sealed entrance so that the disciples could not steal the body and claim that Jesus had risen from the dead. They were authorised to do whatever they wanted to ensure the security of the body in the sepulchre. The tomb was sealed and put under guard.

How did the chief priests and Pharisees know of this foretold resurrection? On the three or four occasions when Jesus had spoken clearly on the subject it was only to the apostles. Two possibilities exist therefore, either Judas had told them when betraying Jesus and they related it as though they heard it directly from Jesus or, more than two years earlier, they rightly understood the implications of the Lord's words after his first cleansing of the temple. At that time Jewish leaders had asked for a sign and Jesus replied, 'Destroy this temple, and in three days I will raise it up' (John 2:19).

If that were the case then they understood more than the apostles who only realised the true meaning *after* the resurrection.

The Saviour's resurrection

Abundant and frequently repeated evidence is given for the bodily resurrection of Jesus. The witnesses were many, varied and competent. They had everything to lose and nothing to gain from bearing false testimony. Their sincerity was proved by the sacrifices, even of life, which their testimony often caused.

128. Women visit the tomb early
Matthew 28:1-8; Mark 16:1-8; Luke 24:1-11; John 20:1-2

The resurrection of Jesus took place on the first day of the week (the day after the Sabbath) well before sunrise. It was during the Feast of Unleavened Bread and this was the day appointed as the Feast of First Fruits, when the first crop of the early (barley) harvest was brought in gratitude to God (Leviticus 23:39).

All the old covenant festivals were designed to represent the life and ministry of the Lord Jesus. Paul noted the significance here when he wrote to the Christians at Corinth, 'now Christ is risen from the dead, and has become the first fruits of those who have fallen asleep... Christ the first fruits, afterward those who are Christ's at his coming' (1 Corinthians 15:20,23).

The resurrection of Christ was a concerted work of the triune Godhead taking place during the night: 'Christ was raised from the dead by the glory of the Father' (Romans 6:4); Jesus was 'declared to be the Son of God with power according to the Spirit of holiness, by the resurrection from the dead' (Romans 1:4); Jesus the Son of God had power to lay down his life and power to take it again (John 10:18).

The resurrection of Jesus is the foundation stone of Christianity for 'if Christ is not risen, then our preaching is empty and your faith is also empty' and 'if Christ is not risen, your faith is futile; you are still in your sins! Then also those who have fallen asleep in Christ have perished' (1 Corinthians 15:14,17-18).

The first people to visit the tomb were loyal women disciples; Mary Magdalene, Mary the mother of James and Joses, Salome wife of Zebedee and mother of James and John, Joanna the wife of Chuza, Herod's steward, and other women (Luke 24:10). It is noteworthy that female disciples were last to leave the cross and first to arrive at the sepulchre. As they made their way to the garden the women wondered who would roll away the stone for them.

They need not have worried for God had intervened with an earthquake and an angel had rolled away the great stone from the entrance of the tomb. The guards had seen the angel whose 'countenance was like lightning, and his clothing as white as snow' (Matthew 28:3), they were terrified and fled. Mary Magdalene ran the half mile and told Peter and John, 'They have taken away the Lord out of the tomb, and we do not know where they have laid him' (John 20:2). Peter and John immediately ran to the tomb. The other women had entered the tomb and two men in shining clothing reassured them that Jesus had risen from the dead. They were told to go quickly and tell his disciples that Jesus had risen and would go before them to Galilee. The women left the garden and made haste to report to the apostles and to the rest.

Meanwhile, having been told of the empty tomb by Mary Magdalene, Peter and John, evidently taking a different route, arrived hastily at the garden and examined the tomb. Mary remained outside weeping. Discovering that the body of the Lord had truly gone they were at a loss to know what was really happening. They were not privileged to see the angels nor to hear the explanation that the Lord had risen. Peter and John returned to the city but Mary Magdalene was left alone in the garden. As she wept she looked inside the tomb and saw two angels who asked why she was weeping. She answered, 'Because they have taken away my Lord, and I do not know where they have laid him' (John 20:13).

Turning round she saw Jesus and, supposing him to be the gardener who had moved the Lord's body, she asked where he had laid him. Jesus then said her name, 'Mary' and she immediately recognised his voice. To her was granted the honour of being the first to see the risen Lord. Mary probably dropped to her knees and held the feet of the Saviour for he said to her, 'Do not cling to me' (John 20:17). The risen Saviour instructed her to report to the apostles, but when she did they did not believe her (Mark 16:11).

Then Jesus made his second resurrection appearance to the other women as they sought out more disciples to tell them that Jesus had risen from the tomb. Jesus said to them, 'Rejoice!' and the women fell to the ground before him, held his feet and worshipped him. When the women told the group of apostles and disciples what had taken place they did not believe them either.

Meanwhile the soldiers set to guard the tomb, terrified by the earthquake, the angel and the missing body, reported back to the chief priests. The priests consulted with the elders and together they concocted a story for the guards, bribing them to say that disciples of Jesus came by night and stole the body while they slept. This is a most ridiculous explanation since Roman soldiers were highly trained and knew they would be court-martialled and executed for sleeping on duty. Yet this story is perpetuated among Jews to this day.

129. Jesus appears on the Emmaus Road
Mark 16:12-13; Luke 24:13-35

That evening, the day of the glorious resurrection of the Saviour, Cleopas and a fellow disciple were walking to Emmaus when they were joined by the risen Lord. They did not recognise him and engaged in conversation with him as though he were a total stranger. Two factors prevented these two from identifying Jesus; his appearance 'in another form' (Mark 16:12) and 'their eyes were restrained, so that they did not know him' (Luke 24:16). A number of reasons may be presented for his appearing incognito: to encourage a profession of their faith to a supposed stranger (Luke 24:19); to bring to light the limits of their faith because they were only 'hoping' (Luke 24:21-24); and to establish that the real ground for their faith was to be the Scriptures (Luke 24:25-27).

Jesus began conversation by asking what they were talking about. Cleopas answered in amazement for he could not imagine anyone coming from Jerusalem being ignorant of the recent events. When pressed Cleopas explained by first giving a fine testimony of Jesus of Nazareth as 'a Prophet mighty in deed and word before God and all the people' (Luke 24:19).

He then outlined the behaviour of the Jewish chief priests and rulers who rejected Jesus and delivered him up to be condemned and crucified. Cleopas and his colleagues had set their hopes on Jesus to redeem Israel. Now it was the third day since his death and some of their women colleagues had been to his tomb early and had come back with a report that they had seen angels who said he was alive. Some of the disciples had gone to the tomb straightaway and found it empty, but had not seen Jesus.

The risen Lord Jesus listened to their conversation and then responded with what we might assume was a gentle but firm rebuke: 'O foolish ones' [referring to their lack of understanding], 'and slow of heart' [referring to their lack of trust], 'to believe in all that the prophets have spoken! Ought not the Christ to have suffered these things and to enter into his glory?' (Luke 24:25-26). The emphasis was upon two words: 'all' and 'ought', that is, the total extent of revelation and the divine necessity of suffering.

When the Old Testament was read the Jews saw only the glory and victory of Messiah. They did not see that the route to these was through suffering.

The Lord was not critical of the disciples for not believing the testimony of the women, nor for their failure to believe the testimony of the angels who said he was alive. Jesus rebuked them for not believing the Old Testament Scriptures! It is evident that the Lord Jesus will not have the faith of his people depend upon any supernatural appearances, nor on the word of angels, nor on the testimony of godly women nor of godly men. He will not ground their faith on experience. He will not even permit their faith to be based upon their personally seeing him! Their faith was to be built on the promises and prophecies of the Old Testament.

So the Lord proceeded to instruct them. He traced through the Scriptures to highlight and elucidate what the Word of God revealed about him as the Christ and Son of God. He had made the same point on a number of occasions, as for example when he challenged the Jews -

> You search the Scriptures, for in them you think you have eternal
> life; and these are they which testify of me (John 5:39).

What an amazing experience to have the Scriptures unfolded before them by the Lord Jesus.

During his three year ministry the Saviour had frequently repeated the necessity of his suffering and death, and the certainty of his rising again (Luke 9:21-22; 44-45; 18:32-33). On the last occasion he added,

> "Behold, we are going up to Jerusalem, and all things that are
> written by the prophets concerning the Son of Man will be
> accomplished"… But they understood none of these things; this
> saying was hidden from them, and they did not know the things
> which were spoken (Luke 18:31,34).

When Jesus taught the parable of The Rich Man and Lazarus (Luke 16:19-31) he spoke of two men dying. The one, the rich man, was in Hades 'tormented in this flame' (Luke 16:24). The other the poor man Lazarus, was in 'Abraham's bosom' (Luke 16:22). The rich man in torment sought relief but could receive none. So he showed concern for his five brothers still alive at home. He requested that Lazarus be sent to the brothers 'lest they also come to this place of torment' (Luke 16:28). Jesus put words into Abraham's mouth, 'They have Moses and the prophets; let them hear them'. but the response came back, 'No, father Abraham; but if one goes to them from the dead, they will repent'. Jesus then expressed the profound truth, 'If they do not hear Moses and the prophets, neither will they be persuaded though one rise from the dead' (Luke 16:31).

In this parable Jesus was once more emphasising the importance of the Old Testament prophecies in substantiating his suffering, death and resurrection and their glorious meaning and significance.[80] The death and resurrection, substantiated by the Old Testament prophecies, forms the vital base for the preaching of the Gospel (Acts 2:22-24; 3:15-16; 13:29-31; 1 Corinthians 15:3-8).

Fulfilled prophecy is far more compelling than accurately recorded history. God requires faith in his prophetic Word concerning the resurrection as distinct from faith in the witnesses to the resurrection. Jesus Christ the Son of God is revealed sufficiently in the Old Testament, faith needs no further revelation, no additional confirmation, no extra miracles.[81] It does however require a work of God (Matthew 16:17; 2 Corinthians 4:6).

The travellers arrived at the village of Emmaus and Jesus gave the impression that he would go further but they encouraged him to stay with them (cf. Revelation 3:20). As they were about to share a meal, the Lord took the bread, blessed and broke it, and gave it to them and suddenly they realised who he was - and he disappeared from their sight. Amazed and delighted they reflected on the journey. They had both had the same special experience which they called 'a burning heart'. It was not a momentary occurrence but continued throughout the Lord's exposition. Their heart was strangely warmed as they heard the Word of God being unfolded to reveal the suffering and triumph of the Lord Jesus Christ (Luke 24:32).

130. Jesus appears in Jerusalem
Luke 24:36-43; John 20:19-25

Imagine their joy as the two disciples hurriedly returned the eight miles to the apostles in Jerusalem. With the betrayal and death of Judas there were now eleven apostles. They were often known as 'the eleven' just as for nearly three years they had been known as 'the twelve' (even when one or two were absent from the group). On this occasion Thomas was absent (John 20:24) and other disciples were present (Luke 24:33). When they arrived, no

---

[80] For example - the death of Christ: Psalm 22; Isaiah 53:5,8; Daniel 9:26; Zechariah 12:10 and the resurrection of Christ: Psalm 16:10; 22:22-31; Isaiah 53:10-11; Hosea 6:2; Jonah 1:17.

[81] For example: Genesis 3:15; 12:3; 22:18; 49:10; Exodus 12:13; Numbers 24:17; Deuteronomy 18:18; 2 Samuel 7:12-13; Psalm 2:2; 22:1,18; 110:1; 118:22; Isaiah 7:14; 9:1-2, 6-7; 11 :10; 42:1; 53; Jeremiah 23:5-6; Daniel 9:24; Micah 5:2; Haggai 2:6-9; Zechariah 9:9 12:10; 13:1; Malachi 3:1

doubt in the dead of night, the apostles first told them that Peter had seen the Lord. Cleopas and his companion then recounted their experience. Suddenly Jesus himself appeared before them and they were terrified. He reassured them of his living reality by inviting them to touch him. At his request they gave him food which he ate before them as further evidence of the reality of his physical resurrection.

Where was the apostle Thomas when the other apostles were all together 'for fear of the Jews'? (John 20:19) Having not been there when the Lord appeared, Thomas remained unconvinced by the testimony of the others. However a week later he was dramatically confronted. The disciples were once again gathered together and this time Thomas was present. Though the doors were shut the Lord Jesus once more came and stood before them. His first words were addressed to Thomas who days before had said -

> Unless I see in his hands the print of the nails, and put my finger into the print of the nails, and put my hand into his side, I will not believe (John 20:25).

When Jesus invited him to put his hand into his side, Thomas declared, 'My Lord and my God!' (John 20:28)

What an outstanding profession of faith and confidence. This is the only time in the Gospels that anyone acknowledged Christ as 'God'.

> Doubting Thomas was the one who gave the strongest and most conclusive testimony to the absolute deity of the Saviour which ever came from the lips of a man![82]

Thomas was responding directly to Jesus since it is recorded, 'Thomas answered and said to him…' Also there is not a hint of correction from the Lord for this confession and acknowledgement of his deity for Thomas is speaking the truth. Furthermore Jesus immediately continued by commending Thomas for his faith but added a vital rider, 'Blessed are those who have not seen and yet have believed' (John 20:29).

All disciples since the last resurrection appearance of Jesus have to trust in the Word of God: 'Faith comes by hearing, and hearing by the word of God' (Romans 10:17); 'we walk by faith, not by sight' (2 Corinthians 5:7) and are united to Jesus our Saviour 'whom having not seen [we] love' (1 Peter 1:8).

Unless the Lord Jesus is God like God the Father there is no mediation, no atonement, no priesthood, no whole work of redemption. He is God and he is man. He is man and therefore can be touched with the feeling of our

---

[82] Arthur W. Pink, *Expositions of the Gospel of John: three volumes unabridged in one* (Grand Rapids, Michigan: Zondervan, 1970), vol. 2, p.299.

infirmities; (Hebrews 4:15) he is God, and therefore 'is able to save to the uttermost those who come to God through him' (Hebrews 7:25). As a human being he can die in the place of another human being; as God he can die for an infinite number of human beings.

131. Jesus appears by the Sea of Galilee
John 21:1-14

The Lord had instructed the apostles, both by an angel and then personally, to meet him in Galilee (Matthew 26:32; 28:7,10). It would be natural for them to go to their own homes in Galilee. It would also seem reasonable for them to return to their occupations and not depend upon the Lord's people to support them. Simon Peter, Thomas Didymus, Nathanael Bartholomew of Cana, James and John and two other disciples met together and Peter announced that he was going fishing. They all accompanied him. After a night fishing they had caught nothing.

At dawn someone on the shore called to them asking if they had caught anything. It was Jesus but they did not recognise him (John 21:4), just like Mary Magdalene had not recognised him at the tomb (John 20:15) nor Cleopas and his colleague who had not recognised him on the Emmaus Road (Luke 24:16). The men had been fishing all night and caught nothing (John 21:3) yet at the word of a stranger they cast the net again on the right side of the boat. They caught fish as the stranger had said and the net was stretched to capacity so that they had difficulty drawing it in.

John knew instinctively that it was the Lord. On hearing this Peter put on his outer garment and plunged into the sea leaving the others to bring the boat and the catch to shore. When they came to the shore a fire was burning and fish cooking and bread prepared. Jesus told them to bring some of their fish and they sat down and enjoyed breakfast with their risen Lord and Master.

This was now the eighth miracle of Jesus recorded in John's Gospel. He explained the reason for such a limited choice from the hundreds which Jesus performed over his three year ministry. The apostle John notes -

> And truly Jesus did many other signs in the presence of his disciples, which are not written in this book; but these are written that you may believe that Jesus is the Christ, the Son of God, and that believing you may have life in his name (John 20:30-31).

We therefore expect to discern some important meaning in this chosen miracle which will glorify the Saviour and stimulate faith in him. To begin with the Lord's instruction was clear, 'Cast the net on the right side of the boat' (John 21:6). There had been a previous occasion when the Lord had performed a similar miracle. The first miraculous catch of fish occurred at the beginning of the Lord's ministry and was associated with the call of the fishermen Peter, Andrew, James and John (Luke 5:1-11). This second occasion took place at the conclusion of his ministry. In each case the men had been fishing all night without catching anything. The first time Jesus said, 'Let down your nets for a catch' (Luke 5:4). The second time he said, 'Cast the net on the right side of the boat, and you will find some' (John 21:6). In the first he called men that they may 'become fishers of men' (Mark 1:17).

The two miraculous catches signify fishing first for people in Israel and then second (on the right or the other side) for people in the nations (the Gentiles). This harmonises with what Jesus said, using different imagery, 'other sheep [among the nations] I have which are not of this fold [that is, of the fold of Israel]; them also I must bring, and they will hear my voice; and there will be one flock and one shepherd' (John 10:16). During his ministry on earth Jesus concentrated upon the Israelites (Matthew 10:6; 15:24). After his death and resurrection and the outpouring of the Holy Spirit, the scope would be widened to embrace all nations (Jew and Gentile). The great commission would be given: 'Go... make disciples of all the nations' (Matthew 28:19).

The numbering of the 'fish' (symbolic of saved Gentiles) is not insignificant. The Church of Jesus Christ will be an exact number known only to God, each one reckoned and accounted for individually, 'a great multitude' (Revelation 7:9). But why note the exact number of fish? Some have suggested that 153 is the number of the different kinds of fish in the sea linking it with Ezekiel 47:1-12 which teaches that ultimately in the Church the 'fish will be of the same kinds as the fish of the Great Sea, exceedingly many' (Ezekiel 47:10). A clearer link may be found elsewhere in the Scriptures. The only other place in the whole of the Bible where the number 153 occurs is in 2 Chronicles 2:17-18 where it is recorded that 153,600 Canaanites were involved in building the temple of Solomon. There may be an intended connection between those Gentiles who shared in the building of the Old Testament physical temple and converted Gentiles who will be built into the New Testament spiritual temple (John 2:21; 1 Peter 2:4-5; 1 Corinthians 3.16; 6:19).

Unlike the parable of The Dragnet (Matthew 13:47-50) there will be no *bad* 'fish' to be thrown away.

132. The public reinstatement of Peter
John 21:15-25

After breakfast the Lord challenged Peter about his priorities. According to Luke and Paul, the risen Saviour had already appeared privately to Peter (Luke 24:34; 1 Corinthians 15:5). There on the shore of the Sea of Galilee Jesus took the opportunity to restore Peter publicly in the eyes of the other apostles and the Church at large. Peter's serious sin in denying the Lord was all the worse because he had been given clear warning by Jesus (Luke 22:31-32). Although it was a prediction of failure it was nevertheless a gracious encouragement too for it foretold the restoration of Peter and instruction to then be an encouragement to his colleagues.

For three days, from that dreadful experience in the courtyard in Jerusalem, Peter would no doubt have been in an agony of spirit remembering all the details of his treachery. On the day of resurrection the angel at the tomb had given instructions to the women to go and tell the Lord's disciples - and Peter - that he was going before them into Galilee. To name Peter in particular was a gracious indication of his restoration to fellowship with the Master. In privacy the Lord ministered to Peter's wounded spirit and broken heart.

It is to be noted that Jesus did not pray on the night of his betrayal for Simon to be kept *from* falling but to be restored *after* falling (Luke 22:32). The fall was necessary, in the providence of God, for Peter to better understand himself, to show him the error of his self-confidence and to humble his proud heart. The need for the devil's 'sifting' was clearly evident in his reply that night, 'Lord, I am ready to go with you, both to prison and to death' (Luke 22:33) and 'Even if all are made to stumble, yet I will not be' (Mark 14:29).

Now on the seashore in Galilee, not many days after the denial, Jesus asked Peter three times (the same number as the denials), 'Do you love me?' Three times Peter responded humbly declaring his deep affection. The Master publicly commended him to the pastoral office of feeding lambs, shepherding sheep and feeding sheep. This was to be achieved by ministering the Word of God appropriately as milk or meat (1 Corinthians 3:2; Hebrews 5:12-14).

The emphasis in the Lord's first question to Peter was placed upon Peter's priorities in love. The question was 'Do you love me more than these?' (John 21:15) Was Jesus referring to the other apostles sitting around the fire? Is the Lord testing how well Peter had come through this period of humbling? Had he been so dramatically changed that he will no longer think of himself as *more* faithful, *more* reliable, *more* self-sacrificing, *more* committed than others?

> For whom the LORD loves he chastens, and scourges every son whom he receives… Now no chastening seems to be joyful for the present, but painful; nevertheless, afterward it yields the peaceable fruit of righteousness to those who have been trained by it' (Hebrews 12:6,11; Proverbs 3:12).

The question may also have been related to the fish, the net, the boat for these represented his occupation. Was Peter being asked if he could willingly give up his means of support for his family and rely solely upon the provision God would supply through his people? Was he ready to abandon his steady income, successful career and financial security to devote himself to preaching the gospel and the pastoral care of God's people, feeding lambs, shepherding and feeding sheep?

The responsibilities of spiritual shepherding laid upon Peter were taken seriously by him and the other apostles. Peter travelled extensively and showed a true love for the people of God. The long life of the apostle John was devoted to the loving-care of the churches in a vast area of Asia Minor. The apostle Paul laboured tirelessly for years promoting the well-being of Christ's Church (2 Corinthians 11:23-29). These three proved to be outstanding spiritual shepherds feeding the sheep, guarding and feeding lambs and protecting the weak and vulnerable. However, the twelve apostles and Paul held a unique office (1 Corinthians 9:1; 2 Corinthians 12:12; Ephesians 2:20). In their place, as shepherds of the flock of God, Christ gave elders (Ephesians 4:11-12). Contrary to the false hierarchies in institutional religion, the men who are elders are also the shepherds [pastors] and also bishops [overseers]. When Paul met with the Ephesian elders (Acts 20:17) at the harbour at Miletus he urged them in their God-given task -

> Take heed to yourselves and to all the flock, among which the Holy Spirit has made you overseers [bishops], to shepherd [to pastor] the church of God which he purchased with his own blood (Acts 20:28).

Here it is clear that elder, pastor [shepherd] and overseer [bishop] all refer to the same individuals. The elders, though they will have differing gifts and experiences, are to exercise a plurality of equals in authority, responsibility, love and care. Peter expressed their responsibility like this -

> The elders who are among you I exhort, I who am a fellow elder and a witness of the sufferings of Christ, and also a partaker of the glory that will be revealed: Shepherd the flock of God which is among you, serving as overseers, not by compulsion but willingly,

not for dishonest gain but eagerly; nor as being lords over those entrusted to you, but being examples to the flock; and when the Chief Shepherd appears, you will receive the crown of glory that does not fade away (1 Peter 5:1-4).

Love for Christ and love for Christians under their care is the basis of all that elders do; in supervision, teaching, pastoral care and in personal counselling.[83]

It is no wonder that elders need Holy Spirit filled colleagues as deacons (Acts 6:3-4; 1 Timothy 3:8-13) to take up the practical tasks in order to free the elders to concentrate on shepherding the flock.

After the third answer Jesus foretold Peter's martyrdom, he would die a violent death by crucifixion and yet in that death he would glorify God (John 21:18-19). The Lord said nothing of the work he would do as a shepherd among the flock, he made no reference to the blessing he would pass on through his writings. It was going to be through suffering that Peter would distinctly glorify God. Similarly when Ananias was sent to counsel Saul of Tarsus, the Lord said -

Go, for he is a chosen vessel of mine to bear my name before Gentiles, kings, and the children of Israel. For I will show him how many things he must suffer for my name's sake (Acts 9:15-16).

Peter asked the Lord about John's future. Jesus indicated that it was not Peter's business. He was urged to concentrate upon his own duty and follow his Master (John 21:22). Jesus said, 'If I will that he remain till I come...' It is the Lord who determines the length and content of our days (Psalm 139:16).

During the next few days the Lord Jesus appeared to over five hundred disciples at once (1 Corinthians 15:6). A few of them had 'fallen asleep' but most were still alive twenty-five years later when Paul wrote his first letter to the Corinthians. What a powerful testimony from such a formidable company - hundreds of personal witnesses. There is no evidence whatsoever that anyone who witnessed the resurrection of Jesus ever recanted, not even among the 500 who gathered in Galilee, in spite of widespread persecution.

---

[83] See Gareth Crossley, *Growing Leaders in the Church: The Essential Leadership Development Resource* (Darlington: Evangelical Press, 2008)

133. The great commission
Matthew 28:16-20; Mark 16:15-18; Luke 24:44-49

The eleven apostles later gathered on the mountain which Jesus had appointed for them to meet (Matthew 28:16). It is difficult to understand how some of those apostles doubted. There may have been something mysterious and supernatural in the appearance of the Lord's glorified body. The disciples in the fishing boat earlier did not immediately recognise him, nor did the two on the Emmaus Road (John 21:4; Luke 24:16).

Upon the mountain Jesus gave the great commission -

> All authority has been given to me in heaven and on earth. Go therefore and make disciples of all the nations, baptising them in the name of the Father and of the Son and of the Holy Spirit, teaching them to observe all things that I have commanded you; and lo, I am with you always, even to the end of the age (Matthew 28:18-20).

The question that is of immediate relevance is this: To whom is the great commission directed? The final clause gives the answer: 'Lo, I am with you always, even to the end of the age'. This phrase makes it clear that the 'you' to whom the promise is given is not solely and exclusively to the eleven disciples. This promise extends to the whole Christian Church throughout history - the entire community of which the eleven were founder members (Ephesians 2:20). It is a promise for us no less than for them. The Lord Jesus will always be with his people.

It is a promise of great comfort. But if the promise extends to us, then the commission with which it is linked must also extend to us. The promise was given to encourage the eleven so that they would not be overwhelmed by the size and difficulty of the task of world evangelism. When Jesus was with his disciples in the region of Caesarea Philippi he told them, 'I will build my church, and the gates of Hades shall not prevail against it' (Matthew 16:18). That process will continue for 'the Lord is not slack concerning his promise, as some count slackness, but is long-suffering toward us, not willing that any should perish but that all should come to repentance' (2 Peter 3:9). He will call and he will save all those chosen 'before the foundation of the world' (Ephesians 1:4), that 'great multitude which no one could number, of all nations, tribes, peoples, and tongues' (Revelation 7:9).

The theme of this great commission is not primarily about evangelism but rather concerning the sovereignty of the Lord Jesus Christ. It is a glorious declaration of his sovereignty and hence a sovereign command to proclaim him to all nations. A good motive for evangelism is the fact that world evangelism is going to be successful! It will achieve what the Saviour wants it to achieve because he, the Sovereign Lord, has *all authority*. In his divine nature as the Son of God he had always possessed *all authority* over everyone and everything in heaven, on earth and in hell, and that from all eternity. All authority has now been 'given' to him as Jesus the God/Man.

Because of his great and glorious achievement at Calvary where he 'humbled himself and became obedient to death, even the death of the cross' God 'has highly exalted him and given him the name which is above every name, that at the name of Jesus every knee should bow, of those in heaven, and of those on earth, and of those under the earth' (Philippians 2:8-10). Jesus the Son of God and now the Son of Man has been given all authority in heaven and on earth.

Jesus has all authority *in heaven,* over all persons and powers there. All that lives and has its being in heaven, angels and archangels, powers, principalities, might, dominion, thrones, and the saints in glory are subject to Christ. All the powers of heaven are at his bidding to perform his will without question. The glorious head of the Church is seated 'at the right hand of the Majesty on high' (Hebrews 1:3) 'far above all principality and power and might and dominion, and every name that is named, not only in this age but also in that which is to come' (Ephesians 1:21).

Jesus also has all authority over all persons and powers *on earth.* All its inhabitants; friend or foe, good or bad, believer or unbeliever. All powers on earth are subject to him. There is no limit to his authority. All the forces of nature and all the skills of men and women are at his disposal. The Lord Jesus is King over a kingdom of power. He is also King over a kingdom of grace. His kingdom of power extends over the whole earth. His kingdom of grace extends over the whole Church. He rules over his kingdom of power for the good of his Church. All things have been put 'under his feet' and he has been given to be 'head over all things to the church' (Ephesians 1:22).

The power and authority is his to evangelise and his to immortalise, to save and to save eternally; to bring to life and to sustain in eternal life. At the end of this present age the Lord Jesus Christ will be able to say once more to the Father, 'Of those whom you gave me I have lost none' (John 18:9). The outcome of evangelism is not arbitrary because there is no limit to the authority of Jesus.

We have been commissioned to 'make disciples of all the nations' (Matthew 28:19) without discrimination, for in the twice-born family of God 'there is neither Jew nor Greek, there is neither slave nor free, there is neither male nor female; for [we] are all one in Christ

Jesus' (Galatians 3:28). Disciples are 'made' by sinners being called to 'repentance toward God and faith toward our Lord Jesus Christ' (Acts 20:21). The gospel must be made known for 'how shall they believe in him of whom they have not heard? And how shall they hear without a preacher?' (Romans 10:14). So we are to 'Go into all the world and preach the gospel to every creature' (Mark 16:15).

Conversion is only the beginning, for making disciples requires that converts are taught and trained as to how the Lord Jesus is to be followed. Christ provides -

> some pastors and teacher, for the equipping of the saints for the work of ministry, for the edifying of the body of Christ, till we all come to the unity of the faith and of the knowledge of the Son of God, to a perfect man, to the measure of the stature of the fullness of Christ (Ephesians 4:11-13).

To be sure, 'in the world [we] will have tribulation', but our Sovereign Lord Jesus Christ has 'overcome the world' (John 16:33). Without him we 'can do nothing' (John 15:5), but with the strength that he alone supplies we 'can do all things' (Philippians 4:13). Consequently we are confident in him, and will be 'steadfast, immovable, always abounding in the work of the Lord, knowing that [our] labour is not in vain in the Lord' (1 Corinthians 15:58). What a wonderful blessing to know that he is always with us 'even to the end of the age' (Matthew 28:20).

After his resurrection and before his ascension the Lord Jesus appeared to his half-brother James (1 Corinthians 15:7). What an amazing transformation had taken place. Less than four months earlier at the time of the Feast of Tabernacles James and the other half-brothers did not believe in Jesus as the Son of God and Messiah (John 7:5). When James became a believer is not recorded but he and at least one other brother are numbered among the apostles, disciples and godly women in the upper room immediately after the ascension (Acts 1:14). James became one of the pillars of the early church (Galatians 2:9) and chairman of the Jerusalem Council of Elders (Acts 15:13; 21:18). James and his brother Jude both have letters which are included in the New Testament Scriptures.

134. Ascension from Bethany
Mark 16:19-20; Luke 24:50-53

Forty days after the glorious resurrection of the Saviour, he appeared for the last time to his eleven apostles and spoke with them in Jerusalem. They were instructed not to leave the city but to wait for 'the promise of the Father' which was the anointing, the baptism of the Holy Spirit (Acts 1:4-5). Jesus then 'led them out as far as Bethany' (Luke 24:50) on the side of the Mount of Olives. They asked him if it was the time when he would restore the kingdom to Israel (Acts 1:6). Jesus said that was a matter entirely for God and not something they should be concerned about, their attention was to be focused on the receipt of power to enable them to be witnesses for him 'in Jerusalem, and in Judea and Samaria, and to the end of the earth' (Acts 1:8). He then 'lifted up his hands and blessed them' and while he blessed them he was carried up into heaven (Luke 24:50-51; Mark 16:19) and 'a cloud received him out of their sight' (Acts 1:9).

While the apostles continued to gaze towards heaven they were challenged by two men (angels?) who said, 'Men of Galilee, why do you stand gazing up into heaven? This same Jesus, who was taken up from you into heaven, will so come in like manner as you saw him go into heaven' (Acts 1:11). So they returned to the city from the Mount of Olives (Olivet) a distance of just under a mile.

The eleven apostles, women disciples, Mary the mother of Jesus (this is the last mention of Mary in the New Testament) and the half-brothers of Jesus met together in the upper room (Acts 1:12-14). It is highly likely that among those godly women some were wives of the apostles, for Peter was married (Mark 1:30) and his wife accompanied him on his journeys, as did the wives of other apostles (1 Corinthians 9:5).

In this group there was a unity of purpose and resolve. They were waiting for the descent of the Holy Spirit promised by the heavenly Father and his beloved Son. These were highly dangerous times for the followers of Jesus. His crucifixion might have opened a floodgate of persecution against all who followed him or spoke of him. Yet the disciples met and continued to meet, they prayed and they continued to pray. There was great commitment and resolve. They prayed to be kept safe from their enemies, faithful to their Lord, spiritually equipped for their task ahead, and successful in the preaching of the glorious gospel of God concerning his Son Jesus Christ our Lord (Romans 1:16-17).

In not many days hence it would be the Feast of Pentecost. Did they anticipate this to be the day appointed by God for power to be given to them? The great harvest would begin with 3,000 converts, penitents who believed in Jesus as the Christ and Son of the living God. Over the ensuing years the promised blessing to Abraham would see unimaginable fulfilment with his descendants being multiplied as the stars of the heaven and as the sand on the seashore (Genesis 22:17), for 'if you are Christ's, then you are Abraham's seed, and heirs according to the promise' (Galatians 3:29). Jesus said, 'I will build my church, and the gates of Hades shall not prevail against it' (Matthew 16:18) and build it he will!

Praise the Lord!

Significant facts

Covenants

A covenant is a contract, a formal agreement or promise between two or more parties: either individuals or groups. In Scripture it is an agreement which establishes a relationship between God and his people. Every covenant of God is designed exclusively by him. The Lord specifies the commitment he will make and also details the conditions that his people are to fulfil to maintain the covenant and enjoy the blessing of God.

Many covenants are recorded in Scripture. Although the word 'covenant' is not used with Adam it is there in the more general sense of a conditional promise, given when the LORD God commanded the man, saying -

> Of every tree of the garden you may freely eat; but of the tree of
> the knowledge of good and evil you shall not eat, for in the day
> that you eat of it you shall surely die (Genesis 2:16-17).

Later a covenant was established with Noah 'and with every living creature' (Genesis 9:8-11). The rainbow is the sign of that covenant (Genesis 9:12-13). A number of highly significant covenants followed. Indeed the Bible is composed of two major covenants, the Old and New Testaments (the word 'Testament' is just another name for 'Covenant'). The Old Testament is basically a history of covenants in which God reveals himself, his character and his will for humanity. He promises wonderful blessings and in return requires faith, love and obedience.

When the Lord chose Abraham, and led him from his homeland and people, he entered into covenant with him to be God to him and bless him with a land, a great nation and a great privilege; for through Abraham 'all the families of the earth shall be blessed' (Genesis 12:1-3; 17:1-8). That covenant continued through Isaac and Jacob and was to form the chief hope of the Israelite nation. When the Lord delivered the Israelites from slavery in Egypt it was this covenant which he was honouring -

> So God heard their groaning, and God remembered his covenant
> with Abraham, with Isaac, and with Jacob. And God looked upon
> the children of Israel, and God acknowledged them (Exodus
> 2:24-25).

On Mount Sinai the Lord distinguished the Israelites from all other nations by giving them the covenant law, the covenant tabernacle and the covenant priesthood. Moses made a record in 'the Book of the Covenant' of all that the Lord had said to him (Exodus 24:4,7). Forty years later, just before the death of Moses and the entry of the Israelites into the promised land, Moses and the people renewed their covenant with God (Deuteronomy 28:1 – 30:20). The continuing history of Israel is a story of frequent disobedience and often of total disregard to their covenantal obligations to worship the Lord only and to obey his law.

Even where there was faithfulness towards God, and an earnest desire to live according to his commands, the requirements of God (the law) were a heavy and unbearable 'yoke on the neck' (Acts 15:10). There was nothing wrong with the law itself, for it 'is holy' and each 'commandment holy and just and good' (Romans 7:12). The problem was that 'it was weak through the flesh' (Romans 8:3). Human nature was so sinfully weak that no one could keep the law of the covenant.

'Jeremiah was even more explicit than other prophets about the fact that disobedience to the covenant would bring the curses of the covenant upon the Israelites.'[84] Judah, like the northern kingdom of Israel before her, had broken that covenant (11:2-10; 31:32). The vast majority of the people had no interest in worshipping or serving the true God. Their lives were filled with corruption. Yet within these dark days of apostasy the light of a new day was prophesied. The Lord will establish a new covenant and this time he will change the hearts of his people so that they will want to keep it -

> Behold, the days are coming, says the LORD, when I will make a new covenant with the house of Israel and with the house of Judah - not according to the covenant that I made with their fathers in the day that I took them by the hand to lead them out of the land of Egypt, my covenant which they broke, though I was a husband to them, says the LORD. But this is the covenant that I will make with the house of Israel after those days, says the LORD: I will put my law in their minds, and write it on their hearts; and I will be their God, and they shall be my people. No more shall every man teach his neighbour, and every man his brother, saying, 'Know the LORD,' for they all shall know me, from the least of them to the greatest of them, says the LORD. For I will forgive their iniquity, and their sin I will remember no more (Jeremiah 31:31-34).

The author of the letter to the Hebrews addressed the Jews who had received the Lord Jesus Christ as Messiah and Saviour. He showed how the New Covenant promises given through the prophet Jeremiah were wonderfully fulfilled in the crucified Son of God. The inadequacies of the Old Covenant and the glories of the New Covenant are spelt out: 'For if that first covenant had been faultless, then no place would have been sought for a second. Finding fault with them, he says: "Behold, the days are coming," says the

---

[84] Gareth Crossley, *The Old Testament Explained and Applied* (Darlington: Evangelical Press, 2002), p.560.

LORD, "when I will make a new covenant with the house of Israel and with the house of Judah"' (Hebrews 8:7-8, quoting Jeremiah 31:31-34).

The New Covenant

The New Covenant totally replaces the Old Covenant (Hebrews 8:13). At its centre is the life and death of the Lord Jesus Christ; in instituting the Lord's Supper, he said, 'This cup is the new covenant in my blood, which is shed for you' (Luke 22:20).

> The New Covenant is a covenant of grace.
>
> It is of grace because it originated in the mysterious love of God for sinners who deserve only his wrath and punishment. Secondly, because it promises salvation, not on the condition of works or anything meritorious on our part, but as an unmerited gift. And, thirdly, because its benefits are secured and applied not in the course of nature, or in the exercise of the natural powers of the sinner, but by the supernatural influence of the Holy Spirit, granted to him as an unmerited gift.'[85]

The Lord Jesus Christ is the 'mediator of a better covenant, which was established on better promises' (Hebrews 8:6). He is the 'one mediator between God and men' (1 Timothy 2:5). The Son of God is called the 'mediator of a better covenant' and the 'surety of a better covenant' (Hebrews 7:22), both phrases meaning that the Lord Jesus Christ is the personal guarantor of the terms of the new and better covenant, secured on the basis of his perfect sacrifice -

> He undertook to answer, as the Surety of the covenant, for all the sins of all those who are to be, and are made partakers of the benefits of it; that is, to undergo the punishment due unto their sins, to make an atonement for them, by offering Himself as a propitiatory sacrifice, redeeming them by the price of His blood from their state of misery and bondage under the law and the curse of it. He also undertook that those who were to be taken into this covenant should receive grace, enabling them to comply with the terms of it, fulfil its conditions, and yield the obedience therein required by God.[86]

---

[85] Charles Hodge, *Systematic Theology* (Grand Rapids, Michigan: Eerdmans, 1977), vol. 2, p.357.

[86] John Owen, *Hebrews: the Epistle of Warning* (Grand Rapids, Michigan: Kregel, 1953 [abridged from eight volumes]), p.129.

Under the New Covenant the laws of God are written on the mind to make us know them, and on our hearts to make us love them, and we receive the indwelling Spirit to enable us to do them (Jeremiah 31:31-34).

Elders

Elders were responsible for the welfare of a tribe, a village, town or larger community. As their name suggests they were normally men of some age being considered mature and experienced enough to make wise decisions and issue sensible instructions. The title of elder as the leader of a group of people was used by Moses in the book of Genesis -

> Joseph went up to bury his father; and with him went up all the servants of Pharaoh, the elders of his house, and all the elders of the land of Egypt, as well as all the house of Joseph... (Genesis 50:7-8).

In Exodus 3:16-17 Moses was instructed to gather together the elders of Israel and inform them first that God was going to lead his people out of Egypt. In Exodus 12:21 when about to give instructions for the Passover, Moses first called for all the elders. In Exodus 24:1 the Lord invited Moses to ascend Mount Sinai with 'Aaron, Nadab and Abihu, and seventy of the elders of Israel, and worship from afar.' These seventy elders assisted Moses with the management of the children of Israel as the estimated 1.7 million made the journey from Egypt to Canaan. In Numbers 11:16-17 the LORD said to Moses -

> 'Gather to me seventy men of the elders of Israel, whom you know to be the elders of the people and officers over them; bring them to the tabernacle of meeting, that they may stand there with you. Then I will come down and talk with you there. I will take of the Spirit that is upon you and will put the same upon them; and they shall bear the burden of the people with you, that you may not bear it yourself alone.'

Elders continued to function as local leaders even years later within the limits imposed by the exile (Ezekiel 8:1). With the return of exiles to Jerusalem the elders had a significant role in encouraging the building of the second temple (Ezra 5:5).

Herodian Dynasty (Family Tree)

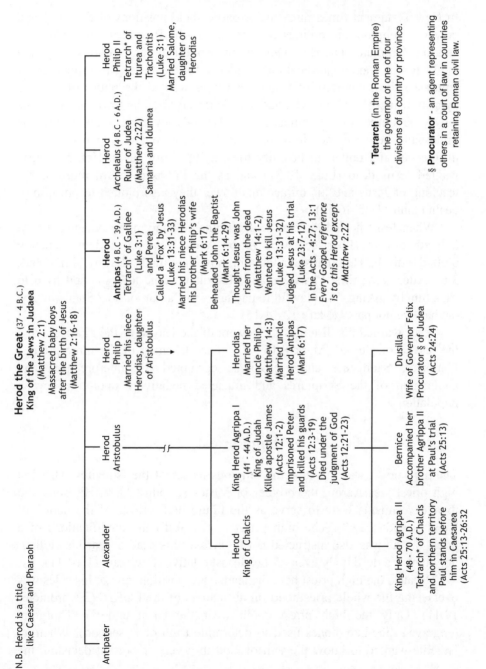

N.B. Herod is a title like Caesar and Pharaoh

Antipater

Alexander

Herod the Great (37 - 4 B.C.)
King of the Jews in Judaea
(Matthew 2:1)
Massacred baby boys after the birth of Jesus
(Matthew 2:16-18)

Herod Philip I
Married his niece Herodias, daughter of Aristobulus

Herod **Antipas** (4 B.C. - 39 A.D.)
Tetrarch* of Galilee
(Luke 3:1) and Perea
Called a 'Fox' by Jesus
(Luke 13:31-33)
Married his niece Herodias his brother Philip's wife
(Mark 6:17)
Beheaded John the Baptist
(Mark 6:14-29)
Thought Jesus was John risen from the dead
(Matthew 14:1-2)
Wanted to kill Jesus
(Luke 13:31-32)
Judged Jesus at his trial
(Luke 23:7-12)
In the Acts - 4:27; 13:1
Every Gospel reference is to this Herod except Matthew 2:22

Herod Archelaus (4 B.C. - 6 A.D.)
Ruler of Judea
(Matthew 2:22)
Samaria and Idumea

Herod Philip II
Tetrarch* of Iturea and Trachonitis
(Luke 3:1)
Married Salome, daughter of Herodias

Herod Aristobulus

Herodias
Married her uncle Philip I
(Matthew 14:3)
Married uncle Herod Antipas
(Mark 6:17)

King Herod Agrippa I (41 - 44 A.D.)
King of Judah
Killed apostle James
(Acts 12:1-2)
Imprisoned Peter and killed his guards
(Acts 12:3-19)
Died under the judgment of God
(Acts 12:21-23)

Bernice
Accompanied her brother Agrippa II at Paul's trial
(Acts 25:13)

Drusilla
Wife of Governor Felix
Procurator § of Judea
(Acts 24:24)

Herod
King of Chalcis

King Herod Agrippa II (48 - 70 A.D.)
Tetrarch* of Chalcis and northern territory
Paul stands before him in Caesarea
(Acts 25:13-26:32)

* **Tetrarch** (in the Roman Empire)
the governor of one of four divisions of a country or province.

§ **Procurator** - an agent representing others in a court of law in countries retaining Roman civil law.

Herodians

In New Testament times three major parties held positions of authority and power in religion and politics over the Jews: the Pharisees, the Sadducees and the Herodians. The Herodians, a minor political non-religious party, and the Pharisees wanted political independence for the Jews. The Sadducees by contrast were supporters of Rome. Pharisees wanted the return of David's dynasty whilst Herodians who had been sincerely friendly towards Herod the Great, favoured the continuation of Herod's dynasty. Agreement was impossible between the Herodians and Pharisees but they put aside their differences and united in hostility towards the Lord Jesus. Herod Antipas wanted Jesus dead (Luke 13:31) and as the Pharisees heard more of the teaching of Jesus and his miraculous power they also plotted to put him to death (John 11:45-46,53).

When Jesus healed the man with a withered hand in the synagogue on a Sabbath day the Pharisees were furious and 'went out and immediately plotted with the Herodians against him, how they might destroy him' (Mark 3:6). After some time Pharisees and Herodians came to Jesus and tried to trick him by asking, 'Is it lawful to pay taxes to Caesar, or not? Shall we pay, or shall we not pay?' (Mark 12:14-15)

Jesus warned his disciples to 'beware of the leaven of the Pharisees and the leaven of Herod' (Mark 8:15). The false teaching of the three groups: Pharisees, Sadducees and Herodians, corrupted the interpretation and application of the Scriptures and impacted negatively upon the Jewish population.

High priest

The high priest was the supreme religious leader of the Israelites. The first high priest was Aaron, the brother of Moses (Exodus 28:1). His sons and their descendants were to serve as the future high priests of the nation of Israel (Exodus 29:9). The high priest had to fulfil the qualifications of a priest but he was also instructed not to uncover his head or tear his clothes, nor go near a dead body even of the closest relative (Leviticus 21:10-11).

Because the high priest held the leadership position, one of his roles was overseeing the whole priesthood 'in all matters of the LORD' (2 Chronicles 19:11). Only the high priest could wear the Urim and the Thummin (engraved dice-like stones used to determine truth or falsehood). When an Israelite wanted to know the will of God in a very important decision, the high priest could be consulted, as when Joshua visited Eleazar (Numbers 27:21). Following the completion of the second temple in 515 B.C. the high priest was in overall charge of temple finances and administration, he collected taxes and maintained order as the recognised political head of the nation.

The Day of Atonement

The Day of Atonement (Yom Kippur) on the tenth day of the seventh month was the annual most solemn celebration for godly Jews. This was the one day in the year when the high priest, and only the high priest, entered behind the great veil in the temple into the Holy of Holies (Holiest of All) to stand before God. For this unique service he put aside the elaborate priestly vestments worn through the year and wore only white linen garments (Leviticus 16:4). Having made a sacrifice for himself and for the people, he then brought the blood and sprinkled it on the mercy seat (Leviticus 16:14; Exodus 25:17-22). He did this to make atonement for himself and the people for all their sins committed during the past year (Exodus 30:10).

It is this particular ceremony that is compared to the ministry of Jesus as our High Priest (Hebrews 9:2-15). It is through the unique function of the Old Covenant high priest that God illustrates the profound work of his Son. In glorious loving self-surrender he sacrificed himself for our sins once for all (Hebrews 9:26; 10:10,12). By entering into the holy presence of God on our behalf, 'he became the author of eternal salvation to all who obey him, called by God as High Priest' (Hebrew 5:9-10).

> For there is one God and one Mediator between God and men, the Man Christ Jesus, who gave himself a ransom for all' (1 Timothy 2:5-6; cf. John 14:6; Acts 4:12).

Through the death and resurrection of the Lord Jesus, his return to the Father and the outpouring of the Holy Spirit, dramatic changes have been brought about. There is no longer any role for an earthly high priest since we now have easy access to the much greater heavenly High Priest. Nor do we need a company of priests to mediate for us by the offering of animal sacrifices. That practice is now obsolete (Hebrews 10:1-10). The priesthood of Aaron and his descendants is superseded by the glorious priesthood of all believers. All those who repent and believe in the Lord Jesus compose -

> a chosen generation, a royal priesthood, a holy nation, his own special people, that you may proclaim the praises of him who called you out of darkness into his marvellous light; who once were not a people but are now the people of God, who had not obtained mercy but now have obtained mercy (1 Peter 2:9-10).

Christianity does not possess a priesthood, *it is a priesthood* (1 Peter 2:9; Revelation 1:6). Every believer in Christ has direct access to God regardless of age, gender, race, or social standing: 'There is neither Jew nor Greek, there is neither slave nor free, there is neither male nor female; for you are all one in Christ Jesus' (Galatians 3:28; cf. Colossians 3:11). For through our wonderful Saviour we all 'have access by one Spirit to the Father' (Ephesians 2:18). We therefore 'have boldness and access with confidence through faith in him' (Ephesians 3:12).

High priests Annas and Caiaphas

In 63 B.C. the Romans captured Jerusalem. The Sanhedrin, the supreme court of the Jews, was allowed to continue running the religious and social life of the nation but the Romans insisted on appointing the high priest. In A.D. 6 the Romans appointed Annas to the office. He was deposed in A.D. 14 by Valerius Gratus, the predecessor of governor Pontius Pilate. Four appointments were made during the succeeding years until in A.D. 17 Caiaphas the son-in-law of Annas was appointed. He was high priest until A.D. 36.

Though officially removed from office Annas remained one of the nation's most influential and powerful men. Five sons (Eleazar, Jonathan, Theophilus, Matthias, and Ananus), Caiaphas his son-in-law, and a grandson followed him in the office of high priest. The Pharisees and also any Jews who had even a slight regard for the law of God, would not accept Caiaphas or any other than Annas as high priest. According to the law of God a high priest was to be appointed for his lifetime (Exodus 40:15; Numbers 35:25); consequently pious Jews would always think of Annas as the true high priest. So although in civic affairs Caiaphas was formally recognised as high priest, in matters of religion Annas took precedence.

This explains why Luke presents a strange anomaly when he locates the timing of the call of John the Baptist as 'while Annas and Caiaphas were high priests' (Luke 3:2). One was high priest by right, the other high priest in fact. The precedence of high priest Annas was evident when the Lord Jesus was arrested and 'they led him away to Annas first, for he was the father-in-law of Caiaphas who was high priest that year' (John 18:13). After the interview, 'Annas sent him bound to Caiaphas the high priest' (John 18:24). Annas was quite obviously the power behind the scenes.

In practice it was Annas who maintained control over the religious and social life of Israel for many years. He and his family network controlled the temple and through the exorbitant prices charged for sacrifices and for the conversion of foreign currencies they were very wealthy. All this financial income was additional to the support prescribed by the law of God.

The extensive power and authority of Annas was also evident after the great day of Pentecost. Peter and John were arrested following the healing of the blind man at the temple gate 'Beautiful'. The two apostles were investigated by 'their rulers, elders, and scribes, as well as Annas the high priest, Caiaphas, John, and Alexander, and as many as were of the family of the high priest... gathered together at Jerusalem' (Acts 4:5-6). Here Luke indicates the precedence of Annas 'the high priest' (not officially high priest) over Caiaphas (the official high priest) who is placed in a subordinate position along with the others.

Judaizers

Judaizers were Pharisees who professed faith in Christ and yet insisted that Gentile believers in Christ must be circumcised and commanded to keep the law of Moses.

After Pentecost and the outpouring of the Holy Spirit a number of Pharisees professed faith in Christ. Some of them began insisting that Gentile believers in Christ must be circumcised and commanded to keep the law of Moses (Acts 15:5). The issue was so serious that a council of apostles and Christian elders gathered to debate the matter thoroughly. The conclusion was drafted in a letter -

> The apostles, the elders, and the brethren, To the brethren who are of the Gentiles in Antioch, Syria, and Cilicia: Greetings. Since we have heard that some who went out from us have troubled you with words, unsettling your souls, saying, 'You must be circumcised and keep the law' - to whom we gave no such commandment - it seemed good to us, being assembled with one accord, to send chosen men to you with our beloved Barnabas and Paul, men who have risked their lives for the name of our Lord Jesus Christ. We have therefore sent Judas and Silas, who will also report the same things by word of mouth. For it seemed good to the Holy Spirit, and to us, to lay upon you no greater burden than these necessary things: that you abstain from things offered to idols, from blood, from things strangled, and from sexual immorality. If you keep yourselves from these, you will do well. Farewell (Acts 15:23-29).

The apostle Paul was an ideal ambassador chosen by God. He was trained as a Pharisee, and his credentials as one were outstanding (Acts 26:5). He called himself 'a Hebrew of Hebrews; concerning the law, a Pharisee; concerning zeal, persecuting the church; concerning the righteousness which is in the law, blameless' (Philippians 3:5–6). But Paul found that his performance of the law could not produce true righteousness. After he placed his trust in Christ's finished work on the cross, he desired to 'be found in him, not having my own righteousness, which is from the law, but that which is through faith in Christ, the righteousness which is from God by faith' (Philippians 3:9).

Some time after the Jerusalem Council, the apostle Peter visited the new church in Antioch. Whilst Peter was mixing with this largely Gentile congregation a number of Judaizers visited the church (Judaizers were Pharisees who professed faith in Christ and yet insisted that Gentile believers in Christ must be circumcised and commanded to keep the law of Moses). Peter was influenced by them to separate from Gentile Christians and eat only with Jews (as according to the Pharisaic tradition). The Law of Moses did not forbid Jews eating with Gentiles but did forbid the eating of certain food (Leviticus 11:1-8). However Peter had been taught earlier, by a vision from heaven, that the food laws of the Old Covenant were no longer in force (Acts 10:10-16).
Writing to the Galatians Paul described how he confronted Peter for his inconsistency in forcing Gentile Christians 'to live as Jews' (literally translated 'to Judaize') -

> ...when I saw that they were not straightforward about the truth of the gospel, I said to Peter before them all, 'If you, being a Jew, live in the manner of Gentiles and not as the Jews, why do you compel Gentiles to live as Jews? We who are Jews by nature, and not sinners of the Gentiles, knowing that a man is not justified by the works of the law but by faith in Jesus Christ, even we have believed in Christ Jesus, that we might be justified by faith in Christ and not by the works of the law; for by the works of the law no flesh shall be justified' (Galatians 2:14-16).

The Roman Catholic Church teaches a doctrine similar to that of the Judaizers of the New Testament in that its doctrine is a mixture of law and grace. At the Council of Trent in the 16th century, the Catholic Church explicitly denied the idea of salvation by faith alone. Catholics have always held that certain sacraments are necessary for salvation.

The issues for the 1st century Judaizers were circumcision and obedience to the law of Moses. The issues for modern-day Roman Catholics are baptism, confession and the grounds of salvation. The works considered necessary may have changed, but both Judaizers and Catholics attempt to merit God's grace through the performance of rituals.

> None are 'justified by the works of the law but by faith in Jesus Christ' (Galatians 2:16).

Pharisees

Pharisees exercised a powerful influence on the people of Israel during the ministry of Jesus and the early church. The historian Josephus (A.D. 37-100), believed by many historians to have been a Pharisee, estimated the total number of Pharisees, before the destruction of Jerusalem and the temple in A.D. 70, to have been around 6,000. They were mostly middle-class businessmen and leaders in the synagogues. They abstained from politics and placed great stress on religious purity. Josephus claimed that Pharisees received the full support and goodwill of the common people, in contrast to the more elite Sadducees, who were from the upper class. Their support among the people gave them a powerful position within the Sanhedrin (the 70-strong High Court of the Jews). Although they were a minority in the Sanhedrin they seem to have had control of the decision-making.

They were known as Pharisees (meaning 'separated') because they separated themselves from all other Jews, aiming at more than ordinary piety and strictness in religion. They traced back their origin to the days following the return of the Jewish exiles from the Babylonian captivity.

They were well-known as legal experts and taught that all Jews should observe all 613 laws in the Torah. Alongside the Torah, which is the written law of Moses in Genesis, Exodus, Leviticus, Numbers and Deuteronomy, the Pharisees were committed to obeying the oral law which they believed God also communicated to Moses on Mount Sinai and which was preserved and developed. These were the Rabbinical teachings of the law and its interpretations that are not recorded in the five books of Moses.

The oral law (known as 'the law of the Rabbis' or 'the tradition of the elders') includes rules for governing worship, for regulating human relationship with God, interpersonal relationships, food laws and laws of the Sabbath, the observance of festivals, rituals, marital relationships, agricultural practices, and civil claims and damages. By observing both these laws (written and oral), they believed that their strict external piety and legalism (excessive adherence to law) would bring about the coming of the Messiah, obtain justification with God, and ensure their entrance into the kingdom of heaven.

The Pharisees who opposed Jesus regarded the oral law as being of equal standing to the written law of Old Testament Scripture. In fact when a conflict arose between the two, they gave precedence to the oral law. Jesus exposed this. Challenged by Pharisees and scribes about transgressing the tradition of the elders over hand washing, he responded with a question -

Why do you also transgress the commandment of God because of your tradition? For God commanded, saying, 'Honour your father and your mother'; and, 'He who curses father or mother, let him be put to death'. But you say, 'Whoever says to his father or mother, "Whatever profit you might have received from me is a gift to God"' - then he need not honour his father or mother'. Thus you have made the commandment of God of no effect by your tradition. Hypocrites! Well did Isaiah prophesy about you, saying: 'These people draw near to me with their mouth, and honour me with their lips, but their heart is far from me. And in vain they worship me, teaching as doctrines the commandments of men' (Matthew 15:3-9).

The elevation of Rabbinic teaching to the level of God's Word in Scripture was a clear violation of the words of Moses -

You shall not add to the word which I command you, nor take from it, that you may keep the commandments of the LORD your God which I command you (Deuteronomy 4:2).

Adding to Scripture is forbidden by God (cf. Revelation 22:18).

The disciples of Jesus were charged with breaking the law of the Sabbath when they plucked ears of corn on a Sabbath Day. With masterly skill Jesus showed the Pharisees that their understanding of the Sabbath was quite wrong. He used five arguments from Old Testament Scripture to make his point conclusive and incontrovertible (Matthew 12:1-14).[87]

Pharisees believed in predestination, acknowledged the immortality of the soul, future rewards and punishments, the existence of good and evil angels, and the resurrection of the body. Many of the doctrines of the Pharisees put them at odds with the Sadducees; however, the two groups managed to set aside their differences at the trial of Jesus. To accomplish his death, the Pharisees and Sadducees united (Mark 14:53; 15:1).

Among the Pharisees were two schools of thought, based on the teachings of two rabbis, Shammai and Hillel. Shammai called for a strict, unbending interpretation of the law on almost every issue, but Hillel taught a looser, more liberal application. Followers of Shammai fostered a hatred for anything Roman, including taxation. Jews who served as tax collectors were debarred from the temple and unacceptable as legal witnesses. Followers of Shammai wanted to break all interaction and trade between Jews and Gentiles. Followers of Hillel took a more liberal attitude and opposed such

---

[87] See section *26. Sabbath day controversies,* p.65.

extreme exclusiveness. Eventually, the two schools within Pharisaism grew so hostile to each other that they refused to worship together.

The clash of conviction between the two parties was brought before Jesus when he was asked by Pharisees testing him, 'Is it lawful for a man to divorce his wife for just any reason?' (Matthew 19:3) They were referring to Deuteronomy 24:1 which permitted a man to divorce a wife when there is the discovery of 'some uncleanness in her'. Rabbi Shammai held that 'some uncleanness in her' meant adultery and adultery alone. Rabbi Hillel taught that if a wife displeased her husband by, for example, spoiling a meal, speaking disrespectfully to him or talking to another man, these were grounds for divorce. Jesus referred back to the creation of woman and the establishment of marriage as being for life. He pointed out that divorce was only allowed because of the hardness of the human heart (Matthew 19:8).

Jesus warned his disciples about the 'leaven' of the Pharisees by which he meant their insidious teaching of human religious tradition which appeared in many guises as legalism, ceremonialism and formalism (the use of forms of worship without regard to inner significance; the basing of ethics on the form of the moral law without regard to intention or consequences). There was an emphasis upon external order and ritual, an insistence upon rules and regulations. Laws of human origin as well as the law of God had to be followed with scrupulous exactness. At times the Pharisees by their traditions made people disobey the commandments of God (Matthew 15:1-9). To the undiscerning, Pharisees gave an appearance of piety, but to Jesus they were 'whitewashed tombs which indeed appear beautiful outwardly, but inside are full of dead men's bones and all uncleanness' (Matthew 23:27).

Whilst many Pharisees hated Jesus and wanted to see him dead there were a few like Nicodemus who rightly considered Jesus 'a teacher who has come from God' and honestly sought answers from him (John 3:1–2). Nicodemus later defended Jesus before the Sanhedrin (John 7:50–51) and was on hand at the Lord's crucifixion to help another Pharisee, Joseph of Arimathea entomb the body of Jesus (John 19:39,38).

Priests

On Mount Sinai God gave Moses instruction for the children of Israel regarding the law, the sacrificial system and the priesthood. The tribe of Levi was exclusively appointed to the priesthood (Numbers 3:12-13). Though all priests were Levites, not all Levites were priests. Only those who descended directly from Aaron (Exodus 29:7-9) were priests authorised to function as mediators between the people and God. They performed animal sacrifices on behalf of the people. Male descendants of Aaron were eligible for service from the age of 30 years to 50 if they were without physical defect and holy in conduct (Leviticus 21:6-8). Priests could not mourn the dead, had to avoid defilement by being near to the dead (except for very close relatives), and could only marry a virgin.

The requirements for ceremonial cleanliness were rigorous in the law of God; the external practices were intended as a reminder of the need for true holiness of heart and mind. Priests served in rotation so that they could each have a turn to minister in the Holy Place and offer sacrifices. Zacharias the father of John the Baptist performed this service (Luke 1:8–9).

Levites, not descended from Aaron, functioned in a variety of other duties. At first they were involved in carrying the ark and the equipment and materials of the tabernacle (Numbers 3:5-9). When the temple was completed it was the Levites who were responsible for its care and services.

No land inheritance was assigned to the tribe of Levi for they were to be sustained by the sacrifices, offerings and gifts of the people (Numbers 18:8-14). In the days of Jesus, priests were known to be wealthy especially the extensive family of High Priest Annas.

There was no king in Israel in the days of Jesus because in 538 B.C. King Cyrus of the Medes and Persians permitted Jews to return from exile to Judea and rebuild the temple *but he did not restore the monarchy* to Judah. Consequently those who governed the temple became the controlling authority over the civil as well as the religious life of the nation. It was around this time that the Sadducees began as a party of the priests. Not all priests were Sadducees, many were Pharisees and many more were not members of any group.

Chief priests

The designation 'chief' seems to have been adopted to distinguish the priests who were appointed to the Sanhedrin, the ruling court of the Jews. Priests were the majority within this council and exercised considerable authority over the Jews within the religious and civil limits prescribed by the Romans. God's law established the office of high priest and that of priests but there is no appointed position for 'chief' priests in the Old Testament.

Conversions not long after the death of Jesus

From the Day of Pentecost the gospel spread rapidly even among the priesthood -

Then the word of God spread, and the number of the disciples multiplied greatly in Jerusalem, and a great many of the priests were obedient to the faith (Acts 6:7).

Resurrection appearances

First Lord's Day (Resurrection Day)

1. Mary Magdalene in the garden (Mark 16:9; John 20:14-18).

2. Mary the mother of James and Joses, Salome and Joanna on the way from the garden (Matthew 28:9; Luke 24:10; Mark 16:1).

3. The apostle Peter (Luke 24:34; 1 Corinthians 15:5).

4. Cleopas and another disciple on the Emmaus Road (Luke 24:13-35; Mark 16:12).

5. The apostles in a room in Jerusalem, Thomas being absent (John 20:19; Luke 24:36-43).

Second Lord's Day

6. The apostles in a room in Jerusalem, Thomas being present (John 20:26-29; Mark 16:14).

Some days later

7. Apostles Peter, Thomas, Nathanael, James, John and two others by the Sea of Galilee (John 21:1-22).

8. Over five hundred in Galilee (1 Corinthians 15:6).

9. James the brother of the Lord (1 Corinthians 15:7).

Forty days after the resurrection

10. The eleven apostles in Jerusalem and on to Bethany for the ascension (1 Corinthians 15:7; Acts 1:2-8; Luke 24:50-51).

Sometime later

11. Saul of Tarsus [Paul] on the Damascus Road (1 Corinthians 15:8).

Sadducees

The Jewish sect of the Sadducees developed over the years from among the priests. They were a religio-political party who were more interested in politics than in religion. Caiaphas was a Sadducee (Acts 5:17) as was his father-in-law Annas and a number of the chief priests. They held the majority of the seats in the Sanhedrin (Supreme Court of the Jews) but tended to yield to the small group of Pharisees in the Sanhedrin because the Pharisees enjoyed the respect of the people. The Sadducees had no appeal to the mass of the people. The general population had little or no respect for them because they were wealthy, upperclass and keen to promote good relations with Rome.

Many of the Sadducees were extremely wealthy gaining a great deal from their control of the temple and its services. Outside of the priesthood they only seem to have attracted to their sect those Jews who were noble or rich. Since their concern was only for this life they were zealous to maintain all the priestly authority and privileges which they claimed came from the Zadok the priest in the days of King Solomon.

The doctrinal convictions of the Sadducees differed markedly from those held by the Pharisees. They said 'that there is no resurrection - and no angel or spirit; but the Pharisees confess both' (Acts 23:8; Matthew 22:23; Mark 12:18–27). Consequently they denied any punishment or reward after death, nor did they believe that God had any involvement in the day to day life of his people. The Sadducees upheld the authority of the written Word of God, especially the five books of Moses (Genesis - Deuteronomy). They rejected the oral law which the Pharisees loved so much.

The Sadducees appear to have had little interest in the ministry of Jesus until he became very popular and then they began to be anxious that the Romans might become concerned by his activities. Some of them joined with Pharisees to test Jesus by asking for a sign from heaven (Matthew 16:1-4). Later they came with a question which aimed to show the foolishness of believing in the resurrection. Jesus answered it simply and clearly (Matthew 22:23-33).[88]

The disquiet of the Sadducees regarding Jesus came to a head following his raising of Lazarus from the dead and a number of their chief priests and Pharisees brought to the Sanhedrin the issue of the Lord's increasing influence. High priest Caiaphas spoke out strongly -

> You know nothing at all, nor do you consider that it is expedient
> for us that one man should die for the people, and not that the
> whole nation should perish (John 11:49-50).

Disguising his true motives under a cloak of nationalism, the crafty Caiaphas was trying to remove a personal obstacle. Jesus posed a great threat to his

---

[88] See section *100. Sadducees and the resurrection,* p.223.

popularity and power, so he argued that if the people followed Jesus the occupying Romans would rise up and destroy the nation.

After the death of the Lord Jesus the Sadducees were greatly annoyed by the preaching of Peter following the healing of the lame beggar at the temple gate. They joined with priests and the captain of the temple in the arrest of Peter and John, being particularly incensed that 'they taught the people and preached in Jesus the resurrection from the dead' (Acts 4:2; cf. 5:17-20).

Sanhedrin

By the time of the Lord's ministry the composition of the governing body for the nation had evolved. Known as the Sanhedrin (a Greek word meaning 'sitting together' hence 'assembly' or 'council') this Supreme Court of the Jews made the ultimate decisions regarding the law. Along with a number of prominent elders the 70 strong council was composed of chief priests, scribes, Sadducees and Pharisees with the high priest usually presiding (Luke 22:66; John 11:47; Acts 23:6).

Alfred Edersheim, a Jewish Christian scholar wrote -

> after the accession of Herod, the Sanhedrin became a shadow of itself. It was packed with Sadducees and Priests of the King's nomination, and with Doctors of the canon-law, whose only aim was to pursue in peace their subtleties; who had not, and, from their contempt of the people, could not have, any real sympathy with national aspirations; and whose ideal heavenly Kingdom was a miraculous, heaven-instituted, absolute rule of Rabbis.[89]

There is no way to ascertain the proportion of each group within the Sanhedrin as there was considerable overlap; the high priest was a Sadducee by conviction and so were most if not all of the chief priests. Likewise many of the scribes were Pharisees by conviction. Three notable Pharisees who were members of the Sanhedrin were Nicodemus, Joseph of Arimathea and Gamaliel (John 3:1; Mark 15:43; Acts 5:34).

The verdict to execute Jesus was passed by the Sanhedrin despite the failure to fulfil the requirements of the law of God through Moses (Deuteronomy 19:15). Jesus was condemned solely for acknowledging himself to be the Son of God (Matthew 26:63-66; 27:1; Mark 14:61-64; Luke 22:70-71).

---

[89] Alfred Edersheim, *The Life and Times of Jesus the Messiah* (Peabody, Massachusetts: Hendrikson, 1993), p.165.

Scribes

The office of scribe traces back 450 years to Ezra the priest and scribe (Ezra 7:11; Nehemiah 8:1) who was an outstanding man of God. Unable to function as a priest whilst exiled in Babylon away from the only God-ordained centre of worship, the temple in Jerusalem, he laboured in teaching, explaining the Word of God to those in exile. In 458 B.C. he led about two thousand exiles on their journey to Jerusalem to join descendants of the 50,000 who undertook the expedition eighty years earlier. This testimony is recorded of him, 'Ezra came up from Babylon; and he was a skilled scribe in the law of Moses, which the LORD God of Israel had given' (Ezra 7:6). He was wholly committed to Scripture for he 'had prepared his heart to seek the law of the LORD, and to do it, and to teach statutes and ordinances in Israel' (Ezra 7:10).

Scribes in ancient Israel were scholarly men whose work was to study the law, transcribe it, and write commentaries. They were also used when the need arose for a written document or when an interpretation of Scripture or a legal point was needed. They taught the people (Mark 1:22) and were widely respected by the community because of their knowledge, dedication, and outward appearance of law-keeping. Every village had at least one scribe.

The scribes took their work seriously and would copy and re-copy the Bible meticulously, even counting letters and spaces to ensure each copy was correct. Hence it can be seen that Jewish scribes were responsible for accurately preserving the Old Testament.

In the days of the Lord Jesus, scribes were often associated with the sect of the Pharisees, many Pharisees were also scribes (see Matthew 5:20; 12:38).

The scribes were responsible for the introduction, development, interpretation and elevation of the oral law which was then adopted by the Pharisees. They became skilled at explaining the letter of the law whilst at the same time ignoring the spirit behind it, often going beyond Scripture and adding, or replacing it by their man-made traditions. Luke refers to scribes as 'teachers of the law' (Luke 5:17) or 'lawyers' (Luke 7:30; 10:25; 11:45; 14:3). Matthew also calls one of the Pharisees a lawyer thereby indicating a scribe who was also a Pharisee (Matthew 22:35).

Their obsession with the oral law, with its corruption of God's law, resulted in many conflicts with Jesus. At the beginning of the Sermon on the Mount, Jesus probably shocked his audience when he declared that the righteousness of the scribes and Pharisees was not enough to get anyone to heaven (Matthew 5:20). A large portion of the Sermon on the Mount was then devoted to what the people had been taught (by the scribes and

Pharisees) and what God actually required (Matthew 5:21-48). Toward the end of Jesus' ministry, he thoroughly condemned both parties, scribes and Pharisees, for their hypocrisy (Matthew 23). They knew the law of God in Scripture, and they often taught it to others, but they did not obey it themselves.

Though the Jews in general had a high regard for their scribes they nevertheless recognised something superior in the teaching of Jesus 'for he taught them as one having authority, and not as the scribes' (Matthew 7:29). Jesus acknowledged the faithfulness of the scribes at times in their teaching yet he was highly critical of their hypocritical behaviour when he said -

> The scribes and the Pharisees sit in Moses' seat. Therefore whatever they tell you to observe, that observe and do, but do not do according to their works; for they say, and do not do (Matthew 23:2-3).

He united scribes with Pharisees when he uttered his dreadful denunciations of those teachers who were 'like whitewashed tombs which indeed appear beautiful outwardly, but inside are full of dead men's bones and all uncleanness' (Matthew 23:27).

It would seem that for most scribes, faith and godliness did not accompany their precision in study and in teaching. Their intellects were clearly engaged but not their hearts. Many were viciously opposed to Jesus and his teaching (Matthew 9:3-7; Mark 11:27-28; Luke 5:30-32; 20:20-26). Scribes were also heavily involved with the chief priests and elders in bringing about the Lord's death (Matthew 26:57; Mark 14:43,53; 15:1,31; Luke 22:1–2).

Sea of Galilee

The Sea of Galilee (Matthew 4:18) is known by many names throughout the Scriptures. In the New Testament it is called 'the Sea of Tiberias' (John 6:1; 21:1); 'the Lake of Gennesaret' (Luke 5:1); 'the sea' (John 6:25); and 'the lake' (Luke 8:22). In Old Testament times it was known as 'the Sea of Chinnereth' (Numbers 34:11); or 'the Sea of Chinneroth' (Joshua 12:3). It is also known today by its Hebrew name Kinneret.

The Sea of Galilee lies almost 200m (700ft) below sea level in the deep Jordan valley and is the lowest freshwater lake on earth and the second-lowest lake in the world (after the Dead Sea). Its length from north to south is about 13 miles (21km) with a width of 7 miles (11km) from east to west, its maximum depth is approximately 43m (140 ft). It is pear shaped, similar to the Continent of Africa, with a distinctive bulge to the west and the narrow end to the south as it flows out as the Jordan River. The water is clear and clean and contains many varieties of fish in great numbers (it is said to contain 54 different species). Encircling most of the sea is a broad pebbly beach with stretches of sand. The mountains to the east and to the west rise to about 600m (2,000 ft.).

The sheltered location and low elevation result in the winters being mild though subject to brief violent storms; the cool air from the uplands rushing down the gorges with great violence and tossing the waters in tempestuous waves. These storms are fairly frequent and extremely dangerous to small boats. Occasionally a tempest breaks over the sea in which a boat could hardly survive - hence the anxiety even of the fishermen disciples when a storm broke out (Mark 4:35-41).

The soil on the level parts around the sea is very fertile producing a good yield of figs, fruits of the vine and vegetables. Since the temperature in the valley is higher than that of the uplands wheat and barley are harvested about a month earlier.

Synagogues

Although the Jews were exiled in the heathen land of Babylon for seventy years it did not extinguish the worship of the one true God. Daniel and his young colleagues were a fine example of faithfulness to God in an alien society. In the days leading up to the return to Israel it is evident that there were many able teachers (scribes) among the Jewish exiles (e.g. Nehemiah 8:7). No doubt these teachers (priests and scribes like Ezra) travelled extensively when and where possible and met privately in homes to instruct the faithful and encourage the worship of the living God.

With the return of the Jews to Israel the practice of meeting in private homes for public worship and religious instruction continued and was eventually superseded by the rise of local synagogues (from the Greek meaning, 'bringing together' that is, an assembly or gathering). Even with the building of the second temple the benefit of local places of worship and instruction continued especially in villages and towns some distance from Jerusalem. Outside Judea, the synagogue was often called a house of prayer. While most Jews could not regularly attend the temple service, they could meet at the synagogue.

Miracles of Jesus recorded in the Gospels

	Matthew	Mark	Luke	John
1. Water turned into wine	-	-	-	2:1-11
2. A nobleman's son healed	-	-	-	4:46-51
3. A miraculous catch of fish	-	-	5:4-7	-
4. A possessed man delivered	-	1:23-28	4:33-37	-
5. Peter's mother-in-law healed	8:14-15	1:29-31	4:38-39	-
6. A leper cleansed	8:2-4	1:40-45	5:12-15	-
7. A paralysed man healed	9:1-8	2:1-12	5:17-26	-
8. A paralytic healed at Bethesda	-	-	-	5:5-9
9. A withered hand restored	12:9-14	3:1-6	6:6-11	-
10. A Centurion's servant healed	8:5-13	-	7:1-10	-
11. The widow of Nain's son raised	-	-	7:11-15	-
12. A possessed mute delivered	12:22	-	11:14	-
13. The stilling the storm	8:24-27	4:37-41	8:23-25	-
14. Gadarene demoniacs healed	8:28-32	5:1-15	8:26-35	-
15. Woman's haemorrhage healed	9:20-22	5:25-34	8:43-48	-
16. The raising of Jairus' daughter	9:23-25	5:38-43	8:51-56	-
17. Two blind men healed	9:27-30	-	-	-
18. A possessed mute delivered	9:32-33	-	-	-
19. The feeding the five thousand	14:19-21	6:41-44	9:16-17	6:11-13
20. Walking on the water	14:25-32	6:46-51	-	6:18-21
21. Healings in Gennesaret	14:34-36	6:53-56	-	-
22. A Syrophoenician girl healed	15:21-28	7:24-30	-	-
23. A deaf-mute healed	-	7:32-35	-	-
24. The feeding the four thousand	15:36-38	8:6-9	-	-
25. A blind man's sight restored	-	8:22-25	-	-
26. A possessed boy delivered	17:14-18	9:17-27	9:38-42	-
27. Money in the fish's mouth	17:27	-	-	-
28. Sight for the man born blind	-	-	-	9:1-7
29. A crippled woman delivered	-	-	13:11-13	-
30. A man healed of dropsy	-	-	14:2-4	-
31. Lazarus raised from the dead	-	-	-	11:39-44
32. Ten lepers healed	-	-	17:12-16	-
33. Restored sight for Bartimaeus	20:30-34	10: 46-52	18:35-43	-
34. Healing the blind and the lame	21:14	-	-	-
35. The dried up fig-tree	-	11:20-21	-	-
36. The ear of Malchus healed	-	-	22:50-51	-
37. A miraculous catch of fish	-	-	-	21:5-6

Parables of Jesus recorded in the Gospels

		Matthew	Mark	Luke	John
1.	The New Cloth on an Old Coat	9:16	2:21	5:36	-
2.	The New Wine in Old Wineskins	9:17	2:22	5:37-38	-
3.	The Building on Rock or Sand	7:24-27	-	6:47-49	-
4.	The Two Debtors	-	-	7:41-43	-
5.	The Sower	13:3-8	4:3-8	8:5-8	-
	The Sower explained	13:18-23	4:14-20	8:11-15	-
6.	The Lamp Under a Basket	-	4:21-22	8:16-17	-
7.	The Seed Growing Secretly	-	4:26-29	-	-
8.	The Wheat and Tares	13:24-30	-	-	-
	The Wheat and Tares explained	13:36-43	-	-	-
9.	The Mustard Seed	13:31-32	4:30-32	13:18-19	-
10.	The Leaven	13:33	-	13:20-21	-
11.	The Hidden Treasure	13:44	-	-	-
12.	The Pearl of Great Price	13:45-46	-	-	-
13.	The Dragnet	13:47-50	-	-	-
14.	The Lost Sheep	18:12-14	-	-	-
15.	Unforgiving Servant	18:23-35	-	-	-
16.	The True Shepherd	-	-	-	10:1-5
17.	The Good Shepherd	-	-	-	10:7-18
18.	The Good Samaritan	-	-	10:30-37	-
19.	The Friend at Midnight	-	-	11:5-8	-
20.	The Rich Fool	-	-	12:16-21	-
21.	The Fruitless Fig Tree	-	-	13:6-9	-
22.	The Seats at a Feast	-	-	14:7-11	-
23.	The Great Supper	-	-	14:15-24	-
24.	The Hasty Builder	-	-	14:28-30	-
25.	The Impetuous King	-	-	14:31-33	-
26.	The Lost Sheep	-	-	15:4-7	-
27.	The Lost Coin	-	-	15:8-10	-
28.	The Lost Son	-	-	15:11-32	-
29.	The Unjust Steward	-	-	16:1-13	-
30.	The Rich Man and Lazarus	-	-	16:19-31	-
31.	The Widow and the Judge	-	-	18:2-8	-
32.	The Pharisee and the Tax Collector	-	-	18:9-14	-
33.	The Labourers in the Vineyard	20:1-16	-	-	-
34.	The Minas	-	-	19:12-27	-
35.	The Two Sons	21:28-32	-	-	-
36.	The Wicked Tenants	21:33-44	12:1-11	20:9-18	-
37.	The Wedding Guests	22:2-14	-	-	-
38.	The Fig Tree	24:32-35	13:28-29	21:29-31	-
39.	The Faithful and Wise Servant	24:45-51	13:34-37	-	-

40.	The Wise and Foolish Virgins	25:1-13	-	-	-
41.	The Talents	25:14-30	-	-	-
42.	The Sheep and Goats	25:31-46	-	-	-
43.	The True Vine	-	-	-	15:1-10

Bible lands in modern times

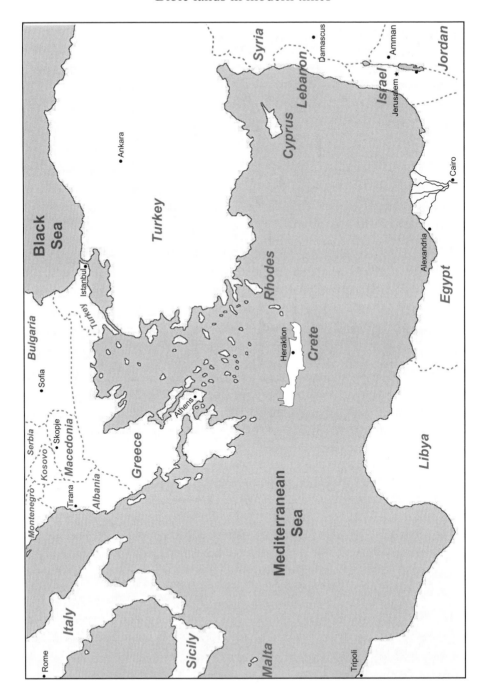

Bible lands in New Testament times

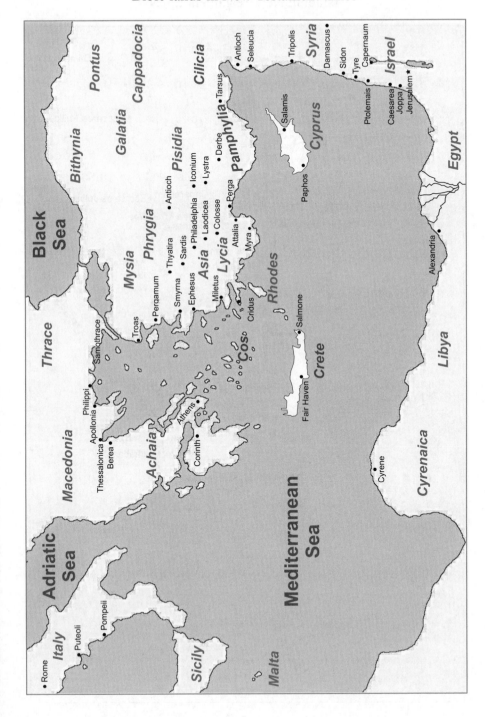

...

Israel in New Testament times

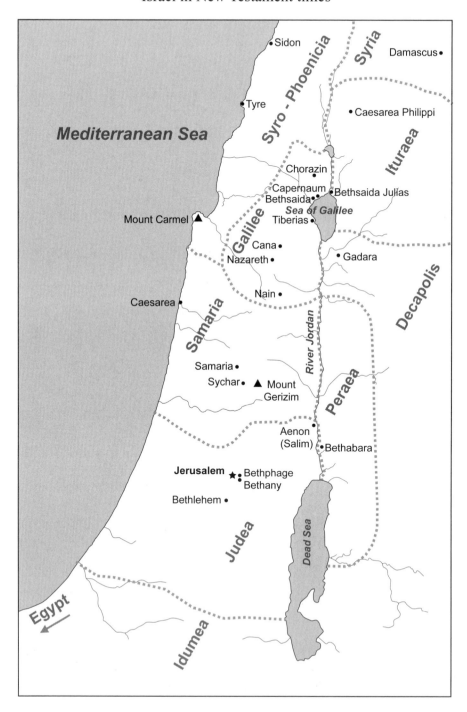

Sea of Galilee in New Testament times

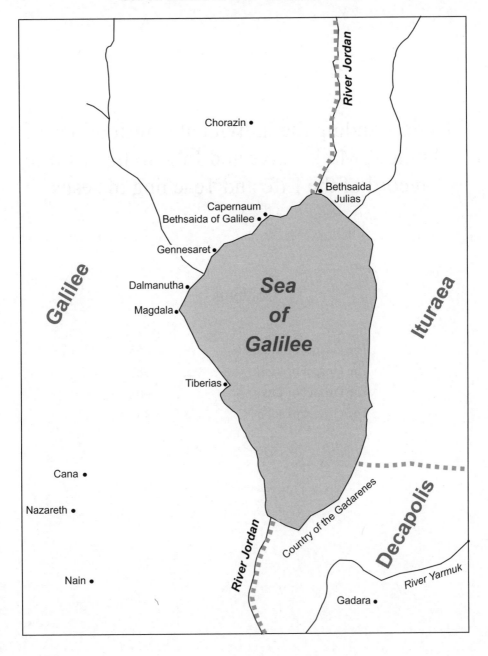

Understanding the individual contributions of Matthew, Mark, Luke and John to the historic record of the Life and Teaching of Jesus

Contents

Understanding
The Gospel of Matthew

Author: the apostle Matthew
(widely accepted)

Theme:
Jesus of Nazareth
the promised King Messiah
has come

Contents

A brief sketch of the author

Although it is nowhere mentioned in Scripture that the apostle Matthew was the author of the book bearing his name, it has been widely accepted through the centuries that he was. 'That Matthew was a skilled literary craftsman no one denies.'[90] The apostle Matthew was a tax collector so would be among the small minority of the population at that time who was able to read and write. He would be fluent in Aramaic and Greek. In his Gospel he demonstrates a clear literary ability as he records an account of the life and ministry of Jesus of Nazareth. Being a Jew his early schooling and mandatory synagogue attendance would have grounded him in the contents and interpretation of the Hebrew Scriptures. At some point he must have rejected his Jewish formative years, to commence working for the Roman overlords. He worked as a tax collector (9:9-11)[91] in or around Capernaum under the jurisdiction of Herod Antipas.

Some scholars suggest that his role among the twelve apostles might have been as note-taker or Christian scribe. The words of Jesus, at the conclusion of a series of parables, would have been particularly pertinent: 'Therefore every scribe instructed concerning the kingdom of heaven is like a householder who brings out of his treasure things new and old' (13:52). Matthew used his talents to good effect.

There were two classes of tax collector, one collected general taxes: ground-tax, income-tax and poll-tax (levied on all persons, bond or free, men from the age of fourteen, and women from the age of twelve, up to the age of sixty-five). The second group were the customhouse officials such as Matthew. They were open to all kinds of corruption and could inflict greater hardship through the imposition of arbitrary taxes.

> There was tax and duty upon all imports and exports; on all that was bought and sold; bridge-money, road-money, harbour-dues, town-dues, etc. The classical reader knows the ingenuity which could invent a tax, and find a name for every kind of exaction, such as on axles, wheels, pack-animals, pedestrians, roads, highways; on admission to markets; on carriers, bridges, ships, and quays; on crossing rivers, on dams, on licences, in short, on

---

[90] Donald Carson and Douglas Moo, *An Introduction to the New Testament.* (Leicester: Inter-Varsity Press, 2005), p.134.

[91] Where the book is not stated the quotation is from Matthew's gospel.

such a variety of objects, that even the research of modern scholars has not been able to identify all the names.[92]

Although Israelites by race, tax collectors served the occupying forces of the despised Romans. Jews hated them as traitors and corruptly becoming rich at the expense of their own people. There were so few in that business that were honest men. Tax collectors were ranked with murderers and robbers, and a Jew was permitted, by the Rabbis, to lie to them if necessary. All tax collectors were banned from the temple, from serving as magistrates or testifying in court.

The attitude towards tax collectors recorded in the gospels is one of contempt. Tax collectors were lumped together with prostitutes (21:31), heathens (18:17), and, most often, blatant sinners (9:10-11). They were as offensive to Jews for their corrupt practices as lepers were for their uncleanness; both were excluded from assembling with the people of God.

At the top of the tax and customs system were the 'publicani,' wealthy men who paid a fixed sum in advance into the Roman state treasury. This gave them the legal right to collect taxes in their designated area. Their profit came from the excess that many of them added to the standard tax. Under the publicani came the chief tax collectors who controlled districts. Zacchaeus, a later convert to faith in Christ, was 'a chief tax collector, and he was rich' (Luke 19:2). The reality of his repentance is shown in his commitment to try to make amends -

> Look, Lord, I give half of my goods to the poor; and if I have taken anything from anyone by false accusation, I restore fourfold. And Jesus said to him, 'Today salvation has come to this house' (Luke 19:8-9).

Working under the chief tax collectors were men like Matthew who dealt directly with the public and took the revenue.

Matthew was also called, 'Levi' by Mark and Luke (Mark 2:14,15; Luke 5:27,29). The name Matthew means 'gift of God,' and 'Levi' means 'attached' (see Genesis 29:34). There is no indication of how Matthew came to have two names. He may have been known as Levi and given the new name Matthew by the Lord Jesus Christ, just like Simon received the new name Peter (Mark 3:16; John 1:42). Alternatively he may have had two names before joining the apostles, as with Thomas Didymus (John 11:16 AV; 'called the Twin' NKJV) and Nathanael Bartholomew.

---

[92] Alfred Edersheim, *The Life and Times of Jesus the Messiah*. (Peabody, Massachusetts: Hendrikson 1993), p.357.

One day, whilst Matthew was sitting in the tax office at Capernaum, Jesus invited him to become a close disciple. Matthew responded wholeheartedly and 'left all, rose up, and followed him' (Luke 5:28). Soon afterwards Matthew prepared a great feast to which he invited his friends and colleagues (Luke 5:29). He wanted to introduce them to the Lord Jesus Christ. It is noteworthy that Matthew, in his Gospel record, made no reference to the grandeur of the feast but simply mentioned the Lord sat at table with his disciples and other guests (9:10). Jesus attended the banquet in spite of the fact that tax collectors were detested by the rest of the Jewish community. When scribes and Pharisees complained about our Lord's association with such people, Jesus simply replied -

> Those who are well have no need of a physician, but those who are sick. I have not come to call the righteous, but sinners, to repentance (Luke 5:31-32).

Matthew the tax collector became one of the twelve apostles of Jesus (9:9). His name appears seventh in two lists of apostles (Mark 3:18; Luke 6:15), and eighth in two others (10:3; Acts 1:13). The last mention of him is among the gathering of apostles and disciples in the upper room prior to the great Day of Pentecost (Acts 1:13).

The Lord Jesus earned a reputation as 'a friend of tax collectors and sinners' (11:19). The appointment of Matthew to rank among the apostles is testimony to that friendship as is our Lord's eagerness to associate with such people (Luke 19:2-10; especially v.5). The parables of The Lost Sheep, The Lost Coin and The Lost Son were addressed to 'the tax collectors and the sinners' who 'drew near to him to hear him' (Luke 15:1). These illustrate the amazing grace of God towards the spiritually lost.

Were it not for the writing of this Gospel, Matthew would have been one of the least known of the apostles. In writing a history of the life, ministry, suffering, death and resurrection of Jesus, he had a clear purpose in mind: to convince the Jews that Jesus of Nazareth was the Messiah promised by God as recorded in the Old Testament Scriptures.

Outline of content in Matthew's Gospel

The birth and infancy of Jesus

1. Genealogy of Jesus through Joseph (legal descent)	1:1-17
2. Joseph told about Mary's child, obedient to God	1:18-25
3. Visit of the wise men from the East	2:1-12
4. Anger of Herod at the birth of the promised King -	
a. Flight of Joseph and the family into Egypt	2:13-15
b. Massacre of infants in and around Bethlehem	2:16-18
c. Herod the Great's death,	
the family of Jesus returns to Nazareth	2:19-23

Preparation for the Lord's ministry

5. John the Baptist, the herald prepares the way	3:1-12
6. Baptism and anointing of Jesus in the River Jordan	3:13-17
7. Temptations of Jesus in the wilderness	4:1-11
8. Beginning of the Galilean ministry	4:12-25

The Sermon on the Mount

9. Characteristics of discipleship	5:1-16
10. Jesus and the law of Moses	5:17-48
11. Piety of Christian disciples	6:1-18
12. Single-minded devotion without worry	6:19-34
13. Judging and discrimination	7:1-6
14. Persevering in prayer: ask, seek, knock	7:7-12
15. The narrow way, obedient heart and solid foundation	7:13-27
16. Response to the Sermon on the Mount	7:28-29

The power of Jesus the Christ

17. Authority over disease: leprosy, paralysis and fever	8:1-17
18. Demands of discipleship	8:18-22
19. Authority over nature: winds and waves obey Jesus	8:23-27
20. Authority over demons	8:28-34
21. Authority to forgive sin	9:1-8
22. Invitation to Matthew, dining with tax collectors	
and sinners and a question of fasting	9:9-17
23. Authority over death and illness	9:18-34
24. Authority to delegate authority -	
a. Compassion of Jesus: harvest great, workers few	9:35-38
b. Appointment of the twelve apostles	10:1-4
c. Sending out the twelve apostles	10:5-42

Opposition to Jesus

Parables of the Kingdom: discovery, entry and commitment

Varied responses to Jesus

Jesus prepares his disciples

Arrival in Jerusalem

Sermon on the last things (Mount of Olives)

The suffering and death of Jesus

The resurrection of Jesus Christ

Context

Matthew the apostle wrote his record of the life and ministry of the Lord Jesus Christ some years after the Lord's death and resurrection. That he wrote some time after the events described is indicated by two incidents in which he made reference to the intervening period. The first was in relation to the thirty pieces of silver returned by Judas with which the chief priests and elders bought the potter's field. Matthew added, 'Therefore that field has been called the Field of Blood *to this day*' (27:7-8). There is also the recording of the lies circulated by the soldiers that the disciples stole the body of Jesus, while the soldiers slept. This saying Matthew reports 'is commonly reported among the Jews *until this day*' (28:13-15).

Some time had passed since the Lord Jesus returned to his heavenly Father at the ascension but how long? The absence of any reference to the fall of Jerusalem (A.D. 70), especially since Matthew records the predictions of Jesus about the destruction of the temple (24:1-2), strongly suggests that he wrote his Gospel before that monumental event took place. Consequently, having evaluated a vast number of scholarly arguments, Carson and Moo conclude: 'On balance... the preponderance of evidence suggests that Matthew was published before 70, but not long before'.[93]

Commencing with the ancestry of Jesus from Abraham through David to Joseph the husband of Mary, Matthew reports the announcement to Joseph of the miraculous conception. His Gospel record then spans the years 4 B.C. to A.D. 30, from the conception to the ascension of the Lord Jesus Christ.

Throughout the book Jesus is presented as the Son of David, the Messiah, King of God's Kingdom.

As Matthew places emphasis upon the fulfilment of Old Testament prophecy, it is fitting that Matthew's Gospel record should stand at the opening of the New Testament.

Distinctive features of Matthew's Gospel

Though Matthew, Mark and Luke have much material in common, each one has a distinctive contribution to make, for all three contain spiritual truths and insights unique to themselves. Matthew arranges his material 'according

---

[93] Donald Carson and Douglas Moo, *An Introduction to the New Testament.* (Leicester: Inter-Varsity Press, 2005), p.156.

to subject-matter rather than in strict chronological sequence.'[94] The most prominent feature is probably his extensive use of the Old Testament in showing the fulfilment of prophecy and in giving numerous quotations.

> In addition to the more than fifty clear quotations, the Gospel contains innumerable single words, phrases, and echoes of the Old Testament. For this reason alone, the Gospel of Matthew served as a natural link between God's people of the old covenant and the new Israel, the church.[95]

Miracles unique to Matthew

1.	Two blind men healed	9:27-31
2.	Healing a demon-possessed mute	9:32-33
3.	A coin found by Peter in a fish's mouth	17:24-27
4.	Healing the blind and lame in the temple	21:14

Parables unique to Matthew

1.	The Wheat and Tares	13:24-30
2.	The Hidden Treasure	13:44
3.	The Pearl of Great Price	13:45-46
4.	The Dragnet	13:47-50
5.	The Unforgiving Servant	18:23-35
6.	The Labourers in the Vineyard	20:1-16
7.	The Two Sons	21:28-32
8.	The Wedding Guests	22:1-14
9.	The Wise and Foolish Virgins	25:1-13
10.	The Sheep and Goats	25:31-46

Incidents unique to Matthew

1.	An angel appears to Joseph in a dream	1:18-25
2.	Visit of the wise men	2:1-12
3.	Flight into Egypt by the family	2:13-15
4.	Slaughter of the innocents	2:16-18
5.	Return to Nazareth	2:19-23
6.	Sermon on the Mount	5:1 - 7:27
7.	Gracious invitation 'Come to me'	11:28-30
8.	Peter walking on the Sea of Galilee	14:28-31
9.	Rebuke of Pharisees 'Woe to you…'	23:1-39

---

[94] Randolph V.G. Tasker, *Matthew, an Introduction and Commentary* (London: Tyndale Press, 1969), p.19.

[95] Robert H. Mounce, *New International Biblical Commentary: Matthew* (Peabody, Massachusetts: Hendrickson Publishers, 1991), pp.3-4.

10. Thirty pieces of silver for Judas	26:15
11. Silver returned: suicide of Judas	27:3-10
12. Dream of Pilate's wife	27:19
13. Appearance of risen saints	27:51-53
14. Guarding of the sepulchre	27:64-66
15. Earthquake	28:2
16. Bribing soldiers	28:12-15
17. Great commission	28.18-20

Teaching unique to Matthew

Matthew presents Jesus as the Teacher. He emphasises the teaching element of the Lord's ministry; pointing out that throughout his three year ministry people were astonished at the Lord's teaching both as to its content and its presentation (7:28-29; 13:54; 22:33). He noted that Jesus saw himself in the role of teacher towards his followers, his 'disciples' (23:8,10; 26:18), and that others viewed him in this way also (8:19; 9:11; 12:38; 17:24; 19:16; 22:16,24,36). When he was not healing or praying, he was teaching.

Matthew draws attention to the fact that at every opportunity Jesus taught in the synagogues of cities and villages in Galilee (4:23; 9:35; 13:54); on mountains (5:1-2; 28:16); in fields (12:1); in houses (13:36-37); in the temple often (21:23; 26:55); and on the Mount of Olives (24:3-4). Before ascending to the Father, he commissioned the disciples to the task of teaching - 'Go... make disciples of all the nations... teaching them to observe all things that I have commanded you' (28:19-20).

Matthew records five major addresses by the Lord Jesus Christ that are not presented in full in the other Gospels -

1. Sermon on the Mount: completeness of Christian character (5:1 - 7:29).
2. Instructions to the twelve apostles: principles for mission (10:1-42).
3. Parables of the Kingdom: discovery, entry and commitment (13:1-52).
4. Characteristics of discipleship: relationships in church (18:1-35).
5. Sermon on the Mount of Olives: the last things (24:3 – 25:46).

Each address is sectioned with a concluding phrase such as: 'when Jesus had ended these sayings...' (7:28; cf. 11:1; 13:53; 19:1; 26:1). Matthew arranged the teaching and events according to their subject-matter rather than presenting them in the strict order of their occurrence. That is why the Gospel has been so useful down the years for reading in worship, instructing new converts, defending the faith and for committing to memory.

1. The Sermon on the Mount (5:1 - 7:29)

Completeness of Christian character

The Sermon on the Mount is the largest single block of Jesus' teaching found in any of the four Gospels. The setting was of huge crowds following Jesus. They gathered from considerable distances all around the district: 'from Galilee, and from Decapolis, Jerusalem, Judea, and beyond the Jordan' (4:25). It was the sight of these enormous crowds which prompted Jesus to ascend a mountain and deliver, what Campbell Morgan called, 'his Manifesto,'[96] that is, our Lord's public declaration of policy and aims for the kingdom of heaven.

The central theme is 'You shall be perfect, just as your Father in heaven is perfect' (5:48). The word 'perfect' does not mean sinless or morally without fault. It means complete in all its parts, mature or full grown. Applied to a follower of Christ it means the completeness of Christian character, which of course, includes high moral principles. Christians are to strive to be more and more like God that they 'may be sons of your Father in heaven' (5:45). As Lloyd-Jones declares -

> This is stupendous, but it is the essential definition of the Christian. The Christian is meant to be like God, he is meant to manifest in his daily life in this cruel world something of the characteristics of God Himself. He is meant to live as the Lord Jesus Christ lived, to follow that pattern and to imitate that example. Not only will he be unlike others. He is meant to be like Christ.[97]

There is an intended contrast between the Old Covenant law given on Mount Sinai and the New Covenant law on this unnamed mountain. There the people were kept away (Exodus 19:12). Here the people draw near (4:25; 5:1; cf. Hebrews 12:18-24). Jesus is seated on a common mountain for he is introducing a new age where 'there is no distinguishing holiness of place now, under the Gospel, as there was under the law; but that it is the will of God that men should pray and praise everywhere, anywhere'.[98] The Old Covenant was written on stone, the New Covenant is written by the Spirit on 'tablets of flesh, that is, of the heart' (2 Corinthians 3:3; cf. Jeremiah 31:33).

---

[96] George C. Morgan, *Great Chapters of the Bible* (London: Marshall, Morgan and Scott, 1946), p.118.

[97] D. Martyn Lloyd-Jones, *Studies in the Sermon on the Mount* (London: Inter-Varsity Fellowship, 1959), vol. 1, pp.313-4.

[98] Arthur W. Pink, *An Exposition of the Sermon on the Mount* (Welwyn: Evangelical Press, 1950), p.11.

The Beatitudes (5:3-12) describe the spiritual awakening and the spiritual virtues of those born of God. Their righteousness goes much deeper than the mere letter of the Old Testament law as taught and practised by the scribes and Pharisees (5:20). Murder and adultery begin in the heart and it is there that sin must be conquered. The law of love requires faithfulness in marriage, truthfulness in undertakings, and generosity of spirit in responding to all hostility and enmity.

In true godliness the giving of charitable gifts, prayer and fasting are personal actions between the individual and God. The underlying concern is wholehearted devotion and dedication to our heavenly Father. Any public display invalidates the virtue and the spiritual blessing. Jesus also forbids 'the self-righteous, hypocritical judging which is false and calls down God's judgment'.[99]

Disciples are urged to keep on asking, seeking, knocking, for God will always graciously respond. The pathway to life has a narrow entry and a difficult way. Christians are to recognise and avoid false teachers and seek to do God's will with sincerity of heart. In the midst of life's uncertain and often turbulent events, Christ and his word provide the only possible stability and security.

The reaction of the congregation to the Sermon on the Mount is noted -

> And so it was, when Jesus had ended these sayings, that the people were astonished at his teaching, for he taught them as one having authority, and not as the scribes (7:28-29).

2. Instructions to the twelve apostles (10:1-42)

Principles for mission

With the appointment and empowering of the twelve apostles, there followed the second major body of teaching as Jesus laid down principles for their mission. They were about to be sent out on their first unaccompanied preaching journey.

An evidence of the power and authority of Jesus is displayed in his ability to grant power and authority to others. The conferring of this authority upon the twelve and later upon the seventy (Luke 10:9,17-20) is the action of deity. As Jesus preached 'the kingdom of heaven is at hand' (4:17) so his disciples were to proclaim the same message (10:7). As he performed miracles of healing and deliverance, so his apostles were to exercise the same ministry. Jesus healed those who suffered from a variety of

---

[99] Richard C.H. Lenski, *The Interpretation of St. Matthew's Gospel* (Minneapolis, Minnesota: Augsburg, 1964), p.288.

illnesses such as leprosy, fever, haemorrhage, blindness, dumbness, and demon-possession. He raised the dead. No-one who was sick, infirm or spiritually oppressed ever left Jesus without being cured. So having travelled around Galilee 'preaching the gospel of the kingdom, and healing all kinds of sickness and all kinds of disease among the people' (4:23; 9:35), he now sends out the twelve with the same power and authority -

> as you go, preach, saying, 'The kingdom of heaven is at hand'.
> Heal the sick, cleanse the lepers, raise the dead, cast out demons.
> Freely you have received, freely give (10:7-8).

When Christ calls his servants, he also equips them for their task. They were to travel through Israel. Their mission was to be restricted to the Jews (10:5-6; cf. 15:24) for the time of worldwide evangelism had not yet come (cf. 28:18-20). The Lord God had promised to visit and to deliver his ancient people Israel (Jeremiah 50:19-20; Ezekiel 34:11-12). This was the priority for the Son of God whilst on earth. Shortly after his death and resurrection, he would commission his disciples to begin in 'Jerusalem, and in all Judea and Samaria' and then move out 'to the end of the earth' (Acts 1:8). The glorious promise to Abraham was to be fulfilled in abundance, 'in you all the families of the earth shall be blessed' (Genesis 12:3).

The apostles were to take no money with them on their journey, not even the smallest coin, no change of clothing nor spare sandals. Only that which was absolutely necessary was to be taken on this assignment. These preachers had a duty to rely upon God for he will provide. At the same time, it was the duty of those who heard to sustain the herald, 'for a worker is worthy of his food' (10:10; cf. 1 Timothy 5:17-18).

Arriving in a city or town they would begin to preach in the street, market square, or (if invited) in the synagogue. They would be able to make enquiry from any interested hearers whether there were those who were 'worthy,' that is, those who, like Simeon, were 'waiting for the Consolation of Israel' (Luke 2:25) or those who, like Anna, 'looked for redemption in Jerusalem' (Luke 2:38).

Jesus was aware that the apostles would receive the same response that he had received. They would be welcomed by some, rejected by others (10:11-14).

3. Parables of the kingdom (13:1-52)

Discovery, entry and commitment

In the third major group of teachings the Lord presented parables concerning the kingdom of heaven. He used parables to reveal truth to believers and to conceal truth from hostile unbelievers (13:10-17). Six of the parables were introduced with the words, 'The kingdom of heaven is like...' The Lord began by setting out the variety of responses in those who hear the gospel (The Sower); the difficulty of distinguishing at times between true and false disciples (The Wheat and Tares); the growth and development of the kingdom of heaven from small beginnings: outwardly (The Mustard Seed) and inwardly (The Leaven); how the priceless kingdom is often discovered (The Hidden Treasure); the King giving his all for his kingdom (The Pearl of Great Price) and gathering and selecting citizens for the kingdom (The Dragnet).

4. Characteristics of discipleship (18:1-35)

Relationships in church

Matthew presents the fourth category of teaching as the response to a question raised by the disciples: 'Who then is greatest in the kingdom of heaven?' (18:1) The Lord took the opportunity to teach how his followers were to behave with humility and respect in their relationships with others. He called a little child to him (no doubt a child present in the home at Capernaum). Having drawn the attention of his disciples to this little one, he took the child in his arms (Mark 9:36). This provided a vivid illustration for his teaching. Humility is the key to entry into the kingdom of heaven (18:3; cf. 5:3) and continual humility must mark out the true follower of Jesus. In this they must be childlike.

Whilst the child was in the midst of them, Jesus emphasised the kindness and care to be taken of such little ones (cf. 19:13-15). They are to be lovingly received and protected from influences which might cause them to stumble. Disciples must also take care themselves not to fall into temptation. If followers of Jesus wander away from the believing community, disciples are to go out of their way to search for them, find them and bring them back home (cf. Luke 15:4).

Church discipline is to be a last resort. Jesus enumerated the steps to be taken to re-establish fellowship and harmony when one believer has sinned against another. The goal throughout is the repentance and restoration of the offender.[100] To ensure a right attitude in any who have been offended, the Lord presents the parable of The Unforgiving Servant. This forcefully illustrates the character of forgiveness by comparing any wrongs we have suffered to the wrongs done by us to God. The extent of God's mercy towards us should move us to extend mercy readily to one another.

---

[100] See: Additional applications, 2. Church discipline, p.384

5. The Sermon on the Mount of Olives (24:3 – 25:46)

Eschatology

Eschatology is the branch of Christian theology concerned with the last things: death, judgment and the final destiny of humanity.

Whilst leaving the temple the disciples drew the Lord's attention to the great structures which had been undergoing renovation and considerable extension over nearly fifty years (cf. John 2:20). No doubt their interest was aroused by him speaking of the city (including the temple) being one day left deserted (23:38; cf. Deuteronomy 28:24,45; 1 Kings 9:7).

After Jesus predicted the total destruction of the temple, the disciples approached him privately on the Mount of Olives to ascertain the time of this catastrophe, the signs of his return and the end of the age. In answer the Lord interwove the judgment of Jerusalem and its utter destruction (an event which occurred in A.D. 70) with the final judgment of the world. He warned of the arrival of false christs and false prophets who will deceive many. He predicted a variety of catastrophes which will cause destruction, suffering and death: widespread wars, 'famines, pestilences, and earthquakes in various places' (24:7).

The Master warned of trials and persecution so severe that 'many will be offended, will betray one another, and will hate one another' (24:10). There will be a falling away of followers and many of those who remain will grow cold in their love for the Lord. Believers are to be constantly alert and on their guard against the temptation to turn away or to follow after false prophets. The hardships will continue to be terrible until the return of Christ when he will gather his people, his elect to himself (24:31).

By the parable of The Fig Tree the Lord urged his disciples to watch out for the early signs of coming destruction to Jerusalem and its temple. Many alive at the time will witness these dreadful events.

In contrast the day and hour of the Saviour's return is unknown. Conditions at that time will be just like the days of Noah. People were then careless at the warnings of a flood. They did not anticipate the sudden tragedy. Life was going on as usual until disaster struck. If a home-owner is warned that his house is going to be burgled, he will be constantly alert to avert the theft even though he may not know just when the visit is to take place. Being warned of these phenomena, disciples of Christ are to live in readiness.

Chapter 24 closes with a parable warning what will happen to servants who are unfaithful in the absence of their master. Jesus consolidated the severe and sober warning using three further parables: the parable of The

Wise and Foolish Virgins (25:1-13); the parable of The Talents (25:14-30); and the parable of The Sheep and Goats (25:31-46). The failure in each case results in exclusion from the blessings of the future life: the foolish virgins are excluded from the marriage feast; the wicked and lazy servant is cast into outer darkness; and the 'goats' who did not respond to the needs of God's people will be sent away to everlasting punishment.

In the first parable external profession is exposed and true godliness rewarded. Among professing believers there are those who are genuine, 'the wise' and those who are false or counterfeit, 'the foolish'. The distinguishing feature is the inward grace implanted by the Holy Spirit: faith working through love, repentance and putting to death the deeds of the flesh. These spiritual graces keep the lamp of true spirituality burning brightly. The object is clearly stated: 'Watch therefore, for you know neither the day nor the hour in which the Son of Man is coming' (25:13). Thus true Christians are prepared for the Saviour's return at any time.

In the parable of The Talents the manner of awaiting the Lord's second advent is set out. In the day when the Son of God returns he will not enter the world through birth in a stable as the son of a lowly carpenter. He will come to sit upon 'the throne of his glory' and pass judgment upon all the nations of the earth (25:31-32). On that day, indolence and sloth will be condemned in the strongest terms. Christians are to be industrious, engaged in doing the will of God.

The Son of God's judgment is serious and inevitable. All humanity will appear before him. All will be judged as to whether they have shown evidence of true faith in Jesus Christ and endeavoured to live in obedience to Christ's commands and in imitation of Christ's example. Those who have given proof of commitment to Christ, 'the righteous', will go away 'into eternal life' (25:46), with all the richness of blessing that the words entail.

Here in Matthew is the great Teacher, with five extended addresses recorded. Jesus is not, however, 'primarily a great religious teacher - His greatest lesson was Himself' (Levertoff).[101]

---

[101] Levertoff in Randolph V.G. Tasker, *Matthew, an Introduction and Commentary* (London: Tyndale Press, 1969), p.19.

Christology

Christology is the branch of Christian theology concerned with the person and work of Christ.

Matthew uses the name 'Christ' (the Greek equivalent of the Hebrew 'Messiah,' and English 'Anointed') seventeen times (Mark seven times, Luke twelve and John twenty).

1. Jesus Christ and the covenants

Unlike Luke and John, Matthew does not state his purpose in writing. A careful reading of the book, however, soon establishes his intention. As with the other three Gospel writers, he wanted to make sure that the truth about Jesus would not be lost. He was especially concerned for the Jews as the opening verse makes clear: 'The book of the genealogy of Jesus Christ, the Son of David, the Son of Abraham' (1:1).

He wanted to establish beyond all doubt that Jesus of Nazareth is the Christ and Son of God, heir to the promises of God's covenants with Abraham and David. Abraham was promised a great nation, a great name, great blessings, divine protection, the land of Canaan, kings among his descendants and a special relationship with God (Genesis 12:1-3; 13:14-17; 15:18; 17:1-8). The Lord also added, 'and in you all the families of the earth shall be blessed' (Genesis 12:3).

These promises were made not just to Abraham but also to his seed (Genesis 26:2-5). Paul later interpreted this as a reference to Christ -

> Now to Abraham and his Seed were the promises made. He does not say, 'and to seeds,' as of many, but as of one, 'and to your Seed,' who is Christ (Galatians 3:16).

The covenant with David was expanded to include an eternal family, kingdom and throne (2 Samuel 7:11-16). The angel Gabriel told Mary that her Son would be the receiver of those special promises -

> He will be great, and will be called the Son of the Highest, and the Lord God will give him the throne of his father David. And he will reign over the house of Jacob forever, and of his kingdom there will be no end (Luke 1:32-33).

Matthew has shown how Jesus of Nazareth fulfilled all the requirements of the promised King Messiah, fulfilling the covenants made with Abraham and with David.

2. Jesus Christ and God

The emphasis in Matthew is that Jesus 'is uniquely the Son of God, enjoying a relationship… that is unparalleled in its intimacy' In three outstanding events he is confessed to be the Son of God (14:33; 16:16; 27:54). To be noted also are the words of heavenly affirmation in 3:17 and 17:5: 'This is my beloved Son, with whom I am well pleased.' For Matthew, Jesus is Emmanuel (1:23), meaning 'God with us' - 'now not only in the sense of one who represents God, but directly, as one who is God with us'.[102]

Matthew notes the constant participation of the Father and the Holy Spirit in the life of the incarnate Son -

- Jesus was conceived by the Holy Spirit (1:18);
- an angel reassured Joseph (1:20);
- the wise men were divinely warned not to return to Herod (2:12);
- the child was delivered from Herod's wicked massacre by an angel's warning (2:13);
- an angel was involved in bringing the family back to Israel (2:19-20);
- God guided the family to Galilee (2:22);
- the Father spoke at the Son's baptism (3:17);
- Jesus was led by the Holy Spirit into the wilderness to be tempted (4:1);
- Jesus was ministered to by angels (4:11);
- Peter's confession of Jesus as 'the Christ, the Son of the living God' (16:16) was said by Jesus to be a direct revelation from the Father (16:17);
- the Father's voice was heard once more at the transfiguration (17:5);
- the stone was rolled away from the tomb by an angel (28:2);
- an angel spoke to the women (28:5).

Matthew highlights how God was involved in the life of Jesus from the beginning to the end, ensuring that the plan so carefully prepared and so distinctly prophesied was fulfilled in the smallest detail.

Not only was God with Jesus but Jesus was also 'God with us' Immanuel (1:23). Time and again the Son of God challenged the Pharisees from the

---

[102] Donald A. Hagner, 'Matthew: Christian Judaism or Jewish Christianity,' in Scot McKnight and Grant R. Osbourne (eds.) *The Face of New Testament Studies: a survey of recent research* (Grand Rapids, MI: Baker Academic, 2004). p.269.

Scriptures. On one occasion he asked a question that any Jewish child would have been able to answer: 'What do you think about the Christ? Whose Son is he?' They said to him, 'The Son of David' (22:42). He then followed with a second question -

> How then does David in the Spirit call him "Lord", saying: 'The LORD said to my Lord, "Sit at my right hand, till I make your enemies your footstool"'? "If David then calls him 'Lord,' how is he his Son?" (22:43-45)

Every Jew knew that Messiah would be descended from David. The Lord's questions would be meaningless unless it is also true that David wrote Psalm 110 and that God actually called this 'son of David' nothing less than David's Lord. In his reign David knew no higher authority than God yet he called the coming descendent, 'Lord' thereby indicating the deity of that descendent. As Hendriksen notes -

> God is speaking to the Mediator. He is promising the Mediator such pre-eminence, power, authority, and majesty as would be proper only for One who, as to his person, from all eternity was, is now, and forever will be God.[103]

In Psalm 110 David, under the inspiration of the Holy Spirit of God, disclosed the humanity and the deity of the Messiah. He is David's Son *and* David's Lord!

Matthew records people recognising his deity and worshipping Jesus -

- the wise men from the East (2:2,11);
- a leper (8:2);
- a ruler whose daughter had just died (9:18);
- his disciples after he had walked on the sea and stilled the storm (14:33);
- a woman of Canaan whose daughter was seriously ill (15:25);
- a number of women seeing Jesus after the resurrection (28:9);
- disciples also when they saw him alive (28:17).

Yet Matthew knew well what Jesus had said in answer to a temptation of Satan: 'It is written, "You shall worship the LORD your God, and him only you shall serve"' (4:10).

That Jesus does not correct any 'worshipper', nor indicate the slightest disapproval, is a further testimony to his deity as the Son of God.

---

[103] William Hendriksen, *The Gospel of Matthew* (Edinburgh: Banner of Truth Trust, 1974), p.812.

3. Jesus Christ and Old Testament prophecy

Matthew's main concern was to demonstrate that Jesus of Nazareth is the fulfilment of the Old Testament prophecies concerning the promised Messiah. The evidence for this is substantial and overwhelming.

In their exhaustive work on the New Testament use of the Old Testament Scriptures Beale and Carson state -

> The Hebrew Scriptures - or Christian Old Testament - permeate Matthew's Gospel. Approximately fifty-five references prove close enough in wording for commentators typically to label them 'quotations,' compared to about sixty-five for the other three canonical Gospels put together.'[104]

Fulfilment of prophecies spanning thousands of years are the strongest proof to the person and work of Jesus of Nazareth. The coming into the world of the Son of God, predicted over a period of 3,500 years, often in considerable detail, and foretold in a multitude of prophecies, indicates the hand of God. No other explanation is possible.

Matthew convincingly demonstrates that the birth, life, teaching, suffering and death of Jesus fulfilled prophecy. For example -

Matthew

1:22-23	Isaiah 7:14	be born of a virgin
2:5-6	Micah 5:2	be born in Bethlehem
2:15	Hosea 11:1	be brought out of Egypt
2:17-18	Jeremiah 31:15	there would be grief over the infants massacred in Ramah
3:3	Isaiah 40:3	be introduced by a herald
4:14-16	Isaiah 9:1-2	minister in Galilee of the Gentiles
8:17	Isaiah 53:4	take away infirmities and sicknesses
11:10	Malachi 3:1	be introduced by a messenger
12:17-21	Isaiah 42:1-4	be a humble, gentle Servant of God, bringing hope to Gentiles
13:14-15	Isaiah 6:9-10	many would not understand his teaching
13:34-35	Psalms 78:2	he would speak in parables
15:7-9	Isaiah 29:13	he would be opposed by hypocrites
21:4-5	Zechariah 9:9	ride humbly into Jerusalem on a donkey
21:42	Psalms 118:22-23	be rejected by some to their own detriment
22:44	Psalms 110:1	was recognised by David as Lord
26:31	Zechariah 13:7	the Shepherd struck and the sheep scattered
26:56	Isaiah 53:7,8,12	be led away, condemned and executed

---

[104] Donald Carson and Douglas Moo [eds], *Commentary on the New Testament Use of the Old Testament* (Grand Rapids, Michigan: Baker Academic, 2007), p.1.

| 27:9-10 | Zechariah 11:12-13 | betrayed for thirty pieces of silver; buying the potter's field |
| 27:35 | Psalms 22:18 | soldiers divide his garments and cast lots |

The expression, 'that it might be fulfilled which was spoken' appears nine times in relation to the Old Testament prophets.

Because of the many Old Testament prophecies and numerous Old Testament quotations it is fitting that Matthew's historic record should appear first in the New Testament. It provides the strongest connection with the promises of God: Old Testament prophecy linked to New Testament fulfilment.

4. Jesus Christ and authority

Through the entire *Gospel of Matthew* constant emphasis is placed on the supreme power and authority of Jesus - 'All authority has been given to me in heaven and on earth' (28:18). Nothing could stand in his way, and his actions and words brought instant compliance.

His authority was supreme[105] -

- over people   4:20,22
- over illness and disease   4:23-24; 9:22, 35; 14:35-36; 15:30-31; 21:14
- over leprosy   8:3
- over paralysis   8:6,13
- over blindness   9:30
- over the individual destinies
    of all human beings   7:21-23; 11:27; 13:40-43
- over wind and waves   8:23-27
- over demons   8:31-32; 15:22,28
- over sin   9:2
- over his mission on earth   10:1
- over the temple   12:3-6
- over his own destiny   16:21; 20:17-19; 26:45-46
- over space, time and the future   18:19-20; 28:20; 26:64
- over nature   21:18-19

It is fitting that the response of so many to his authority and majesty was to fall down and worship him (8:2; 9:18; 14:33; 15:25; 28:9,17).

---

[105] Adapted from: Walter A. Elwell and Robert W. Yarbrough, *Encountering the New Testament (Encountering Biblical Studies): A Historical and Theological Survey* (Grand Rapids, Michigan: Baker Academic, 2013), p.82.

Jesus' authority was not that of despotic power, but of divine love;
it was used to alleviate human suffering, not to impose an arbitrary
or impersonal will.[106]

- Jesus is the Lord of the Sabbath (12:8);
- He will come again 'on the clouds of heaven with power and
  great glory' (24:30);
- He is the supreme revealer of the Father (11:27);
- He is the Son of God (3:17; 8:29; 14:33; 16:16; 17:5; 26:63-64;
  27:54);
- He is full of wisdom and mighty miraculous power (13:54).

There is no limit to the authority of Jesus Christ. In the great commission
Jesus sends out his followers with a task to make disciples of all the nations.
The One who gives the command declares: 'All authority has been given to
me in heaven and on earth' (28:18). Universal authority has been given to the
Lord Jesus Christ by God the Father on the basis of his unique and perfect
work on the cross of Calvary. In a prophecy in the second psalm, David
records God saying to his Son, 'Ask of me, and I will give you the nations
for your inheritance' (Psalms 2:8). The Son has evidently asked; the Father
has granted; the inheritance has to be brought in. Consequently disciples of
Jesus are commissioned to go and find his people. With the authority of
Jesus behind them, they cannot fail. The Church will be built and the gates of
hell cannot prevent it (16:18).

Jesus Christ has all authority over all persons and powers in heaven. All
that lives and has its being in heaven: angels and archangels, powers,
principalities, might, dominion, thrones, and the saints in glory are subject to
Christ. All the powers of heaven are in his hand to perform his will without
question. The Glorious Head of the Church is seated 'at the right hand of the
Majesty on high' (Hebrews 1:3) 'far above all principality and power and
might and dominion, and every name that is named, not only in this age but
also in that which is to come' (Ephesians 1:21). He also has all authority
over all persons and powers on earth. All its inhabitants; friend or foe, near
or far, good or bad, believer or unbeliever. All powers on earth are subject to
him. There is no limit to his authority. All the forces of nature and all the
skills of men and women are at his disposal.

He is King over a kingdom of power and he is King over a kingdom of
grace. His kingdom of power extends over the whole earth. His kingdom of

---

[106] Walter A. Elwell and Robert W. Yarbrough, *Encountering the New Testament
(Encountering Biblical Studies): A Historical and Theological Survey* (Grand
Rapids, Michigan: Baker Academic, 2013), p.82.

grace extends over the whole church. He rules over his kingdom of power for the good of his kingdom of grace. All things have been put 'under his feet' and he has been given to be 'head over all things to the church' (Ephesians 1:22).

5. Jesus Christ and 'the kingdom'

In his role as the herald of the Lord, John the Baptist cried, 'Repent, for the kingdom of heaven is at hand' (3:2). The Lord Jesus began his preaching ministry with the same theme, 'Repent, for the kingdom of heaven is at hand' (4:17). The expression, 'the kingdom' appears fifty-five times in Matthew's Gospel. Thirty-two of these appear as 'the kingdom of heaven,' five appear as 'the kingdom of God' or the 'Father's kingdom', six as 'the kingdom' and three as 'the kingdom of the Son of Man'. In the person of Jesus Christ the kingdom has drawn near (4:17). He is 'the gospel [good news] of the kingdom' (24:14). Ten times Jesus introduced a parable with the expression, 'The kingdom of heaven is like...'

Jesus, the Son of Man, is the King of heaven's kingdom (12:28; 13:41; 25:31,34). Four times the designation, 'the King of the Jews' occurs in relation to Jesus (2:2; 27:11,29,37). Even the Gentile wise men of the East journeyed hundreds of miles in search of the One 'who has been born King of the Jews' (2:2). In the Lord's final hours as he was being sentenced to death and delivered for crucifixion, Pilate asked him, 'Are you the King of the Jews?' Jesus answered, 'It is as you say' (27:11).

Jesus was frequently addressed by the Messiah-King title, 'the Son of David': by two blind men on two separate occasions (9:27; 20:30); by the Canaanite woman pleading for the healing of her daughter (15:22); by the crowds as Jesus entered Jerusalem (21:9); and by children in the temple (21:15). When Jesus healed one who was 'demon-possessed, blind and mute... all the multitudes were amazed and said, "Could this be the Son of David?"' (12:23)

The nature of Christ's kingship stands in sharp contrast to that displayed in the kingdoms of the world. Though he was prophesied as 'the lion of the tribe of Judah' (Revelation 5:5; Genesis 49:9-10); he was also prophesied as the gentle, sensitive and peace-loving Servant of God (12:15-21; cf. Isaiah 42:1-3) who would behave like a lamb (Isaiah 53:7; cf. Revelation 5:5-6). Prophecy speaks too of Messiah as God's servant David who would feed his people and be their shepherd (Ezekiel 34:23). Ellicott comments -

> The name of David is here put simply, as in Ezekiel 34:24, Ezekiel 37:24-25, Jeremiah 30:9; Hosea 3:5, instead of the more usual

designations of the Messiah as the Son, the Branch, the Offspring of David; but there can be no possible doubt of the meaning…[107]

Consequently it is as a loving shepherd that this King will exercise his rule (2:6). This -

> King will exercise His Kingship, caring for all the members of the flock, leading them rather than lording it over them, and taking pity on them when they are harassed and helpless [see 9:36].[108]

The imagery of a lion and a lamb represents Christ as an invincible ruler who has a heart full of compassion. Whilst he is too powerful to be defeated, stands strongly against all opposition and fearlessly defends his own people, he is also the most gracious, loving, considerate and compassionate Saviour. The lion was seen when Jesus, driven by his personal holiness and righteousness, publicly condemned the hypocrisy, corruption and wickedness of the scribes and Pharisees (23:1-39). It was displayed when he 'went into the temple of God and drove out all those who bought and sold in the temple, and overturned the tables of the money changers and the seats of those who sold doves'.

His lion-like zeal for the honour of God and his shepherd's love for his people were expressed in his declaration at the time when he said to them, 'It is written, "My house shall be called a house of prayer", but you have made it a "den of thieves"' (21:12,13).

Matthew delights in the compassionate aspect of our Lord's kingly rule for he alone records two occasions when Jesus, in dispute with the Pharisees quoted Hosea where the Lord says, 'I desire mercy and not sacrifice' (9:13; 12:7; Hosea 6:6).

> In the character of King Jesus there is in fact a remarkable combination of strength and condescension, a unique blending of humility, loving-kindness, gentleness, magnanimity, tenderness and compassion, as is made abundantly clear in many passages in the Gospel of Matthew where there are no parallels in the other Gospels.[109]

Born in royal-Bethlehem, he lived most of his life at Nazareth in Galilee. The Jews of Judea despised the people of the North. This they spoke of as, 'Galilee of the Gentiles' (4:15; Isaiah 9:1). To be known as a Nazarene (2:23)

---

[107] See his argument for understanding the passage spiritually rather than literally in *Ellicott's Commentary for English Readers* biblehub.com Ezekiel 34:23

[108] Randolph V.G. Tasker, *Matthew, an Introduction and Commentary* (London: Tyndale Press, 1969), p.21.

[109] *Ibid.,* p.22.

was to be singled out, rejected and despised. Whilst no Old Testament prophet ever prophesied that Messiah would be called a Nazarene, many told how the Jews would despise him (cf. Psalms 22:6; Isaiah 49:7; 53:3). He is 'King of kings and Lord of Lord's,' yet is known as 'the carpenter's son' (13:55).

His humility was beyond question. The basis upon which he made his invitation to those 'who labour and are heavy laden' was his assurance that he was 'gentle and lowly in heart' (11:28,29).

Though gentle and humble to those who respond to his invitation, he is nevertheless the King who is ultimately intolerant of wickedness and evil in any form. King Jesus will one day judge the nations and separate them as sheep from goats (25:31-46). Matthew alone includes mercy as the neglected element in the attitude of the Pharisees (23:23; cf. Luke 11:42). Jesus will however have no mercy upon those who have been unmerciful and unforgiving (18:21-35).

6. Jesus Christ the King of Israel and the world

The opening family tree traces the birth of Jesus back to Abraham, the father of the Jewish nation, showing that Jesus is indeed the Son of Abraham and the Son of David just as God had promised. Matthew introduces Jesus using these titles 'the Son of David, the Son of Abraham' (1:1) thus emphasising that Jesus is the promised Messiah (Christ) of the Jews.

Jesus was sent not to destroy but to fulfil the law and the prophets of the Old Testament (5:17) and be unique in the history of the people of Israel (9:33). Christianity is the true continuation of the religion of the Old Covenant, true Judaism.

The mission of Jesus whilst on earth concentrated almost exclusively upon the nation of Israel. Matthew alone has the words of Jesus to his disciples, 'Do not go into the way of the Gentiles, and do not enter a city of the Samaritans. But go rather to the lost sheep of the house of Israel' (10:5-6); and later to the Canaanite woman, 'I was not sent except to the lost sheep of the house of Israel' (15:24).

Jesus presented himself as the King of the Jews by the fulfilment of prophecy, by his sinless life, by his miracles, and by his teaching with astonishing authority (7:29). In spite of all the evidence the leaders of the Jews rejected him, even at times asserting that he was motivated and empowered by the vilest of evil spirits (12:24). In response to this wholesale rejection Jesus gave a sober warning: the 'next public sign-miracle for that

Jewish generation would be the sign of the prophet Jonah, a disguised allusion to His coming death and resurrection'.[110]

Matthew sees this warning as the turning point in the Lord's ministry. A new focus is announced. Jesus is to build his Church (16:18). So henceforth he will concentrate upon private instruction, teaching and preparing his disciples (16:21).

Whilst he is the promised Messiah (Christ) to Israel (1:1,18; 2:4; 16:16,20; 22:42; 23:8; 26:63-64), he is, at the same time, the Saviour of the nations. He came to be a blessing also to Gentiles (the non-Jewish world). Matthew, along with Mark and Luke, pays particular attention to the ministry of the Lord Jesus in Galilee. When Jesus moved his home base from Nazareth to Capernaum, Matthew alone records a fulfilment of prophecy occurring in 'Galilee of the Gentiles' (4:14-16; cf. Isaiah 9:1-2).

It was Gentiles, wise men from the East, who were the first to acknowledge Jesus (2:2). It was a Gentile, a Roman centurion, whose faith outshone that found in Israel (8:10). Jesus said that many Gentiles would 'come from east and west, and sit down with Abraham, Isaac and Jacob in the kingdom of heaven' (8:11). It was another Gentile, a woman of Canaan, whose faith was so highly commended by Jesus (15:28). At the cross a Gentile, a Roman centurion, testified to the sonship of Christ: 'Truly this was the Son of God!' (27:54)

There were clear warnings to Israel. The parable of The Wicked Tenants alerted Jews to the loss of their privileged position. Unworthy tenants would be removed and the land entrusted to a new people who would bear fruit for God (21:33-45).

Matthew's deep concern for the Jews does not blind him or prejudice him against Gentiles. He concludes his Gospel with the fullest record of the great commission in which the task set for those believing Israelites is to 'make disciples of all the nations [Gentiles]' (28:19). The mission of Jesus is worldwide.

Additional applications

1. Church membership

Matthew is the only Gospel writer to record the Lord speaking of the church by name. The first occurred in the region of Caesarea Philippi, on the northern border of Israel, after the inspired confession by the apostle Peter

---

[110] Robert G. Gromacki, *New Testament Survey* (Grand Rapids, Michigan: Baker, 1974), p.72.

that Jesus was 'the Christ, the Son of the living God'. The Lord responded, 'I will build my church, and the gates of Hades shall not prevail against it' (16:16,18).

The word 'church' translates a Greek word which is a combination of two words basically meaning 'out' and 'to call.' The 'church' is therefore a company of those who have been 'called out' to follow Christ as his disciples. Jesus makes it clear that this is a spiritual work done by God alone. The whole-hearted confession that Jesus is 'the Christ, the Son of the living God' (16:16) is evidence of a spiritual revelation by the 'Father who is in heaven' (16:17). The Father reveals the Son and the Son reveals the Father (11:25-27).

As the Lord's eight Beatitudes show, this work of God is evidenced in the transformed lives of believers as they are poor in spirit, those who mourn over sin, who are meek, who hunger and thirst for righteousness, who are merciful, pure in heart, peacemakers and often persecuted (5:3-10). These are 'the marks of a true disciple of Christ' (David Dickson).[111] As Martyn Lloyd-Jones asserts -

> Read the Beatitudes, and there you have a description of what every Christian is meant to be. It is not merely the description of some exceptional Christians... It is His description of every single Christian.[112]

All these characteristics are meant to be in evidence in the lives of all Christians. They confirm the reality of faith in Jesus as 'the Christ, the Son of the living God' (16:16). The church is the universal company of believers who have a common faith in the person and work of Christ, that is, in his deity and in the salvation he has achieved for his people.

Whilst adding to the church is a work of God alone, it is the responsibility of those who believe to make Christ and his salvation known to others. Consequently the building of the church is to be achieved by members of the church making disciples through preaching the gospel and instructing them in the teachings of Christ (28:19-20). The people of God may be sure that he will build his church on the rock-solid fact of his messiahship and that the forces of hell will not be able to prevent it. Believers are 'living stones' who have come to Christ, the chief cornerstone, to be 'built up a spiritual house' (1 Peter 2:4-6). Those who hear and obey

---

[111] David Dickson, *A Brief Exposition of the Evangel of Jesus Christ According to Matthew*, Edinburgh, Banner of Truth Trust, 1981, p.43.

[112] D. Martyn Lloyd-Jones, *Studies in the Sermon on the Mount* (London: Inter-Varsity Fellowship, 1959), vol. 1, p.33.

the words of Jesus, build their lives on a sure foundation able to weather any storm (7:24-25).

2. Church discipline

Jesus granted Peter and the apostles the right to exercise authority over the church. The 'keys of the kingdom' are placed into their hands (16:19). By the preaching of the Gospel the door is opened to all who believe. When anyone receives the promise of the Gospel with true faith, all their sins are forgiven by God through the merit of Christ's sacrificial death. As John Calvin declares -

> it is a wonderful consolation to godly souls that they know that the news of salvation brought to them by some little mortal man is ratified before God. Let the ungodly ridicule the doctrine which is preached at God's command if they like. They will feel at the last that it was really and truly God who was threatening them by the mouth of men.[113]

The church has the authority over the kingdom of heaven to confirm or exclude entrance to it (16:19). The Lord set out the procedure for the discipline of professing believers by a local church, including expulsion from the church of any who would not repent of sin (18:15-17). When problems arise between believers there are clear steps to be taken. Jesus had already dealt with how an offender should seek to resolve a difficulty -

> if you bring your gift to the altar, and there remember that your brother has something against you, leave your gift there before the altar, and go your way. First be reconciled to your brother, and then come and offer your gift (Matthew 5:23-24).

The onus is upon a believer, whether guilty of a misunderstanding, misdemeanour, or sin to do all in his or her power to achieve reconciliation and therefore maintain harmony and unity in the local church. When conscious that 'your brother has something against you' (5:23) action has to be taken immediately to remove the problem. Reconciliation (with repentance) is essential. The church must not tolerate unresolved issues among brethren. Action has to be taken in three decisive steps.

Step one involves a private and secret meeting (18:15). No one else is to be consulted. No other person is to be informed. The elders are not to be notified. It is to be a private meeting one-to-one, face-to-face. This should resolve the problem. If not, then step two is to be taken. One or two others

---

[113] John Calvin, *A Harmony of the Gospels Matthew, Mark and Luke,* (Edinburgh: Saint Andrew Press, 1972), p.188.

are to be invited to be witnesses. On the basis of the Old Testament Scriptures, every word is established 'by the mouth of two or three witnesses' (18:16; Deuteronomy 19:15). If this fails to result in repentance and reconciliation, then the local church is to be informed, and together members will urge repentance. If this exhortation fails then the final step is the expulsion of the offender (18:17). This is the last resort.

If these instructions had been obeyed in evangelical churches in our own day, local churches would be healthier. The gospel would not have been so blasphemed among unbelievers on account of the sinful behaviour allowed by the church and in the church (cf. Romans 2:17-24; Titus 2:2-15; 3:1-2,9-11; 1 Timothy 6:1-2). Sadly, when discipline is exercised at this level these days, the offender often leaves and finds a ready welcome in another company of believers who have no concern to enquire whether the newcomer is in good standing or not.[114]

Conclusion

Matthew emphasises that the coming of Jesus cannot be understood as just another event in history. 'It is the supreme event in history, planned and prophesied by God centuries before it ever occurred.'[115]

Matthew's historic record is the story of King Jesus Christ, the promised Messiah, as prophesied in the unique self-disclosure of God to his people in Old Testament Scriptures. It concerns the ancestry and birth of Jesus, how men and women searched for, found and worshipped him. It records details of his forerunner John the Baptist, his baptism, the Holy Spirit's anointing and his temptations in the wilderness, the calling of apostles, the content and manner of his preaching and teaching, his law and commandments, his works and words, and his teaching in parables.

The power of Jesus the Christ over nature and disease is abundantly demonstrated by Matthew: describing how the Lord multiplied vast quantities of bread and fish, stilled a storm, walked on the storm-tossed Sea of Galilee, withered a fruitless fig-tree, healed leprosy with a touch and command, restored sight to the blind and speech to the dumb, delivered the demon-possessed and raised the dead.

The Master's skill in teaching and preaching is presented distinctly: by prose, parables, examples and illustrations. Lengthy sermons by this master

---

[114] Where sin or error is of a public nature the procedure is different (see 1 Corinthians 5:1-5; Galatians 2:11-14; 1 Timothy 5:20).

[115] Walter A. Elwell and Robert W. Yarbrough, *Encountering the New Testament (Encountering Biblical Studies): A Historical and Theological Survey* (Grand Rapids, Michigan: Baker Academic, 2013), p.80.

of communication are recorded: instructing, correcting, refuting, reassuring, inviting and comforting.

Matthew shows the Saviour's commitment and unwavering determination to fulfil the task entrusted to him by his Father. It is displayed in his triumphant though humble entry into Jerusalem, by allowing himself to be taken prisoner and by subjecting himself to all the horrific events leading to his trial, sentence and crucifixion. These are clearly recorded and culminate with his glorious resurrection and bodily appearances and the final commission to his followers.

The Jewish people mostly rejected Jesus as king. They wanted a political king who would overthrow the Romans and re-establish the extensive rule and power of King David. They had no desire for a spiritual king who calls people to repentance and righteousness.

Jesus is God's King (Psalm 2:6), God's Son (Psalm 2:7).

Blessed are all those who put their trust in him (Psalm 2:12).

Understanding
The Gospel of Mark

Author: John Mark

Theme:
Jesus, the supreme Servant of God
shows that
discipleship means service

Contents

A brief sketch of the author

John Mark was known almost entirely by his surname Mark (Acts 12:12,25; and 15:37). He was the cousin of Barnabas who accompanied Paul on his early missionary journeys, and the son of Mary. Mary was a wealthy woman living in Jerusalem whose substantial home was a meeting point for a congregation of believers (Acts 12:12). Perhaps it was the house where the Last Supper was held (14:12-17),[116] also where the disciples gathered after the resurrection and where the Holy Spirit came upon them on the Day of Pentecost (Acts 1:13; 2:1-2).[117]

There is a strong possibility that Mark may have mentioned himself in connection with the arrest of the Lord Jesus when he wrote -

> Now a certain young man followed him, having a linen cloth thrown around his naked body. And the young men laid hold of him, and he left the linen cloth and fled from them naked (14:51-52).

Mark is the only one of the four Gospel writers to record this incident; in all likelihood no one else knew about it! Is he recording his own personal connection with the Lord Jesus? To do this in his historic account would be like the apostle John in referring to himself without mentioning his name (John 18:15-16; 19:26-27; 20:2-8; 21:7, 20-24).

It would be difficult to see any other reason for including this event. If the upper room where Jesus ate the last supper were in fact the family home of John Mark, then it would be quite feasible to suppose that he, a teenager, was woken before midnight as the Lord and his disciples left the house to go to the Garden of Gethsemane.[118] Throwing a robe around his body, he would follow at a discrete distance, eventually almost to be apprehended by temple police; only managing to escape capture by slipping from his robe which had been grabbed by his assailant. To record this incident would be pertinent in showing his connection with the Lord and his apostles.

Although John Mark is not mentioned some months later, when Peter visited the home following his release from prison (Acts 12:12), it is reasonable to suppose that he was present, and that he was already a believer

---

116 Where the book is not stated the quotation is from Mark's gospel.
117 J. Gresham Machen, *The New Testament: an introduction to its literature and history* (Edinburgh: Banner of Truth Trust, 1976), p.200.
118 William Hendriksen, *The Gospel of Mark*, Edinburgh: Banner of Truth Trust, 1975, pp.3-13.

and well known to the apostle. Peter writes of him as, 'Mark my son' (1 Peter 5:13) indicating his affection and their close association. The apostle was most likely the agent in John Mark's conversion to Christ.

During the severe famine of AD. 44-45 Barnabas and Paul visited Jerusalem bringing aid from believers in Antioch to believers in Judea (Acts 11:27-30). When Paul and Barnabas returned to Antioch they took John Mark (the cousin of Barnabas, Colossians 4:10) along with them (Acts 12:25). Commissioned by the church at Antioch, Paul and Barnabas set out on their first missionary journey accompanied by John Mark. These servants of God sailed to the Island of Cyprus. At Salamis Paul and Barnabas 'preached the word of God in the synagogues of the Jews' and John Mark was there to assist (Acts 13:5). Travelling across Cyprus they came to Paphos. Here there was an encounter with Elymas the sorcerer and the conversion of Proconsul Sergius Paulus (Acts 13:6-12).

Leaving the Island of Cyprus the party sailed north to Perga in the district of Pamphylia on the southwestern Mediterranean coast of Asia Minor (modern day Turkey)[119]. From Perga the plan was to press north to Antioch in Pisidia (not to be confused with Antioch in Syria). Mark did not continue with the expedition but returned home to Jerusalem (Acts 13:13).

No explanation is given for Mark's withdrawal from the missionary enterprise. He may have gone home through fear because the road from Perga to Antioch was notorious for bandits and robbers. He may have gone home because it was becoming increasingly obvious that Paul rather than his cousin Barnabas was heading the team. It might well have been for religious considerations; Mark had been raised as a Jew and Paul's emphasis in seeking to reach Gentiles may have caused him disquiet. Alternatively he may have simply been homesick (a suggestion made by Chrysostom, a leader in the Early Church, c. A.D. 347-407).

Paul and Barnabas, having completed their first missionary journey, returned to Antioch in Syria. After some time Paul suggested a return visit to the towns and cities where they had preached the gospel. 'Barnabas was determined to take with them John called Mark' (Acts 15:37). Paul strongly disagreed reminding Barnabas that John Mark had left them prematurely on their first journey. Each man held to his firm conviction. No compromise could be reached. The difference was so pronounced that separation was the only recourse. Lenski's comment is apposite -

> 'A clash occurred' …. We need not overdraw the picture and speak
> of passionate and bitter words, of hot tempers and anger. Paul and

---

[119] See map, 'Bible lands in New Testament times', p.351.

Barnabas were not men of that common, cheap type. This clash was one between incompatible convictions, Barnabas being sure that Mark would prove fit for the task, Paul equally convinced that he would not prove fit. Neither insulted the other nor did anything regrettable. But because they had such opposite convictions in regard to Mark, the two men separated and divided the field, Barnabas going to Cyprus and taking Mark along with him, Paul taking the rest of the field on the mainland. Barnabas and Paul evidently agreed on this division.[120]

There is no reason whatsoever to suppose that the relationship between Paul and Barnabas was damaged. One positive outcome of the separation was a doubling of the missionary endeavour, Paul taking Silas, and Barnabas taking John Mark. Barnabas is not mentioned again in *The Acts of the Apostles*. There is but one later reference to him in Paul's first letter to the Corinthians (1 Corinthians 9:6).

Nothing further is heard of John Mark for twelve years until in A.D. 63, when Paul, imprisoned in Rome, wrote to the Colossians. It is a surprise to learn that John Mark was with him -

Aristarchus my fellow prisoner greets you, with Mark the cousin of Barnabas (about whom you received instructions: if he comes to you, welcome him), and Jesus who is called Justus. These are my only fellow workers for the kingdom of God who are of the circumcision; they have proved to be a comfort to me (Colossians 4:10-11).

Around the same time Paul also wrote a letter to Philemon in which he referred to John Mark among his 'fellow labourers' (Philemon 24).

When the apostle Paul was released from prison in Rome he continued travelling among the churches. Peter was in 'Babylon'[121] around that time, for it was from that city he wrote the letter we now know as The First Letter of Peter. In that letter Peter indicates Mark's presence with him and the strong bond that existed between them (1 Peter 5:13). There is a strong tradition that Mark drew upon the apostle Peter for much of the information

---

[120] Richard C.H. Lenski, *The Interpretation of The Acts of the Apostles* (Minneapolis, Minnesota: Augsburg, 1961), p.634.

[121] Opinion differs as to whether this is Babylon on the Euphrates or a metaphorical symbol for Rome. See: Richard C.H. Lenski, *The Interpretation of The Epistles of St. Peter, St. John and St. Jude* (Minneapolis, Minnesota: Augsburg, 1966), 231; and John Calvin, *The Epistle of Paul The Apostle to the Hebrews and The First and Second Epistles of St. Peter* (Edinburgh: Saint Andrew Press, 1972), pp.322-3.

recorded in his gospel narrative.[122] Who better placed than Peter to remember the words and works of the Lord Jesus Christ?

Mark was not only close to the apostle Peter, for it is clear that the bond that developed with the apostle Paul was also very close - as colleague and friend. When Paul was imprisoned in Rome for a second time he wrote to Timothy saying, 'Get Mark and bring him with you, for he is useful to me for ministry' (2 Timothy 4:11).

Whatever the problems may have been in the first weeks of the first missionary journey, it is evident that they had long been forgotten by the apostle Paul. John Mark's earlier behaviour was relegated to the past and proved no hindrance to a full and useful ministry in the service of the Lord.

Tradition states that Mark visited Egypt and established churches in Alexandria. It is commonly held that he died as a Christian martyr during the reign of Emperor Nero.

John Mark's greatest contribution, under God, was to gather information from Peter, Barnabas and Paul, together with other apostles and eye-witnesses of Jesus Christ that he had opportunity to listen to, question and record. From this he was able to produce a concise history of the life, ministry, suffering, death and resurrection of the Lord Jesus Christ which we now know as 'The Gospel of Mark.'

---

[122] Papias, an elder in the church in Hierapolis (14 miles from Laodicea and near Colossae - Colossians 4:13), writing in the first half of the 2nd Century quoted an earlier church leader indicating that Mark attended Peter and recorded his preaching and teaching about the Lord Jesus, see: J. Gresham Machen, *The New Testament: an introduction to its literature and history* (Edinburgh: Banner of Truth Trust, 1976), pp.198-9.

Outline of content in Mark's Gospel

Introduction to the Gospel

Northern and Perean ministry

Ministry in Jerusalem

Jesus' final week in Jerusalem

The resurrection of Jesus

Context

Mark's close connection with the apostles Peter and Paul is highly significant. Mark could not have been so closely associated with both men had there not been a fundamental agreement between them on the life and teaching of the Lord Jesus and the doctrine of the Church. Furthermore this intimate bond with these two great apostles as disciple, assistant and friend enhances immeasurably his fitness to write a Gospel record. From Peter he would receive authoritative information concerning the life and teaching of the Lord Jesus. From Paul he would gain insight as to what and how to communicate to Gentiles.

Clement of Alexandria, and other Early Church Fathers, describe the impression made by the powerful preaching of Peter. According to them, those who heard the apostle were keen to possess a written record and requested Mark, Peter's companion, to produce such an account.[123] A further pointer to the sanction of an apostle behind this account is seen in the vivid portrayal of the disciples in its pages as Carson and Moo remark -

> While found in all four gospels, the picture of the disciples as cowardly, spiritually blind, and hard of heart is particularly vivid in Mark. This, it is held, points to an apostolic viewpoint, for only an apostle would have been able to criticise the Twelve so harshly.[124]

Mark's Gospel is the shortest of the four, being just over half the size of Matthew's record. He omits any mention of the early ministry of Jesus in Judea and his successive visits to Jerusalem during the Galilean ministry.

Mark evidently wrote his historic record before the fall of Jerusalem in A.D. 70, otherwise he would have mentioned that event. Just when and where the book was written, interesting as these questions might be to academic scholarship, are not likely to have a significant impact on understanding its contents.[125]

---

[123] Robert Lee, *The Outlined Bible: an outline and analysis of every book in the Bible* (London: Pickering and Inglis, no date), Analysis No.41.

[124] Donald Carson and Douglas Moo, *An Introduction to the New Testament* (Leicester: Inter-Varsity Press, 2005), p.176.

[125] For a summary of past and present scholarship see: Donald Carson and Douglas Moo, *An Introduction to the New Testament* (Leicester: Inter-Varsity Press, 2005), pp.177-182.

From the subject matter it is evident that, unlike Matthew who wrote for Jewish readers, Mark was concerned to address Gentiles, especially the Romans. In consequence the genealogy of Christ, fulfilled prophecy and references to the Mosaic law are not included. There are very few references to the Old Testament; Jewish words are interpreted (3:17; 5:41; 7:11,34; 15:22,34) and Jewish customs are explained (7:3-4; 14:12; 15:42). That the readers were unfamiliar with the geography of Israel is indicated by Mark's stating that the Jordan was a river (1:5; cf. Matthew 3:5; Luke 3:3), and the Mount of Olives was situated 'opposite the temple' (13:3; cf. Matthew 24:3).

> Unlike standard biographies, Mark's Gospel states nothing about Jesus' birth, upbringing and appearance; and it specifies neither the length of His public ministry, nor His age at the time of His crucifixion. About a third of the record is devoted to a description of the eight days between Jesus' entry into Jerusalem on the colt, and His resurrection.[126]

A further factor pointing to a Roman Gentile readership is the emphasis adopted by Mark. Most Romans showed little interest in doctrine or teaching. They were concerned with action. Mark's approach is admirably suited to this interest since he presents the life of the Lord Jesus as that of an ideal servant or perfect workman for God, displaying power in miraculous acts of mercy.

Mark brings out the characteristic features of the service of the Saviour, and the manner in which he served. In Mark there is more about the Lord's deeds than about his teaching. The powerful actions of Jesus would arrest the attention. Mark frequently uses the word translated 'immediately' (thirty-six times NKJV) and 'forthwith' (three times NKJV) which reinforces the sense of activity. By comparison this word is only found eleven times in Matthew and only once in Luke. Mark discloses the true nature of Christ as the Son of God, then brings out the details of the greatest composite miracle - his suffering, death and resurrection.

Distinctive features of Mark's Gospel

Mark recounts the facts of the life of Jesus in a simple and most dramatic manner. He writes of the impact made by the Son of God upon the minds and hearts of those who heard him: they were 'astonished at his teaching' (1:22; 11:18; cf. 6:2; 10:26), 'amazed' (1:27; 2:12; 6:51; 9:15; 10:32) and 'astonished beyond measure' at his power (7:37).

---

[126] Stephen S. Short, 'The Gospel According to Mark,' in George C.D. Howley (ed.), *New Testament Commentary* (Pickering and Inglis, 1969), p.178.

Mark presents interesting details which Matthew and Luke do not mention. He writes as one informed by an eye-witness. He notes that the paralysed man was 'carried by four' (2:3); that when Jesus was in a boat with his disciples, before the storm broke, 'he was in the stern, asleep on a pillow' (4:38). Mark alone gives the Aramaic words with which Jesus awakened the daughter of Jairus (5:41). He notes the condition of the grass upon which the five thousand sat to eat and that they sat 'in ranks, in hundreds and in fifties' (6:39-40). He also provides much more detail about the healing of the boy with a deaf and dumb spirit (9:14-29).

Matthew and Mark both include Jesus calling a little child and setting him in the midst of the disciples (Matthew 18:2) but only Mark adds the detail, 'And when he had taken him in his arms, he said to them...' (9:36). Similarly Mark adds that when the disciples rebuked mothers for bringing their little children to Jesus 'he took them up in his arms, laid his hands on them, and blessed them' (10:16; cf. Matthew 19:13-15; Luke 18:15-17). When Jesus and his apostles were on his last journey to Jerusalem, Mark alone notes, 'Jesus was going before them' (10:32; cf. Matthew 20:17; Luke 18:31). In that simple statement there is a dramatic indication of Jesus' commitment on the one hand and loneliness on the other.

Mark is the only Gospel writer who notes the specific reference to Peter by the angel in his instruction to the women at the tomb (16:7). As a close friend and companion of the apostle it is understandable that he would make this inclusion. The apostle Peter would have special reason for it to be recorded after his dreadful denial of Jesus.

Miracles unique to Mark

1.	The healing of a deaf-mute	7:32-35
2.	The healing of a blind man at Bethsaida	8:22-25

Twenty miracles are recorded by Mark in contrast to only five full-scale parables.

Parable unique to Mark

1.	The seed growing secretly	4:26-29

Mark presents only five parables of Jesus (Matthew has nineteen, Luke has twenty-seven). Only one parable is found in Mark which is not in the other three gospels: the parable of The Seed Growing Secretly. It adds to the parable of The Sower (Mark 4:3-9) in which Jesus was answering the question why so many who heard the gospel did not become genuine Christians. Was the fault in the teacher (the sower), the teaching (the seed) or the taught (the soil)? The answer identified four conditions of heart in those who heard. Only one condition indicated genuine and permanent results and that was the good ground, the heart that was responsive in receiving the word and bearing fruit. The problem does not lie in the teacher or the teaching. The problem lies in the heart of the hearer.

In the parable of The Seed Growing Secretly, Jesus indicated the unseen working of God. A Christian may proclaim the gospel to others yet have no influence over its effectiveness. If and when that word sprouts and grows 'he himself does not know how' (4:27; cf. Ecclesiastes 11:6). The power of germination (regeneration) belongs to the Lord alone (John 1:13; 3:5). As the apostle Paul was later to point out to the Christians at Corinth: 'I planted, Apollos watered, but God gave the increase' (1 Corinthians 3:6). James makes the same point when he writes, 'Of his own will he [the Lord] brought us forth by the word of truth' (James 1:18).

Christology

Christology is the branch of Christian theology concerned with the person and work of Christ.

Mark presents Jesus as the Son of God, the Son of Man, the supreme authority, the king of the kingdom of God, and the heavenly servant.

1. Jesus the Son of God

Though Mark emphasises the servanthood of Christ in his humanity, he does not neglect to record proofs of the Saviour's deity. In the opening sentence Jesus is introduced as 'the Son of God' (1:1). At his baptism the Father declared, 'You are my beloved Son, in whom I am well pleased' (1:11). Demons, possessed with partial supernatural knowledge, recognised him saying, 'You are the Son of God' (3:11). Other demons identified him as, 'Son of the Most High God' (5:7). On the mount of transfiguration, again the Father spoke in unique terms about Jesus, 'This is my Beloved Son. Hear him!' (9:7) At the crucifixion it is a Gentile, a Roman centurion, who witnessing the event, confessed, 'Truly this man was the Son of God!' (15:39)

2. Jesus the Son of Man

Mark records the Saviour frequently referring to himself as 'the Son of Man' (2:10,28; 8:31 and ten more). Whilst Mark does not neglect that Jesus knew physical hunger as the Son of Man (11:12), his Gospel sheds more light than the others on the emotional aspects of his humanity. Mark indicates that when a leper came to Jesus pleading to be healed, the Lord was 'moved with compassion' (1:41). When, on a Sabbath, about to heal a man with a withered hand, he looked at the scribes and Pharisees 'with anger, being grieved by the hardness of their hearts' (3:5). Faced with rejection by the villagers among whom he had lived from boyhood, 'he marvelled because of their unbelief' (6:6). It was as he was about to heal a deaf mute by the Sea of Galilee, that, 'looking up to heaven, he sighed' (7:34). When challenged by Pharisees, following the feeding of the four thousand, 'he sighed deeply in his spirit' (8:12). When the disciples rebuked mothers for bringing little children to him, 'he was greatly displeased' (10:14). Only Mark records the reaction of Jesus to the rich young ruler, who 'looking at him, loved him' (10:21).

3. Jesus the supreme authority

Early in the ministry of Jesus the people were astonished at his authority in word and deed, '...they were astonished at his teaching, for he taught them as one having authority, and not as the scribes' (1:22); and 'What is this? ... For with authority he commands even the unclean spirits, and they obey him' (1:27). This reaction from the crowd rapidly spread throughout Galilee with the result that everyone wanted to meet him (1:28, 32-33, 37). They 'came to him from every direction' (1:45).

Jesus also demonstrated his authority over sin (2:1-12); the Sabbath (2:28); nature (4:35-41; 6:47-51); disease (5:25-34); death (5:22-24, 35-43); unscriptural tradition (7:1-13); and over the temple in Jerusalem (11:15-18).

In the final confrontation with the high priest and the Jewish council, Jesus declared his authority to be supreme. When -

> again the high priest asked him, saying to him, 'Are you the Christ, the Son of the Blessed?' Jesus said, 'I am. And you will see the Son of Man sitting at the right hand of the Power, and coming with the clouds of heaven' (Mark 14:61-62).

4. Jesus the King of the Kingdom of God

Although the expression 'the kingdom' appears fifty-five times in Matthew, it is only found fourteen times in Mark, five of which are located in 10:13-27. In each case it is in the full title, 'the kingdom of God'. Before presenting the parable of The Sower, Mark records the introductory words of Jesus to his disciples: 'To you it has been given to know the mystery of the kingdom of God; but to those who are outside, all things come in parables...' (4:11).

This explains not only the subject of this parable, but the subject of all parables (4:13). The kingdom of God is not understood by everyone

(4:11-12); it grows without anyone knowing how (4:27); almost imperceptibly from insignificant beginnings, like a mustard seed (4:30-32).

This was the situation during the lifetime of Jesus on earth. The 'kingdom of God' was 'at hand' (1:15). In the person of Jesus Christ God's kingdom had come right there and then to the people. They must change their thinking about their sin, acknowledge and confess it, and turn in full trust and commitment to the Lord. In other words, they are to 'repent and believe in the gospel' (1:15).

Jesus predicted, that soon 'the kingdom of God' would be 'present with power' (9:1). The future culmination will be an occasion of great celebration (14:25). In the meantime a true and sincere love for God and for others will mark out citizens of the kingdom (12:28-34).

The principles associated with the kingdom of God will challenge attitudes towards children (10:13-16); towards wealth (10:17-27); will require self-denial (28-31) and courage to stand out from the crowd (15:43). For the kingdom of God is a mystery (4:11), not in the sense of something secret that is difficult or impossible to understand or explain, but in that it challenges and opposes every natural human valuation. As long as people continue to have their minds set on earthly things (8:33) they will never understand, still less become part of the kingdom of God.

5. Jesus the heavenly Servant

The ministry of Jesus began after he was baptised by John in the River Jordan and anointed by the Holy Spirit for his ministry of service for God. Immediately he was driven into the wilderness by the Holy Spirit (1:9-12) where he was tempted for almost six weeks. As the promised Servant of God (Isaiah 42:1) Jesus prayed, taught, healed and trained disciples to carry on his work. He used his own life of service as an example to his followers. Disciples of Jesus must model themselves upon their Master.

Mark records three occasions when the Lord predicted his own suffering and death, bringing out the implications for his followers in the cost of discipleship.

occasion	first	second	third
Jesus predicted his death	8:31	9:31	10:32-34
The disciples misunderstood	8:32-33	9:32	10:35-40
Jesus taught the cost of discipleship	8:34-38	9:35-37	10:41-45

Discipleship means service and service often means suffering: 'For whoever desires to save his life will lose it, but whoever loses his life for my sake and the gospel's will save it' (8:35). Jesus was severely tested right from the commencement of his ministry. Incidentally Mark is the only one to record that at his temptations he 'was with the wild beasts' (1:13).

The service of Jesus was characterised:

- *in healing the sick and demon-possessed* with tender and loving care: 'Jesus, moved with compassion, stretched out his hand and touched [the leper], and said to him, "I am willing; be cleansed." As soon as he had spoken, immediately the leprosy left him, and he was cleansed' (Mark 1:41-42).

- *in teaching* with illustrations drawn from everyday life such as the parable of The Sower (4:3-8,13-20) and the parable of The Wicked Tenants (12:1-8). The Lord's teaching was given in clear familiar language so that 'the common people heard him gladly' (12:37). He taught the truth in love, as with the rich young ruler (10:17-22).

- *in feeding the hungry:* 'I have compassion on the multitude, because they have now continued with me three days and have nothing to eat. And if I send them away hungry to their own houses, they will faint on the way; for some of them have come from afar' (8:2-3).

- *in pastoral concern:* 'And Jesus, when he came out, saw a great multitude and was moved with compassion for them, because they were like sheep not having a shepherd. So he began to teach them many things' (6:34).

- *in receiving little children:* 'Then they brought little children to him, that he might touch them; but the disciples rebuked those who brought them. But when Jesus saw it, he was greatly displeased and said to them, "Let the little children come to me, and do not forbid them; for of such is the kingdom of God. Assuredly, I say to you, whoever does not receive the kingdom of God as a little child will by no means enter it." And he took them up in his arms, laid his hands on them, and blessed them' (10:13-16).

- *in resisting pressure from others* and persisting in fulfilling his ministry for God: ' "Is it lawful on the Sabbath to do good or to do evil, to save life or to kill?" But they kept silent. And when he had looked around at them with anger, being grieved by the hardness of their hearts, he said to the man, "Stretch out your hand." And he stretched it out, and his hand was restored as whole as the other. Then the Pharisees went out and immediately plotted with the Herodians against him, how they might destroy him' (3:4-6).

- *in recognising the service of others:* 'Now John answered him, saying, "Teacher, we saw someone who does not follow us casting out demons in your name, and we forbade him because he does not follow us." But Jesus said, "Do not forbid him, for no one who works a miracle in my name can soon afterward speak evil of me. For he who is not against us is on our side. For whoever gives you a cup of water to drink in my name, because you belong to Christ, assuredly, I say to you, he will by no means lose his reward' (9:38-41).

Likewise, when 'one poor widow came and threw in two mites, which make a quadrans. So he called his disciples to himself and said to them, "Assuredly, I say to you that this poor widow has put in more than all those who have given to the treasury; for they all put in out of their abundance, but she out of her poverty put in all that she had, her whole livelihood" (12:42-44).

- *in accepting the inconvenience of service:* 'Then the multitude came together again, so that they could not so much as eat bread' (3:20).

- *in concern for fellow workers:* 'And he said to them, "Come aside by yourselves to a deserted place and rest a while"' (6:31).

- *in self-sacrifice:* 'For even the Son of Man did not come to be served, but to serve, and to give his life a ransom for many' (10:45).

There could be no greater example than the Lord Jesus as One who served God faithfully to the end.

He is still the heavenly servant serving, for after his ascension the apostles obeying his instruction, 'went out and preached everywhere, the Lord working with them and confirming the word through the accompanying signs' (16:20).

Additional applications

1. Discipleship means service with self-denial

The Father anointed the Lord Jesus with the Holy Spirit for his ministry and service (1:10). In like manner the Son of God anoints his followers with the Holy Spirit to empower and equip them for their ministry and service (1:8). That service is characterised by a true spirit of self-denial: 'Whoever desires to come after me, let him deny himself, and take up his cross, and follow me' (8:34). What a great example Jesus gives. As he contemplated his approaching rejection, suffering and death, he prayed in the Garden of Gethsemane: 'Abba, Father, all things are possible for you. Take this cup away from me; nevertheless, not what I will, but what you will' (14:36).

Right thinking and right faith must issue in right living. Right living meant following Jesus' way, the way of the cross.[127]

2. Discipleship means service with humility

Another feature of Christian service highlighted in Mark's Gospel is humility. A question which, on more than one occasion, had been the topic of conversation and cause of dispute among the twelve, was 'Who would be the greatest?' (9:34). Jesus dealt with this issue at length pointing out that greatness in the kingdom is measured by humble service. Again he referred to his own example -

> whoever desires to become great among you shall be your servant. And whoever of you desires to be first shall be slave of all. For even the Son of Man did not come to be served, but to serve, and to give his life a ransom for many (10:43-45).

Humility will be evident when followers of Christ are prepared, when appropriate, to take a back seat (9:35) and serve everyone else first. It will also appear in their attitude towards children (9:37).

3. Discipleship means service with confidence

Followers of the Master are not to be ashamed of him nor embarrassed to acknowledge their allegiance to him. 'For whoever is ashamed of me and my words in this adulterous and sinful generation, of him the Son of Man also will be ashamed when he comes in the glory of his Father with the holy angels' (8:38). Their confidence is to be in the Lord not in themselves.

Mark presents the apostles as illustrations of the nature of discipleship for Christians of every generation, race and age. At times they were good examples: in the way in which they responded to the call of Jesus and left everything to follow him (1:18,20; 2:14; 10:28); in their participation in his ministry (3:14-15; 6:7,12-13,30); and in the insight Jesus shared with them (4:11). Nevertheless Mark does not gloss over their mistakes, weakness and failure: their faithlessness (4:38-40; 9:14-29); their selfish ambition (9:34; 10:35-45); and their abandonment of Jesus after the arrest in Gethsemane when 'they all forsook him and fled' (14:50).

At that point the time and energy devoted to training men for ministry must have appeared as utterly wasted. Yet Jesus had given a glimmer of hope for the future. Predicting the desertion of the disciples on the very eve of his betrayal, Jesus said -

---

[127] Robert A. Guelich, *Word Biblical Commentary: Mark 1-8* (Nashville, Tennessee: Thomas Nelson, 1989), p.xlii.

> All of you will be made to stumble because of me this night, for it is written: 'I will strike the Shepherd, and the sheep will be scattered.' But after I have been raised, I will go before you to Galilee (14:27-28).

One day, after that notable Pentecost and the outpouring of the Holy Spirit, they would set forth in a new and dynamic manner, to put into practice all that their Master taught and all that he exemplified. The fruit of his labours over the three years preparation would be the foundation of his new people, the Church of Christ. They would become so courageous and confident in their Master as to turn 'the world upside down' (Acts 17:6).

Conclusion

Upon the arrival of Jesus the Son of God, a monumental change was taking place in God's dealings with his people. The work of God would no longer focus upon Jerusalem, the temple or its priesthood, but upon 'the stone which the builders rejected' that had been made 'the chief corner-stone' (12:10). He, the Lord Jesus Christ, is the foundation stone, of the new temple 'not made with hands' (Hebrews 9:11).

In a vivid and lucid style Mark records the life and work of the Lord Jesus. It is ideally suited to evangelistic endeavour. Mark presents Christology and discipleship: who Jesus is and what it means to follow him.

Since his purpose in writing was that Gentiles would repent and believe in Jesus as the Son of God he launches into his account omitting the wonderful events surrounding the birth of Christ; the family tree; the profound teaching of the early ministry in Judea; the extended sermons such as the Sermon on the Mount and the intimate sermons to his apostles, especially those delivered in the upper room. Important as these things are, they come in second place to the information which will lead to conversion. Once sinners have repented and believed in Christ they can progress to the deeper things recorded by others - and be richly blessed.

In Mark there is a disciple of Jesus, committed to telling the facts of the life of the Saviour in the simplest and most dramatic manner. He launches straight into the heart of his message. Declaring the Lord's historic credentials through the person and witness of John the Baptist, he reveals Jesus as the receiver and transmitter of the Holy Spirit of God. The rapid pace is set. The brief history is recounted at great speed. So many of the events and reactions occur 'immediately'. And, whilst it is ideally suited for evangelism in demonstrating the deity of Christ and declaring his sacrificial death, it also instructs believers in the significance of Christ's person and ministry.

Understanding
The Gospel of Luke

Author: Luke

Theme:

Jesus, the perfect Man
has come to seek and
to save that which was lost

Contents

A brief sketch of the author

Little is known about Luke and yet what is known presents a picture of a fine Christian character.

From the introduction to the third Gospel it would appear that Luke was not with Jesus during his earthly ministry. According to his own testimony he made a careful examination and enquiry of those who were 'eyewitnesses and ministers of the word' (Luke 1:2). Drawing on the various narratives he formed 'an orderly account' for the benefit of the 'most excellent Theophilus' so that he would know the solid historic foundation upon which his faith was built (Luke 1:3-4). As Trenchard observes -

> God chose a man of culture, with a wide interest in contemporary history, master of an excellent Hellenistic Greek, a fine storyteller and an exact historian, to write a wonderfully selective account of the great happening from the birth of John the Baptist until Paul's first imprisonment in Rome.[128]

Luke (an abbreviated form of the name Lucanus) was a Gentile not a Jew. In his letter to the Colossians the apostle Paul distinguishes Luke from the Jews who were with him 'who are of the circumcision' (Colossians 4:10-14). Though a Gentile he was clearly well acquainted with the festivals, customs, practices, opinions and prejudices of the Jews.

It is likely that he was a Jewish proselyte, a Gentile by birth and education, but one who had come to worship and serve the true God and therefore a convert to Judaism. This would mean that Paul, in Colossians 4 is distinguishing Luke from those who were Jews by birth. One of the reasons for supposing Luke to have been a proselyte is related to the outcry of the Jews against Paul in Jerusalem. On that occasion they accuse Paul of taking a Gentile into the temple at Jerusalem. They name the Gentile as Trophimus the Ephesian (Acts 21:29). Since Luke was present with Paul at the time it is surprising that the Jews did not name him also - unless he was a Gentile proselyte.

Paul spoke of Luke in the warmest terms as 'the beloved physician' (Colossians 4:14). He was with Paul during his first imprisonment in Rome, a worthy 'fellow-labourer' (Philemon 24) and stood by him during the second Roman imprisonment when all others were away (2 Timothy 4:11).

---

[128] Ernest H. Trenchard, 'The Acts of the Apostles,' in: George C.D. Howley (ed.) *New Testament Commentary.* Pickering and Inglis, 1969), p.289.

Luke's journey with Paul from Philippi to Jerusalem

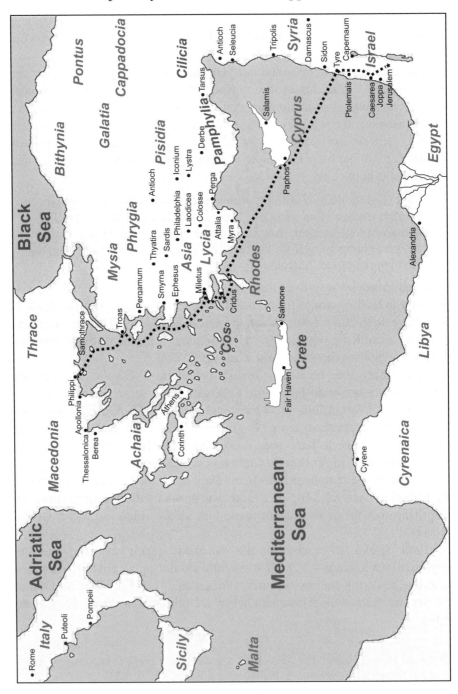

Luke accompanied the apostle Paul on a number of his missionary journeys. These are easily determined from the way in which Luke at times wrote 'we', 'us' and 'our' instead of 'they', 'them' and 'their'. By this method it may be concluded that Luke joined Paul at Troas on his second missionary journey (Acts 16:10; cf. v.8), and sailed with Paul, Silas and Timothy over to Samothrace, Neapolis and onto the main land at Philippi.

Following the conversion of Lydia in the city and the subsequent spiritual delivery of a fortune-telling slave girl, an uproar broke out against Paul and Silas. The two servants of the Lord were beaten and thrown into prison. The Lord graciously used these two to bring the Philippian jailer and all his household to saving faith in Christ. When Paul and Silas were about to be quietly released, Paul told of his Roman citizenship and insisted that the magistrate came personally to release them. Hearing they were Romans, and knowing instantly of the seriousness of the treatment they had received when they were punished without trial, the magistrate soon arrived and politely pleaded with them to leave the city.

Nothing further is heard of Luke for over four years until he met with Paul again in the city of Philippi. Here Luke joined Paul for the journey to Jerusalem (see map on previous page).

The apostle was 'hurrying to be at Jerusalem, if possible, on the Day of Pentecost' (Acts 20:16). Paul expressed the spiritual motivation for his trip to Israel's capital - 'I go bound in the spirit to Jerusalem, not knowing the things that will happen to me there, except that the Holy Spirit testifies in every city, saying that chains and tribulations await me' (Acts 20:22-23; cf. 21:4,11-13). Nevertheless he does not explained the reason behind the urgency. Does he want to be in the Jerusalem at this particular festival time because that is the largest annual gathering of pilgrims to the city? It would present a golden opportunity for winning souls for Christ. Does he want to consolidate his position with the rest of the apostles? Maybe his major concern was to give an account of his missionary journey.

Timothy, Sopater, Aristarchus, Secundus and Gaius had already gone ahead from Macedonia to Troas and were waiting for Paul and Luke there.

They all met up and stayed on in Troas for a week (Acts 20:4-6). Here during the rather lengthy preaching of the apostle Paul, Eutychus fell asleep and fell to his death from the third storey of the building. The Lord raised him from death through the agency of the apostle Paul.

From Troas Luke sailed with Paul to Miletus. Paul sent a message to the elders of the Ephesian Church to meet him there (Acts 20:17). After conversation and an emotional parting, Paul and Luke took a ship bound for Phoenicia and disembarked in the port of Tyre in Syria. Finding believers in the city they stayed seven days and then departed for Jerusalem staying for some time on the way in Caesarea at the home of Philip the evangelist (Acts 21:8).

Once in Jerusalem they were warmly greeted by the brethren. Luke was with Paul when he met up with James, the brother of the Lord, and the other elders of the church in Jerusalem. Paul gave a detailed report of those things which God had done among the Gentiles through his ministry. And when they heard it, they glorified the Lord' (Acts 21:19-20).

Luke was present a week or so later when a commotion was stirred up against Paul. Jews from Asia accused him of teaching everywhere against the Jews, the law of Moses and against Jerusalem. Furthermore they accused him of taking Gentiles into the temple (Acts 21:28). The hostility was so great that Paul was delivered from death only by the intervention of the commander of the garrison who brought soldiers and centurions to control the mob. For his own safety Paul was arrested and within a short while secretly moved under a large army escort to the garrison in Caesarea (Acts 23:23-24). Paul was kept in prison for over two years (Acts 24:27) and when the time came for him to be taken under escort to Rome, Luke was there to travel with him (see map on next page). Luke himself describes Paul setting out under arrest for Rome. He tells the story in the first person plural strongly supporting the idea that Luke was present throughout (Acts 27:1f.).

It appears from recorded practices of the time, that when an arrested prisoner was on his way to trial at Rome he was allowed to be accompanied by two slaves. Luke may have acted as Paul's slave so that he could be his companion to Rome and to prison. As 'the beloved physician' (Colossians 4:14) his professional skills and experience would be invaluable to his friend who suffered from 'a thorn in the flesh' (2 Corinthians 12:7), if indeed that was a physical disability rather than a spiritual malady.

If Luke remained in Jerusalem during Paul's imprisonment in Caesarea it would have given him ample opportunity to meet with apostles, eyewitnesses and elders and to continue his research for his Gospel record (1:1). Contact with Silas would furnish him with details about the church in Jerusalem. Time spent with Timothy would enable the gathering of information about Paul's activity when Luke had been absent. Then there is the time he spent with Paul himself, a good friend and trusted colleague. Luke was often in ideal circumstances for collecting information for his *Gospel Record* and for preparing his account for *The Acts of the Apostles*.

Luke does not seem to have been a preacher or an evangelist. He was a man who made his contribution in terms of personal service. Luke's education and medical training would also equip him to undertake careful research. This was the skill that the Holy Spirit stimulated and enhanced to make him a most useful and faithful biblical historian.

Luke accompanied Paul (under arrest) to Rome

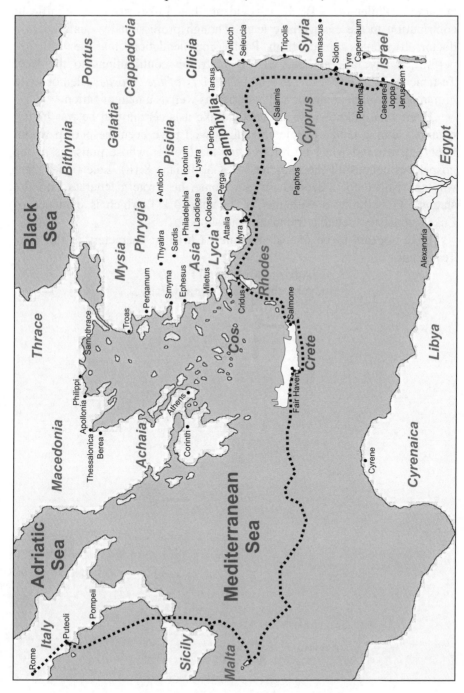

Writing from prison to Philemon, his 'beloved friend and fellow labourer' (Philemon 1) Paul referred to Luke also as his 'fellow labourer' (Philemon 24). It is evident that Luke made a significant contribution to the evangelistic team. Though professionally qualified as a doctor, it would appear, from Paul's commendation, that he willingly performed any task at hand. His two written contributions to the New Testament, *The Gospel of Luke* and *The Acts of the Apostles*, demonstrate him to be a proficient author and historian as well as a man of action.

From what is known about Doctor Luke it is certain that he was highly regarded among God's people and might well have been the person whom Paul had in mind when he referred to 'the brother whose praise is in the gospel throughout all the churches' (2 Corinthians 8:18). Later when Paul was imprisoned for a second time in Rome, he wrote a letter to Timothy stating: 'Only Luke is with me' (2 Timothy 4:11), which is evidence of Luke's consistent reliable friendship and support.

Luke appears to be one of the finest Christian characters in the New Testament.

<blockquote>
A friend loves at all times,
and a brother is born for adversity.
Proverbs 17:17
</blockquote>

Outline of content in Luke's Gospel

Ministry in Samaria and Judea

Last journey of Jesus to Jerusalem

Ministry in Samaria and Galilee -

The Lord's last week in Jerusalem

Prophecies given by Jesus

The suffering and death of Jesus

Context

The testimony of the Early Church Fathers is uniform that this Gospel 'was written by Luke, the companion of Paul, and was therefore regarded by them as really the gospel which Paul preached'.[129] There is general agreement that Luke used three sources in his research: the Gospel of Mark, material used by Matthew but not included in Mark, and word-of-mouth testimony by 'eyewitnesses and ministers of the word' (1:2).[130]

Luke's Gospel and his other book, *The Acts of the Apostles* were produced during the lifetime of the apostles Peter, John and Paul and were received during their lives as inspired books of sacred authority. For example, Paul wrote to Timothy: 'Let the elders who rule well be counted worthy of double honour, especially those who labour in the word and doctrine. For the Scripture says, 'You shall not muzzle an ox while it treads out the grain,' and, 'The labourer is worthy of his wages' (1 Timothy 5:17-18). The first quotation is taken from Deuteronomy 25:4. The second is only found in the Gospel of Luke where Luke recorded these words of the Lord Jesus (10:7). Paul is indicating that the Gospel writings of Luke are on a par with the writings of the Old Testament Scriptures!

Luke wrote more of the New Testament literature by volume than any other, including Paul.

Of the three synoptic writers (Matthew, Mark and Luke), Luke contains the highest proportion of material unique to himself. Over 50% of the content is found exclusively in Luke (Matthew has about 40% exclusive to himself and Mark has only 10% exclusive to himself).[131]

The first four verses bear a marked difference in style and vocabulary to the rest of the gospel. Here there is a classical literary style, where he is reporting his sources with a style and vocabulary that are Hebrew and Aramaic.[132]

Luke addressed both his *Gospel* and *The Acts of the Apostles* to Theophilus, a man of high rank as the title 'most excellent' (1:3) indicates.

---

[129] Albert Barnes, *A Popular Family Commentary on the New Testament: being notes practical and explanatory, Vol. 2 Luke and John* (London: Gresham Publishing Co. no date), p.iii.

[130] Where the book is not stated the quotation is from Luke's gospel.

[131] Robert G. Gromacki, *New Testament Survey* (Grand Rapids, Michigan: Baker, 1974), p.113.

[132] Aramaic is a Syrian dialect predominant in the Near East from the 6th century B.C. It gradually replaced Hebrew as the language of the Jews.

Whether this man was an earnest seeker or a devout believer is not clear. He was most probably a Gentile, a recent convert, and keen to know as much as possible about the life and teaching of the Lord Jesus Christ. Alternatively, since Theophilus means 'lover of God', this may be Luke's way of addressing his record to anyone who loves God, whether a recent convert or a mature believer.

Luke is writing as to a personal friend. A product of exhaustive research this historic record was intended to combat the spread of false gospels and misleading accounts of the life of Christ - 'that you may know the certainty of those things in which you were instructed' (1:4). The emphasis throughout is upon the humanity of the Lord Jesus Christ. The cry of the centurion at the cross encapsulates the essence of Luke's Gospel, 'Certainly this was a righteous Man!' (23:47) Jesus is the perfect Man, fully human and fully divine, for he is the Son of Man as well as the Son of God.

In The Gospel of Luke we see the compassionate love of the Saviour. As a doctor Luke was deeply interested in the cure of illness and the relief of suffering. The parable of The Good Samaritan and the parable of The Lost Son are only recorded by this author. As a humanitarian he was sympathetically concerned for the poor and the distressed. It is the gospel for needy outcasts. Fallen-women are raised and hated tax collectors are loved, for Jesus is 'the Son of Man' who 'has come to seek and to save that which was lost' (19:10).

Nevertheless the spiritual dimension is by no means overlooked or undervalued. Jesus is presented as One whose priorities were spiritual, demanding total commitment from his followers. He clashed with the religious leaders and was severe in his denunciation of their abuses. He was intolerant of every kind of evil.

Luke includes a genealogy of Jesus. There are marked differences between this genealogy and that presented by Matthew (Matthew 1:1-17). Matthew, being concerned to show Jesus as the promised Messiah of the Jews, begins the ancestral line at Abraham. Luke, being concerned for the worldwide implications, goes back to Adam. Matthew's genealogy is the legal lineage of Jesus through Joseph. Luke's is the personal lineage of Jesus through his mother Mary.

Luke follows the framework of Mark's Gospel: preparation for ministry, Galilean ministry, journey to Jerusalem, crucifixion and resurrection. Luke adds to this framework: two chapters at the beginning concerning the prophecies and births of John the Baptist and Jesus, information at the cross, and a chapter on the resurrection appearances not found in the other Gospels. The journey to Jerusalem is expanded to almost ten chapters (9:51-19:27); Mark has one (chapter 10-11); Matthew has two (chapters 19 and 20).

Luke shows a special interest in the early life of the Lord Jesus and in Mary his mother. He may have spoken to Mary in person on more than one occasion during his visits to Israel as he accompanied the apostle Paul. From Mary it is likely that Luke received all the accurate personal details of those early days: the announcement of the birth of John the Baptist (1:13-20); the announcement of the birth of Jesus (1:28-35); the visit of Mary to Elizabeth (1:39-41); Elizabeth's greeting to Mary (1:42-45) along with Mary's response (1:46-55); and the prophecy of Zacharias (1:68-79).

Luke may also have heard at first hand from Mary about the necessity of the journey to Bethlehem in Judea for the birth of the Lord Jesus (2:1-7); the angel's appearance to the shepherds and the great heavenly chorus (2:8-20); the circumcision of Jesus (2:21); his presentation in the temple and the prophecy of Simeon (2:22-35); the meeting with Anna the prophetess (2:36-38); and Jesus at twelve years of age engrossed in conversation with teachers in the temple (2:41-50).

It is highly likely that Luke used the two years when Paul was incarcerated at Caesarea to gather material for his Gospel from eye-witnesses and from documents in Israel. He would be able to discuss his findings, and his own recollections, with the apostle Paul. Having then achieved a 'perfect understanding of all things from the very first' he would be able to produce 'an orderly account' (1:3).

Distinctive features of Luke's Gospel

Luke highlights the connection between the history of Christ and secular history. There are, for example, details explaining the journey of Joseph and Mary to Bethlehem when 'a decree went out from Caesar Augustus... while Quirinius was governing Syria' (2:1-5). There are seven more verifiable facts presented to pinpoint the beginning of our Lord's ministry -

- the fifteenth year of the reign of Tiberius Caesar;
- Pontius Pilate governor of Judea;
- Herod tetrarch of Galilee (tetrarch is the title of a ruler over one of four divisions of a Roman province);
- Philip tetrarch of Iturea and Trachonitis;
- Lysanias tetrarch of Abilene;
- Annas and Caiaphas high priests;
- the preaching of John the Baptist in the wilderness (3:1-2).

Jesus is part of concrete human history. Luke is a genuine and careful Greek historian. He provides Theophilus with historical certainty.

Luke begins his account with the new prophecies given in the year before the birth of Jesus. In announcing the coming of the Messiah the long silent voice of prophecy speaks again by an angel of the Lord in the temple. How fitting that the story of the Lord's incarnation should begin there at the time of sacrifice. In all, nine new prophetic declarations are recorded by Luke, then at the end of his Gospel record he draws to a conclusion with the emphasis of Jesus having fulfilled the old messianic prophecies of the Old Testament. Just before his departure, the Lord Jesus said to his disciples -

> These are the words which I spoke to you while I was still with you, that all things must be fulfilled which were written in the law of Moses and the Prophets and the Psalms concerning me (Luke 24:44).

This the Saviour has wonderfully and perfectly achieved.

Contemporary prophecies unique to Luke

Luke writes in contrast to Matthew, who set the incarnation of the Son of God in the context of Old Testament prophecy, and to Mark who makes no reference to prophecy. Luke alone records nine contemporary prophetic declarations -

1. Announcement of the birth of John the Baptist	1:13-20
2. Announcement of the birth of Jesus	1:28-35
3. Elizabeth's greeting to Mary	1:42-45
4. Mary's response	1:46-55
5. The prophecy of Zacharias	1:68-79
6. The angel's proclamation to the shepherds	2:10-11
7. The praise of the heavenly chorus	2:14
8. The revealed promise to Simeon	2:26
9. The prophecy of Simeon	2:29-35

Miracles unique to Luke

1. The first great catch of fish	5:1-11
2. The widow of Nain's son brought back to life	7:11-17
3. A crippled woman restored to health	13:10-17
4. The healing of a man suffering from dropsy	14:1-6
5. Ten lepers healed	17:11-19
6. The healing of the ear cut off by Peter	22:50-51

Parables unique to Luke

1. The Two Debtors	7:41-43
2. The Good Samaritan	10:30-37

3. The Friend at Midnight	11:5-8
4. The Rich Fool	12:16-21
5. The Fruitless Fig Tree	13:6-9
6. The Seats at a Feast	14:7-11
7. The Great Supper	14:15-24
8. The Hasty Builder	14:28-30
9. The Impetuous King	14:31-33
10. The Lost Sheep (similar to Matthew 18:12-13)	15:4-7
11. The Lost Coin	15:8-10
12. The Lost Son	15:11-32
13. The Unjust Steward	16:1-13
14. The Rich Man and Lazarus	16:19-31
15. The Widow and the Judge	18:1-8
16. The Pharisee and the Tax Collector	18:9-14

Incidents unique to Luke

1. Zacharias serves in the temple	1:5-23
2. Mary visits her cousin Elizabeth	1:39-56
3. Joseph and Mary go to Bethlehem, Jesus born	2:1-9
4. Jesus at twelve with teachers in the temple	2:41-52
5. A sinful woman of the city	7:36-50
6. The return of the seventy disciples	10:17-24
7. Mary and Martha: issue over preparing a meal	10:38-42
8. Zacchaeus, a chief tax collector	19:1-10

The Lord's attitude to prayer

Luke presents the Lord Jesus as a praying Messiah.[133] There are also two parables of Jesus regarding prayer which are unique to Luke - The Widow and the Judge (18:1-8) and The Friend at Midnight (11:5-8).These emphasise the importance of persistence and insistence in prayer.

Women in Luke's Gospel

Luke sees the birth of Christ from Mary's perspective (whereas Matthew presents it from Joseph's viewpoint). He records how Anna gave thanks to God when she saw the Christ (2:36-38); and how the Lord raised to life the widow's son at Nain and 'presented him to his mother' (7:14-15). Later, when the Lord was engaged in his extensive ministry in Galilee, Luke notes the presence and practical support provided by godly women -

> Now it came to pass, afterward, that he went through every city and village, preaching and bringing the glad tidings of the

---

[133] See later section: Christology 1. The prayer life of Jesus, p. 427.

> kingdom of God. And the twelve were with him, and certain women who had been healed of evil spirits and infirmities - Mary called Magdalene, out of whom had come seven demons, and Joanna the wife of Chuza, Herod's steward, and Susanna, and many others who provided for him from their substance (8:1-3).

Luke pays particular attention to note the names of the women. Joanna, for example, had been healed by Jesus. Her husband Chuza was a steward to Herod Antipas (8:3). Consequently he was a wealthy man holding a position of power and status. Joanna was therefore well placed to provide material support for the Lord and his apostles. She was no doubt among the women at the cross (23:49) and certainly one of the first to witness the empty tomb (24:10).

Luke makes mention of women almost as many times as Matthew and Mark combined. He discloses how Jesus praised Mary (the sister of Lazarus) when she wanted to listen to him and learn of spiritual realities (10:38-42); and how he healed a woman who had been severely crippled for eighteen years (13:10-13). The Lord has a high regard for women as is seen in the parables recorded by Luke (13:20-21; 15:8-10; 18:1-8). It was women who stood at the cross whilst the Saviour suffered (23:49). It was women who went early to the tomb to minister to the Lord's body (24:1).

Luke has a particular concern for the fallen and despised. He is the only one who reports the Lord's loving concern for them as demonstrated in his dealing with a sinful woman of the city. She, discovering where Jesus was having a meal, came in, stood by him, inadvertently wet his feet with her tears and proceeded to wipe them away with her hair. She then poured expensive perfumed oil on his feet (7:36-50). The Pharisee host was most perturbed. How gentle and kind the Saviour was in support of her action. Defending her against criticism he wonderfully vindicated her and testified to her deep love. He praised her for her loving generosity.

Luke was also the only one to note the time spent with despised Zacchaeus leading to the Lord declaring, 'Today salvation has come to this house, because he also is a son of Abraham; for the Son of Man has come to seek and to save that which was lost' (19:9-10).

Luke empathises individual people. Names are presented which are not found elsewhere: Zacharias, Elizabeth, Simeon, Anna, Zacchaeus and Cleopas.

Teaching unique to Luke

The ministry of the Holy Spirit

Luke shows a special interest in the work of the Holy Spirit -

- Zacharias was promised that his son would 'be filled with the Holy Spirit, even from his mother's womb' (1:15);
- it was the Holy Spirit who overshadowed Mary at the conception of Jesus (1:35);
- her cousin Elizabeth was 'filled with the Holy Spirit' (1:41-45);
- Elizabeth's husband Zacharias was also 'filled with the Holy Spirit, and prophesied' (1:67);
- the Holy Spirit enlightened Simeon and led him to the temple so that he recognised Jesus as the promised Messiah (2:26-32);
- Jesus was the One promised who would baptise with the Holy Spirit (3:16);
- he was anointed by the Holy Spirit at his baptism (3:22);
- filled with the Holy Spirit to accomplish his ministry (4:1);
- led by the Holy Spirit into the wilderness to be tempted by the devil (4:1-2).
- after the testing for forty days and forty nights he returned to Galilee 'in the power of the Spirit' (4:14);
- his preaching ministry began in the synagogue at Nazareth when he read a prophecy from the prophet Isaiah (61:1-2) and summed up his whole Spirit-empowered ministry. Jesus testified -

> The Spirit of the LORD is upon me, because he has anointed me to preach the gospel to the poor; he has sent me to heal the brokenhearted, to proclaim liberty to the captives and recovery of sight to the blind, to set at liberty those who are oppressed; to proclaim the acceptable year of the LORD (4:18-19).

Having read the prophecy the Lord then declared -

> Today this Scripture is fulfilled in your hearing (4:21).

When the seventy disciples returned from their mission -

- 'Jesus rejoiced in the Spirit' (10:21);
- he promised the Holy Spirit to all God's children who asked for him (11:13);
- he warned of the dreadful consequences of blasphemy against the Holy Spirit (12:10).

In *The Acts of the Apostles* Luke continues the same emphasis upon the ministry of the Holy Spirit as the Spirit directs and enables the servants of God in their worldwide mission (Acts 1:2, 5, 8, 16; 2:4, 33, 38; 4:8, 31, etc.). The Lord Jesus Christ who began his glorious ministry here on earth, now continues that ministry from heaven through the Holy Spirit (Acts 1:1-2).

Christology

1. The prayer life of Jesus

Luke especially notes Jesus as a praying Messiah. There are eight references to the Lord praying which are not found in the other three Gospel accounts.

1.	Jesus prayed as he was being baptised	3:21
2.	In the wilderness after healing a great number	5:15-16
3.	All night before he appointed the twelve apostles	6:12-16
4.	Alone, before challenging the disciples	9:18-22
5.	On the mount of transfiguration	9:28-29
6.	For Peter that his faith would not fail	22:32
7.	At Calvary for those who crucified him	23:34
8.	As he committed his Spirit to the Heavenly Father	23:46

Luke recalls the connection between the Master's prayers and major events in his ministry, like his baptism and his transfiguration (3:21; 9:29). The Lord prayed when important decisions had to be taken, such as the appointment of the twelve or when he was about to draw forth the great confession that he is 'the Christ of God' (6:12; 9:20).

How reassuring it is too that Jesus prayed for Peter that his faith should not fail and then encouraged him, once restored, to strengthen his brethren (22:32). The Saviour knew Peter would falter and yet his prayers would bring Peter through. What a Saviour!

Then as Jesus was being crucified, another amazing prayer burst from his lips: 'Father, forgive them, for they do not know what they do' (23:34). Once again, even in the utmost agony, he fulfils a messianic prophecy. Isaiah predicted that, at the very time when he would bare the sin of many, Christ would make intercession for the transgressors (Isaiah 53:12).

> He speaks his first word from the cross, and *probably* while the nails were being driven… There is nothing of wrath. He threatens not, nor invokes vengeance… There is nothing of accusation or lament, no invocation of help - *Save Me!* … When we examine and analyse it, this first word from the cross discloses … the *perfect love* of the holy Son of man, maintained and approved even unto death: for the cry which went up to God has for its *presupposition* that He as man retains nothing but forgiveness and love… the word points us to *atoning love* - and that too, of the

Father himself, as it is revealed through the *Son*... (Stier's italics).[134]

2. The Saviour of the world

Luke presents Jesus as the Saviour of the world; in order to validate this, the Lord's ancestry is traced back beyond Abraham to Adam (3:34-38; cf. Matthew 1:1-2). The coming of the Lord was for all; both Jew and Gentile were addressed by his message. At our Lord's birth the angels announced 'good tidings of great joy which will be to all people' and God's 'peace, goodwill toward men' (2:10,14). Simeon declared Jesus as 'a light to bring revelation to the Gentiles' (2:32).

Luke alone records our Lord's reference to Old Testament Gentiles who experienced the grace of God -

- the widow of Zarephath (4:25-26; cf. 1 Kings 17:8-24);
- Naaman the Syrian (4:27; cf. 2 Kings 5:1-14);
- the Queen of the South (11:31; cf. 1 Kings 10:1-13; 2 Chronicles 9:1-12);
- the men of Nineveh (11:32; cf. Jonah 3:1-5).

Luke alone records the healing of ten lepers with only one, a Samaritan, returning to give thanks (17:16) the remaining nine presumably being Jews. In the parable of The Good Samaritan, alone found in Luke, Jesus presented a despised enemy of Israel to illustrate genuine love and care in the face of the disinterested and uncaring Jews, depicted by the priest and the levite (10:25-37).

At his ascension the Saviour gave instruction 'that repentance and remission of sins should be preached in his name to all nations, beginning at Jerusalem' (24:47).

3. The Man of human sympathy

People matter immensely to the Lord. Luke highlights that the godly and the spiritually lost are a concern upon the Saviour's heart. With Mark and Matthew, Luke records the call of Matthew and the subsequent shared meal with 'a great number of tax collectors and others' (5:29). The scribes and Pharisees were incensed by his associating with tax collectors and sinners but Jesus made his mission clear, he had not come 'to call the righteous, but

---

[134] Rudolf Stier, *The Words of our Lord Jesus* (Edinburgh: T. & T. Clark, 1885), vol. 7, pp.428-30.

sinners to repentance' (5:32). His purpose is to give hope to the fallen and despised.

The parables of The Lost Sheep, The Lost Coin, and the Lost Son, only found in Luke's Gospel, show the Lord's love for the lost and answers the critical spirit of the Pharisees and scribes who said, 'This man receives sinners and eats with them' (15:2). These parables also reveal;

- the effort the shepherd takes in searching for his lost sheep 'until he finds it' (15:4);
- his subsequent rejoicing that he has found what was lost;
- the diligence of the seeker in carefully sweeping the house 'until she finds it,' and the Lord's subsequent 'joy in the presence of the angels of God over one sinner who repents' (15:8,10);
- the love and patience of the father waiting for the return of his son, the great mercy and grace with which he is welcomed home and how 'they began to be merry' (15:24).

These powerfully illustrate the love of the Son, the Holy Spirit and the Father, in reassuring sinners that there is hope and a warm welcome to any who turn in repentance to the Lord. The Triune Godhead takes pleasure in the salvation of a sinner. How reminiscent of the gospel found in the Old Covenant -

> Seek the LORD while he may be found, call upon him while he is near. Let the wicked forsake his way, and the unrighteous man his thoughts; let him return to the LORD, and he will have mercy on him; and to our God, for he will abundantly pardon (Isaiah 55:6-7).

> The LORD your God in your midst, the Mighty One, will save; he will rejoice over you with gladness, he will quiet you with his love, he will rejoice over you with singing (Zephaniah 3:17).

The way in which the Lord Jesus dealt with women was quite exceptional. Unlike the Jewish Rabbis of his day and generation, he showed great respect and treated them with dignity. All four Gospel writers record the welcome which Jesus gave to the presence of women among his followers but it is Luke who emphasises the point. Jesus also cared deeply about the plight of suffering women.

Luke is the only one to record his tenderness and compassion for the bereaved in the raising back to life of the widow of Nain's son (7:11-15). Jesus, like the Father, 'relieves the fatherless and widow' (Psalm 146:9). As a physician, Luke paid particular note to the condition of the woman with a haemorrhage, noting that 'a woman, having a flow of blood for twelve years, who had spent all her livelihood on physicians and could not be healed by any, came from behind and touched the border of his garment. And immediately her flow of blood stopped' (8:44-45).

Additional applications

1. Prayer

This Gospel has more on the subject of prayer than any of the other three Gospels. Luke especially emphasises the prayer life of Jesus. At the Lord's baptism, it was 'while he prayed' (3:21) that he was anointed by the Holy Spirit. After healing a leper he 'withdrew into the wilderness and prayed' (5:16). Before appointing the twelve apostles he spent a whole night in prayer (6:12). It was whilst 'he was alone praying' that his disciples joined him and he raised the question, 'Who do the crowds say that I am?' (9:18) which resulted in the great confession of the apostle Peter that Jesus is 'The Christ of God.'

In preparation for the transfiguration, Jesus took three apostles and 'went up on the mountain to pray' (9:28), and it was 'as he prayed' that 'the appearance of his face was altered, and his robe became white and glistening' (9:29). When the seventy returned from their mission Jesus prayed and thanked the Father for granting spiritual illumination (10:21).

It was the Lord's regular practice in prayer which prompted the request of one of his disciples, for it was 'as he was praying in a certain place, when he ceased, that one of his disciples said to him, 'Lord, teach us to pray' (11:1). In response the Lord taught them, and the world, a pattern for prayer (11:2-4).

At the celebration of the Passover in the upper room, Jesus warned his disciples that they would all be made to stumble because of him that night. Peter protested and declared his allegiance to Christ even to death. Jesus predicted Peter's threefold denial and Luke alone records the reassurance given - 'But I have prayed for you' (22:32). Only Luke's record contains the two prayers of Jesus on the cross (23:34,46).

Jesus is a wonderful example as a man of prayer. It is most startling and challenging that the all-holy, righteous, only-begotten Son of God should pray so much. How much more, therefore, should we sinners by nature pray and plead with God for ourselves, our brothers and sisters in Christ and the lost.

Luke alone records the parable of The Widow and the Judge, 'that men always ought to pray and not lose heart' (18:1-8). The parable of The Friend at Midnight, teaches persistent prayer to God - asking, seeking and knocking

(11:5-10), and the parable of The Pharisee and the Tax Collector shows that self-righteousness is a great blockage to prayer and acceptance before God (18:9-14). Jesus is a most helpful teacher on the subject of prayer (11:1-4). This gospel is a great encouragement to prayer.

2. The right use of money

Three parables unique to Luke relate to the use of money and possessions - The Rich Fool (12:13-21); The Unjust Steward (16:1-13); and the Rich Man and Lazarus (16:19-31).

In the first, a rich farmer is concerned to store more and more of his yearly produce with an eye to an extremely comfortable retirement. Unfortunately for him he dies before reaching retirement and thus gains no benefit. 'So is he who lays up treasure for himself, and is not rich toward God' (12:21). Expressed in a slightly different way, Jesus also said -

> No servant can serve two masters; for either he will hate the one and love the other, or else he will be loyal to the one and despise the other. You cannot serve God and mammon (16:13; cf. Matthew 6:24).

Though the components of the parable of The Unjust Steward (16:1-13) are very difficult to interpret, the clear challenge to every Christian is found in the criticism implied in the conclusion -

> For the sons of this world are more shrewd in their generation than the sons of light. And I say to you, make friends for yourselves by unrighteous mammon, that when you fail, they may receive you into an everlasting home (16:8-9).

As stated by Jesus, unbelievers are often wiser than believers in the use of money and possessions. Evidently there are lessons to learn even from the ungodly. From this parable disciples of Christ are taught firstly, to learn wisdom, not the wisdom of the world (James 3:13-16) but 'the wisdom that is from above' which 'is first pure, then peaceable, gentle, willing to yield, full of mercy and good fruits, without partiality and without hypocrisy' (James 3:17).

Then, secondly Christians are encouraged to invest in the future (16:9). One distinct way in which to 'make friends for yourselves by unrighteous mammon' is to give generously to the support of evangelists, ministers of the gospel and missionaries. When John Wesley preached on this subject his three points were: 'Gain all you can; save all you can; give all you can!'

From a human perspective, the financial support towards the conversion of sinners is the finest way to make new friends with money! Money and possessions are not sinful in themselves. They are however a great responsibility. Those who use them well for the benefit of others will have gone a long way in discharging that duty. We are stewards answerable to God (12:42; cf. 1 Corinthians 4:2).

Even the parable of The Good Samaritan contains a generous use of finance on behalf of another needy soul (10:35). The principles of Christian giving are further developed by the apostle Paul as he commends the churches of Macedonia for their sacrificial giving (2 Corinthians 8 and 9).

The third parable relating to the use of money, shows a beggar called Lazarus (meaning, 'one who has received mercy') and an unnamed rich man (16:19-31). The rich man knows the name of the beggar at his gate (16:20,24) but has totally disregarded him. Lazarus is his neighbour yet he has no love or mercy for him. Pharisees are present at the telling of the parable. They are known to be 'lovers of money' (16:14) and Paul will later record, the 'love of money is a root of all kinds of evil' (1 Timothy 6:10).

In all three parables relating to riches the overriding principle is clear: 'Take heed and beware of covetousness, for one's life does not consist in the abundance of the things he possesses' (12:15). Money and possessions are to be used for the glory of God and the good of others (1 Timothy 6:17-19). Financial investment is best made in the spiritual bank of heaven -

> provide yourselves money bags which do not grow old, a treasure in the heavens that does not fail, where no thief approaches nor moth destroys. For where your treasure is, there your heart will be also (12:33-34).

3. The cost of discipleship

As with Matthew and Mark, Luke records the Lord's three predictions of his suffering, rejection and death (9:22; 9:44; 18:31-33; cf. Matthew 16:21; 17:22-23; 20:18-19; Mark 8:31; 9:31; 10:33-34). All three writers include the challenge following the first prediction. In it Jesus indicated the cost of following him: wholehearted commitment in self-denial, cross-bearing and discipleship (9:23-26; Matthew 16:24-28; Mark 8:34-38).

Luke recounts the further sacrifices required. Presenting it in the starkest terms, the Lord desires total devotion to himself, with a hatred of father and mother, wife and children, brothers and sisters, and one's own life (14:26). This cannot be taken literally, since Jesus never violated or contradicted the law of God (cf. Matthew 5:17-18; 22:37-40; Ephesians 5:28-29). He is showing in the most forceful manner that devotion and loyalty to him must always have priority over every other relationship. As Jesus said on another occasion -

He who loves father or mother *more than me* is not worthy of me.
And he who loves son or daughter *more than me* is not worthy of
me (Matthew 10:37, emphasis added).

In two parables, unique to Luke's Gospel, Jesus emphasises the importance
of carefully considering the cost of discipleship. In the parable of The Hasty
Builder (Luke 14:28-30) the meaning is abundantly clear. Only a foolish
person starts building without working out the expenses involved. To half-
finish a building brings embarrassment and humiliation. Through the parable
of The Impetuous King (Luke 14:31-33) the point is driven home - think
carefully, consider the cost of discipleship: whole-hearted, life-long
commitment to Christ. Nothing less will do.

Conclusion

The Gospel of Luke begins and ends with rejoicing in Jesus. The angel
Gabriel encouraged Mary to rejoice when he announced the miracle which
was about to take place within her (1:28-33). She was highly favoured by
God. Her Son would receive the divinely given name of Jesus, meaning
'Jehovah is salvation' which indicated the significance of his coming. Mary
was told of her Son's absolute greatness; his divine sonship; the successor of
all the glorious promises to David; and of whose kingdom there would be no
end. *The Gospel of Luke* amplified and expanded these great themes rising
ever upward in a grand crescendo to the death, resurrection and ascension of
Jesus the Christ, Son of the living God.

At the close of the Lord's thirty-three years on earth the eleven apostles
were filled with great joy as they saw the ascension of Christ. In the previous
three years they had witnessed the living reality of the incarnate Son of God.

They were to testify to his deep love for the despised and rejected; his
gentleness towards the weak; his tenderness with the fallen and forlorn; his
compassion towards those who suffered in body, mind or spirit; his grit and
determination in fulfilling the commission entrusted to him by the heavenly
Father; and throughout all he displayed sinlessness and righteousness in
every situation and circumstance.

Luke gathered these testimonies together, checked his sources, carefully
arranged his material, and presented 'an orderly account' to the 'most
excellent Theophilus' (1:3). God however intended that the results of Luke's
research would have a much wider readership. The gospel must go to the
world! As the Son of God, the servant of God, had prophetically testified -

And now the LORD says, who formed me from the womb to be
his Servant, to bring Jacob back to him, so that Israel is gathered
to him (for I shall be glorious in the eyes of the LORD, and my

God shall be my strength), indeed he says, 'It is too small a thing that you should be my Servant to raise up the tribes of Jacob, and to restore the preserved ones of Israel; I will also give you as a light to the Gentiles, that you should be my salvation to the ends of the earth' (Isaiah 49:5-6).

Understanding
The Gospel of John

Author: the apostle John

Theme:

Confidence in the deity
of Jesus of Nazareth,
the only begotten Son of God

Contents

A brief sketch of the author

John was the son of Zebedee (Mark 10:35). Zebedee was a fisherman on the Sea of Galilee and appears to have been prosperous for he employed a number of others (Mark 1:20). Following the trade of his father, John along with his brother James, was also a fisherman on the Sea of Galilee. They had a close working relationship with another fisherman Simon (Luke 5:7,10).

Whether John's father was a believer is not stated but there is no doubt about the spiritual state of his mother. John's mother Salome was the sister of Mary, the mother of Jesus (19:25;[135] cf. Matthew 27:56; Mark 15:40). Hence Salome was the Lord's aunt. John and Jesus were therefore cousins although John never mentioned this familial tie.

Salome was a godly devout woman, found among those women who willingly and gladly provided practical support for Jesus and his disciples (Matthew 27:55-56; Mark 15:40-41). She was also one of the women who went to the tomb with spices early on resurrection morning intending to anoint the body of the Lord (Mark 16:1). Since spices were expensive to buy this may be a further indication that Salome and Zebedee were reasonably wealthy.

Brought up to respect the law, there would be periodic visits to Jerusalem from the age of thirteen. John would become familiar with the rituals of the temple, with the sacrifices, the incense, the altar, and the priestly robes.

John was probably younger than his brother James, whose name usually preceded his (Mark 1:29; 5:37; 9:2; 10:35; 14:33; Luke 9:54). John was not taught in the schools of the Jewish Rabbis (Acts 4:13) but in the wilderness by John the Baptist. He was among the young men who gathered around the Baptist to study the Old Testament, especially the prophecies concerning the Messiah. These disciples (1:35) were well-taught by their mentor.

The Baptist, enlightened by the Holy Spirit, understood and interpreted the great themes of prophecy and how they converged and found their fulfilment in the promised One of God (Genesis 3:15). John, the son of Zebedee, along with his colleagues, knew 'of whom Moses in the law, and also the prophets, wrote' (1:45), that he was 'Messiah [which is translated, the Christ]' (1:41), 'the Son of God! …the King of Israel!' (1:49; cf. v.34), and 'the Lamb of God who takes away the sin of the world!' (1:29).

---

[135] Where the book is not stated the quotation is from John's gospel.

The Baptist knew himself to be the herald of the Lord (1:23) who was commissioned to introduce Messiah and reveal him to Israel (1:31). His students were prepared and ready for John to identify the Messiah in person.

The Baptist knew that to identify Jesus as 'the Lamb of God' (1:36) would result in his disciples transferring their allegiance immediately to the greater teacher, Jesus of Nazareth. That was precisely what the Baptist intended, for he would later say of Jesus, 'He must increase, but I must decrease' (3:30). The Baptist knew his God-given calling and responsibility. Humbly he acknowledged his role, preparing men by teaching them the content and interpretation of Old Testament Scripture, thus equipping them for their service to Christ. Once he had achieved his God-given responsibilities, he was ready to depart this life.

The apostle John's first glorious encounter with the Saviour was fixed firmly in his mind, for 'it was about the tenth hour' (1:39), that is, four o'clock in the afternoon. That little personal touch in the Gospel account strongly indicates the author's presence. The unnamed disciple of John the Baptist among those who went from the Baptist and became disciples of Christ, was John (1:35,40); for it would be strange for him to give the names of the others: Andrew, Simon Peter, Philip and Nathanael (1:40,41,43,45) and purposely omit just one, unless it were his own. Hengstenberg notes -

> That the other disciple was John, was recognised even in the age of the Church Fathers; e.g., by Chrysostom. It is favourable to this view, that the Evangelist [the apostle John] elsewhere loves to conceal himself, cf. 20:2, not from a general shyness of coming forward personally... but from fear that, by making his personality prominent, he might injure the historic objectivity...[136]

Once introduced to Jesus, John became a devoted and loyal disciple. When the Lord Jesus appointed his twelve apostles, John was among the chosen band. It was in connection with that appointment that Jesus identified a particular trait in John and his brother James. The Lord named the two of them 'Boanerges, that is, "Sons of Thunder"' (Mark 3:17). This 'implies natural vehemence, fiery zeal, and passionate intensity'.[137]

This spirit was clearly evident when the brothers were ready to call down fire from heaven on a Samaritan village which would not welcome Jesus (Luke 9:54). The same fiery zeal was displayed when John rebuked someone for casting out demons in the Master's name because he was not of

---

[136] Ernest W. Hengstenberg, *Commentary on the Gospel of St John* (Minneapolis, Minnesota: Klock and Klock, 1980), vol. 1, p.93.

[137] William H. Van Doren, *Gospel of John: expository and homiletical* (Grand Rapids, Michigan: Kregel, 1981), p.xi.

their group (Mark 9:38). The brothers' enthusiasm and eagerness was demonstrated yet again when they joined their mother Salome in asking for the most honoured places in the kingdom of Christ - 'Grant us that we may sit, one on your right hand and the other on your left, in your glory' (Mark 10:37; cf. Matthew 20:20).

Their intense fervour knew no bounds when they boldly declared they were ready to drink of the Saviour's cup and be baptised with his baptism (Mark 10:38-39). It would only be a few years later that James followed the Lord in 'drinking the cup that he drank'. He was to be the first apostolic martyr (Acts 12:2).

By contrast his brother John was to be the last apostle to leave this world. His strong feelings, his intense passion for the cause of Christ, was to drive him, once controlled through the indwelling Spirit and fashioned by grace, through years of pastoral labour among the seven churches of Asia Minor, through persecution and to banishment on the Isle of Patmos (Revelation 1:9). 'John's subsequent humility, gentleness, and love were the fruit of Christ abiding in him and he in Christ.'[138]

The friendship between the apostle John and the apostle Peter is clearly seen on numerous occasions, sometimes with one or two others but often just the two of them (Mark 5:37; Matthew 17:1; Mark 13:3; Luke 22:8; Matthew 26:37; John 20:2-3; 21:7; Acts 3:1ff.). Though among the twelve apostles of Christ, and good friends, they nevertheless displayed strikingly different personalities. Judged from their writings, and the history of the Gospels, 'Peter showed his love more by outward, busy action; John, by inward quiet devotion. Peter loved the Lord in His official dignity as the Messiah and King. John loved Him in His personal character as the source of spiritual light and life'.[139]

The apostle John, author of this Gospel, never used his own name nor the personal pronoun to indicate himself. He spoke of himself throughout as 'the disciple whom Jesus loved' (13:23; 19:26; 20:2; 21:7); as 'another disciple' and 'the other disciple' (18:15,16). There can be no doubt about his identity since John provided clear confirmation at the end of his record -

> Then Peter, turning around, saw the disciple whom Jesus loved following, who also had leaned on his breast at the supper... This is the disciple who testifies of these things, and wrote these things; and we know that his testimony is true (21:20,24).

---

[138] William H. Van Doren, *Gospel of John: expository and homiletical* (Grand Rapids, Michigan: Kregel, 1981), p.xi.

[139] *Ibid.*, p.x.

Up to the very end John had spoken of himself in the third person, but in the final words he revealed himself so that greater weight may be attached to one who was an eyewitness, who personally knew all that he wrote about.

The apostle John was one of the three invited by Jesus into the sick room of Jairus's daughter (Mark 5:37); he was one of the three invited to accompany the Lord to the mount of transfiguration (Matthew 17:1). John was together with Peter, James and Andrew, on the Mount of Olives talking privately with Jesus (Mark 13:3); John and Peter were the two apostles asked to prepare the Passover meal (Luke 22:8). It was the apostle John who reclined in the closest position to the Lord at the supper in the upper room (13:23-24) to whom Peter quietly motioned that he might ask a private question of the Lord (13:24). John, again with Peter and James, accompanied Jesus further into the Garden of Gethsemane to witness the agonising prayer only a few hours before the horror of Calvary (Matthew 26:37).

When Jesus was arrested 'Peter followed him at a distance to the high priest's courtyard' (Matthew 26:58). John added information not found elsewhere. None of the other three Gospel writers mentioned another disciple following with Peter -

> And Simon Peter followed Jesus, and so did another disciple. Now that disciple was known to the high priest, and went with Jesus into the courtyard of the high priest. But Peter stood at the door outside. Then the other disciple, who was known to the high priest, went out and spoke to her who kept the door, and brought Peter in (18:15-16).

For John to have intimate knowledge of these things suggests that he was there and he is here again referring to himself.[140]

With Peter he was concerned to know what was to befall the Lord Jesus. Being known to the high priest 'the other disciple' gained access into the court of the high priest. How he was known to the high priest is not stated. He also knew the name of the servant who lost his ear (18:10), and the relative of Malchus who challenged Peter (18:26). 'The other disciple' was sufficiently known by the servants of the high priest to secure the admittance of Peter to the courtyard.

That a fishmonger should be known by the servants here is not at all surprising. Galilee supplied the fish for the whole country with the exception

---

[140] For reasons in favour of John as the unnamed disciple see: William Hendriksen, *A Commentary on the Gospel of John* (London: Banner of Truth Trust, 1959), vol. 1, pp.3-31, vol. 2, pp.390-1. For reasons against see: Arthur W. Pink, *Expositions of the Gospel of John: three volumes unabridged in one* (Grand Rapids, Michigan: Zondervan, 1970), vol. 3, p.178.

of the Mediterranean Coast. Fish was brought into Jerusalem through the Fish Gate (Nehemiah 3:3; Zephaniah 1:10). That a fishmonger was known by the high priest is however rather surprising, though Zebedee's wealth and Salome's family ties may account for the connection, and social barriers may not have been so strong in first-century Israel.

'The other disciple' would witness the interrogation of the Lord before Annas. Peter remains in the courtyard whilst he presses on into the council chamber. 'Of the apostolic band John alone goes through the terrors of that night with any measure of firmness.'[141]

John was present at the cross when Jesus committed responsibility for his mother Mary into his care, and 'from that hour that disciple took her to his own home' (19:27). It would appear that John had a family home in Jerusalem, for John could not have shown hospitality towards the mother of Jesus or taken her to his own home if he had lived alone. There is no way of knowing for certain if John's family had a house in Jerusalem as well as one in Capernaum but from the crucifixion of Christ there is no record of John being connected with a home in Galilee. He certainly lived for some years in Judea during the earliest period of the Christian Church (Acts 8:14; Galatians 2:1,9).

Jesus lovingly spared his mother from witnessing the further agony of her son on the cross: the three hours of terrible darkness, that heart-rending cry, 'My God, my God, why have you forsaken me?' (Matthew 27:46), and his death. John, however, returned to the cross after escorting Mary away. Whether or not he heard the cry, 'I thirst!' and/or 'It is finished!' (19:28,30), he was certainly back to witness the piercing of the Saviour's side after his death (19:31-35).

The prophecy of Simeon, so many years before, was now being fulfilled. A sword pierced through Mary's soul (Luke 2:35). Can there be any greater grief to a woman than to watch one of her own children dying in agony? The disciple whom Jesus loved was there to console the mother whom Jesus loved. The day following, was a Sabbath Day of shared grief.

On the first day of the new week, Peter and John responded to the distress of Mary Magdalene as she reported the disappearance of the Lord's body (20:1-2). Running to the tomb, John was first to arrive but Peter was the first to enter. Throughout the coming weeks John was to witness a number of appearances of the risen Lord (20:19, 26; 21:1-2; Luke 24:36). Fishing on the Sea of Galilee he was the first to recognise Jesus as he walked

---

141 William H. Van Doren, *Gospel of John: expository and homiletical* [1872] {Grand Rapids, Michigan: Kregel, 1981), p.xii.

by the shore (21:7). Peter, however, plunged into the water to meet the Lord. Later, after breakfast, Peter showed concern about John's future (21:20-21).

John spent the ten days between the Lord's ascension and the Day of Pentecost in the company of his fellow apostles and disciples who 'continued with one accord in prayer and supplication, with the women and Mary the mother of Jesus, and with his brothers' (Acts 1:14). Participating in the great blessings resulting from the outpouring of the Holy Spirit, John witnessed the conversion of 3,000 Jews, and the rapid growth of the Christian Church.

Sometime later, when Peter and John attended the temple together, they met a man lame from birth (Acts 3:1-2). In consequence of the healing of that man 'in the name of Jesus Christ of Nazareth,' Peter and John were arrested and brought before the Jewish Council (Acts 4:3-7). Though threatened these two apostles were not to be silenced from boldly preaching about the Lord Jesus Christ (Acts 4:19-20). Upon their release they returned to the company of believers and rejoiced in the sovereign rule of the Lord.

Two or three years later a spiritual awakening occurred in Samaria under the preaching of Philip the evangelist. Apostles Peter and John were sent from Jerusalem to investigate. When they arrived they prayed for the converts and the blessing of the New Covenant was granted to those who believed, for 'they received the Holy Spirit' (Acts 8:17). Taking their journey back to Jerusalem Peter and John demonstrated their evangelistic fervour by 'preaching the gospel in many villages of the Samaritans' (Acts 8:25). John, who would have called down fire upon the Samaritans (Luke 9:52-54), was now eager to embrace Samaritans in brotherly love.

Fourteen years after the crucifixion and resurrection of Christ, King Herod Agrippa I 'stretched out his hand to harass some from the church' (Acts 12:1). John's brother, the apostle James, was the first apostle to be martyred. Having killed James and seeing that it pleased the Jews, Herod took action to arrest and imprison the apostle Peter. In the providence of God this apostle was miraculously rescued and returned to the company of believers.

Six years later (A.D.50) John, together with Peter and James the brother of the Lord, were visited by the apostle Paul in Jerusalem. Writing of their meeting, Paul described these three as 'pillars' of the church (Galatians 2:9). John would no doubt have been involved in the Jerusalem Council as they debated the great question: 'Is faith in Jesus Christ alone sufficient for salvation?' The issue arose from the conversion of Gentiles. Their relationship to the law of Moses was a matter of debate. Some members of the council said, 'It is necessary to circumcise them, and to command them to keep the law of Moses' (Acts 15:5). The council however accepted the resolution of James, 'not [to] trouble those from among the Gentiles who are turning to God' (Acts 15:19). In other words, they would not be required to submit to circumcision nor obedience to the Mosaic law. Faith alone in Christ alone was the conclusion of the Jerusalem Council.

There is no mention of John in Jerusalem at the time of Paul's last visit (e.g. Acts 21:18).

When John wrote his epistles he said that he was writing about a person whom he had heard, seen, looked upon and handled (1 John 1:1-3). He was confident that what he was writing could withstand historical investigation. The same note was sounded in *The Gospel of John* (20:30-31).

As an act of severe persecution, John was transported to the Isle of Patmos (Revelation 1:9) probably condemned to work in the salt mines. There the Lord appeared to him in majestic glory and gave him a message for 'the seven churches which are in Asia' (Revelation 1:11). That which was sent to comfort, encourage and warn the churches in Asia Minor, was to become a great blessing to the wider church throughout succeeding generations.

One aspect of John's character which shines from his Gospel, his letters and the Book of Revelation is his consuming passion for the honour of the Lord Jesus Christ. He flames into indignation against anything that would challenge it.

> In all his writings there is a most beautiful blending of tenderness and firmness, of the most gracious ministry of love and the most unsparing denunciation of evil.[142]

> In this Gospel, Jesus Christ is presented as the One whom we are to believe; in John's Epistles the One whom we are to love; and in the Revelation the One for whom we are to wait.[143]

---

142 August Van Ryn, *Meditations in John* (Chicago: Moody Bible Institute, 1949), 20.

143 Robert Lee, *The Outlined Bible: an outline and analysis of every book in the Bible* (London: Pickering and Inglis, no date), Analysis No.43.

Outline of content in John's Gospel

The incarnation and early disciples

The initial ministry of Jesus

The opposition to Jesus

f. Sorrow at his departure: joy at his return	16:16-24
g. Comfort and reassurance	16:25-33
18. Prayer by Jesus -	
a. For the Son of God to be glorified	17:1-5
b. For the safekeeping of his disciples	17:6-16
c. For the sanctification of his disciples	17:17-19
d. For the uniting of all believers	17:20-23
e. For all his people to join him in glory	17:24-26

The betrayal, arrest and crucifixion of Jesus

19. Betrayal and arrest in the Garden of Gethsemane	18:1-11
20. Religious trial before Jewish leaders -	
a. Taken to high priest Annas	18:12-14
b. Peter's first denial in the courtyard	18:15-18
c. Jesus before high priest Annas	18:19-24
d. Peter's second and third denials in the courtyard	18:25-27
21. Civil trial before Pilate	18:28 - 19:16
22. The crucifixion of Jesus -	
a. Crucified between two others	19:17-18
b. Pilate's inscription on the cross	19:19-22
c. Soldiers cast lots for his clothing	19:23-24
d. John entrusted with the care of the mother of Jesus	19:25-27
e. The death of Jesus - "It is finished!"	19:28-30
f. A soldier pierces his side with a sword	19:31-37
g. The Lord's body laid in Joseph's tomb	19:38-42

The resurrection of Jesus

23. The empty tomb	20:1-10
24. Appearances of the risen Jesus -	
a. Appearance to Mary Magdalene	20:11-18
b. Appearance to the disciples (Thomas absent)	20:19-25
c. Appearance to the disciples (Thomas present)	20:26-29
d. John's purpose in selecting eight miraculous signs	20:30-31
e. Eighth miraculous sign: a large catch of 153 fish	21:1-14
f. Reinstatement of Peter to pastoral responsibilities	21:15-23
25. Authentication of John's testimony and Gospel	21:24-25

Context

The apostle John clearly sets out his aim in writing a record of the life and teaching of the Lord Jesus Christ. His purpose is evangelistic. Within the book there is a theological defence of the deity and humanity of Jesus Christ. This is presented with the clear goal to draw out the response of whole-hearted faith. By receiving the facts about the person and work of the Lord Jesus Christ the reader 'may believe that Jesus is the Christ, the Son of God, and that believing... may have life in his name' (20:31).

Whilst the aim is a declared missionary purpose, that it may be the means of winning new converts to faith in Christ, it also conveys truth which will confirm and strengthen the faith of those who already believe. It is a book upon which the Christian may feed the mind and warm the heart. It is the deepest and most profound of the four Gospels. It has often been symbolised by the eagle (Revelation 4:7) for this is the only creature that can rise into the highest heaven and look directly into the sun and not be blinded by its brilliance.

It is a penetrating disclosure of the Word who was God and who became flesh. Here is beautifully displayed 'the glory as of the only begotten of the Father, full of grace and truth' (1:1,14). For many Christians it is the most precious and beloved book in the Bible. Some of the most widely known and best-loved texts in the Word of God are from this Gospel (3:16; 6:35; 11:25; 14:1-4,6). As James Boice observes -

> John 3:16 has probably been the means by which more persons have come to know Jesus Christ as their Saviour and Lord than any other single portion of Scripture.[144]

There is a marked contrast between this Gospel and the first three. Matthew portrays Jesus as the Son of David, the Messiah/King; Mark presents Jesus as the Servant of God; and Luke emphasises the humanity of the Saviour. John however reveals Jesus as the eternal, pre-existent Son of God, the One who is God yet distinct from God - God with God (1:1). The One who became a human being and revealed God (1:18), whom to see is like seeing the Father (14:9). So much in John depends upon the record of the other three Gospels. He assumes his readers have knowledge of the history revealed by them and throughout he confirms their testimony.

---

[144] James M. Boice, *The Gospel of John: an expositional commentary* (Grand Rapids, Michigan: Zondervan 1985), p.17.

In this Gospel there is a profound insight into the One who was promised in the Old Testament Scriptures. As August Van Ryn asserts -

> John writes from a heart capable of the deepest feelings - feelings set in motion by the love of Christ and love for Christ. Our gracious Lord used such a one to write of Him to stir the same deep emotions, the same unyielding loyalty in our souls.[145]

Distinctive features of John's Gospel

It would seem that John was familiar with the other Gospels and did not see the necessity to repeat everything but rather to give more detail on things of major significance and mention matters which had been omitted.

John gives no account of the birth of Jesus nor of his baptism, although he clearly presupposes a knowledge of Christ's baptism on the part of his readers. There is no word about the healing of anyone possessed by an evil spirit. Neither are the institution of the Lord's Supper, the prayer in Gethsemane, nor the ascension included.

Yet John shows a detailed knowledge of things that the other Gospels omit. For example, John records the early ministry of Jesus in Jerusalem and Judah. John alone provides an account of the changing of the water into wine in Cana of Galilee (2:1-11). He alone discloses the interviews of Jesus with Nicodemus (3:1-21) and the woman of Samaria (4:1-26). From him we learn of the raising of Lazarus (11:1-44) and the Master washing the feet of his disciples (13:1-15). Only in John do we find the great sermons on the Bread of Life (6:26-59), the Good Shepherd (10:1-30) and the Holy Spirit, the Spirit of Truth, the Comforter (interspersed throughout chapters 14-16). No one else includes the Lord's prayer in the upper room (17:1-26).

This apostle shows that the Lord's ministry lasted close to three years, not one year as might at first be thought from reading the other Gospels.

John is the most selective of the four Gospel writers. More than ninety percent of his content is only found here. Since the three other Gospels were already in existence, John filled in some important gaps in the account of the Lord's ministry (to some of which he was the only eyewitness), yet concentrated upon drawing out the profound depth of spiritual meaning and significance. Facts so often plainly detailed in the Synoptics (the Gospels of Matthew, Mark and Luke) are interpreted in John.

Where the other Gospels refer to 'scribes' or 'Pharisees,' John uses the term 'Jews'. It occurs over sixty times in this Gospel compared to only five

---

[145] August Van Ryn, *Meditations in John* (Chicago: Moody Bible Institute, 1949), p.20.

times in each of the other three. In John's Gospel the term 'Jews' represents the leaders of the nation of Israel, those determined enemies and haters of Jesus of Nazareth. The focus of their hostility is not upon God himself, since the Jews already believed in God, 'the issue was whether they would believe that Jesus was the Messiah and Son of God. Thus Jesus' relationship with God becomes the inevitable focal point'.[146]

God is presented in John's Gospel primarily in two ways: as the One who sent Jesus (e.g. 5:37) and as the Father of the Son (e.g. 5:17-23).

Miracles unique to John

Only eight miracles were recorded by John, of these six were unique to his Gospel. John called them 'signs' because they are miracles with a special meaning or message attached to them. For example, the man born blind who received his sight (John 9:1) is a powerful illustration of the spiritual blindness with which all humanity begins life. It follows and illustrates the Lord's revelation as being 'the light of the world' (8:12).

These miraculous signs also possess a profound significance in relation to the person of Jesus Christ. They reveal the 'glory' of Jesus and lead to faith (2:11). Their full meaning is only understood by those who believe (11:40; 12:37).

John reveals that he chose the eight 'signs' with a specific purpose in mind -

> And truly Jesus did many other signs in the presence of his disciples, which are not written in this book; but these are written that you may believe that Jesus is the Christ, the Son of God, and that believing you may have life in his name (20:30-31).

These miraculous signs show the power of Christ's Word, and of *his* Word alone. As mentioned six are only found in this Gospel, the two exceptions being the feeding of the five thousand and walking on water.[147]

1. Turning water into wine in Cana of Galilee	2:1-11	
2. Healing the nobleman's son in Capernaum	4:46-54	
3. Healing the paralysed man at Bethesda	5:1-15	
4. Feeding the five thousand in Bethsaida	6:1-14	
5. Walking on the Sea of Galilee	6:15-21	
6. Healing in Jerusalem of the man born blind	9:1-41	

---

[146] Andreas I. Köstenberger, *Encountering John: the gospel in historical, literary, and theological perspective* (Grand Rapids: Baker Academics, 2002), p.39.

[147] cf. Matthew 14:13-33; Mark 6:33-51; Luke 9:11-17.

7. Raising Lazarus from the dead in Bethany   11:1-44

8. The great catch of fish at the Sea of Tiberias[148]   21:4-11

The first seven 'signs' were performed during the Lord's ministry, the last one after his death and resurrection. Jesus often accompanied miracles with teaching, as in the case of the feeding of the five thousand (6:1-14) being followed by the sermon on himself as the True Bread from Heaven (6:22-40). The healing of the man born blind leads to teaching on spiritual blindness and sight (9:39-41) and the raising of Lazarus powerfully illustrates Jesus as 'the resurrection and the life' (11:25).

Parable unique to John

The True Vine   15:1-10

Teaching unique to John

Within the sections listed below are many teachings unique to John -

1. The new birth   3:1-21
2. Jesus the giver of the water of life   4:6-29
3. The defence of his sonship and deity   5:19-47
4. Jesus the Bread of Life   6:22-63
5. Jesus the truth that makes free   8:12-59
6. Jesus the Good Shepherd   10:1-30
7. Final instructions in the upper room   13:1 - 16:33
8. The High Priestly Prayer   17:1-26 [149]

John included none of the Lord's parables. 'Rather is there a collection of discourses in which the relation of the Father to the Son is worked out with theological precision.'[150]

Pneumatology (concerning the Holy Spirit)

Of all the Gospels, John has the most explicit teaching about the Holy Spirit. When Jesus returns to the Father in heaven, the Father will send the Holy Spirit in the name of Jesus (14:26). The Spirit is the heavenly Helper the Paraclete, the One sent alongside to assist in whatever way may be required

---

[148] See the chapter on Significant facts: 'The Sea of Galilee' p.345.

[149] Although this is prayer not teaching, it contains valuable instruction within it.

[150] David J. Ellis, 'The Gospel according to John,' in: George C.D. Howley [ed] *New Testament Commentary* (Pickering and Inglis, 1969), p.251.

(14:16,26; 15:26; 16:7). He is 'the Spirit of truth who proceeds from the Father' (15:26); 'the Spirit of truth, whom the world cannot receive' (14:17), 'the Holy Spirit' (14:26).

The New Covenant blessings of the Holy Spirit are dependent upon Jesus being glorified (7:39), in other words, the gift of the Holy Spirit to believers is conditional upon the suffering, death, resurrection and ascension of the Son of God. It is a great advantage to believers for Christ to depart so that the Holy Spirit may come (16:7).

The activities of the Holy Spirit include: indwelling believers (14:17; cf. Ezekiel 36:27), and being with them forever (14:16); ensuring the apostles have a clear understanding and an accurate recall of the teaching of Jesus (14:25-26); bearing witness to Christ (15:26); glorifying him (16:14); guiding believers 'into all truth' with reference to Christ (16:13); convicting 'the world of sin, and of righteousness and of judgment' (16:8-11); and granting further revelations of 'things to come' (16:13-14).

Christology

John's first chapter presents eight great titles for Jesus of Nazareth. He is the Word (v.1); the Life (v.4); the Light (v.7); the Lamb of God (v.29); the Messiah [Christ] (v.41); the Son of God (v.49); the King of Israel (v.49); and the Son of Man (v.51). Each designation links Jesus with Old Testament prophecy and Old Testament teaching.

1. Jesus: the Word

The Word who was God and with God (1:1) became a human being (1:14). He is God's self-disclosure (1:18), the perfect communication of God the Father. As the Word he is the Messenger *and* the Message.

> And the Word became flesh and dwelt among us, and we beheld
> his glory, the glory as of the only begotten of the Father, full of
> grace and truth (1:14).

The word 'dwelt' translates a Greek word which means literally 'to tent' or 'to tabernacle'. To write of 'glory' in connection with 'tabernacle' immediately relates to the first tabernacle in the wilderness where God promised to display the glory of his presence among his people (Exodus 29:43-46). In the person of Jesus this is supremely achieved.

His glory is the glory of deity. John made a particular point of noting his personal experience of seeing this (beholding his glory) in Jesus on the mount of transfiguration (1:14).

The living Word will be successful in achieving the entirety of his God-given commission -

> For as the rain comes down, and the snow from heaven, and do not return there, but water the earth, and make it bring forth and bud, that it may give seed to the sower and bread to the eater, so shall my word be that goes forth from my mouth; it shall not return to me void, but it shall accomplish what I please, and it shall prosper in the thing for which I sent it (Isaiah 55:10-11).

This was primarily fulfilled in the Word which is Jesus Christ and secondarily through the Gospel and Words of God.

2. Jesus: the Life

This follows logically from what has been said in the opening verses of the first chapter of John's Gospel. As the Son of God was intimately involved in the creation of life in the beginning then he must be the fountain of life. As David declared -

> For with you is the fountain of life; in your light we see light (Psalm 36:9).

When Adam was created from 'the dust of the ground' he did not become 'a living being' until God 'breathed into his nostrils the breath of life' (Genesis 2:7). God is life: Jesus Christ is life.

As Moses drew to the close of his long ministry he warned the children of Israel -

> I call heaven and earth as witnesses today against you, that I have set before you life and death, blessing and cursing; therefore choose life, that both you and your descendants may live; that you may love the LORD your God, that you may obey his voice, and that you may cling to him, for he is your life' (Deuteronomy 30:19-20).

Only through God can be found an existence which really deserves the name of life.

In John's gospel we see that the eternal Son of God is the giver of physical life (1:3) so too he is the giver of spiritual life. As the Spirit of God breathed into the dead in the valley of dry bones (Ezekiel 37:9-10), so Jesus breathes life into those who are physically dead (11:25) and those who are spiritually dead (5:39-40). He grants abundant life (10:10), and eternal life (6:54). God the Father gives life, the Son of God gives life and the Holy Spirit gives life. No distinction is ever drawn between the power and perfections of the three Holy Persons.

Jesus is life, for 'in him was life' (1:4). He is 'the resurrection and the life' (11:25); 'the way, the truth, and the life' (14:6), 'that whoever believes in him should not perish but have eternal life' (3:15); he came 'that they may have life, and that they may have it more abundantly' (10:10). He who believes in Jesus 'though he may die, he shall live. And whoever lives and believes in [him] shall never die' (11:25-26). He is 'the Bread of life' whoever comes to him will never hunger (6:35). He is 'the Bread of God... who... gives life to the world' (6:33); He is 'the living bread which came down from heaven, if anyone eats of this bread, he will live forever' (6:51). Jesus 'will raise him up at the last day' (6:54).

In Proverbs, where there is such an intimate relation between Wisdom and the Word,[151] Wisdom is said to be 'a tree of life to those who take hold of her' (Proverbs 3:18). Wisdom declares -

> For whoever finds me finds life, and obtains favour from the LORD; but he who sins against me wrongs his own soul; all those who hate me love death (Proverbs 8:35-36).

All who are without Christ lack life before God. They are dead and damned.

3. Jesus: the Light

In the Old Testament real life is connected with true light (Psalms 36:9). Prophecy declares that the chosen Servant of the Lord (Isaiah 42:1-4) will be given by God 'as a light to the Gentiles, to open blind eyes' (Isaiah 42:6-7). In other words, to bring them to salvation -

> Indeed he [the LORD] says, 'It is too small a thing that you should be my Servant to raise up the tribes of Jacob, and to restore the preserved ones of Israel; I will also give you as a light to the Gentiles, that you should be my salvation to the ends of the earth' (Isaiah 49:6).

The Son of God is the great illuminator, the One who enlightens -

> For you will light my lamp; the LORD my God will enlighten my darkness... For who is God, except the LORD? And who is a rock, except our God? (Psalms 18:28,31)

John records that Christ is 'the true light which gives light to every man coming into the world' (1:9). Whilst he is in the world he is 'the light of the world' (9:5; cf. 8:12; 12:46), He enlightens and leads all who follow him on

---

[151] Ernest W. Hengstenberg, *Commentary on the Gospel of St John* [1865], (Minneapolis, Minnesota: Klock and Klock, 1980), vol. 1, p.25.

a clear path. Many however 'loved darkness rather than light, because their deeds were evil' (3:19).

4. Jesus: the Lamb of God

The symbol of a lamb forms a major theme throughout the Bible. From Abel (Genesis 4:4) and the prophecy of Abraham (Genesis 22:8) to the Passover (Exodus 12:3-10); and from the prophecy of Isaiah (Isaiah 53:7) to identification by John the Baptist (1:29,36); Jesus is 'the Lamb of God who takes away the sin of the world' (1:29). He 'is indeed the Christ, the Saviour of the world' (4:42). A further confirmation that Jesus is the perfect Lamb of God was demonstrated on the cross. He was as a lamb 'without blemish' (Exodus 12:5); 'a lamb without blemish and without spot' (1 Peter 1:19). For in him there is no sin (8:46; cf. Hebrews 4:15; 1 Peter 2:22; 2 Corinthians 5:21; 1 John 3:5).

When soldiers broke the legs of the two thieves crucified with Jesus, they did not break his legs. John sees this as another prophecy fulfilled. Quoting from the institution of the Passover he writes, 'these things were done that the Scripture should be fulfilled, 'Not one of his bones shall be broken' (19:36; cf. Exodus 12:46; Numbers 9:12; Psalms 34:20).

5. Jesus: the Messiah (Christ)

John makes much of this title. This is the title by which Andrew spoke of Jesus when he addressed his brother Simon (1:41). The same by which the woman of Samaria declared her belief in the promises of Moses (4:25,29) and the Samaritans of Sychar declared their faith in Jesus as 'the Saviour of the world' (4:42). It was the Messiah for whom godly Jews longed - 'him of whom Moses in the law, and also the prophets, wrote' (1:45). It was Moses who wrote the Pentateuch, the first five books of the Old Testament in which the promises and prophecies of Messiah stretched back to Genesis 3:15.

Peter's grand confession declared Jesus to be 'the Christ, the Son of the living God' (6:69) as did Mary the sister of Lazarus, saying he is the Christ 'who is to come into the world' (11:27). Seeing and believing these two great truths about Jesus result in eternal life (20:31).

Moses was referring to the Messiah when he recorded the promise of God concerning a great Prophet -

> I will raise up for them a Prophet like you from among their brethren, and will put my words in his mouth, and he shall speak to them all that I command him. And it shall be that whoever will not hear my words, which he speaks in my name, I will require it of him (Deuteronomy 18:18-19).

The woman of Samaria no doubt had this promise in mind when saying to the Lord Jesus 'Sir, I perceive that you are a prophet' (4:19). She followed this by declaring her confidence in the promised Messiah -

'I know that Messiah is coming' [who is called Christ]. 'When he comes, he will tell us all things.' Jesus said to her, 'I who speak to you am he' (4:25-26).

When five thousand were miraculously fed with bread and fish, they declared of Jesus, 'This is truly the Prophet who is to come into the world' (6:14). Others, hearing him speak in the temple came to the same conclusion, 'Truly this is the Prophet' (7:40).

6. Jesus: the Son of God

John uses this designation of Jesus many times in his Gospel account: Jesus is 'the Only Begotten of the Father' (1:14); 'the Only Begotten Son' (1:18); 'his Only Begotten Son' (3:16); 'the Only Begotten Son of God' (3:18); 'the Son of God' (1:34, 49; 5:25; 9:35; 10:36; 11:4, 27; 19:7; 20:31); 'the Son of the living God' (6:69). Often Jesus spoke of himself simply as, 'the Son' (3:35, 36; 5:19, 20, 21, 22, 23, 26; 6:40; 8:36; 14:13); 'his Son' (3:17); or, when addressing the Father, as 'your Son' (17:1). Throughout there is but one conclusion, 'the Son' means 'the Son of the living God.'

The 'Father-Son' relationship is the key to understanding Jesus as presented here by John (e.g. 5:16-30; 10:27-39; 14:7-31). This intimate bond is seen to shape every word and action of Jesus.

The Son of God coming into the world is the supreme gift of God the Father -

For God so loved the world that he gave his only begotten Son, that whoever believes in him should not perish but have everlasting life. For God did not send his Son into the world to condemn the world, but that the world through him might be saved (3:16-17).

Jesus gently challenged the Samaritan woman -

If you knew the gift of God, and who it is who says to you, 'Give me a drink,' you would have asked him, and he would have given you living water (4:10).

Jesus is the eternal, uncreated Son of God (1:1). As such he is the perfect revelation and representative of God the Father (1:18; 10:30; 14:9). In John's Gospel the deity of Jesus is plain for all to see. The Son of God had no hesitation in using the special name of God of himself. To the Jews he said -

'Most assuredly, I say to you, before Abraham was, I am.' Then they took up stones to throw at him; but Jesus hid himself and went out of the temple, going through the midst of them, and so passed by (8:58-59).

The Jews knew that Jesus was taking to himself the special name of God which was revealed to Moses at the burning bush -

Then Moses said to God, 'Indeed, when I come to the children of Israel and say to them, "The God of your fathers has sent me to you," and they say to me, "What is his name?" what shall I say to them?' And God said to Moses, 'I am who I am.' And he said, 'Thus you shall say to the children of Israel, "I am has sent me to you"' (Exodus 3:13-14).

The Jews would not accept that Jesus was the Son of God, Immanuel, God with us. They were not prepared to enquire into his true identity. In their blindness they were determined to stone him for what they concluded was the worst kind of blasphemy. However Jesus was not simply indicating an amazing connection with the living God, that he is God like God when he said 'before Abraham was, I am'. Jesus was revealing more than that. As the Son of God, *he was the One who spoke to Moses* from the burning bush!

The One who is now Jesus, is the Son of God who existed before Abraham, before creation, for he is the Eternally Ever-Living God. He is the Word who 'was with God, and the Word [who] was God. He was in the beginning with God. All things were made through him, and without him nothing was made that was made' (1:1-3). The Son of God reveals his true eternal identity when he says, 'Before Abraham was, I am' (8:58). 'Here was a full disclosure of His glory: the affirmation that He was none other than the Eternal One'.[152]

The Scriptures of the Old and New Testaments confirm this. Moses recorded his personal experience at the burning bush: 'the Angel of the LORD appeared to him' and 'God called to him from the midst of the bush' (Exodus 3:2,4; cf. Acts 7:30,35).

The Angel of the LORD appears in the pages of Scripture in such a way that his deity cannot be denied. On each occasion it is the Son of God appearing momentarily in human form before his incarnation -

- appearing to Abraham's wife's maid Hagar, he is called 'the Angel of the LORD' four times (Genesis 16:7,9,10,11). Moses the historian identified him as 'the LORD [YHWH] who spoke to

---

152 Arthur W. Pink, *Expositions of the Gospel of John: three volumes unabridged in one* (Grand Rapids, Michigan: Zondervan, 1970), vol. 2, p.56.

her' (Genesis 16:13). Hagar spoke of him as 'God' (Genesis 16:13).

- Moses recorded the testimony of Jacob: 'Then the Angel of God spoke to me in a dream, saying... "I am the God of Bethel"' (Genesis 31:11,13).

- when Jacob blessed Joseph, he spoke of the 'God, before whom my fathers Abraham and Isaac walked, the God who has fed me all my life long to this day' as 'the Angel who has redeemed me from all evil' (Genesis 48:15,16).

- this is further confirmed by the prophet Hosea, who declares of Jacob, 'He took his brother by the heel in the womb, and in his strength he struggled with God. Yes, he struggled with the Angel and prevailed' (Hosea 12:3-4).

There are many more examples showing that the Angel of the Lord in the Old Testament is deity.

John records another incident of the Lord asserting his unique relationship with the Father. Challenged at Bethesda for healing a paralysed man on the Sabbath, Jesus justified his action by saying -

'My Father has been working until now, and I have been working.' Therefore the Jews sought all the more to kill him, because he not only broke the Sabbath, but also said that God was his Father, making himself equal with God (John 5:17-18).

When confronted by those who came to arrest him, was it simply the Lord's courage which caused such a physical reaction in them, or the words he used?

Jesus therefore, knowing all things that would come upon him, went forward and said to them,'Whom are you seeking?' They answered him, 'Jesus of Nazareth.' Jesus said to them, 'I am.' ... Now when he said to them, 'I am,' they drew back and fell to the ground (18:4-6).

In the seven 'I am' sayings (Greek literally, 'I, I am') which the apostle John alone records, the connection with the name of God is unmistakable -

1. I, I am the bread of life   6:35
2. I, I am the light of the world   8:12; 9:5
3. I, I am the door   10:7
4. I, I am the good shepherd   10:11,14
5. I, I am the resurrection and the life   11:25
6. I, I am the way, the truth and the life   14:6
7. I, I am the true vine   15:1

In the days of Ezekiel the prophet, God gave a promise that he would personally search for his sheep and seek them out, 'feed them in good pasture... seek what was lost and bring back what was driven away, bind up the broken and strengthen what was sick' (Ezekiel 34:14,16). Jesus Christ fulfils God's personal promise as the 'good shepherd' who knows his sheep (10:14); and 'gives his life for the sheep' (10:11). His sheep know his voice and they follow him (10:27). He gives them eternal life and no one can take them from him (10:28). God, the good shepherd, has come in Jesus. He is 'Immanuel, God with us' (Matthew 1:23).

The deity of Jesus is shown too in John's Gospel by his supernatural knowledge: seeing Nathanael under the fig tree (1:48); predicting his own death and resurrection (2:19; 12:23-24), and the death of Lazarus (11:14); anticipating Peter's threefold denial (13:38); 'knowing all things that would come upon him' (18:4); and foretelling the nature of Peter's death (21:18-19).

Referring to his pre-existence, Jesus the Son of God prayed in the upper room -

> And now, O Father, glorify me together with yourself, with the glory which I had with you before the world was (17:5).

There are other proofs of deity which are not immediately obvious, yet once seen are overwhelmingly convincing. When recording the unbelief of the Jews, despite the convincing proof of the many miracles Jesus performed, John saw a fulfilment of the prophecy of Isaiah 6:10 -

> He has blinded their eyes and hardened their hearts, lest they should see with their eyes, lest they should understand with their hearts, and turn, so that I should heal them (12:40).

John then adds the telling remark -

> These things Isaiah said when he saw his glory and spoke of him' (12:41).

John is continuing to speak about Jesus from 12:37 to the end of the chapter. Hengstenberg explains it this way -

> John 'beheld Christ in the Jehovah of the Old Testament. - Isaiah saw "the Lord" sitting on His throne. He says in v.5, "Mine eyes have seen the King, the Lord of hosts." But according to the tenor of the Old Testament, all visible manifestation, all revelation of the Lord, is made through - His Angel, the brightness of his glory; and this was seen manifest in Christ in the flesh, - "And spake of Him;" thus that also refers to Christ, which in v.40 was quoted

from Isaiah as the Lord's own act. It was He, therefore, who blinded the eye of the Jews...[153]

Pink explains blinding the eyes of the people and hardened their hearts in this way -

> ... it is important to mark the *order* of ... two statements: in 12:37 they *did not* believe; ... in 12:39, they *could not* believe. The most attractive appeals had been made: the most indubitable [unquestionable] evidence had been presented: yet they despised and rejected the Redeemer. They *would not* believe; in consequence, God gave them up, and now they *could not* believe.[154]

Hendriksen in this way -

> 'The terrible consequences of hardening ourselves against the solemn admonitions and warnings that come to us is here pointed out. Again ... *the fault lies not in any sense with God!* He is the God of love. He is not a cruel monster who deliberately and with inward delight prepares people for everlasting damnation. On the contrary, he earnestly warns, proclaims the Gospel, and states - as Jesus did repeatedly during his earthly ministry - what will happen if people believe, also what will happen if they do not. He even *urges* them to walk in the light. But when people, of their own accord and after repeated threats and promises, reject him and spurn his messages, then - and not until then - he hardens them, *in order* that those who were *not willing* to repent may not *be able* to repent.[155]

Pink further comments -

> A striking testimony is this to the absolute Deity of Christ. The prediction quoted in the previous verse [v.40] is found in Isaiah 6. At the beginning of the chapter the prophet sees "Jehovah sitting upon *a* throne, high and lifted up, and his train filled the temple." Above the throne stood the seraphim, with veiled face, crying, "Holy, holy, holy, is the Lord of hosts." ... And here the Holy Spirit tells us in John 12, "These things said Isaiah, when he saw *his* glory, and spake of him" - the context makes it unmistakably

---

153 Ernest W. Hengstenberg, *Commentary on the Gospel of St John* (Minneapolis, Minnesota: Klock and Klock, 1980), vol. 2, p.127.

154 Arthur W. Pink, *Expositions of the Gospel of John: three volumes unabridged in one* (Grand Rapids, Michigan: Zondervan, 1970), vol. 2, p.281.

155 William Hendriksen, *The Gospel of John* (London: Banner of Truth Trust, 1974), p.212.

plain that the reference is to the Lord Jesus. One of the sublimest descriptions of the manifested Deity found in all the Old Testament is here applied to Christ.[156]

As Isaiah recoiled with a sense of uncleanness he confessed: 'my eyes have seen the King, the LORD [Yahweh] of hosts' (Isaiah 6:5). The clear implication is that Isaiah saw a vision of the Son of God (who became Jesus), the One who was God like the Father is now God like us (1:14).

Again, at the cross, John notes yet another fulfilment of Scripture - 'They shall look on him whom they pierced' (19:37). In the original context, it is God who is speaking -

> And I will pour on the house of David and on the inhabitants of Jerusalem the Spirit of grace and supplication, then they will look on me whom they pierced. Yes, they will mourn for him as one mourns for his only son, and grieve for him as one grieves for a firstborn (Zechariah 12:10).

This is yet another proof that Jesus is God like the Father.

Finally, when the apostle Thomas was presented with unassailable proof of the deity of Jesus, he yielded wholeheartedly to him with the words, 'My Lord and my God!' (20:28). The Saviour acknowledged this with his reply and added a word of encouragement to all those who were to follow -

> Thomas, because you have seen me, you have believed. Blessed are those who have not seen and yet have believed (20:29; cf. 1 Peter 1:8).

7. Jesus: the King of Israel

King David received an amazing promise. Descended as he was from Judah (Genesis 49:10), he was to be in the Messianic line, in other words, the Son of God would be born as a descendant of David -

> When your days are fulfilled and you rest with your fathers, I will set up your seed after you, who will come from your body, and I will establish his kingdom. He shall build a house for my name, and I will establish the throne of his kingdom forever... Your throne shall be established forever (2 Samuel 7:12-13,16).

John the Baptist well knew the connections of the prophecies and promises of God. They would converge in One Man - Messiah the King and Son of God. Hence Nathanael, a student of John the Baptist, could conclude, when faced with the supernatural knowledge of Jesus, 'You are the Son of God!

---

[156] Arthur W. Pink, *Expositions of the Gospel of John* (Grand Rapids, Michigan: Zondervan, 1970), vol. 2, p.282-3.

You are the King of Israel!' (1:49) It is unlikely that any of the Jews, who dined in the field and were fed at the Lord's hand, had spiritual understanding when they sought to 'take him by force to make him king' (6:15). However, there would no doubt be genuine believers among those who cried out, '"Blessed is he who comes in the name of the LORD!" The King of Israel!' as Jesus entered Jerusalem for the last time (12:13; cf. Psalms 118:26). The prophecy of the coming King was being fulfilled: 'Behold, your King is coming, sitting on a donkey's colt' (12:15; cf. Zechariah 9:9).

The mockery of the soldiers in the Praetorium at Jerusalem was particularly offensive because Jesus was indeed the King of the Jews. Platting a crown out of long-spiked thorns, pressing it down upon his head and draping a purple robe around the Saviour, 'they said, "Hail, King of the Jews!" And they struck him with their hands' (19:3). Pilate, seeking to appeal to the crowd, said to the Jews, 'Behold your King!' (19:14), only to hear the God-dishonouring retort, 'We have no king but Caesar!' (19:15). Finally, whatever Pilate's motive in writing it, the testimony on the cross was clear for all to see; the placard read, 'Jesus of Nazareth, the King of the Jews' (19:19; cf. v.21).

Jesus left Pilate in no doubt about the nature of his kingdom -

> "My kingdom is not of this world. If my kingdom were of this world, my servants would fight, so that I should not be delivered to the Jews; but now my kingdom is not from here." Pilate therefore said to him, "Are you a king then?" Jesus answered, "You say rightly that I am a king. For this cause I was born, and for this cause I have come into the world, that I should bear witness to the truth. Everyone who is of the truth hears my voice" (18:36-37).

8. Jesus: the Son of Man

The title 'Son of God' refers to our Lord's deity, whilst the title 'Son of Man' depicts his humanity. There was good reason for John to emphasise both. By the time he wrote his Gospel record the Christian Church was being invaded by the heresy of the Docetics who believed that deity was by necessity totally removed from any kind of human component. Hence, for them, believing in the deity of the Son of God inevitably meant that he could not have become a human being (see John's unequivocal denunciation of this in 1 John 4:2-3; 2 John 7).

John highlights the true humanity of Jesus: he came from Nazareth (1:45); attended a wedding (2:2); travelled with his mother and brothers (2:12); was weary (4:6); asked for a drink of water (4:7); walked across the

Sea of Galilee (6:1); was known as a child in his village (6:42); was challenged by his siblings (7:3); spat on the ground to make mud for a blind man's eyes (9:6); wept over the death of Lazarus (11:35); washed his disciples' feet (13:5); was thirsty on the cross (19:28); died (19:30); his body was pierced (19:34), and laid in a tomb (19:42), and even after his resurrection the nail marks were evident in his hands (20:20,27).

In the details describing the final hours of his death, none could doubt the true humanity of Jesus. The Word that was God became flesh (1:1,14) not in appearance only but entering truly and fully into human existence and experience.

Only One who was God and Man could be the Mediator between heaven and earth. Only One who was truly human could suffer and die in the place of other human beings.

Eleven times, in this Gospel, Jesus is recorded as referring to himself as 'the Son of Man.' In the first, when addressing Nathanael, the Lord identified himself with Jacob's dream of a ladder between heaven and earth. He said, '…hereafter you shall see heaven open, and the angels of God ascending and descending upon the Son of Man' (1:51).

It illustrates what Jesus said much later in the upper room, shortly before his death -

> I am the way, the truth, and the life. No one comes to the Father except through me (John 14:6).

Again, in the second occurrence of this title Son of Man, Jesus links back to an Old Testament event (3:13-14). This time it is to an occasion during the Israelites' wilderness journey and proved a fitting prelude to what is probably the most widely known verse of the Bible - John 3:16. Around 1440 B.C. the Israelites were journeying in the wilderness around the land of Edom and became very discouraged. They grumbled against the Lord and against Moses. In consequence the Lord sent venomous snakes among the people and many were bitten and died. Crying to the Lord, Moses was given the remedy. A bronze snake was to be erected on a pole in the centre of the camp. Anyone bitten by a snake was simply to look at the bronze snake and they would be healed (Numbers 21:4-9).

Jesus showed how this incident illustrated his saving work: (i) the people sinned against God; (ii) God brought judgment; (iii) the remedy was to believe the promise of God and look at the bronze snake; (iv) and the spiritual meaning - 'There is life for a look at the Crucified One.'

> … even so must the Son of Man be lifted up, that whoever believes in him should not perish but have eternal life (3:14-15).

Is this the only occasion in Scripture when the Lord Jesus is represented by something usually regarded as evil? The snake (serpent) was the agent in the Fall of humanity (Genesis 3:1-6). That 'serpent of old' is a name for 'the Devil and Satan' (Revelation 12:9; 20:2). Why then, would the Lord God use something associated with evil to represent his Holy Son? The answer is found in the amazing transaction on Calvary's cross -

> For he [the Father] made him [the Son] who knew no sin to be sin
> for us, that we might become the righteousness of God in him
> (2 Corinthians 5:21).

The Saviour identified with the uncleanness and rebellion of his people. He, though remaining entirely holy throughout, nevertheless took responsibility for our sins, as though *he* were guilty, in order to deliver *us* from the penalty, the power and (one day) the presence of sin. By his self-sacrifice at Calvary he paid our debt in full.

As the Son of Man the Lord Jesus will judge all humanity (5:22,26-27); give everlasting nourishment to all who come to him (6:27,53); die that others may live (12:24); and in dying be glorified together with his Father (13:31).

Beside the eight great titles for Jesus of Nazareth which are present in the first chapter of John's Gospel, two more are worthy of highlighting from John's Gospel. Jesus is the Teacher and Jesus is supremely the One sent by the Father.

9. Jesus: the Teacher

The Prophet promised through Moses will be a greater teacher than Moses. Response to his words will be a matter of life and death. Two of the first disciples of Jesus, Andrew and a colleague, addressed Jesus as 'Rabbi (which is to say, when translated, Teacher)' when they first met the Lord (1:38). Scribes and Pharisees addressed Jesus as 'Teacher' (8:4). When Martha told her sister Mary that Jesus had arrived, as they mourned the death of their brother Lazarus, she simply said, 'The Teacher has come and is calling for you' (11:28). After the resurrection Mary Magdalene showed her respect and devotion for Jesus when she addressed him as, 'Rabboni!' [which is to say, Teacher] (20:16).

It would seem that this was the most natural term for close friends and disciples to use in addressing the Lord Jesus. The Saviour emphasised the point when he spoke to the disciples in the upper room saying, 'You call me Teacher and Lord, and you say well, for so I am' (13:13).

Throughout his ministry Jesus taught frequently in synagogues (6:59) and often in the temple (7:28; 8:2). Indeed he readily acknowledged this when at his trial before the Sanhedrin. When the high priest asked him about his disciples and doctrine -

> Jesus answered him, "I spoke openly to the world. I always taught in synagogues and in the temple, where the Jews always meet, and in secret I have said nothing. Why do you ask me? Ask those who have heard me what I said to them. Indeed they know what I said (18:20-21).

Jesus is 'a teacher come from God' (3:2) as Nicodemus acknowledged in the early days of the Lord's ministry. At that stage Nicodemus little knew the extent of the Lord's knowledge and insight. This Teacher possesses skill and expertise which is way beyond anything he, or any other, could have known or understood. He is the revealer of the ultimate truth about God and creation. This is 'Christ Jesus, who became for us wisdom from God - and righteousness and sanctification and redemption - that, as it is written, "He who glories, let him glory in the LORD"' (1 Corinthians 1:30-31).

10. Jesus: the One sent by the Father

John presents Jesus as the Word, the Life, the Light, the Lamb of God, the Christ, the Son of God, the King of Israel, the Son of Man and the Teacher. Undergirding all these appellations of the Master there is the golden thread that he is the One sent by God (3:34; 5:23-24, 30; 5:36-38; 6:29, 38-40, 44, 57; 7:16, 18, 28-29, 33; 8:16, 18, 26, 29, 42; 9:4; 10:36; 11:42; 12:44, 49; 13:20; 14:24; 15:21; 16:5; 17:3, 8, 18, 21, 23, 25; 20:21). These may be highlighted by a quotation from the high priestly prayer of Jesus -

> For I have given to them the words which you have given me, and they have received them, and have known surely that I came forth from you; and they have believed that you sent me (John 17:8).

Emphasised throughout John's Gospel is 'the glory as of the only begotten of the Father, full of grace and truth' (1:14). For example, the Son of God manifested his glory on earth by his first miracle in Cana of Galilee (2:11); in the raising of Lazarus (11:4; 40); in his death upon the cross (17:5); his glory was revealed in a vision in the Old Testament Scriptures (12:41) and it will be seen again after the great resurrection (17:24). Yet the Son never tried to seek his own glory (8:50), but the glory of the One who sent him (7:18).

Additional applications

1. Faith

Faith is shown to be fundamental in *The Gospel of John*. The verb 'to believe' occurs over sixty-five times in John, more often than in all the other

Gospels combined. Those who believe: are the children of God (1:12); are not condemned (3:18) have everlasting life (3:36); will always be fully satisfied (6:35); will never die (11:26); will not continue in darkness (12:46); believe also in God the Father (12:44).

Those who do not believe in Jesus are condemned already (3:18). They shall not see life but are continually subject to the wrath of God (3:36).

John is concerned to show not only the need to believe but also to emphasise the object of that faith. Here he puts on record what Jesus calls people to believe in -

- Old Testament Scripture   2:22; 5:46-47
- the name of Jesus   2:23
- the words of Jesus   8:45-46
- the works of Jesus   14:11
- Jesus as the One sent by God   6:29; cf. 12:44
- Jesus himself   3:18; 4:39; 10:42; 12:42, etc.
- Jesus as the Son of God   9:35-38
- Jesus as the Messiah   11:27; 20:31
- the unique relationship
    between the Father and the Son   14:10

To illustrate and enforce the vital necessity of faith, John provides many examples of those who believed in Jesus -

- John the Baptist when seeing Jesus anointed   1:34
- the disciples of Jesus in seeing his first miracle   2:11
- many in Jerusalem seeing his miracles   2:23
- Samaritans in Sychar hearing his teaching   4:39-42
- the nobleman and his household seeing the healing   4:50,53
- many in Jerusalem seeing his 'signs'   7:31
- many in Jerusalem hearing his words   8:30
- many hearing the testimony of the Baptist
                        then seeing Jesus   10:42
- Martha just before the raising of Lazarus   11:27
- many after the raising of Lazarus in Bethany   11:45
- many secret believers among the Jewish leadership   12:42

A problem exists in being able to distinguish temporary, or superficial faith, from real saving faith. Early in his ministry when he was present in Jerusalem for the Passover John records that 'many believed in his name when they saw the signs which he did. But Jesus did not commit himself to them, because he knew all men, and had no need that anyone should testify of man, for he knew what was in man (2:23-25). Again following the feeding of the five thousand and the sermon on the Bread of Life 'many of his disciples went back and walked with him no more' (6:66).

These people started off believing, impressed by his miracles, but then turned away when Jesus disclosed the cost of discipleship. A similar situation was described by Jesus as the seed that fell on stoney ground in the parable of The Sower. There the gospel was believed by some until the difficulties of persecution or the demands of following Jesus became evident. True faith demonstrates itself in nothing less than whole-hearted devotion and loving obedience even when we do not fully understand the teaching of Jesus. Like Peter we will respond, when questioned about our loyalty, 'Lord, to whom shall we go? You have the words of eternal life. Also we have come to believe and know that you are the Christ, the Son of the living God' (6:68-69).

Jesus is the Son of God and Son of Man. He is true deity and true humanity. John's account of the ministry, death and resurrection of Jesus was written to convince readers that Jesus was both divine and human and draw forth true faith.

> John wanted to show that Jesus was not merely an appearance of God (similar to those in the Old Testament) or a man in whom dwelt the spirit of Christ. He intended to demonstrate that Jesus was both God and man and that within His single person was a perfect union of the two natures.[157]

This was not simply of academic interest but designed to convince readers of the true identity of Jesus bringing the response of faith to receive the gift of eternal life -

> For God so loved the world that he gave his only begotten Son, that whoever believes in him should not perish but have everlasting life (John 3:16).

Jesus was sent from the Father to die as the only Saviour of sinners, and to draw out faith to participate in that great blessing. A lasting promise was clearly issued, summed up in the words of Jesus -

> Blessed are those who have not seen and yet have believed (John 20:29).

---

[157] Robert G. Gromacki, *New Testament Survey* (Grand Rapids, Michigan: Baker, 1974), p.134.

2. Love

John's Gospel overflows with love. It is the amazing love of God to the world which is so overwhelming. He loved so much as to give his Only Begotten Son (3:16). This was costly in the extreme since God had such a deep love for his Son from 'before the foundation of the world' (17:24). Throughout his life on earth Jesus was conscious of the Father's love (17:26), he knew that the Father had 'given all things into his hand' (3:35) and revealed 'all things that he himself does' (5:20). The Saviour was particularly conscious of the Father's love as he fulfilled his commission and laid down his life (10:17). The Father's love to the Son was beautifully mirrored in the love of the Son to the Father. Jesus was concerned that the world would know the love he had for the Father through the testimony of his disciples (14:31), and know too that he was sent by the Father who loves the disciples as much as he loves his Son (17:23; cf. 16:27).

The same love of the Father for the Son is the love which the Son of God has for his disciples and the love that he would have them experience (17:26) constantly (15:9). This love knows no limit for 'having loved his own who were in the world, he loved them to the end' (13:1). Indeed: 'Greater love has no one than this, than to lay down one's life for his friends' (15:13). The friends of Jesus are those who love him and obey him (15:14).

Disciples, being so loved by the Father and his Son, respond with wholehearted devotion and love. Their genuine love is expressed in obedience to Jesus, his commandments (14:15) and his word (cf. 14:24) and results in the sweetest communion with the Saviour (14:21) and with the Father (14:23). It is loving obedience that enables disciples to abide in the love of Christ (15:10). In their love they rejoice in the work of Jesus as he goes to prepare a place for them in the Father's house (14:28,2).

Those who reject Jesus have no love of God in them (5:42). They love 'darkness rather than light' (3:19). They do not love Jesus the Son of God, so God is not their Father (8:42). By contrast those loved by Jesus are no longer loved by the world (15:19).

The Lord's disciples not only love him but should also love each other. This he commands (15:17), for this mutual love will distinguish his true disciples (13:35). It is a 'new commandment' in that there is a qualification; Jesus has added the words, 'as I have loved you' (13:34; 15:12).

Here then is the love of God mutually experienced by the Father and the Son and shared with all true disciples who themselves seek to demonstrate this unique love towards each other. It is the Gospel of love in which John points to some disciples who are very conscious of being loved by the Saviour. He writes of the love of Jesus for Martha, Mary and their brother

Lazarus (11:5). They knew they were loved (11:3). The Lord's love was evident at the tomb of Lazarus when 'Jesus wept' (11:35, cf. v.36). John, the author of this Gospel also knew that he was loved by Jesus, for he identified himself as 'the disciple whom Jesus loved' (21:20, 24; cf. 13:23; 19:26; 20:2). Carson and Moo explain in this way -

> When a New Testament writer thinks of himself as someone whom Jesus loves, it is *never* to suggest that other believers are *not* loved or are somehow loved less... those who are most profoundly aware of their own sin and need, and who in consequence most deeply feel the wonders of the grace of God that has reached out and saved them, *even them*, are those who are most likely to talk about themselves as the objects of God's love in Christ Jesus. Those who do not think of themselves in such terms ought to [Ephesians 3:14-21].[158]

Conclusion

The writers of the Synoptic Gospels (Matthew, Mark and Luke) faithfully present the facts of the life and ministry of the Lord Jesus Christ. John provides more of the interpretation. In the providence of God he was well prepared for this responsibility having spent time with John the Baptist pouring over the Old Testament Scriptures, learning the profound significance of the prophecies and their convergence in the promised Messiah of God. Three years followed under the personal tutelage of the Saviour. The experiences of the teaching, healings, nature miracles, barbaric crucifixion and glorious resurrection prepared John for a life of service in evangelism and pastoral ministry. Years of reflection, prayer, conversation and meditation in the Scriptures and upon the words of Jesus, led to this monumental contribution to the Word of God. The Holy Spirit, as promised by the Saviour, guided John through the writing to ensure that this too was God-breathed Scripture.

John presents Jesus as the Word, the Life, the Light, the Lamb of God, the Christ, the Son of God, the King of Israel, the Son of Man and the Teacher. Jesus is the One sent by God to be 'the Christ, the Saviour of the world' (4:42). To participate in this glorious salvation sinners are urged to believe in Jesus as 'the Christ, the Son of God' (20:31) in order that they may know the blessing of eternal life (3:15-16). True faith demonstrates itself in nothing less than whole-hearted devotion and loving obedience.

---

[158] Donald Carson and Douglas Moo, *An Introduction to the New Testament* (Leicester: Inter-Varsity Press, 2005), p.241.

In the face of the holiness and sinlessness of his life, the excellent morality and spirituality of his teaching, the vast number and variety of his miracles of compassion - the chief priests, Pharisees and scribes, together with the mass of the population of Israel, did not believe in him.

> He came to his own, and his own did not receive him. But as many as received him, to them he gave the right to become children of God, to those who believe in his name, who were born, not of blood, nor of the will of the flesh, nor of the will of man, but of God (John 1:11-13).

Under God, the apostle John makes a unique contribution to our knowledge and understanding of the Man from heaven, Jesus the Christ, the Son of God.

Overall Conclusion

Matthew, Mark, Luke and John are four amazing testimonies of the life and teaching of the Lord Jesus Christ. Each one is Holy Spirit inspired and a vital part of the Scriptures which are 'profitable for doctrine, for reproof, for correction, for instruction in righteousness,' that every Christian 'may be complete, thoroughly equipped for every good work' (2 Timothy 3:16,17).

God influenced everything from the beginning of creation towards the coming of his eternal Son as the solution to all the ills and calamities of the whole of humanity.

The life, teaching and saving work of the Lord Jesus are the pinnacle of God's momentous demonstration of love and mercy, the unique highpoint of all history. Everything before it flowed relentlessly to it and everything after streams irresistibly from it.

The four Gospels brim with the grace and truth of God as they declare the wonder of the 'perfect man', the 'one Mediator between God and men, the Man Christ Jesus, who gave himself a ransom for all' (Ephesians 4:13; 1 Timothy 5:5-6).

As we read and study the life and teaching of Jesus we can readily understand the thrill and delight which the Father felt towards his Beloved Son (e.g. Matthew 3:17; 17:5; John 12:28). How wonderful too that -

> God also has highly exalted him and given him the name which is above every name, that at the name of Jesus every knee should bow, of those in heaven, and of those on earth, and of those under the earth, and that every tongue should confess that Jesus Christ is Lord, to the glory of God the Father (Philippians 2:9-11).

Let the world rejoice -

Jesus Christ is Lord, to the glory of God the Father!

.

Chart of the Four Gospels

	Matthew	Mark	Luke	John
Introduction				
1. Prologues	1:1	1:1	1:1-4	-
e. The deity of the Son	-	-	-	1:1-2
f. The work of the Son	-	-	-	1:3-5
g. The herald of Jesus	-	-	-	1:6-8
h. The rejection of Jesus	-	-	-	1:9-11
i. The acceptance of Jesus	-	-	-	1:12-13
j. The incarnation of Christ	-	-	-	1:14-18
2. Introducing John and Jesus				
a. John the Baptist foretold	-	-	1:5-25	-
b. Birth of Jesus told to Mary	-	-	1:26-38	-
c. Mary visits cousin Elizabeth	-	-	1:39-45	-
d. Mary's hymn of praise	-	-	1:46-56	-
e. Birth foretold to Joseph	1:18-25	-	-	-
f. Birth of John the Baptist	-	-	1:57-66	-
g. Zacharias prophesies	-	-	1:67-80	-
3. The genealogies of Jesus	1:2-17	-	3:23-38	-
The birth and childhood of Jesus				
4. The birth of Jesus (Bethlehem)	-	-	2:1-7	-
5. Shepherds in the fields	-	-	2:8-21	-
6. Jesus taken to the temple -				
a. Simeon sees God's salvation	-	-	2:22-35	-
b. Anna rejoices	-	-	2:36-38	-
7. Wise men from the East	2:1-12	-	-	-
8. Flight to Egypt; the massacre	2:13-18	-	-	-
9. Herod's death; family returns	2:19-23	-	2:39-40	-
10. Jesus at twelve with teachers	-	-	2:41-52	-
The preparation for ministry				
11. John the Baptist preaching	3:1-12	1:2-8	3:1-18	-
12. The baptism of Jesus	3:13-17	1:9-11	3:21-22	-
13. The temptations of Jesus	4:1-11	1:12-13	4:1-13	-
14. John's testimony about Jesus	-	-	-	1:19-34
15. The first disciples of Jesus	-	-	-	1:35-51
16. First miracle: water to wine	-	-	-	2:1-12
The early Judean ministry				
17. First cleansing of the temple	-	-	-	2:13-25
18. Conversation with Nicodemus	-	-	-	3:1-21
19. John the Baptist's final testimony	-	-	-	3:22-36
20. Herod imprisons John	14:3-5	6:17-20	3:19-20	-
21. The woman of Samaria	-	-	-	4:1-42

	Matthew	Mark	Luke	John
The great Galilean ministry				
22. Jesus begins to preach	4:12,17	1:14-15	4:14-15	4:43-45
23. The nobleman's son healed	-	-	-	4:46-54
24. Jesus rejected in Nazareth	13:54-58	6:1-6	4:16-30	-
25. Jesus moves to Capernaum	4:13-16	1:21-22	4:31-32	-
26. Peter, Andrew, James, John called	4:18-22	1:16-20	5:1-11	-
27. Demon-possessed delivered	-	1:23-28	4:33-37	-
28. Peter's mother-in-law healed	8:14-17	1:29-34	4:38-41	-
29. Jesus preaches around Galilee	4:23	1:35-39	4:42-44	-
30. Leper cleansed	8:2-4	1:40-45	5:12-16	-
31. Four friends of a paralysed man	9:1-8	2:1-12	5:17-26	-
32. Matthew called	9:9-13	2:13-17	5:27-32	-
33. A question of fasting	9:14-17	2:18-22	5:33-39	-
34. Healing at the Pool of Bethesda	-	-	-	5:1-47
35. Sabbath Day controversies -				
a. Plucking grain	12:1-8	2:23-28	6:1-5	-
b. A withered hand	12:9-14	3:1-6	6:6-11	-
36. Multitudes healed	12:15-21	3:7-12	-	-
37. Great harvest; few labourers	9:35-38	-	-	-
38. Twelve apostles appointed	10:1-4	3:13-19	6:12-16	-
39. Multitudes gather	4:24-5:2	-	6:17-19	-
40. The Sermon on the Mount -				
a. The beatitudes	5:3-12	-	6:20-26	-
b. Salt and light	5:13-16	-	-	-
c. Jesus fulfils law and prophets	5:17-20	-	-	-
d. Murder & anger without cause		5:21-26	-	-
e. Adultery and the look to lust	5:27-30	-	-	-
f. Divorce - except immorality	5:31-32	-	-	-
g. Oaths - let your Yes be Yes	5:33-37	-	-	-
h. Turn the other cheek	5:38-42	-	6:29-31	-
i. Love your enemies	5:43-44	-	6:27-28; 32-36	
j. Be perfect as your Father	5:45-48	-	-	-
k. Charitable deeds	6:1-4	-	-	-
l. When you pray…	6:5-8	-	-	-
m. Our Father in heaven…	6:9-13	-	-	-
n. Forgive and be forgiven	6:14-15	-	-	-
o. When you fast…	6:16-18	-	-	-
p. Laying up treasure in heaven	6:19-21	-	-	-
q. Serve God not mammon	6:22-24	-	-	-
r. Devotion without worry	6:25-32	-	-	-
s. Seek first the kingdom of God	6:33-34	-	-	-
t. Judge not	7:1-6	-	6:37-38; 41-42	
u. Can the blind lead the blind?	-	-	6:39-40	
v. Persevere - ask, seek, knock	7:7-12	-	-	-
w. Narrow gate and difficult way	7:13-14	-	-	-
x. False prophets	7:15-20	-	6:43-45	-
y. Saying and doing	7:21-23	-	6:46	-

	Matthew	Mark	Luke	John
z. The house on the rock	7:24-27	-	6:47-49	-
41. People's responses	7:28-29	-	-	-
42. Jesus heals centurion's servant	8:1,5-13	-	7:1-10	-
43. A widow's son restored to life	-	-	7:11-17	-
44. John sends disciples to Jesus	11:2-19		7:18-35	-
45. Jesus critical of the Galileans	11:20-30	-	-	-
46. A sinful woman from the city	-	-	7:36-50	-
47. Jesus evangelises through Galilee	-	-	8:1-3	-
48. Demon-possessed mute healed	12:22-30	3:20-27	11:14-23	-
49. Blasphemy against the Spirit	12:31-37	3:28-30	-	-
50. Jesus rebukes seeking signs	12:38-42	-	11:29-36	-
51. Return of an unclean spirit	12:43-45	-	11:24-28	-
52. Jesus and his true family	12:46-50	3:31-35	8:19-21	-
53. Parables of the kingdom -				
a. The Sower	13:1-9	4:1-9	8:4-8	-
b. The purpose of parables	13:10-17	4:10-12	8:9-10	-
c. The Sower explained	13:18-23	4:13-20	8:11-15	-
d. The Lamp Under a Basket	-	4:21-25	8:16-18	-
e. The Seed Growing Secretly	-	4:26-29	-	-
f. The Wheat and Tares	13:24-30	-	-	-
g. The Mustard Seed	13:31-32	4:30-32	13:18-19	-
h. The Leaven	13:33		13:20-21	-
i. The reason for parables	13:34-35	4:33-34	-	-
j. Wheat and Tares explained	13:36-43	-	-	-
k. The Hidden Treasure	13:44	-	-	-
l. The Pearl of Great Price	13:45-46	-	-	-
m. The Dragnet	13:47-50	-	-	-
54. New Covenant scribes	13:51-53	-	-	-
55. Jesus stills the storm	8:18,23-27	4:35-41	8:22-25	-
56. The Gadarene demoniacs healed	8:28-34	5:1-20	8:26-39	-
57. The woman's haemorrhage healed and daughter of Jairus restored	9:18-26	5:21-43	8:40-56	-
58. Two blind men healed	9:27-31	-	-	-
59. Demon-possessed mute healed	9:32-34	-	-	-
60. The twelve apostles sent out	10:1,5-42	6:7-11	9:1-6	-
61. The death of John the Baptist	14:1-12	6:14-29	9:7-9	-
62. Return of apostles	-	6:30-32	9:10	-
63. Feeding 5,000 (Bethsaida Julias)	14:13-21	6:33-44	9:11-17	6:1-14
64. Walking on the Sea of Galilee	14:22-33	6:45-52	-	6:15-21
65. The sick at Gennesaret healed	14:34-36	6:53-56	-	-
66. The sermon on the Bread of Life	-	-	-	6:22-71
67. Scribes and Pharisees rebuked	15:1-20	7:1-23	6:39-40	

Northern and Perean ministry

68. Syrophoenician's daughter	15:21-28	7:24-30	-	-
69. Various healings	15:29-31	-	-	-

	Matthew	Mark	Luke	John
70. A deaf-mute healed	-	7:31-37	-	-
71. Feeding 4,000 (Decapolis)	15:32-39	8:1-10	-	-
72. Pharisees/Sadducees seek a sign	16:1-4	8:11-13	-	-
73. Warning of leaven of Pharisees, Sadducees and Herodians	16:5-12	8:14-21	-	-
74. A blind man healed at Bethsaida		8:22-26	-	-
75. Peter's confession of Christ	16:13-20	8:27-30	9:18-20	-
76. Lord's suffering: 1st prediction	16:21	8:31	9:21-22	-
77. Peter rebukes Jesus	16:22-23	8:32-33	-	-
78. Cost of discipleship	16:24-28	8:34-9:1	9:23-27	-
79. The transfiguration	17:1-13	9:2-13	9:28-36	-
80. Demon-possessed boy	17:14-21	9:14-30	9:37-43	-
81. Lord's suffering: 2nd prediction	17:22-23	9:31-32	9:44-45	-
82. The coin in the fish's mouth	17:24-27	-	-	-
83. The greatest in the kingdom	18:1-5	9:33-37	9:46-48	-
84. A stranger casting out demons	-	9:38-41	9:49-50	-
85. Causes of offences and surgery	18:6-9	9:42-50	-	-
86. Care for little ones (lost sheep)	18:10-14	-	-	-
87. Forgiveness between believers	18:15-17	-	-	-
88. Binding and loosing	18:18-20	-	-	-
89. Frequency of forgiveness	18:21-22	-	-	-
90. Parable of Unforgiving Servant	18:23-35	-	-	-

The later Judean ministry

	Matthew	Mark	Luke	John
91. Setting out for the feast	-	-	-	7:1-10
92. Rejection by Samaritans	-	-	9:51-56	-
93. Cost of discipleship	8:19-22	-	9:57-62	-
94. The seventy sent out by the Lord	-	-	10:1-16	-
95. Teaching at the Feast of Tabernacles	-	-	-	7:11-53
96. The woman taken in adultery	-	-	-	8:1-11
97. Jesus the light of the world	-	-	-	8:12-59
98. The man born blind	-	-	-	9:1-41
99. The 'door' and 'good shepherd'	-	-	-	10:1-21
100. Return of the seventy disciples	-	-	10:17-24	-
101. Parable of The Good Samaritan	-	-	10:25-37	-
102. Martha and Mary differ	-	-	10:38-42	-
103. Disciples taught to pray	-	-	11:1-4	-
104. Parable of The Friend at Midnight	-	-	11:5-13	-
105. Criticism of scribes and Pharisees	-	-	11:37-54	-
106. Warning against covetousness	-	-	12:1-12	-
107. Parable of The Rich Fool	-	-	12:13-21	-
108. Avoiding worry about life	-	-	12:22-34	-
109. Prepared for the master's return	-	-	12:35-48	-
110. Interpreting the times	-	-	12:49-59	-
111. Repentance is essential for all	-	-	13:1-5	-

	Matthew	Mark	Luke	John
112. Parable of The Fruitless Fig-Tree	-	-	13:6-9	-
113. Woman with a disabling spirit	-	-	13:10-17	-
114. The Feast of Dedication	-	-	-	10:22-39
115. Journey to Bethabara (Perea)	-	-	-	10:40-42

The Peraean ministry

	Matthew	Mark	Luke	John
116. Strive to enter the narrow gate	-	-	13:22-30	-
117. The Lord rebukes Herod	-	-	13:31-33	-
118. Jesus mourns over Jerusalem	-	-	13:34-35	-
119. Dinner with a prominent Pharisee	-	-	14:1-6	-
120. Parable of The Seats at a Feast	-	-	14:7-15	-
121. Parable of The Great Supper	-	-	14:16-24	-
122. The cost of discipleship	-	-	14:25-35	-
123. Parables of Lost Sheep, Coin, Son	-	-	15:1-32	-
124. Parable of The Unjust Steward	-	-	16:1-13	-
125. Jesus rebukes the Pharisees	-	-	16:14-18	-
126. Parable of Rich Man and Lazarus	-	-	16:19-31	-
127. Jesus warns of offences	-	-	17:1-4	-
128. Faith and duty	-	-	17:5-10	-
129. The raising of Lazarus	-	-	-	11:1-45
130. Reaction against Jesus	-	-	-	11:46-57
131. The final journey to Jerusalem	19:1-2	10:1	17:11	-
132. The healing of ten lepers	-	-	17:12-19	-
133. Predicting the Lord's return	-	-	17:20-37	-
134. Parable of Widow and the Judge	-	-	18:1-8	-
135. Parable of Pharisee/Tax Collector	-	-	18:9-14	-
136. Jesus answers about divorce	19:3-12	10:2-12	-	-
137. Jesus receives little children	19:13-15	10:13-16	18:15-17	-
138. The rich young ruler	19:16-22	10:17-22	18:18-23	-
139. Reward for those who leave all	19:23-30	10:23-31	18:24-30	-
140. Parable of Labourers in Vineyard	20:1-16	-	-	-
141. Lord's suffering: 3rd prediction	20:17-19	10:32-34	18:31-34	-
142. James and John make a request	20:20-28	10:35-45	-	-
143. Blind Bartimaeus	20:29-34	10:46-52	18:35-43	-
144. Hospitality with Zacchaeus	-	-	19:1-10	-
145. Parable of The Minas	-	-	19:11-28	-
146. Mary anoints Jesus	26:6-13	14:3-9	-	12:1-11

The Lord's final week in Jerusalem

	Matthew	Mark	Luke	John
147. The triumphal entry	21:1-11	11:1-11	19:29-44	12:12-19
148. Fruitless leafy fig-tree	21:18-22	11:12-14	-	-
149. Second cleansing of the temple	21:12-13	11:15-19	19:45-48	-
150. Healing in the temple	21:14-17			
151. The dried up fig-tree		11:20-26	-	-
152. The authority of Jesus	21:23-27	11:27-33	20:1-8	-
153. Parable of The Two Sons	21:28-32	-	-	-

	Matthew	Mark	Luke	John
154. Parable of Wicked Vinedressers	21:33-46	12:1-12	20:9-19	-
155. Parable of Marriage of The King's Son and a missing garment	22:1-14	-	-	-
156. Paying taxes to Caesar	22:15-22	12:13-17	20:20-26	-
157. Sadducees and the resurrection	22:23-33	12:18-27	20:27-39	-
158. First and great commandment	22:34-40	12:28-34	-	-
159. David's Son; David's Lord	22:41-46	12:35-37	20:40-44	-
160. Scribes and Pharisees rebuked	23:1-39	12:38-40	20:45-47	-
161. The widow's mites	-	12:41-44	21:1-4	-
162. Greeks request to meet Jesus	-	-	-	12:20-50

Prophecies of Jesus given to his disciples

163. Jesus reveals the future -				
a. Destruction of the temple	24:1-2	13:1-2	21:5-6	-
b. Signs of the times	24:3-14	13:3-13	21:7-19	-
c. Destruction of Jerusalem	24:15-29	13:14-25	21:20-26	-
d. Jesus will come with power	24:30-31	13:26-27	21:27-28	-
164. Parable of The Fig Tree	24:32-41	13:28-32	21:29-33	-
165. Watch and pray in readiness	24:42-44	13:33-37	21:34-38	-
166. Parable of The Faithful Servant	24:45-51	-	-	-
167. Parable of The Ten Virgins	25:1-13	-	-	-
168. Parable of The Talents	25:14-30	-	-	-
169. Parable of The Sheep and Goats	25:31-46	-	-	-

The Passover meal and betrayal

170. Judas agrees to betray Jesus	26:1-5	14:1-2	22:1-6	-
	26:14–16	14:10-11		-
171. Preparation for the Passover	26:17-19	14:12-16	22:7-13	-
172. Sitting at table	26:20	14:17	22:14-16	13:1-2
173. Jesus washes disciples' feet	-	-	-	13:3-17
174. A betrayer among them	26:21-25	14:18-21	22:21-23	13:18-29
175. Institution of Lord's Supper	26:26-29	14:22-25	22:17-20	-
176. Judas leaves	-	-	-	13:30-36
177. Disciples discuss greatness	-	-	22:24-30	
178. The last sermons of Jesus -				
a. The way, truth and life	-	-	-	14:1-14
b. Promise of the Comforter	-	-	-	14:15-31
c. Parable of The True Vine	-	-	-	15:1-10
d. New commandment of Jesus	-	-	-	15:11-17
e. Hatred of the world	-	-	-	15:18-27
f. Warning of persecution	-	-	-	16:1-4
g. Work of the Holy Spirit	-	-	-	16:5-15
h. Sorrow turned to joy	-	-	-	16:16-22
i. Prayer in the Son's name	-	-	-	16:23-26
j. Christ has overcome	-	-	-	16:27-33

	Matthew	Mark	Luke	John
179. Prayer of the great High Priest				
a. for God to glorify his Son	-	-	-	17:1-5
b. for the apostles and disciples	-	-	-	17:6-19
c. for his Church universal	-	-	-	17:20-26
180. Peter warned	26:30-35	14:26-31	22:31-34	13:37-38
181. Disciples to take supplies			22:35-38	-

The suffering and death of the Saviour

	Matthew	Mark	Luke	John
182. Grief in Garden of Gethsemane	26:36-46	14:32-42	22:39-46	18:1
183. Betrayal and arrest	26:47-56	14:43-52	22:47-53	18:2-12
184. Jesus taken before Annas	-	-	-	18:13-14,
	-	-	-	18:19-23
185. Trial before the Sanhedrin	26:57-68	14:53-65	22:63-65	18:24
186. Peter's denial	26:58-75	14:54-72	22:54-62	18:15-18,
	-	-	-	18:25-27
187. Condemned by Sanhedrin	27:1	15:1	22:66-71	-
188. Jesus before Pilate (1st time)	27:2,11-14	15:2-5	23:1-7	18:28-38
189. Judas hangs himself	27:3-10	-	-	-
190. Jesus before Herod	-	-	23:8-12	-
191. Jesus before Pilate (2nd time)	27:15-26	15:6-15	23:13-25	18:39-
				19:15
192. Mocked by soldiers	27:27-30	15:16-19	-	-
193. Delivered to be crucified	27:31-34	15:20-23	23:26-33	19:16-17
194. Crucifixion: six hours agony	27:35-56	15:24-41	23:34-49	19:18-30
195. The Lord's side is pierced	-	-	-	19:31-37
196. His body placed in a tomb	27:57-61	15:42-47	23:50-56	19:38-42
197. The tomb sealed	27:62-66	-	-	-

The Saviour's resurrection

	Matthew	Mark	Luke	John
198. Women visit the tomb early	28:1-8	16:1-8	24:1-11	20:1-2
199. Peter and John at the tomb	-	-	24:12	20:3-10
200. Jesus appears to Mary	-	16:9-11	-	20:11-18
201. Jesus appears to other women	28:9-10	-	-	-
202. Guards report the missing body	28:11-15	-	-	-
203. Jesus appears on Emmaus Road	-	16:12-13	24:13-35	-
204. Jesus appears in Jerusalem	-	-	24:36-43	20:19-25
205. Jesus appears again in Jerusalem		16:14	-	20:26-31
206. Jesus appears by Sea of Galilee		-	-	21:1-14
207. The public reinstatement of Peter		-	-	21:15-25
208. The great commission	28:16-20	16:15-18	24:44-49	-
209. Ascension from Bethany	-	16:19-20	24:50-53	-

Also by the same author

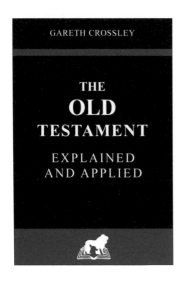

GARETH CROSSLEY

THE
OLD
TESTAMENT

EXPLAINED
AND APPLIED

This is an overview of the thirty-nine books of the Old Testament. The aim of this book is to present a glimpse of the contents of each Old Testament book so that the overall plan and purpose of God might be clearly perceived. It shows how from the beginning of time God was laying the foundation for the salvation of his people. This book identifies the predictions that are made about the glorious Saviour's life and death throughout the Old Testament. It shows also how feasts, festivals and sacrifices teach the value of Christ's death centuries before it happened.

Jesus Christ the Son of God is the grand subject, the central theme, of the Old Testament. When the Lord is challenged about his claims to unique sonship he presents, as one of a number of proofs, the content of Old Testament Scripture. Indeed on the great day of his resurrection he refers to the Old Testament as *the* abiding proof of his Person and Work.

'The best of its kind. As one who has taught Old Testament for more than a decade, I have read more than my fair share of such books, looking for the one to use for classes and to recommend to others. This is that book.'
Dr Benjamin Shaw, Associate Professor of Old Testament, Greenville Presbyterian Seminary, IN. US

'I can say with no reservations, this is THE BEST REVIEW OF THE OLD TESTAMENT that I have ever come across! Every Bible Student and every Pastor should order this book and use it. There is nothing out there that is any better in my opinion!"
D.J. Dickey, Pastor Emeritus, Glencullen Baptist Church, Portland, OR, US

'Having used the book profitably for a year in the classroom as a high school Bible teacher, I would especially commend it to students at this level or new Christians and it will prove a valuable resource for Sabbath Schools, church libraries or homeschooling families.'
David Whitla, Snr Pastor, Southside Reformed Presbyterian Church, IN, US

'This superb overview of the Old Testament is the best for the general reader that I have seen to date. Buy it, and you will not need another Old Testament Survey.   John Brentnall, Editor, Peace and Truth Magazine, UK

email: sales@RevealingChrist.org   website: RevealingChrist.org

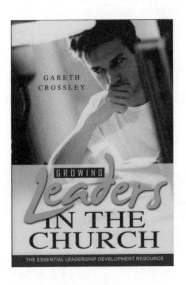

Growing Leadership in the Church is a leadership development resource designed to equip present and future church leaders in the practical issues of church life. The format depends upon close interaction between trainers and trainees.

Thirteen chapters cover pertinent issues including Pastoral oversight, Personal life, Pastoral counselling, Preaching and teaching, Missionary endeavour.

Each chapter has many subdivisions for example -

Pastoral counselling
> What is counselling?
> Is counselling Biblical?
> Ungodly counsel
> Theory and practice
> Counselling in the Bible
> The art of listening
> Applying Scripture
> Case studies